PROGRAMMING IN CLIPPER

The Definitive Guide to the Clipper dBASE Compiler

PROGRAMMING IN CLIPPER

The Definitive Guide to the Clipper dBASE Compiler

Stephen J. Straley

Addison-Wesley Publishing Company, Inc.
Reading, Massachusetts   Menlo Park, California   New York
Don Mills, Ontario   Wokingham, England   Amsterdam   Bonn   Sydney
Singapore   Tokyo   Madrid   Bogotá   Santiago   San Juan

DEDICATION

To my Mom, Aunt Pat, Sharon and Robert, and especially to Nicole -
hang on to dreams and ideas, for one day they will become reality.

A New York Communications Systems Book.

Many of the designations used by manufacturers and sellers to distinguish their products are claimed as trademarks. Where those designations appear in this book, and
Addison-Wesley was aware of a trademark claim, the designations have been printed
in initial caps or all caps.

dBASE II and dBASE III are registered trademarks of Ashton-Tate, Inc.
dBASE III Plus is a trademark of Ashton-Tate, Inc.
WordStar is a trademark of MicroPro International Corporation.
Lotus 1-2-3 is a trademark of Lotus Development Corporation.
SideKick is a trademark of Borland International, Inc.
Scrabble is a trademark of Selchow & Righter, Inc.
Plink86 is a trademark of Phoenix Software Associates, LTD.
Viewgen is a trademark of Software Tools Development Corporation.
HiLite is a trademark of Software Enhancement Technology.
Quickcode is a trademark of Fox & Geller, Inc.
Genifer is a trademark of Bytel Corporation.
Novell Netware is a trademark of Novell, Inc.
PC Net II is a trademark of AST Research, Inc.
3COM Ethernet is a trademark of 3Com Corporation.
Clipper and Nantucket are trademarks of Nantucket Corporation.

Library of Congress Cataloging-in-Publication Data

Straley, Stephen J.
  Programming in Clipper.

  Includes index.
  1. Compilers (Computer programs) 2. Clipper
(Computer program) 3. dBASE III (Computer program)
I. Title
QA76.76.C65S77 1987   005.4'53   87-19316

A B C D E F G H I J -HA- 8987
First printing, October 1987

ABOUT THE AUTHOR: STEVE STRALEY

Stephen J. Straley, formerly the senior support engineer at Nantucket, Inc., was directly involved in the early development stages of Clipper. For over a year, he traveled across the country meeting with computer users, teaching and demonstrating the many aspects of the compiler. He is part owner of a software development and consulting firm in southern California and on the East Coast, which specializes in application development using Clipper and the C language.

ACKNOWLEDGMENTS

Brian Russell is a man with practical ideas for the "programming whiz-kid" in all of us. To give mere acknowledgement to a man who gave me the key for new insights and wonders is not just. Personally, I thank him for myself and for all of us who use his "child." As it matures, so do we!

Phil Kimble, Roger Clay, Steve Hilbourne and Fred Ho are the backbone of this book; Cheryll Webber is the guardian of our sanity. The daily use and direction of this product is attributable to these individuals, who are the remaining force in the Technical Support Division of Nantucket, Inc. Never will there be a finer group of individuals dedicated to stretching the compiler to unimaginable parameters, finding answers to daily questions, solving problems with the product, and interfacing with the company and the market.

SPECIAL OFFER

Source Code Disk for
PROGRAMMING IN CLIPPER

We have prepared a 5-1/4" diskette to save you the time it takes to type in the examples and programs provided by Steve Straley. This disk will also save you the time it takes to find and correct the inevitable typing errors which keep programs from running properly.

The disk contains, in addition to the various examples and source code fragments, a complete *Code Generator*, a *Menu Generator* and a sample *Call Tracking* application. Just compile them and use them to help you in your own program development. This disk is an invaluable tool for every Clipper programmer.

The Source Code Disk is only available from New York Communications Systems, Inc. To order, photocopy or clip out the coupon below.

New York Communications Systems, Inc.
P.O. Box 20024
New York, NY 10017-0001

YES! Please send me _____ copies of the Source Code Disk for
PROGRAMMING IN CLIPPER at only $19.95 each.
(New York residents add $1.65 sales tax.)

__Check enclosed __VISA __MasterCard __American Express
Account No. _____
Exp. Date _____ Signature _____
Name _____
Company _____
Address _____
City _____ State _____ Zip _____

(Please allow 4-6 weeks for delivery.)

B001

TABLE OF CONTENTS

PREFACE

My main objectives in writing this book were to remove some of the mystique surrounding compilers, to help change the thought patterns of first-time users of a compiler, and to provide helpful tips in programming. While this book assumes a basic fa-
miliarity with dBASE II or dBASE III, it is also useful for readers who have never
used the dBASE interpreters. Personally, I hope to offer a new way of thinking to
those programming in the dBASE III language. Please take note of that last phrase,
"...the dBASE III language." With the advent of the Clipper compiler, dBASE III
leaves the confines of database management and takes its first steps toward becoming
a true high-level language for microcomputers.

Currently, there is some confusion in explaining the differences between dBASE III
and Clipper. While advertising agencies are eager to label Clipper as a compiler, we
must pay equal attention to dBASE III as an interpreter. One goal of this book is to
bridge the gap between the two and to show how each relates to the real world and to
the other. Sometimes, there will be cases where the application involved should be
designed and executed under the environment of dBASE III. Also, there will be times
where the code must execute under both systems. However, there will be more situations calling for the use of Clipper. The demand on the developer is to identify which
system is appropriate for each application. These chapters will enable you to make in-
formed decisions.

Once you understand how a compiler is basically different from an interpreter, it will
be clear how the coding in the respective environments will ultimately differ. The
guidelines and examples we give for working in the two environments will be your
tools for success. The examples should help change bad coding techniques to more
structured, disciplined methods. No specialized university degrees are required, just
effort and determination. Effort in training yourself to "do it better" and determination within yourself to find "the better way" will both pay off.

dBASE III allows many techniques that it should not allow if it is ever to be considered a structured language. Programming with dBASE III can be compared to
programming with BASIC. A few years ago I heard that most BASIC and dBASE III
programmers write "spaghetti code," a group of syntactically correct words and
phrases jumbled together and thrown against the "wall of execution." If the jumbled
code executes, the rule is "Don't touch it and walk away quietly." If it does not work
and falls off the wall, then programmers run over, twist the few pieces that fell off the
wall and throw them up again.

Structured programming emphasizes purpose and meaning; routines are not just
thrown together haphazardly. The notion of modular coding is the key. Structured
coding is like building a wall, with each brick carefully laid, on top of another. The
bricks on top rely on the brick below, yet each brick is small, clear, and well-defined in
itself.

Clipper's power lies in its ability to understand the plate of spaghetti as well as the carefully constructed wall of bricks.

Look at Clipper as a foreign language. Suppose you had the chance to go to a foreign land and stay there on your own. One of the first requirements for survival would be learning the local language. There would be no better way to do this than to listen to the natives and practice speaking with them.

Reading textbooks without practical direction and examples is no different from trying to learn a foreign language in a classroom environment, where your survival is not dependent on understanding. For many individuals, understanding Clipper is vital to surviving in the world of microcomputers. This world is based on speed, portability, and money. Using Clipper is essential if one is to survive in the current market atmosphere.

No matter what your experience level is with dBASE or Clipper, this book provides ample coding examples to illustrate theories, rules, and principles. I hope that these programming samples provide additional insight which may ultimately reduce confusion and save you time and money. Granted, for some these sections may cover areas already understood, but reviewing them never wastes time. For others with little or no experience in application development or in using Clipper, the ground rules at the beginning of most chapters should be helpful. Following these are sample codes, illustrating the points being discussed. If after reviewing the section containing the sample coding, the concepts are not clear, stop. Reread the code first, then the theory, and then try to duplicate the situation yourself on your computer. Even if things do not work out initially, keep trying; persist and you will prevail. Eventually, you'll see the light and create bigger and better applications.

Use this book not only as a learning guide to Clipper, but as a reference text as well. A small function, procedure, or even a suggestion in tackling a problem may be initially overlooked. Keep referring to the chapters pertaining to your code. If something is finally found, time is ultimately saved in finishing your application. If time can be saved, money is earned. If money is earned, you have survived.

So now onto the world of Clipper, the first true dBASE III compiler. Prepare yourself for a language finally geared to the belief that anything is possible . . . for a computer. Happy Clipping!

HOW TO USE THIS BOOK

Some will view this text as a guide to the Clipper/dBASE III language. Others will look for specific commands and techniques unique to the compiler, while still others will search for the one or two pieces of additional insight which will solve their problems. Whatever your reasons are for using this book, read it all! No one section is more important than another.

The main theme I have tried to stress is better programming. The compiler allows the implementation of coding principles and techniques previously impossible or inconvenient. For the most part there are two types of users of the compiler: those converting old dBASE III applications to Clipper to increase their speed, and those who have already converted and are now using the compiler to take advantage of its advanced features. In either case, clean coding and the expanded possibilities of structured programming are the main focuses of this book.

If you pick up this text simply to get additional background on one or two commands, you will miss other advantages of the book. There are many sections that can be looked at as a programming cookbook, but theories and techniques are implied recipes. They need to be reread, felt, simmered, and experienced in order to fully realize their thrust. This book should serve as a locksmith to the Clipper language. It can make the keys and can define the lock, but it actually takes a breathing soul to turn the keys inside of that lock in order to gain access. Expand your thinking to beyond the "now." Take the commands and concepts of "now" and apply them to future dreams and ideas. With some effort those ideas and dreams can become practical applications sitting on someone's desk in the future.

HOW TO USE CLIPPER

Frequently, the programming examples in the text should be compiled in order to see how they appear in final form. The following is the normal syntax for compiling and linking:

```
C>clipper <filename>
The Clipper Compiler, Winter '85
Copyright (c) 1985, 1986 Nantucket, Inc., All Rights Reserved.

Compiling <filename>.PRG
Code size:541    Symbols:160    Constants:896

C>plink86
PSA Linkage Editor (Nantucket Clipper) Version 1.46.c
Copyright (C) 1984 by Phoenix Software Associates Ltd.

=>fi <filename>
=>lib \<path>\clipper
=>;

<FILENAME>.EXE (119 K)
```

NOTE: All subsequent examples of program code or screen output will use the typeface shown above.

If there is any variation in this syntax, the sequence of compiling and/or linking will be given.

So look at the commands, definitions, and theories for rules. The restrictions are only in your own capabilities!

CHAPTER ONE

Interfacing dBASE and Clipper

CLIPPER and dBASE II

dBASE II emerged when programmers were just beginning to introduce database management systems to microcomputers. Since those days, dBASE II has stabilized, while system capacities have increased and new standards have gradually evolved. Consequently, there are bound to be some differences between dBASE II and Clipper. These differences are not only in command structure and syntax, but also in the mechanical constructs and theoretical approaches as well.

Most of the practical differences between Clipper and dBASE II parallel the differences between dBASE II and dBASE III. An immediate difference between dBASE II and Clipper is the expanded command and function base in Clipper. Another difference is in coding techniques. Because of greater capabilities in Clipper, code can be greatly condensed to accomplish the same task. Outlined in detail are some of the more significant differences and the trouble areas to avoid.

BASIC FILE CONSTRUCT

There is a difference between those dBASE II database files converted to dBASE III via dCONVERT and normal dBASE III/Clipper database files. If a dBASE II file has been converted via dCONVERT, a symptom of "Clippered" applications is that data in the database will be shifted by one character. For example, displayed fields will suddenly appear to contain a character from the previous field. Additionally, SEEKs and FINDs will no longer work. Due to the shift in the character position in a dBASE II dCONVERTED to dBASE III, the indexes built will be based on an incorrect record construct. To get around this problem, do the following:

1) Create a duplicate structure of the database with a temporary name either in dBASE III or in Clipper's CREATE utility program.

2) Append the records from the old dCONVERTED database to the newly generated database. This may be accomplished either through the dBASE III interpreter or through a small compiled program.

3) Erase the old file and rename the newly appended file with the old file's name.

4) Reindex all pertinent index files.

Below are layouts of the basic file headers of a true dBASE III file, a Clipper database file and, finally, a dBASE II-dCONVERTED-dBASE III database file. To examine these yourself, use the following procedure (be sure that DEBUG is either in the same directory as your .dbf files or in your DOS path):

```
C>DEBUG <filename.dbf>
```

A hyphen will appear. Enter the letter "D" and a carriage return. The beginning of the header of the entered file will show across the screen. After a few lines, another hyphen will appear. To exit from DEBUG, just enter the letter "Q."

dBASE III database file:

```
C>debug dbase.dbf
-d
1D45:0100  03 56 03 16 00 00 00 00-42 00 0B 00 00 00 00 00  .V......B.......
1D45:0110  00 00 00 00 00 00 00 00-00 00 00 00 00 00 00 00  ................
1D45:0120  4F 4E 45 00 00 00 00 00-00 00 00 43 00 00 00 00  ONE........C....
1D45:0130  0A 00 00 00 00 00 00 00-00 00 00 00 00 00 00 00  ................
1D45:0140  0D 00 1A EA 00 00 00 00-2E 8F 06 56 77 2E 8F 06  ...j.......Vw...
1D45:0150  58 77 E8 21 F0 EA 00 00-00 00 2E 8F 06 68 77 2E  Xwh!pj.......hw.
1D45:0160  8F 06 6A 77 E8 27 F0 EA-00 00 00 00 2E 8F 06 7A  ..jwh'pj.......z
1D45:0170  77 2E 8F 06 7C 77 E8 2D-F0 EA 00 00 00 00 2E 8F  w...|wh-pj......
-Q
```

CLIPPER database file:

```
C>debug clipper.dbf
-d
1D45:0100  03 56 03 16 00 00 00 00-42 00 0B 00 00 00 00 00  .V......B.......
1D45:0110  00 00 00 00 00 00 00 00-00 00 00 00 00 00 00 00  ................
1D45:0120  4F 4E 45 00 00 00 00 00-00 00 00 43 00 00 00 00  ONE........C....
1D45:0130  0A 00 00 00 00 00 00 00-00 00 00 00 00 00 00 00  ................
1D45:0140  0D 00 1A 01 00 00 02 00-00 00 41 63 6B 6E 6F 77  .........Acknow
1D45:0150  6C 65 2E 00 28 00 00 00-01 00 02 00 0F 00 0D 01  le..(...........
1D45:0160  41 00 63 00 6B 00 6E 00-6F 00 77 00 6C 00 65 00  A.c.k.n.o.w.l.e.
1D45:0170  64 00 67 00 6D 00 65 00-6E 00 74 00 73 00 0D 00  d.g.m.e.n.t.s...
-q
```

dBASE II dCONVERTED dBASE III database file:

```
C>debug II.DBF
-d
1D45:0100  03 56 03 18 00 00 00 00-21 04 0B 00 00 00 00 00  .V......!.......
1D45:0110  00 00 00 00 00 00 00 00-00 00 00 00 00 00 00 00  ................
1D45:0120  4F 4E 45 00 00 00 00 00-00 00 00 43 00 00 00 00  ONE........C....
1D45:0130  0A 00 00 00 00 00 00 00-00 00 00 00 00 00 00 00  ................
1D45:0140  0D 00 00 00 00 00 00 00-00 00 00 00 00 00 00 00  ................
1D45:0150  00 00 00 00 00 00 00 00-00 00 00 00 00 00 00 00  ................
1D45:0160  0D 00 00 00 00 00 00 00-00 00 00 00 00 00 00 00  ................
1D45:0170  00 00 00 00 00 00 00 00-00 00 00 00 00 00 00 00  ................
-q
```

The first two headers are virtually identical. Note the first four bytes which contain the dBASE III database marker and the next three pertaining to the date of the last update. Also note that if either of the first two databases were to contain a memo field, the first byte would be an 83, not an 03.

Now compare either of these two headers with the header of the dCONVERTED database. Notice that the ninth and tenth bytes are different. These point to the beginning positions of the fields in the file. While both the dBASE III and Clipper headers contain a 42 00, the dCONVERTED file contains a 21 04. This small difference is magnified when indexing because the index process is then based on an incorrect database header.

MODIFY COMMAND

Clipper is external to any text editor. dBASE II has the ability to build and modify command files within itself. These ASCII files may be compiled by Clipper. However, there are occasional problems.

A major problem is that the wraparound symbol is acknowledged by the interpreter and not by the compiler. In MODIFY COMMAND <filename>, if a command line extends beyond the width of a screen, a CHR(141) is placed at the end of the line and the input is continued onto the next line. This extra character must be removed! Try using a true text editor for programming, such as EDIX, PMATE, or EX EDITOR. Notice the reference to text editor. There are some editors which leave high seventh-order bit markers, better known as high-byte markers. Avoid using word processors (such as WordStar in the document mode and SideKick's editor) which may have a tendency to leave formatting characters in the text itself.

BASIC COMMANDS

In Clipper there are additional commands and changes in basic syntax from dBASE II. Examples of this are the symbols for true and false which are changed from a simple **T** or **F** in dBASE II to a **.T.** or a **.F.** in Clipper. There are also many new functions in Clipper, which under dBASE II would require many lines of extra coding, but need only one or two command lines in Clipper (e.g., date conversions and string conversions). dCONVERT does not completely convert program files in dBASE II to program files which can be compiled. It may be extremely slow, but ultimately it may be to your advantage to completely recode a dBASE II application into code which will work efficiently in Clipper. Only you can decide if the time needed for such a project will ultimately pay off.

If you recode, you will obtain valuable experience in learning the proper syntax and structure for the compiler, as well as the practical experience of applying the additional commands and functions in Clipper and dBASE III. The experience will pay dividends in the future.

SEPARATE WORK AREAS

One significant difference between dBASE II and Clipper is in file handling. In dBASE II only two selectable areas are available; in Clipper there are ten. Clipper has greater capacity in the files: longer length character fields, a memo field, more fields per database, and more records per database, to name just a few. Take some

time to familiarize yourself with the new commands and look over the section comparing Clipper to dBASE III.

RELATIONS

The concept of *relations* was introduced in dBASE III. In dBASE II, for example, if
information on a customer were separated into two files, the only way to print information from both files is to store the vital information to be printed in one file in
memory variables. You then switch work areas or USE a new file, find the proper
record, and then display all information, from both memory variables and fields. Or,
you could have linked two files that were indexed on the same field and selected information from the primary or secondary file. However, this awkwardness can be
avoided with Clipper and dBASE III by setting relations from one file into another.
Relations are those "hooks" which can tie two or more databases together based on
certain key fields. As the database pointer in the main or parent database moves, so
do the pointers in its children. Information from all files can be displayed without the
use of memory variables. Because of this connection, we say that the databases relate
to one another based on certain key elements, fields.

MEMORY VARIABLES

Under dBASE II, only 64 memory variables can be used at any one time. It may seem
impossible to use all 64 memory variables, yet it happens. As our applications and
sophistication grew, so did the number of memory variables used. Eventually, all 64
variables were assigned and used. The two ways around this problem were to save
some or all of those variables to a temporary memory file on disk and restore them
later, or to join a couple of variables together, especially string variables, and parse
them out at the time needed. Indeed, there is a limit to the number of memory variables based on the amount of available memory on the machine running your application. With Clipper, the number of memory variables allowed may be as great as 2,048.
It is highly doubtful that an application will ever need more than 2,048 variables.

With the Autumn '86 release of Clipper, memory variables longer than 255 bytes may
be saved to a .MEM file.

CLEAR GETS

This command, which normally is placed immediately after a READ command, com-
pletes the READ and clears all GETS, preparing the system for the next set of
@...SAY/GET. Under the compiler, no CLEAR GETS command is necessary; the
READ command will clear out all GETs before the next set.

Using CLEAR GETS can be useful, although it is not necessary after a READ command. The CLEAR GETS command can highlight variable input. Below is a piece of

code using the CLEAR GETS and READ commands. Go through the program at least twice and notice how the CLEAR GETS command affects the screen.

```
********************
* Name          CLEARGET.prg
* Date          March 22, 1986
* Notice        Copyright 1986, Stephen J. Straley
* Note          This program shows how CLEAR GETS works.
*
********************

STORE 0 TO a,b,c,d,e,f,g
DO WHILE .T.
   CLEAR
   SET DELIMITER OFF
   SET INTENSITY ON
   @ 3,10 SAY "Number of hours worked: " GET a PICT "##"
   @ 4,10 SAY "      Pay rate one hour: " GET b PICT "##.##"
   @ 5,10 SAY " Amount to be deducted: " GET c PICT "###.##"
   @ 6,10 SAY "            Federal Tax: " GET d PICT "###.##"
   @ 7,10 SAY "              State Tax: " GET e PICT "###.##"
   @ 8,10 SAY "              Local Tax: " GET f PICT "###.##"
   @ 9,10 SAY "          Amount of Pay: " GET g PICT "###.##"
   CLEAR GETS
   SET DELIMITER ON
   SET INTENSITY OFF
   @ 12,10 SAY "          How many hours worked? " GET a PICT "##"
   READ
   @ 13,10 SAY "What is the pay rate per hour? " GET b PICT "##.##"
   READ
   @ 14,10 SAY "How much extra to be deducted? " GET c PICT "###.##"
   READ
   @ 15,10 SAY "          What is the Federal Tax? " GET d PICT "###.##"
   READ
   @ 16,10 SAY "          What is the State Tax? " GET e PICT "###.##"
   READ
   @ 17,10 SAY "          What is the Local Tax? " GET f PICT "###.##"
   READ
   g = a * b - c - d - e - f
   STORE .T. TO loop
   @ 20,10 SAY "       Do you want to continue? " GET loop
   READ
   IF .NOT. loop
      EXIT
   ENDIF
ENDDO
* End of File
```

Notice that there is no READ before the first CLEAR GETS. To distinguish between prompt and variable, the DELIMITERS and INTENSITY are set to highlight all GETS without a DELIMITER on them. Therefore, in this sample, the prompts are displayed in one fashion, while the GETS are displayed (highlighted) in another. If the GETS were not CLEARED before the first READ, the prompt would wait for input by the user on the first GET. Since the first seven GETS are only being used for display purposes and not for input, the CLEAR GETS command is used to clear out those seven GETS and wait only for input on the eighth GET. In dBASE III, CLEAR GETS is also allowed; not so in the compiler!

TO SEEK OR TO FIND

One of the biggest misjudgments by the developers of dBASE II was in the implementation of the FIND. It was never really planned that things to be "found" would first be stored in a variable. It was assumed that it was the contents of the variable and not the variable's name that were being searched for. To get the concept to work under dBASE II, a macro symbol was needed in front of the variable so its contents, not the variable name, were searched for with the FIND command. In dBASE III and in the compiler, the implementation of the SEEK command was added. In Clipper the SEEK command is preferred over the use of the FIND command. The SEEK command automatically looks at the value (or contents) of the memory variable and searches for that in the database. The FIND command is now reserved strictly for the interpreted and interactive environment.

A NAME BY ANY OTHER NAME...

File names under the compiler must follow the following conventions:

1)   No hyphens are allowed in the name of the root file name.

2)   The file cannot begin with a character other than a letter.

3)   Program file extensions can only be either .PRG, or .FMT. (If using CLiP files, which will be explained later, .FMT is ignored.)

SUMMING IT UP

Other than these overt differences, the biggest difference between Clipper and dBASE II is in theory. Under the compiler, applications normally programmed in dBASE II would look and act totally different. The only way to get a better feel for this contrast is to look over some of the sample codes, the discussions on some of the unique features in the compiler, the sample applications and, ultimately, to practice!

CLIPPER and dBASE III

No list of the differences between dBASE III and Clipper can really be complete. Many of the important variations are very subtle and will only surface when practicing the basics in the compiled environment. As opposed to the obvious differences between Clipper and dBASE II, the differences here are more in theory or practice. Keep in mind that while Clipper supports the syntax and basic structure of code of the dBASE III language, the environment is totally different.

What makes Clipper so powerful is that the compiler can take code running under the interpreter and make some logical, structured order of it, while allowing for a whole new branch of structured programming to flourish. This dual role allows for two totally different types of users: those individuals seeking to gain an improvement in performance and execution, and those looking for power beyond the limits of the interpreter. And what a difference! There will come a time for any developer to make a decision between the two environments. Clipper expands the realm of possibilities. The ideas and concepts of tomorrow may be programmed today. A good example of this is the left trim function (LTRIM()).

Prior to its implementation in Clipper (and later in dBASE III), there was a strong need for the left trim function (LTRIM()) in many applications. A user-defined function was the answer to the problem. There was no need to wait for the publishers to "get with it." Additionally, there were a few nice functions in dBASE III Plus, such as ABS(), MAX(), and MIN(), not supported in Clipper prior to the Autumn '86 version. With just a few creative functions and procedures, most of those commands were simulated in Clipper. The point is that old versions of the compiler can be just as useful as new versions and do not restrict creativity.

A decision must be made whether to use Clipper or dBASE III. With the power of Clipper, the possibilities are endless. It is far less complicated to code for one environment than for both. dBASE III allows for many faults whereas Clipper does not. Clipper is more structured and restrictive than dBASE III. All of this is true only because of the differences in the fundamental natures of the products. One is an interpreter, and one is a compiler. In the following chapters, one goal is to help you decide between the two products. dBASE III is meant for users wanting on-site query and on-the-fly report generating; Clipper is meant for programmers!

MEMORY VARIABLES

Clipper supports up to 2,048 active memory variables, while dBASE III can only support 256 active variables. Also, internal to Clipper, string memory variables can have a length of 32,000 bytes as opposed to 255 bytes for dBASE III. The point to keep in mind here is that while Clipper has this internal capacity, these variables cannot be saved directly to a memory file because Clipper maintains compatibility with dBASE

III memory files. Remember, dBASE III can only handle variables with a length of 255. In order for a string memory variable to be SAVEd to a memory file in Clipper, the string must be parsed out to separate memory variables, each with a length no greater than 255 bytes per string variable. When RESTORing from a memory file remember to concatenate all of the previously parsed variables into one memory variable which is the sum of all of the string variables involved.

```
********************
* Name         PARSE.prg
* Date         February 13, 1986
* Notice       Copyright 1986, Stephen J. Straley
* Note         This sample program will save a screen to
*              a memory variable, then parse that variable into
*              a few memory variables, then SAVE those variables to
*              a MEMORY FILE, RESTORE that file, and eventually,
*              flash the screen back.  To be used with the WINTER 85
*              version as well as earlier versions.
*
********************

STORE SPACE(4000) TO ascr
CALL _scrsave WITH ascr
FOR x = 1 TO 16
    temp = LTRIM(STR(x))
    ascr&temp = SUBSTR(ascr,(x-1)*250+1,250)
NEXT
RELEASE ascr
SAVE ALL LIKE ascr* TO Scrfile

NOTE > Now to restore from the file....

CLEAR
? "Now for the restoration...."
RESTORE FROM Scrfile
ascr = ""
FOR x = 1 TO 16
    temp = LTRIM(STR(x))
    ascr = ascr + ascr&temp
NEXT
WAIT
CALL _scrrest WITH ascr
a 23,00 SAY ""              && To reposition the cursor to the bottom of the screen
* End of File
```

With the Autumn '86 version of Clipper, you can save the screen memory variable directly to a .MEM file without having to parse it into many 255-byte memory variables. One thing to keep in mind is that this .MEM file cannot be looked at by dBASE III. If you should try and RESTORE a .MEM file in dBASE that has in it a memory variable longer than 255 bytes, the following error message will be displayed by dBASE III:

```
. RESTORE FROM Memory
Memory Variable file is invalid.
                    ?
RESTORE FROM Memory
    .
```

So for the sake of maintaining a sense of compatibility, you may opt to limit the size of your memory variables to 255 bytes with the newest version of Clipper.

FIELDS

Clipper allows 1024 fields per file while dBASE III allows only 256. This expansion must be carefully looked at for every application if maintaining compatibility is in any way a factor. Many times, databases can be consolidated by taking advantage of the extra capacity. However, an incompatibility with dBASE III might be the net result. If you decide to take this step, be consistent and code your procedures, program files, and user defined functions for the compiler as well. It will serve no purpose to maintain compatible *code* between dBASE III and Clipper while the *databases* are incompatible.

Another feature of fields in Clipper is an extended capacity in the length of a character field. The compiler will support a character field length of over 32,000 bytes whereas dBASE III will only support 255 byte-long character fields. Again, look at the application closely to see if using this added feature will be an advantage or a nightmare. A quick example of an advantageous situation would be the following:

Let us say a compiled system would generate a series of variables to be saved from the application. In an accounting system, these values might be the last check number printed, the posting account number for the package, and other system-wide information. Saving these variables to a memory file would mean that the file could be accessed and modified from dBASE III. In order to avoid this, there is the other option of saving the variables to a temporary database. The problem with this approach is that dBASE III could have access to the information, thus allowing it to be modified at will when it should be left alone.

A solution to this problem would be to create a one-character field database which would have a length of 255 bytes. Now the trick is to parse all of the important information in one long character string and replace the character *field* with the character *string*. Since the developer would know the length of each piece of information, it could all be saved together as one. When executing the application, the program would have to take the database, look at the field, and separate out the important information into separate memory variables. The advantage to this solution is that the information would be saved according to changes dictated by the system. dBASE III cannot be used to modify any of the information because the expanded character field cannot be read by the interpreter.

So you see, incompatibility may or may not be a disadvantage. It all depends upon your specific need. Look over your situation carefully and choose wisely!

INDEX FILES

At the outset, let me state clearly that index files made under Clipper are totally incompatible with dBASE III, and index files made under DBASE III are incompatible with Clipper.

There is no limit in Clipper to the number of index files you can have open on a file at one time. Under dBASE III, the limit is 7 index files per database file. While Clipper has no limit, DOS is still restricted to 20 files open at one time. If you were to allow for the standard 5 files for the operating system and one for the application or program itself, and one more for the database, that would leave 13 possible files that can be opened at one time. Below is an example of this in action. Included is a structure for the database we are using in this example. Add data and note that the last index is updated with the rest.

For this example, we will use a database named MULTY.DBF:

```
Structure for database: C:MULTY.dbf    Number of data records:   0
Date of last update     : 07/03/86

Field  Field Name  Type       Width   Dec
    1  FIRST_NAME  Character     20
    2  LAST_NAME   Character     20
    3  INITIALS    Character      3
    4  SERIAL_NO   Numeric        8
    5  PURCHASED   Date           8
    6  COMPANY     Character     30
    7  CITY        Character     25
    8  STATE       Character      2
    9  PHONE       Character     10
```

```
********************
* Name       SAMPINDX.prg
* Date       MAY 19, 1986
* Notice     Copyright 1986, Stephen J. Straley
* Note       This demonstrates how the indexes are updated,
*            when there are more than 7 index files
*            open at the same time.  The name of the database
*            is MULTY.DBF
*
********************

USE Multy
? "Test one"
INDEX ON initials TO Multy1
? "Test two"
```

```
INDEX ON serial_no TO Multy2
? "Test three"
INDEX ON purchased TO Multy3
? "Test four"
INDEX ON first_name TO Multy4
? "Test five"
INDEX ON company TO Multy5
? "Test six"
INDEX ON city TO Multy6
? "Test seven"
INDEX ON state TO Multy7
? "Test eight"
INDEX ON phone TO Multy8
? "Test nine"
INDEX ON last_name TO Multy9
? "Now opening them all"
USE Multy INDEX Multy1, Multy2, Multy3, Multy4, Multy5, Multy6, Multy7,
Multy8, Multy9
CLEAR
TEXT

    Try putting in at least three entries and pay strict attention to
    the last name.  Try putting the last names out of order, like a
    "T" record before a "J" record and before a "B" record.  This sample
    program would list the records in order of the last name, yet
    the last name index was the 9th open index file.

ENDTEXT
WAIT
CLEAR
DO WHILE .T.
   STORE "Y" TO cont
   CLEAR
   @ 5,5 SAY "Continue? " GET cont
   READ
   IF UPPER(cont) = "N"
      EXIT
   ENDIF
   CLEAR

   APPEND BLANK
   @  5, 5 SAY "Initials   " GET initials
   @  6, 5 SAY "Serial No  " GET serial_no
   @  7, 5 SAY "Purchased  " GET purchased
   @  8, 5 SAY "First Name " GET first_name
   @  9, 5 SAY "Company    " GET company
   @ 10, 5 SAY "City       " GET city
   @ 11, 5 SAY "State      " GET state
   @ 12, 5 SAY "Phone      " GET phone
   @ 13, 5 SAY "Last Name  " GET last_name
   READ
ENDDO
CLEAR
```

```
USE Multy INDEX Multy9
LIST last_name
* End of File
```

In addition to the differences with the extension defaults (.NDX for dBASE III index files and .NTX for Clipper index files), there are other differences as well.

There are two basic reasons why the index file structure under Clipper is different from dBASE III's index file structure:

1) Under dBASE III, pages (see the explanation of pages below) may be lost during certain update operations (i.e. replacing key fields); in addition empty pages may take space without function.

2) Under dBASE III, pages are allocated and, upon change, the entire page is moved. Under the compiler, a page has an accompanying table, which is in essence a mini-index, and the table is updated accordingly.

Now, let's look at the implications of this.

The first problem to overcome is to make certain that updates to the key would not corrupt the index file, especially as the file size increased. Second, the dBASE III indexing in multiples of four with SET EXACT ON was looked at seriously and circumvented with a new algorithm. This last problem is known by all dBASE III users who have fallen into this trap. More important than these basic underlying reasons was the issue of speed and how to handle it. What came about was an improved algorithm, but before explaining how the new algorithm is used by the compiler, let us look at how indexes are viewed under the interpreter.

In dBASE III, the basic construct of an index is held in what is commonly referred to as a *page*. This is no more than a 256-byte block of memory that the interpreter will look at one time to analyze. Now, let us say that we have two keys, the first being X in size and a second larger one, Y in size. On the first pass, the key is updated and X is placed into a page. Since it is the first key, it is very simple to enter. When we come to the second pass, we see that Y is in front of X. A complete shift takes place while a temporary page is established for Y and a final page is established consisting of Y in front of X (note the diagram):

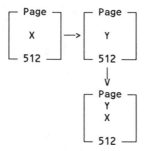

What transpires is the movement of the pages in memory and the creation of an extra page which is left dangling. The first level of pages serves no use, for all intents and purposes, since it is the second level page that contains the actual index order. This constant shifting and managing of the pages of memory will have two effects:

1) Large index files with huge amounts of repetitively indexed data become astronomical in size.

2) Indexing is slow as the pages are adjusted. Memory is not used efficiently.

With the development of dBASE III Plus, the indexing scheme remained the same with one minor twist: the buffering techniques were changed to allow more memory (up to 640K of RAM) to be used by the indexing algorithm. Since indexing on machines with larger memories can now be accomplished entirely in RAM memory, the operation is relatively quick. Unfortunately, there is **no** increase in speed on those machines with less available memory!

Incidentally, very few applications do nothing but indexing; for example, screen formatting, printer output, and calculations are common parts of programs. So if the entire RAM is used for indexing, applications using other commands will slow down as buffers are flushed and the definitions of the commands are loaded into memory.

With the preceding information in mind, let us look at the algorithm the compiler employs.

Clipper also has pages. However, these pages are larger than those in dBASE III. A page of memory is 1024 bytes, or 1K. This will allow a larger amount to be viewed at one time, which is one way of being more efficient. Additionally, the page is broken up into two parts: a *front half* and a *back half*. The front half is basically a mini-index routine. It is a series of pointers, or a table of pointers, indicating the order of the keys inside of the page itself. The back half of the page actually holds the key of the index.

Using the same example as above, on the first pass key X and the header of the index file are analyzed, and it is determined that there is nothing in the file. Key X is placed in the back half of the page and the pointer in the front half is also updated. Now the second key, Y, is analyzed and compared to the first key, X. The size is also examined to ensure that it is still under one full page (otherwise an entire new page would be created). It is then placed behind the key in the back half of the page. However, the pointer to it is placed in front of the pointer of key X. Since pointers are smaller than keys, this change can take place within the page of memory, and not create a secondary page to hold the change. The keys are generally left alone and only the pointers are updated, as described, so indexing is faster, and memory is used more efficiently. This is most noticeable when large database and index keys are being updated constantly. The following diagram shows what transpires during this operation:

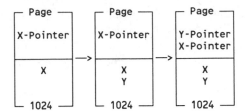

Note that the updating occurs entirely within a page of memory, indexing is rapid and space is used efficiently. The trick occurs at the moment of indexing. The algorithm links all of the different tables together, pointing to the various keys inside of the pages. The pointer in the header is the address point of the first index in the b-tree operation.

Below is a listing of the two headers of similar index files, the first being in Clipper and the second in dBASE III. The important things to note are the completely different header structure and the contents of the header.

CLIPPER index file:

```
C>debug clipper.ntx
-d
1D45:0100  06 00 01 00 00 04 00 00-00 00 00 00 12 00 0A 00  ...............
1D45:0110  00 00 32 00 19 00 6F 6E-65 00 00 00 00 00 00 00  ..2...one.......
1D45:0120  00 00 00 00 00 00 00 00-00 00 00 00 00 00 00 00  ...............
1D45:0130  00 00 00 00 00 00 00 00-00 00 00 00 00 00 00 00  ...............
1D45:0140  00 00 00 00 00 00 00 00-00 00 00 00 00 00 00 00  ...............
1D45:0150  00 00 00 00 00 00 00 00-00 00 00 00 00 00 00 00  ...............
1D45:0160  00 00 00 00 00 00 00 00-00 00 00 00 00 00 00 00  ...............
1D45:0170  00 00 00 00 00 00 00 00-00 00 00 00 00 00 00 00  ...............
-q
```

dBASE III index file:

```
C>debug dbase.ndx
-d
1D45:0100  01 00 00 00 02 00 00 00-00 00 00 00 0A 00 19 00  ...............
1D45:0110  00 00 14 00 00 00 00 00-6F 6E 65 20 00 73 00 FF  ........one.s..
1D45:0120  FF FF 2E 00 28 00 00 00-01 00 02 00 04 00 0D 01  ....(..........
1D45:0130  42 00 69 00 6F 00 73 00-0D 00 05 00 B4 00 08 00  B.i.o.s....4...
1D45:0140  00 00 00 01 00 00 02 00-00 00 41 63 6B 6E 6F 77  ..........Acknow
1D45:0150  6C 65 2E 00 28 00 00 00-01 00 02 00 0F 00 0D 01  le..(..........
1D45:0160  41 00 63 00 6B 00 6E 00-6F 00 77 00 6C 00 65 00  A.c.k.n.o.w.l.e.
1D45:0170  64 00 67 00 6D 00 65 00-6E 00 74 00 73 00 0D 00  d.g.m.e.n.t.s...
-Q
```

Immediately obvious is the initial byte. In the dBASE III index structure, the initial byte is set to 01 while in Clipper it is set to 06. Also note that the beginning byte containing the key expression for the index file is located at byte 25 in dBASE III and at byte 23 in Clipper. If these headers were to be displayed further, you could see that the beginning of the file would begin further down in the file in Clipper than in dBASE III. This is due to the larger page size being implemented.

RELATIONS

Unlike the interpreter which is limited to one relation per database file, Clipper will allow a series of relations to be established -- up to eight "children" relating to a single "parent." Only one parent file may be established at a given time. Relations are vital for cross-referencing and report generating. Listed below is a fragment which shows how possible multi-child relations can be established.

```
CLEAR
a 5,0,23,79 BOX "*"
a 7,5 SAY "One moment while all files are initialized"

file4 = "PRHIST"      && A History File
file3 = "PRCHECK"     && A Check File
file2 = "PREMPLOY"    && An Employee Master File
file1 = "PRTIME"      && A Timecard file


***********************************
* This section sets up all files *
***********************************

SELECT 4
USE &file4. INDEX Prhist_a
SELECT 3
USE &file3. INDEX Prchk_a.dat
ZAP
SELECT 2
USE &file2. INDEX Premp_a.dat
SELECT 1
USE &file1. INDEX Prtime_a.dat
SELECT 1
**************************************************************************
* This section adds the checks to be processed to the check file, based *
* completely on the number of timecards in the timecard file.           *
**************************************************************************
DO WHILE .NOT. EOF()
   a 21, 5 SAY "Now adding employee number " + TRIM(employee) + ;
   " to the check file"
   temp_emp = employee
   SELECT 3
   APPEND BLANK
   REPLACE employee WITH temp_emp
   SELECT 1
   SKIP
ENDDO
*********************************************************
* This section sets up final relation and then goes    *
* on to calculate both federal/state/and local taxes   *
*********************************************************

a 21, 5 SAY SPACE(73)
SELECT 3
```

```
GO TOP
SET RELATION TO employee INTO &file2., TO employee INTO &file1.

***********************************************
* Both files are indexed on employee as is *
* the parent file as well.                  *
***********************************************

@ 7, 5 SAY SPACE(73)

DO WHILE .NOT. EOF()

   ****************************************************************
   * Calculate base pay                                          *
   *    AMT_REG_P is set to salary rate (if a salary employee)   *
   *    else is set to the hourly rate X the number of           *
   *    straight hours worked                                    *
   ****************************************************************
   IF &file2.->salaried
      REPLACE amt_reg_p WITH &file2.->pay_rate_s
   ELSE
      REPLACE amt_reg_p WITH &file1.->stra_time * &file2.->pay_rate_h
   ENDIF

   *****************************************************************************
   * Calculate Overtime pay, Total Gross Pay, and Exempted Pay               *
   *                                                                         *
   * Temp_pay is first the hourly rate X the rate for overtime X the         *
   *    number of overtime hours worked.                                     *
   * Temp_pay is then added to hourly rate X the rate for double time        *
   *    X the number of double time hours worked.                            *
   * Temp_pay is finally added to the hourly rate X the rate for triple      *
   *    time X the number of triple time hours worked.                       *
   *    AMT_OVR_P is then set to Temp_pay                                     *
   *    AMT_VAC_P is set to the hourly pay rate X the rate for vacation time *
   *    X the number of vacation hours worked                                *
   *    AMT_SIC_P is set to the hourly pay rate X the hours of sick time     *
   *    AMT_GRO_P is set to the regular pay + the overtime pay + vacation    *
   *    pay + the sick pay                                                   *
   *    Temp_pay is then set to the tips + the bonus + any misc. pay -       *
   *    any gross pay deduction (master employee record)                     *
   *    AMT_TGR_P is set to the gross pay(AMT_GRO_P) + temp_pay(all else)     *
   *    AMT_EXP_P is set to the amount of exempted pay                       *
   *****************************************************************************

   temp_pay = &file2.->pay_rate_h * prover * &file1.->half_time
   temp_pay = temp_pay + &file2.->pay_rate_h * prdouble * &file1.->doub_time
   temp_pay = temp_pay + &file2.->pay_rate_h * prtriple * &file1.->trip_time
   REPLACE amt_ovr_p WITH temp_pay, amt_vac_p WITH &file2.->pay_rate_h *
prvaca * &file1.->vaca_time
   REPLACE amt_sic_p WITH &file2.->pay_rate_h * &file1.->sick_time
   REPLACE amt_gro_p WITH amt_reg_p + amt_ovr_p + amt_vac_p + amt_sic_p
   temp_pay = &file1.->tips + &file1.->bonus + &file1.->misc_pay -
&file>gross_pay
```

```
    REPLACE amt_tgr_p WITH amt_gro_p + temp_pay, amt_exp_p WITH &file1.-
>exem_pay
ENDDO
CLOSE DATABASES
```

In this sample fragment of code from a possible payroll section, everything is based on the contents of a check file. Based on related information in the employee master file and the employee's timecard file, the check will be cut. The concept is that relations are not only important for report generating (i.e., a database with the invoice header relating to a secondary database with the detail information or line item). Obtaining vital information for calculating purposes is just as important.

CUSTOMIZED HELP

An application in Clipper may be designed with a built-in help system. This feature can give dBASE III systems an extremely polished look and feel. If you take the viewpoint that manuals are never really read, then the on-line help feature may be a viable method to save time in document preparation and to provide an accessible reference. For further information, please refer to Chapter 13, Clipper's Help Utility.

USER DEFINED FUNCTIONS

Possibly the greatest feature of Clipper, the User Defined Functions (UDF's) enable the programmer to create, develop, expand, and manipulate data in just about any situation. UDF's allow the experienced programmer to develop features that may not be available in Clipper and to have the ability to implement new features immediately, without update fees or problems.

PROCEDURES AND PROCEDURE FILES

If it is not a function, it is a procedure. Being a compiler, Clipper treats programming in two lights: functions and procedures. Any operation that performs a **task** is considered by the compiler to be a *procedure*; anything that **returns a value** is a *function*. Keeping this in mind, program recursion is fully supported in Clipper. For further details, please refer to Chapter 8, Clipper Procedures.

NOTES FOR MEMOS AND STRINGS

Clipper has increased the functionality of memo fields and strings. Unlike the interpreter, a memo in Clipper may be edited on the entire screen or a portion of the screen. Indeed, under the compiler a memo can act like a memo: a note pad taking very little space on the screen, with a border as well. Under Clipper, strings may be treated and edited as memos as well.

MACRO SUBSTITUTION

An extensive effort was made to expand the use of macros in Clipper and their interface with the flow of any application. Some of the new advantages include the use of macros in a DO WHILE...ENDDO loop as well as the use of recursive macros. Clipper includes the standard uses for macros in the place of constants, variable names, literals, and most full expressions. However, one limitation of macros under Clipper is prohibition of the use of a macro in a command line. Since the compiler needs to know the full command at the time of compilation, macros must be avoided and the command must be spelled out. Significant cases are commas inside of a macro being used in conjunction with the LIST command, and full screen addressing completely in a macro. For further information on the differences, please refer to Chapter 11, Macros and Arrays.

ARRAYS AND MATRIXES

One of the most powerful tools of the Clipper language is its ability to handle arrays. This concept is totally new to the structure of the dBASE III language and is only available with the compiler. Equally useful is the ability to handle matrixes or multi-dimensional arrays, and macro substitution in conjunction with arrays.

INTERFACING WITH OTHER LANGUAGES

Another added feature of the compiler is the ability to interface with and use routines and modules written in other languages, such as Assembler and C.

CONTROL KEYS

The compiler contains an extended ability to SET specific keys depending upon their ASCII value, and to DO specific tasks, programs, functions or procedures. Not only is on-line help available, but with enhanced flexibility and control of the keyboard, entire applications can be organized and executed with minimal keystrokes.

MORE FUNCTIONS AND MORE COMMANDS

Appealing to the needs of many developers, the compiler adds several new functions which both speed up applications and make coding techniques extremely simple. Under the compiled environment, what might have taken numerous lines of code will now take just one or two. Along with additional functions are a few additional commands: CALL, BOX, SAVE SCREEN, FUL. TEXT, etc. All of these are designed with one intent: to expand the capabilities and capacity of the language.

SAVING SCREENS

Another added feature of the compiler is the capability of saving screens to memory variables, to temporary memory files, or even to databases. Menu drawing, which became very fast under the compiler, now can be virtually instantaneous.

CLIPPER VARIABLE

Clipper also can distinguish between variable dBASE III code (code which may contain commands not supported by the compiler) and Clipper code. When the PUBLIC variable CLIPPER is declared, it is considered to be *true* under the compiler, while under the interpretive environment it is considered *false*. Therefore, any code inside a logical test of the compiler (IF CLIPPER) will execute properly. Conversely, that same code would be ignored and the alternative code would be executed under the interpreter. This allows developers to code in parallel for both environments without maintaining two separately coded applications.

PARAMETER PASSING FROM DOS

Parameters can now be passed directly into an application from the operating system. With this flexibility, chaining a series of programs is within the realm of possibilities. In the Autumn '86 version of Clipper, you are allowed to pass more than just one parameter to a Clipper application from DOS.

BASIC CODING TECHNIQUES

This is the most difficult feature of the compiler to explain and understand but once you master it, many of the frustrations of working with an interpreter can be eliminated. Modular coding, expanded ideas, and program recursion are all features of the compiler. The main concept to grasp is that if it is possible, no matter how difficult, it is more feasible with the compiler than with the interpreter. Coding and programming with Clipper is an adventure into the world of possibilities!

DIFFERENCES

Along with the advantages of the compiler, the features **not** supported by the compiler should be understood. Most of these are not supported because by their nature they are better suited to an interpreter rather than a compiler. You will get a better understanding of this as we discuss the differences between a compiler and an interpreter. Suffice it to say that in many circumstances the interpreter takes care of a great many things for the programmer. Many times, these commands are really in control of the programmer, and not vice versa. A compiler is very literal and precise; an interpreter does just that—it interprets meaning and is placed between developer and code. Following is a list of those features not supported by Clipper. There are a few commands which have been simulated under the compiler's environment and are marked with an asterisk (*). They are discussed in Appendix F, Simulating dBASE III Commands.

ASSIST	HELP	BROWSE *	RETURN TO MASTER *
INSERT	SET	LIST STATUS	LIST STRUCTURE *
CREATE REPORT	CREATE LABEL	LIST MEMORY	DISPLAY STATUS
SET DEBUG	CHANGE	LIST FILES	DISPLAY STRUCTURE *
SET ECHO	SET HELP	DISPLAY FILES	DISPLAY MEMORY
SET MENU	SET STEP	MODIFY LABEL	MODIFY COMMAND
SET SAFETY	SET HEADING	MODIFY REPORT	MODIFY STRUCTURE
SET TALK	EDIT *		

In addition, there are many routines taken for granted in the interpreter that are not supported by the compiler. For example, one file might have a 1-byte *character* field that contains nothing but "Y" or "N". In comparison, a second database file might have a field with the same name as our character field, except its data type is *logical*. Let's set up a situation to copy from one file to the other. The code might look like this:

```
USE Two
APPEND FROM One
```

dBASE III's front end checks and handles the files as they are COPYing / APPEND-ing. The one character "Y" or "N" would be appended by dBASE III to the logical field (the same holds true for character fields which look like a date field). The interpreter will automatically handle the conversion to a date field. If we try to copy from one file to the other under the compiler, the following error message would be displayed on the screen:

```
proc:TEST line:2  Type conflict in REPLACE                QUIT? (Q/A/I)
```

These situations, if overlooked during coding, will cause problems during execution. The best advice when converting a system from dBASE III to Clipper is to rethink the mechanics of the system. Take the flow of the application to the very bare essence and work from there. Yes, it once worked in dBASE III, but that is not the reason for running with the compiler. Get a feeling for the constraints of the compiler and see if your code fits!

CLIPPER & dBASE III Plus

CHANGE IN HEADERS

When dBASE III Plus was released, there was an unexpected change in the structure of the header of database files. This obviously caused a great deal of consternation to Clipper users. However, the situation was resolved in the Winter '85 release and compatibility was restored. Below are headers of the dBASE III file and a dBASE III Plus file. The fourth byte was changed from a 16 to an 18. The result is a shift in position of records being displayed, reported, and even indexed. The solution is either to use the Winter '85 or later release of the compiler or use dBASE III to create the databases. Once created, the system will function as planned.

dBASE III Header:
```
C>debug dbase.dbf
-d
1D45:0100 03 56 03 16 00 00 00 00-42 00 0B 00 00 00 00 00 00  .V.....B.......
1D45:0110 00 00 00 00 00 00 00 00-00 00 00 00 00 00 00 00  ................
1D45:0120 4F 4E 45 00 00 00 00 00-00 00 00 43 00 00 00 00 00  ONE........C....
1D45:0130 0A 00 00 00 00 00 00 00-00 00 00 00 00 00 00 00  ................
1D45:0140 0D 00 1A EA 00 00 00 00-2E 8F 06 56 77 2E 8F 06  ...j.......Vw...
1D45:0150 58 77 E8 21 F0 EA 00 00-00 00 2E 8F 06 68 77 2E  Xwh!pj.......hw.
1D45:0160 8F 06 6A 77 E8 27 F0 EA-00 00 00 00 2E 8F 06 7A  ..jwh'pj.......z
1D45:0170 77 2E 8F 06 7C 77 E8 2D-F0 EA 00 00 00 00 2E 8F  w...|wh-pj......
-q
```

dBASE III Plus Header:
```
C>debug plus.dbf
-d
1D45:0100 03 56 03 18 00 00 00 00-41 00 0B 00 00 00 00 00 00  .V.....A.......
1D45:0110 00 00 00 00 00 00 00 00-00 00 00 00 00 00 00 00  ................
1D45:0120 54 48 52 45 45 00 00 00-00 00 00 43 00 00 00 00 00  THREE......C....
1D45:0130 0A 00 00 00 00 00 00 00-00 00 00 00 00 00 00 00  ................
1D45:0140 0D 1A 1A EA 00 00 00 00-2E 8F 06 56 77 2E 8F 06  ...j.......Vw...
1D45:0150 58 77 E8 21 F0 EA 00 00-00 00 2E 8F 06 68 77 2E  Xwh!pj.......hw.
1D45:0160 8F 06 6A 77 E8 27 F0 EA-00 00 00 00 2E 8F 06 7A  ..jwh'pj.......z
1D45:0170 77 2E 8F 06 7C 77 E8 2D-F0 EA 00 00 00 00 2E 8F  w...|wh-pj.....
```

Notice the value of the 9th byte. In dBASE III, the value is 42, yet in dBASE III Plus, the value is dropped by one position to 41. This is the shift in the header previously described.

SINGLE/USER ENVIRONMENT

While most of the additional commands were brought on by the advent of dBASE III Plus, the main thrust of that program is to provide a multi-user environment. An entire section of this text is devoted to the discussion of Clipper and the world of multi-user programs. However, the main thrust of this book is using the compiler for single-user applications.

dBASE and CLIPPER COMMANDS

As with all vital products, enhancements are continuously introduced for dBASE III. An important feature of Clipper is its ability to stay compatible with these enhancements and to provide continued support for the dBASE III language, regardless of the number of commands and functions already built in. Below is a list of commands in dBASE III and Clipper, and an indicator of how Clipper supports the commands, using the following key: not at all (N), fully support (F), available in extended routines (E), or may be simulated (S). The dBASE III + column identifies those commands supported by dBASE III Plus. The next four columns are for the Winter '85 release of Clipper and the last four are for the Autumn '86 release.

COMMAND	dBASE III+:	CLIPPER WINTER 1985 OPTIONS				CLIPPER AUTUMN 1986 OPTIONS			
		N:	F:	E:	S:	N:	F:	E:	S:
?	X		X				X		
??	X		X				X		
@CLEAR	X		X				X		
@GET	X		X				X		
@SAY	X		X				X		
@TO	X	X					X		
ACCEPT	X		X				X		
APPEND	X	X				X			
APPEND BLANK	X		X				X		
APPEND FROM	X		X				X		
ASSIST	X	X	X			X			
AVERAGE	X		X				X		
BROWSE	X				X			X	X
CALL	X		X				X		
CANCEL	X		X				X		
CHANGE	X	X				X			
CLEAR	X		X				X		
CLEAR ALL	X		X				X		
CLEAR FIELDS	X	X				X			
CLEAR GETS	X		X				X		
CLEAR MEMORY	X		X				X		
CLEAR TYPEAHEAD	X				X		X		
CLIPPER			X				X		
CLOSE	X		X				X		
CONTINUE	X		X				X		
COPY FILE	X		X				X		
COPY STRUCTURE	X		X				X		
COPY TO STRUCTURE EXTENDED	X		X				X		
COUNT	X		X				X		
CREATE	X		X				X		
CREATE LABEL				X					X

COMMAND	dBASE III+:	CLIPPER WINTER 1985 OPTIONS				CLIPPER AUTUMN 1986 OPTIONS			
		N:	F:	E:	S:	N:	F:	E:	S:
CREATE QUERY	X	X				X			
CREATE REPORT					X				X
CREATE SCREEN	X	X				X			
CREATE VIEW	X	X				X			
CREATE VIEW FROM ENVIRONMENT	X	X				X			
DELETE	X		X				X		
DECLARE			X				X		
DIR	X		X				X		
DISPLAY	X		X				X		
DISPLAY HISTORY	X	X				X			
DISPLAY MEMORY	X	X				X			
DISPLAY STATUS	X	X				X			
DISPLAY STRUCTURE	X				X				X
DO	X		X				X		
DO CASE	X		X				X		
DO WHILE	X		X				X		
EDIT	X				X				X
EJECT	X		X				X		
ERASE	X		X				X		
EXIT	X		X				X		
EXPORT	X	X				X			
EXTERNAL			X				X		
FIND	X		X				X		
GO	X		X				X		
HELP	X	X				X			
IF	X		X				X		
IMPORT	X	X				X			
INDEX ON	X		X				X		
INPUT	X		X				X		
INSERT	X	X				X			
JOIN	X		X				X		
KEYBOARD			X				X		
LABEL	X		X				X		
LIST	X		X				X		
LIST HISTORY	X	X				X			
LIST MEMORY	X	X				X			
LIST STATUS	X	X				X			
LIST STRUCTURE	X				X				X
LOAD	X	X				X			
LOCATE	X		X				X		
LOOP	X		X				X		
MENU TO			X				X		
MODIFY COMMAND	X	X				X			
MODIFY LABEL	X	X				X			
MODIFY QUERY	X	X				X			
MODIFY REPORT	X	X				X			
MODIFY SCREEN	X	X				X			
MODIFY STRUCTURE	X	X				X			
MODIFY VIEW	X	X				X			
NOTE	X		X				X		

COMMAND	dBASE III+:	CLIPPER WINTER 1985 OPTIONS N:	F:	E:	S:	CLIPPER AUTUMN 1986 OPTIONS N:	F:	E:	S:
ON ERROR / ESCAPE / KEY	X	X				X			
PACK	X		X				X		
PARAMETERS	X		X				X		
PRIVATE	X		X				X		
PROCEDURE	X		X				X		
PUBLIC	X		X				X		
QUIT	X		X				X		
READ	X		X				X		
RECALL	X		X				X		
REINDEX	X		X				X		
RELEASE	X		X				X		
RENAME	X		X				X		
REPLACE	X		X				X		
REPORT	X		X				X		
RESTORE	X		X				X		
RESTORE SCREEN			X				X		
RESUME	X	X				X			
RETRY	X	X				X			
RETURN	X		X				X		
RUN	X		X				X		
SAVE	X		X				X		
SAVE SCREEN			X				X		
SEEK	X		X				X		
SELECT	X		X				X		
SET	X		X				X		
SET ALTERNATE on/OFF	X		X				X		
SET ALTERNATE TO	X		X				X		
SET BELL ON/off	X		X				X		
SET CATALOG ON/off	X	X				X			
SET CATALOG TO	X	X				X			
SET CENTURY on/OFF	X	X					X		
SET COLOR ON/off	X	X				X			
SET COLOR TO	X		X				X		
SET CONFIRM on/OFF	X		X				X		
SET CONSOLE ON/off	X		X				X		
SET DATE	X			X			X		
SET DEBUG on/OFF	X	X				X			
SET DECIMALS TO	X		X				X		
SET DEFAULT TO	X		X				X		
SET DELETED on/OFF	X		X				X		
SET DELIMITERS on/OFF	X		X				X		
SET DELIMITERS TO	X		X				X		
SET DEVICE TO SCREEN	X		X				X		
SET DOHISTORY on/OFF	X	X				X			
SET ECHO on/OFF	X	X				X			
SET ESCAPE ON/off	X		X				X		
SET EXACT on/OFF	X		X				X		
SET EXCLUSIVE ON/off	X	X					X		
SET FIELDS ON/off	X	X				X			
SET FIELDS TO	X	X				X			
SET FILTER TO	X		X				X		

COMMAND	dBASE III+:	CLIPPER WINTER 1985 OPTIONS				CLIPPER AUTUMN 1986 OPTIONS			
		N:	F:	E:	S:	N:	F:	E:	S:
SET FIXED on/OFF	X		X				X		
SET FORMAT TO	X		X				X		
SET FUNCTION TO	X		X				X		
SET HEADING ON/off	X	X				X			
SET HELP ON/off	X	X				X			
SET HISTORY TO	X	X				X			
SET INDEX TO	X		X				X		
SET INTENSITY ON/off	X		X				X		
SET KEY TO			X				X		
SET MARGIN TO	X		X				X		
SET MEMOWIDTH TO	X	X				X			
SET MENUS ON/off	X	X				X			
SET MESSAGE TO			X				X		
SET ORDER TO	X	X					X		
SET PATH TO	X		X				X		
SET PRINT TO	X	X				X			
SET PRINT on/OFF	X		X				X		
SET PRINTER TO	X	X					X		
SET PROCEDURE TO	X		X				X		
SET RELATION TO	X		X				X		
SET SAFETY ON/off	X	X				X			
SET SCOREBOARD ON/off			X				X		
SET STATUS ON/off	X	X				X			
SET STEP on/OFF	X	X				X			
SET TALK ON/off	X	X				X			
SET TITLE ON/	X	X				X			
SET TYPEAHEAD TO	X	X				X			
SET UNIQUE on/OFF	X		X				X		
SET VIEW TO	X	X				X			
SKIP	X		X				X		
SORT	X		X				X		
STORE	X		X				X		
SUM	X		X				X		
SUSPEND	X	X				X			
TEXT	X		X				X		
TOTAL	X		X				X		
TYPE	X		X				X		
UNLOCK	X	X					X		
UPDATE	X		X				X		
USE	X		X				X		
USE...EXCLUSIVE	X	X					X		
WAIT	X		X				X		
ZAP	X		X				X		

FUNCTIONS	dBASE III+:	CLIPPER WINTER 1985 OPTIONS				CLIPPER AUTUMN 1986 OPTIONS			
		N:	F:	E:	S:	N:	F:	E:	S:
&	X		X				X		
&&	X		X				X		
ABS()	X				X		X		

FUNCTIONS	dBASE III+:	CLIPPER WINTER 1985 OPTIONS				CLIPPER AUTUMN 1986 OPTIONS			
		N:	F:	E:	S:	N:	F:	E:	S:
ALIAS()		X					X		
ASC()	X		X				X		
AT()	X		X				X		
CDOW()	X		X				X		
CHR()	X		X				X		
CMONTH()	X		X				X		
COL()	X		X				X		
DATE()	X		X				X		
DAY()	X		X				X		
DBF()	X				X				X
DELETED()	X		X				X		
DISKSPACE()	X				X				X
DOW()	X		X				X		
DTOC()	X		X				X		
DTOS()			X				X		
EMPTY()			X				X		
EOF()	X		X				X		
ERROR()	X	X				X			
EXP()	X	X				X			
FCOUNT()					X		X		
FIELD()	X	X				X			
FIELDNAME()			X				X		
FILE()	X		X				X		
FKLABEL()	X				X				X
FKMAX()	X				X				X
FLOCK()	X	X					X		
FOUND()			X				X		
GETENV()	X	X						X	
HARDCR()					X		X		
IIF()	X		X				X		
INDEXKEY()		X					X		
INKEY()	X		X				X		
INT()	X		X				X		
ISAPLHA()	X				X				X
ISCOLOR()	X				X				X
ISLOWER()	X				X				X
ISUPPER()	X				X				X
LASTKEY()			X				X		
LEFT()	X				X		X		
LEN()	X		X				X		
LOCK()	X	X					X		
LOG()	X		X				X		
LOWER()			Ä				X		
LTRIM()	X		X				X		
LUPDTE()	X				X			X	
MAX()	X				X		X		
MEMOEDIT()			X				X		
MEMOREAD()		X					X		
MEMORY(0)		X					X		
MEMOWRIT()		X					X		
MESSAGE()	X	X					X		

FUNCTIONS	dBASE III+:	CLIPPER WINTER 1985 OPTIONS				CLIPPER AUTUMN 1986 OPTIONS			
		N:	F:	E:	S:	N:	F:	E:	S:
MIN()	X				X		X		
MOD()	X				X				X
MONTH()	X		X				X		
NDX()	X				X				X
NETERR()	X	X					X		
NETNAME()	X	X					X		
OS()	X				X				X
PCOL()	X		X				X		
PCOUNT()		X					X		
PROCLINE()			X				X		
PROCNAME()	X						X		
PROW()	X		X				X		
READKEY()	X	X				X			
READVAR()			X				X		
RECCOUNT()	X								
LASTREC()			X				X		
RECNO()	X		X				X		
RECSIZE()	X				X			X	
REPLICATE()	X		X				X		
RIGHT()	X				X		X		
RLOCK()	X	X					X		
ROUND()	X		X				X		
ROW()	X		X				X		
RTRIM()	X	X					X		
SECONDS()			X				X		
SELECT()			X				X		
SETPRC()		X					X		
SPACE()	X		X				X		
SQRT()	X		X				X		
STR()	X		X				X		
STUFF()	X				X				X
SUBSTR()	X		X				X		
TIME()	X		X				X		
TRANSFORM()	X		X				X		
TRIM()	X		X				X		
TYPE()	X		X				X		
UPDATED()			X				X		
UPPER()	X		X				X		
VAL()	X		X				X		
VERSION()	X				X				X
WORD()			X				X		
YEAR()	X		X				X		

Most of these commands and functions were introduced in either dBASE II or in dBASE III. However, there are a few that are new in dBASE III Plus. As dBASE III Plus becomes more established in the market, more and more routines will be developed in Clipper to support it. The point here is that the change is easy and can be simulated with any version of the compiler.

RESERVED WORDS IN CLIPPER

Like most languages or compilers, Clipper has a list of reserved words. Using these words may produce strange results in your applications. Therefore, avoid using these words either for memory variables, function names, file names, or even procedure names. In addition, the underscore character "_" is not allowed as the beginning character of a variable, function, or procedure name.

$START$	CXNDPB	FOPEN	MOVMEM	STPBLK
	CXNDPH	FORKL		STPCHR
ALLMEM	CXNDPL	FORKLP	OPEN	STPCPY
ATOF	CXNM8	FORKV		STRCAT
	CXS55	FORKVP	POW	STRCMP
BDOS	CXS88	FREOPEN	POW2	STRCPY
BLDMEM	CXS_55	FREXP		STRCSPN
	CXT5		RBRK	STRLEN
CLOSE	CXV05	GETENV	READ	STRNCAT
CREAT	CXV25	GETMEM	REMOVE	STRNCMP
CXA38	CXV52	GETML	RENAME	STRNCPY
CXA55	CXV53		RLSMEM	STRSPN
CXA_55	CXV54	HEADER*	RLSML	STSCMP
CXC33	CXV83		RSTMEM	SYSTEM
CXC55	CXVDF	IEXEC		
CXC88	CXVFD		SBRK	UNLINK
CXC_55	CXV_45	LDEXP	SETMEM	
CXD33	CXV_54	LOG	SIZMEM	WAIT
CXFNM4	ERRNO	LOG10	SORT	WINTER85
CXFNM5	EXCEPT	LSBRK	STBCPY	WRITE
CXFXT4	EXIT	LSEEK	STCCPY	
CXFXT5	EXP		STCI_D	
CXM33		MATHERR	STCIS	XCEXIT
CXM55	FABS	MKEXT	STCISN	XCOVF
CXM_55	FCLOSE	MKNAME	STCI_D	
CXN5	FMOD	MODF	STCU_D	

* reserved word in Autumn '86 version

CLIPPER AND THE REST OF THE WORLD

With the entire computer industry constantly changing, it is extremely difficult to predict future developments. Those in the industry appear to belong to one of two groups: the 20 percent group which is comfortable with new ideas and new technologies, and the 80 percent group which waits to see what IBM does. The scenario has been and probably always will be the same. The problem is that the two groups are never completely in sync with each other. However, there are those rare instances when a product or a group of products seem to bridge the gap between the two. Clipper is one such product. While it establishes a new approach to database management practice on microcomputers, it is compatible with the current standards (dBASE III and IBM) yet at the same time looks towards the future by interfacing with Lattice C and the UNIX operating system.

Some of the old conceptions of what a database manager should and should not be do not apply to Clipper. In the industry there are often simple solutions to many problems. But what about the future, other languages, other capabilities? After all, the entire world does not program in dBASE III alone.

To allow for this, any routine which is supported by Lattice C, version 2.15 may be linked directly into the program with very little effort. Most of the C library is contained in the compiler's library; it becomes simply a question of addressing those routines. This also explains some of the capabilities of the compiler. In many instances it acts like dBASE III; in many more it acts like C. Second, the compiler can work with those ASSEMBLY routines which do many things including invoking direct interrupts, manipulating buffers and screen I/O, as well as locking records and files. Many developers who know the operating system/machine specific to their needs can program these tools to coexist with their applications. It is practical to have those routines interact with Clipper routines. Because of the advent of the CALL command (which dBASE III Plus enabled), these approaches are now possible.

Many programmers now use the C language. To have the flexibility to use such a language for many machine level tasks while programming in Clipper makes for a very bright and profitable future!

WORD PROCESSING VS. TEXT EDITING

Many programs are written in dBASE III's pseudo (MODIFY COMMAND) text editor. With this editor, problems will occur with lines longer than one screen. DBASE III has a tendency to place a soft carriage return marker (CHR(141)) in the file, which will really confuse Clipper when compiling.

Regardless of the reason, almost all word-processors and dBASE III's editor should **not** be used for programming in Clipper! Use programming specific text editors such as Pmate, EDIX, Norton's Editor, EC, XyWrite, BRIEF, and WordStar in the non-document mode. Avoid using RAM resident editors such as Popcorn and SideKick.

CHAPTER TWO

Compiling

EXAMINING CLIPPER AS A COMPILER

To help us understand compilers, let's start with some definitions:

Compiler: A programming routine that enables a computer to convert a pro-
              gram expressed in pseudo-code language into machine language, or
              another pseudo-code language for later translation.

Compilation: The end results of a compile.

Pseudo-Code: A program requiring a conversion of code for use by the computer.
              This code is independent of the hardware; it is also called symbolic
              code.

Now for a more practical interpretation of the definitions:

A compiler is a program, such as dBASE III, WordStar, or Lotus 1-2-3. Each of these
can also be called a *programming routine*. Clipper is indeed a programming routine,
but what does it do? According to the definition, a compiler allows the computer to
"convert a program expressed in pseudo-code into machine language." For example,
dBASE III programs are written in a form of pseudo-code. They are text files that
need to be translated to a language the computer can understand before they can be
run. A compiler takes the files containing pseudo-code and translates those instructions into machine language. There are several theories on compilers. Here is a brief
overview relevant to the Clipper compiler.

Clipper is a *two-pass* compiler. The first pass generates *tokens*, and the second pass
generates *code*. A *token* is a logical symbol generated by the compiler for a logical
group or entity. It consists of one or more lines of code (e.g. a STORE command, a
FOR...NEXT command, etc.). These symbols can be more easily understood by Clipper than a line of code.

Think of the first pass as a scan for code which can be interpreted all at one time. A
STORE command is simple and can be symbolically represented with one token.
Similarly, a simple counting FOR...NEXT loop, consisting of four or five lines, may be
represented by a single token. Compilers, in theory, act like people. There is only so
much information we can process at one time. In our thought process we break things
down automatically into logical chunks of information that we know we can process at
one time. This does not mean that we have processed the information, just that we
have broken it down to be processed. To us these breaks may be represented by
sentences, paragraphs, or even pages, but to the compiler, the breaks are represented
by a symbol or a token.

The second pass is the code-generating pass. On this pass the compiler will actually make a secondary file containing machine language code representing the pseudo-code it was fed. The compiler then refers to the tokens generated by the first pass and begins to break up the code logically for the second pass. If there is a token which is not understood, an error occurs. What happens then is that the second pass is out-of-sync with the first pass (or the tokens). This out-of-sync condition is known as a *phase error*. This is like threading a motion picture projector with film that has torn holes on one side. One side of the film might slip. Eventually the two sides will not be parallel. If enough tension is placed on the film itself, a rip will occur. That rip is comparable to a phase error. We will discuss solutions to this in later sections of this book.

As we said, dBASE III programs are a form of "pseudo-code." The compiler translates words or commands into a code that the computer can understand directly ("machine language"). How is that any different from dBASE III? The difference between Clipper and dBASE III is that dBASE III does this with an *interpreter*.

Interpreter: A program that translates a stored program expressed in pseudo-code into machine language and performs the operations as they are translated.

dBASE III translates programs into a language the computer can understand and **performs the operations as they are translated**. This is a clear case where more is **not** better. With an interpreter, code is read, translated, and executed one line at a time, resulting in a direct one-to-one relationship for every line of code. A compiler, on the other hand, prepares code to be executed later. It translates the code for the machine.

Think of a human interpreter and what happens in a typical scenario. The interpreter listens to what is being said, translates it into a different language, then conveys the same thoughts in the second language. This is a slow and cumbersome process. Consider how much faster the communication process would be if, instead of needing an interpreter, you were able to speak directly in another language.

Let us set up an example of code and see how the differences between compiling and interpreting are magnified. Consider the following fragment:

```
STORE 1 TO looping
DO WHILE looping <= 500
   @ 10,10 SAY looping
   STORE looping + 1 TO looping
ENDDO
```

The compiler would take these six lines of code and make an equivalent set of machine language instructions. These instructions would tell the computer to display a variable 500 times, incrementing it by 1 each time at a certain position on the screen. However, the interpreter works differently. On the first pass the interpreter reads every line and acts accordingly. Finally, when it finishes the first pass and gets to the

"ENDDO" command, it loops back to the beginning of the "DO WHILE..." command, rereads it, evaluates the expression and then proceeds. From here, the interpreter would then read the next two lines **again**, translate and perform them, and then continue. Have any of these lines been changed? No! So why is there a need to REREAD them? There is no reason. What were six lines of simple code have suddenly grown to 2002 lines of code. (We get 2002 lines this way: The basic format of the loop consists of 4 lines. Multiply this by 499, the number of repetitions after the initial pass, and the result is 1996. Add the first six lines of code to 1996 and we have 2002.)

The compiler is more efficient. The translation of pseudo-code to machine code is the same as with interpreting. However, compiling a program is only half the process necessary to make a program file in dBASE III run without the aid of an interpreter. The next step is called LINKING.

The compiler takes the words in a dBASE III application and makes a secondary file with an .OBJ extension (better known as an object file) which consists of the now converted machine language words. Think of a dictionary for a moment. Every dictionary entry has basically two parts: the first is the listing of the word and the second is the corresponding definition of that word. The object file is no more than the listing of the word, the first part of the dictionary with the spellings, the pronunciations, and the etymologies. These words do not "do" anything; they are just ordered and translated into a common language that the computer can understand.

The other half of our dictionary entry, the half containing what the words mean, must be added to the words in order to get them to perform properly. The definitions for all of the dBASE III words are grouped together in what is called a library file (a file with a .LIB extension). In order to function properly, these words need to be tied together or *linked* with their appropriate definitions located in the Clipper library file. This is the purpose of a linker and is further discussed in Chapter 3. Remember that while a compiler condenses code to a level understood by the computer, this is only half of the necessary operation. The compilation must be linked to the proper definitions found in a library file. A linker and a library file are vital.

COMPILING WITH CLIPPER

There are certain things we need to cover specifically regarding the Clipper compiler. The Clipper compiler is a true compiler. However, it reflects certain aspects which are unique to the dBASE III language and certain rules about compiling with Clipper may not be applicable to other compilers. First, think like a compiler. The error checking routines prominent in an interpreter are not present, so the control of the process is the responsibility of the developer or programmer. The code is going to be translated to its literal value at the time of compilation. The compiler will not look at values of variables and understand those values to mean "bring in this definition from the library when I link." It does not work like that. A good example of this would be the following:

```
STORE "@ 2,3 SAY 'Hello there..'" TO prompt
&prompt
```

That line will work with the interpreter but **not** with the compiler. The compiler does not interpret the meaning of the variable PROMPT when it is translating your code. All that the compiler will do is set up an address point labeled "prompt" to hold a certain value at the time of execution. The compiler library knows to move a certain value into that address because you specifically told it to with the STORE command. However, on the second line there is no command, just a macro. The compiler translates this line of code to expand the macro at the time of execution. It does not know that an "@ SAY...GET..." command will be executed so it does not pull that routine from the library into your executable file. Your application will not run as it did before, due to the differences between the interpreter (which allows for these programming maneuvers) and the compiler (which does not).

Let's look at another example, one in which we wish to branch off from a main menu to go to sub-menus with the branching choice made by the user. Many times program names are generic root names with numbers attached to them in order to have them correspond to the options chosen by the users. Here is some sample code:

```
@ 20,15 SAY "Enter Choice: " GET option PICT "9"
READ
DO Submenu&option
```

This is a perfectly legitimate command in both dBASE III and Clipper, but when compiling these three lines of code, we must think like a compiler and not rely on the interpreter. This will probably compile and link properly, but when you execute those lines of code you will receive an error message. Why? Again, the macro is not interpreted when it is being compiled. Therefore it does not tell the compiler to go out to the disk drive and look for and compile all of the possible options obtained from the macro. In other words, the compiler will not assume you want to have programs "SUBMENU1", "SUBMENU2", "SUBMENU3" and "SUBMENU4" compiled. You must think ahead and compile those programs yourself (using CLiP files which we will discuss in the next sections) and link them into your main file with the Clipper library. There are certain guidelines we must follow in order to have our applications compile, link, and execute properly.

Another consideration in using the Clipper compiler is the use of names for program files and procedures. The same routine for field verification and validity is used for files as for fields. That's why file and procedure names can't contain hyphens or start with numbers. Fields can't have them and neither can files! Make file names describe the operation with clear labels. The same is true for procedures and functions. If a symbol for separation is required or desired, then use the underscore and avoid the hyphen. Finally, if numbers are also needed, put them closer to the end of the routine's name. Whatever technique you use, **be consistent**.

CLIPPER SWITCHES

Let's take a look at the switches available with the compiler, what they do and how they are activated. Be careful when compiling these switches, especially the -n and the -l options. Do not mix object files which were compiled with a particular switch with other object files which were not. Also be very careful never to mix object files compiled with different compiler versions. People tend to forget to recompile all of their files when updating from one Clipper version to the next. The result is that they forget some object files and don't realize the mistake until the program hangs.

Switches:

    -n   Enhanced Native Code
    -l   No Line Numbers
    -s   Syntax Check on Program Source

When using switches make sure that you use lower case rather than upper case letters. If you use upper case letters, the compiler will tell you there was an illegal switch call, ignore it, and compile as if no switch had been called. Furthermore, use the switches **after** the name of the program being compiled, or **after** the name of the CLiP file being compiled. Also, if more than one switch is desired, chain the letters together or separate each switch with an additional space and hyphen like this:

                    C>Clipper Myfile -n -l
or
                    C>Clipper Myfile -nl
or (for CLiP files)
                    C>Clipper @Myfile -n

Using the **-s** switch tells the compiler to go through the file(s) mentioned and check for syntax problems. All illegal syntax is flagged just as if you were trying to compile without the switch. The only difference is that the compiler **will not** generate object code. This saves time because the second pass through your application is totally avoided.

The second switch is the **-l** option or the line number switch. Using this switch will strip the reference bits for line numbers associated with your source code. This will lower the size of the object file by 3 bytes per source line.

Finally, the **-n** option switch stands for the enhanced native code option. Using this feature, Clipper will compile true native code, optimizing your application. The net results will slightly increase the size of the object files as well as increase the final execution speed of the application. For most applications, this option is not necessary. This option is somewhat beneficial when developing test programs and small utility programs.

ERROR MESSAGES

Errors can and will occur, especially with large applications. It can be frustrating to sit in front of a screen and jot down every error spotted by the compiler. Depending on the nature of the error, in most cases the type of error or problem must be noted as well as the line number and module in which the error occurred. These notes would then be referenced when fixing the program errors. Magnify this routine a hundredfold for large applications. Taking notes manually is not efficient. Let the computer do the work for you! Port the errors out to an alternate file by using the DOS switch, the greater than sign (>). Using this switch in conjunction with the Clipper compiler will redirect all error messages to a disk file with the name you give it. An example of this would be as follows:

```
C>Clipper Myfile > Errors.lst
```

The compiler is called up, the source code read in, and if any compiler errors are found, they are redirected to a file called "ERRORS.LST." This file can then be printed or viewed on the screen. With some text editors which provide split screen editing, the trouble spots can be on the screen at the same time as the source code. Use whatever tools are available to you, including your operating system, in order to save time and energy!

COMMON PROBLEMS

Below are listed some common problems that occur when trying to compile either a small program or a large application using Clipper. Each problem is defined and followed by a brief explanation and the way to solve the problem, if any exists. Use these solutions when you are trying to compile your own programs.

Command Syntax In Macros

Unlike dBASE III, any statement that would be considered part of the syntactical structure of the command will not work in a macro under Clipper. A good example is the following:

```
STORE "@ 5,10 SAY 'Hello Federal...'" TO command
&command
```

The compiler does not evaluate the macro at the time of compilation. A compiler error would point to the macro and would look like the following:

```
^ ASSIGNMENT error
```

Instead, place the '@ 5,10 SAY' literally in the file for the compiler to see and to compile. So now the command lines read:

```
      STORE "Hello world..." TO command
      a 5,10 SAY command
```

Another error with macros is trying to put commas in the macro, especially if a field listed is being generated. An example is:

```
      STORE "field_one, field_two, field_three" TO listing
      LIST &listing
```

Under Clipper, these lines would indeed compile and link with no apparent problems. When you try to run it, however, you would only get the listing of "field_one" -- the other fields would be lost. Again, since the macro is not being evaluated (interpreted) at the time of the compilation, it does not know whether to allow for one field or two fields, let alone three fields. Since the commas are viewed as part of the command syntax of the command line, problems will arise if you are trying to do this sort of statement. Solutions for this problem are either to replace the commas with plus signs or store the name of each field to be listed to its own separate variable or macro. For the latter option, if there are three fields to be listed, there must be three separate macros. The command would look like this:

```
      STORE "field_one" TO list_one
      STORE "field_two" TO list_two
      STORE "field_three" TO list_three
      LIST &list_one., &list_two., &list_three
```

Using the Nantucket Batch File to Compile

A batch file was provided with the compiler and quite often people use this batch file to get their .PRG files turned into .EXE files. Often, a problem arises with its use. When the batch file is called with the file name of the application along with the .PRG extension, problems occur such as in the following:

```
C>CL keys.prg
The Clipper Compiler, Winter '85
Copyright (c) 1985, 1986 Nantucket Inc., All Rights Reserved.

Compiling KEYS.PRG
Code size:177        Symbols:80            Constants:224

C>plink86 FI keys.prg
PSA Linkage Editor (Nantucket Clipper) Version 1.46.c
Copyright (C) 1984 by Phoenix Software Associates Ltd.

Warning 7:    Unknown record type 2A in File KEYS.PRG

Fatal error 41
Premature end of file at offset 5422 in File KEYS.PRG

C>
```

Does it look familiar? Even the words "fatal error" sound so dreadful and final. Nevertheless, all is not lost. The problem here is not with the compiler, but with the way the batch file works with the linker. Notice that Clipper compiled the program with no errors and produced a code size message which means that an object file was indeed generated.

Take a look at the line where the linker is being called. Notice that the file name is passed to the linker exactly as it was passed to the batch file, including the .PRG extension. That is the problem. Clipper will always assume you are initially trying to compile a .PRG file; it does not need to be passed that extension by the batch file and it will ignore it. However, the linker assumes it is getting a file with a .OBJ extension (which is what Clipper will produce after a successful compilation). The problem is that the batch file is passing the .PRG extension to the linker and the linker is trying to link your ordinary text file with the library of machine language routines. You can see why this is indeed a fatal error.

To get rid of this problem, just remove the .PRG extension when using the batch file to compile and to link your applications.

External Programs Needed but NOT Compiled

Consider the following piece of code:

```
STORE "0" TO choice
@ 10,10 SAY "<1> Enter Transaction"
@ 11,10 SAY "<2> Edit Transaction"
@ 12,10 SAY "<3> Scan Transaction"
@ 13,10 SAY "<4> Delete Transaction"
@ 14,10 SAY "What is Choice? " GET choice PICT "9" VALID(choice $"1234")
READ
DO Trans&choice
```

Here is an example of a macro not being evaluated during the compiling process. Clipper will not know from the last command line to go out to the disk and compile "Trans1.prg", "Trans2.prg", "Trans3.prg" and "Trans4.prg" with your application. You will have to compile those four programs separately and link them to your main files; otherwise, you will assuredly get an error message when you run the program.

Another problem occurs when utilizing on-line help with a program file called HELP.PRG. Since this file is called by striking the F1 key and not by a direct DO command, Clipper will not know to compile it with your application. Program files containing nothing but user-defined functions also fall into the category of being needed and being referenced but not compiled and, worse yet, not linked.

The only way to avoid these situations is to plan ahead! If HELP.PRG is referenced, if a function in a user-defined function file is called, or if a macro can call a program/procedure file at any time, those files **must** be compiled and linked with your application.

Phase Errors

This is the most difficult error to explain. Clipper makes two passes through a file. The first pass translates commands into tokens. The second pass uses those tokens to generate appropriate machine code. A phase error occurs when the tokens generated on the first pass are not understood by the code generated on the second pass. This can be quite confusing because many things may cause this problem ranging from bad memory chips to high-bit graphic characters in a program file. In either case check for the following conditions:

1.   Remove any RAM-resident programs when compiling.

2.   Check your computer's expansion boards.

3.   Avoid using word-processors which may leave high-bit characters in the file, specifically those used for word wrap and hyphen marking.

Symbol Redefinition Error

This problem occurs when a procedure file has the same name as a procedure within that file. Simply change the name of either the procedure file or the name of the procedure within that file and the error should go away.

Unbalanced Conditions

Many times the compiler will yield an error message "Unbalanced DO WHILE" or "Unbalanced ENDDO" when in fact all DO WHILEs and ENDDOs match up. Whenever this condition occurs, check not only for all DO WHILEs, but all IFs, DO CASEs and corresponding ENDDOs, ENDIFs, and ENDCASESs. All must match and must follow standard operating procedures. Because dBASE III is an interpreter and only holds roughly 1K worth of source code information, it is quite possible to have an unbalanced condition in dBASE III that still works. Clipper, however, will pick up on this and report it.

Mixing Clipper Switches

While this error occurs during the linking of your application (and is described in detail in Chapter 3), the problem is listed here because of the cause. If the enhanced native code option is chosen for some modules and not for others and these are linked together, a major catastrophe occurs. Choose a standard code option for your compilations and stick to it. A suggested approach is compiling all programs without any switch until they are completely developed and tested. Then recompile using the switches you want.

Using a Word Processor

As I said earlier, word processors can cause problems. Don't confuse a *word processor* with a *text editor*; there is a big difference. A text editor just edits text. With a word processor, text files are normally formatted for output to the printer, including wraparounds, soft carriage returns, bold-facing routines, etc. Codes inserted for these functions are not understood by the compiler. Even dBASE III's MODIFY COMMAND automatically wraps a word around from one side of the screen to the next. Take a look at a dBASE III procedure file by using DOS to TYPE it to the console; look at the odd graphic characters throughout. DBASE III knows to ignore these characters because it wrote them, but Clipper does not ignore them. Make sure that there are no high-bit characters embedded in your code.

Sometimes symptomatic error messages appear on the last line of the code, even on a simple READ. Adding a line of code, even a remark line, only moves the error message one line further down. Other times, phase errors occur. All of these errors may indicate a high-bit character inside the text file. WordStar in document mode and Borland's SideKick are notorious for causing these situations.

The best way to avoid this condition is to use a text editor rather than a word processor for your coding.

Too Many Constants / Too Many Symbols

This problem occurs when too much code is compiled at one time. There is a process in the compiling referred to as *parsing*. Parsing involves making a reference pointer for commands, statements, variables and their respective names -- in fact, just about everything that is referenced by the compiler. From the parsing process, the tokens are generated into logical segments to be handled at one time. However, the parser has a size limitation. It is like a Scrabble board, with each parse a tile to be placed on the board. Every new and unique parse requires the placement of a new tile. Eventually, there comes a point when the board is filled with little tiles, and yet there is more code to be parsed. That's when you get this error message. From that point on, nothing is compiled properly.

The solution is to learn how to use CLiP files to break your application into a number of separate compiles. Generally, the program files can be placed in two or more separate CLiP files. These then create separate compiled (object) files. Consider the process carefully. Each time the compiler is called upon initially, it generates three tables: one for the code, one for the symbols, and one for the constants. Each unique symbol, code, and constant marker in your files generates a unique code to be placed in the appropriate table.

Eventually, one or more of the tables gets filled. Sometimes, changing code alleviates the problem. This solution works only in cases where the compilation is extremely close to completion. The most likely table to fill up first is the constant table followed by the symbol table. The problem is knowing how many more codes will be placed in the table. There is no way to determine that ahead of time. Therefore, the simplest solution is to break up the programs into separate compiles and join them together through the linking step. To accomplish this task, we employ what are termed CLiP files.

CLiP FILES

The following diagram shows the flow of operation of an application:

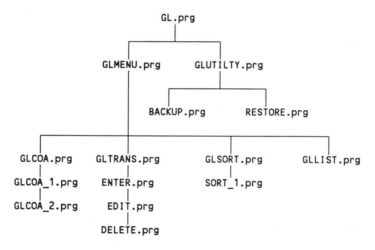

In this structure, GL.prg calls both GLMENU.prg and GLUTILTY.prg, which in turn call their respective sub-routines. Now let's say that you tried to compile this. Clipper would go down the list of program names that it recognizes, pull them into one object file and try to compile it all. If there is too much to compile at one time, an error message referring to "Too Many <Constants> <Symbols>" would appear. If you want to use overlays, separate object files would need to be generated for the code to be properly structured for the linker.

To compile the files individually or in preselected groups, we create CLiP files, which are ordinary text files with .CLP extensions. The CLiP file contains the names of the programs (without the .PRG extentions) to be compiled exclusively. It doesn't matter if a program calls another program (sub-routine) or procedure. Only those programs listed in the CLiP file will be compiled. Referring back to the example above, let's make three unique CLiP files.

First, create a text file called GL.CLP, which contains the following list of programs without extensions:

```
GL
GLMENU
GLUTILTY
BACKUP
RESTORE
```

Close the file and create another text file called GLCOA.CLP. Inside of this file will be the names of the following programs:

```
GLCOA
GLCOA_1
GLCOA_2
GLTRANS
ENTER
EDIT
DELETE
```

Finally, close that file and create yet another file called FINAL.CLP. Inside this text file will be the following file names:

```
GLSORT
GLSORT_1
GLLIST
```

Keep in mind that all files listed in a CLiP file must have a .PRG extension; format files and procedure files with an extension other than .PRG must be renamed before you compile the CLiP file.

Compile each CLiP file by using the following command line syntax:

```
C>CLIPPER @GL
C>CLIPPER @GLCOA
C>CLIPPER @FINAL
```

The result will be three separate object (.OBJ) files with the names of the associated CLiP files. Note that the major difference on the command line between a massive compile (looking at GL.PRG and compiling its sub-routines) and the CLiP file is the additional character (the @ sign). This special character tells the compiler that there is a CLiP file with the following name and to compile each listed program file collectively, yet exclusive to the list, no matter what else is called by a listed program. After the compilation of these CLiP files there would be three new files created on the disk:

```
GL.OBJ
GLCOA.OBJ
FINAL.OBJ
```

Notice that it does not matter what is being compiled inside the CLiP file. The name of the CLiP file can be anything as long as the extension is .CLP. The compiler takes the name of the CLiP file and uses that as the name of the object file. In this example, the last CLiP file is called FINAL.CLP for a good reason. Sometimes we compile code which has problems in it, and these problems may not surface until we try to run our application. It can be frustrating to change one or two lines of code in GLLIST.PRG, for example. Once we have made the necessary changes, we have to recompile and relink our application. By using CLiP files properly, we can isolate code which is clean from that which we are still trying to finish.

In this example, all we have to do once we change the desired lines of code in GLLIST.PRG is to recompile the FINAL.CLP file by itself and then link it with the remaining two files previously compiled. This method is very helpful in saving time and energy when trying to get an application up and running. The final step is to link all the object files with the library. To do this, you need to either build a LiNK file or use PLINK86 interactively. The LiNK file is just a text file with a .LNK extension in which you put the commands for PLINK86. An example follows:

GL.LNK

```
    FI GL
    FI GLCOA
    FI FINAL
    LIB CLIPPER
```

To activate the linker with this link file you would type in the following:

```
C>PLINK86 @GL
```

The default name of the executable file will be the name of the first object file seen by the linker. In the above example, it would be GL.EXE. Further information on the linker is available in Chapter 3.

After the linker connects the three object files with the Clipper library, the executable file is created. The .PRG file which normally begins the application MUST BE the first file in the list of files in the first linked CLiP (now converted to object) file.

The following program demonstrates one way of automating the writing of CLiP files. Study this code and, if you choose, type it in and compile it. You will find that you use it often in your development work. In addition, this program demonstrates how to use contextual help, user defined functions, and program flow and development. Much of the explanatory help repeats what has been covered above; if you choose, you need not include it in your program.

```
********************
* Name          COMPILE.prg
* Date          AUGUST 1, 1986
* Notice        Copyright 1986, Stephen J. Straley
* Note          This program will check the directory for files, write
*               CLiP files, and then write a batch file for the compile.
*               An extensive HELP module is included to demonstrate the
*               compiler in process and the advantages of CLiP
*               files.
*
********************

SET SCOREBOARD OFF
scrframe = CHR(201) + CHR(205) + CHR(187) + CHR(186) + CHR(188) + CHR(205) +;
           CHR(200) + CHR(186) + CHR(32)
scrbar    = CHR(204) + REPLICATE(CHR(205),78) + CHR(185)
scrlin    = CHR(186)
STORE SPACE(4000) TO scr_page1, scr_page2

DO Scrinit
DO Input_it
CLOSE DATABASES
DO Port_it1
CLOSE DATABASES
DO Port_it2
CLOSE DATABASES
DO Port_it3
CLOSE DATABASES
DO Choice
DO Exiting


********************

PROCEDURE Scrinit

   **************************************************************************
   * This Procedure will initialize the screen with the main menu message  *
   * save it to an array for future display, and then display a brief      *
   * opening message.                                                      *
   **************************************************************************
   CLEAR
   @ 0,0,20,79 BOX SUBSTR(scrframe,1,8)
   @ 4,0 SAY scrbar
   FOR x = 1 TO 3
      @ x,1 SAY REPLICATE(CHR(219),78)
   NEXT
   @ 1,5 SAY " COMPILE "
   @ 1,75 - LEN(" Version 1.00 ") SAY " Version 1.00 "
   @ 3,40 - LEN(" The Clipper Utility Program - Main Menu ")/2 SAY " The Clipper
Utility Program - Main Menu "
   CALL _scrsave WITH scr_page1
   @ 10,5 SAY "The following program was designed to make CLiP Files out of all"
   @ 12,5 SAY "program, format, and procedure files available to the program on
the"
```

```
     @ 14,5 SAY "registered directory/drive.  If you are unsure what CLiP files are
or"
     @ 16,5 SAY "their purpose, please strike FUNCTION KEY 1 (F1) for a descrip-
tion."
     STORE "Y" TO continue
     @ 18,25 SAY "Would you like to continue? " GET continue PICT "!" VALID(continue
$"YN")
     READ
     IF continue = "N"
        @ 23,0 SAY ""
        QUIT
     ENDIF


********************

PROCEDURE Input_it

     **************************************************************************
     * This routine will take a directory of all PRG, PRC, and FMT files in *
     * the current directory.                                               *
     **************************************************************************

     @ 0,0 CLEAR
     @ 4,0,20,79 BOX SUBSTR(scrframe,1,8)
     CALL _scrsave WITH scr_page2
     @ 10,10 SAY ""
     ?? "Reading Disk Information"
     @ 11,10 SAY ""
     IF .NOT. FILE("*.PRG")
        ?? "There are no Program Files Available on drive"
     ELSE
        RUN DIR *.PRG > CAPTURE.TXT
     ENDIF
     @ 12,10 SAY ""
     IF .NOT. FILE("*.PRC")
        ?? "There are no Procedure Files Available on drive"
     ELSE
        ?? "Procedure FIles Present.  Make a note to Rename them *.PRG"
        RUN DIR *.PRC >>CAPTURE.TXT
     ENDIF
     @ 13,10 SAY ""
     IF .NOT. FILE("*.FMT")
        ?? "There are no Format Files Available on drive"
     ELSE
        ?? "Format FIles Present.  Make a note to Rename them *.PRG"
        RUN DIR *.FMT >>CAPTURE.TXT
     ENDIF
```

```
********************

PROCEDURE Port_it1

   ********************************************************************
   * This procedure will take the captured file and port it into a *
   * raw data base.                                                 *
   ********************************************************************

   CREATE Template
   USE Template
   APPEND BLANK
   REPLACE field_name WITH "TEMP", field_type WITH "C", field_len WITH 80
   USE
   CREATE Port1 FROM Template
   ERASE Template
   USE Port1
   APPEND FROM Capture.txt SDF
   USE

********************

 PROCEDURE Port_it2

   ****************************************************************
   * This procedure takes the ported database in PORT1.DBF,   *
   * sorts it into a secondary database by root file name and *
   * extension, and notes if it is going to be a major file   *
   * (a file at the head of a CLiP file).                     *
   ****************************************************************

   CREATE Template
   USE Template
   APPEND BLANK
   REPLACE field_name WITH "ROOT", field_type WITH "C", field_len WITH 8
   APPEND BLANK
   REPLACE field_name WITH "EXT", field_type WITH "C", field_len WITH 3
   APPEND BLANK
   REPLACE field_name WITH "MAJOR", field_type WITH "L", field_len WITH 1
   USE
   CREATE Port2 FROM Template
   ERASE Template

********************

 PROCEDURE Port_it3

   *************************************************
   * This will port between the two files created by *
   * Procedures Port_it1 and Port_it2             *
   *************************************************

   SELECT 2
   USE Port2
```

```
SELECT 1
USE Port1
DO WHILE .NOT. EOF()
   IF SUBSTR(temp,1,1) # " "
      SELECT 2
      APPEND BLANK
      REPLACE root  WITH SUBSTR(A->temp,1,8), ext WITH SUBSTR(A->temp,10,3)
      REPLACE major WITH .F.
      SELECT 1
   ENDIF
   SKIP
ENDDO
```

****

PROCEDURE Choice

```
*************************************************************************
* This procedure branches off into 2 directions, depending upon the   *
* response of the user.  If a "Y" is entered. then every PRG, PRC,    *
* and/or FMT file is set up to be compiled individually.  Otherwise, *
* the program will branch off to prompt the user to enter which       *
* files to compile together.                                          *
*************************************************************************

CALL _scrrest WITH scr_page1
STORE "Y" TO input
@ 10,15 SAY "Would you like to compile every file separately? " GET input PICT
"!" VALID(input $"YN")
READ
IF input = "Y"
   DO Separate
ELSE
   DO Indiv
ENDIF
```

****

PROCEDURE Indiv

```
**********************************************************************
* This is the procedure that allows for a selective compiling list *
**********************************************************************

SELECT 1
USE Port2
COPY STRUCTURE TO Port4
screen_no = 0
SET MESSAGE TO 22
DO WHILE screen_no >= 0
   CALL _scrrest WITH scr_page1
   position  = RECNO()
   down      = 6
```

```
over      = 5
option    = 1
count     = 1
ending    = LASTREC()
IF EOF()
   DO Exiting
ENDIF
DO WHILE count <= 30
   DO CASE
   CASE ext = "PRG"
      info = "This is a Program File"
   CASE ext = "PRC"
      info = "This is a Procedure File"
   OTHERWISE
      info = "This is a Format File"
   ENDCASE
   IF DELETED()
      info = info + " --- FILE ALREADY SELECTED/USED"
   ENDIF
   info = SPACE(5) + info
   @ down, over PROMPT root MESSAGE CENTRING(info)
   over = over + 15
   IF over > 70
      down = down + 2
      over = 5
   ENDIF
   count = count + 1
   SKIP
   IF EOF()
      EXIT
   ENDIF
ENDDO
@ down, over PROMPT "Write File" MESSAGE CENTRING("Selected Files will be
now written")
over = over + 15
IF over > 70
   down = down + 2
   over = 5
ENDIF
IF .NOT. EOF()
   @ down, over PROMPT "Next Screen" MESSAGE SPACE(78)
ENDIF

SET KEY -1 TO Review
SET KEY 24 TO Downprmt
SET KEY  5 TO Upprmt

MENU TO option

SET KEY -1 TO
SET KEY 24 TO
SET KEY  5 TO
```

```
      DO CASE
      CASE option = 0
         screen_no = screen_no - 1
         IF screen_no >= 0
            GO position
            SKIP - 30
         ENDIF
      CASE option = 32
         screen_no = screen_no + 1
         count = 1
         CALL _scrrest WITH scr_page1
      CASE option = count
         DO Writfile
         screen_no = 0
      OTHERWISE
         GO (screen_no * 30 + option)
         IF DELETED()
            RECALL
         ELSE
            DELETE
         ENDIF
         GO position
         count = 1
      ENDCASE
   ENDDO


*******************

PROCEDURE Writfile

   *****************************************************
   * This Procedure starts to write the chosen files *
   * out to disk in the form of the CLiP file.       *
   *****************************************************

   SET FILTER TO DELETED()
   GO TOP
   rec_count = 0
   DO WHILE .NOT. EOF()
      rec_count = rec_count + 1
      SKIP
   ENDDO
   IF rec_count > 32 .OR. rec_count = 0
      IF rec_count > 32
         a_mess = LTRIM(STR(rec_count)) + " is too many files in " + ;
                  "a CLiP file. Unselect " + LTRIM(STR(32 - rec_count)) + ;
                  " files. "
      ELSE
         a_mess = "An empty file can not be written.  Any Key to Continue.."
      ENDIF
      @ 22,0 SAY CENTRING(a_mess)
      qw = INKEY(0)
      SET FILTER TO
```

```
         GO TOP
         RETURN
      ENDIF
      COPY TO Port3
      STORE .F. TO Abort_it
      DO Outfile
      IF Abort_it
         RETURN
      ENDIF
      USE Port2
      PACK
      GO TOP


********************

PROCEDURE Outfile

      *******************************************************************
      * In this procedure, the user is given the choice of which    *
      * of the selected files will head the list, after which the   *
      * CLiP file will be named.                                    *
      *******************************************************************

      option = 0
      down_out = 6
      over_out = 5
      USE Port3
      CALL _scrrest WITH scr_page1
      @ 3,1 SAY REPLICATE(CHR(219),78)
      @ 3,26 SAY "CLiP File Selection Menu"
      DO WHILE .NOT. EOF()
         visual = TRIM(root) + ."" + ext
         @ down_out, over_out PROMPT visual
         over_out = over_out + 15
         IF over_out > 70
            down_out = down_out + 2
            over_out = 5
         ENDIF
         SKIP
      ENDDO
      MENU TO option
      IF option = 0
         STORE .T. TO Abort_it
         RETURN
      ENDIF
      GO option
      REPLACE major WITH .T.
      DO Finalout
```

```
********************

PROCEDURE Finalout

   ********************************************************
   * This is the routine that actually writes the CLiP *
   * file in the order assigned by Outfile.             *
   ********************************************************

   LOCATE FOR major = .T.
   outfile = TRIM(root) + ."CLP"
   SET ALTERNATE TO &outfile
   @ 11,20,14,60 BOX scrframe
   @ 12,21 SAY SUBSTR(CENTRING("Now creating " + outfile),21,38)
   @ 13,21 SAY SUBSTR(CENTRING(" Listing " + TRIM(root) + ."" + ext),21,38)
   SET CONSOLE OFF
   SET ALTERNATE ON
   ? TRIM(root)
   SET ALTERNATE OFF
   SET CONSOLE OFF
   GO TOP
   DO WHILE .NOT. EOF()
      IF .NOT. major
         @ 13,21 SAY SUBSTR(CENTRING(" Listing " + TRIM(root) + ."" + ext),21,38)
         SET CONSOLE OFF
         SET ALTERNATE ON
         ? TRIM(root)
         SET ALTERNATE OFF
         SET CONSOLE OFF
      ENDIF
      IF ext = "PRC" .OR. ext = "FMT"
         ths_is_in = TRIM(root) + ."" + ext
         ths_is_out = TRIM(root) + ."PRG"
         RENAME &ths_is_in. TO &ths_is_out
      ENDIF
      SKIP
   ENDDO
   GO option
   SELECT 2
   USE Port4
   APPEND BLANK
   REPLACE root WITH A->root, ext WITH A->ext, major WITH A->major
   SELECT 1
   ZAP


********************

PROCEDURE Separate

   ****************************************
   * This routine will separate all files *
   * into individual CLiP files.          *
   ****************************************
```

```
    USE Port2
    REPLACE ALL major WITH .T.
    @ 12,01 SAY SUBSTR(CENTRING("Manipulating Data FIle for Output"),1,78)
    COPY TO Port4
    GO TOP
    SET CONSOLE OFF
    DO WHILE .NOT. EOF()
        outfile = TRIM(root) + ."CLP"
        a_mess = "Now working with " + TRIM(root) + ."'" + ext
        @ 12,01 SAY SUBSTR(CENTRING(a_mess),1,78)
        SET ALTERNATE TO &outfile
        SET ALTERNATE ON
        ? root
        SET ALTERNATE OFF
        CLOSE ALTERNATE
        SKIP
        @ 12,20 SAY SPACE(40)
    ENDDO
    SET CONSOLE ON


********************


PROCEDURE Exiting


    ****************************************************************
    * This routine gives the option to write a batch file that *
    * automatically compiles the selected CLiP files.          *
    ****************************************************************

    CLOSE DATABASES
    CALL _scrrest WITH scr_page1
    STORE "Y" TO input, ynput
    @ 10,15 SAY "Would you like a BATCH file to compile your CLP files? " GET input
PICT "!" VALID(input $"YN")
    READ
    @ 10,15 SAY SPACE(60)
    IF input = "Y"
        @ 10,15 SAY "Would you like to PAUSE between every compile? " GET ynput PICT
"!" VALID(ynput $"YN")
        READ
        @ 10,15 SAY SPACE(60)
        batch = SPACE(8)
        @ 10,15 SAY "Enter desired name of batch file: " GET batch PICT "!!!!!!!!!"
        READ
        batch = IF(LEN(TRIM(batch)) = 0, "CLIPCOMP.BAT", TRIM(batch) + ."BAT")
        USE Port4
        GO TOP
        @ 10,01 SAY SUBSTR(CENTRING("Now Writing " + batch + " to drive"),1,78)
        SET ALTERNATE TO &batch
        SET CONSOLE OFF
        DO WHILE .NOT. EOF()
            a_mess = "Now Writing for Clipper @" + TRIM(root)
            @ 12,1 SAY SUBSTR(CENTRING(a_mess),1,78)
```

```
                SET ALTERNATE ON
                ? "CLS"
                ? "CLIPPER @" + TRIM(root)
                IF ynput = "Y"
                    ? "PAUSE"
                ENDIF
                SET ALTERNATE OFF
                SKIP
            ENDDO
            CLOSE ALTERNATE
            @ 10,1 SAY SPACE(78)
            @ 12,1 SAY SPACE(78)
            a_mess = "Run Batch File, "
        ELSE
            a_mess = "Compile CLiP Files, "
        ENDIF
        a_mess = a_mess + "then run 'LINKIT' to determine Link Structure"
        @ 11,1 SAY SUBSTR(CENTRING(a_mess),1,78)
        @ 13,1 SAY SUBSTR(CENTRING("Thank you for running COMPILE.  A product of NOS
Development"),1,78)
        ERASE Capture.txt
        ERASE Template.dbf
        ERASE Port1.dbf
        ERASE Port2.dbf
        IF FILE("Port3.dbf")
            ERASE Port3.dbf
        ENDIF
        @ 23,00 SAY ""
        QUIT


********************

 PROCEDURE Review

    ***************************************************************
    * This procedure will display all selected files for group *
    * CLiP files.  This routine is called by the striking of   *
    * the F2 key.  Because it was called by the SET KEY TO      *
    * command, the parameters listed below are never used, yet  *
    * are necessary for the procedure to function properly.     *
    ***************************************************************

    PARAMETER p, l, v

    SAVE SCREEN
    CALL _scrrest WITH scr_page2
    down_rev = 6
    over_rev = 5
    SET FILTER TO DELETED()
    GO TOP
    DO WHILE .NOT. EOF()
        @ down_rev, over_rev SAY root
        over_rev = over_rev + 15
```

```
      IF over_rev > 70
         down_rev = down_rev + 2
         over_rev = 5
      ENDIF
      SKIP
   ENDDO
   a_mess = "All Files Listed.  Any Key to Return to Main Menu"
   @ 22,00 SAY CENTRING(a_mess)
   qw = INKEY(0)
   SET FILTER TO
   GO position
   RESTORE SCREEN


********************

PROCEDURE Help

   *******************************************************
   * This is the HELP routine called by pressing F1.   *
   *******************************************************

   PARAMETERS aa, bb, cc

   SAVE SCREEN
   DO CASE
   CASE aa = "SCRINIT"
      @ 0,0 CLEAR
      TEXT
CLiP FILES... are text files with .CLP extensions.  Inside of these text
               files are the names of the programs we wish to compile, either
               individually or in a group of files.  Consider the following
               file layout:


                         GL.prg
               ┌───────────┴───────────┐
          GLMENU.prg              GLUTILITY.prg
                            ┌───────────┴───────────┐
                       BACKUP.prg              RESTORE.prg

  ┌───────────┬───────────────┐               ┌───────────────┐
GLCOA.prg   GLTRANS.prg              GLSORT.prg              GLLIST.prg
  │           │                        │
GLCOA_1.prg  ENTER.prg              SORT_1.prg
  │           │
GLCOA_2.prg  EDIT.prg
              │
           DELETE.prg         (Any Key to Continue...or Q to Quit)
ENDTEXT
qw = INKEY(0)
IF qw = ASC("Q") .OR. qw = ASC("q")
   RESTORE SCREEN
   RETURN
```

```
ENDIF
@ 0,0 CLEAR
@ 0,00 SAY "CLiP FILES"
@ 2,00 SAY CENTRING("In the previous listed structure, GL.prg calls both
GLMENU.prg and")
@ 4,00 SAY CENTRING("GLUTILITY.prg, which in turn call their respective sub-
routines.  Now let's")
@ 6,00 SAY CENTRING("say you tried compiling this application by starting everyth-
ing off with")
@ 8,30 SAY "C>"
@ ROW(),COL() SAY "C"
  qw = INKEY(.5)
@ ROW(),COL() SAY "L"
  qw = INKEY(.5)
@ ROW(),COL() SAY "I"
  qw = INKEY(.5)
@ ROW(),COL() SAY "P"
  qw = INKEY(.5)
@ ROW(),COL() SAY "P"
  qw = INKEY(.5)
@ ROW(),COL() SAY "E"
  qw = INKEY(.5)
@ ROW(),COL() SAY "R"
  qw = INKEY(.5)
@ ROW(),COL()+1 SAY "G"
  qw = INKEY(.5)
@ ROW(),COL() SAY "L"
  qw = INKEY(.5)
@ 10,00 SAY CENTRING("From this, one at a time, each program(sub-routine) would be
called in and")
@ 12,00 SAY CENTRING("compiled.  Eventually, your screen may look like this...")
@ 14,00 SAY "Compiling GL.PRG         "
DO Counting WITH 150
@ 15,00 SAY "Compiling GLMENU.PRG   "
DO Counting WITH 76
@ 16,00 SAY "Compiling GLUTILTY.PRG"
DO Counting WITH 252
@ 17,00 SAY "Compiling GLCOA.PRG    "
DO Counting WITH 56
@ 18,00 SAY "Compiling GLCOA_1.PRG "
DO Counting WITH 32
@ 19,00 SAY "Compiling GLCOA_2.PRG "
DO Counting WITH 89
@ 20,00 SAY "Compiling GLTRANS.PRG "
DO Counting WITH 162
@ 21,00 SAY "Compiling ENTER.PRG    "
DO Counting WITH 52
@ 22,00 SAY "Too Many Constants          Press Any Key for Next Screen or 'Q' to
Quit..."
  qw = INKEY(0)
 IF qw = ASC("Q") .OR. qw = ASC("q")
    RESTORE SCREEN
    RETURN
```

```
ENDIF
@ 0,0 CLEAR
TEXT
CLiP FILES
```

Note: At this point in the compiling process, the compiler is informing us that
           too much is being compiled. Technically speaking, the compiler estab-
           lishes a point of reference in a special table for every constant ("STORE
           0.00 TO a, STORE 1 TO b, etc.). Once this special table is full, the
           compiler can't compile any more source code during this particular pass.

From this point on, every line of this program and following programs would produce
the same error and bogus object code. The solution is to break up the amount of
code the compiler has to see at one time. To do this, you have to use CLiP files.
CLiP files are also necessary in preparing your application to be broken up for
overlays.

CLiP files are no more than ordinary text files with a .CLP extension. Inside a
CLiP file, place the name of the program you wish to compile exclusively. It does
not matter if a program calls another program (sub-routine). Only those programs
listed in the CLiP file will be compiled together making a single .OBJ file. CLiP
files may contain just one name of a program, or an entire group. Making the right
decision is difficult when it pertains to overlays. This program will help
decipher that for you. Let's make 3 unique .CLP files.

Return to the example program: Any Key to Continue or 'Q' to Quit..."

```
ENDTEXT
qw = INKEY(0)
IF qw = ASC("Q") .OR. qw = ASC("q")
   RESTORE SCREEN
   RETURN
ENDIF
@ 0,0 CLEAR
TEXT
CLiP FILES
```

Inside GL.CLP, list the following programs:	GL
	GLMENU
	GLUTILTY
	BACKUP
	RESTORE

Inside GLCOA.CLP, list the following programs:	GLCOA
	GLCOA_1
	GLCOA_2
	GLTRANS
	ENTER
	EDIT
	DELETE

Inside FINAL.CLP, list the following programs:	GLSORT
	GLSORT_1
	GLLIST

So now there are an additional 3 files on your directory with the names of the programs we wish to compile.
                              Any Key to Continue or 'Q' to Quit
```
ENDTEXT
qw = INKEY(0)
IF qw = ASC("Q") .OR. qw = ASC("q")
   RESTORE SCREEN
   RETURN
ENDIF
@ 0,0 CLEAR
TEXT
CLiP Files
```

Now compile each CLiP file in the following manner:

```
        C>CLIPPER @GL
        C>CLIPPER @GLCOA
        C>CLIPPER @FINAL
```

The result would be three separate .OBJ files with the names of the associated .CLP
files. So now on the disk there would be three new files created after the three
compiles:

```
        GL.OBJ
        GLCOA.OBJ
        FINAL.OBJ
```

Notice that no matter what is being compiled inside of the .CLP files, the name of
the CLiP file can be anything. Keep in mind that the compiler will take the name
of the CLiP file and use that as the name of the .OBJ file. In this example, the
last .CLP file is called FINAL.CLP for a good reason.

                              Any Key to Continue or 'Q' to Quit...
```
ENDTEXT
qw = INKEY(0)
IF qw = ASC("Q") .OR. qw = ASC("q")
   RESTORE SCREEN
   RETURN
ENDIF
@ 0,0 CLEAR
TEXT
CLiP Files
```

Sometimes, we compile code which has problems in it, and these problems may not
surface until we try to run our application. It can be frustrating to change one
or two lines of code in GLLIST.prg, for example. Once we have made the necessary
changes, we would have to recompile and re-link our application together. By using
CLiP files, we can isolate code which is "clean" from that which we are still
trying to finish. In this example, all we would have to do once we changed the
desired lines of code in GLLIST.PRG is to recompile the FINAL.CLP file by itself,
and then to link it with the two files previously compiled. This method is very
helpful in saving time and energy when trying to get an application up and running.

Finally, CLiP files are the only method by which to break up program, procedure, and format files into logical sections for an overlay scheme. The linker which comes with Clipper does not automatically figure out the best overlay scheme for your system. It can't. Consider your system. Is it the same exact system as your clients? Probably not. Therefore, it is up to you to logically break up the programs into separate compiles and to link them together in an order best suited for your environment.

```
                        Any Key to Continue...
ENDTEXT
   CASE aa = "CHOICE"
       @ 0,0 SAY CENTRING("If you want each and every PRG, FMT, and PRC file avail-
able")
       @ 1,0 SAY CENTRING("to be compiled individually (separated and placed in in-
dividual CLiP")
       @ 2,0 SAY CENTRING("files, then answer 'Y' to this question.  Otherwise, you
may choose")
       @ 3,0 SAY CENTRING("selectively which files to compile together.  Any Key to
Continue...")
   CASE aa = "OUTFILE"
       @ 0,0 SAY CENTRING("The below listed files were chosen to be compiled to-
gether.  Please now")
       @ 1,0 SAY CENTRING("select which file will head the list of the compile.
This means that")
       @ 2,0 SAY CENTRING("the name of the CLiP file will take the name of the
first file in")
       @ 3,0 SAY CENTRING("the list.  RETURN for selected file; ESC key for first
in list.")
   OTHERWISE
       @ 0,0 SAY CENTRING("To choose a file to join a list, move the cursor key to
that file name")
       @ 1,0 SAY CENTRING("and strike the RETURN key.  To move to a previous menu,
strike the ESC")
       @ 2,0 SAY CENTRING("key.  If there is no previous screen, the ESC key will
return to the")
       @ 3,0 SAY CENTRING("DOS prompt.    Any Key to Return...")
   ENDCASE
   qw = INKEY(0)
   RESTORE SCREEN


********************

PROCEDURE Counting

   ****************************************************
   * This procedure will just simulate a compiling *
   * process.  It is used in the HELP routine.     *
   ****************************************************

   PARAMETER end_count

   posit = ROW()+1
   FOR qw = 1 TO end_count
```

```
      @ posit,00 SAY "Line " + LTRIM(STR(qw))
    NEXT


********************

PROCEDURE Downprmt

    ****************************************************
    * This procedure simulates going down 5 prompts *
    ****************************************************

    PARAMETER p, l, v

    KEYBOARD REPLICATE(CHR(4),5)


********************

PROCEDURE Upprmt

    **************************************************
    * This procedure simulates going up 5 prompts *
    **************************************************

    PARAMETER p, l, v

    KEYBOARD REPLICATE(CHR(19),5)


********************

FUNCTION Centring

    ********************************************************
    * This function centers any string passed to        *
    * it and pads the string with blanks to the left and *
    * to the right to make a string of 80 characters.    *
    ********************************************************

    PARAMETER string

    temp = (80 - LEN(string))/2
    IF INT(LEN(string)/2) = LEN(string)/2
       RETURN(SPACE(temp) + string + SPACE(temp))
    ELSE
       RETURN(SPACE(temp) + string + SPACE(temp)) + " "
    ENDIF
* End of File
```

In Summary

The fundamental point of this chapter is that there are very big differences between an interpreter and a compiler. As developers, we can use those differences to our advantage, while as managers we can go after the similarities for functionality. The differences, both big and small, must be understood.

It is normal to question why an application which worked under the interpreter fails to compile, but the answer isn't always simple. For example, consider a program which has 85 consecutive IF statements but one ENDIF is missing, or a DO program inside an IF statement where the terminating ENDIF is located in a program being called. Because the interpreter can handle only so much source code at one time, it is possible that both cases would function with apparent ease under the interpreter; however, this would not be the case under the compiler. Is the compiler wrong for not allowing faulty coding? Is the interpreter wrong? The main point is that there **is** a difference, and you must code accordingly.

MEMORY REQUIREMENTS AND CLIPPER

Memory Boundaries

Clipper automatically requires an additional 64K of memory above the given load size of the program in order to execute. (The load size is provided by Plink86 after a successful link.) This additional memory is needed to handle some of the basic commands as well as most of the conditional statements and macro substitutions. However, to take advantage of larger systems, the compiler will attempt to take hold of more memory, provided the additional memory is not being used by another program or by the system. The amount of extra memory that Clipper takes is directly proportional to the amount available above the minimum 64K the compiler demands. Developers who do not allow for this may plan a system or an overlay scheme around the 64K requirement. This can become a special problem for those applications which are programmed to RUN another program. If the Clipper program is loaded in first, and additional memory is free, the application will try to take more than just the 64K minimum. Then when it comes time to RUN a word-processor, for example, an "insufficient memory" message will appear, even when all calculations show that there should be enough memory for both programs.

Consider the following program fragment:

```
CLEAR
RUN C:COMMAND
WAIT
```

Once the program cleared the screen and reloaded DOS, we ran CHKDSK to check the amount of available memory. Here are the results:

Test.exe = 128,076 bytes + 71,536 Req. = 199,612 bytes Minimum required

Memory	Machine I	Machine II	Machine III
Before	480,672	544,464	358,800
During	233,872	297,600	123,136
Taken	246,800	246,864	234,664

Notice that Machine III has almost 200K less available to run a program than does Machine II. Interestingly, the same program used **more memory on Machine II than on Machine III**. The program automatically used a proportional amount of the extra memory. Also notice that the amount taken on all three machines is not even close to the minimum amount required by the program. On the larger machine an additional 47K was taken by the application.

This is just a small example of a situation that may cause large troubles. Be careful when designing, coding, and linking the application. The minimum amounts quoted are just that, minimums, and should not be used as the absolute figures when calculating a memory management scheme. Following is an additional diagram of the internal memory mechanisms for a computer with 256K of RAM available:

```
┌─────────────────────────────────────────┐
│                                         │
│  64K for DOS                            │
│                                         │
├─────────────────────────────────────────┤
│                                         │
│  128K for Clipper.lib                   │
│                                         │
├─────────────────────────────────────────┤
│  64K for memory variables               │
│              buffers                     │
│              memory management           │
└─────────────────────────────────────────┘
```

In this configuration, only 16K is allotted for index buffering and only 500 memory variables (roughly) will be allowed. However, on a machine with more RAM available, the following memory schematic would pertain:

```
┌─────────────────────────────────────────┐
│                                         │
│   64K for DOS                           │
│                                         │
├─────────────────────────────────────────┤
│                                         │
│                                         │
│   128K for Clipper.lib                  │
│                                         │
│                                         │
├─────────────────────────────────────────┤
│                                         │
│   128K for memory variables             │
│            buffers                      │
│            memory management            │
│                                         │
├─────────────────────────────────────────┤
│   64K for miscellaneous memory          │
│            values (e.g. screens)        │
│                                         │
└─────────────────────────────────────────┘
```

In this scheme, the larger allocation for memory variables, buffers, and basic memory management means a faster indexing routine and over 2000 memory variables. Also, the additional 64K for miscellaneous memory variables allows faster execution and performance.

Clipper and Memory - Autumn '86

A few words on the memory management in the Autumn '86 release of Clipper are in order. There are four items to be aware of when developing an application with this release of Clipper:

1) The number of memory variables.
2) The number of buffers used for INDEXing.
3) The need to RUN other programs within a Clipper application.
4) The amount of free memory pool to be used for data manipulation.

Unless specifically directed otherwise, Clipper will automatically allocate values to each of these four areas. However, if you wish to control the environment under which Clipper will operate, you must use a DOS "SET" command.

If no SET command is issued, Clipper will allocate all available memory in the following order:

1) **First,** the size of the executable (.EXE) program is loaded into memory.

2) **Second,** 24K bytes are set aside for "free memory pool." This area is used for data manipulation.

3)   **Third,** 20 percent of the remaining available memory will be used for allocating memory variables.

4)   **Fourth,** after memory variables have been allocated, 33 percent of the remaining memory will be set aside for the RUN command and for index buffers. This value will always be at least 16K bytes.

5)   **Fifth,** the rest of the available memory will be added to the free memory pool. This value will be added to the previously established 24K bytes. If you have an expanded memory system, then a Clipper application will automatically make use of the extra memory. However, keep in mind that a Clipper application will allocate up to 1 megabyte for buffers, depending on the amount of that memory which is actually available. Also, if there is any expanded memory available, then the Clipper application will automatically require a minimum of 16K bytes from the expanded memory system.

Modifying the Memory of Autumn '86 Applications

As stated before, the memory configuration can be altered to better fit each application's requirements and needs. To do so, you must issue a SET command at DOS, either directly or through a batch file, preferably AUTOEXEC.BAT. The command syntax would be as follows:

```
SET CLIPPER= [vXXX;] [rXXX;] [eXXXX;] [xXXX;]
```

Make sure that you do not place an extra space between the word "CLIPPER" and the equal sign. If you do, this command will be ignored by your applications. Now here is what each of the four parameters mean:

1.   The "v" parameter:

This parameter is used to restrict the amount of memory that will be allocated for a memory variable table to "XXX" Kilobytes.

If not specified, a Clipper application will automatically allocate 20 percent of the available memory, up to a maximum of 44 K.

Since Clipper will allow up to 2048 memory variables and each memory variable will take up 22 bytes for a position in the memory table, the maximum usage would be 43.95 K.

However, programs converted from dBASE III applications won't use more than 256 variables. Here is how to figure out how much space should be allocated for the memory table:

256 memory variables X 22 bytes = 5652 bytes / 1024 = 5.5 Kilobytes

To implement this, use the following SET command:

```
SET CLIPPER= v006;
```

By doing this, you would have freed roughly 38K bytes from the allocated memory.

If you set the "v" parameter to more than 44K bytes (or v044), your application will allocate the memory accordingly but Clipper will not recognize it, and the memory would be wasted.

2.   The "r" parameter:

This parameter is used to allocate space for both the RUN command and for indexing buffers. If you try to RUN a program that allocates for itself as much available memory as possible, the space used for the indexing buffers will be given up to the external program.

Once the external program returns control back to the Clipper application, the space will be reassigned to the indexing buffers.

If more memory is requested by the "r" parameter than the amount of available memory left in the free pool, the following error message will appear:

```
proc:<startup> line:  System error not enough memory    QUIT? (Q/A/I)
```

The maximum number allowed for this parameter is equal to the free pool of memory less the number entered for the "v" parameter. If expanded memory is available, then the "r" parameter will be used only for the RUN command while the space required by the indexing buffers will be moved to the expanded memory area. Of course, this is dependent on the "e" parameter.

3.   The "e" Parameter:

This parameter is used to specify the maximum amount of expanded memory the application will use. If no parameter is issued, the application will allocate all available expanded memory up to a maximum of one megabyte.

If the expanded memory is present and available, the application will use this memory space for indexing buffers.

The minimum number allowed for this parameter is 16K bytes. The command would look like this:

```
SET CLIPPER= e016;
```

4.   The "x" Parameter:

This parameter is used to exclude a specified amount of memory from being allocated and is primarily used to test various restrictions and environments under
which the application will run; you can restrict your application from taking advantage of all the available memory present at the time the application is executed.

For instance, to make a 640K system look like a 512K machine, the value in the
"x" parameter would be 128.

No matter how much memory is blocked from your application allocation process, the RUN command can still use this area of memory.

All of these parameters can be evaluated from within a program by using the GETE()
function. By checking for the word "CLIPPER" in your environmental table, you can
see if there is enough memory to actually RUN a command, thus preserving the integrity of the system. If you are manipulating large memory variable strings, you can
test to see the amount of available memory and restrict the size of the memory variables accordingly.

Again, all of these options first became available with the Autumn '86 version of the
compiler.

CHAPTER THREE

Linking

PLINK86

BASIC COMMANDS

Below is a list of some of the commands available in PLINK86. Along with each command is a brief description of its purpose. For further details on how these commands can be used in linking your application, please refer to the section on Overlay Management.

FILE / FI

The FILE command tells the linker that what follows is the name of the object file to be linked. When this command is used, the file extension (.OBJ) is assumed. FI is an abbreviation for the FILE command.

OUTPUT

The OUTPUT command labels the file created by the linker at the end of linking. The output file will have an .EXE extension. If no label is given, then the root name of the executable file will be the name of the first object file in the link list. The .EXE extension will still be assigned.

LIB

The LIB command identifies which run-time libraries need to be linked with the given object modules. The version of PLINK86 provided with the compiler automatically assumes that the library to be linked will be CLIPPER.LIB. If there are other files to be linked, such as OVERLAY.LIB for the creation of overlays, they need to be specified.

MAP

The MAP command is used to obtain reports which detail the memory map location of the program symbols, codes, and constant tables, as well as all library routines intrinsic to Clipper and/or PLINK86. The basic format for the MAP command is:

   MAP = <filename> flag1,... , flagn.

Map Flags:

   G -   This flag will produce a file of all global public symbols. They are listed in alphabetical order with their assigned addresses.

   S -   This flag will produce a file that contains a map of all the sections in input order. The report contains the following headings:

Maddr -   memory address where section will be loaded.

Msize -   memory space used by the section.

Daddr -   address where section is stored within disk file.

Dsize -   disk space used by the section.

Lev -   the level number of this section. A zero indicates a section that is not overlayed that will reside in the main memory module.

Ov# -   Overlay number of this section. A zero indicates the main or "root" section. A non-zero indicates a section loaded by the overlay loader.

Fth -   Overlay number of "father" section within the overlay structure. A zero indicates an overlay which has no ancestors.

Pload -   Pre-Load flag. A "Yes" indicates that the overlay will be loaded by the loader before execution of the actual program due to its level of zero.

A -   This flag will print all reports. If no flag is given, this report is the default report.

M -   This flag will print a report on the modules. Each module and its segments are listed in input order. Listed under each segment are its symbols and addresses. Common blocks and absolute symbols are listed separately in front of the report.

E -   This flag will print a report of the error messages and warning messages that are normally displayed to the screen. Messages generated by the VERBOSE command are not part of this report.

WIDTH

This statement will change the page width of the memory map reports. The default value is 80.

HEIGHT

This statement will change the number of lines per page for the memory map reports. The default value is 65 lines.

NWIDTH

This statement changes the width of symbol names and other identifiers printed in the map. The default is nine characters.

VERBOSE

This command will display the current operation of the linker while it is in session. The last line on the screen is used for the display. Do not use this command if redirecting the output to file or printer.

BEGINAREA

This command is used to initiate the beginning of an area for an overlay. The word BEGIN can be used as an abbreviation for this command.

ENDAREA

This command is used to conclude an area for an overlay. The word END can be used as an abbreviation for this command.

SECTION

This command separates the following object module files to be contained in an internal overlay.

SECTION INTO

This command separates the following object module files to be contained in an external overlay file. This file will have an .OVL extension.

OVERLAY

This command specifies the names of the segment classes which can remain in the overlay structure.

DEBUG

This command will display to the screen the name of the overlay section that is currently being executed.

WARNING ERRORS

If any of the following error messages appear, the linking process will finish, but there is no guarantee that your application will run.

Error
Number: Cause:

1   There are several causes for this error condition. One cause is that the address being referenced is lower in memory than the segment register addressing it. In theory it is like a variable which has not been initialized at a higher level or made PUBLIC being called by a lower program. This is not a common error message. Also see ERROR 10, below.

2   Under the operating system, the designated stack location of the application is kept in the header of the executable file. This is then used to set the SS and SP registers when the program is called and executed. The linker looks for a stack segment marked as either SS or SP by the compiler or assembler.

If it is found, the eventual address is placed in the header. If it is not found, zeroes are placed in the header at that location, and the program will not function correctly. This can be avoided if the SS and SP registers are set by the application itself. Even then the application could halt if such an interruption occurs before it has had a chance to establish a valid stack. In normal compiling of Clipper or dBASE code, this error should not appear.

3   A *group* is a collection of segments that must reside within 64K of memory space. Sixteen-bit addresses can then be used to access objects within the group. A part of the group cannot be accessed if the group is too large; the group size must then be reduced. Even if the segment is less than 64K, verify with the memory map that segments have not been separated by intervening segments from another group. If this error message occurs, and the segment is close to 64K, reduce the segment even further, to around 40K, to make certain it will link.

This is similar to large .OBJ modules. Sometimes, when there is too much compiling, the code/symbol/constant tables may exceed their 32K limit. If this should occur, the amount compiled at one time must be reduced. The same theory holds true for linking.

Also, this situation often occurs when attempting to link assembly language modules with high-level language modules. The class and segment names used in assembly language code should match those used in the high-level language code.

4   The module name given in the MODULE command was not found in any of the linked files.

5   The 8086 processor uses a dual addressing scheme, making the offset portion of a long address relative to the physical segment selected by the paragraph. Though the offset can be determined at linkage, the paragraph address, being an absolute address point in memory, must be adjusted according to where the operating system loads the application into memory. The linker outputs a long address relative to the start of the program and continues linking.

6   Relevant only for CP/M-86.

7   The given module contains a record type unfamiliar to the linker. The entire record will be skipped. Included with this will be FATAL ERROR 41, which means that the linker is looking for a file that follows standard relocatable object module format and one of the files given to the linker does not follow this rule. This is a common error when developers try to use BATCH files which not only call the compiler, but call the linker as

well. If this is the case, check to see if file extensions are being used. Predictably, the .PRG extension is given with the file name, which Clipper does not mind. However, that file extension will be passed to the linker. Instead of linking in the newly compiled .OBJ file, the batch file is telling the linker to use the .PRG file. Make sure that no file extensions are used with batch files unless absolutely necessary. Let the compiler and the linker assume their default values.

8   Each record in an object file will contain a check field at the end for validation purposes. This message indicates that the checksum value was bad; linking will continue, however. If object files are patched, the checksum must be changed to reflect the possible change in the file size.

9   PLINK86 reached the end of the record and found that the number of bytes processed is different from the specified size. Each record in an object file is preceded by the record size. This is the source of the discrepancy.

10   A reference to the named modules was made to the given target object and assumed that the segment register to be used for the access will point to the given frame object.

        The target cannot be accessed as desired if a 16-bit address is being used and the target is more than 64K bytes away from a frame (or an 8-bit address with a distance greater than 256 bytes). The address actually used will be wrapped around to fit into the required offset size. If there is a group larger than 64K, make it smaller for proper access.

11   There may be only one definition for each public global symbol in the program being linked. Another definition was found for the named symbol, either in another module or created by the DEFINE command. The linker will ignore the duplicate definition, retain the first one, and continue linking. However, to insure that the application's integrity is maintained, the duplication should be found and removed.

        This is a frequent error if either of the following things should happen:

        a.   You compile a user defined function library and some of the same functions are defined and compiled at the end of another program module. When these two files are linked and a reference is made to one of those user defined functions, the linker sees two symbols for the same call.

        b.   Sometimes, developers use the same set of procedure names in different procedure files. For example, a procedure named "ADDTHEM" may be defined in procedure file "POLICY" and defined again in procedure file "CODES". Each version of "ADDTHEM" would be slightly different depending on which SET PROCEDURE TO file is being used. Since the compiler makes no distinction between program files and procedures, one of the "ADDTHEM" procedures will have to be changed and all subsequent and relative calls similarly changed to fit the new name.

12   The named public segment was assigned to more than one group. One module placed the segment in one group, while another module placed the same segment in another group. System integrity will be in question if this occurs.

13   The name segment was first defined as a public segment and then later redefined as a common block, or the other way around. All definitions of the segment should be changed to be the same type.

14   A duplicate stack segment was defined within the named module. The linker will use the last stack definition made to specify the stack in the executable file's header. If this stack segment is empty or too small, the application will, in all probability, halt during execution.

Verify that all stack segment definitions use the same name and class name, for they will be combined into one segment having the same size.

FATAL ERRORS

Many errors are the result of a series of previously reported errors, usually in the compiling process. These errors are sometimes ignored and compiling continues. If a batch file is used, the error does not stop all processing until the process invokes the linker. Below is a listing of the possible error messages and, where applicable, the probable cause.

**Error
Number: Cause:**

1   "@" files are nested too deeply for the linker. The linker will only accept three "@" files at any given time. If there are any loops, each loop will count as a legitimate pass.

2   There was a disk error while attempting to read the designated "@" file. Try to rebuild the file.

3   The file name entered after the "@" was not found on the specified drive or directory.

5   The expression given has too many characters for input. The maximum
           number of characters allowed in an expression is 64.

6   There was an invalid digit in a number. Valid digits depend on the radix
           being used (the default for addresses is hex and for everything else, it is
           decimal).

10   Invalid file name was given.

11   The linker was expecting a statement. A key word which begins a command
           statement should be present. With some versions of the compiler, the batch
           file (CL.BAT) that was provided with the compiler was missing the letters
           "FI." Here is what it looked like:

```
clipper %1
plink86 %1
```

           It should have been:

```
clipper %1
plink86 FI %1
```

14   The linker was expecting an identifier. A section, segment, module, or sym-
           bol name must be entered.

15   Expecting " = "

16   A value was expected. At this point a 16-bit quantity must be given.

17   No files were given to link. The FI statement must be used and at least one
           file must be linked.

18   The ")" was expected at the end of a CLASS statement. If a list of segment
           names is used, the names must be enclosed in parentheses.

WORK FILE ERRORS

Error
Number: Cause:

30   The given work file cannot be created, probably due to lack of space in the
           disk directory.

31   There was an I/O error while writing the work file.

32   There was an I/O error while reading the work file.

33   There was an I/O error while attempting to reposition the work file (doing
           an **lseek**, for example).

34   Too many object modules (symbols, segments, groups) are defined.
           Basically, the program being created is too large for the linker to handle as
           specified.

INPUT OBJECT FILE ERRORS

**Error
Number: Cause:**

41   A premature end of input file was found. This error occurs when compiling
           and linking with the help of a batch file, normally CL.BAT. If an extension
           is given with the batch file, the compiler accepts both the main name and
           the file (.PRG) extension. However, the file name and extension of .PRG
           were passed to the linker, which will try to link the .PRG file instead of the
           .OBJ file to the library. Just remove the file extension when using the batch
           file. The compiler will assume .PRG extensions, and the linker will assume
           .OBJ extensions.

42   There was a fatal read error in object file input.

43   PLINK86 could not locate the named object file. When an object file can-
           not be located, the linker will ask for the name prefix such as a drive or path
           name. If using batch files, the linker will just abort operation and not
           prompt the user for the correct response.

OUTPUT FILE ERRORS

**Error
Number: Cause:**

45   The linker cannot create the output file on the disk. Check to see if the disk
           directory is full or if the disk is write protected.

46   The output file type given is not valid. If this option is used, the output file
           must be either an .EXE or .CMD type.

47   Fatal disk write error has occurred. Either this is due to the disk being full
           or write protected, or there is some type of hardware error.

48   Fatal disk read error while output to file. Probably due to an unrecoverable
           hardware error or the disk is full or write protected.

49   The output file cannot be closed. Check to see if the disk is write protected or if a hardware error has occurred.

50   The memory map cannot be created because the disk directory is full or the disk is write protected.

MISCELLANEOUS ERRORS

Error
Number: Cause:

51   Undefined symbols are present. The linker will list the symbols that are undefined, meaning that there was no reference to a library routine containing the definition. The name of the object file in which the symbol was initially compiled will be given with the symbol name. Only the name of the object file will be listed. If several program files are compiled collectively to make up one object file, the reason for the error could be in any one of those files.

For example, let's say we misspell the function SPACE() as SAPCE() in a program module named OVER.PRG. OVER.PRG was called in and compiled by UNDER.PRG and both are in an object file labeled UNDER.OBJ. Clipper will make a symbol for SAPCE(), assuming that it will be a user defined function and will be defined later. Therefore, the compiler will not report an error. Since it is only a misspelling, there will not be a user defined function so labeled and no matching symbol will be present either in another object file or in the library. Here is what linking would look like:

```
C>plink86 fi under lib \dbase\clipper
PSA Linkage Editor (Nantucket Clipper) Version 1.46.c
    Copyright (C) 1984 by Phoenix Software Associates Ltd.


    Can't find file CLIPPER.LIB.
    Enter new file name prefix (drive:  or path name/)
    or . to quit =>\dbase\

    Can't find file CLIPPER.LIB.
    Enter new file name prefix (drive:  or path name/)
    or . to quit =>\dbase\

    The following 1 symbols are undefined:

    Symbol SAPCE was accessed from Module UNDER File UNDER

    Fatal error 51
    Undefined symbols exist
```

Note: just correct the spelling, recompile, and relink.

52   The linker is informing the user that the specified symbol is self-defined.
            Generally this error occurs when the DEFINE command was used to define
            a symbol relative to another symbol, which was in turn used to define an-
            other symbol. Finally, the chain of references goes back to the original sym-
            bol, completing the circle. In actuality, no symbol ever gets defined.

54   There is not enough available memory to execute the linker. The minimum
            amount of memory required to run PLINK86 is 256K of RAM.

57   There is a problem with the OVERLAY.LIB file.

58   The stack segment is too large for the linker to handle. The largest segment
            can be no greater than 64K bytes. Remember that the stack segments which
            are defined in each module are concatenated by PLINK86 similar to the
            way public segments are concatenated.

INTEL FORMAT OBJECT FILE ERRORS

These errors are caused by problems with the format of the input structure of the object files given to the linker. Normally this implies that the input file is trying to use a
feature that the linker will not support. Clipper is not subject to this error. However,
since object files compiled outside Clipper can be linked in, it may apply to those.

**Error
Number: Cause:**

61   An LTL segment appeared in an Intel module. Unfortunately PLINK86
            does not support these for input.

62   A REGINT (register initialize) record specified a register to be initialized
            in a way unsupported by the executable file format. The linker will only
            support CS:IP (the program starting address point) and SS:SP (the stack
            pointer). These may be pre-initialized with a REGINT record.

63   A LIDATA subrecord has a repeat count of zero which is strictly disal-
            lowed by the standards of the INTEL format.

64   An Intel format object library file was used which has an illegally built li-
            brary index. A possible solution would be to rebuild the library.

65   Plink86 does not support an absolute starting address in the given module.
            The linker will only support a starting address which is given relative to
            some segment.

66   The given module uses a group element type which is not supported by

PLINK86. At present, the linker will only support segments which are included in groups (group component descriptor code = FFH).

70 An invalid location was specified for a fixup. The LOC field must be greater than 4 for all segments relative for a fixup.

71 An invalid location was specified for a fixup. The LOC field must be greater than 1 for all segments self-relative to the fixup.

73 A frame specification type is unsupported by PLINK86. Normally, this frame type is either 6 or 7.

PROGRAM STRUCTURE ERRORS

Error
Number: Cause:

80 Overlays are nested too deeply. Check the structure of the overlays being generated and remove a level.

81 There are too many ENDAREA statements. There are more ENDAREA statements than the number of BEGINAREA statements that have not yet been closed.

82 An unbalanced situation exists between BEGINAREA and ENDAREA. Treat these two statements like a DO WHILE...ENDDO loop or a FOR...NEXT loop.

83 The program being linked will not fit into a 1-megabyte address space.

DOS and MSLINK LINKERS

COMMANDS AND SYNTAX

Review your DOS manual concerning the LINK program provided with your operating system. If you use the MicroSoft Linker, refer to that manual for the specific commands and syntax.

The default allotted segment size with MicroSoft Linker version 3.05 has decreased, but it can be increased by command. In order to link any Clipper application with this linker, use the following format:

```
mslink %1 ,,,\path\/se:1024,,;
```

The %1 is used for a batch file, passing the name of the program to be compiled and linked. The \path\ tells the linker where CLIPPER.LIB is located, and the remaining characters are needed to increase the segment size. In this example, the segments have been set to the maximum size, 1024 bytes.

OVERLAY MANAGEMENT WITH PLINK86

OVERLAY BASICS

An overlay is simply a section of the application which is organized so that it will use the same memory area as another section of the application. No special programming commands are necessary to establish an overlay; this is accomplished by the linker. The theory is that since portions of large applications will share the same memory area, the overall memory requirements on a system will be lessened. The disadvantage in using overlays is the immediate increase of execution time due to an increase of I/O needed to load each overlay from the disk drive.

Try to link your application as is, without the use of overlays. Even if the application is larger than 640K, get a benchmark from which to start. Avoid using overlays if you can; they slow down an application and are difficult to manage. If you do decide to use overlays, establish a series of test programs to compile and to link, or follow the examples in the **call tracking** application located in Appendix I.

There are no simple rules for utilizing overlays. Two points must first be made:

1) Overlay management is never the total solution.
2) Make sure when planning for the implementation of overlays that you consider the computer system on which the application will run.

Overlay Management is Never the Total Solution

Just adding a few extra statements to the linker and creating overlays is not the total solution. Three factors affect overlay management:

a) The way we Code
b) The way we Compile
c) The way we Link

Obviously, linking has a direct effect on the memory scheme of the application. The compiling and coding are equally important, but are more difficult to plan and handle. The linking and compiling are handled after the application has been coded and at least one attempt has been made at creating an overlay. After one attempt, a good developer can adjust the overlay via the coding, compiling, or even linking techniques. All three methods are elaborated upon later in this chapter.

Plan the Application for the Computer on Which it Will Run

Some applications may never run due to the restrictions of a machine's memory, the capacity of the disk, the restriction of the operating system, the execution speed, or a combination of all four. Quite often, and usually after a few attempts with overlays, a decision must be made whether or not to use overlays. Sometimes, the amount of time necessary to create the ideal overlay scheme is not cost effective.

MEMORY REQUIREMENTS

Every application has a specific memory requirement. That requirement fluctuates from system to system and from application to application. Below are ten factors which determine the amount of RAM required by any one specific application on any one machine. Once this base is established, each of these factors may be manipulated to decrease the amount of memory required.

1) The size of any required program file that will remain in the main load module (i.e. code, symbol, and constant size)

2) The Code Size (from the compiler) of the object files that may reside in an overlay

3) The Symbol Size (from the compiler) of the object files that may reside in an overlay

4) The Constant Size (from the compiler) of the object files that may reside in an overlay

5) The size of any outside programs which may be executed

6) The size of any "called" routine which will be linked in with the application

7) The size of any RAM resident program or RAM drive

8) The required amount of memory needed for macros and memory variables

9) The required memory for the basic Clipper library

10) The size of the operating system

The following is a brief discussion of each of the ten memory size issues:

1)   The Size of the Object File in the Main Load Module:

This pertains to the specific size of the constant, symbol, and code tables for those modules which must reside in the main load module. An example of these types of modules would be the HELP program, the main calling program, a user-defined function library, or even a special chaining program. Any module which needs to be accessed by an overlay module should reside in the main load module.

2)   The Code Size of the Object File for Overlays:

After every compilation, the compiler will generate three numbers, the first of which pertains to the size of the code table generated by the compiler. The compiler takes source code and generates intermediate code that represents the commands being issued. For example, for a simple STORE command, a series of push, move, and pop instructions would be generated.

3)   The Symbol Size of the Object File for Overlays:

The second number reported after compilation is the size of the symbol table. A symbol is a reference to a greater part. The compiler will generate a symbol for procedure or function names, memory variables, macros, etc., which refers to the item. This reference is either linked to its definition or is expanded to its true value.

4)   The Constant Size of the Object File for Overlays:

The last number reported is the size of the constant table. A constant is a quote or a value (for example). The prompt messages in an @SAY, @GET or @PROMPT are all constants, while the STORE 0 TO x command would generate some room in the constant table for the zero.

5)   The Size of Any Outside Executed Programs:

In some cases, a CHKDSK command is needed or perhaps the Mode command has to be used to change printer direction. In these cases, DOS is reloaded, and the size is figured into the memory size one more time. Additionally, any program which is called upon to execute via the RUN command must be calculated. The main program remains in memory while the secondary application is loaded into memory on top of the original. The main program is still in control even though the secondary application is executing. Upon completion of processing, the second application will turn control of the system back to the original program. However, the secondary program or application will not load if there is not enough room for **both** programs to fit in memory. Keep in mind that compiled applications initially try to grab as much memory as possible proportional to the amount available. **Because** of this, it is **very** difficult to design applications which will RUN another large application (such as a word processor).

6)   The Size of any Called Programs:

In some applications, special programs may be written in 'C' or in Assembler to be linked in with Clipper applications. These routines increase the size of the application.

7)   The Size of RAM Resident Programs:

Some utility programs can reside in the background until called upon, at which time they execute as prescribed. They take space away from the amount of RAM available to the application. Some of these programs are not clean in the way they interface with the operating system. This means that errors may occur even if there is enough available RAM memory for both the compiled application and the background program. It is not advisable to run Clipper programs concurrently with active RAM resident programs.

8)   The Size of the Macro Library and Memory Variables:

Along with the basic memory size as quoted by PLINK86, an additional 64K minimum is needed for memory variables and macro substitutions. If the system has more than 64K available, the application will take as much memory as possible, proportional to the amount available. For more information on this see Chapter 14, Programming Structure and Application Layout.

9)   The Size of the Clipper Library:

Every application, even the simplest one-line program, will yield a high-load module. This is because the Clipper library is loaded into the executable file. For example, in a program with only a one-line CLEAR command, the object file size is 532 bytes, yet the executable size is 128,524 bytes. The entire library is not linked into the file; some commands, if used, will link in more code. For example, if in place of our CLEAR command a REPORT FORM <filename> is used, the object file would be 567 bytes with an executable file of 140,668 bytes. The basic library file size is roughly 128K and cannot be decreased.

10)   The Size of DOS:

This is the simplest factor to calculate, but remember that each version of DOS is different. Verify the version of DOS on the computer for which the application is being designed, not the machine on which the application is being developed, compiled, and linked. The way to determine the RAM size required by your version of DOS is to run the DOS program CHKDSK when no other programs or devices are loaded.

```
C>chkdsk

 10592256 bytes total disk space
   258048 bytes in 6 hidden files
   147456 bytes in 32 directories
  9576448 bytes in 530 user files
    12288 bytes in bad sectors
   598016 bytes available on disk

   524288 bytes total memory
   480672 bytes free
```

In this example, the amount of available memory on the machine is 512K. However, after the DOS has been loaded into the system, the amount available to run programs is 470K. On this particular machine, DOS required almost 43K.

THE WAY WE CODE

Too often, this is the most overlooked factor in attempting to minimize RAM overhead and maximize overlay efficiency. Developers can get caught up in their own coding techniques, which may be the very root of many problems in creating the perfect overlay structure.

With PLINK86, we are allowed to have the constants of an overlay move with the overlay, rather than reside in the main load module. If we can tailor our coding to have more constants than symbols, our main load module will be smaller while our overlays grow. However, this may not be really necessary. Main load modules and overlay modules can also be reduced in size if we simply make better use of memory variables, reusing stale ones, or recoding a specific section of code. The way we code plays a subtle yet significant role in our memory management scheme. Below are just a few samples relating to this topic.

Command Differences

Let's code a simple loop to count from 1 to 500. First we will use a DO WHILE loop; then we will do the same thing with a FOR command.

Sample One:

```
STORE 1 TO x
DO WHILE x <= 500
   STORE x + 1 TO x
ENDDO
```

Sample Two:

```
FOR x = 1 TO 500
NEXT
```

	Sample One:	Sample Two:
Code Size:	59	66
Symbol Size:	48	48
Constant Size:	64	48

Notice that even though there are fewer lines of code in Sample Two, the code size is 7 bytes larger. On the other hand, the constant size for Sample One is 16 bytes larger than Sample Two, yielding a total of 9 more bytes than the first sample. Multiplying these figures over entire applications, the numbers become significant. This type of information is also critical when choosing an overlay structure. Since constants move in and out with their corresponding overlay sections, it may be beneficial to have a larger constant size which resides only in the overlay. On the other hand, if multiple sections and overlays are nested, the corresponding code sizes and constant sizes will move with one another. Therefore, the overall smaller code or constant size in Sample Two may be more usable.

Literals or Macros?

Sometimes commands and their respective conditions may be stated in more than one fashion. For example, conditional clauses can reside in a macro rather than being entered as a literal. The following two samples establish a simple SET FILTER command, the first using a literal structure and the second a macro substitution.

Sample One:

```
USE Test
SET FILTER TO SUBSTR(name,1,3)="STE" .AND.;
    LEN(TRIM(SUBSTR(phone,10,4)))<>0
```

Sample Two:

```
USE Test
STORE "SUBSTR(name,1,3)="STE" .AND. ;
   LEN(TRIM(SUBSTR(phone,10,4)))<>0" TO test
SET FILTER TO &test
```

	Sample One:	Sample Two:
Code Size:	62	45
Symbol Size:	80	64
Constant Size:	144	128

In the first sample, the literal command is larger on all sections which suggests that the second method of coding is more efficient than the first, especially when developing with the intent of using overlays. However, due to the nature of the command and the fact that the macro will be expanded for every record in TEST.DBF, the second example may slow down execution speed drastically. If a large database is to be used, and execution time is a major concern, then code the routine as a literal. If the size of the application is of supreme concern, and if the file in use is relatively small, then the macro is more appropriate.

Just Bad Code

Bad code not only affects the readability and flow of the application but the memory scheme as well. Below are two samples of a testing situation inside HELP, each checking for the name of the program and for the memory variable involved. The first sample uses nested IF commands while the second uses a more structured DO CASE flow.

Sample One:

```
IF p = "ONE"
   IF v = "TEST"
   ELSE
      IF v = "NEW"
      ELSE
         IF v = "THIS"
         ELSE
         ENDIF
      ENDIF
   ENDIF
ELSE
   IF p = "TWO"
      IF v = "A"
      ELSE
         IF v = "B"
         ELSE
            IF v = "C"
            ELSE
            ENDIF
         ENDIF
      ENDIF
   ELSE
      IF v = "X"
      ELSE
         IF v = "Y"
         ELSE
            IF v = "Z"
            ELSE
            ENDIF
         ENDIF
      ENDIF
   ENDIF
ENDIF
```

Sample Two:

```
DO CASE
CASE p = "ONE"
   DO CASE
   CASE v = "TEST"
   CASE v = "NEW"
   CASE v = "THIS"
```

```
      OTHERWISE
      ENDCASE
CASE p = "TWO"
   DO CASE
   CASE v = "A"
   CASE v = "B"
   CASE v = "C"
   OTHERWISE
   ENDCASE
OTHERWISE
   DO CASE
   CASE v = "X"
   CASE v = "Y"
   CASE v = "Z"
   OTHERWISE
   ENDCASE
ENDCASE
```

	Sample One:	Sample Two:
Code Size:	317	302
Symbol Size:	64	64
Constant Size:	208	208

Obviously, the code in the first sample is larger by 15 bytes. This might seem insignificant in this test environment. However, in a real HELP procedure or over an entire application, this difference will magnify and may present a problem.

Simply having the computer wait for a keystroke from the operator to signal it to continue can be a challenge to code. As with all functions, this routine returns a value, and that value can either be stored to a memory variable, displayed on the screen, or hidden in some fashion. Depending how we code even the simplest wait routine, our application space and speed can increase or decrease. Here are a few more samples:

Sample One:

```
CLEAR
a 10,10 SAY "Any Key to continue..."
temp = INKEY(0)
```

Sample Two:

```
CLEAR
a 10,10 SAY "Any Key to continue..."
SET CONSOLE OFF
?? INKEY(0)
SET CONSOLE ON
```

Sample Three:

```
CLEAR
@ 10,10 SAY "Any Key to continue..."
IF INKEY(0) <> 0
ENDIF
```

	Sample One:	Sample Two:	Sample Three:
Code Size:	42	51	51
Symbol Size:	48	32	32
Constant Size:	96	96	96

The major difference to note is that in Sample One a temporary memory variable is used in conjunction with the INKEY() function. In the other samples the INKEY() function is either being displayed or tested. With the temporary variable the code size is less than the other two. However, the symbol size is greater, while the constants remain the same. Symbols are important to the main load module of an application, while the code size is important to the overlay modules. If less symbol size is important, Sample Three is preferred to Sample Two because it has fewer command lines.

THE WAY WE COMPILE

The way we compile our applications also plays a very important role in the final memory scheme. First consider the following samples of code:

Sample One:

```
********************
* Name      CODESIZE.prg
* Date      August 29, 1986
* Author    Stephen Straley
* Notes     This is the first tested file in the compiling example.
*
********************

CLEAR
@ 10,10 SAY "Do you want to continue (Y/N) ? "
IF VERIFY()
   @ 12,10 SAY "O.k.  I continued...."
ELSE
   @ 12,10 SAY "Program Terminated"
ENDIF

********************
* Name      FUNC.prg
* Date      April 29, 1986
* Author    Stephen Straley
* Notes     This is the function library that goes
*           with TEST.prg to illustrate how to compile.
*
********************
```

```
FUNCTION Verify

    SET CONSOLE OFF
    WAIT TO intemp
    SET CONSOLE ON
    IF UPPER(intemp) = "Y"
       ?? " Yes"
       RETURN(.T.)
    ENDIF
    ?? "  No"
    RETURN(.F.)
```

Each file was compiled separately, yielding the following code/symbol/constant sizes.

	CODESIZE.PRG:	FUNC.PRG:	COMBINED:
Code Size:	96	97	193
Symbol Size:	48	64	112
Constant Size:	167	112	279

When these two object files are linked together, the final executable file size is 129,036 bytes.

Now we'll try compiling the two files together with the aid of a CLiP (.CLP) file. The file (called TEST.CLP) will look like this:

```
                    Test
                    Func
```

And the compiling command would be: CLIPPER @Test

The resulting code/symbol/constant sizes are:

Sample Two:

	TEST.PRG / FUNC.PRG
Code Size:	193
Symbol Size:	80
Constant Size:	272

When this file is linked with the library, the final executable file size is 128,988 bytes.

The only major difference in this test situation is that the symbol size decreased by 32 bytes; however, the size of the executable file decreased by 48 bytes. Obviously, the linker has less overhead to add in order to handle the fewer symbols in the second test.

Let's try one more example, one in which we code the user defined function directly in with the test program. The file would look like this:

Sample Three:

```
********************
* Name      TESTSIZE.prg
* Date      August 29, 1986
* Author    Stephen Straley
* Notes     This file includes the user defined function.
*
*******************

CLEAR
@ 10,10 SAY "Do you want to continue (Y/N) ? "
IF VERIFY()
   @ 12,10 SAY "O.k.  I continued...."
ELSE
   @ 12,10 SAY "Program Terminated"
ENDIF

FUNCTION Verify

   SET CONSOLE OFF
   WAIT TO intemp
   SET CONSOLE ON
   IF UPPER(intemp) = "Y"
      ?? " Yes"
      RETURN(.T.)
   ENDIF
   ?? "  No"
   RETURN(.F.)
```

In this test example, the code/symbol/constant sizes are:

	TEST.PRG
Code Size:	181
Symbol Size:	64
Constant Size:	247

This results in a final executable file size of 128,924 bytes.

On all three sections–code, symbols, and constants–the size decreases and the final decrease in the executable file size was proportional.

In the second example, the compiler establishes a separate code and constant table for each file in the CLiP file, while the symbol size is reduced. Again, symbols always remain in the main load module with references to global memory variables, macros, and functions or procedures. In Sample Three, when the two programs and functions were combined into one file, all factors reduced in size. The compiler will handle most of the management of code, symbol, and constants if the information is present.

The point of this can best be seen in major applications, not in test programs. Most applications require similar items: a help file, a procedure library, a function library, and so on. Since there is no real limit to the number of procedures in a procedure file (since program files are in essence procedures, and since user defined functions can reside within a procedure file), it is obvious that we can combine specific files into one large file. This file can be compiled once, saving on all fronts: code size, symbol size, and constant size.

Compiling plays a direct role in determining file sizes. And only because of certain system criteria are we restricted from compiling with complete freedom.

THE WAY WE LINK

The most important factor in memory requirements is the way we link our applications with each other and with outside routines, outside libraries, the overlay library, and the Clipper library. Overlays help overcome large memory requirements of an application. In other words, overlays would be unnecessary if every microcomputer had a minimum of 640K of memory and every application required far less. But since this is not the situation, the creation, understanding, and utilization of overlays is crucial.

An overlay is a partitioned section of memory used to swap different sections of the application in and out according to need. This allows available memory to be used more efficiently. Specific procedures or program files can share the same section of memory, thus reducing the overall demand on RAM. Up to this point, we have stressed that many factors play a major role in how we can link and what the results will be when we do link.

In discussing both coding and compiling, we made several references to the code, symbol and constant sizes. These three values play an important role in what we can do with overlays. With the linker we also control where these tables reside with the main load module and even within the overlays themselves. The next section looks carefully at the relationships of memory requirements, overlay and main load module sizes, as well as code, symbol and constant sizes.

The next few sections center on the application source code called "MENU GENERATOR". There is one more example of small differences in coding and compiling. Using the MENU GENERATOR as the example, note the following figures:

```
Compiled in one Program File:                           143,400 bytes

Compiled in one CLiP File:                              144,204 bytes

Compiled in separate CLiP Files and LINKed by one LiNK file:  148,256 bytes
```

SOME COMMON RULES

1. Important files should remain in the main load module.

    Quite often this rule is ignored, and subsequent run-time errors, especially the EXEC SEQUENCE ERROR, will occur. Be very careful that any function or procedure library, help utility, screen driver, or any other object file pertinent to the operation of the application is linked to the main object file. This constitutes the main load module. A pertinent file is a file that may be called upon by any program, in or out of an overlay, regardless of its section. Clearly, a HELP file would fall into this classification, for the user should be allowed to call upon it at **any** point in the application without causing a major disturbance to the overlay scheme and memory manager.

2. Never have sections call other sections within the same overlay.

    If a section manages to call another section of code within the same overlay, then an EXEC SEQUENCE ERROR will occur and the system will automatically stop running. Overlay files can call other overlay file, but not sections within the same overlay. In mapping the execution of your applications, be careful to follow sibling branches, and verify that they do not call the same level of sibling at any time.

3. Never calculate an overlay based upon the directory size of the object file.

    Use the three table sizes generated after each compilation: the code, symbol, and constant sizes. With every overlay, PLINK86 adds additional bytes to the load module in order to handle the overlay scheme. For the first overlay used, add an additional 20 bytes; for every subsequent overlay add 16 bytes.

4. Never assume that the application will fit in 256K with the use of overlays.

    In some cases it just cannot be accomplished. Every overlay generates additional overhead with the linker and in many cases a Catch 22 scenario develops. In this situation we use overlays to reduce overhead but due to the increase of linkage overhead needed to handle those overlays, the system will still not execute under a certain memory requirement.

5. The LOAD size is not the EXE size.

    At the end of a successful linkage, PLINK86 will generate a number for the basic load module size. It does not mean that this is the memory requirement for that application. All that number includes are the sizes of the library(s) and object file(s) used. Therefore, the basic memory overhead to handle macros and memory variables has not been included, nor has the size of the operating system. As a general rule, add an additional 100K to this generated number to arrive at the approximate memory requirement for that application.

CODE, CONSTANT, AND SYMBOL TABLES

Code, constant, and *symbol* table sizes are generated at the completion of every successful compilation. Each number plays a significant role in the size of our main load module and has equal importance in the overlay size. More than the size of the largest section in an overlay determines its overall size. Each number refers to a specific function of your code.

The code section is that table which equates the specific steps or commands as written in the dBASE III language and converts them to tokens or symbols representing those actions. Of course, these tokens are linked to the library with regard to their specific machine-level action. The smallest code section size will be 12 bytes. Both the main load module and overlay modules have a certain area set aside for the code section or table.

The constant table is that table of the specific data that never changes. Examples of constant tables are the string of a SAY, a PROMPT, and a specific value assigned to a variable. These constants are a part of the overlay file, yet they may move in and out of memory with the overlay itself. The smallest constant section table size is 32 bytes. Depending on how it is linked, either the main load module or overlay module has a designated area established for this table.

The symbol table refers to functions, program names, memory variables, and macro substitutions. This table is often ignored in calculating the memory requirement of an application. The smallest symbol table size generated by the compiler will be 32 bytes. The symbol table always remains in the main load module, regardless of the size and number of overlays.

Depending on many factors, the linker loads extra overhead in with the application to handle the designated overlay scheme as well as the compiling scheme. For example, more overhead is needed to link many object files together than is required for just a couple of object files. Remember that a user defined function generates a symbol to the compile. If many .PRG files are separated, preventing one massive object file, each object file has an identical symbol every time the UDF is used. At link time the linker consolidates these identical symbols the best it can. This process takes up extra overhead. The solution is to compile larger amounts at one time, such as all .PRG files that make use of unique symbols. This allows the compiler to generate a more efficient symbol table. The table below illustrates this:

.PRG:	A:	B:	C:	D:	E:
Symbol:	UNIQUE()	"hello"	DO A	READ	UNIQUE()
	TRIM()	x =	"bye"	DO A	LTRIM()
	DATE()	SET KEY TO	STR()	SET FORMAT TO	DATE()
	x =	TRANSFORM()	CHR()	SET ALTERNATE	?
				ON	
	"hello"	STR()	DAY()	??	QUIT
	x =	SET KEY TO	"bye"		DATE()
	x =				

If each .PRG file were compiled separately, the code/symbol/constant tables would look something like this:

.PRG:	A:	B:	C:	D:	E:
Symbol:	UNIQUE()	"hello"	DO A	READ	UNIQUE()
	DATE()	x =	"bye"	DO A	LTRIM()
	"hello"	SET KEY TO	STR()	SET FORMAT TO	DATE()
	TRIM()	TRANSFORM()	CHR()	SET ALTERNATE	?
				ON	
	x =	STR()	DAY()	??	QUIT

Regardless of the number of symbols stuffed in the table, the minimum sizes of the table are set in advance. Each is unique. The minimum size of the code table is 12 bytes, the symbol table size 32 bytes, and the constant table size 32 bytes. Below is a screen dump of a compile on an empty .PRG file named TEST.PRG:

```
C:\>clipper test
The Clipper Compiler, Winter '85
Copyright (c) 1985, 1986 Nantucket Inc., All Rights Reserved.

Compiling TEST.PRG
Code size:12   Symbols:32   Constants:32
```

The way to get around the extra overhead used by the linker would be to combine each of those table markers into one, combining like markers and reordering them within one unique table. If you were to compile all of these different .PRG files into one massive program file allowing the compiler to make one pass, the resulting .OBJ table would look something like this:

A:

```
UNIQUE()
TRIM()
DATE()
x =
"hello"
SET KEY TO
TRANSFORM()
STR()
DO A
"bye"
```

```
CHR( )
DAY( )
READ
SET FORMAT TO
?
??
LTRIM( )
SET UNIQUE ON
QUIT
```

It is clear that this table is more consolidated and there would be less work for the linker. Allowing the compiler to cross reference and establish some sort of pre-link order to the tables also saves some overhead.

The linker adds extra overhead to move more symbols out of overlay files and down to the main load module. This amount fluctuates and cannot be specifically calculated. Just be aware of it and allow for it. Unfortunately, there is nothing you can do to prevent this extra overhead from being added. Not all situations require one massive compile. Sometimes, more frequently in larger applications, the amount of space used by the linker for the overlays and reshuffling is far less than that used by one huge load module from one massive compile and link.

Here are a few key figures (all are approximations) to use when designing an overlay scheme:

The basic Clipper library (without REPORT/LABEL commands)	126,200
Additional bytes to support REPORT/LABEL commands	12,000
Size of DOS (varies)	36,000
Partitioned area for memory variables	64,000
TOTAL..	238,200

A series of linking techniques is shown in the next section, each with a small diagram of its internal workings and a brief description of the technique. The examples refer to the MENU GENERATOR application. The eleven program files of MENU GENERATOR were compiled separately using CLiP files. Below is a list of the object files and their code, symbol, and constant sizes. All figures shown below refer to the number of bytes per table, not kilobytes. These numbers will be referred to in all subsequent overlaying techniques we discuss.

Object File	Code Size	Symbol Size	Constant Size
Cmenu.obj	1968	608	3600
Startoff.obj	747	80	496
Begin.obj	328	320	192
Promptng.obj	736	576	320

Menuentr.obj	1108	432	752
Menudraw.obj	726	528	272
Move_cur.obj	655	336	224
Drawbox.obj	385	128	208
Movetitl.obj	380	176	106
Moveesc.obj	380	176	106
Finished.obj	1071	544	1024

In the next two sections, each linking will show the LiNK file used, any memory map that may be pertinent, the file sizes, a diagram of how the memory scheme is laid out, and a summary of the theory involved.

INTERNAL OVERLAYS

In this series of overlays and linking options it is assumed that the entire file, including overlays, fits on a 360K floppy drive. Therefore, with internal overlays the only hurdles to overcome are those pertaining to memory. External overlays will be covered in the next section.

Sample One:

This LiNK file will link all eleven object modules together to make one executable file with no overlays. This link file was the one used to quote a file size of 148,256K.

```
      Command at DOS:    PLINK86 @One

   Name of LiNK file:    One.lnk

   Contents of file:     FI Cmenu
                         FI Startoff
                         FI Begin
                         FI Promptng
                         FI Menuentr
                         FI Menudraw
                         FI Move_cur
                         FI Drawbox
                         FI Movetitl
                         FI Moveesc
                         FI Finished
                         LIB \DBASE\Clipper

           Load Size:    139,264

      Directory Size:    148,352
```

Here the library file is located in the subdirectory labeled DBASE. Notice that the load module that starts the entire application is located at the top of the link list. Without the OUTPUT command, PLINK86 takes the name of this object file as the name of the application. It is generally advisable when using CLiP files and compiling exclusively (compiling a specific set of program files, regardless of the number of program files that the file may call) that the root name of the CLiP file be that of the first program file in the CLiP list. It then follows that the application root name is the first listed name in the link list.

CMENU.EXE via One.lnk:

```
      Total Symbols     3904
    Total Constants     7300
         Total Code     8484
    Clipper Library   119576
```

Sample Two:

The following is a LiNK file that has the main program in the main load module and every other program in one overlay in multiple sections. The additional overhead listed in the overlay file is used to handle the multiple sections within that overlay. The size of the overlay, including basic overhead, is based on the largest code section within the overlay and the largest constant section within the same overlay.

```
    Command at DOS:     PLINK86 @Two

   Name of LiNK file:   Two.lnk

   Contents of file:    FI Cmenu
                        LIB \DBASE\CLIPPER
                        BEGIN
                           SECTION FI Startoff
                           SECTION FI Begin
                           SECTION FI Promptng
                           SECTION FI Menuentr
                           SECTION FI Menudraw
                           SECTION FI Move_cur
                           SECTION FI Drawbox
                           SECTION FI Movetitl
                           SECTION FI Moveesc
                           SECTION FI Finished
                        END

        Load Size:      137,216

    Directory Size:     151,408
```

It is impossible to have programs call other programs in different SECTIONs within the same overlay area. Therefore, this link would eventually yield an EXEC SEQUENCE ERROR and abort the program. However, for the purpose of this demonstration the following is a sample of how the overlay would be viewed, if it were possible to execute.

CMENU.EXE via Two.lnk:

Start	Begin	Prmpt	MenuE	MenuD	MvCur	DrBox	MoveT	MoveE	Finis	Overlay Size
										Code Size
747	328	736	1108	726	655	385	380	380	1071	1108

Overhead

6016

```
        Overlay Handling        20
        CMENU code size       1968
        Total Constants      7300
          Total Symbols      3904
        Clipper Library    119576
```

Sample Three:

This sample is basically the same as Sample Two except that the overlay does not have any SECTIONs within it. Thus, the amount of overhead used by the linker is less. Also, the overlay sizes for each type (code and constants) are combined for each (excluding the figures for CMENU which is calculated in the main load module).

```
     Command at DOS:      PLINK86 @Three

     Name of LiNK file:   Three.lnk

     Contents of file:    FI Cmenu
                          LIB \DBASE\CLIPPER
                          BEGIN
                            FI Startoff
                            FI Begin
                            FI Promptng
                            FI Menuentr
                            FI Menudraw
                            FI Move_cur
                            FI Drawbox
                            FI Movetitl
                            FI Moveesc
                            FI Finished
                          END

          Load Size:      142,336

     Directory Size:      151,120
```

In this sample the SECTION command has been removed and all of the remaining object files are put together in one overlay. All of the symbols are in the main load module, yet the code and constant sizes are combined. Because there is no SECTION command, any program in any module may call and DO any other program in any other module.

CMENU.EXE via Three.lnk:

	Startoff
	Begin
	Promptng
	Menuentr
Remaining Code Sizes	Menudraw
	Move_cur
3700	Drawbox
	Movetitl
	Moveesc
	Finished
(3052)	Overhead

```
Overlay Handling        20
CMENU constant size   3600
   Total Constants    7300
   Total Symbols      3904
   Clipper Library  119576
```

Sample Four:

This sample is the same as the previous one except for the additional command, OVERLAY NIL, $CONSTANTS. This command moves the constant data up from the main load module to the overlay module. Since there is only one overlay, the effect is the same except the .EXE file is a little smaller. The linker will now require less to handle the file.

```
Command at DOS:     PLINK86 @Four

Name of LiNK file:  Four.lnk

Contents of file:   FI Cmenu
                    LIB \DBASE\CLIPPER
                    OVERLAY NIL, $CONSTANTS
                    BEGIN
                       FI Startoff
                       FI Begin
                       FI Promptng
                       FI Menuentr
                       FI Menudraw
                       FI Move_cur
                       FI Drawbox
                       FI Movetitl
                       FI Moveesc
```

```
                    FI Finished
                END

    Load Size:      142,336

Directory Size:     151,072
```

CMENU.EXE via Four.lnk:

	Startoff
Remaining Constant Sizes	Begin
	Promptng
6516	Menuentr
	Menudraw
	Move_cur
Remaining Code Sizes	Drawbox
	Movetitl
3700	Moveesc
	Finished
(3052)	Overhead

```
    Overlay Handling        20
CMENU constant size       3600
   CMENU code size        1968
     Total Symbols        3904
 Clipper Library        119576
```

USING MULTIPLE SECTIONS

This section of the discussion on linking introduces the subject of multiple sections and overlaying the file. Because of the recursive program calling, it is difficult to make an overlay file with many sections in it and not have problems. Therefore, in order to save on space and strive for multiple sections, more than one overlay must be established. Using a diagrammed map of the system is a handy way to show the proper way of setting up the linkage.

Sample One:

Consider the following link file:

```
FI Cmenu
MAP = Ten a
LIB \Dbase\Clipper
BEGIN
   SECTION FI Moveesc
   SECTION FI Movetitl
   SECTION FI Finished
END
```

```
BEGIN
   SECTION FI Menudraw, Promptng
   SECTION FI Move_cur
   SECTION FI Drawbox
END
BEGIN
   SECTION FI Menuentr
   SECTION FI Startoff
END
BEGIN
   SECTION FI Begin
END
```

Following is the memory map that the linker provides.

Groups:

Name	Address	Size	DSalloc
DGROUP	1EFF0	3130	

Segments:

Section : Maddr=0, Msize=1B3B0, Daddr=1C00, Lev=0, Ovly#=0

Name	Addr	Size	Name	Addr	Size
CMENU.NIL	0	15F	CENTER.NI	160	3A
SHORT.NIL	1A0	27	VERIFY.NI	1D0	6B
PROCHEAD.	240	39	HELP.NIL	280	4A4
DOITAGAIN	730	2E	CHAINA.NI	760	24
CHAINB.NI	790	29	$START.NI	7C0	DF
$INTERFAC	89F	6F4	$INTERFAC	F93	8B
$DRIVERS.	101E	54F	EXEC.C.NI	156D	136B
_PROG.NIL	28D8	1CA	NDEBUG.C.	2AA2	B
SYMSYS.C.	2AAD	523	CTERM.C.N	2FD0	915
STACK.C.N	38E5	12B1	DB.C.NIL	4B96	4B00
OPS.C.NIL	9696	261E	STERM.C.N	BCB4	377E
SET.C.NIL	F432	BCB	CSUPPORT.	FFFD	1861
MACRO.C.N	1185E	36A	$HACKJOB.	11BC8	271
_PROG.NIL	11E39	5D	_PROG.NIL	11E96	2DD
_PROG.NIL	12173	0	_PROG.NIL	12173	0
_PROG.NIL	12173	0	_PROG.NIL	12173	120
INDEX.C.N	12293	27E9	RPAR.C.NI	14A7C	1D4B
_PROG.NIL	167C7	6A	_PROG.NIL	16831	5DB
_PROG.NIL	16E0C	15	NATION.C.	16E21	19C
_PROG.NIL	16FBD	41	_PROG.NIL	16FFE	1D
_PROG.NIL	1701B	6A	_PROG.NIL	17085	38
_PROG.NIL	170BD	2E	_PROG.NIL	170EB	25
_PROG.NIL	17110	0	_PROG.NIL	17110	0
_PROG.NIL	17110	A59	_PROG.NIL	17B69	1B
_PROG.NIL	17B84	12F	_PROG.NIL	17CB3	41
_PROG.NIL	17CF4	2D	_PROG.NIL	17D21	1E
_PROG.NIL	17D3F	456	_PROG.NIL	18195	9A
_PROG.NIL	1822F	1D	_PROG.NIL	1824C	33

```
_PROG.NIL   1827F   2D    _PROG.NIL   182AC   A8
_PROG.NIL   18354   C     _PROG.NIL   18360   C
_PROG.NIL   1836C   C4    _PROG.NIL   18430   41A
_PROG.NIL   1884A   178   _PROG.NIL   189C2   92
_PROG.NIL   18A54   4C    _PROG.NIL   18AA0   3C
_PROG.NIL   18ADC   15    _PROG.NIL   18AF1   423
_PROG.NIL   18F14   106   _PROG.NIL   1901A   A0
_PROG.NIL   190BA   43    _PROG.NIL   190FD   AF
_PROG.NIL   191AC   15    _PROG.NIL   191C1   0
_PROG.NIL   191C1   E     _PROG.NIL   191CF   84
_PROG.NIL   19253   164   _PROG.NIL   193B7   5B
_PROG.NIL   19412   11F   _PROG.NIL   19531   F9
_PROG.NIL   1962A   50    _PROG.NIL   1967A   24
_PROG.NIL   1969E   20    _PROG.NIL   196BE   32
_PROG.NIL   196F0   1A4   _PROG.NIL   19894   0
_PROG.NIL   19894   21    _PROG.NIL   198B5   3E
_PROG.NIL   198F3   58    _PROG.NIL   1994B   2CD
_PROG.NIL   19C18   34    _PROG.NIL   19C4C   2AE
_PROG.NIL   19EFA   241   _PROG.NIL   1A13B   A8
_PROG.NIL   1A1E3   17F   _PROG.NIL   1A362   0
_PROG.NIL   1A362   B     _PROG.NIL   1A36D   12
_PROG.NIL   1A37F   1B    _PROG.NIL   1A39A   7B
_PROG.NIL   1A415   9C    _PROG.NIL   1A4B1   34
_PROG.NIL   1A4E5   EB    _PROG.NIL   1A5D0   2B
_PROG.NIL   1A5FB   28    _PROG.NIL   1A623   6B
_PROG.NIL   1A68E   125   _PROG.NIL   1A7B3   7C
_PROG.NIL   1A82F   EA    $OVTB$.OV   1A920   128
OVDATA.OV   1AB00   1EC   OVCODE.OV   1ACF0   6B6
```

```
Section : Maddr=1B3B0, Msize=170, Daddr=1CFD0, Lev=1, Ovly#=1
    MOVEESC.N   1B3B0   161

Section : Maddr=1B3B0, Msize=170, Daddr=1D150, Lev=1, Ovly#=2
    MOVETITL.   1B3B0   161

Section : Maddr=1B3B0, Msize=420, Daddr=1D2E0, Lev=1, Ovly#=3
    FINISHED.   1B3B0   207   FINISHED_   1B5C0   208

Section : Maddr=1B7D0, Msize=550, Daddr=1D720, Lev=1, Ovly#=4
    MENUDRAW.   1B7D0   2A5   PROMPTNG.   1BA80   29C

Section : Maddr=1B7D0, Msize=260, Daddr=1DC80, Lev=1, Ovly#=5
    MOVE_CUR.   1B7D0   25F

Section : Maddr=1B7D0, Msize=160, Daddr=1DEF0, Lev=1, Ovly#=6
    DRAWBOX.N   1B7D0   15A

Section : Maddr=1BD20, Msize=3C0, Daddr=1E060, Lev=1, Ovly#=7
    MENUENTR.   1BD20   3BD

Section : Maddr=1BD20, Msize=2C0, Daddr=1E430, Lev=1, Ovly#=8
    STARTOFF.   1BD20   2BB
```

```
Section : Maddr=1C0E0, Msize=140, Daddr=1E700, Lev=1, Ovly#=9
    BEGIN.NIL  1C0E0     136

Section : Maddr=1C220, Msize=5F00, Daddr=1F0F0, Lev=0, Ovly#=10, Pre-Loaded

    $EXPR.$EX  1C220       0    $EXPR.$EX  1C220       0
    $EXPR.$EX  1C220       0    $EXPR.$EX  1C220      27
    $EXPR.$EX  1C250      13    $EXPR.$EX  1C270      26
    $EXPR.$EX  1C2A0       0    $EXPR.$EX  1C2A0       0
    $EXPR.$EX  1C2A0      39    $EXPR.$EX  1C2E0       0
    $EXPR.$EX  1C2E0       0    $MDATA.$M  1C2E0      B0
    $SYMSTART  1C390       0    $SYMBOLS.  1C390     260
    $SYMBOLS.  1C5F0      B0    $SYMBOLS.  1C6A0      B0
    $SYMBOLS.  1C750     220    $SYMBOLS.  1C970     210
    $SYMBOLS.  1CB80     240    $SYMBOLS.  1CDC0     150
    $SYMBOLS.  1CF10      80    $SYMBOLS.  1CF90     1B0
    $SYMBOLS.  1D140      50    $SYMBOLS.  1D190     140
    $SYMEND.$  1D2D0       2    $CONSTANT  1D2E0     E30
    $CONSTANT  1E110      A0    $CONSTANT  1E1B0      A0
    $CONSTANT  1E250     400    $CONSTANT  1E650     110
    $CONSTANT  1E760     140    $CONSTANT  1E8A0      E0
    $CONSTANT  1E980      D0    $CONSTANT  1EA50     2F0
    $CONSTANT  1ED40     1F0    $CONSTANT  1EF30      C0
    DATA.DATA  1EFF0    2D70    $LIB_TABL  21D60     33C
    STACK.DAT  220A0      80
```

The basic load module from this is 139,424 bytes. Look at the "Section : Maddr =" points in the map for each individual overlay. For the first overlay, the beginning address point is at 1B3B0 and the ending address point is 1B7CF. The difference between the two is 41F hex or 1055 bytes. This is close to the number for the largest code module (FINISHED) which was 1071 (the code size for that object file). Obviously, this overlay must allow for the largest section's code value. The remaining two object files, MOVEESC and MOVETITL, are both smaller than FINISHED so the overlay will accommodate the relative code, constant and symbol size of FINISHED.obj.

In the next overlay area the ending address point minus the beginning address point yields a total overlay area of 1,359 bytes. Look at the sections involved. There are four object files comprising three sections. The total of the code values generated by the compiler from the two object files in the first section is 1,426 bytes. This figure is larger than the code size of MOVE_CUR,obj (655) and DRAWBOX.obj (385). Therefore, this overlay is the size of the largest section, which is the combination of MENUDRAW and PROMPTING.

These overlays sit on top of one another. The basic picture for this linkage would be something like this:

Overlay BEGIN	319 bytes
Overlay MENUENTR STARTOFF	959 bytes

Overlay MENUDRAW + PROMPTING
        Move_cur
        Drawbox
	1,426 bytes

Overlay MOVEESC
        MOVETITL
        FINISHED
	1,071 bytes

Symbols/Expressions/Constants Clipper.lib Code: CMENU	~ 135,000 bytes

We can reduce some of the main load size by moving the $CONSTANTS out of the preload section and into the overlay in which each $CONSTANT belongs. For instance, according to the table chart, the symbol size for CMENU.OBJ is 608. In the previous memory map the first $CONSTANT symbol has a value of hex E30. When converted to decimal, it equals 3,632. This is close to the compiled figure of 3600. The next $CONSTANT size has a value of A0. This equates to 160 which is roughly the constant size of either MOVETITL.OBJ or MOVEESC.OBJ. In our link list the second object file linked into the system in the first overlay area is MOVEESC.OBJ. There is a definite pattern to these numbers and where they reside in the memory map.

In order to move the corresponding $CONSTANT symbols to their respective places, an additional linking command needs to be issued BEFORE the first overlay area.

OVERLAY NIL, $CONSTANT

The following example shows how this command would look in the link list:

```
FI Cmenu
MAP = Ten2 a
LIB \Dbase\Clipper
OVERLAY NIL, $CONSTANTS
BEGIN
    SECTION FI Moveesc
    SECTION FI Movetitl
    SECTION FI Finished
END
BEGIN
    SECTION FI Menudraw, Promptng
    SECTION FI Move_cur
    SECTION FI Drawbox
```

```
END
BEGIN
   SECTION FI Menuentr
   SECTION FI Startoff
END
BEGIN
   SECTION FI Begin
END
```

The corresponding memory map looks like this:

Groups:

Name	Address	Size	DSalloc
DGROUP	1EAE0	3130	

Segments:

Section : Maddr=0, Msize=1C1B0, Daddr=1C00, Lev=0, Ovly#=0

Name	Addr	Size	Name	Addr	Size
CMENU.NIL	0	15F	CENTER.NI	160	3A
SHORT.NIL	1A0	27	VERIFY.NI	1D0	6B
PROCHEAD.	240	39	HELP.NIL	280	4A4
DOITAGAIN	730	2E	CHAINA.NI	760	24
CHAINB.NI	790	29	$START.NI	7C0	DF
$INTERFAC	89F	6F4	$INTERFAC	F93	8B
$DRIVERS.	101E	54F	EXEC.C.NI	156D	136B
_PROG.NIL	28D8	1CA	NDEBUG.C.	2AA2	B
SYMSYS.C.	2AAD	523	CTERM.C.N	2FD0	915
STACK.C.N	38E5	12B1	DB.C.NIL	4B96	4B00
OPS.C.NIL	9696	261E	STERM.C.N	BCB4	377E
SET.C.NIL	F432	BCB	CSUPPORT.	FFFD	1861
MACRO.C.N	1185E	36A	$HACKJOB.	11BC8	271
_PROG.NIL	11E39	5D	_PROG.NIL	11E96	2DD
_PROG.NIL	12173	0	_PROG.NIL	12173	0
_PROG.NIL	12173	0	_PROG.NIL	12173	120
INDEX.C.N	12293	27E9	RPAR.C.NI	14A7C	1D4B
_PROG.NIL	167C7	6A	_PROG.NIL	16831	5DB
_PROG.NIL	16E0C	15	NATION.C.	16E21	19C
_PROG.NIL	16FBD	41	_PROG.NIL	16FFE	1D
_PROG.NIL	1701B	6A	_PROG.NIL	17085	38
_PROG.NIL	170BD	2E	_PROG.NIL	170EB	25
_PROG.NIL	17110	0	_PROG.NIL	17110	0
_PROG.NIL	17110	A59	_PROG.NIL	17B69	1B
_PROG.NIL	17B84	12F	_PROG.NIL	17CB3	41
_PROG.NIL	17CF4	2D	_PROG.NIL	17D21	1E
_PROG.NIL	17D3F	456	_PROG.NIL	18195	9A
_PROG.NIL	1822F	1D	_PROG.NIL	1824C	33
_PROG.NIL	1827F	2D	_PROG.NIL	182AC	A8
_PROG.NIL	18354	C	_PROG.NIL	18360	C
_PROG.NIL	1836C	C4	_PROG.NIL	18430	41A
_PROG.NIL	1884A	178	_PROG.NIL	189C2	92

```
_PROG.NIL  18A54    4C   _PROG.NIL  18AA0    3C
_PROG.NIL  18ADC    15   _PROG.NIL  18AF1   423
_PROG.NIL  18F14   106   _PROG.NIL  1901A    A0
_PROG.NIL  190BA    43   _PROG.NIL  190FD    AF
_PROG.NIL  191AC    15   _PROG.NIL  191C1     0
_PROG.NIL  191C1     E   _PROG.NIL  191CF    84
_PROG.NIL  19253   164   _PROG.NIL  193B7    5B
_PROG.NIL  19412   11F   _PROG.NIL  19531    F9
_PROG.NIL  1962A    50   _PROG.NIL  1967A    24
_PROG.NIL  1969E    20   _PROG.NIL  196BE    32
_PROG.NIL  196F0   1A4   _PROG.NIL  19894     0
_PROG.NIL  19894    21   _PROG.NIL  198B5    3E
_PROG.NIL  198F3    58   _PROG.NIL  1994B   2CD
_PROG.NIL  19C18    34   _PROG.NIL  19C4C   2AE
_PROG.NIL  19EFA   241   _PROG.NIL  1A13B    A8
_PROG.NIL  1A1E3   17F   _PROG.NIL  1A362     0
_PROG.NIL  1A362     B   _PROG.NIL  1A36D    12
_PROG.NIL  1A37F    1B   _PROG.NIL  1A39A    7B
_PROG.NIL  1A415    9C   _PROG.NIL  1A4B1    34
_PROG.NIL  1A4E5    EB   _PROG.NIL  1A5D0    2B
_PROG.NIL  1A5FB    28   _PROG.NIL  1A623    6B
_PROG.NIL  1A68E   125   _PROG.NIL  1A7B3    7C
_PROG.NIL  1A82F    EA   $CONSTANT  1A920   E30
$OVTB$.OV  1B750   128   OVDATA.OV  1B900   1EC
OVCODE.OV  1BAF0   6B6
```

```
Section : Maddr=1C1B0, Msize=210, Daddr=1DDD0, Lev=1, Ovly#=1
    MOVEESC.N  1C1B0   161   $CONSTANT  1C320    A0

Section : Maddr=1C1B0, Msize=210, Daddr=1DFF0, Lev=1, Ovly#=2
    MOVETITL.  1C1B0   161   $CONSTANT  1C320    A0

Section : Maddr=1C1B0, Msize=820, Daddr=1E220, Lev=1, Ovly#=3
    FINISHED.  1C1B0   207   FINISHED_  1C3C0   208
    $CONSTANT  1C5D0   400

Section : Maddr=1C9D0, Msize=7A0, Daddr=1EA60, Lev=1, Ovly#=4
    MENUDRAW.  1C9D0   2A5   PROMPTNG.  1CC80   29C
    $CONSTANT  1CF20   110   $CONSTANT  1D030   140

Section : Maddr=1C9D0, Msize=340, Daddr=1F210, Lev=1, Ovly#=5
    MOVE_CUR.  1C9D0   25F   $CONSTANT  1CC30    E0

Section : Maddr=1C9D0, Msize=230, Daddr=1F560, Lev=1, Ovly#=6
    DRAWBOX.N  1C9D0   15A   $CONSTANT  1CB30    D0

Section : Maddr=1D170, Msize=6B0, Daddr=1F7A0, Lev=1, Ovly#=7
    MENUENTR.  1D170   3BD   $CONSTANT  1D530   2F0

Section : Maddr=1D170, Msize=4B0, Daddr=1FE60, Lev=1, Ovly#=8
    STARTOFF.  1D170   2BB   $CONSTANT  1D430   1F0

Section : Maddr=1D820, Msize=200, Daddr=20320, Lev=1, Ovly#=9
    BEGIN.NIL  1D820   136   $CONSTANT  1D960    C0
```

```
Section : Maddr=1DA20, Msize=41F0, Daddr=20DD0, Lev=0, Ovly#=10, Pre-Loaded
```

$EXPR.$EX	1DA20	0	$EXPR.$EX	1DA20	0
$EXPR.$EX	1DA20	0	$EXPR.$EX	1DA20	27
$EXPR.$EX	1DA50	13	$EXPR.$EX	1DA70	26
$EXPR.$EX	1DAA0	0	$EXPR.$EX	1DAA0	0
$EXPR.$EX	1DAA0	39	$EXPR.$EX	1DAE0	0
$EXPR.$EX	1DAE0	0	$MDATA.$M	1DAE0	B0
$SYMSTART	1DB90	0	$SYMBOLS.	1DB90	260
$SYMBOLS.	1DDF0	B0	$SYMBOLS.	1DEA0	B0
$SYMBOLS.	1DF50	220	$SYMBOLS.	1E170	210
$SYMBOLS.	1E380	240	$SYMBOLS.	1E5C0	150
$SYMBOLS.	1E710	80	$SYMBOLS.	1E790	1B0
$SYMBOLS.	1E940	50	$SYMBOLS.	1E990	140
$SYMEND.$	1EAD0	2	DATA.DATA	1EAE0	2D70
$LIB_TABL	21850	33C	STACK.DAT	21B90	80

All of the $CONSTANTs have been moved. The first went to the section of the map before the first overlay (that $CONSTANT is for CMENU.OBJ). Each section in the overlay has the corresponding $CONSTANT size. The last address for the file is now 21B90 hex, or 138,128 bytes. This is a decrease in file size of 1,296 bytes. Where the extra bytes went is easy to explain. By moving the $CONSTANT tables in with the overlay, the overlay increases by the size of the largest $CONSTANT map. The overlay, parsed by many sections, now has two basic parts: a part of memory to house the largest code module, and a part to house the largest constant module. Looking at the first overlay, the largest $CONSTANT table is FINISHED.OBJ. Therefore, the remaining two object files' constants size can fit inside the first one. With this approach the overlay module grows by about 1024 bytes, but the overall application saves about 212 bytes. A diagram of the memory scheme shows the following:

Overlay BEGIN	Code: 310 Constants: 192	511 bytes
Overlay MENUENTR STARTOFF	Code: 909 Constants: 752	1,711 bytes
Overlay MENUDRAW+PROMPTNG Move_cur Drawbox	Code: 1,345 Constants: 592	1,951 bytes
Overlay MOVEESC MOVETITL FINISHED	Code: 1,039 Constants: 1,024	2,079 bytes
Symbols / Expressions		
Clipper.lib		~ 131,876 bytes
Constants + Code of CMENU		

The topmost overlay size is (1DA20 - 1) - 1D820 hex which is 1FF or 511 decimal. This is obviously bigger than the code size for BEGIN.OBJ. It is the combination of the code size and the constant size for BEGIN.OBJ, which is 520. Always allow for a small variance in the calculations. In the second overlay the largest code section is from MENUENTR.OBJ, as is the largest constant section. Using the same method for calculating the overlay size, we find that the overlay is roughly 1711 bytes, while the combined code and constant size for MENUENTR.OBJ is 1860. This is well within the range of tolerance. The total of all of the constant sizes from the files which are saved within the other constants' tables is:

FILE	BYTES
Startoff.obj	496
Drawbox.obj	208
Move_cur.obj	224
Movetitl.obj	106
Moveesc.obj	106
TOTAL.................	1,140

This is very close to the difference between the first and second links.

Going back to the first example, look at the basic code sizes of the sections, remembering that the overlay size is based on the size of the largest code table in a section. If only some SECTION commands were issued, then the overlay size is based on the code size of the object file outside of the SECTION within the same overlay, plus the size of the largest SECTION's code size. However, in this example, look at the code size of the first overlay. Note that FINISHED.OBJ is the largest and the other two SECTIONs (MOVEESC.OBJ and MOVEESC.OBJ) can move in and out of the space set aside for FINISHED.OBJ.

Suppose we move FINISHED.OBJ down with MENUENTR.OBJ and STARTOFF.OBJ. First, the first overlay would decrease in size relative to the largest section code size. Since both remaining files (MOVEESC.OBJ and MOVETITL.OBJ) are the same in code size, their overlay would not establish room for either of their respective sizes. Looking at the overlay which now contains FINISHED.OBJ, we see that the size of MENUENTR.OBJ and FINISHED.OBJ are approximately equal in size. Therefore, in theory, the overlay should not be much bigger than it already is. Make sure that the object file being moved (FINISHED.OBJ) is not called by any of the other object files in other sections of the new overlay. Since in this case neither procedure MENUENTR nor procedure STARTOFF makes any calls to FINISHED we can place FINISHED.OBJ in a separate section in this overlay. Looking at the link file we would see:

```
FI Cmenu
MAP = Ten a
LIB \DBASE\Clipper
```

```
BEGIN
   SECTION FI Moveesc
   SECTION FI Movetitl
END
BEGIN
   SECTION FI Menudraw, Promptng
   SECTION FI Move_cur
   SECTION FI Drawbox
END
BEGIN
   SECTION FI Menuentr
   SECTION FI Startoff
   SECTION FI Finished
END
BEGIN
   SECTION FI Begin
END
```

Here is the map generated by this link:

```
Groups:

    Name         Address  Size  DSalloc
    DGROUP       1EDA0    3130

Segments:

    Section :  Maddr=0, Msize=1B3B0, Daddr=1C00, Lev=0, Ovly#=0

        Name        Addr    Size    Name        Addr    Size
        CMENU.NIL      0     15F    CENTER.NI    160      3A
        SHORT.NIL    1A0      27    VERIFY.NI    1D0      6B
        PROCHEAD.    240      39    HELP.NIL     280     4A4
        DOITAGAIN    730      2E    CHAINA.NI    760      24
        CHAINB.NI    790      29    $START.NI    7C0      DF
        $INTERFAC    89F     6F4    $INTERFAC    F93      8B
        $DRIVERS.   101E     54F    EXEC.C.NI   156D    136B
        _PROG.NIL   28D8     1CA    NDEBUG.C.   2AA2       B
        SYMSYS.C.   2AAD     523    CTERM.C.N   2FD0     915
        STACK.C.N   38E5    12B1    DB.C.NIL    4B96    4B00
        OPS.C.NIL   9696    261E    STERM.C.N   BCB4    377E
        SET.C.NIL   F432     BCB    CSUPPORT.   FFFD    1861
        MACRO.C.N   1185E    36A    $HACKJOB.   11BC8    271
        _PROG.NIL   11E39     5D    _PROG.NIL   11E96    2DD
        _PROG.NIL   12173      0    _PROG.NIL   12173      0
        _PROG.NIL   12173      0    _PROG.NIL   12173    120
        INDEX.C.N   12293    27E9    RPAR.C.NI   14A7C    1D4B
        _PROG.NIL   167C7     6A    _PROG.NIL   16831    5DB
        _PROG.NIL   16E0C     15    NATION.C.   16E21    19C
        _PROG.NIL   16FBD     41    _PROG.NIL   16FFE     1D
        _PROG.NIL   1701B     6A    _PROG.NIL   17085     38
        _PROG.NIL   170BD     2E    _PROG.NIL   170EB     25
        _PROG.NIL   17110      0    _PROG.NIL   17110      0
```

```
       _PROG.NIL   17110    A59    _PROG.NIL   17B69    1B
       _PROG.NIL   17B84    12F    _PROG.NIL   17CB3    41
       _PROG.NIL   17CF4    2D     _PROG.NIL   17D21    1E
       _PROG.NIL   17D3F    456    _PROG.NIL   18195    9A
       _PROG.NIL   1822F    1D     _PROG.NIL   1824C    33
       _PROG.NIL   1827F    2D     _PROG.NIL   182AC    A8
       _PROG.NIL   18354    C      _PROG.NIL   18360    C
       _PROG.NIL   1836C    C4     _PROG.NIL   18430    41A
       _PROG.NIL   1884A    178    _PROG.NIL   189C2    92
       _PROG.NIL   18A54    4C     _PROG.NIL   18AA0    3C
       _PROG.NIL   18ADC    15     _PROG.NIL   18AF1    423
       _PROG.NIL   18F14    106    _PROG.NIL   1901A    A0
       _PROG.NIL   190BA    43     _PROG.NIL   190FD    AF
       _PROG.NIL   191AC    15     _PROG.NIL   191C1    0
       _PROG.NIL   191C1    E      _PROG.NIL   191CF    84
       _PROG.NIL   19253    164    _PROG.NIL   193B7    5B
       _PROG.NIL   19412    11F    _PROG.NIL   19531    F9
       _PROG.NIL   1962A    50     _PROG.NIL   1967A    24
       _PROG.NIL   1969E    20     _PROG.NIL   196BE    32
       _PROG.NIL   196F0    1A4    _PROG.NIL   19894    0
       _PROG.NIL   19894    21     _PROG.NIL   198B5    3E
       _PROG.NIL   198F3    58     _PROG.NIL   1994B    2CD
       _PROG.NIL   19C18    34     _PROG.NIL   19C4C    2AE
       _PROG.NIL   19EFA    241    _PROG.NIL   1A13B    A8
       _PROG.NIL   1A1E3    17F    _PROG.NIL   1A362    0
       _PROG.NIL   1A362    B      _PROG.NIL   1A36D    12
       _PROG.NIL   1A37F    1B     _PROG.NIL   1A39A    7B
       _PROG.NIL   1A415    9C     _PROG.NIL   1A4B1    34
       _PROG.NIL   1A4E5    EB     _PROG.NIL   1A5D0    2B
       _PROG.NIL   1A5FB    28     _PROG.NIL   1A623    6B
       _PROG.NIL   1A68E    125    _PROG.NIL   1A7B3    7C
       _PROG.NIL   1A82F    EA     $OVTB$.OV   1A920    128
       OVDATA.OV   1AB00    1EC    OVCODE.OV   1ACF0    6B6

Section :  Maddr=1B3B0, Msize=170, Daddr=1CFD0, Lev=1, Ovly#=1
       MOVEESC.N  1B3B0    161

Section :  Maddr=1B3B0, Msize=170, Daddr=1D150, Lev=1, Ovly#=2
       MOVETITL.  1B3B0    161

Section :  Maddr=1B520, Msize=550, Daddr=1D2E0, Lev=1, Ovly#=3
       MENUDRAW.  1B520    2A5    PROMPTNG.   1B7D0    29C

Section :  Maddr=1B520, Msize=260, Daddr=1D840, Lev=1, Ovly#=4
       MOVE_CUR.  1B520    25F

Section :  Maddr=1B520, Msize=160, Daddr=1DAB0, Lev=1, Ovly#=5
       DRAWBOX.N  1B520    15A

Section :  Maddr=1BA70, Msize=3C0, Daddr=1DC20, Lev=1, Ovly#=6
       MENUENTR.  1BA70    3BD

Section :  Maddr=1BA70, Msize=2C0, Daddr=1DFF0, Lev=1, Ovly#=7
       STARTOFF.  1BA70    2BB
```

```
Section : Maddr=1BA70, Msize=420, Daddr=1E2D0, Lev=1, Ovly#=8
     FINISHED. 1BA70    207    FINISHED_  1BC80    208

Section : Maddr=1BE90, Msize=140, Daddr=1E700, Lev=1, Ovly#=9
     BEGIN.NIL 1BE90    136

Section : Maddr=1BFD0, Msize=5F00, Daddr=1F0F0, Lev=0, Ovly#=10, Pre-Loaded

     $EXPR.$EX 1BFD0     0     $EXPR.$EX  1BFD0     0
     $EXPR.$EX 1BFD0     0     $EXPR.$EX  1BFD0    13
     $EXPR.$EX 1BFF0    26     $EXPR.$EX  1C020     0
     $EXPR.$EX 1C020     0     $EXPR.$EX  1C020    39
     $EXPR.$EX 1C060     0     $EXPR.$EX  1C060    27
     $EXPR.$EX 1C090     0     $MDATA.$M  1C090    B0
     $SYMSTART 1C140     0     $SYMBOLS.  1C140   260
     $SYMBOLS. 1C3A0    B0     $SYMBOLS.  1C450    B0
     $SYMBOLS. 1C500   210     $SYMBOLS.  1C710   240
     $SYMBOLS. 1C950   150     $SYMBOLS.  1CAA0    80
     $SYMBOLS. 1CB20   1B0     $SYMBOLS.  1CCD0    50
     $SYMBOLS. 1CD20   220     $SYMBOLS.  1CF40   140
     $SYMEND.$ 1D080     2     $CONSTANT  1D090   E30
     $CONSTANT 1DEC0    A0     $CONSTANT  1DF60    A0
     $CONSTANT 1E000   110     $CONSTANT  1E110   140
     $CONSTANT 1E250    E0     $CONSTANT  1E330    D0
     $CONSTANT 1E400   2F0     $CONSTANT  1E6F0   1F0
     $CONSTANT 1E8E0   400     $CONSTANT  1ECE0    C0
     DATA.DATA 1EDA0  2D70     $LIB_TABL  21B10   33C
     STACK.DAT 21E50    80
```

The diagram for this file is as follows:

```
┌─────────────────────────────────────┐
│ Overlay BEGIN                        │     319 bytes
├─────────────────────────────────────┤
│ Overlay MENUENTR                     │
│         STARTOFF                     │   1,055 bytes
│         FINISHED                     │
├─────────────────────────────────────┤
│ Overlay MENUDRAW + PROMPTING         │
│         Move_cur                     │   1,426 bytes
│         Drawbox                      │
├─────────────────────────────────────┤
│ Overlay MOVEESC                      │
│         MOVETITL                     │     367 bytes
├─────────────────────────────────────┤
│ Symbols/Expressions/Constants        │
│                                      │
│ Clipper.lib                          │  ~ 135,000 bytes
│                                      │
│ Code: CMENU                          │
└─────────────────────────────────────┘
```

The difference between the two linked files is 592 bytes (take the last address points in each memory map, 220A0 and 21E50, and subtract the second from the first). The difference between the code size of FINISHED.OBJ and MOVEESC.OBJ (or

MOVETITL.OBJ) is roughly 691 bytes. The overlay now containing FINISHED.OBJ increased by 96 bytes. Subtract the 96 bytes gained from the 691 bytes saved and the net result is a total saving of 596 bytes. This shows that the space is being better utilized in this linking scheme than in the first.

If possible keep similar sizes together in as many sections as necessary. However, remember that the linker will add bytes for each additional section and for each overlay. In many cases, when the code is broken down to many separate overlays or sections, the number of bytes added by the linker offsets the number of bytes saved by an elaborate linking scheme. Fortunately, this is not the case here. Above all, make sure that the sections in an overlay do not call any other section within the same overlay.

To finish this example, here is the LiNK file and memory map of the previous example with the additional command OVERLAY NIL, $CONSTANTS. The use of this command allows the constant tables to be out of the pre-load section and in their respective overlays. Since constants pertain only to the code used in the overlay, it is beneficial to do this. After looking at the command syntax, note the preceding memory map and the one following, especially the overlays and the pre-load section.

```
FI Cmenu
MAP = Ten6 a
LIB \DBASE\Clipper
OVERLAY NIL, $CONSTANTS
BEGIN
    SECTION FI Moveesc
    SECTION FI Movetitl
END
BEGIN
    SECTION FI Menudraw, Promptng
    SECTION FI Move_cur
    SECTION FI Drawbox
END
BEGIN
    SECTION FI Menuentr
    SECTION FI Startoff
    SECTION FI Finished
END
BEGIN
    SECTION FI Begin
END
```

Once again, here is the memory map:

```
Groups:

    Name        Address  Size  DSalloc
    DGROUP      1E640    3130

Segments:
```

Section : Maddr=0, Msize=1C1B0, Daddr=1C00, Lev=0, Ovly#=0

Name	Addr	Size	Name	Addr	Size
CMENU.NIL	0	15F	CENTER.NI	160	3A
SHORT.NIL	1A0	27	VERIFY.NI	1D0	6B
PROCHEAD.	240	39	HELP.NIL	280	4A4
DOITAGAIN	730	2E	CHAINA.NI	760	24
CHAINB.NI	790	29	$START.NI	7C0	DF
$INTERFAC	89F	6F4	$INTERFAC	F93	8B
$DRIVERS.	101E	54F	EXEC.C.NI	156D	136B
_PROG.NIL	28D8	1CA	NDEBUG.C.	2AA2	B
SYMSYS.C.	2AAD	523	CTERM.C.N	2FD0	915
STACK.C.N	38E5	12B1	DB.C.NIL	4B96	4B00
OPS.C.NIL	9696	261E	STERM.C.N	BCB4	377E
SET.C.NIL	F432	BCB	CSUPPORT.	FFFD	1861
MACRO.C.N	1185E	36A	$HACKJOB.	11BC8	271
_PROG.NIL	11E39	5D	_PROG.NIL	11E96	2DD
_PROG.NIL	12173	0	_PROG.NIL	12173	0
_PROG.NIL	12173	0	_PROG.NIL	12173	120
INDEX.C.N	12293	27E9	RPAR.C.NI	14A7C	1D4B
_PROG.NIL	167C7	6A	_PROG.NIL	16831	5DB
_PROG.NIL	16E0C	15	NATION.C.	16E21	19C
_PROG.NIL	16FBD	41	_PROG.NIL	16FFE	1D
_PROG.NIL	1701B	6A	_PROG.NIL	17085	38
_PROG.NIL	170BD	2E	_PROG.NIL	170EB	25
_PROG.NIL	17110	0	_PROG.NIL	17110	0
_PROG.NIL	17110	A59	_PROG.NIL	17B69	1B
_PROG.NIL	17B84	12F	_PROG.NIL	17CB3	41
_PROG.NIL	17CF4	2D	_PROG.NIL	17D21	1E
_PROG.NIL	17D3F	456	_PROG.NIL	18195	9A
_PROG.NIL	1822F	1D	_PROG.NIL	1824C	33
_PROG.NIL	1827F	2D	_PROG.NIL	182AC	A8
_PROG.NIL	18354	C	_PROG.NIL	18360	C
_PROG.NIL	1836C	C4	_PROG.NIL	18430	41A
_PROG.NIL	1884A	178	_PROG.NIL	189C2	92
_PROG.NIL	18A54	4C	_PROG.NIL	18AA0	3C
_PROG.NIL	18ADC	15	_PROG.NIL	18AF1	423
_PROG.NIL	18F14	106	_PROG.NIL	1901A	A0
_PROG.NIL	190BA	43	_PROG.NIL	190FD	AF
_PROG.NIL	191AC	15	_PROG.NIL	191C1	0
_PROG.NIL	191C1	E	_PROG.NIL	191CF	84
_PROG.NIL	19253	164	_PROG.NIL	193B7	5B
_PROG.NIL	19412	11F	_PROG.NIL	19531	F9
_PROG.NIL	1962A	50	_PROG.NIL	1967A	24
_PROG.NIL	1969E	20	_PROG.NIL	196BE	32
_PROG.NIL	196F0	1A4	_PROG.NIL	19894	0
_PROG.NIL	19894	21	_PROG.NIL	198B5	3E
_PROG.NIL	198F3	58	_PROG.NIL	1994B	2CD
_PROG.NIL	19C18	34	_PROG.NIL	19C4C	2AE
_PROG.NIL	19EFA	241	_PROG.NIL	1A13B	A8
_PROG.NIL	1A1E3	17F	_PROG.NIL	1A362	0
_PROG.NIL	1A362	B	_PROG.NIL	1A36D	12
_PROG.NIL	1A37F	1B	_PROG.NIL	1A39A	7B

```
    _PROG.NIL   1A415     9C    _PROG.NIL   1A4B1     34
    _PROG.NIL   1A4E5     EB    _PROG.NIL   1A5D0     2B
    _PROG.NIL   1A5FB     28    _PROG.NIL   1A623     6B
    _PROG.NIL   1A68E    125    _PROG.NIL   1A7B3     7C
    _PROG.NIL   1A82F     EA    $CONSTANT   1A920    E30
    $OVTB$.OV   1B750    128    OVDATA.OV   1B900    1EC
    OVCODE.OV   1BAF0    6B6
```

Section : Maddr=1C1B0, Msize=210, Daddr=1DDD0, Lev=1, Ovly#=1
```
    MOVEESC.N   1C1B0    161    $CONSTANT   1C320     A0
```

Section : Maddr=1C1B0, Msize=210, Daddr=1DFF0, Lev=1, Ovly#=2
```
    MOVETITL.   1C1B0    161    $CONSTANT   1C320     A0
```

Section : Maddr=1C3C0, Msize=7A0, Daddr=1E220, Lev=1, Ovly#=3
```
    MENUDRAW.   1C3C0    2A5    PROMPTNG.   1C670    29C
    $CONSTANT   1C910    110    $CONSTANT   1CA20    140
```

Section : Maddr=1C3C0, Msize=340, Daddr=1E9D0, Lev=1, Ovly#=4
```
    MOVE_CUR.   1C3C0    25F    $CONSTANT   1C620     E0
```

Section : Maddr=1C3C0, Msize=230, Daddr=1ED20, Lev=1, Ovly#=5
```
    DRAWBOX.N   1C3C0    15A    $CONSTANT   1C520     D0
```

Section : Maddr=1CB60, Msize=6B0, Daddr=1EF60, Lev=1, Ovly#=6
```
    MENUENTR.   1CB60    3BD    $CONSTANT   1CF20    2F0
```

Section : Maddr=1CB60, Msize=4B0, Daddr=1F620, Lev=1, Ovly#=7
```
    STARTOFF.   1CB60    2BB    $CONSTANT   1CE20    1F0
```

Section : Maddr=1CB60, Msize=820, Daddr=1FAF0, Lev=1, Ovly#=8
```
    FINISHED.   1CB60    207    FINISHED_   1CD70    208
    $CONSTANT   1CF80    400
```

Section : Maddr=1D380, Msize=200, Daddr=20320, Lev=1, Ovly#=9
```
    BEGIN.NIL   1D380    136    $CONSTANT   1D4C0     C0
```

Section : Maddr=1D580, Msize=41F0, Daddr=20DD0, Lev=0, Ovly#=10, Pre-Loaded

```
    $EXPR.$EX   1D580      0    $EXPR.$EX   1D580      0
    $EXPR.$EX   1D580      0    $EXPR.$EX   1D580     13
    $EXPR.$EX   1D5A0     26    $EXPR.$EX   1D5D0      0
    $EXPR.$EX   1D5D0      0    $EXPR.$EX   1D5D0     39
    $EXPR.$EX   1D610      0    $EXPR.$EX   1D610     27
    $EXPR.$EX   1D640      0    $MDATA.$M   1D640     B0
    $SYMSTART   1D6F0      0    $SYMBOLS.   1D6F0    260
    $SYMBOLS.   1D950     B0    $SYMBOLS.   1DA00     B0
    $SYMBOLS.   1DAB0    210    $SYMBOLS.   1DCC0    240
    $SYMBOLS.   1DF00    150    $SYMBOLS.   1E050     80
    $SYMBOLS.   1E0D0    1B0    $SYMBOLS.   1E280     50
    $SYMBOLS.   1E2D0    220    $SYMBOLS.   1E4F0    140
    $SYMEND.$   1E630      2    DATA.DATA   1E640   2D70
    $LIB_TABL   213B0    33C    STACK.DAT   216F0     80
```

The basic load size is 216F0 hex, or 136,994 bytes, or 134K when PLINK86 is finished linking.

The remaining modules in the PRE-LOAD section of the file (the $SYMBOLS, the $EXPR) can not be added to the OVERLAY NIL command, or the program would no longer function. One of the reasons $SYMBOLS cannot be moved is that once a program starts up, if there is a symbol that connects it to another symbol (e.g. DO Proca) and that connecting symbol has no reference point in the pre-load, but is now in the overlay, the program stops running. It is similar to giving someone an outdated roadmap when important landmarks have been moved. The programs stop running because they get lost, and you are forced to start again. Other than $CONSTANTS, nothing should be moved out of the pre-loaded section of the file into the overlays.

NESTING OVERLAYS

The reason for nesting overlays has two parts. First, with multiple overlay areas, extra memory is sometimes wasted because each overlay sits on top of the previous overlay area. Second, space is often wasted inside an overlay, due to smaller sections. A nested overlay may be able to reside in that empty area, thus filling up space set aside for other assigned sections and overlays.

The problem with nesting overlays lies in the SECTION command. Suppose we look at the same layout of files that we had in the previous example. The use of the SECTION command allows object files to be moved in and out of the same overlay area. If a file in a nested overlay branches off a SECTIONed file in a lower level overlay, and a call is made to a lower level SECTIONed file, major problems will occur. The following examples will show the problems involved, the advantages of nesting overlays, and the ultimate solution. First, look at the following two LiNK files and note the advantages each has over non-nested overlay files, as well as over one another.

Example One:

```
FI Cmenu
MAP = Ten7 a
LIB \DBASE\Clipper
BEGIN
    SECTION FI Menuentr
    SECTION FI Finished
    SECTION FI Startoff
    BEGIN
        SECTION FI Menudraw, Promptng
        SECTION FI Move_cur
        SECTION FI Drawbox
        BEGIN
            SECTION FI Moveesc
            SECTION FI Movetitl
            BEGIN
```

```
            SECTION FI Begin
        END
      END
    END
  END
```

The following is the memory map.

Groups:

Name	Address	Size	DSalloc
DGROUP	1E990	3130	

Segments:

Section : Maddr=0, Msize=1B3B0, Daddr=1C00, Lev=0, Ovly#=0

Name	Addr	Size	Name	Addr	Size
CMENU.NIL	0	15F	CENTER.NI	160	3A
SHORT.NIL	1A0	27	VERIFY.NI	1D0	6B
PROCHEAD.	240	39	HELP.NIL	280	4A4
DOITAGAIN	730	2E	CHAINA.NI	760	24
CHAINB.NI	790	29	$START.NI	7C0	DF
$INTERFAC	89F	6F4	$INTERFAC	F93	8B
$DRIVERS.	101E	54F	EXEC.C.NI	156D	136B
_PROG.NIL	28D8	1CA	NDEBUG.C.	2AA2	B
SYMSYS.C.	2AAD	523	CTERM.C.N	2FD0	915
STACK.C.N	38E5	12B1	DB.C.NIL	4B96	4B00
OPS.C.NIL	9696	261E	STERM.C.N	BCB4	377E
SET.C.NIL	F432	BCB	CSUPPORT.	FFFD	1861
MACRO.C.N	1185E	36A	$HACKJOB.	11BC8	271
_PROG.NIL	11E39	5D	_PROG.NIL	11E96	2DD
_PROG.NIL	12173	0	_PROG.NIL	12173	0
_PROG.NIL	12173	0	_PROG.NIL	12173	120
INDEX.C.N	12293	27E9	RPAR.C.NI	14A7C	1D4B
_PROG.NIL	167C7	6A	_PROG.NIL	16831	5DB
_PROG.NIL	16E0C	15	NATION.C.	16E21	19C
_PROG.NIL	16FBD	41	_PROG.NIL	16FFE	1D
_PROG.NIL	1701B	6A	_PROG.NIL	17085	38
_PROG.NIL	170BD	2E	_PROG.NIL	170EB	25
_PROG.NIL	17110	0	_PROG.NIL	17110	0
_PROG.NIL	17110	A59	_PROG.NIL	17B69	1B
_PROG.NIL	17B84	12F	_PROG.NIL	17CB3	41
_PROG.NIL	17CF4	2D	_PROG.NIL	17D21	1E
_PROG.NIL	17D3F	456	_PROG.NIL	18195	9A
_PROG.NIL	1822F	1D	_PROG.NIL	1824C	33
_PROG.NIL	1827F	2D	_PROG.NIL	182AC	A8
_PROG.NIL	18354	C	_PROG.NIL	18360	C
_PROG.NIL	1836C	C4	_PROG.NIL	18430	41A
_PROG.NIL	1884A	178	_PROG.NIL	189C2	92
_PROG.NIL	18A54	4C	_PROG.NIL	18AA0	3C
_PROG.NIL	18ADC	15	_PROG.NIL	18AF1	423
_PROG.NIL	18F14	106	_PROG.NIL	1901A	A0

```
_PROG.NIL   190BA     43   _PROG.NIL   190FD     AF
_PROG.NIL   191AC     15   _PROG.NIL   191C1      0
_PROG.NIL   191C1      E   _PROG.NIL   191CF     84
_PROG.NIL   19253    164   _PROG.NIL   193B7     5B
_PROG.NIL   19412    11F   _PROG.NIL   19531     F9
_PROG.NIL   1962A     50   _PROG.NIL   1967A     24
_PROG.NIL   1969E     20   _PROG.NIL   196BE     32
_PROG.NIL   196F0    1A4   _PROG.NIL   19894      0
_PROG.NIL   19894     21   _PROG.NIL   198B5     3E
_PROG.NIL   198F3     58   _PROG.NIL   1994B    2CD
_PROG.NIL   19C18     34   _PROG.NIL   19C4C    2AE
_PROG.NIL   19EFA    241   _PROG.NIL   1A13B     A8
_PROG.NIL   1A1E3    17F   _PROG.NIL   1A362      0
_PROG.NIL   1A362      B   _PROG.NIL   1A36D     12
_PROG.NIL   1A37F     1B   _PROG.NIL   1A39A     7B
_PROG.NIL   1A415     9C   _PROG.NIL   1A4B1     34
_PROG.NIL   1A4E5     EB   _PROG.NIL   1A5D0     2B
_PROG.NIL   1A5FB     28   _PROG.NIL   1A623     6B
_PROG.NIL   1A68E    125   _PROG.NIL   1A7B3     7C
_PROG.NIL   1A82F     EA   $OVTB$.OV   1A920    128
OVDATA.OV   1AB00    1EC   OVCODE.OV   1ACF0    6B6
```

```
Section :  Maddr=1B3B0, Msize=3C0, Daddr=1CFD0, Lev=1, Ovly#=1
     MENUENTR.  1B3B0    3BD

Section :  Maddr=1B3B0, Msize=420, Daddr=1D3B0, Lev=1, Ovly#=2
     FINISHED.  1B3B0    207   FINISHED_   1B5C0    208

Section :  Maddr=1B3B0, Msize=2C0, Daddr=1D7E0, Lev=1, Ovly#=3
     STARTOFF.  1B3B0    2BB

Section :  Maddr=1B670, Msize=550, Daddr=1DAC0, Lev=2, Ovly#=4
     MENUDRAW.  1B670    2A5   PROMPTNG.   1B920    29C

Section :  Maddr=1B670, Msize=260, Daddr=1E020, Lev=2, Ovly#=5
     MOVE_CUR.  1B670    25F

Section :  Maddr=1B670, Msize=160, Daddr=1E290, Lev=2, Ovly#=6
     DRAWBOX.N  1B670    15A

Section :  Maddr=1B7D0, Msize=170, Daddr=1E400, Lev=3, Ovly#=7
     MOVEESC.N  1B7D0    161

Section :  Maddr=1B7D0, Msize=170, Daddr=1E580, Lev=3, Ovly#=8
     MOVETITL.  1B7D0    161

Section :  Maddr=1B940, Msize=140, Daddr=1E700, Lev=4, Ovly#=9
     BEGIN.NIL  1B940    136

Section :  Maddr=1BBC0, Msize=5F00, Daddr=1F0F0, Lev=0, Ovly#=10, Pre-Loaded

     $EXPR.$EX  1BBC0      0   $EXPR.$EX   1BBC0     39
     $EXPR.$EX  1BC00     27   $EXPR.$EX   1BC30      0
```

$EXPR.$EX	1BC30	13	$EXPR.$EX	1BC50	26
$EXPR.$EX	1BC80	0	$EXPR.$EX	1BC80	0
$EXPR.$EX	1BC80	0	$EXPR.$EX	1BC80	0
$EXPR.$EX	1BC80	0	$MDATA.$M	1BC80	B0
$SYMSTART	1BD30	0	$SYMBOLS.	1BD30	260
$SYMBOLS.	1BF90	1B0	$SYMBOLS.	1C140	220
$SYMBOLS.	1C360	50	$SYMBOLS.	1C3B0	210
$SYMBOLS.	1C5C0	240	$SYMBOLS.	1C800	150
$SYMBOLS.	1C950	80	$SYMBOLS.	1C9D0	B0
$SYMBOLS.	1CA80	B0	$SYMBOLS.	1CB30	140
$SYMEND.$	1CC70	2	$CONSTANT	1CC80	E30
$CONSTANT	1DAB0	2F0	$CONSTANT	1DDA0	400
$CONSTANT	1E1A0	1F0	$CONSTANT	1E390	110
$CONSTANT	1E4A0	140	$CONSTANT	1E5E0	E0
$CONSTANT	1E6C0	D0	$CONSTANT	1E790	A0
$CONSTANT	1E830	A0	$CONSTANT	1E8D0	C0
DATA.DATA	1E990	2D70	$LIB_TABL	21700	33C
STACK.DAT	21A40	80			

This example's basic load size is 21A40 or 137,792 bytes. The basic rule to follow is that the code size of a nested overlay is added to the basic code size of the file or section from which the nested overlay branched. Using this LiNK file, the code size of BEGIN.OBJ is added to that of MOVETITL.OBJ. To determine the size of the overlay area in which MOVETITL.OBJ resides, compare the two sections. When MOVETITL.OBJ is called, BEGIN.OBJ is included and the two of them are bigger than MOVEESC.OBJ. Some loading time is also saved. Whenever BEGIN.OBJ is in operation, MOVETITL.OBJ. is ready to be executed in memory. If BEGIN did in fact call upon MOVETITL, the computer would not have to load another module or take any extra time to execute.

To get a better understanding of how nested overlay areas work and the amount of space taken by the main overlay, let's review a memory diagram of the overlay scheme.

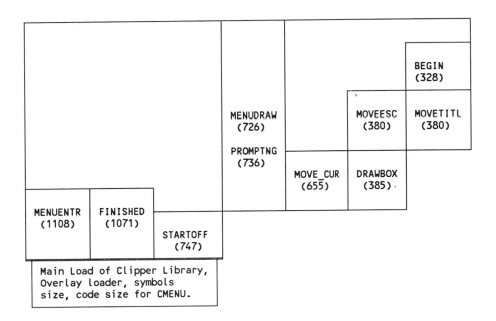

The size of the overlay is determined by the size of STARTOFF, MENUDRAW, and PROMPTNG–approximately 2209 bytes. If we turn to the memory map, the relative address points for the overlay area are approximately 2063 bytes. This difference is attributable to the linker's ability to condense and consolidate the various tables. Notice that regardless of the size of any other overlay or sectioned area, the entire overlay is based upon the size of STARTOFF, MENUDRAW, and PROMPTNG. It is evident that there is wasted space. It is possible to move the order of object files in the LiNK file to increase the SECTION sizes, even those SECTIONS with branch-off overlays. To get a better understanding of this, study the following LiNK file and map file, comparing them with the previous ones.

```
FI Cmenu
MAP = Ten8 a
LIB \DBASE\Clipper
BEGIN
    SECTION FI Startoff
    SECTION FI Finished
    SECTION FI Menuentr
    BEGIN
        SECTION FI Drawbox
        SECTION FI Move_cur
        SECTION FI Menudraw, Promptng
        BEGIN
            SECTION FI Moveesc
            SECTION FI Movetitl
            BEGIN
                SECTION FI Begin
            END
```

```
        END
    END
END
```

And this is the memory map:

```
Groups:

Name        Address  Size  DSalloc
DGROUP      1ED40    3130

Segments:

Section :  Maddr=0, Msize=1B3B0, Daddr=1C00, Lev=0, Ovly#=0

    Name        Addr    Size    Name        Addr    Size
    CMENU.NIL   0       15F     CENTER.NI   160     3A
    SHORT.NIL   1A0     27      VERIFY.NI   1D0     6B
    PROCHEAD.   240     39      HELP.NIL    280     4A4
    DOITAGAIN   730     2E      CHAINA.NI   760     24
    CHAINB.NI   790     29      $START.NI   7C0     DF
    $INTERFAC   89F     6F4     $INTERFAC   F93     8B
    $DRIVERS.   101E    54F     EXEC.C.NI   156D    136B
    _PROG.NIL   28D8    1CA     NDEBUG.C.   2AA2    B
    SYMSYS.C.   2AAD    523     CTERM.C.N   2FD0    915
    STACK.C.N   38E5    12B1    DB.C.NIL    4B96    4B00
    OPS.C.NIL   9696    261E    STERM.C.N   BCB4    377E
    SET.C.NIL   F432    BCB     CSUPPORT.   FFFD    1861
    MACRO.C.N   1185E   36A     $HACKJOB.   11BC8   271
    _PROG.NIL   11E39   5D      _PROG.NIL   11E96   2DD
    _PROG.NIL   12173   0       _PROG.NIL   12173   0
    _PROG.NIL   12173   0       _PROG.NIL   12173   120
    INDEX.C.N   12293   27E9    RPAR.C.NI   14A7C   1D4B
    _PROG.NIL   167C7   6A      _PROG.NIL   16831   5DB
    _PROG.NIL   16E0C   15      NATION.C.   16E21   19C
    _PROG.NIL   16FBD   41      _PROG.NIL   16FFE   1D
    _PROG.NIL   1701B   6A      _PROG.NIL   17085   38
    _PROG.NIL   170BD   2E      _PROG.NIL   170EB   25
    _PROG.NIL   17110   0       _PROG.NIL   17110   0
    _PROG.NIL   17110   A59     _PROG.NIL   17B69   1B
    _PROG.NIL   17B84   12F     _PROG.NIL   17CB3   41
    _PROG.NIL   17CF4   2D      _PROG.NIL   17D21   1E
    _PROG.NIL   17D3F   456     _PROG.NIL   18195   9A
    _PROG.NIL   1822F   1D      _PROG.NIL   1824C   33
    _PROG.NIL   1827F   2D      _PROG.NIL   182AC   A8
    _PROG.NIL   18354   C       _PROG.NIL   18360   C
    _PROG.NIL   1836C   C4      _PROG.NIL   18430   41A
    _PROG.NIL   1884A   178     _PROG.NIL   189C2   92
    _PROG.NIL   18A54   4C      _PROG.NIL   18AA0   3C
    _PROG.NIL   18ADC   15      _PROG.NIL   18AF1   423
    _PROG.NIL   18F14   106     _PROG.NIL   1901A   A0
    _PROG.NIL   190BA   43      _PROG.NIL   190FD   AF
    _PROG.NIL   191AC   15      _PROG.NIL   191C1   0
```

_PROG.NIL	191C1	E	_PROG.NIL	191CF	84
_PROG.NIL	19253	164	_PROG.NIL	193B7	5B
_PROG.NIL	19412	11F	_PROG.NIL	19531	F9
_PROG.NIL	1962A	50	_PROG.NIL	1967A	24
_PROG.NIL	1969E	20	_PROG.NIL	196BE	32
_PROG.NIL	196F0	1A4	_PROG.NIL	19894	0
_PROG.NIL	19894	21	_PROG.NIL	198B5	3E
_PROG.NIL	198F3	58	_PROG.NIL	1994B	2CD
_PROG.NIL	19C18	34	_PROG.NIL	19C4C	2AE
_PROG.NIL	19EFA	241	_PROG.NIL	1A13B	A8
_PROG.NIL	1A1E3	17F	_PROG.NIL	1A362	0
_PROG.NIL	1A362	B	_PROG.NIL	1A36D	12
_PROG.NIL	1A37F	1B	_PROG.NIL	1A39A	7B
_PROG.NIL	1A415	9C	_PROG.NIL	1A4B1	34
_PROG.NIL	1A4E5	EB	_PROG.NIL	1A5D0	2B
_PROG.NIL	1A5FB	28	_PROG.NIL	1A623	6B
_PROG.NIL	1A68E	125	_PROG.NIL	1A7B3	7C
_PROG.NIL	1A82F	EA	$OVTB$.OV	1A920	128
OVDATA.OV	1AB00	1EC	OVCODE.OV	1ACF0	6B6

Section : Maddr=1B3B0, Msize=2C0, Daddr=1CFD0, Lev=1, Ovly#=1
    STARTOFF. 1B3B0   2BB

Section : Maddr=1B3B0, Msize=420, Daddr=1D2B0, Lev=1, Ovly#=2
    FINISHED. 1B3B0   207 FINISHED_ 1B5C0   208

Section : Maddr=1B3B0, Msize=3C0, Daddr=1D6E0, Lev=1, Ovly#=3
    MENUENTR. 1B3B0   3BD

Section : Maddr=1B770, Msize=160, Daddr=1DAB0, Lev=2, Ovly#=4
    DRAWBOX.N 1B770   15A

Section : Maddr=1B770, Msize=260, Daddr=1DC20, Lev=2, Ovly#=5
    MOVE_CUR. 1B770   25F

Section : Maddr=1B770, Msize=550, Daddr=1DEA0, Lev=2, Ovly#=6
    MENUDRAW. 1B770   2A5 PROMPTNG. 1BA20   29C

Section : Maddr=1BCC0, Msize=170, Daddr=1E400, Lev=3, Ovly#=7
    MOVEESC.N 1BCC0   161

Section : Maddr=1BCC0, Msize=170, Daddr=1E580, Lev=3, Ovly#=8
    MOVETITL. 1BCC0   161

Section : Maddr=1BE30, Msize=140, Daddr=1E700, Lev=4, Ovly#=9
    BEGIN.NIL 1BE30   136

Section : Maddr=1BF70, Msize=5F00, Daddr=1F0F0, Lev=0, Ovly#=10, Pre-Loaded

$EXPR.$EX	1BF70	0	$EXPR.$EX	1BF70	0
$EXPR.$EX	1BF70	27	$EXPR.$EX	1BFA0	39
$EXPR.$EX	1BFE0	0	$EXPR.$EX	1BFE0	0
$EXPR.$EX	1BFE0	13	$EXPR.$EX	1C000	26

$EXPR.$EX	1C030	0	$EXPR.$EX	1C030	0
$EXPR.$EX	1C030	0	$MDATA.$M	1C030	B0
$SYMSTART	1C0E0	0	$SYMBOLS.	1C0E0	260
$SYMBOLS.	1C340	50	$SYMBOLS.	1C390	220
$SYMBOLS.	1C5B0	1B0	$SYMBOLS.	1C760	80
$SYMBOLS.	1C7E0	150	$SYMBOLS.	1C930	210
$SYMBOLS.	1CB40	240	$SYMBOLS.	1CD80	B0
$SYMBOLS.	1CE30	B0	$SYMBOLS.	1CEE0	140
$SYMEND.$	1D020	2	$CONSTANT	1D030	E30
$CONSTANT	1DE60	1F0	$CONSTANT	1E050	400
$CONSTANT	1E450	2F0	$CONSTANT	1E740	D0
$CONSTANT	1E810	E0	$CONSTANT	1E8F0	110
$CONSTANT	1EA00	140	$CONSTANT	1EB40	A0
$CONSTANT	1EBE0	A0	$CONSTANT	1EC80	C0
DATA.DATA	1ED40	2D70	$LIB_TABL	21AB0	33C
STACK.DAT	21DF0	80			

Based on the ending address points, the link file is approximately 944 bytes larger. Looking at the link file and the resulting diagram, it is easy to see where the increase took place.

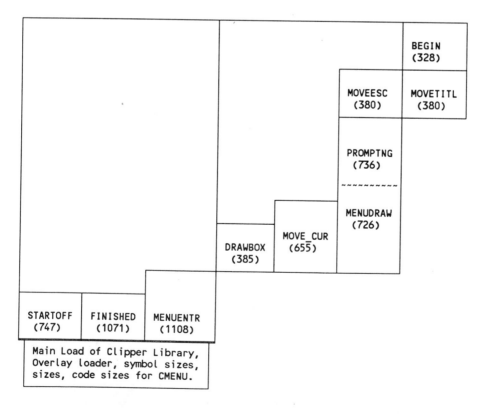

The overlay size is based upon the combined sizes of five files: MENUENTR, MENUDRAW, PROMPTNG, MOVETITL, and BEGIN. The combined code size is 3278 bytes. The increase in size, using this LiNK file instead of the previous LiNK file, is roughly 1069 bytes. Compared with the figure generated by the linker, this makes sense. Notice that just a few files were changed in order, not in content. The result was a general increase in the size of the overlay file. Even though this link is still just 135K, it can be made smaller. Of course, both LiNK files can be decreased in size with the addition of the OVERLAY NIL, $CONSTANTS command.

With this linking method, there is one problem. If this program is run as linked, an EXEC SEQUENCE ERROR will occur. As stated before, files in one SECTION within the same overlay cannot call files from other SECTIONs. The LiNK file and the map diagram relating to the flow of operation, indicate that immediately after CMENU starts, BEGIN is called. Once BEGIN is called and loaded, STARTOFF, DRAWBOX, and MOVETITL are also loaded. After BEGIN executes, the flow branches either to STARTOFF or to MENUENTR. If the files are not present, then STARTOFF is called. This is no problem because STARTOFF is loaded in with BE-GIN. However, if the database files are present and STARTOFF is skipped, then MENUENTR is called. This presents a major problem. Even though BEGIN is call-ing MENUENTR, BEGIN resides with STARTOFF. This means that in essence STARTOFF is calling MENUENTR leading to the EXEC SEQUENCE ERROR.

Nesting overlays depends on the method of compiling or program calling used, espe-cially if the SECTION command is used in conjunction with them. Be careful! Many problems can occur other than an EXEC SEQUENCE ERROR. For example, memory variables can get lost, resulting in UNDEFINED VARIABLES or TYPE CONFLICT errors. The program can just stop executing and the cursor will hang in the upper left corner of the screen.

One point should be made clear. Nesting overlays is only advantageous when 1) there is a clear route to and from programs; 2) recursive program calling is not utilized; and 3) the SECTION command is used at the highest level in the program. If several files have been compiled, labeled A through F, and files A, B, and C all require file D, then a possible LiNK option would be:

```
BEGIN
    FILE D
    BEGIN
        SECTION FILE A
        SECTION FILE B
        SECTION FILE C
    END
    SECTION FILE E
    SECTION FILE F
END
```

The constraints for this linkage are as follows:

1)   Files A, B, and C cannot call one another, nor can they call on Files E and F.

2)   Files A, B, and C all require File D to be loaded in order to execute properly.

3)   The size of the overlay is determined by one of the following:
    a)   D + E
    b)   D + F
    c)   D + the largest section in the nested overlay (A, B, or C). Notice that file D
         is included in all calculations. You may choose to SECTION file D, which
         would alter the calculations as follows;

        i)   E
        ii)   F
        iii)   D + the largest section in the nested overlay (A, B, or C)

4)   All files are called from the main load file which is not shown in the LiNK file.

Nesting overlays can be quite useful, because there is extra code added to the executable file which handles each and every overlay. The amount added is less for
nested overlays than with multiple overlays. Unnested overlays sit on top of one another, while nested overlays reside in one large overlay. The same module should not
be placed into two different overlays. By nesting overlays, you can "factor out" duplicate routines without having to place them in the main load module.

EXTERNAL OVERLAYS

As with internal overlays, external overlays are used in order to save space, both in
memory and on disk. The only advantage external overlays have over internal overlays
is that all relative code (or constant) information is placed on the disk and removed
from the .EXE file. This does not mean that the amount of RAM memory decreases,
just the actual file size. The main program still needs to partition the proper memory
area to hold the overlay as it comes in and out of RAM.

The disadvantage of external overlays is protection. For example, an overlay file may
be copied improperly to the disk drive or may be accidentally erased. Both examples
are impossible with internal overlays, for all overlays reside within the executable file.
The overlays may not actually be loaded from the disk drive, as would be expected
with external overlays. At least with internal overlays, a file will always be intact.

The only time it is imperative to use external overlays is when disk file size is para-
mount. Since with internal overlays, the code resides within the executable file, the
.EXE file may grow to an astronomical size. The executable file may even become

larger than 360K. In order to transfer the file from one machine to another, in such a case, the external overlay scheme is vital. Here are some examples to show how external overlays actually work.

First, let's review briefly the LiNK files to be used for the comparison.

```
Internal Overlay:                  External Overlay:

FI Cmenu                           FI Cmenu
MAP = Two a                        MAP = Two a
LIB \DBASE\Clipper                 LIB \DBASE\Clipper
BEGIN                              BEGIN
  SECTION FI Startoff                SECTION INTO Cmenover FI Startoff
  SECTION FI Begin                   SECTION INTO Cmenover FI Begin
  SECTION FI Promptng                SECTION INTO Cmenover FI Promptng
  SECTION FI Menuentr                SECTION INTO Cmenover FI Menuentr
  SECTION FI Menudraw                SECTION INTO Cmenover FI Menudraw
  SECTION FI Move_cur                SECTION INTO Cmenover FI Move_cur
  SECTION FI Drawbox                 SECTION INTO Cmenover FI Drawbox
  SECTION FI Movetitl                SECTION INTO Cmenover FI Movetitl
  SECTION FI Moveesc                 SECTION INTO Cmenover FI Moveesc
  SECTION FI Finished                SECTION INTO Cmenover FI Finished
END                                END
```

Each "INTO < filename >" clause places the code tables for the object files in the external overlay. The filename "Cmenover" entered may be up to eight characters long and will have a file extension, .OVL, which denotes that the file is an overlay file. The following is a directory stamp of the overlay generated by the linker.

```
C>dir *.ovl

Volume in drive C has no label
Directory of  C:\FW\WORK

CMENOVER OVL    6272   5-12-86   3:58p
         1 File(s)  12718080 bytes free
```

The total of the code table sizes of the object modules involved with the overlay file is a relative code size of 6516 bytes. Allowing for the linker to condense the code tables and for organizing the object files, this compares nicely with a directory file size for the overlay of 6272 bytes. As will be shown, the overlay file size increases if the constant tables are also moved into the overlay. Following are the memory maps:

Internal Overlay:

```
Groups:

Name      Address  Size  DSalloc
DGROUP    1E5A0    3130
```

Segments:

Section : Maddr=0, Msize=1B3B0, Daddr=1C00, Lev=0, Ovly#=0

Name	Addr	Size	Name	Addr	Size
CMENU.NIL	0	15F	CENTER.NI	160	3A
SHORT.NIL	1A0	27	VERIFY.NI	1D0	6B
PROCHEAD.	240	39	HELP.NIL	280	4A4
DOITAGAIN	730	2E	CHAINA.NI	760	24
CHAINB.NI	790	29	$START.NI	7C0	DF
$INTERFAC	89F	6F4	$INTERFAC	F93	8B
$DRIVERS.	101E	54F	EXEC.C.NI	156D	136B
_PROG.NIL	28D8	1CA	NDEBUG.C.	2AA2	B
SYMSYS.C.	2AAD	523	CTERM.C.N	2FD0	915
STACK.C.N	38E5	12B1	DB.C.NIL	4B96	4B00
OPS.C.NIL	9696	261E	STERM.C.N	BCB4	377E
SET.C.NIL	F432	BCB	CSUPPORT.	FFFD	1861
MACRO.C.N	1185E	36A	$HACKJOB.	11BC8	271
_PROG.NIL	11E39	5D	_PROG.NIL	11E96	2DD
_PROG.NIL	12173	0	_PROG.NIL	12173	0
_PROG.NIL	12173	0	_PROG.NIL	12173	120
INDEX.C.N	12293	27E9	RPAR.C.NI	14A7C	1D4B
_PROG.NIL	167C7	6A	_PROG.NIL	16831	5DB
_PROG.NIL	16E0C	15	NATION.C.	16E21	19C
_PROG.NIL	16FBD	41	_PROG.NIL	16FFE	1D
_PROG.NIL	1701B	6A	_PROG.NIL	17085	38
_PROG.NIL	170BD	2E	_PROG.NIL	170EB	25
_PROG.NIL	17110	0	_PROG.NIL	17110	0
_PROG.NIL	17110	A59	_PROG.NIL	17B69	1B
_PROG.NIL	17B84	12F	_PROG.NIL	17CB3	41
_PROG.NIL	17CF4	2D	_PROG.NIL	17D21	1E
_PROG.NIL	17D3F	456	_PROG.NIL	18195	9A
_PROG.NIL	1822F	1D	_PROG.NIL	1824C	33
_PROG.NIL	1827F	2D	_PROG.NIL	182AC	A8
_PROG.NIL	18354	C	_PROG.NIL	18360	C
_PROG.NIL	1836C	C4	_PROG.NIL	18430	41A
_PROG.NIL	1884A	178	_PROG.NIL	189C2	92
_PROG.NIL	18A54	4C	_PROG.NIL	18AA0	3C
_PROG.NIL	18ADC	15	_PROG.NIL	18AF1	423
_PROG.NIL	18F14	106	_PROG.NIL	1901A	A0
_PROG.NIL	190BA	43	_PROG.NIL	190FD	AF
_PROG.NIL	191AC	15	_PROG.NIL	191C1	0
_PROG.NIL	191C1	E	_PROG.NIL	191CF	84
_PROG.NIL	19253	164	_PROG.NIL	193B7	5B
_PROG.NIL	19412	11F	_PROG.NIL	19531	F9
_PROG.NIL	1962A	50	_PROG.NIL	1967A	24
_PROG.NIL	1969E	20	_PROG.NIL	196BE	32
_PROG.NIL	196F0	1A4	_PROG.NIL	19894	0
_PROG.NIL	19894	21	_PROG.NIL	198B5	3E
_PROG.NIL	198F3	58	_PROG.NIL	1994B	2CD
_PROG.NIL	19C18	34	_PROG.NIL	19C4C	2AE
_PROG.NIL	19EFA	241	_PROG.NIL	1A13B	A8
_PROG.NIL	1A1E3	17F	_PROG.NIL	1A362	0

```
      _PROG.NIL   1A362      B    _PROG.NIL   1A36D      12
      _PROG.NIL   1A37F     1B    _PROG.NIL   1A39A      7B
      _PROG.NIL   1A415     9C    _PROG.NIL   1A4B1      34
      _PROG.NIL   1A4E5     EB    _PROG.NIL   1A5D0      2B
      _PROG.NIL   1A5FB     28    _PROG.NIL   1A623      6B
      _PROG.NIL   1A68E    125    _PROG.NIL   1A7B3      7C
      _PROG.NIL   1A82F     EA    $OVTB$.OV   1A920     138
      OVDATA.OV   1AB00    1EC    OVCODE.OV   1ACF0     6B6
```

Section : Maddr=1B3B0, Msize=2C0, Daddr=1CFD0, Lev=1, Ovly#=1
```
      STARTOFF.   1B3B0    2BB
```

Section : Maddr=1B3B0, Msize=140, Daddr=1D2A0, Lev=1, Ovly#=2
```
      BEGIN.NIL   1B3B0    136
```

Section : Maddr=1B3B0, Msize=2A0, Daddr=1D3F0, Lev=1, Ovly#=3
```
      PROMPTNG.   1B3B0    29C
```

Section : Maddr=1B3B0, Msize=3C0, Daddr=1D6A0, Lev=1, Ovly#=4
```
      MENUENTR.   1B3B0    3BD
```

Section : Maddr=1B3B0, Msize=2B0, Daddr=1DA70, Lev=1, Ovly#=5
```
      MENUDRAW.   1B3B0    2A5
```

Section : Maddr=1B3B0, Msize=260, Daddr=1DD30, Lev=1, Ovly#=6
```
      MOVE_CUR.   1B3B0    25F
```

Section : Maddr=1B3B0, Msize=160, Daddr=1DFA0, Lev=1, Ovly#=7
```
      DRAWBOX.N   1B3B0    15A
```

Section : Maddr=1B3B0, Msize=170, Daddr=1E110, Lev=1, Ovly#=8
```
      MOVETITL.   1B3B0    161
```

Section : Maddr=1B3B0, Msize=170, Daddr=1E290, Lev=1, Ovly#=9
```
      MOVEESC.N   1B3B0    161
```

Section : Maddr=1B3B0, Msize=420, Daddr=1E420, Lev=1, Ovly#=10
```
      FINISHED.   1B3B0    207    FINISHED_   1B5C0     208
```

Section : Maddr=1B7D0, Msize=5F00, Daddr=1F0F0, Lev=0, Ovly#=11, Pre-Loaded

```
      $EXPR.$EX   1B7D0      0    $EXPR.$EX   1B7D0       0
      $EXPR.$EX   1B7D0      0    $EXPR.$EX   1B7D0      26
      $EXPR.$EX   1B800     39    $EXPR.$EX   1B840      13
      $EXPR.$EX   1B860      0    $EXPR.$EX   1B860       0
      $EXPR.$EX   1B860      0    $EXPR.$EX   1B860       0
      $EXPR.$EX   1B860     27    $MDATA.$M   1B890      B0
      $SYMSTART   1B940      0    $SYMBOLS.   1B940     260
      $SYMBOLS.   1BBA0     50    $SYMBOLS.   1BBF0     140
      $SYMBOLS.   1BD30    240    $SYMBOLS.   1BF70     1B0
      $SYMBOLS.   1C120    210    $SYMBOLS.   1C330     150
      $SYMBOLS.   1C480     80    $SYMBOLS.   1C500      B0
      $SYMBOLS.   1C5B0     B0    $SYMBOLS.   1C660     220
```

$SYMEND.$	1C880	2	$CONSTANT	1C890	E30
$CONSTANT	1D6C0	1F0	$CONSTANT	1D8B0	C0
$CONSTANT	1D970	140	$CONSTANT	1DAB0	2F0
$CONSTANT	1DDA0	110	$CONSTANT	1DEB0	E0
$CONSTANT	1DF90	D0	$CONSTANT	1E060	A0
$CONSTANT	1E100	A0	$CONSTANT	1E1A0	400
DATA.DATA	1E5A0	2D70	$LIB_TABL	21310	33C
STACK.DAT	21650	80			

External Overlay:

Groups:

Name	Address	Size	DSalloc
DGROUP	1E5A0	3130	

Segments:

Section : Maddr=0, Msize=1B3B0, Daddr=1C00, Lev=0, Ovly#=0

Name	Addr	Size	Name	Addr	Size
CMENU.NIL	0	15F	CENTER.NI	160	3A
SHORT.NIL	1A0	27	VERIFY.NI	1D0	6B
PROCHEAD.	240	39	HELP.NIL	280	4A4
DOITAGAIN	730	2E	CHAINA.NI	760	24
CHAINB.NI	790	29	$START.NI	7C0	DF
$INTERFAC	89F	6F4	$INTERFAC	F93	8B
$DRIVERS.	101E	54F	EXEC.C.NI	156D	136B
_PROG.NIL	28D8	1CA	NDEBUG.C.	2AA2	B
SYMSYS.C.	2AAD	523	CTERM.C.N	2FD0	915
STACK.C.N	38E5	12B1	DB.C.NIL	4B96	4B00
OPS.C.NIL	9696	261E	STERM.C.N	BCB4	377E
SET.C.NIL	F432	BCB	CSUPPORT.	FFFD	1861
MACRO.C.N	1185E	36A	$HACKJOB.	11BC8	271
_PROG.NIL	11E39	5D	_PROG.NIL	11E96	2DD
_PROG.NIL	12173	0	_PROG.NIL	12173	0
_PROG.NIL	12173	0	_PROG.NIL	12173	120
INDEX.C.N	12293	27E9	RPAR.C.NI	14A7C	1D4B
_PROG.NIL	167C7	6A	_PROG.NIL	16831	5DB
_PROG.NIL	16E0C	15	NATION.C.	16E21	19C
_PROG.NIL	16FBD	41	_PROG.NIL	16FFE	1D
_PROG.NIL	1701B	6A	_PROG.NIL	17085	38
_PROG.NIL	170BD	2E	_PROG.NIL	170EB	25
_PROG.NIL	17110	0	_PROG.NIL	17110	0
_PROG.NIL	17110	A59	_PROG.NIL	17B69	1B
_PROG.NIL	17B84	12F	_PROG.NIL	17CB3	41
_PROG.NIL	17CF4	2D	_PROG.NIL	17D21	1E
_PROG.NIL	17D3F	456	_PROG.NIL	18195	9A
_PROG.NIL	1822F	1D	_PROG.NIL	1824C	33
_PROG.NIL	1827F	2D	_PROG.NIL	182AC	A8
_PROG.NIL	18354	C	_PROG.NIL	18360	C
_PROG.NIL	1836C	C4	_PROG.NIL	18430	41A
_PROG.NIL	1884A	178	_PROG.NIL	189C2	92

```
        _PROG.NIL  18A54    4C   _PROG.NIL  18AA0    3C
        _PROG.NIL  18ADC    15   _PROG.NIL  18AF1   423
        _PROG.NIL  18F14   106   _PROG.NIL  1901A    A0
        _PROG.NIL  190BA    43   _PROG.NIL  190FD    AF
        _PROG.NIL  191AC    15   _PROG.NIL  191C1     0
        _PROG.NIL  191C1     E   _PROG.NIL  191CF    84
        _PROG.NIL  19253   164   _PROG.NIL  193B7    5B
        _PROG.NIL  19412   11F   _PROG.NIL  19531    F9
        _PROG.NIL  1962A    50   _PROG.NIL  1967A    24
        _PROG.NIL  1969E    20   _PROG.NIL  196BE    32
        _PROG.NIL  196F0    1A4  _PROG.NIL  19894     0
        _PROG.NIL  19894    21   _PROG.NIL  198B5    3E
        _PROG.NIL  198F3    58   _PROG.NIL  1994B   2CD
        _PROG.NIL  19C18    34   _PROG.NIL  19C4C   2AE
        _PROG.NIL  19EFA   241   _PROG.NIL  1A13B    A8
        _PROG.NIL  1A1E3   17F   _PROG.NIL  1A362     0
        _PROG.NIL  1A362     B   _PROG.NIL  1A36D    12
        _PROG.NIL  1A37F    1B   _PROG.NIL  1A39A    7B
        _PROG.NIL  1A415    9C   _PROG.NIL  1A4B1    34
        _PROG.NIL  1A4E5    EB   _PROG.NIL  1A5D0    2B
        _PROG.NIL  1A5FB    28   _PROG.NIL  1A623    6B
        _PROG.NIL  1A68E   125   _PROG.NIL  1A7B3    7C
        _PROG.NIL  1A82F    EA   $OVTB$.OV  1A920   140
        OVDATA.OV  1AB00   1EC   OVCODE.OV  1ACF0   6B6
```

```
   Section :  Maddr=1B3B0, Msize=2C0, Daddr=10, Lev=1, Ovly#=1
      STARTOFF.  1B3B0    2BB

   Section :  Maddr=1B3B0, Msize=140, Daddr=2E0, Lev=1, Ovly#=2
      BEGIN.NIL  1B3B0    136

   Section :  Maddr=1B3B0, Msize=2A0, Daddr=430, Lev=1, Ovly#=3
      PROMPTNG.  1B3B0    29C

   Section :  Maddr=1B3B0, Msize=3C0, Daddr=6E0, Lev=1, Ovly#=4
      MENUENTR.  1B3B0    3BD

   Section :  Maddr=1B3B0, Msize=2B0, Daddr=AB0, Lev=1, Ovly#=5
      MENUDRAW.  1B3B0    2A5

   Section :  Maddr=1B3B0, Msize=260, Daddr=D70, Lev=1, Ovly#=6
      MOVE_CUR.  1B3B0    25F

   Section :  Maddr=1B3B0, Msize=160, Daddr=FE0, Lev=1, Ovly#=7
      DRAWBOX.N  1B3B0    15A

   Section :  Maddr=1B3B0, Msize=170, Daddr=1150, Lev=1, Ovly#=8
      MOVETITL.  1B3B0    161

   Section :  Maddr=1B3B0, Msize=170, Daddr=12D0, Lev=1, Ovly#=9
      MOVEESC.N  1B3B0    161

   Section :  Maddr=1B3B0, Msize=420, Daddr=1460, Lev=1, Ovly#=10
      FINISHED.  1B3B0    207  FINISHED_  1B5C0    208
```

```
Section :  Maddr=1B7D0, Msize=5F00, Daddr=1D870, Lev=0, Ovly#=11, Pre-Loaded
```

$EXPR.$EX	1B7D0	0	$EXPR.$EX	1B7D0	0
$EXPR.$EX	1B7D0	0	$EXPR.$EX	1B7D0	26
$EXPR.$EX	1B800	39	$EXPR.$EX	1B840	13
$EXPR.$EX	1B860	0	$EXPR.$EX	1B860	0
$EXPR.$EX	1B860	0	$EXPR.$EX	1B860	0
$EXPR.$EX	1B860	27	$MDATA.$M	1B890	B0
$SYMSTART	1B940	0	$SYMBOLS.	1B940	260
$SYMBOLS.	1BBA0	50	$SYMBOLS.	1BBF0	140
$SYMBOLS.	1BD30	240	$SYMBOLS.	1BF70	1B0
$SYMBOLS.	1C120	210	$SYMBOLS.	1C330	150
$SYMBOLS.	1C480	80	$SYMBOLS.	1C500	B0
$SYMBOLS.	1C5B0	B0	$SYMBOLS.	1C660	220
$SYMEND.$	1C880	2	$CONSTANT	1C890	E30
$CONSTANT	1D6C0	1F0	$CONSTANT	1D8B0	C0
$CONSTANT	1D970	140	$CONSTANT	1DAB0	2F0
$CONSTANT	1DDA0	110	$CONSTANT	1DEB0	E0
$CONSTANT	1DF90	D0	$CONSTANT	1E060	A0
$CONSTANT	1E100	A0	$CONSTANT	1E1A0	400
DATA.DATA	1E5A0	2D70	$LIB_TABL	21310	33C
STACK.DAT	21650	80			

Notice that the load module for the first LiNK file is exactly the same as that of the second LiNK file. Also the address points in memory where the external overlay is brought into the main program are the same as in the internal overlay. Clearly, the only advantage to external overlays is the disk space used.

The best approach is to develop the application to run on a hard-disk system. Even if external overlays are used, they can be loaded onto the hard disk and executed. The real use for external overlays is when you need to distribute an application that is larger than 360 kilobytes. Develop the proper overlay technique and link accordingly. Note the respective file sizes and then add a small chaining routine to the main program that will prompt the user for the appropriate disk and check for the necessary overlay file. If you use this technique, don't let the internal mechanisms of the linker display its message:

```
PLINK86 Overlay Loader - Can't find file CMENOVER.OVL.
Enter file name prefix (X: or path name/) or '.' to quit=>
```

This is not very user-friendly! The best way to avoid this is to add a FILE() function looking for the existence of the overlay file itself. If it appears, then have the application continue by chaining to that overlay. If it does not appear, simply add some code which prompts the user to either exit the program or to insert a new disk. Keep in mind that even functions can be called in an external overlay. If any of these functions are called, the existence of the overlay file must be checked prior to the actual function call. Following is the overlay file size for the same LiNK file. Notice the sizes of the files moved into the external overlay.

```
C>dir *.ovl

Volume in drive C has no label
Directory of  C:\PROJECT\PROGRAMS\TEST

CMENOVER OVL    10080    5-13-86    8:31a
       1 File(s)     290816 bytes free
```

Subtracting the size of the old overlay file from this new figure shows an increase in size of 3808 bytes. The constant sizes, not including the constant size for CMENU.OBJ, are 3700 bytes. The extra file size exists because code was added by the linker to handle the constants separately from the code tables. The overlay file increased in size because the constant tables were moved out of the main load module and into the overlay file. The executable file decreased by 3856 bytes.

With PLINK86, version 1.46.c., if external overlays are used, even though you may have a path set to a subdirectory containing the OVERLAY.LIB, the linker will not find it. If the linker cannot find the OVERLAY.LIB file on the currently logged directory, PLINK86 will generate the following message:

```
Can't find file OVERLAY.LIB.
Enter new file name prefix (drive:  or path name/)
or . to quit =>
```

Just type in the subdirectory name containing the OVERLAY.LIB file. You may have to do this once or twice. To completely avoid the problem simply copy the OVERLAY.LIB file into the same subdirectory in which you are currently working.

A CHAINING PROGRAM

There are two types of chaining programs: one allows a program in an overlay section to go to another program in the same overlay, while the second checks for an overlay file on the disk drive and prompts the user accordingly.

Chaining to other overlay files depends entirely on each application and on programming techniques. In many cases memory variables are saved to a memory file containing the drive designators for both program and data drives. In this case only the name of the overlay would vary from program to program. This program should be written as a procedure and should reside in the main load module.

Chaining to other sections, though not directly possible and not recommended, is a bit more tricky. It is not as simple as adding an extra command line. Procedural considerations must be foreseen, and memory variables dependent on both procedures (the one chaining to the other) must be PUBLIC to both. A possible example would be the following:

```
********************

PROCEDURE Chainto

    PARAMETERS goto_prog, ret_prog

    DO &goto_prog
    DO &ret_prog
```

Keep in mind that when returning to the original calling program, the chain goes back to the beginning of the procedure or program file which originally made the call to the CHAINTO procedure. The reason for this is that the control of the original calling program is washed out of memory as the second section in the overlay comes into memory. Without the returning program parameter, the RETURN does not know where to go and an EXEC SEQUENCE ERROR or similar memory related error occurs. Programs utilizing a chaining program must be coded accordingly. Conditional testing for flag set and reset by the chaining program jumps the execution of a procedure or program file from the beginning to some other point within the application.

Finally, if it is necessary to use a chaining program, make sure that the procedure for the chain resides in the main load module. Otherwise, an EXEC SEQUENCE ERROR may occur (which is the reason why you program for the chaining in the first place).

USING THE MAP

A memory map showing all of the entry points of an application is available through a command in PLINK86 or is automatically available in Microsoft's 3.05 LINK program. These entry points are either the dBASE programs, the internal Clipper routines, or Lattice C routines. The areas used for data, constants, etc. are shown. Below is an example of a memory map from the application called CREATE.prg located in the **application** section of this text. It was linked with MicroSoft's LINK, version 3.05.

```
         Start  Stop   Length Name              Class
       ┌─ 00000H 000A6H 000A7H CREATE
   P   │  000B0H 00147H 00098H FIRST
   r   │  00150H 0043AH 002EBH SECOND
   o   │  00440H 00A86H 00647H THIRD
   c   │  00A90H 00D74H 002E5H FOURTH
   e   │  00D80H 0172EH 009AFH FIFTH
   d   │  01730H 018ACH 0017DH SIXTH
   u   │  018B0H 0198BH 000DCH SEVENTH
   r   │  01990H 01AA7H 00118H EIGHT
   e   │  01AB0H 01F55H 004A6H NINE
   s   │  01F60H 022D1H 00372H TEN
       │  022E0H 022EEH 0000FH CREATE1
   a   │  022F0H 026DBH 003ECH ELEVEN
   n   │  026E0H 02773H 00094H TWELVE
   d   │  02780H 02CD5H 00556H THIRTEEN
       └  02CE0H 02FEDH 0030EH FOURTEEN
```

02FF0H	03185H	00196H	FIFTEEN
03190H	032DCH	0014DH	SIXTEEN
032E0H	033BDH	000DEH	SEVENTEEN
033C0H	0348DH	000CEH	EIGHTEEN
03490H	035EFH	00160H	NINETEEN
035F0H	03766H	00177H	TWENTY
03770H	03825H	000B6H	TWENTY1
03830H	03868H	00039H	PROCHEAD
03870H	038A8H	00039H	FUNCHEAD
038B0H	0391AH	0006BH	VERIFY
03920H	039FEH	000DFH	$START
039FFH	040F2H	006F4H	$INTERFACE
040F3H	0417DH	0008BH	$INTERFACE
0417EH	054E8H	0136BH	EXEC.C
054E9H	05A37H	0054FH	$DRIVERS
05A38H	05CA8H	00271H	$HACKJOB
05CA9H	07509H	01861H	CSUPPORT.C
0750AH	087BAH	012B1H	STACK.C
087BBH	0ADD8H	0261EH	OPS.C
0ADD9H	0F8D8H	04B00H	DB.C
0F8D9H	0FDFBH	00523H	SYMSYS.C
0FDFCH	11B46H	01D4BH	RPAR.C
11B47H	12711H	00BCBH	SET.C
12712H	1271CH	0000BH	NDEBUG.C
1271DH	14F05H	027E9H	INDEX.C
14F06H	1526FH	0036AH	MACRO.C
15270H	15B84H	00915H	CTERM.C
15B85H	19302H	0377EH	STERM.C
19303H	1949EH	0019CH	NATION.C
1949FH	194B3H	00015H	_PROG
194B4H	1967DH	001CAH	_PROG
1967EH	196BEH	00041H	_PROG
196BFH	19728H	0006AH	_PROG
19729H	19785H	0005DH	_PROG
19786H	19A62H	002DDH	_PROG
19A63H	19A63H	00000H	_PROG
19A63H	19A63H	00000H	_PROG
19A63H	19A63H	00000H	_PROG
19A63H	19B82H	00120H	_PROG
19B83H	1A15DH	005DBH	_PROG
1A15EH	1A18AH	0002DH	_PROG
1A18BH	1A5A4H	0041AH	_PROG
1A5A5H	1A5B0H	0000CH	_PROG
1A5B1H	1A5F1H	00041H	_PROG
1A5F2H	1AA47H	00456H	_PROG
1AA48H	1AA65H	0001EH	_PROG
1AA66H	1AA98H	00033H	_PROG
1AA99H	1ABC7H	0012FH	_PROG
1ABC8H	1ABD3H	0000CH	_PROG
1ABD4H	1AC97H	000C4H	_PROG
1AC98H	1ACB2H	0001BH	_PROG
1ACB3H	1AE2AH	00178H	_PROG
1AE2BH	1AEBCH	00092H	_PROG
1AEBDH	1AF08H	0004CH	_PROG
1AF09H	1AFB7H	000AFH	_PROG
1AFB8H	1AFE4H	0002DH	_PROG
1AFE5H	1B08CH	000A8H	_PROG
1B08DH	1B0A9H	0001DH	_PROG
1B0AAH	1BB02H	00A59H	_PROG
1BB03H	1BB9CH	0009AH	_PROG
1BB9DH	1BBB9H	0001DH	_PROG
1BBBAH	1BCBFH	00106H	_PROG
1BCC0H	1BCFBH	0003CH	_PROG

Functions

Clipper Routines

Lattice C Routines

```
          1BCFCH 1BD65H 0006AH _PROG
          1BD66H 1BD9DH 00038H _PROG
          1BD9EH 1BDCBH 0002EH _PROG
          1BDCCH 1BDF0H 00025H _PROG
          1BDF1H 1BDF1H 00000H _PROG
          1BDF1H 1BDF1H 00000H _PROG
          1BDF1H 1BE90H 000A0H _PROG
          1BE91H 1BEA5H 00015H _PROG
          1BEA6H 1C2C8H 00423H _PROG
          1C2C9H 1C30BH 00043H _PROG
          1C30CH 1C33DH 00032H _PROG
          1C33EH 1C4E1H 001A4H _PROG
          1C4E2H 1C645H 00164H _PROG
          1C646H 1C6A0H 0005BH _PROG
          1C6A1H 1C7BFH 0011FH _PROG
          1C7C0H 1C8B8H 000F9H _PROG
          1C8B9H 1C908H 00050H _PROG
          1C909H 1C92CH 00024H _PROG
          1C92DH 1C94CH 00020H _PROG
          1C94DH 1C96DH 00021H _PROG
          1C96EH 1C9ABH 0003EH _PROG
          1C9ACH 1CA03H 00058H _PROG
          1CA04H 1CCD0H 002CDH _PROG
          1CCD1H 1CD04H 00034H _PROG
          1CD05H 1CFB2H 002AEH _PROG
          1CFB3H 1D1F3H 00241H _PROG
          1D1F4H 1D1FEH 0000BH _PROG
          1D1FFH 1D1FFH 00000H _PROG
          1D1FFH 1D20CH 0000EH _PROG
          1D20DH 1D290H 00084H _PROG
          1D291H 1D291H 00000H _PROG
          1D291H 1D338H 000A8H _PROG
          1D339H 1D4B7H 0017FH _PROG
          1D4B8H 1D4CCH 00015H _PROG
          1D4CDH 1D4CDH 00000H _PROG
          1D4CDH 1D568H 0009CH _PROG
          1D569H 1D583H 0001BH _PROG
          1D584H 1D5FEH 0007BH _PROG
          1D5FFH 1D632H 00034H _PROG
          1D633H 1D71DH 000EBH _PROG
          1D71EH 1D748H 0002BH _PROG
          1D749H 1D770H 00028H _PROG
          1D771H 1D7DBH 0006BH _PROG
          1D7DCH 1D7EDH 00012H _PROG
          1D7EEH 1D912H 00125H _PROG
          1D913H 1D98EH 0007CH _PROG
          1D98FH 1DA78H 000EAH _PROG
          1DA80H 1DA98H 00019H $EXPR          $EXPR
  M       1DAA0H 1DAA0H 00000H $EXPR          $EXPR
  e       1DAA0H 1DABFH 00020H $MDATA         $MDATA
  m       1DAC0H 1DAC0H 00000H $SYMSTART      $SYMSTART
  o       1DAC0H 1DD5FH 002A0H $SYMBOLS       $SYMBOLS
  r       1DD60H 1DF4FH 001F0H $SYMBOLS       $SYMBOLS
  y       1DF50H 1DF51H 00002H $SYMEND        $SYMEND
          1DF60H 2343FH 054E0H $CONSTANTS     $CONSTANTS
  S       23440H 2669FH 03260H $CONSTANTS     $CONSTANTS
  e       266A0H 29413H 02D74H DATA           DATA
  g       29420H 2975BH 0033CH $LIB_TABLE     DATA
  .       29760H 297DFH 00080H STACK          DATA

          Origin   Group
          266A:0   DGROUP
```

To determine the precise load module size, take the last map figure (297DF) and subtract the stack figure (80). To this number, add 1000 for the allotted internal stack in Clipper and convert the Hex number to decimal. The result is the basic load module.

$$297DF - 80 + 1000 = 2A75F \text{ Hex} = 173,919 \text{ bytes}$$

Here is the memory map for the same file, which is generated by **PLINK86**

```
Groups:

Name        Address  Size  DSalloc
DGROUP       266A0   3130
```

```
Segments:

Section : Maddr=0, Msize=297D0, Daddr=2400, Lev=0, Ovly#=0
```

Name	Addr	Size	Name	Addr	Size
CREATE.NI	0	A7	FIRST.NIL	B0	98
SECOND.NI	150	2EB	THIRD.NIL	440	647
FOURTH.NI	A90	2E5	FIFTH.NIL	D80	9AF
SIXTH.NIL	1730	17D	SEVENTH.N	18B0	DC
EIGHT.NIL	1990	118	NINE.NIL	1AB0	4A6
TEN.NIL	1F60	372	CREATE1.N	22E0	F
ELEVEN.NI	22F0	3EC	TWELVE.NI	26E0	94
THIRTEEN.	2780	556	FOURTEEN.	2CE0	30E
FIFTEEN.N	2FF0	196	SIXTEEN.N	3190	14D
SEVENTEEN	32E0	DE	EIGHTEEN.	33C0	CE
NINETEEN.	3490	160	TWENTY.NI	35F0	177
TWENTY1.N	3770	B6	PROCHEAD.	3830	39
FUNCHEAD.	3870	39	VERIFY.NI	38B0	6B
$START.NI	3920	DF	$INTERFAC	39FF	6F4
$INTERFAC	40F3	8B	EXEC.C.NI	417E	136B
_PROG.NIL	54E9	1CA	NDEBUG.C.	56B3	B
$DRIVERS.	56BE	54F	SYMSYS.C.	5C0D	523
CTERM.C.N	6130	915	STACK.C.N	6A45	12B1
DB.C.NIL	7CF6	4B00	OPS.C.NIL	C7F6	261E
STERM.C.N	EE14	377E	SET.C.NIL	12592	BCB
CSUPPORT.	1315D	1861	MACRO.C.N	149BE	36A
$HACKJOB.	14D28	271	_PROG.NIL	14F99	5D
_PROG.NIL	14FF6	2DD	_PROG.NIL	152D3	0
_PROG.NIL	152D3	0	_PROG.NIL	152D3	0
_PROG.NIL	152D3	120	INDEX.C.N	153F3	27E9
RPAR.C.NI	17BDC	1D4B	_PROG.NIL	19927	6A
_PROG.NIL	19991	5DB	_PROG.NIL	19F6C	15
NATION.C.	19F81	19C	_PROG.NIL	1A11D	41
_PROG.NIL	1A15E	1D	_PROG.NIL	1A17B	6A
_PROG.NIL	1A1E5	38	_PROG.NIL	1A21D	2E
_PROG.NIL	1A24B	25	_PROG.NIL	1A270	0
_PROG.NIL	1A270	0	_PROG.NIL	1A270	A59
_PROG.NIL	1ACC9	1B	_PROG.NIL	1ACE4	12F
_PROG.NIL	1AE13	41	_PROG.NIL	1AE54	2D

_PROG.NIL	1AE81	1E	_PROG.NIL	1AE9F	456
_PROG.NIL	1B2F5	9A	_PROG.NIL	1B38F	1D
_PROG.NIL	1B3AC	33	_PROG.NIL	1B3DF	2D
_PROG.NIL	1B40C	A8	_PROG.NIL	1B4B4	C
_PROG.NIL	1B4C0	C	_PROG.NIL	1B4CC	C4
_PROG.NIL	1B590	41A	_PROG.NIL	1B9AA	178
_PROG.NIL	1BB22	92	_PROG.NIL	1BBB4	4C
_PROG.NIL	1BC00	3C	_PROG.NIL	1BC3C	15
_PROG.NIL	1BC51	423	_PROG.NIL	1C074	106
_PROG.NIL	1C17A	A0	_PROG.NIL	1C21A	43
_PROG.NIL	1C25D	AF	_PROG.NIL	1C30C	15
_PROG.NIL	1C321	0	_PROG.NIL	1C321	E
_PROG.NIL	1C32F	84	_PROG.NIL	1C3B3	164
_PROG.NIL	1C517	5B	_PROG.NIL	1C572	11F
_PROG.NIL	1C691	F9	_PROG.NIL	1C78A	50
_PROG.NIL	1C7DA	24	_PROG.NIL	1C7FE	20
_PROG.NIL	1C81E	32	_PROG.NIL	1C850	1A4
_PROG.NIL	1C9F4	0	_PROG.NIL	1C9F4	21
_PROG.NIL	1CA15	3E	_PROG.NIL	1CA53	58
_PROG.NIL	1CAAB	2CD	_PROG.NIL	1CD78	34
_PROG.NIL	1CDAC	2AE	_PROG.NIL	1D05A	241
_PROG.NIL	1D29B	A8	_PROG.NIL	1D343	17F
_PROG.NIL	1D4C2	0	_PROG.NIL	1D4C2	B
_PROG.NIL	1D4CD	12	_PROG.NIL	1D4DF	1B
_PROG.NIL	1D4FA	7B	_PROG.NIL	1D575	9C
_PROG.NIL	1D611	34	_PROG.NIL	1D645	EB
_PROG.NIL	1D730	2B	_PROG.NIL	1D75B	28
_PROG.NIL	1D783	6B	_PROG.NIL	1D7EE	125
_PROG.NIL	1D913	7C	_PROG.NIL	1D98F	EA
$EXPR.$EX	1DA80	19	$EXPR.$EX	1DAA0	0
$MDATA.$M	1DAA0	20	$SYMSTART	1DAC0	0
$SYMBOLS.	1DAC0	2A0	$SYMBOLS.	1DD60	1F0
$SYMEND.$	1DF50	2	$CONSTANT	1DF60	54E0
$CONSTANT	23440	3260	DATA.DATA	266A0	2D70
$LIB_TABL	29410	33C	STACK.DAT	29750	80

As with the previous map, take the last address point (29750) and subtract the 80 hex from it for the stack brought in by the linker. Then add 1000 hex for Clipper's stack, and convert this figure to decimal for the basic load module linking with PLINK86.

$$29750 - 80 + 1000 = 2A6D0 \text{ Hex} = 173,776 \text{ bytes}$$

QUIT TO VERSUS CHAINING BIG PROGRAMS

When developing an application, don't forget that the environment of the compiler is different from that of the interpreter. The syntax and structure look the same as dBASE III, but Clipper is still a more powerful language. Think of Clipper as a set of the dBASE III language. Programs which once chained from one program file to another, to word processors, or to other applications, may not do so under the compiled environment. Your program files are now totally memory resident. This takes up more memory than the same files did in the interpreter's environment.

Some recoding and rethinking may be necessary to make the program function as before. Below are just a few examples of how to accomplish this.

THE QUIT_TO BATCH FILE

One way to get programs to chain together is through the aid of a batch file. Below is one such example:

```
* Procedure: QTO.PRG
* Author ..: Barry Grant
* Date ....: 05-29-85, modified 06-26-85 by Ray Love
* Notes ...: Based on a routine by Tom Rettig from the "Advanced
*            Programmer's Guide", copyright (c) 1985 Luis Castro,
*            Jay Hansen, and Tom Rettig, Published by Ashton-Tate.
*
* This program allows programs to call one another by starting
* execution with a batch file then modifying that batch file to
* call the next program.  This is done by passing the name of the
* next program to the procedure QUIT_TO.   For example,
*
*    DO Quit_to WITH Next
*
* where the contents of next is the program to execute.  The called
* routines can return by using the same procedure.  To exit the
* batch file, pass "GOTO END" to QUIT_TO.
*
* -IMPORTANT-
* The length of the memory variable passed to QUIT_TO must always
* be 8 characters.  The file pointer used by DOS must find the
* instruction GOTO START at the same location in the batch file
* every time.
*
* Any memory variables that need to be passed may be SAVEd to a
* .MEM file.
*
* This example uses the names START.BAT for the batch file and
* MAIN.EXE for the initial program to execute.  The file START.BAT
* contains the following:
*
*    ECHO OFF
*    MAIN
*    GOTO START
*    :START
*    GOTO END
*    GOTO START
*    :END
*    ECHO ON
```

```
PROCEDURE QUIT_TO

PARAMETERS program

    SET ALTERNATE TO START.BAT
    SET ALTERNATE ON
    SET CONSOLE OFF
    ? "ECHO OFF"
    ? "MAIN"
    ? "GOTO START"
    ? ":START"
    ? program
    ? "GOTO START"
    ? ":END"
    ? "ECHO ON"
    SET ALTERNATE TO
    SET CONSOLE ON
    QUIT


* The following three programs demonstrate the use of QUIT_TO.
* Compile separately, create START.BAT, and enter "START" at the
* DOS prompt.

* MAIN.prg
* Notes ...: Main menu of a procedure to call other programs.

    SET PROCEDURE TO QTO
    DO WHILE .T.
       CLEAR
       @ 10,30 SAY "M A I N   M E N U"
       @ 12,30 PROMPT " 1.    Program 1 "
       @ 13,30 PROMPT " 2.    Program 2 "
       @ 14,30 PROMPT " 3.     QUIT    "
       MENU TO choice
       DO CASE
       CASE choice = 1
          * Add spaces to make next string 8 character long...
          next = "TEST_1  "
       CASE choice = 2
          next = "TEST_2  "
       OTHERWISE
          next = "GOTO END"
       ENDCASE
       DO QUIT_TO WITH next
    ENDDO
    * EOF MAIN.PRG

    * TEST_1.prg

    SET PROCEDURE TO QTO
    CLEAR
    WAIT "This is TEST_1.PRG   Press any key to return to MAIN."
    next = "MAIN    "
```

```
DO QUIT_TO WITH next
* EOF TEST_1.prg

* TEST_2.prg
SET PROCEDURE TO QTO
CLEAR
WAIT "This is TEST_2.prg   Press any key to return to MAIN."
next = "MAIN     "
DO QUIT_TO WITH next
* EOF TEST_2.prg
```

COMING BACK TO THE MAIN PROGRAM

A major concern in chaining two or more large applications together is the inability to leave one program to run another and then to return to the correct position in the original application. If the RUN command is invoked, the line immediately following it will be executed once control is regained by the original program. However, with large applications this is not that easy. The original program will remain in memory while the RUN command will try to load the second application (or program) on top of the first one. In most environments, the second program will not be able to be loaded into memory either because of file size, restricted memory size, or both. This is a common problem in applications that call up an external word processor.

The major problem with a batch file fix is the inability to get back to the exit point of the original application without being forced to go through the entire menu scheme as if starting up the program for the first time. The following example demonstrates a solution to this problem with the batch file fix and some minor recoding.

```
*********************
* Name       CHAINIT.prg
* Date       September 21, 1986
* Notice     Copyright 1986, Stephen J. Straley
* Note       This example shows how, with minor coding, a program
*            can exit to another program and reenter the application
*            close to the exit point.
*
*********************

***********************************************************************
* This section of code is needed in order to check the disk       *
* to see if the system/environment file is out there. If it is,   *
* then chain to that procedure; otherwise, go directly to the     *
* Main Menu.                                                       *
***********************************************************************
CLEAR
IF FILE("ALLMEM.MEM")
   RESTORE FROM Allmem
   ERASE Allmem.mem
   DO &goproc
```

```
ENDIF
DO Aamen1

*********************

PROCEDURE Aamen1

DO WHILE .T.
   CLEAR
   scrframe = CHR(201) + CHR(205) + CHR(187) + CHR(186) + ;
              CHR(188) + CHR(205) + CHR(200) + CHR(186) + CHR(32)
   STORE 0 TO option
   @ 6, 12, 16, 55 BOX scrframe
   @ 5, 29 SAY "Main Menu"
   @ 8, 14 PROMPT " Account Charts "
   @ 10, 14 PROMPT " Transactions "
   @ 12, 14 PROMPT " Postings "
   @ 14, 14 PROMPT " Reports "
   @ 8, 38 PROMPT " Listings "
   @ 10, 38 PROMPT " Other Systems "
   @ 12, 38 PROMPT " Utilities "
   @ 14, 38 PROMPT " End of Period "
   @ 17, 27 SAY "ESC to RETURN"
   MENU TO option
   DO CASE
   CASE option = 1
      DO Aamen11
   CASE option = 2
      *************************
      * Do sub-procedure here *
      *************************
   CASE option = 3
      *************************
      * Do sub-procedure here *
      *************************
   CASE option = 4
      *************************
      * Do sub-procedure here *
      *************************
   CASE option = 5
      *************************
      * Do sub-procedure here *
      *************************
   CASE option = 6
      *************************
      * Do sub-procedure here *
      *************************
   CASE option = 7
      *************************
      * Do sub-procedure here *
      *************************
   CASE option = 8
      DO Aamen18
```

```
      CASE option = 0
         @ 19, 15 SAY "All Files Closed, Returning to Operating System"
         QUIT
      ENDCASE

   ENDDO

   ********************

   PROCEDURE Aamen18

   DO WHILE .T.
      STORE 0 TO option1
      @ 15, 40, 22, 65 BOX scrframe
      @ 17, 46 PROMPT " Month End "
      @ 18, 46 PROMPT " Quarter End "
      @ 19, 46 PROMPT " Year End "
      @ 21, 47 SAY "ESC to RETURN"
      MENU TO option1
      DO CASE
      CASE option1 = 1
         *************************
         * Do sub-procedure here *
         *************************
      CASE option1 = 2
         *************************
         * Do sub-procedure here *
         *************************
      CASE option1 = 3
         *************************
         * Do sub-procedure here *
         *************************
      CASE option1 = 0
         EXIT
      ENDCASE

   ENDDO

   ********************

   PROCEDURE Aamen11

   DO WHILE .T.
      STORE 0 TO option2
      @ 8, 32, 20, 54 BOX scrframe
      @ 8, 39 SAY "Sub-Menu"
      @ 10, 33 PROMPT " 1> Enter Accounts "
      @ 13, 33 PROMPT " 2> Edit Accounts "
      @ 16, 33 PROMPT " 3> Scan Accounts "
      @ 19, 33 PROMPT " 4> Delete Accounts "
      @ 21, 37 SAY "ESC to RETURN"
      MENU TO option2
      DO CASE
```

```
   CASE option2 = 1
      *************************
      * Do sub-procedure here *
      *************************
   CASE option2 = 2
      *************************
      * Do sub-procedure here *
      *************************
   CASE option2 = 3
      *************************
      * Do sub-procedure here *
      *************************
   CASE option2 = 4
      DO Aamen114
   CASE option2 = 0
      EXIT
   ENDCASE

ENDDO

********************

PROCEDURE Aamen114

DO WHILE .T.
   STORE 0 TO option3
   a 17, 13, 21, 33 BOX scrframe
   a 18, 18 PROMPT " Quit File "
   a 19, 18 PROMPT " Go to Top "
   a 21, 17 SAY "ESC to RETURN"
   MENU TO option3
   DO CASE
   CASE option3 = 1
      goproc = PROCNAME()
      SAVE TO Allmem
      QUIT
   CASE option3 = 2
      DO Aamen1
   CASE option3 = 0
      EXIT
   ENDCASE

ENDDO
* End of CHAINIT
```

This example has five major considerations:

1)   The number of variables stored to one MEMory file is still limited to 254
     variables. If more variables exist, additional files will have to be created to
     properly save the environment.

2)   It doesn't get to the exact point of departure. However, with additional
      coding, this too may be simulated.

3)   Files must be reopened, relations reestablished, and record pointers prop-
      erly positioned when returning to the main application.

4)   Screen variables (those variables which contain the screen mapping) may be
      saved to the memory file. However, proper parsing must take place.

5)   The routine must be able to exit to the top level routine and not be expected
      to pop to the procedure immediately preceding the routine.

CHAINING THE PROGRAMS...WITH A FLAIR!

There is yet another way to circumvent the chaining problem. Many developers don't
want to start their application via the batch file approach. They want the chaining to
be managed entirely from within their programs. The problem is that there is no command in Clipper or in dBASE III that is equivalent to dBASE II's QUIT TO command.

If a CANCEL or a QUIT command is given, then memory is released, but everything
is turned over to the operating system. To chain from the operating system, a batch
file would have been generated prior to running the application which is, as we stated,
not the intent. On the other hand, if a RUN command is issued, then the application
remains in memory and there may be insufficient memory space as the other program
is loaded.

The solution to the problem is not simple and not clean. It may cause problems and
user interfacing difficulty. The solution consists of a batch file approach and the technique of saving the environment to a MEMory file. If the AUTOEXEC.BAT is saved
to a temporary file and then changed with the proper chaining calls followed by a
cold-boot, then the first application could chain to the second program, clear out
memory space for it, and save the environmental conditions for reentry.

Keep in mind that if this is done there will be considerable lag time as the computer
goes through the booting process and chains to the second application. If the second
application is anything other than a program with the capabilities of writing batch files,
the AUTOEXEC.BAT file must have the name of the original calling program's name
in it as well. Also, upon reentry of the original program, the old AUTOEXEC.BAT
file must be restored. When the program has completed processing, one more cold-
boot must be activated in order to reset the system to its original condition.

Below is an example of just that process:

```
********************
* Name          AMENU.prg
* Date          August 21, 1986
* Notice        Copyright 1986, Stephen J. Straley
* Note          This is the first application.  Try this under a 256K
*               environment space.
*
********************

   CLEAR
   STORE .F. TO reboot
   IF FILE("ALLMEM.MEM")
      RESTORE FROM Allmem
      ERASE Allmem.mem
      RUN CD\
      RUN DEL Autoexec.bat
      RUN REN Autoexec.tem Autoexec.bat
      RUN CD\FW\WORK\TEST      && The name of the sub-directory for program
      DO &goproc
      STORE .T. TO reboot
   ENDIF
   DO Aamen1


   ********************

   PROCEDURE Aamen1

   DO WHILE .T.
      CLEAR
      scrframe = CHR(201) + CHR(205) + CHR(187) + CHR(186) + ;
                 CHR(188) + CHR(205) + CHR(200) + CHR(186) + CHR(32)
      STORE 0 TO option
      @ 6, 12, 16, 55 BOX scrframe
      @ 5, 29 SAY "Main Menu"
      @ 8, 14 PROMPT " Account Charts "
      @ 10, 14 PROMPT " Transactions "
      @ 12, 14 PROMPT " Postings "
      @ 14, 14 PROMPT " Reports "
      @ 8, 38 PROMPT " Listings "
      @ 10, 38 PROMPT " Other Systems "
      @ 12, 38 PROMPT " Utilities "
      @ 14, 38 PROMPT " End of Period "
      @ 17, 27 SAY "ESC to RETURN"
      MENU TO option
      DO CASE
      CASE option = 1
         DO Aamen11
      CASE option = 2
         ************************
         * Do sub-procedure here *
         ************************
      CASE option = 3
```

```
      **************************
      * Do sub-procedure here *
      **************************
   CASE option = 4
      **************************
      * Do sub-procedure here *
      **************************
   CASE option = 5
      **************************
      * Do sub-procedure here *
      **************************
   CASE option = 6
      **************************
      * Do sub-procedure here *
      **************************
   CASE option = 7
      **************************
      * Do sub-procedure here *
      **************************
   CASE option = 8
      DO Aamen18
   CASE option = 0
      @ 19, 15 SAY "All Files Closed, Returning to Operating System"
      IF reboot
         RUN Coldboot
      ELSE
         QUIT
      ENDIF
   ENDCASE

ENDDO

********************

PROCEDURE Aamen18

DO WHILE .T.
   STORE 0 TO option1
   @ 15, 40, 22, 65 BOX scrframe
   @ 16, 12 SAY ""
   @ 17, 46 PROMPT " Month End "
   @ 18, 46 PROMPT " Quarter End "
   @ 19, 46 PROMPT " Year End "
   @ 21, 47 SAY "ESC to RETURN"
   MENU TO option1
   DO CASE
   CASE option1 = 1
      **************************
      * Do sub-procedure here *
      **************************
   CASE option1 = 2
      **************************
      * Do sub-procedure here *
      **************************
```

```
        CASE option1 = 3
            *************************
            * Do sub-procedure here *
            *************************
        CASE option1 = 0
            EXIT
        ENDCASE

ENDDO

********************

PROCEDURE Aamen11

DO WHILE .T.
        STORE 0 TO option2
        @ 8, 32, 20, 54 BOX scrframe
        @ 8, 39 SAY "Sub-Menu"
        @ 10, 33 PROMPT " 1> Enter Accounts "
        @ 13, 33 PROMPT " 2> Edit Accounts "
        @ 16, 33 PROMPT " 3> Scan Accounts "
        @ 19, 33 PROMPT " 4> Delete Accounts "
        @ 21, 37 SAY "ESC to RETURN"
        MENU TO option2
        DO CASE
        CASE option2 = 1
            *************************
            * Do sub-procedure here *
            *************************
        CASE option2 = 2
            *************************
            * Do sub-procedure here *
            *************************
        CASE option2 = 3
            *************************
            * Do sub-procedure here *
            *************************
        CASE option2 = 4
            DO Aamen114
        CASE option2 = 0
            EXIT
        ENDCASE

ENDDO

********************

PROCEDURE Aamen114

DO WHILE .T.
        STORE 0 TO option3
        @ 17, 13, 21, 33 BOX scrframe
        @ 18, 10 SAY ""
```

```
      a 18, 18 PROMPT " Quit File "
      a 19, 18 PROMPT " Go to Top "
      a 21, 17 SAY "ESC to RETURN"
      MENU TO option3
      DO CASE
      CASE option3 = 1
         goproc = PROCNAME()
         SAVE TO Allmem
         CLEAR ALL
         RUN CD\
         RUN REN AUTOEXEC.BAT AUTOEXEC.TEM
         SET CONSOLE OFF
         TEXT TO FILE Autoexec.bat
cd\fw\work\test
BMENU
AMENU
         ENDTEXT
         RUN Coldboot
      CASE option3 = 2
         DO Aamen1
      CASE option3 = 0
         EXIT
      ENDCASE

   ENDDO
* End of AMENU.prg
```

And now for the second program...

```
********************
* Name          BMENU.prg
* Date          September 21, 1986
* Notice        Copyright 1986, Stephen J. Straley
* Note          This is just a simple subprogram that checks the
*               amount of memory available
*
********************

   CLEAR
   ? "I am in BBMENU..."
   RUN chkdsk
   WAIT
* End of BMENU
```

This technique works because there is a program called COLDBOOT residing on the main directory. For a listing of the COLDBOOT program, please refer to the section in Chapter 10, Assembly and C Routines and the CALL Command.

CHAPTER FOUR

Commands

This chapter includes explanations of all the CLIPPER commands. If you are converting code from dBASE III to Clipper solely for the sake of increasing speed, take particular note of the different ways the two environments use the same commands. However, if you are converting an application with the intent of marketing it (which means protecting the source code as well), take note of the additional commands, for they can greatly enhance your product.

The listing for each command includes the command *name*, proper *syntax*, *description*, *command type*, any *variances* and one or more *samples*. If a command is labeled *standard*, then it works like the standard dBASE III command. If the command is somewhat different or enhanced under Clipper, the command is labeled *enhanced*. If the command is unique to the Autumn '86 version of Clipper, the command will begin with "Autumn 86: Special Command." However, if only a clause or a small variance is unique in the Autumn '86 version, that clause or variance will follow the words "Autumn 86:".

The following notation is used in describing the commands:

< expC >:	a character expression, normally a string.
< expL >:	a logical expression, either .T. or .F.
< expD >:	a date expression.
< expN >:	a numeric expression (a number or a formula).

@

Syntax:	@ < row,column > [SAY < exp > [PICTURE < clause >]] [GET < exp > [PICTURE < clause >] [RANGE < exp,exp] [VALID < exp >]] [CLEAR]
Description:	Used to display information to the screen or to the printer at specific locations. The CLEAR clause will clear the portion of the screen beginning at the < row,column > position continuing across from that column marker and panning down from that row marker.
Command:	dBASE Standard.
Variance:	The implementation of the VALID option is new. With the VALID option, the program can test for immediate input validation. The @ command is not completed until the expression in the VALID option is true. Escape is possible if ESCAPE is SET ON and the key is entered.

Autumn 86:   A few new picture functions have been added:

@E -   Numeric input in European Format.

@) -   For negative numbers (credit balances), the leading spaces
            are not displayed within the parentheses.

@K -   Allows a suggestion value to be seen within the GET area
            but it will be cleared if any key, including the **Enter** key, is
            struck.

@S < expN > Will allow horizontal scrolling of the field or variable
             < expN > characters wide.

Sample:
```
CLEAR
STORE "A" TO input
a 10,10 SAY "I only want you to enter in any of the"
a 11,10 SAY "  first three letters of the alphabet."
a 15,10 SAY "Enter character " GET input PICT "aK !";
        VALID( input$"ABC" )
a 20,10 SAY "Very good..."
WAIT
a 10,10 CLEAR
```

@...TO   (Autumn 86 Special Command)

Syntax: @ < row,column > [CLEAR] TO < row2, column2 > [DOUBLE]

Description: Used to draw a single or double line box, or to clear an area of the
                screen.

Command: dBASE Standard.

Autumn 86:   This command was implemented in the Autumn '86 version.

![< expC >]

Syntax: ![< expC >]

Description: Introduced in Clipper - Winter '85. This operator is equivalent to
                the .NOT. operator. It offers additional compatibility with other lan-
                guages some developers may be acquainted with.

Command: Clipper enhanced.

Variance: This operator may not be used in place of the < > sign. For that op-
                 eration, as well as the other mathematical operators as well, maintain
                 the standard conventions.

                 The ! operator must not have a blank space between it and < expC >
                 or else it will be interpreted as being a RUN command.

Sample: `IF !EOF()        && In Place of IF .NOT. EOF()`

                 The following would **not** be legal:

                 `IF test !="Sample"  && in place of IF test <> "Sample"`

! (See RUN)

?

Syntax: ? < expression list >

Description: This operator displays and evaluates the value of an expression. The
                 single question mark will issue a carriage return and line feed **before**
                 the expression is displayed / evaluated. A question mark without an
                 expression list will generate a blank line.

Command: dBASE Standard.

Samples: `? RECNO()   && Will display the current record number`
                 `? last_name && Will print out the contents of the`
                 `             && last_name field.`
                 `? DATE() = DATE()  && Will display a .T. for this true`
                 `             && expression.`

??

Syntax: ?? < expression list >

Description: This operator displays and evaluates the value of an expression. The
                 double question mark will **not** issue a carriage return and line feed
                 before the expression is displayed/evaluated. All that will be dis-
                 played/evaluated will be the expression either on the screen, to the
                 printer, or to an alternate file.

Command: Standard

Samples:
```
?? RECNO()   && Will display the current record number
?? last_name && Will print out the contents of the
                && last_name field.
?? DATE() = DATE()  && Will display a .T. for this true
                    && expression.
```

= =

Syntax: < expression > = = < expression >

Description: Similar to SET EXACT ON; however, this operator will look for a perfect match: same characters, length, and value on both sides of the equation. SET EXACT ON evaluates characters, not value.

Command: Clipper enhanced.

Variance: Below is a list of examples showing the use of the = = operator with SET EXACT ON and with SET EXACT OFF and what each would yield. If there should ever be a case when two variables do not match but are equal (e.g., X = 0 and Y = 0, but X < > Y) or there is a case where -0 = 0, then use the double equal sign.

Sample:
```
SET EXACT ON      "Test this" = "Test this "        && True

"Test this " = "Test this"  && True
SET EXACT OFF     "Test this" = "Test this "  && False
"Test this " = "Test this"  && True
SET EXACT ON      "Test this" == "Test this "  && False
"Test this " == "Test this" && False
SET EXACT OFF     "Test this" == "Test this "  && False
"Test this " == "Test this" && False
```

ACCEPT

Syntax: ACCEPT [< prompt message >] TO < memvar >

Description: Prompts the user for specific input. All data input by the user is treated as character type. Therefore, if numeric input is desired in conjunction with this command, the VALue() of the string must be converted. The prompting message will appear to the left-most side of the screen; the cursor immediately follows the string, waiting for input.

The memory variable does not have to be initialized prior to the issuance of this command. If the memory variable does exist, then that value will be replaced by the new input.

If the **Enter** key is hit without any value for the memory variable, the memory variable will then be set to a NULL value with LEN() of 0.

A maximum of 255 characters can be entered into the variable with the ACCEPT command.

Command: Standard.

Sample:
```
********************
* Name          ACCEPT.prg
* Date          August 3, 1986
* Notice        Copyright 1986, Stephen J. Straley
* Note          Demonstrates the ACCEPT command
**********************

test = 4
FOR x = 1 TO 2
   CLEAR
   ACCEPT "What is the variable: " TO test
   ? test
   ? LEN(test)
   WAIT
NEXT
* End of File
```

APPEND BLANK

Syntax: APPEND BLANK

Description: This command places a blank record at the end of the file and positions the record pointer/counter to that blank record. All character fields are filled with spaces, numeric fields have a value of zero (0), logical fields are set to a value of .F. (false), and date fields are set to a value of " / / ". From this point, data entry may be performed with a series of @... SAY... GET on the fields that were just opened.

Command: dBASE Standard.

Autumn 86:   Attempts to APPEND and lock a new record whenever SET EXCLUSIVE is OFF. If another user has locked the file on which the APPEND BLANK is to be performed, the NETERR() function will return a .T.

Sample:

```
********************
* Name       APPEND.prg
* Date       August 3, 1986
* Notice     Copyright 1986, Stephen J. Straley
* Note       This program will demonstrate the use of the
*            APPEND BLANK command.  There are a few other
*            commands mixed in, but study to the main thrust
*            of this program.
*
*******************

CREATE Temp
USE Temp
APPEND BLANK
REPLACE field_name WITH "CHARACT", field_len WITH 15, field_type
WITH "C"
APPEND BLANK
REPLACE field_name WITH "NUMERIC", field_len WITH 10, field_type
WITH "N"
APPEND BLANK
REPLACE field_name WITH "DATE", field_len WITH 8, field_type WITH
"D"
APPEND BLANK
REPLACE field_name WITH "logic", field_len WITH 1, field_type WITH
"L"
USE
CREATE Append FROM Temp
ERASE Temp
USE Append
CLEAR
APPEND BLANK
? "Positioned on record: "
?? RECNO()
?
? "Character field is set to: "
?? charact
? LEN(charact)
? "Numeric field is set to: "
?? numeric
? "Date field is set to: "
?? date
? "Logical field is set to: "
?? logic
WAIT
CLEAR
a 10,10 SAY "Input the character field: " GET charact
a 12,10 SAY "  Input the numeric field: " GET numeric
a 14,10 SAY "     Input the date field: " GET date
a 16,10 SAY "  Input the logical field: " GET logic
READ
USE
ERASE Append
* End of File
```

APPEND FROM

Syntax: APPEND [scope][FIELDS < field list >] FROM < file name >
                  [FOR/WHILE < condition >][SDF/Delimited]

Description: Allows records to be added to the currently selected/open database
                  from one database.

Command: dBASE Standard.

Variance: The APPEND FROM command in Clipper supports a field list.
                  This list is an optional argument. The word "FIELDS" must be pres-
                  ent if this option is used. If used, when the data from the FROM
                  database is brought in, only fields listed in the < fields list > are
                  appended. The scope of the appended records may also be
                  specified.

Sample: `APPEND Record 10 FIELDS name, city, state FROM Alter`

AVERAGE

Syntax: A V E R A G E < f i e l d l i s t > T O < m e m v a r l i s t >
                  [FOR/WHILE < condition >]

Description: Enables an average of specified fields to be calculated based on a
                  specific condition in the currently selected and open database.

Command: dBASE Standard.

Variance: Both arguments (the < field list > and the < memvar list >) are
                  mandatory.

Sample: `AVERAGE myage, yourage, ourage TO a_age, b_age, c_age;`
                  `FOR myage > 20`

BOX

Syntax: @ < top,left,bottom,right > BOX < string >

Description: The BOX command is used mainly for drawing boxes quickly and ef-
                  ficiently, especially in the implementation of frames for screen
                  designs. The string parameter of the BOX command either must be
                  a string of nine characters or a null string. If the null string is passed
                  to the BOX command, the area specified by the four coordinates is

cleared. Otherwise, the string being passed represents the characters designated for: 1) the top left corner; 2) the line across the top; 3) the top right corner; 4) the line down the right side; 5) the bottom right corner; 6) the line across the bottom; 7) the bottom left corner; 8) the line up the left side; and, 9) the character to fill the space framed by the box.

Command: Clipper enhanced.

Sample:

```
*********************
* Name          BOXES.prg
* Date          August 4, 1986
* Notice        Copyright 1986, Stephen J. Straley
* Note          This program will draw many boxes using the
*               BOX command.
*********************

frame = CHR(201) + CHR(205) + CHR(187) + CHR(186) + ;
        CHR(188) + CHR(205) + CHR(200) + CHR(186) + ;
        CHR(32)
STORE  1 TO top
STORE  0 TO left
STORE 22 TO bottom
STORE 79 TO right
FOR x = 1 TO 10
   a top, left, bottom, right BOX frame
   STORE top + 1 TO top
   STORE left + 3 TO left
   STORE bottom - 1 TO bottom
   STORE right - 3 TO right
NEXT
a 11,35 SAY "FINISHED!"
a 23,00 SAY ""
* End of File
```

CALL

Syntax: CALL <process> [WITH <parameter list>]

Description: This command gives you access to separately compiled and/or assembled routines. These routines must be linked in at the same time as the other object files produced by Clipper. All CALLed programs **must conform to the following rules**:

1)   They must follow C language calling and parameter passing conventions.
2)   They must be in the "Intel 8086 relocatable object file format" with the .OBJ file extension.

3)   They must be available to the Linker.

4)   The library of the compiler of the calling program must be available to the Clipper linker. Remember that additional run-time support will be necessary for any language other than Assembly language.

5)   Up to seven parameters may be passed to the CALLed routine.

6)   The FAR process is necessary for CALLed programs.

7)   All data references consist of 4 byte pointers of the form SEG-MENT:OFFSET. They are on top of the stack in the order passed. All data types are passed by reference.

8)   CALLed programs must preserve the BP, SS and DS registers.

9)   Character strings are passed by reference and are null terminated.

10)   Data item lengths must be preserved.

11)   Numeric variables are passed as 8 byte floating point representation. They maintain a 53 bit characteristic and an 11 bit exponent biased by 1023.

Command: Clipper enhanced.

Autumn 86:   [WITH WORD(< expN >)] has been added. This will convert numeric parameters from type double to type int, reducing the overhead of the CALLed routine. If the value of the numeric expression expressed in the WORD function does not exceed plus or minus 32K, there is no need to pass a larger parameter.

Sample: See Chapter 10, Assembly and C Routines and the CALL command.

CANCEL

Syntax: CANCEL

Description: Just as effective as the QUIT command, this command stops the execution of a procedure/command file as well as the program and returns to the operating system.

Command: dBASE Standard.

Sample:
```
********************
* Name          CANCEL.prg
* Date          August 4, 1986
* Notice        Copyright 1986, Stephen J. Straley
* Note          This will show the CANCEL command stopping
*               the execution of the program within a
*               subroutine off the main program.
********************
```

```
CLEAR
DO WHILE .T.
   to_quit = .F.
   ? "Currently in the main section of the program..."
   DO Subroute
ENDDO

PROCEDURE Subroute

   @ ROW()+1, 5 SAY "Do you want to Cancel? " GET to_quit
   READ
   IF to_quit
      CANCEL
   ENDIF
* End of File
```

CLEAR

Syntax: CLEAR

Description: This command clears the screen and positions the cursor at
                 ROW = 0, COL = 0, or the upper left-most corner of the screen.

Command: dBASE Standard.

Variance: This command **cannot** be used in your Help.prg file. If used, it will
                 clear all GET/READs from the calling program. To get around this
                 problem, issue an @ 0,0 CLEAR command to clear the screen.

CLEAR ALL

Syntax: CLEAR ALL

Description: This command clears all memory variables from the system, closes all
                 open databases and associated indexes and releases any SET RELA-
                 TION TO command. It SELECTs work area 1.

Command: dBASE Standard.

CLEAR GETS

Syntax: CLEAR GETS

Description: Used in conjunction with associated @ SAY/GET commands, a
                  CLEAR GETS command releases all GET statements prior to this
                  command.

Command: dBASE Standard.

Variance: In Clipper, the addition of the 'S' on GETS is required for the com-
                  piler to function properly.

Notes: This command is used to help display a memory variable pertinent to
                  the system in reverse video if the normal attributes of the screen are
                  maintained.

Sample:
```
********************
* Name          ANOTHGET.prg
* Date          August 4, 1986
* Notice        Copyright 1986, Stephen J. Straley
* Note          This program demonstrates how CLEAR GETS can
*               be used as a display command on GETs rather
*               than an input command.
*********************

STORE 0 TO testvar1
STORE "This is a test" TO testvar2
CLEAR
@ 01,10 SAY "There is this way..."
@ 04,10 SAY " The first variable: "
@ ROW(),COL()+1 SAY testvar1
@ 05,10 SAY "The second variable: "
@ ROW(),COL()+1 SAY testvar2
@ 10,10 SAY "Now there is this way..."
@ 14,10 SAY " The first variable: " GET testvar1
@ 15,10 SAY "The second variable: " GET testvar2
CLEAR GETS
@ 23,00 SAY ""
* End of File
```

CLEAR MEMORY

Syntax: CLEAR MEMORY

Description: This command releases/clears all memory variables from the system.

Command: dBASE Standard.

CLOSE

Syntax: CLOSE < file type >

Description: The CLOSE ALTERNATE command closes an open alternate file.

               The CLOSE DATABASES command closes all open databases and
               all associated indexes.

               The CLOSE INDEX command closes all open index files which are
               currently in use.

               The CLOSE FORMAT/PROCEDURE command closes all open
               FORMAT/PROCEDURE files. Keep in mind that format files are
               treated no differently from any other program file or procedure file.
               In a compiled application, there is no real distinction between a pro-
               gram file and open format and procedure files.

Command: dBASE Standard.

CONTINUE

Syntax: CONTINUE

Description: This command resumes a search initiated by a LOCATE FOR com-
               mand, continuing to search for records which meet the search
               criteria. If a CONTINUE is successful in its search, the record
               pointer is placed on that record; otherwise, the EOF() marker is set
               to .T. (true) and the record pointer is placed on the last record.

Command: dBASE Standard.

COPY FILE

Syntax: COPY FILE < source file > TO < destination file >

Description: The COPY FILE command makes an exact copy of < source file >
                    with the name < destination file >. Both file names **must** have the
                    file extension included as well as the drive\directory designator if it
                    is any different from that of the default drive\directory.

                    The COPY FILE command will not work on a currently open file.

Command: dBASE Standard.

Variance: If used as noted, a DOS message (1 file(s) copied) will appear on the
                    screen immediately following the completion of this command. This
                    is because Clipper uses DOS for the copying and DOS messages ap-
                    pear as well. To avoid this, send the output of the messages to a
                    NUL device in the following way:

                    ```
                    COPY FILE <source file> TO <destination file>>NUL
                    ```

                    The > NUL must appear immediately after the name of the destina-
                    tion file, without any blank spaces.

                    Below are a few samples both with the additional clause and without.

Sample: ```
                    COPY FILE Mainfile.dbf TO Temp.dbf
                    COPY FILE Mainfile.dbt TO Temp.dbt>NUL
                    USE Mainfile
                    COPY FILE C:\DBASE\Myprog.prg TO A:\Myprog.bak>NUL
                    ```

## COPY STRUCTURE

Syntax:             COPY STRUCTURE TO < filename > [FIELDS < field list >]

Description:        The COPY STRUCTURE command only copies the structure of the
                    currently active database to < filename >.

Command:            dBASE Standard.

Variance:           The < field list > cannot be in a macro substitution. The fields must
                    be either in separate variables or coded as literals in the pro-
                    gram/procedure file. As with all other similar commands, the
                    < filename > must include the drive/directory designator if the file
                    being generated is not to be on the default drive/directory. If no file
                    extension is given, the file is assumed to carry a .DBF extension.
                    ```

If the FIELDS <field list> option is not included, the entire structure of the active database will be copied to the TO <filename>.

Sample: USE Mainfile
               COPY STRUCTURE TO Temp
               USE Temp

COPY TO <filename>

Syntax: COPY TO <filename> [<scope>] [FIELDS <field list>] [FOR
               <condition>] [WHILE <condition>] [SDF/DELIMITED WITH
               BLANK/<delimiter>]

Description: The COPY TO <filename> command copies the currently selected
               database to another database or to an alternate text file. The copied
               file can consist of selected fields within the selected database, and/or
               can be copied with a specific condition. The FOR and WHILE
               clauses may be used together. IF the SDF/DELIMITED clause is
               used, the COPied file will be an ASCII text file.

Command: dBASE Standard.

Sample: USE Hist

               COPY TO Nufi FIELDS last_name, total_hours;
                   FOR total_hours > 40

COPY TO STRUCTURE EXTENDED

Syntax: COPY TO <filename> STRUCTURE EXTENDED

Description: The COPY TO STRUCTURE EXTENDED command creates a
               new database consisting of only four fields: field_name, field_type,
               field_len, and field_dec. Fields of the open database become
               records in the structure extended database.

Command: dBASE Standard.

Notes: If used, this command can allow databases to be modified structural-
               ly within an application, especially if used in conjunction with the
               CREATE FROM command.

Sample:
```
********************
* Name            COPYSTRU.prg
* Date            August 3, 1986
* Notice          Copyright 1986, Stephen J. Straley
* Note            This will take the database MULTY.DBF and
*                 convert the fields to records in
*                 CONVERTD.DBF
*********************

USE Multy
COPY TO Convertd STRUCTURE EXTENDED
CLEAR
USE Convertd
LIST field_name, field_type, field_len, field_dec
```

COUNT

Syntax: COUNT [< scope >][FOR/WHILE < condition >] TO < mem-var >

Description: This command counts how many records in the currently active and open database file meet a specific condition and stores that figure to a memory variable.

Command: dBASE Standard.

Variance: The COUNT command must store the final figure of its operation to a memory variable.

Sample:
```
USE Phonbook
COUNT FOR state = "CA" .AND. TRIM(city) = "San Diego";
TO how_many
CLEAR
a 10,10 SAY "I know "
?? LTRIM(STR(how_many))
?? " People in San Diego, California"
```

CREATE

Syntax: CREATE < database file name >

Description: This command allows an application to create the necessary databases without a pre-existing template/empty database or an available template/empty structure extended database.

Command: Clipper enhanced.

Notes: Using the CREATE command results in a new file consisting of four
                fields: field_name, field_type, field_len, and field_dec. In essence, a
                STRUCTURE EXTENDED file will be created from scratch,
                without the previous existence of a database. Records may then be
                added and, from this, new databases established.

Sample:
```
********************
* Name        PRINIT.prg
* Date        August 4, 1986
* Notice      Copyright 1986, Stephen J. Straley
* Note        This will create the history file for a
*             payroll program.
**********************

STORE "C:" TO scrdata
IF !FILE(scrdata + "Prhist.dat")
   CREATE Template
   USE Template
   APPEND BLANK
   REPLACE field_name WITH "EMPLOYEE", field_type WITH "C",;
           field_len WITH 15
   APPEND BLANK
   REPLACE field_name WITH "PERIOD", field_type WITH "N",;
           field_len WITH 1
   APPEND BLANK
   REPLACE field_name WITH "HOURS", field_type WITH "N",;
           field_len WITH 8, field_dec WITH 4
   APPEND BLANK
   REPLACE field_name WITH "MARRIED", field_type WITH "L",;
           field_len WITH 1
   GO TOP
   CLEAR
   LIST field_name, field_type, field_len, field_dec
   USE
   file = scrdata + "PRHIST.DAT"
   CREATE &file. FROM Template
   ?
   ? "File created..."
   ERASE Template
   ?
   ? "Template erased..."
ENDIF
* End of File
```

CREATE FROM

Syntax: CREATE < newfile > FROM < structure extended file >

Description: The CREATE FROM command forms a new database file based on the contents of a structure extended file.

Command: dBASE Standard.

Variance: Issue a CLOSE DATABASES or a USE command immediately following this command if the newly created file is to be opened. With the CREATE FROM command, records in a structure extended database file are converted to be the actual structure for the file specified by the < newfile > parameter. To initially CREATE the structure extended file, refer to the CREATE command or the COPY STRUCTURE EXTENDED command.

Sample: See PRINIT.prg in the CREATE command

DECLARE

Syntax: DECLARE < memvar > [< expN >] [, < array list >]

Description: This command establishes an array named < memvar > of < expN > items. The items may be of any type and may be mixed. Keep in mind that arrays are always private. The brackets ([]) around < expN > must be included when working with arrays.

A few other things to keep in mind when using arrays are:

1)   The LEN() function will return the number of items in the array if the array name is the only parameter used; otherwise it will return the LEN of the element addressed.

2)   The TYPE() function will always return an "A" indicating an array type if the array name without element numbers is passed to the function.

3)   Establishing a memory variable with the same name as an array will destroy the array and release the contents of the array; an array cannot be saved to an external file (SAVE TO < memfile >).

4)   Arrays cannot be passed as a parameter with the CALL command.

5) Arrays may be used with macros but with limited usage (see samples below).

6) Arrays may be passed to procedures with the following regulations:

   a) DO <procedure> WITH (<memvar>[<expN>])
      passing element to procedure by value;

   b) DO <procedure> WITH (memvar)
      passing the entire array by reference by just passing the name of the array to the procedure.

7) The memory space required by an array is considered to be dynamic (it grows as items are added, much like a MEMO FILE) and follows the following formula:

   a) The array itself is 22 bytes times the number of elements to be stored in it.

   b) If an element to be added to the array is longer in width than 22 bytes, an address is added in place of the element which refers to the actual position in memory where that element resides.

Command: Clipper enhanced.

Sample:

```
********************
* Name          SAMPARRY.prg
* Date          August 4, 1986
* Notice        Copyright 1986, Stephen J. Straley
* Note          This program will initialize the months and
*               the days of the week to two memory
*               variables, and pass them to procedures.
********************

DECLARE month_a[12], day_a[7], date_a[50], numb_a[25],
hodge_a[100]

***************************************
* The following initializes the arrays *
***************************************

FOR x = 1 TO 50
   DO CASE
   CASE x <= 7
      day_a[x]   = CDOW(DATE() + (1 *x))
      month_a[x] = CMONTH(DATE() + (30 * x))
      numb_a[x]  = x * 324
```

```
      date_a[x]   = DATE() + x * 84
   CASE x > 7 .AND. x <= 12
      month_a[x] = CMONTH(DATE() + (30 * x))
      numb_a[x]  = x * 324
      date_a[x]   = DATE() + x * 84
   CASE x > 12 .AND. x <= 25
      numb_a[x]  = x * 324
      date_a[x]   = DATE() + x * 84
   CASE x > 25
      date_a[x]   = DATE() + x * 84
   ENDCASE
NEXT
CLEAR


****************************************************
* This section displays the values of the arrays *
****************************************************

a 01,05 SAY "Days of the week are ... "
FOR x = 1 TO 7
   ? day_a[x]
   hodge_a[x] = day_a[x]
NEXT
WAIT
CLEAR

a 01,05 SAY "Months of the year are ... "
FOR x = 1 TO 12
   ? month_a[x]
   hodge_a[x + 7] = month_a[x]
NEXT
WAIT
CLEAR

STORE 1 TO temp_col
STORE 3 TO temp_row

a 01,05 SAY "A random set of 25 numbers are ... "
FOR x = 1 TO 25
   a temp_row, temp_col SAY numb_a[x]
   DO Chngescr
   hodge_a[x + 19] = numb_a[x]
NEXT
WAIT
CLEAR

STORE 1 TO temp_col
STORE 3 TO temp_row

a 01,05 SAY "A random of 50 dates are ... "
FOR x = 1 TO 50
   a temp_row, temp_col say date_a[x]
   DO Chngescr
```

```
         hodge_a[x + 44] = date_a[x]
NEXT
WAIT
CLEAR

STORE 1 TO temp_col
STORE 3 TO temp_row

a 01,05 SAY "The total is ... "
FOR x = 1 TO 100
   a temp_row, temp_col SAY hodge_a[x]
   DO Chngescr
NEXT
WAIT
CLEAR

************************************************************
* This follow displays information using the LEN() and *
* TYPE() functions.                                     *
************************************************************

a 10,15 SAY "The following will show the depth "
?? "of each array ... "
a 12,10 SAY "The number of elements in the Month Array    "
?? LEN(month_a)
a 13,10 SAY "The number of elements in the Day Array      "
?? LEN(day_a)
a 14,10 SAY "The number of elements in the Number Array   "
?? LEN(numb_a)
a 15,10 SAY "The number of elements in the Date Array     "
?? LEN(date_a)
a 16,10 SAY "The number of elements in Hodge Podge Array "
?? LEN(hodge_a)
a 20,10 SAY "The type of the arrays are ...              "
?? TYPE("month_a")
WAIT
CLEAR
STORE "" TO in_temp

************************************************************
* This section passes the array to a procedure by value *
************************************************************

DO Passarry WITH month_a[3]
a 14,10 SAY "Month_a[3] is out of the procedure and equal to: "
a 14,60 SAY month_a[3]
WAIT

************************************************************
* This section passes the array by value yet shows how to *
* reassign the value back to the array.                   *
************************************************************
```

```
DO Passarry WITH month_a[3]
month_a[3] = in_temp
@ 14,10 SAY "Month_a[3] is out of the procedure and equal to: "
@ 14,60 SAY month_a[3]
WAIT


***************************************************************
* This section passes the entire array to a procedure by *
* reference.                                             *
***************************************************************

DO Anotarry WITH numb_a
CLEAR

STORE 3 TO temp_row
STORE 1 TO temp_col
@ 01,05 SAY "The numbers are now set to ... "
FOR x = 1 TO 25
   @ temp_row, temp_col SAY numb_a[x]
   DO Chngescr
NEXT

********************

PROCEDURE Passarry

   PARAMETERS in_val

   CLEAR
   @ 04,23 SAY "The value of the passed array is ... "
   @ 04,60 SAY in_val
   @ 06,23 SAY "Let us change the value ... " GET in_val
   READ
   @ 08,23 SAY "The new value is ... "
   @ 08,60 SAY in_val
   @ 10,20 SAY ""
   in_temp = in_val
   WAIT

********************

PROCEDURE Anotarry

   PARAMETERS b

   CLEAR
   temp_col = 1
   temp_row = 3
   @ 01,05 say "You may edit this Number Array ... "
   FOR x = 1 TO 25
      @ temp_row, temp_col GET b[x]
      DO Chngescr
   NEXT
   READ
```

```
********************

PROCEDURE Chngescr

   temp_col = temp_col + 15
   IF temp_col > 65
      temp_col = 1
      temp_row = temp_row + 1
   ENDIF
* End of File
```

DELETE

Syntax: DELETE [< scope >][FOR < condition >][WHILE < condition >]

Description: The DELETE command marks a record(s) in the currently open
                and active database for future deletion. Without any conditional
                clause accompanying the DELETE command, only the current
                record is marked for deletion. Both a FOR condition and a WHILE
                condition may exist simultaneously; however, the FOR condition will
                take precedence.

                Records are noted as DELETEd with an asterisk located in the first
                position on the screen/printer/file (used in conjunction with the
                DISPLAY and LIST commands).

Command: dBASE Standard.

Sample:
```
GO 5
DELETE   && this command will mark record 5 for deletion.

GO TOP
DELETE ALL FOR state = "CA" WHILE SUBSTR(phone,1,2) = "(2"
*
* All records in the state of CA and with a phone number
* starting with a "(2" will be marked for deletion.
*
```

DIR

Syntax: DIR [< drive >][< path >][< skeleton >]

Description: The DIR command displays the file names, number of records, size
                of the file in bytes, and date of last update for all databases on the
                designated drive/path. Not only database information but general
                file information as well may be displayed.

If no <skeleton> is passed, a search for .DBF files will be made. Other files may be displayed by using DOS wild cards in the <skeleton> as in the DOS DIR command.

Command: dBASE Standard.

Sample:
```
DIR
DIR *.*
DIR *.NTX
DIR *.PRG
DIR A:\ONE\*.*
```

DISPLAY

Syntax: DISPLAY [OFF][scope] FIELDS <field list> [FOR/WHILE <condition>]

Description: This command allows the contents of fields to be displayed.

Command: dBASE Standard.

Variance: To display any field, the FIELDS clause is mandatory; the field names are not displayed as a header and there is no automatic pausing after each 20 lines.

Autumn 86:   [TO PRINT/TO FILE <filename>] is an additional clause for the DISPLAY command.

Sample:
```
DISPLAY FIELDS name, city, state FOR state = "CA"
```

DO

Syntax: DO <file name> [WITH <parameter(s)>]

Description: This command begins execution of a program file or procedure.

Command: dBASE Standard.

Variance: Since the application is compiled, just the name of the file is required to begin execution of that program/procedure. At the conclusion of the program/procedure, control is returned to the calling program. In the case of the top level program, control will be returned to DOS. There is, in theory, no restriction to the number of consecutive DOs;

therefore, Clipper supports recursive programming. However, an
unlimited number of recursive DOs will cause your application to fail
because of the finite size of the internal stack.

Any number of parameters may be passed to a program file or to a
procedure, by reference or by value. If a parameter is passed by
reference, the parameter is passed without parentheses and the
called routine can change the value of the parameter which may be
accessed by higher level routines. If a parameter is passed by value,
it is contained within parentheses and only the value of the parameter is passed to the program/procedure; even if that value is
changed, the original value of the variable is retained in the calling
program.

Sample: 1. This sample demonstrates recursive programming.

```
*********************
* Name           RECURSE.prg
* Date           August 4, 1986
* Notice         Copyright 1986, Stephen J. Straley
* Note           This program will demonstrate recursive
*                program calling.
*********************

CLEAR
x = 1
DO Sub1 WITH (x)

*********************

PROCEDURE Sub1

   PARAMETERS y

   ?? y
   ?? SPACE(5)
   IF y > 10
      CANCEL
   ENDIF
   y = y + 1
   DO Sub1 WITH (y)
* End of File
```

2. This sample demonstrates the two methods of passing parameters.

```
*********************
* Name           PASSING.prg
* Date           August 4, 1986
* Notice         Copyright 1986, Stephen J. Straley
* Note           This program will demonstrate passing
*                variables to a sub-routine.
*********************
```

```
                    STORE 0 TO x, y
                    CLEAR
                    DO Readj WITH x, (Y)        && pass x by reference
                    ? x                         && pass Y by value
                    ? y

                    ********************

                    PROCEDURE Readj

                       PARAMETERS a, y

                       a = a + 5
                       y = y + 15
                       ? a
                       ? y
                       WAIT
                    * End of File
```

DO CASE

Syntax: DO CASE
               CASE < condition >
                   < commands >
               CASE < condition >
                   < commands >
               CASE < condition >
                   < commands >
               OTHERWISE
                   < commands >
               ENDCASE

Description: The DO CASE command allows for structured programming control
               that selects a specific set of commands to perform based upon the
               evaluation of < condition >.

               The ENDCASE statement terminates the DO CASE structure.

               The DO CASE commands should be used if more than two sets of
               actions are to be taken. Otherwise, an IF...ELSE...THEN command
               would be appropriate.

               The OTHERWISE statement allows the program to take an
               alternate path of action when all CASE statements evaluate false.

               DO CASEs may be nested.

Command: dBASE Standard.

Sample:
```
DO CASE
 CASE option = 1
    DO Enter
 CASE option = 2
   DO CASE
   CASE subopt = 1
      DO Brnchoff
   CASE subopt = 2
      DO Whichway
   OTHERWISE
      DO Thisway
   ENDCASE
 CASE option = 3
   DO Edit
 CASE option = 4
   DO Append
OTHERWISE
   DO Scan
ENDCASE
```

DO WHILE

Syntax: DO WHILE < condition >
                < commands >
                ENDDO

Description: The DO WHILE command allows command statements within the
                DO WHILE and associated ENDDO statement to be repeated so
                long as the condition specified by the DO WHILE command
                remains true.

                The ENDDO statement must terminate the structure of the DO
                WHILE command; this does not terminate the flow of operation of
                the DO WHILE command. If the condition prescribed by the DO
                WHILE command evaluates true (.T.), the subsequent commands
                will be executed; otherwise, those commands within the structure of
                the DO WHILE command will be skipped and the command follow-
                ing the associated ENDDO statement will be executed.

                Macro substitution is permissible within the confines of the DO
                WHILE command.

                DO WHILEs may be nested.

Command: dBASE Standard.

Sample:
```
STORE 0 TO looping
DO WHILE looping <> 501
   ?? looping
   ?? SPACE(10)
   looping = looping + 1
ENDDO
?
? "All finished..."

CLEAR
DO WHILE .T.
  ? DATE()
  input = "Y"
  @ ROW()+1,0 SAY "Do you want to go on? " GET input;
              PICT "!" VALID(input$"YN")
  READ
  IF input = "N"
     EXIT
  ENDIF
ENDDO
```

EJECT

Syntax: EJECT

Description: The EJECT command issues a form feed command to the printer. If
                the printer is not properly hooked up to the computer, an error will
                not be generated and the command will be ignored.

Command: dBASE Standard.

ERASE

Syntax: ERASE < file name >

Description: The ERASE command removes a file from the disk directory. The
                use of wild card characters (*) as parameters are permitted with this
                command.

Command: dBASE Standard.

Sample:
```
ERASE Temp.dbf
ERASE Temp.*
ERASE *.ntx
```

EXIT

Syntax: **EXIT**

Description: The EXIT command stops the execution of commands within a DO
              WHILE...ENDDO loop and transfers execution to the command
              statement immediately following the appropriate ENDDO.

Command: dBASE Standard.

Sample:
```
CLEAR
DO WHILE .T.
   ? DATE()
   input = "Y"
   a ROW()+1,0 SAY "Do you want to go on? " GET input;
                PICT "!" VALID(input$"YN")
   READ
   IF input = "N"
      EXIT
   ENDIF
ENDDO
?
? "All finished..."
```

EXTERNAL

Syntax: **EXTERNAL** < procedure list >

Description: This command is used to declare a symbol during compiling for later
              use by the PLINK86 linker. This allows procedures to be placed in
              overlays and still be called with a macro.

Command: Clipper enhanced.

Sample:
```
EXTERNAL Program1, Program2, Program3
which_one = "2"
* Program2 would be in an overlay
DO Program&which_one
```

FIND

Syntax: **FIND** < expC > / < expN >

Description: The FIND command searchs the active, indexed database for the
              first record with a matching key as specified by the character expres-
              sion or numeric expression.

Command: dBASE Standard.

Variance: A search for criteria stored in a variable specified by the user at run-
                time should use the SEEK command. Use the FIND command for
                literal FINDs, such as FIND "CA".

                When searching for a match based on the contents of a memory vari-
                able, the FIND command may only be used in conjunction with the
                MACRO (&) function. If leading blanks are present, quotations
                must surround the macro substitution.

                The FIND command will rewind the record pointer and start the
                search from the top of the indexed database file.

                If no match occurs, then EOF() is set to .T. and FOUND() is set to
                .F.

Sample: ```
                USE Phonbook Index Namebook
                FIND "Jones"
                ? "The record was " + IF(FOUND(), "found!", "not found...")
                ```

## FOR...NEXT

Syntax:         FOR < memvar > = < expN > TO < expN > [STEP < expN >]
                     < commands >
                NEXT

Description:    This command allows looping for a range of values, where the value
                of < memvar > may increment or decrement by the amount of the
                STEP expression at each loop.

                While the memory variable and expressions are mandatory, the
                STEP operator is optional and may increment or decrement < mem-
                var >.  If the STEP clause is not used, a STEP of + 1 is assumed.

Command:        Clipper enhanced.

Sample:         ```
                **************************************************
                * This routine will initialize 20 memory variables
                **************************************************

                FOR x = 1 TO 20
                   STORE LTRIM(STR(x)) TO value
                   STORE 0.00 TO temp&value
                NEXT
                ```

FUNCTION

Syntax: FUNCTION < name >
                    < commands >
                RETURN(< value >)

Description: This command initializes User Defined Functions. As with proce-
                dures, functions may or may not have parameters passed to them.

Command: Clipper enhanced.

Sample: Refer to Chapter 12, Designing User Defined Functions (UDFs).

GO / GOTO

Syntax: GO/GOTO < exp > /TOP/BOTTOM

Description: The GO/GOTO command places the record pointer in the currently
                selected area at the specified record / location in the database.

Command: Clipper enhanced.

Variance: GOTO RECORD < exp > is not supported. The record pointer
                may be placed at a specific record by including that record number
                in the GO/GOTO command, or the record pointer may be placed at
                the logical TOP or logical BOTTOM of the file.

                With an index file open, the logic of the TOP and BOTTOM options
                are dictated by the order prescribed by the index file in use. Only the
                first index file in a series will affect the logical order of the active
                database. Specifying the record number affects the database direct-
                ly, ignoring the index file.

Command: Standard

Sample:
```
USE Temp
GO 1
? "I am at record "
?? RECNO()

USE Temp INDEX Temp
GO TOP
```

```
*
* This position will be in logical order based on the
* order of the index file.  It may be different from
* the actual order in the database.
? "I am at record "
?? RECNO()
```

IF

Syntax:
```
IF <condition>
      <commands>
[ELSE]
      <commands>
ENDIF
```

Description: The IF command allows a branching depending on <condition> in a structured programming environment.

Command: dBASE Standard.

Notes: Nested IF commands are permissible within the same procedure, function, or program file. All IF commands must terminate with a corresponding local ENDIF.

Under the compiler, all IF and corresponding ENDIFs are counted. There may be an extreme situation where an ENDIF is missing and is able to run under the interpreter, but the compiler will flag this as an error.

Sample:
```
CLEAR
STORE SPACE(8) TO indate
a 10,10 SAY "Enter Date: " GET indate PICT "99/99/99"
READ
indate = CTOD(indate)
IF DATE() = indate
   a 15,10 SAY "Hey, you picked today's date.."
ELSE
   a 15,10 SAY "Sorry, the date you chose is not today."
ENDIF
```

INDEX ON

Syntax: INDEX ON <key expression> TO <file name>

Description: The INDEX command creates a file; contained in the head of that file is the key structure specified by <key expression>. This key structure is associated with the database which was open at the time the INDEX command was invoked. The main purpose is to build a series of keys which will instruct the compiler to put some order to the database, either alphabetically, chronologically, numerically, or any combination thereof. The index is no more than a file pointer to the record numbers in the database, in the order set by the key.

Command: dBASE Standard.

Variance: Clipper builds the key based on a blank record. If a TRIM() is performed, a null results. Therefore, if a TRIM() is necessary, allowance must be made for the largest possible data that might be in the key field. However, this is only half of the problem, since the compiler performs implicit SEEKs on non-primary indexes. This means that Clipper, when executing, could alter the index keys, especially where REPLACE or READ is involved. To solve this, explicit control must be forced onto the compiler. To accomplish this, the key expression must include the padding of the calculated length of the key expression. As a result, the key expression will always equal the maximum value that key can ever hold.

The following code would accomplish this:

```
SUBSTR(<expC> + SPACE(<number>), 1, <number>)
```

This string < expC > is padded with blank spaces for length < number >, and a SUBSTR of this is taken, beginning at position 1 of string < expC > to < number >. Example:

```
INDEX ON SUBSTR(TRIM(last_name) + ", " +;
TRIM(first_name) + " " + middle +;
SPACE(LEN(last_name + ", ") + ;
LEN(first_name + " ") +;
LEN(middle)), 1, LEN(last_name) + ;
2 + LEN(first_name) + 1 + LEN(middle))
```

Unless otherwise instructed, Clipper will assume an index file extension of .NTX.

An index key may be a field, an expression, a function, or any combination thereof.

Logical and memo fields **cannot** be part of a key expression.

INDEXing is in ascending order.

Keys must be built on similar types: in joining numeric, date and character fields to an index, the appropriate function must be used in order to convert them all to one type.

Sample:
```
USE Phonbook
INDEX ON DTOC(date_ent) + STR(age) + last_name TO Phon1

* This would build an index in date order, followed by
* the order of the string representation of the age
* field, then followed by the order of the last_name
* field.
```

INPUT

Syntax: INPUT [< expC >] TO < memvar >

Description: The INPUT command accepts user-entered data from the keyboard.
                 The INPUT can be of any data type and is completed by striking the
                 Enter key.

Command: dBASE Standard.

Notes: The < expC > is the prompt for the INPUT command. This is an
                 optional clause. If a memory variable is used in place of the charac-
                 ter string, the content of the memory variable is used as the prompt.

                 If a character string is INPUT, the variable must be pre-initialized.
                 Otherwise, an undefined variable message will appear at run-time.

                 Mathematical expressions are legal.

Variance: If nothing is entered, the old value of the variable is retained,
                 whereas in dBASE III the INPUT message is repeated until a valid
                 response is entered.

Sample:
```
DO WHILE .T.
   CLEAR
   INPUT "[Enter in something ]" TO value
   ?
   ? value
   ? TYPE("value")
   ?
   ?
   WAIT
ENDDO
```

JOIN

Syntax: JOIN WITH < alias > TO < new filename > FOR < condition >
                 [FIELDS < field list >]

Description: The JOIN command creates a new database based on two open databases by merging specified records and fields to that new file.

Command: dBASE Standard.

Notes: If not specified, the <new filename> will assume the default drive\directory and .DBF extension. If there are common fields in both open databases, the desired field is specified with the use of the Alias->field syntax. To specify a field in the currently open and selected database, only the name of the field without an Alias-> clause is required. If no FIELDS clause is specified, the field assignment will begin with the active database. The fields from the second file are then added until the 1024 field limit has been reached.

Duplicate field names will not appear in the created database file.

The record pointer is set at the top of the file in the current area. Each record in the secondary file is then evaluated for the FOR <condition>. If the FOR <condition> is **true**, the record is added to the new file. When all of the records in the second file are looked at, the record pointer in the current area is advanced one record and the process is repeated. This continues for all of the records in the currently active database.

Sample:
```
********************
* Name          JOINIT.prg
* Date          August 4, 1986
* Notice        Copyright 1986, Stephen J. Straley
* Note          This is a small procedure that will create
*               three databases: two for entry and one to
*               be joined.  The case established is purely
*               hypothetical and was created to show how
*               the command works.
*
********************

CREATE Temp
APPEND BLANK
REPLACE field_name WITH "EMPLOYEE", field_type WITH "C", ;
        field_len WITH 10
APPEND BLANK
REPLACE field_name WITH "AGE", field_type WITH "N", ;
        field_len WITH 3
APPEND BLANK
REPLACE field_name WITH "HOURLY", field_type WITH "L", ;
        field_len WITH 1
USE
CREATE Master FROM Temp
CREATE Temp
```

```
                    APPEND BLANK
                    REPLACE field_name WITH "PERSON", field_type WITH "C", ;
                            field_len WITH 10
                    APPEND BLANK
                    REPLACE field_name WITH "WAGE", field_type WITH "N", ;
                            field_len WITH 8, field_dec WITH 2
                    APPEND BLANK
                    REPLACE field_name WITH "DATE_IN", field_type WITH "D", ;
                            field_len WITH 8
                    USE
                    CREATE Second FROM Temp
                    CLOSE DATABASE
                    SELECT 2
                    USE Second
                    SELECT 1
                    USE Master
                    DO WHILE .T.
                       STORE SPACE(10) TO in_name
                       CLEAR
                       @ 05,05 SAY "Enter Name of Person:  " GET in_name
                       READ
                       IF LEN(TRIM(in_name)) = 0
                          EXIT
                       ENDIF
                       APPEND BLANK
                       REPLACE employee WITH in_name
                       @ 07,05 SAY "      Enter age: " GET age
                       @ 09,05 SAY "Hourly Employee: " GET hourly
                       READ
                    ENDDO
                    CLEAR
                    SELECT 2
                    DO WHILE .T.
                       STORE SPACE(10) TO in_name
                       CLEAR
                       @ 03,25 SAY "Enter either a different name from before or"
                       @ 04,25 SAY "    the same ... for testing, mix it up!"
                       @ 07,05 SAY "  Enter name: " GET in_name
                       READ
                       IF LEN(TRIM(in_name)) = 0
                          EXIT
                       ENDIF
                       APPEND BLANK
                       REPLACE person WITH in_name
                       @ 09,05 SAY "Enter wage: " GET wage
                       @ 11,05 SAY "Enter date: " GET date_in
                       READ
                    ENDDO
                    CLEAR
                    @ 01,05 SAY "Here is the first database: "
                    SELECT 1
                    FOR x = 1 to 3
                       ? FIELDNAME(x)
```

```
NEXT
?
? "There are " + LTRIM(STR(LASTREC())) + ;
   " records in the database."
WAIT
CLEAR
@ 01,05 SAY "Here is the second database: "
SELECT 2
FOR x = 1 TO 3
   ? FIELDNAME(x)
NEXT
?
? "There are " + LTRIM(STR(LASTREC())) + ;
   " records in the database."
WAIT
CLEAR
@ 01,05 SAY "Now Joining to make Third.dbf"
SELECT 1
JOIN WITH Second TO Third FOR A->employee <> B->person ;
     FIELDS A->employee, B->wage, A->age, B->date_in
USE Third
FOR x = 1 TO 4
   ? FIELDNAME(x)
NEXT
?
? "There are " + LTRIM(STR(LASTREC())) + ;
   " records in the database."
WAIT
GO TOP
LIST fields employee, wage, age, date_in
* End of File
```

KEYBOARD

Syntax: KEYBOARD < expC >

Description: This command stuffs the Clipper input buffer with < expC >. It may
                 be used to simulate "RETURN TO MASTER" by stuffing several
                 character strings together, simulating key strokes which would leave
                 lower levels to return to higher ones.

Command: dBASE Standard.

Sample:
```
FOR x = 1 TO 2
   STORE SPACE(35) TO input
   CLEAR
   @ 1, 5 SAY "Press the ESC key for keyboard stuff..."
   IF INKEY(0) = 27
      KEYBOARD "Hi there, this is a test..."
```

```
            ENDIF
            @ 10,10 GET input
            READ
        NEXT
```

LABEL

Syntax: LABEL FORM < file name > [< scope >][SAMPLE] [TO PRINT]
                [FOR/WHILE < condition >] [TO FILE < file name >]

Description: The LABEL command allows labels to be printed based on the
                format outlined in a .LBL file on the disk.

Command: dBASE Standard.

Variance: Contents of a LABEL field **must** be a valid expression. Clipper will
                ignore anything following a comma in a label.

Sample:
```
* In Clipper
TRIM(last_name) + " " + first_name

* In dBASE III
last_name, first_name
```

Notes:

1)   Drive designators must be included if files reside any where
      other than the default drive, and file extensions must be in-
      cluded if the extension is anything **other** than .LBL.

2)   Both the FOR and WHILE conditions may be used in the
      LABEL command. If not specified, all records are assumed.

3)   The SAMPLE option is used to print test labels.

4)   The TO FILE option is used to send the labels to a standard
      ASCII text file.

LIST

Syntax: LIST [OFF] [scope] < field list > [FOR < condition >]
                [WHILE < condition >] [TO PRINT/TO FILE < filename >]

Description: The LIST command displays the contents of a database.

Command:	dBASE Standard.
Variance:	The TO PRINT and the TO FILE options have been added to the syntax of the command.
Notes:	The OFF option turns off the display of record numbers.
	Both the FOR condition and the WHILE condition may be present in the command line; the FOR condition will take precedence over the WHILE condition.
Sample:	

```
USE Employees
LIST OFF last_name, first_name FOR state = "CA";
        WHILE age <= 50 TO FILE Output
*
* A list of records with just the last name and first name
* will be printed to an alternate file with the name of
* "OUTPUT.TXT".  Only those records with fields (state =
* "CA") and (age <= 50) will be printed.
```

LOCATE

Syntax:	LOCATE [< scope >] FOR < condition > [WHILE < condition >]
Description:	The LOCATE command searches the open and selected database for the first record that meets the condition specified.
Command:	dBASE Standard.
Notes:	The LOCATE command does not require an INDEX file to be in USE.
	The LOCATE command rewinds the record pointer to the top of the file and searches sequentially, unless otherwise specified by a scope or a WHILE condition.
	If a NEXT scope is used, the limit of the search will be bound by the specified number in the NEXT clause.
	If no match is made, then EOF() is set to .T. and FOUND() is set .F.
	If a match is made, the record pointer remains on the record number which satisfied the condition specified.

To search further, without moving back to the top of the file, the
CONTINUE command is invoked.

Sample:
```
USE Phonbook
LOCATE FOR state = "CA" .AND. prefix = "(714)"
? phone_num
WAIT
CONTINUE
? EOF()
```

LOOP

Syntax: LOOP

Description: The LOOP command immediately jumps to the beginning of the cur-
                rent DO WHILE... ENDDO loop. Any command or series of com-
                mands following the LOOP command are ignored.

Command: dBASE Standard.

Notes: Good structured program techniques dictate avoidance of this com-
                mand; however, there are cases where nothing but a LOOP com-
                mand can be used. Be very careful in planning program flow and use
                false (DO WHILE .NOT. ...ENDDO) conditions to avoid a LOOP
                command, if possible, rather than TRUE (DO WHILE...ENDDO)
                conditions. Also use the EXIT command to escape from the DO
                WHILE. Below is an example which shows two options.

Sample:
```
********************
* Name          LOOPING.prg
* Date          August 5, 1986
* Notice        Copyright 1986, Stephen J. Straley
* Note          Sample 1 demonstrates the use of the LOOP
*               command and Sample 2 show a way to avoid it.
*
********************

* Sample Procedure # 1
*
STORE .T. TO looping
DO WHILE looping
   CLEAR
   @ 10,10 SAY "<First Pass> Would you like the time? (Y/N) "
   SET CONSOLE OFF
   WAIT TO temp
   SET CONSOLE ON
   IF UPPER(temp) = "N"
      STORE .F. TO looping
```

```
         LOOP
      ENDIF
      a 12,10 SAY "The time is ... "
      ?? TIME()
      ?
      ?
      WAIT
   ENDDO
   *
   * Sample Procedure # 2 ... the second way...
   *
   DO WHILE .T.
      CLEAR
      a 10,10 SAY "<Second Pass> Would you like the time? (Y/N) "
      SET CONSOLE OFF
      WAIT TO temp
      SET CONSOLE ON
      IF !UPPER(temp) = "N"
         a 12,10 SAY "The time is ... "
         ?? TIME()
         ?
         ?
         WAIT
      ELSE
         EXIT
      ENDIF
   ENDDO
   * End of File
```

MENU TO

Syntax: MENU TO < memvar >

Description: The MENU TO command allows the creation of menu prompts and
               options with greater ease and efficiency.

               This command is to be used in conjunction with the PROMPT com-
               mands. Think of the MENU TO command as you do a READ on a
               GET command. It is vital to initialize the < memvar >.

               MENU TO < memvar > highlights the first PROMPT command
               and will allow the cursor to move from PROMPT command to
               PROMPT command. MENU TO also places in the < memvar > the
               numeric value of the PROMPT command selected. The values are
               determined by the order of the PROMPT commands.

               There can be a maximum of 32 PROMPT commands per MENU
               TO command.

User defined HELP can be activated from within a series of PROMPT/MENU TO commands. The parameter passed to the HELP.PRG as the input variable (input_var) is the <memvar> created by the MENU TO command.

Command: Clipper enhanced.

Sample: See PROMPT ... MESSAGE Command

NOTE / * / &&

Syntax: NOTE/* <text>
                <command line> && <text>

Description: The NOTE/*/&& commands allow text to be entered into the pro-gram/procedure code that can be used to describe the action being taken by the procedure or command.

                This command should be used extensively for the sake of properly commenting the intent of a procedure or program file. However, do not bog down your application with redundant comment or unneces-sary notations.

Command: dBASE Standard.

Variance: Clipper strips all comment lines out of the code/text file so they do not appear in the object file. However, 3 bytes are reserved for prop-erly noting the line number of the command line(s) which contained the notation/comment.

                Because comment lines do not slow down the process of a compiled application, they should be used more rather than less, which is the tendency under dBASE III.

                Blank lines are also omitted when compiling and only take up 3 bytes of space to trace the line numbers; therefore, a good practice to fol-low would be to use blank lines to help the readability of a program, procedure, or function.

                Note: Use the following as a guide for different ways to comment a program.

                *   <Formatting and General Notation> Used for headings, procedure and function separations, distinct differences in program flow from one section to another.

NOTE   < Section Notation, Less General Notation > To general-
          ly note the purpose of the following or preceding section
          of code, yet maintain the basic flow of the entire program,
          procedure, or function.

&&   < Line Notation, Specific Commenting > To comment
          directly on a line, generally stating the purpose or intent of
          a specific command on that line.

Sample:

```
********************
* Name           NOTES.prg
* Date           August 5, 1986
* Notice         Copyright 1986, Stephen J. Straley
* Note           This will show the different ways to
*                comment a program.  Notice that the
*                asterisk (*) is generally used for the
*                header of a program/procedure or
*                function, while the NOTE command is
*                directly in the flow of the program, and
*                the double macro symbol (&&) is in the
*                command line itself.
*
********************

STORE 1 TO counter

NOTE > Initialize a counter to 1 and use the counter to <
NOTE > go until it reaches 500 <

CLEAR
DO WHILE counter <= 500

   @ 10,15 SAY "The current count is: " GET counter PICT "###"
   CLEAR GETS
   STORE counter + 1 TO counter    && Increment the value
   *                                   of counter
ENDDO
* End of File
```

PACK

Syntax: PACK

Description: The PACK command removes from the currently open and selected
                database those records that were previously marked for deletion.

Command: dBASE Standard.

Notes: With the use of the PACK command, all open indexes are automati-
                  cally REINDEXed.

PARAMETERS

Syntax: PARAMETERS

Description: The PARAMETERS command assigns local variables with the
                  names given. The values in those variables will be either referenced
                  or valued as determined by the calling program.

Command: dBASE Standard.

Variance: If a PARAMETER is established for a variable and none is passed
                  to it, then the variable is set to a null value. A passed PARA-
                  METER may be any legitimate expression including formulas,
                  character strings, etc.

Autumn 86:   More than one parameter may be passed to a program directly from
                  DOS.

Sample: Refer to PARAM.prg in the section on parameters in Chapter 8,
                  Clipper Procedures.

PROMPT ... MESSAGE

Syntax: @ <row>,<col> PROMPT <expC> [MESSAGE <expC>]

Description: The PROMPT...MESSAGE command places menu selections on
                  the screen, highlights menu choices, and allows the cursor to be
                  moved via the cursor pad or direct input.

Command: Clipper enhanced.

Notes: 32 PROMPTs per MENU command are allowed. If the MESSAGE
                  clause is used, the SET MESSAGE TO command must be used if a
                  row position other than 0 is desired.

                  The order of the PROMPT is important, for it is the order that is
                  evaluated once a menu item is chosen.

                  The **Enter** key will return the value of the current highlighted bar.
                  The **PgUp** key will immediately move the highlighted bar to the first

PROMPT; the **PgDn** key will immediately move the highlighted bar to the last PROMPT. Striking the ESC key will cause a value of 0 to be passed to the variable in the MENU TO command.

The HELP.prg and all subsequently established SET KEY TO commands work in conjunction with the MENU TO command. The input variable passed to the procedure will be the variable in the MENU TO command.

A User Defined Function may be used to center the MESSAGE string.

Each < expC > in the PROMPT command should have unique beginning characters. As well as having the cursor keys move to the appropriate choices, striking the first letter in < expC > will complete the MENU TO command and move the highlight to the appropriate PROMPT area. Preceding spaces and tabs are ignored as the first character in < expC >.

Sample:

```
********************
* Name           SET_MESS.prg
* Date           August 5, 1986
* Notice         Copyright 1986, Stephen J. Straley
* Note           This procedure will simulate a possible
*                menu using the SET MESSAGE TO command at
*                line 24. CENTRING is a user defined function
*                which centers the message.
*
********************

STORE 1 TO menu_choic
SET MESSAGE TO 24
DO WHILE menu_choic <> 0
   CLEAR
   @  1,25 PROMPT "1> Enter Account Information" ;
           MESSAGE CENTRING("This is for general accounts")
   @  3,25 PROMPT "2> Enter Special Information" ;
           MESSAGE CENTRING("This is for the Special Accounts")
   @  5,25 PROMPT "3> Enter Transactions" ;
           MESSAGE "This will be for all accounts"
   @  7,25 PROMPT "4> Balance Normal Accounts"
   @  9,25 PROMPT "5> Balance Special Accounts" ;
           MESSAGE CENTRING("This Requires a PASSWORD")
   @ 11,25 PROMPT "6> Special Utility Sub-Menu"
   @ 13,25 PROMPT "7> End of Period Processing"
   @ 15,25 PROMPT "0> EXIT TO OPERATING SYSTEM"
   @ 18,00 SAY;
     CENTRING("Please choose an option by moving the cursor")
   @ 19,00 SAY;
     CENTRING("or striking the appropriate number")
```

```
              MENU TO menu_choic
              IF menu_choic = 8
                 QUIT
              ENDIF
              @ 22,10 SAY "Five Seconds will elapse or Any Key to Continue."
              IF INKEY(5) = 32
              ENDIF
           ENDDO

           FUNCTION Centring

              PARAMETERS string

              STORE (80 - LEN(string)) / 2 TO temp
              IF 2 * temp + LEN(string) < 80
                 RETURN(SPACE(temp) + string + SPACE(temp) + " ")
              ENDIF
              RETURN(SPACE(temp) + string + SPACE(temp))
           * End of File
```

PROCEDURE

Syntax: PROCEDURE < procedure name >

Description: A PROCEDURE is a group of commands that perform a specific task.

Command: dBASE Standard.

Notes: The names of procedures may be up to 10 characters long and follow the same format as do fields. Procedure files still follow the 8 character format.

Variance: Procedure Files **must** have a unique name; they may not be the same as a procedure.

                 A procedure **may** be included at the bottom of a program file.

Sample:
```
********************
* Name        ATTHEBOT.prg
* Date        August 5, 1986
* Notice      Copyright 1986, Stephen J. Straley
* Note        This small routine will show that a
*             procedure may reside at the end of the
*             program which calls it.  This
*             technique will keep unusual routines
*             with the "mother" program.
*
********************
```

```
DO WHILE .T.
   STORE 0 to temprow, tempcol
   CLEAR
   a 10,12 SAY "What row do you want?     " GET temprow ;
           RANGE 0,21
   READ
   a 12,12 SAY "What column do you want? " GET tempcol ;
           RANGE 0,65
   READ
   IF temprow = 0 .AND. tempcol = 0
      EXIT
   ENDIF
   DO Theverybot WITH temprow, tempcol
   a 22,00 SAY ""
   WAIT
ENDDO

********************

PROCEDURE Theverybot

   PARAMETERS at_this, at_that

   CLEAR
   FOR x = 1 TO 500
      a at_this, at_that SAY x
   NEXT
* End of File
```

PUBLIC Clipper

Syntax: PUBLIC Clipper

Description: The PUBLIC Clipper command is used to allow one set of source
                     code to work both in Clipper and in dBASE III without modification.

Command: Clipper enhanced.

Notes: At the beginning of any application/program, declare one variable as
                     PUBLIC and call that variable "Clipper". However, **do not** assign
                     this variable a value. Under dBASE III, variables without value
                     automatically assume a .F. value. This is true as well with all vari-
                     ables under Clipper except the one variable titled "Clipper", which
                     assumes the value of .T.

                     Therefore, code that will only work with the compiler and that code
                     which is specific to dBASE III can be isolated by an IF statement.

Sample: ********************
                * Name   CLIPVAR.prg
                * Date   August 6, 1986
                * Notice   Copyright 1986, Stephen J. Straley
                * Note   To demonstrate the use of the CLIPPER
                *   variable in a "real" situation.
                *
                ****

```
CLEAR
PUBLIC Clipper

IF Clipper
   @ 5,10,20,70 BOX REPLICATE(CHR(177), 9)
ELSE
   STORE  5 TO temprow
   STORE 10 TO tempcol
   DO WHILE temprow <= 20
      DO WHILE tempcol <= 70
         @ temprow, tempcol SAY CHR(177)
         STORE tempcol + 1 TO tempcol
      ENDDO
      STORE 10 TO tempcol
      STORE temprow + 1 TO temprow
   ENDDO
ENDIF
* End of File
```

QUIT

Syntax: QUIT

Description: The QUIT command closes all open files, clears all memory vari-
                ables, and returns control to the operating system.

Command: dBASE Standard.

Notes: All compiled programs should have at least one safe method/flow in
                which the QUIT command is executed. This will insure that once the
                application is through executing all database files and index files are
                closed safely.

Sample:
```
CLEAR
@ 10,10 SAY "Do you want to continue? "
SET CONSOLE OFF
WAIT TO temp
SET CONSOLE ON
IF UPPER(temp) <> "Y"
   QUIT
```

```
ENDIF
DO Go_on
```

READ

Syntax: READ

Description: The READ command activates all current @...GETs invoked since
                 the last CLEAR, CLEAR ALL, CLEAR GETS or READ.

Command: dBASE Standard.

Variance: The [SAVE] option is not supported.

Notes: This command is used in full screen entry/editing modes. Since
                 dBASE interactive commands for editing are not supported by the
                 compiler, the use of APPEND BLANK, and @...GET, READ is the
                 manner by which data is entered and edited.

Sample:
```
STORE SPACE(10) TO name
CLEAR
a 10,10 SAY "Enter the name: " GET name
READ
STORE 1 TO a,b,c,
a 14,10 SAY "Enter a number: " GET a
a 15,10 SAY "   and again..: " GET b
a 16,10 SAY " and one more.: " GET c
READ
```

RECALL

Syntax: RECALL < scope > [[FOR]/[WHILE] < condition >]

Description: The RECALL command un-marks those records marked for dele-
                 tion and reactivates them in the current and open database.

Command: dBASE Standard.

Variance: Both the FOR < condition > clause and the WHILE < condition >
                 clause can be in use at the same time. The FOR < condition > will
                 take precedence over the WHILE clause.

Notes: Unless specified by the < scope > clause or the FOR/WHILE
                 < condition > clauses, the RECALL command will only affect the
                 current record.

Once records have been marked for deletion and the PACK or the ZAP command has been issued, the RECALL command will have no effect on the database.

A general RECALL command will have no effect on the database if that database is under the restraints of the SET DELETED ON command. Under this condition, all records for RECALL must be specified.

Sample:

```
USE Phonbook
GO 5
RECALL
USE Temp
RECALL ALL FOR state = "CA"
```

REINDEX

Syntax: REINDEX

Description: The REINDEX command rebuilds all of the active index files in the currently open and selected area.

Command: dBASE Standard.

Notes: In effect this command is an easier way to update an index file based on the current information in the database once the index files have been created. It would be equivalent to the INDEX ON < expC > TO < filename > command.

Sample:

```
USE Phonbook INDEX Phon1
REINDEX

NOTE \ another way to do the same is the following \
USE Phonbook
SET INDEX TO Phon1
REINDEX
```

RELEASE

Syntax: RELEASE < memory variable >
                RELEASE < memory variable list >
                RELEASE ALL [LIKE/EXCEPT < skeleton >]

Description: The RELEASE command deletes from memory a memory variable(s) and reallocates memory space for future use.

Command: dBASE Standard.

Notes: If the < skeleton > clause is used, a question mark (?) and an asterisk (*) are treated just as they are in DOS: a ? will mask a single character; an * will mask one or more characters. Since Clipper has an expanded capacity to handle memory variables, you may not find it necessary to invoke this command.

Sample:
```
STORE "Hi There" TO prompt
STORE 1 TO position
STORE "Returning to Operating System" TO depart
RELEASE ALL LIKE p*
* The only memory variable left will be depart
RELEASE ALL
* No more memory variables are present
```

RENAME

Syntax: RENAME < filename.1 > TO < filename.2 >

Description: The RENAME command changes the name of the first < filename > to that of the second < filename >.

Command: dBASE Standard.

Notes: Both < filename >s must include the file extension. Included with the < filename > must be the drive\directory designator if either is other than the default drive\directory.

                The new < filename > cannot be that of an existing file on the same designated drive\directory.

                Open files cannot be RENAMEd.

                This command can be used in conjunction with the FILE() function in order to simulate file locking.

Sample:
```
IF FILE(Mainfile.dbf)
   RENAME Mainfile.dbf TO Temp.dbf
   USE Temp
ELSE
   CLEAR
   @ 10,25 SAY "That file is already in use."
   @ 12,25 SAY "   Any Key to Continue."
   tkey = INKEY(0)
ENDIF
```

REPLACE

Syntax: REPLACE [<scope>] <field> WITH <exp> [, <field> WITH <exp> ...] [FOR <condition>] [WHILE <condition>]

Description: The REPLACE command changes the contents of specified fields in the active database.

Command: dBASE Standard.

Variance: A FOR clause and a WHILE clause may exist simultaneously with the FOR option taking precedence over the WHILE option.

Autumn 86: Values may be REPLACED into another area, so long as an open database is active in that area.

In order to call that area, use the ALIAS of that area:

```
SELECT 2
USE History
SELECT 1
USE Timecard
REPLACE history->prev_quart WITH timecard->reg_hours * 40
```

Notes: Unless otherwise specified by the scope, the FOR clause, or the WHILE clause, only the current record is affected by the REPLACE command.

The field and the expression must be of the same data type.

Each REPLACE on a key field with the indexed file open will update the index.

Sample:
```
USE Phonbook INDEX Namebook
REPLACE first_name WITH "Nomad"

********************************************************
* Now replace all state fields in the proper index    *
* file with "CA" for the phone number prefix = (213) *
********************************************************

USE Phonbook INDEX Statbook
REPLACE ALL state WITH "CA" FOR prefix = "(213)"
```

REPORT FORM

Syntax:	REPORT FORM < file name > [< scope >] [FOR < condition >] [W H I L E < c o n d i t i o n >] [P L A I N] [H E A D I N G < expC >][NOEJECT] [TO PRINT] [TO FILE < file name >]
Description:	The REPORT FROM command allows forms to be printed based on the format outlined in a .FRM file on the disk.
Command:	dBASE Standard.
Variance:	If an attempt is made to run a REPORT FORM with a division on a field/variable where the divisor is zero or is left blank, a run-time error will occur stating such. A user defined function can be written and implemented to overcome this problem. See the UDF **DIVIDE0()** in Chapter 12, designing user defined functions (UDFs).
Notes:	The default extension for the FORM file is .FRM, while the default extension for the TO file for output is .TXT.
	Both the FOR < condition > and WHILE < condition > may be used with the FOR option taking precedence over the WHILE option.
	The PLAIN option causes the report to print without page numbers or a system date. The HEADING option with a character expression defines an extra heading that is printed on the page line of each page. NOEJECT option in conjunction with the TO PRINT option will suppress the initial form feed.

RESTORE FROM

Syntax:	RESTORE FROM < filename > [ADDITIVE]
Description:	The RESTORE FROM command retrieves from disk a memory variable file and activates all memory variables stored in that file.
Command:	dBASE Standard.
Variance:	There is virtually no limit on the allocated space for active memory variables since many machines cannot handle the expanded capacity of the compiler.
Autumn 86:	This version allows memory variables longer in length than 255 bytes to be RESTORED from a .MEM file. Thus, full screens previously

saved with the SAVE SCREEN or the CALL command can be saved completely to a memory file without being parsed into 255 character substrings.

Notes: Unless otherwise specified, the < filename > will be assumed to have a .MEM file extension.

If the RESTORE FROM command is used without the ADDITIVE clause, all currently active memory variables are deleted and only those memory variables in the memory file will be present.

In order to maintain all current memory variables, the ADDITIVE clause must be included with the RESTORE FROM command. If there are any memory variables with the same name as a memory variable in the RESTOREd memory file, the memory variable in the system is overwritten by the variable from the file.

Sample:

```
STORE 1 TO x
? x
SAVE TO Temp
STORE 5 TO x
? x
RESTORE FROM Temp
? x
```

RESTORE SCREEN

Syntax: RESTORE SCREEN

Description: The RESTORE SCREEN command brings back a screen which was previously saved in memory.

Command: Clipper enhanced.

Notes: This command was included to help design applications with a more polished look to them. It is especially handy when used in conjunction with a HELP.PRG file: the original screen can be saved in memory while the help screen is displayed to the user.

Using this command is a one-shot situation. Once the screen is RESTOREd, it can not be RESTOREd again without being SAVEd again. Screens which have been saved to memory variables by using the CALL command can be restored repeatedly by using those variables in conjunction with the CALL command to the Clipper library.

Review the SAVE SCREEN command for further information.

Addition: Using the CALL variation can be **extremely** hazardous to anything
                 else that is residing in memory whenever this command is CALLed.
                 For a complete description of the complications using these CALL
                 routines, see SAVE SCREEN, below, and DRAWMEN1.prg in the
                 section on Windowing for Menus and Submenus in Chapter 14.

Autumn 86:   [FROM <memvar>] was added with this version. This is as effec-
                 tive as the sample listed below.

Sample:
```
CALL _scrrest WITH screen[1] && available in all releases
* This sample shows how to RESTORE a screen directly from a
* memory variable.

tempscr = screen[1]
RESTORE SCREEN FROM tempscr
* Again, this syntax is only available in the Autumn '86
* release.
```

RETURN

Syntax: RETURN

Description: The RETURN command restores control to the program or proce-
                 dure which originally called the current program or procedure. If
                 there is no program file or procedure to return control to, control is
                 returned to DOS.

Command: dBASE Standard.

Variance: RETURN TO MASTER is not supported; however, with a combina-
                 tion of KEYBOARD and RETURN commands, this command may
                 be simulated.

Sample:
```
********************
* Name          RETURNTO.prg
* Date          August 5, 1986
* Notice        Copyright 1986, Stephen J. Straley
* Note          To show the use of RETURN and the simulation of
*               a RETURN TO MASTER.
*
********************

DO WHILE .T.
   CLEAR
   STORE "2" TO option
   a 0,0 SAY "Top Level"
   a 5,10 SAY "Exit to the system .......   1"
```

```
      @ 6,10 SAY "Go down next level .......   2"
      @ 8,10 SAY "Enter option ............   " GET option ;
             PICT "X" VALID(option$"12")
      READ
      IF option = "2"
         DO Down1
      ELSE
         EXIT
      ENDIF
   ENDDO

   ********************

   PROCEDURE Down1

      DO WHILE .T.
         CLEAR
         STORE "2" TO option
         @ 0,0 SAY "Level One"
         @ 5,10 SAY "Return to Top Level ......   1"
         @ 6,10 SAY "Go down next level .......   2"
         @ 8,10 SAY "Enter option ............   " GET option ;
                PICT "X" VALID(option$"12")
         READ
         IF option = "2"
            DO Down2
         ELSE
            RETURN
         ENDIF
      ENDDO

   ********************

   PROCEDURE Down2

      CLEAR
      STORE "2" TO option
      @ 0,0 SAY "Level Two"
      @ 5,10 SAY "Return to Master ..........   1"
      @ 6,10 SAY "Return to Previous Level ...  2"
      @ 8,10 SAY "Enter option ..............   " GET option ;
             PICT "X" VALID(option$"12")
      READ
      IF option = "1"
         KEYBOARD "1"
      ENDIF
      RETURN
   * End of File
```

RUN / (!)

Syntax: RUN < filename >
                 ! < filename >

Description: The RUN/! command executes a program from a currently running
                 Clipper application.

Command: dBASE Standard.

Notes: When the RUN command has completed execution of the given file,
                 control is returned to the application on the command line immedi-
                 ately following the RUN command.

                 In order for the RUN command to execute, the total of the amount
                 of memory of the initial application, the amount of memory loaded
                 by COMMAND.COM, and the amount of memory for the program
                 to be RUN must be at least 100K less than the allotted memory of
                 the machine.

                 COMMAND.COM must be available on the drive and directory
                 path of the initial application performing the actual "RUN".

Sample:
```
DO WHILE .T.
   STORE "Today's Date is " + CDOW(date()) + ;
         ", " + CMON(date()) TO prompt
   STORE prompt + " " + STR(DAY(date()),2) + ;
         ", " + STR(YEAR(date()),4) TO prompt
   @ 14,40-LEN(prompt)/2 SAY prompt
   @ 18,25 SAY "Is this the Correct Date?  "
   SET CONSOLE OFF
   WAIT TO temp
   SET CONSOLE ON
   IF UPPER(temp) = "Y"
      mdate = date()
      @ 18,0 SAY SPACE(80)
      @ 18,29 SAY "Enter Date:  " GET mdate
      READ
      mdate = DTOC(mdate)
      RUN DATE &mdate
   ELSE
      EXIT
   ENDIF
ENDDO
```

SAVE SCREEN

Syntax: SAVE SCREEN

Description: This command SAVEs a screen in memory.

Command: Clipper enhanced.

Notes: This command was included to help design applications with a more polished look to them. It is especially handy when used in conjunction with a HELP.PRG file: the original screen can be saved in memory while the help screen is displayed to the user. For restoring the screen, review the RESTORE SCREEN command.

Remember to allow an additional 4K of RAM to be used by the application for the screen you want to keep in memory (2000 characters possible on the screen plus 1 attribute byte for each character).

Using this command is a one-shot situation. That is, one cannot save screens to databases or even to memory variables with this command. To do so, you must CALL the Clipper library. If you do CALL _scrsave, you must consider the following:

1) The amount of space needed for every screen saved will be 4000 bytes.

2) Screens can not be saved directly to arrays or databases. Temporary variables must be established and the arrays or databases must be replaced by the values of the variables.

Addition: Using the CALL _scrsave variation can be **extremely** hazardous to anything else that is residing in memory when this command is CALLed. For example, let us say that a database is open with three index files and a screen is saved. On the surface this is simple. However, for the sake of this example, let us say that you do not allot enough space for the temporary variable ("tempscr") and you CALL the library subroutine to save the screen to that variable. The result might be corrupted index files, database header problems, or even an application that once worked, working no longer. **Be very careful!** I can't stress this point enough. Remember, you are dealing with RAM when using this feature and many other "things" reside in RAM as well: databases, indexes, memory variables, macros, DOS, and even your application!

Autumn 86:   [TO < memvar >] has been added with this version. It is now the
                same as the CALL command as shown below.

Sample 1:
```
STORE SPACE(4000) TO tempscr
CALL _scrsave WITH tempscr        && This is available in all
STORE tempscr TO screen[1]        && releases
```

Sample 2:
```
STORE SPACE(4000) TO tempscr      && This form is available in
SAVE SCREEN WITH tempscr          && the Autumn '86 release.
STORE tempscr TO screen[1]
```

SAVE TO

Syntax: SAVE TO < filename > [ALL LIKE/EXCEPT < skeleton >]

Description: The SAVE TO command stores all or part of the current set of
                memory variables to a designated file.

Command: dBASE Standard.

Autumn 86:   Memory variables of character type and longer than 255 bytes may
                be saved to a memory file without any program parsing.

Notes: If the < filename > does not include the drive\directory designator,
                the default drive\designator is assumed.

                Unless otherwise specified, the file extension for all memory files is
                .MEM.

                With the use of the < skeleton > clause, a question mark (?) repre-
                sents a single character, while an asterisk (*) represents one or more
                characters.

                If the ALL LIKE/EXCEPT clause is not used, all current memory
                variables are saved to the designated file.

Sample:
```
STORE "!" TO this
STORE "ə" TO that
STORE "#" TO what
SAVE ALL LIKE th* TO Memfile
NOTE This memory file will contain only this and that.
```

SEEK

Syntax: SEEK < expression >

Description: The SEEK command searches for the first record in a database file
                     with a key of an open index file that matches < expression > .

Command: dBASE Standard.

Variance: Should be used instead of the dBASE command: FIND &expression.

Notes: The SEEK command always "rewinds" the database pointer and
                     starts the search from the top of the file.

                     Macro substitution is not required when the expression being
                     searched for is contained in a memory variable.

                     If the search is unsuccessful, then FOUND() is set to .F. and EOF()
                     is set to .T.

                     If a file is indexed on more than one field, the expression must refer
                     to the first field only.

Sample:
```
STORE SPACE(10) TO search_name
CLEAR
a 10,10 SAY "Enter Name to search for: " GET search_name
READ
USE Phonbook Index Namebook
SEEK search_name
a 12,10 SAY IF(FOUND(), "Yes I found it", "Nope, not here")
```

SELECT

Syntax: SELECT < expN >
                     SELECT < expC >

Description: The SELECT command moves through ten separate work areas.
                     These areas allow ten separate databases to be opened and accessed
                     at the same time.

Command: dBASE Standard.

Autumn 86:   SELECT 0 will now select the first unused area.

Notes: Without any command, the initial SELECTed area is 1.

The range of valid work areas is 1 through 10 (or A through J). If the alias name is used to SELECT the area, it will take precedence over the letter representation.

Record pointers are not connected between work areas unless a SET RELATION TO command has been previously used.

Information from another previously SELECTED area may be obtained provided the letter of the work area precedes the name of the field in question, using the syntax A->field_name.

Alias->field_name is supported; however, the specific work area should be used in place of the file/alias name whenever referring to another selected area/database.

Sample:
```
SELECT 1
USE Temp
SELECT 2
USE Mainfile
IF A->name = name
    ?? "The name in the TEMP is the name in MAINFILE"
ELSE
    ?? "The name in the TEMP is NOT the name in MAINFILE"
ENDIF
```

SET ALTERNATE TO

Syntax: SET ALTERNATE TO [<filename>]

Description: The SET ALTERNATE TO command creates a text file for the SET ALTERNATE ON command to port to.

Default: No file set

Command: dBASE Standard.

Notes: The file name must include a drive\directory designator if it is other than the default drive\directory.

If no file extension is specified, .TXT will be used.

Not using the <filename> clause will close the ALTERNATE file. You may also issue a CLOSE ALTERNATE command.

Until the alternate file is closed there is a risk of losing information which is to be added to the file due to an improper flush of the buffers.

SET ALTERNATE

Syntax: SET ALTERNATE ON/OFF

Description: The SET ALTERNATE ON/OFF command actually tells the computer that the information that follows is to be appended to the alternate file, provided the information is not being displayed using the @...SAY/GET commands.

Default: OFF

Command: dBASE Standard.

Notes: The SET ALTERNATE ON command will redirect all non-full screen entries and displays to the named file.

                    The file created by the SET ALTERNATE commands is an ASCII text file.

Sample:
```
SET ALTERNATE TO Text
? "Hi there"
SET ALTERNATE ON
? "I said 'Hi there...'"                    && This goes to Text.txt
CLEAR
a 10,10 SAY "This should print out here..." && This doesn't
WAIT
SET ALTERNATE OFF
CLOSE ALTERNATE
```

SET CENTURY (Autumn 86 Special Command)

Syntax: SET CENTURY ON/OFF

Description: The SET CENTURY ON/OFF command allows the input and the display of dates within the century prefix. It will be in standard MM/DD/YYYY format. Autumn 86 version supports all dates in the range of 01/01/0100 thru 12/31/2999.

Default: OFF

Command: Clipper Enhanced - Autumn 86

SET COLOR TO

Syntax: SET COLOR TO [< standard > [, < enhanced > [< border >]]]

Description: This command changes the colors displayed on the screen.

Default: Normal.

Command: dBASE Standard.

Autumn 86:   [, < unselected >] is a new clause which is to follow the optional
                   [< border >] clause. This allows the current and selected GET to be
                   displayed in a different color than all other unselected gets.

Variance: The < standard > is used by all output created by commands such as
                   @ SAY and ?. The < enhanced > section of this command affects
                   the GET portion of the command.

                   Macros are supported with this command; unlike other cases, these
                   macros can contain commas and slashes (which normally are con-
                   sidered part of the syntactical structure of the command). Options
                   such as the "+" and the "*" are also supported with letters rather
                   than numbers and will only affect the foreground of the screen.

                   Keep in mind that if numbers are used to represent the desired
                   colors rather than letters, the number to the left of the slash is writ-
                   ten to the *high order 4 bits* of the color attribute byte, while the num-
                   ber to the right of the slash is written to the *low order 4 bits* of the
                   color attribute byte. In other words, to get best results, make sure
                   you use numbers less than 8 with the SET COLOR TO command.

                   To reset the screen to the original default values, use SET COLOR
                   TO without parameters.

                                        Guide:

Color	Number	Letter
Black	0	N
Blue	1	B
Green	2	G
Cyan	3	BG
Red	4	R
Magenta	5	RB
Brown	6	GR
White	7	W
Underline		U - Monochrome Only
Inverse		I
Blank		X

Sample:
```
********************
* Name      COLOR.prg
* Date      August 5, 1986
* Notice    Copyright 1986, Stephen J. Straley
* Note      This sample program shows the
*           SET COLOR TO command in operation.
*
▲▲▲▲▲▲▲▲▲▲▲▲▲▲▲▲▲▲▲▲▲

STORE SPACE(30) TO input
CLEAR
DO WHILE .T.
   @ 10,10 SAY "Leave Blank to QUIT"
   @ 12,10 SAY "Set Color to what? " GET input
   READ
   IF EMPTY(input)
      EXIT
   ENDIF
   SET COLOR TO &input
ENDDO

CLEAR
SET COLOR TO
SET COLOR TO 7/7, 0/0
STORE SPACE(10) TO password
@ 10,22 SAY "And now to set the screen to hide input"
@ 11,22 SAY "    for the sake of a password!"
@ 14,22 SAY "Enter Password => " GET password
READ
@ 16,22 SAY "The password was &password."

SET COLOR TO
* End of File
```

SET CONFIRM

Syntax: SET CONFIRM ON/OFF

Description: With the SET CONFIRM ON command, the Enter key is required
                 to end each and every GET.

                 Otherwise, once a GET is filled with the proper number of desig-
                 nated characters (either by the attributes of the variable or by the
                 PICTURE clause), the cursor automatically advances to the next
                 GET. If the READ is completed, the flow of the program will con-
                 tinue.

Default: OFF

Command: dBASE Standard.

Sample:
```
STORE SPACE(15) TO test1, test2
SET CONFIRM ON
@ 2,10 SAY "Enter 20 characters to test1: " GET test1
@ 3,10 SAY "                        test2: " GET test2
READ
SET CONFIRM OFF
@ 2,10 SAY "Enter 20 characters to test1: " GET test1
@ 3,10 SAY "                        test2: " GET test2
READ
```

SET CONSOLE

Syntax: SET CONSOLE ON/OFF

Description: The SET CONSOLE command turns the screen either off or on for
                screen display other than @...SAY commands.

Default: ON

Command: dBASE Standard.

Notes: The SET CONSOLE command will not affect output to a printer.

                This command is normally used to shut off the screen so that those
                commands which route some type of a message back to the screen
                can be handled by other programming techniques and commands.

Sample:
```
@ 10,10 SAY "Press Any Key to Continue or Q to Quit..."
SET CONSOLE OFF
WAIT TO temp
SET CONSOLE ON
IF UPPER(temp) = "Q"
    RETURN
ENDIF
```

SET DECIMALS TO

Syntax: SET DECIMALS TO < expN >

Description: The SET DECIMALS TO command establishes the number of
                decimal places that Clipper will display in mathematical calculations,
                functions, memory variables, and fields.

Default: 2

Command: dBASE Standard.

Variance: In some functions, dBASE III will assume the decimal place by the
                number of places in the passed parameter. In Clipper, all results are
                bound by the SET DECIMALS TO command.

                The SET DECIMAL TO command will only apply to calculations in-
                volved with division, the SQRT(), LOG(), and EXP() functions.

Sample: ```
                ? LOG(1)
                SET DECIMALS TO 4
                ? LOG(1)
                ```

## SET DEFAULT TO

Syntax:         SET DEFAULT TO < disk drive >

Description:    The SET DEFAULT TO command changes the drive used for read-
                ing and writing of database, index, memory, and alternate files.

Default:        < current logged drive >

Command:        dBASE Standard.

Notes:          Because of the compiled environment, the SET DEFAULT TO
                command does not pertain to format files, procedure files and other
                program files in the manner that it would under the interpreter. This
                is due to the fact that the compiler will compile the format and pro-
                cedure files in with the main program files and they will be included
                in the final executable program.

Sample:         ```
                SET DEFAULT TO B
                USE Phonbook
                ```

SET DELETED

Syntax: SET DELETED ON/OFF

Description: The SET DELETED command is, in essence, a filter placed on the
                database to mask out those records marked for deletion. A SET
                DELETED ON command is just as effective as a SET FILTER TO
                .NOT. DELETED().

Default: OFF

Command: dBASE Standard.

Notes: Whether SET DELETED ON or OFF is used in conjunction with
                the INDEX and REINDEX command, all records are included.

                If the SET DELETED command is ON, then RECALL ALL does
                not recall any records.

Sample: ```
                USE Temp
                DISPLAY ALL
                SET DELETED ON
                DISPLAY ALL
                ```

## SET DELIMITERS

Syntax:         SET DELIMITERS ON/OFF

Description:    The SET DELIMITERS ON command allows specific characters to
                delimit field area input.  See SET DELIMITERS TO.

Default:        OFF

Command:        dBASE Standard.

Notes:          If left OFF, the fields are delimited by reverse video or highlighting.

## SET DELIMITERS TO

Syntax:         SET DELIMITERS TO [ < expC > ][DEFAULT]

Description:    The SET DELIMITERS TO command changes the characters
                which delimit the area before and after field or variable input.

Default:        ::

Command:        dBASE Standard.

Notes:          The character string expressed in < expC > may be either one or two
                characters.  If only one character is used, then that character is used
                both before and after field/variable input areas.  If two characters
                are entered, then the first character represents the character before
                the field, and the second character is used after the field.
                ```

If the DEFAULT clause is used in place of < expC > the characters are reset to "::".

No matter what the DELIMITERS are SET TO, if the SET DELIMITERS OFF command is in effect, no delimiters are used. SET DELIMITERS ON must be used before SET DELIMITERS TO.

Sample:
```
SET DELIMITERS ON
SET DELIMITERS TO "[]"
STORE 0 TO value
CLEAR
a 10,10 SAY "Get value: " GET value
READ
```

SET DEVICE TO

Syntax: SET DEVICE TO < PRINT/SCREEN >

Description: The SET DEVICE TO command determines where the @...SAY command will be displayed (either the screen or the printer).

Default: SCREEN

Command: dBASE Standard.

Notes: If the SET DEVICE TO PRINT is used in conjunction with a series of @...GET commands, the values for the GETS will all be ignored. If a position command requires that the printer either back up on the paper in column position or in row position, a page eject is issued.

This command is not to be confused with the SET PRINT ON command. This command is only connected with @...SAY commands.

Sample:
```
CLEAR
a 10,10 SAY "Hi there..."
SET DEVICE TO PRINT
a 10,10 SAY "I am over here now..."
EJECT
SET DEVICE TO SCREEN
a 12,10 SAY "I am now here..."
```

SET ESCAPE

Syntax: SET ESCAPE ON/OFF

Description: The SET ESCAPE ON command allows an ALT-C to terminate the execution of the program and ignores VALID. If the SET ESCAPE OFF command is issued, ALT-C will **not** terminate an operation and no escape from a READ is possible.

Default: ON

Command: Clipper enhanced.

Notes: This command may be used to offer alternate escape routes from an application.

                Though it *is* an option, allowing a user to ALT-C inside an application is **extremely** dangerous to the integrity of the open and active databases and indexes.

                If SET ESCAPE is off and an ALT-C is entered, Clipper issues the (Q/A/I) error message.

SET EXCLUSIVE   (Autumn 86: Special Command)

Syntax: SET EXCLUSIVE ON/OFF

Description: The SET EXCLUSIVE ON/OFF command determines the way in which the database and related memo and index files are opened.

                ON means non-shared file access; OFF means shared files.

Default: ON

Command: Autumn 86 version ONLY

SET EXACT

Syntax: SET EXACT ON/OFF

Description: The SET EXACT command determines how much of a comparison will be performed between two character expressions.

Default: OFF

Command: dBASE Standard.

Variance: Index files with key fields NOT in multiples of four bytes may now be
                found with the SET EXACT command ON. In some applications,
                where the key wasn't precisely in a multiple of four bytes, items un-
                der the interpreter were rarely found with a SEEK or a FIND.

Notes: The SET EXACT OFF command makes a character by character
                comparison and allows for a match to be made if the short string is to
                the right of the equal sign. For example:

```
? "Monday" = "Monday Night Bowling"     .F.
? "Monday Night Bowling" = "Monday"     .T.
```

                With SET EXACT ON, both sides of the equation are evaluated and
                must be equal. Therefore, the second test would now yield a .F. to
                the screen.

                The SET EXACT ON command is equivalent to the $==$ operator
                for string evaluations. For most numeric evaluations, the $==$ oper-
                ator is preferred.

SET FILTER TO

Syntax: SET FILTER TO [< expression >]

Description: The SET FILTER TO command masks a database so that only those
                records that meet the condition prescribed by the < expression >
                will be shown.

Default: No filter set

Command: dBASE Standard.

Notes: Using the SET FILTER TO command without an expression will
                turn off the filter on the active database and allow all records to be
                accessed.

                If the SET FILTER TO command is used, a GO TOP command
                should follow immediately. GO TOP will reposition the record
                pointer to the top of the newly FILTERed database.

The SET FILTER TO command will only apply to the currently open and active database. A separate and unique FILTER may be set for each open area.

Sample: Consider the follow database:

```
File: Main.dbf
Record #        Name        Age
    1          Stephen       26
    2          Ray           36
    3          Cheryll       34
    4          Barry         45
    5          David         27
    6          Steve         29
    7          Stan          88
    8          Marilyn       36
    9          Rita          19
   10          Terri         22
```

Now issue the following commands:

```
SET FILTER TO SUBSTR(name,1,2) = "St" .OR. age = 22
GO TOP
```

The database, if displayed, would now look like this:

```
File: Main.dbf
Record #        Name        Age
    1          Stephen       26
    6          Steve         29
    7          Stan          88
   10          Terri         22
```

SET FIXED

Syntax: SET FIXED ON/OFF

Description: The SET FIXED command activates a system-wide fixed placement on the number of decimal places shown for all numeric output.

Default: OFF

Command: dBASE Standard.

Notes: The number of decimal places that are FIXED are determined by the default or set value of the SET DECIMAL TO command.

SET FORMAT TO

Syntax: SET FORMAT TO < file name >

Description: The SET FORMAT TO command selects a custom format which
                has been previously stored in a format (.fmt) file.

Default: No file.

Command: dBASE Standard.

Variance: Files with a .FMT extension will not be recognized if CLiP files are
                used to compile an application. Files with a .FMT extension must be
                renamed to .PRG files in order to be puled in by the compiler.

                The SET FORMAT TO command does not automatically CLEAR
                the screen upon entry of the format file.

Sample: `SET FORMAT TO Editscr`

SET FUNCTION

Syntax: SET FUNCTION < expN > TO < expC >

Description: The SET FUNCTION TO command allows each function key to be
                re-programmed to represent a character expression.

Default: No keys set

Command: dBASE Standard.

Variance: Unlike dBASE III, the character expression is not limited to 30
                characters. Additionally, function keys cannot be set to commands,
                but can call procedures, functions and programs. < expC > can also
                contain Control characters, such as CTL-C.

Notes: The < expN > represents the numeric value for the function key as
                depicted by the INKEY() function. Function key 1 is set to HELP if
                it is available; function keys 2 through 10 are accessed by pressing the
                appropriate key; function keys 11 through 20 are accessed by press-
                ing SHIFT plus the key; function keys 21 through 30 are combined
                with CONTROL; and function keys 31 through 40 are combined with
                the ALT key. Also see the SET KEY command.

Sample:
```
DO WHILE .T.
   CLEAR
   a 0,10 SAY "Strike a Key..."
   qw = INKEY(0)
   IF qw = 28
      LOOP
   ELSE
      IF qw = 32
         EXIT
      ENDIF
   ENDIF
   a 4,9,21,71 BOX REPLICATE(CHR(219), 9)
   STORE "" TO test
   SET FUNCTION qw TO MEMOEDIT(test,5,10,20,70,.T.)
ENDDO

DO WHILE .T.
   CLEAR
   STORE SPACE(500) TO test
   a 10,0 GET test
   READ
   IF LEN(TRIM(test)) = 0
      EXIT
   ENDIF
   WAIT
ENDDO
```

SET INDEX

Syntax: SET INDEX TO [< file list >]

Description: This command opens an index file to the active and open database.
                   If more than one file is listed in < file list >, the order of the data-
                   base will be determined by the first index file in the < file list >. All
                   file operations will be based on the first index file; however, all index
                   files in the < file list > will be updated if the database is updated.

Default: None.

Command: dBASE Standard.

Variance: While macros are supported with the SET INDEX TO command,
                   the rule remains that syntax verbs are unsupported in macros. In
                   other words, the use of commas in a macro in conjunction with the
                   SET INDEX TO command is **not** supported. Each file being listed
                   must be in a separate macro; it is suggested that the macro be "dot
                   terminated" before the use of a comma.

Sample: STORE "C:" TO drive
                 STORE "Time_a.dat" TO file1
                 USE Time
                 SET INDEX TO &drive.&file1., &drive.Time_b.dat

SET INTENSITY

Syntax: SET INTENSITY ON/OFF

Description: The SET INTENSITY command sets the field input color to either
                 highlighted (inverse video) or normal color.

Default: ON

Command: dBASE Standard.

Notes: Rather than using the SET DELIMITER TO command and estab-
                 lishing a set of delimiters, the video attributes may be used instead.
                 For most data entry procedures, this is more effective.

Sample: STORE SPACE(10) TO sample
                 CLEAR
                 @ 10,10 SAY "Enter with Intensity: " GET sample
                 READ
                 SET INTENSITY OFF
                 @ 12,10 SAY "Enter without Intensity: " GET sample
                 READ

SET KEY TO

Syntax: SET KEY < expN > TO [< proc >]

Description: This command is used where < expN > is equal to the value given by
                 INKEY() for any keyboard key and < proc > is a procedure.
                 Through Winter '85, extended codes had not been converted. As a
                 result, compatibility with dBASE III was maintained.

Default: No Key SET except F1 to HELP.PRG, if HELP.PRG is present.

Command: Clipper enhanced.

Notes: The < proc > is the name of the procedure or program that will be
                 called whenever the designated key is entered.

Special program control may be used in conjunction with the SET KEY command. For example, additional GETS may be added to the current and active READ by setting a key to a procedure with a few additional GETS. Once in the READ if the specially assigned KEY is pressed, the additional GETS are added to the stack, and thus made available to the current READ. All cursor control and movement will work between previously displayed GETs and those added with the SET KEY TO command.

Regardless of use, three parameters are passed to the procedure. Therefore, any procedure that may be called by the use of the SET KEY TO command **must** have the PARAMETER command with the calling program name (p), the line number of the READ or MENU TO command (l), and the input variable name of either the GET or the MENU TO command (v).

Sample:

```
********************
* Name        SET_KEY.prg
* Date        August 6, 1986
* Notice      Copyright 1986, Stephen J. Straley
* Note        This shows the use of the SET KEY command
*
********************

SET KEY 28 TO One_cnt
SET KEY -1 TO Two_cnt
SET KEY -2 TO Three_cnt
SET KEY -3 TO Four_cnt
SET KEY -4 TO Five_cnt
SET KEY -5 TO Six_cnt
DO WHILE .T.
   CLEAR
   TEXT

       F1 will count to 600 by one
       F2 will count to 600 by two
       F3 will count to 600 by three
       F4 will count to 600 by four
       F5 will count to 600 by five
       F6 will count to 600 by six

       Enter 'QUIT' to exit program

   ENDTEXT
   STORE "    " TO temp_var
   @ 20,20 SAY "Strike a key or type QUIT to exit -> " GET ;
           temp_var
   READ
   IF UPPER(TRIM(temp_var)) = "QUIT"
      QUIT
```

```
      ENDIF
   ENDDO

********************

PROCEDURE One_cnt

   PARAMETERS p, l, v

   CLEAR
   FOR x = 1 TO 600
      @ 12,25 SAY "Total count: "
      ?? x
   NEXT
   WAIT

********************

PROCEDURE Two_cnt

   PARAMETERS p, l, v

   CLEAR
   FOR x = 1 TO 600 STEP 2
      @ 12,25 SAY "Total count: "
      ?? x
   NEXT
   WAIT

********************

PROCEDURE Three_cnt

   PARAMETERS p, l, v

   CLEAR
   FOR x = 1 TO 600 STEP 3
      @ 12,25 SAY "Total count: "
      ?? x
   NEXT
   WAIT

********************

PROCEDURE Four_cnt

   PARAMETERS p, l, v

   CLEAR
   FOR x = 1 TO 600 STEP 4
      @ 12,25 SAY "Total count: "
      ?? x
   NEXT
   WAIT
```

```
********************

PROCEDURE Five_cnt

   PARAMETERS p, l, v

   CLEAR
   FOR x = 1 TO 600 STEP 5
      @ 12,25 SAY "Total count: "
      ?? x
   NEXT
   WAIT

********************

PROCEDURE Six_cnt

   PARAMETERS p, l, v

   CLEAR
   FOR x = 1 TO 600 STEP 6
      @ 12,25 SAY "Total count: "
      ?? x
   NEXT
   WAIT
* End of File
```

SET MARGIN TO

Syntax: SET MARGIN TO < expN >

Description: The SET MARGIN TO command adjusts the left hand margin for
               all printed output according the value expressed in the < expN >.

Default: 0

Command: dBASE Standard.

Notes: Once a SET MARGIN TO is set and after printing has occurred, the
               margin must be reestablished at 0 in order for all video display to ap-
               pear in the proper positions.

Sample:
```
SET DEVICE TO PRINT
@ 10,10 SAY "The margin is set to 0"
SET MARGIN TO 5
@ 15,10 SAY "Now it is set to 5"
```

```
SET DEVICE TO SCREEN
@ 15,10 SAY "It is off position..."
SET MARGIN TO 0
@ 15,10 SAY "It is now on position."
```

SET MESSAGE TO

Syntax: SET MESSAGE TO <expN>

Description: This command is designed to work with the MENU TO and
                 PROMPT commands. With the SET MESSAGE TO command,
                 choose a line number between 1 and 24 inclusive where a special
                 prompt message will appear every time the cursor is placed on a
                 PROMPT option. By using the SET MESSAGE TO line number
                 option, every prompt to the screen may have an additional message
                 giving more information to the user regarding that menu choice.

Default: 24

Command: Clipper enhanced.

Notes: Keep in mind that the SET MESSAGE TO <expN> does not set
                 the message that will be displayed; that happens in the PROMPT
                 command. All the SET MESSAGE TO <expN> command will do
                 is establish the line number on which the additional message will ap-
                 pear whenever the MESSAGE clause is used with the PROMPT
                 command.

Sample: Refer to the PROMPT ... MESSAGE command.

SET ORDER TO   (Autumn 86: Special Command)

Syntax: SET ORDER TO [<expN>]

Description: The SET ORDER TO command selects a new active index from the
                 index list. If <expN> is 0 the current index list order will be
                 maintained.

Default: 1

SET PATH TO

Syntax: SET PATH TO < expC >

Description: This command will change the system PATH.

Default: None set.

Command: dBASE Standard.

Variance: Using this command in conjunction with a continuation marker (a
                 semicolon) is not supported. The entire path must be entered on
                 one line.

Sample: `SET PATH TO C:\EDP, C:\EDP\STATION1,C:\EDP\STATION2`

SET PRINT

Syntax: SET PRINT ON/OFF

Description: The SET PRINT command directs all output that is not controlled
                 by the @...SAY command to the printer as well as the console.

Default: OFF

Command: dBASE Standard.

Notes: In order to prevent output from being displayed on the screen when
                 it should go exclusively to the printer, the SET CONSOLE OFF
                 command may have to be invoked as well, especially when using ?
                 and ?? to display information.

Sample:
```
? "This is a test"
SET PRINT ON
? "This is another test with both..."
SET CONSOLE OFF
? "This is only printing on the printer..."
```

SET PRINTER TO   (Autumn 86 Special Command)

Syntax: SET PRINTER TO [< device > / < filename >]

Description: If you are redirecting the full screen output to a file, the SET
                 DEVICE TO PRINT command is also required. This command is
                 extremely useful when used in conjunction with the SET KEY TO
                 command in order to trap screen messages and program location.

Default: OFF

Command: Autumn 86 Enhancement.

Sample:
```
SET DEVICE TO PRINT
SET PRINTER TO Screen.txt
a = 1
a 5,10 SAY "This is a test, so enter a value -> " GET a
READ
SET PRINTER TO                 && This closes the printer file.
SET PRINTER TO LPT1
a 10,10 SAY "This is now going to line printer 1"
SET PRINTER TO
SET DEVICE TO SCREEN
```

SET PROCEDURE TO

Syntax: SET PROCEDURE TO < filename >

Description: The SET PROCEDURE TO command allows a series of proce-
                 dures which are contained in a .PRG file to be pulled into the
                 application and used accordingly.

Default: None set.

Command: dBASE Standard.

Variance: There is no maximum number of procedures allowed in a PROCE-
                 DURE file.

                 The PROCEDURE < filename > must not have the same name as
                 any name of a procedure.

                 The PROCEDURE file does not constitute an open file during run-
                 time.

Further detailed information regarding procedures and their functions under Clipper is in Chapter 8, Procedures.

Sample: SET PROCEDURE TO Proclist
                  DO Proclis1

SET RELATION TO

Syntax: SET RELATION TO < key exp >/RECNO()/ < expN > INTO
                  < alias >
                  [,TO < key exp >/RECNO()/ < expN > INTO < alias > ...]

Description: The SET RELATION TO command links two or more database
                  files according to a key expression that is common to all files.

Variance: Up to eight child RELATIONs are supported from one mother file.

Notes: The SET RELATION command will link the currently selected
                  database file to an open file in another area.

                  The second, and subsequent files are identified by their aliases.

                  With the key expression option, the key must be contained in the
                  selected database, and the linked file(s) must be indexed on the key
                  expression. Whenever the active file is repositioned, the linked file is
                  searched for the first record matching the key expression from the
                  active file.

                  With the RECNO() option, the files may be linked by record num-
                  bers.

                  If a matching record cannot be found in the linked file, the linked file
                  is positioned to the end of the file and a blank record is appended.

Sample: CLEAR
                  a 5,0,23,79 BOX "*"
                  a 7,5 SAY "One moment while all files are initialized"

                  file4 = "PRHIST"   && A History File
                  file3 = "PRCHECK"   && A Check File
                  file2 = "PREMPLOY"   && An Employee Master File
                  file1 = "PRTIME"   && A Timecard File

```
***************************************************************
* This section sets up all files and subsequent relations  *
***************************************************************

SELECT 4
USE &file4. INDEX Prhist_a
SELECT 3
USE &file3. INDEX Prchk_a.dat
ZAP
SELECT 2
USE &file2. INDEX Premp_a.dat
SELECT 1
USE &file1. INDEX Prtime_a.dat
SELECT 1


********************************************************************
* This section adds checks to be processed to the check file,    *
* based on the number of timecards in the timecard file.         *
********************************************************************
DO WHILE .NOT. EOF()
  @ 21, 5 SAY "Now adding employee number " + TRIM(employee) + ;
  " to the check file"
  temp_emp = employee
  SELECT 3
  APPEND BLANK
  REPLACE employee WITH temp_emp
  SELECT 1
  SKIP
ENDDO
*******************************************************
* This section sets up final relation and then goes  *
* on to calculate both federal/state/and local taxes *
*******************************************************
@ 21, 5 SAY SPACE(73)
SELECT 3
GO TOP
SET RELATION TO employee INTO &file2., TO employee INTO &file1.
*********************************************************
* Both files are indexed on employee and the parent    *
* file has a similar field as well.                    *
*********************************************************
@  7, 5 SAY SPACE(73)

DO WHILE .NOT. EOF()
```

```
******************************************************************
* Calculate base pay                                             *
*   AMT_REG_P is set to salary rate (if a salary employee)       *
*            else is set to the hourly rate X the number of      *
*            straight hours worked                               *
******************************************************************
   IF &file2.->salaried
     REPLACE amt_reg_p WITH &file2.->pay_rate_s
   ELSE
      REPLACE amt_reg_p WITH &file1.->stra_time * &file2.-
>pay_rate_h
   ENDIF


******************************************************************
* Calculate Overtime pay, Total Gross Pay, and Exempted Pay      *
*                                                                *
* Temp_pay is first the hourly rate X the rate for overtime X    *
*     the number of overtime hours worked.                       *
* Temp_pay is then added to hourly rate X the rate for           *
*     double time X the number of double time hours worked.      *
* Temp_pay is finally added to the hourly rate X the rate for    *
*     triple time X the number of triple time hours worked.      *
* AMT_OVR_P is then set to Temp_pay.                             *
* AMT_VAC_P is set to the hourly pay rate X the rate for         *
*     vacation time X the number of vacation hours worked.       *
* AMT_SIC_P is set to the hourly pay rate X the hours of         *
*     sick time.                                                 *
* AMT_GRO_P is set to the regular pay + the overtime pay +       *
*     vacation pay + the sick pay.                               *
* Temp_pay is then set to the tips + the bonus + any misc.       *
*     pay - any gross pay deduction (master employee record)     *
* AMT_TGR_P is set to the gross pay(AMT_GRO_P) +                 *
*     temp_pay(all else)                                         *
* AMT_EXP_P is set to the amount of exempted pay                 *
******************************************************************

   temp_pay = &file2.->pay_rate_h * prover * &file1.->half_time
    temp_pay = temp_pay + &file2.->pay_rate_h * prdouble * &file1.-
>doub_time
    temp_pay = temp_pay + &file2.->pay_rate_h * prtriple * &file1.-
>trip_time
   REPLACE amt_ovr_p WITH temp_pay, amt_vac_p WITH &file2.-
>pay_rate_h * prvaca * &file1.->vaca_time
   REPLACE amt_sic_p WITH &file2.->pay_rate_h * &file1.->sick_time
   REPLACE amt_gro_p WITH amt_reg_p + amt_ovr_p + amt_vac_p +
amt_sic_p
    temp_pay = &file1.->tips + &file1.->bonus + &file1.->misc_pay -
&file1.->gross_pay
   REPLACE amt_tgr_p WITH amt_gro_p + temp_pay, amt_exp_p WITH
&file1.->exem_pay
ENDDO
CLOSE databases
```

SET UNIQUE

Syntax: SET UNIQUE ON/OFF

Description: The SET UNIQUE command determines whether all records with
                  the same value on a key expression will be included in the index file.

                  An index created with SET UNIQUE ON will create an index based
                  solely on each unique value within the database. Only the first
                  record with duplicate keys will be included in the new index file.

Default: OFF

Command: dBASE Standard.

Variance: Under dBASE III, the index file based on SET UNIQUE ON will be
                  smaller than the original file; under Clipper, the second index file
                  based on the unique field will be the same size as the original index
                  file, due to the manner in which Clipper handles indexing.

SKIP

Syntax: SKIP [expN] [ALIAS < expN > / < expC >]

Description: The SKIP command moves the record pointer in either the active
                  database or in any other open database.

Command: Clipper enhanced.

Variance: The ALIAS clause allows the pointer in another pre-opened area,
                  not currently selected, to be moved without having to go directly to
                  the selected area and move the pointer. The pointer will be reposi-
                  tioned in that file by using either the ALIAS number < expN > or
                  the ALIAS name < expC >.

Sample:
```
SKIP ALIAS 2
* The old way to do the same would have been
* SELECT 2
* SKIP
* SELECT 1
```

```
SKIP 5 ALIAS Employee
* The old way to do the same would have been
* SELECT Employee
* SKIP 5
* SELECT 1
```

SORT

Syntax: SORT < scope > TO [< newfile >] ON < field >
               [/A][/C][/D][, < field2 >][/A][/C][/D] [FOR < condition >]
               [WHILE < condition >]

Description: The SORT command copies the currently selected database to
               < newfile > with the records in alphabetical, chronological, or
               numerical order as specified by the ON < field > clause.

Command: dBASE Standard.

Variance: The /D option will not work on date fields.

Notes: The < newfile > will have a .dbf extension unless otherwise specified.

               A file cannot be SORTed to itself or any other open file.

               The switches mean the following:

                   /A = ASCENDING order
                   /D = DESCENDING order
                   /C = Ignore CASE

               Combining switches is valid: /AC or /CD, etc...

               To SORT on multiple fields, the most important key must be
               specified first. Separate field names with commas. This cannot be
               used in macro substitution.

               SORTing is not allowed on memo fields or logical fields.

               SORT does not work with substring functions or complex expres-
               sions.

Sample: USE Phonbook
               SORT ON state, city, prefix /C TO Newbook
```
```

STORE

Syntax: STORE <expression> TO <memory variable>/<memory variable list>

Description: The STORE command initializes a memory variable(s) to a specific value.

                   Acceptable alternate syntax would be:

                   <memory variable> = <expression>

Command: dBASE Standard.

Notes: With the alternative syntax, only one variable can be initialized to an expression at one time. The primary syntax structure should be used if a series of variables needs to be initialized to one value.

                   If a memory variable has the same name as an active field name, the field name will take precedence over the memory variable unless the memory variable is explicitly specified as M-> <memory variable>.

Sample:
```
STORE 0 TO memvar1, memvar2, memvar3, memvar4

memvar1 = 0
memvar2 = 0
memvar3 = 0
memvar4 = 0
STORE 5 TO M->last_name  && where there is also an active
*                                  field named last_name.
```

SUM

Syntax: SUM <field list> TO <memvar list> [FOR/WHILE <condition>]

Description: The SUM command sums to a <memvar> the values of fields in a database, depending upon the condition set.

Command: dBASE Standard.

Variance: With this command, the memory variable or the memory variable list is mandatory, and the lists on each side of the TO section maintain a one-to-one relationship.

Sample: USE Example
                SUM amount_owe, past_due TO owe_amount, due_amount ;
                    FOR state = "CA" WHILE .NOT. priority

TEXT

Syntax: TEXT [TO PRINT/TO FILE < filename >]
                    < commands >
                ENDTEXT

Description: The TEXT command prints large quantities of information without
                using the @...SAY command.

Command: dBASE Standard.

Variance: The [TO PRINT/TO FILE] clauses allow the TEXT/ENDTEXT to
                print to the printer or to an alternate file. This feature is useful for
                uniform report writing; with one routine you can send TEXT/
                ENDTEXT to screen, to printer, or to a file for output/format at a
                later time.

TOTAL ON

Syntax: TOTAL ON < key field > TO < newfile > [< scope >] FIELDS
                < field list > [FOR < condition >] [WHILE < condition >]

Description: The TOTAL command is used to sum numeric fields in the currently
                selected database file and send the results TO a second database file.
                The numeric fields in the second database will contain the total for
                all records that have the same key value as the fields in the original
                database.

Command: dBASE Standard.

Variance: The FIELDS clause must be included in the TOTAL ON command.

Notes: The currently selected database file must be either INDEXed or
                SORTed on the key to be TOTALed.

                The second database name must have a drive designator if the file is
                to be written to a drive\directory other than the default drive\
                directory. Unless specified, a .DBF extension will be given the
                < newfile >.

The structure of the secondary database is identical to that of the selected database. Memo fields are not copied to the new file.

All records are TOTALed to the < newfile > unless specified by the scope, or a FOR < condition >, a WHILE < condition >, or both.

All records with the same value in the specified key field will be condensed to a single record in the secondary database.

Sample:
```
USE Phonbook INDEX Statbook
TOTAL ON state TO A:Summary FIELDS owe, paid FOR owe > 0

* This will produce a secondary database called A:Summary.dbf
* which will have in it two fields: the amount owed and the
* amount paid.  This database will have a record for each state
* which will be a total of the monies owed and paid.
```

TYPE

Syntax: TYPE < file name > [TO PRINT]/[TO FILE < filename >]

Description: The TYPE command types out the contents of an ASCII file.

Command: dBASE Standard.

Variance: The DOS redirectional option is not supported. In order to get output to a printer, use the TO PRINT option and use the TO FILE option rather than setting an alternate file.

Sample:
```
* The Following is LEGAL under Clipper *
*
TYPE Results.txt TO PRINT            && goes to the printer
TYPE Results.txt                     && goes to the screen
TYPE Results.txt TO FILE Outfile.txt && goes to a file

* The Following is NOT LEGAL under Clipper *
*
TYPE Results.txt >PRN
TYPE Results.txt >Outfile.txt
```

UNLOCK   **(Autumn 86 Special Command)**

Syntax: UNLOCK [ALL]

Description: The UNLOCK command releases the file or record lock in the
                     selected work area. If the [ALL] clause is used, all current locks in
                     all work areas will be removed.

Command: Autumn 86 version only - Networking Command

UPDATE ON

Syntax: UPDATE ON < key field > FROM < Alias > REPLACE < field >
                     WITH < exp > [, < field2 > WITH < exp > ...] RANDOM

Description: The UPDATE command uses data from an existing file and changes
                     data records accordingly in the currently selected database. The
                     alterations are made by matching records in the two database files on
                     a single key field.

Command: dBASE Standard.

Variance: The RANDOM clause must be used; this saves Clipper from having
                     to open an index file for the FROM database.

Notes: The file being UPDATEd must be the currently selected database
                     and must be either SORTed or INDEXed on the key field; the
                     FROM (< Alias >) file must be in one of the unselected work areas
                     and it may be in any order.

                     The key field must have the same name in both files.

                     If the REPLACE expression involves a field in the secondary file, the
                     field listed in the FROM statement must be identified as ALIAS-
                     > character field.

Sample:
```
SELECT 2
USE Statbook
SELECT 1
USE Phonbook INDEX Namebook
UPDATE ON state FROM Statbook REPLACE B->paid WITH ;
        B->paid + paid
```

USE

Syntax: USE [< file name >][INDEX < index file list >]
                   [ALIAS < expC >]

Description: The USE command opens an existing database in the selected work
                   area.

Command: dBASE Standard.

Autumn 86:   EXCLUSIVE [ALIAS < alias name >] will set the specified file to
                   be USED EXCLUSIVEly by the user, thus locking it from USE by
                   all other users.

Notes: If the database file contains an associated memo file, that file is
                   opened automatically.

                   Depending on the number of previously open files, there is no limit
                   to the number of index files to be opened at one time.

                   Without any parameter, the USE command will close the active
                   database, associated memo file, and all open index files. The USE
                   command in this fashion will also flush all buffers associated with
                   that file.

                   Unless otherwise specified, a file extension of .DBF will be assumed.
                   If the file extension is .DBF, it is recommended that no file extension
                   be used either as a literal or in a macro substitution.

                   If no ALIAS clause is used, the alias for the selected work area/file
                   will be the root name of the file itself.

                   Issuance of the USE command without any associated INDEX files
                   will place the record pointer at the top of the file. If the INDEX
                   clause is used, the record pointer is positioned at the first logical
                   record based on the first index file listed in the INDEX file list.

Sample: USE Temp

                   * The record pointer is positioned at 1
                   * The ALIAS is set to "TEMP"

                   USE

                   * Closes the active database Temp and flushes the
                   * buffers accordingly.

```
USE Temp INDEX Temp1.dat, Temp2, Temp3 ALIAS Test

* The file Temp.dbf is opened and any associated memo
* file will be opened as well.
*
* The record pointer will be positioned at the first
* logical record in the database as dictated by the
* file "Temp1.dat".  The remaining index files are
* assumed to have an extension of ",NTX".
*
* The ALIAS of the file is set to "TEST"
```

WAIT

Syntax: WAIT [< expC >][TO < memvar >]

Description: The WAIT command pauses all processing/execution until any key
                  is pressed.

Command: dBASE Standard.

Notes: < expC > is any string to be used as a prompt message. If none is
                  used, the default prompt of "Press any key to continue..." will be
                  used.

                  If the TO clause is added, the value of the key pressed is stored to
                  < memvar >. This is character type and does not need to be
                  initialized prior to the issuance of this command.

Sample:
```
WAIT "Press any key to continue or Q to quit..." TO input
IF UPPER(input) = "Q"
    RETURN
ENDIF
```

ZAP

Syntax:	ZAP
Description:	The ZAP command removes all records from the active database.
Command:	dBASE Standard.
Notes:	If the ZAP command is issued, **all** records within the database, whether marked for deletion or not, will be completely removed. All open indexes will be re-initialized as well.
| Sample: | ```
USE Temp INDEX Temp1.dat, Temp2, Temp3
ZAP
``` |
```

CHAPTER FIVE

Functions

This chapter describes all Clipper functions. The format used is identical to that used in the previous chapter describing Clipper commands. Each function summary includes *syntax, description, function type, variances*, and one or more *code samples*. All functions also are identified as either enhanced by Clipper, following the dBASE III standard, or simulated by programming. (Some of the simulated functions, e.g., VERSION(), do not seem to have any meaningful purpose; nevertheless, they are included here as a reference.)

Autumn 86 Notes:

Functions may now be issued without an associated command. In other words, if the function really performs an operation (e.g., INKEY(0) and SETPRC(5,10)), it may be issued on a command line by itself.

```
Example:    ? "Press Any Key to Continue..."
            INKEY(0)
            RETURN
```

Additionally, I have included **all** of the functions available in the Autumn '86 release. These functions include those within the compiler/library, and those in the EXTENDDB file, the EXTENDA file, and the EXTENDC file. Notes within the description of the functions provide linking information.

The following notation is used in describing the function:

      <expC>: a character expression, normally a string.
      <expL>: a logical expression, either .T. or .F.
      <expD>: a date expression.
      <expN>: a numeric expression (a single number, a complete numeric expression, or a formula).

& - MACRO SUBSTITUTION

Syntax: & < character string >

Description: This function allows the value of a memory variable to be evaluated and, where necessary, acted upon.

Function: Standard.

Variance: MACRO substitutions in Clipper must conform to the requirements of a compiler. Keep in mind that the MACROs in your application do not have any values during the time of compiling. They are marked for future reference and a place for them is reserved in memory, but they are not looked at and interpreted. Therefore, commands and the syntax of commands cannot be included in the MACRO. The compiler must see each command and compile it accordingly for linking with the library. Also, you must not use a MACRO in conjunction with a function (e.g. @ 2,3 SAY &FIELD-NAME(2)).

However, MACROs can be used in DO WHILE loops and the parameters of commands may be within the MACRO, as long as no part of the syntactical structure of the command is included (i.e., you cannot use a MACRO with a LIST command and have the listed fields separated with commas).

As with dBASE, a period (.) immediately following a macro will preclude the possibility of an extra space being added.

One last thing concerning macro substitution: while Clipper is still restricted to a line length of 255 characters, Clipper is also restricted to no more than 15 iterations or parses per macro. Anything more than that will yield a macro expansion error. To avoid this, break up the number of logical parses to a macro and add an additional macro for anything greater than 15 parses.

Sample:

```
file4   = "PRTIME"
file2   = "PREMPLOY"
file1   = "PRCHECK"
scrdata = "C:"
SELECT 4
USE &scrdata.&file4..dat INDEX &scrdata.Prtime_a.dat
SELECT 2
USE &scrdata.&file2..dat INDEX &scrdata.Premp_a.dat
SELECT 1
USE &scrdata.&file1..dat INDEX &scrdata.Prchk_a.dat
SET RELATION TO employee INTO &file4., ;
              TO employee INTO &file2.
```

ABS()

Syntax: ABS(<expN>)

Pass: <numeric expression>
Return: <numeric expression>

Description: The ABS() function yields the absolute value of a numeric expression.

Function:	Standard - Autumn '86.
Autumn 86:	Prior to this version, this function was simulated.
Sample:	`? ABS(-5)    && This will yield a 5`

ADEL()

Syntax:	ADEL(< expC >, < expN >)
Pass:	< character expression >, < numeric expression >
Return:	nothing

Description: This function deletes an element in an array named < expC > at the < expN > position. All array elements lower in the array list from the given numeric expression will move up one position in the array. In other words, the old sixth array element will now become the fifth element. However, the length of the array will remain unchanged, with an undefined element at the end of the array list.

Function: Clipper enhanced - Autumn '86 only.

Autumn 86: In order to use this function, the DBU.LIB library file must be linked in with your application and must appear in your link list after CLIP-PER.LIB.

Sample:

```
********************
* Name      ADELTEST.prg
* Date      December 1, 1986
* Notice    Copyright 1986, Stephen J. Straley
* Note      This sample program demonstrates how the ADEL()
*           function will delete an element from an array list.
*
*           In order for this function to work, the Autumn '86
*           version must be used and the DBU.LIB file
*           must be linked in with the CLIPPER.LIB.
*
********************

CLEAR
DECLARE counter[10]
FOR x = 1 TO 10
   counter[x] = x
NEXT
a 1,5 SAY "Here is a list of numbers..."
?
FOR x = 1 TO 10
```

```
      ? counter[x]
NEXT
?
WAIT "Press any key to DELETE the 5th element in array list"
CLEAR
ADEL(counter, 5)
@ 1,5 SAY "Here is the new list..."
?
? "The number of elements in the array is "
?? LEN(counter)
?
FOR x = 1 TO 10
   ? counter[x]
NEXT
?
?
TEXT
Notice that the length of the array remained at 10 while there
are only 9 elements showing on the screen.  Also notice that
the 5th element was removed from the array and that all lower
elements moved up one position within the array.
ENDTEXT
* End of File
```

ADIR()

Syntax:	ADIR(<expC> [,<expC>])
Pass:	<character expression> [, <character expression>]
Return:	<numeric expression>

Description: This function returns the number of files which match a pattern specified by the first <expC> on the currently logged disk\ directory. The pattern specified may be "*.ext", or even "*.*".

The second <expC> is used for the name of a previously declared array. If this is used, the names of all files matching the pattern of the first <expC> will be inserted into this array.

Function: Clipper enhanced - Autumn '86 only.

Autumn 86: In order to use this function, the DBU.LIB library file must be linked in with your application and must appear in your link list after CLIPPER.LIB.

Sample:

```
********************
* Name        ADIRTEST.prg
* Date        December 1, 1986
* Notice      Copyright 1986, Stephen J. Straley
* Note        This sample program first demonstrates how the ADIR()
*             function will yield the number of matching elements
*             on the current logged disk\directory.  It then
*             shows how to load those matching file names into an
*             array, which eventually gets displayed back to the
*             screen.
*
*             In order for this function to work, the Autumn '86
*             version must be used and the DBU.LIB file
*             must be linked in with the CLIPPER.LIB.
*
********************

    CLEAR

    DECLARE dir_files[ADIR("*.*")]

    ADIR("*.*", dir_files)

    @ 2, 10 SAY "The number of file(s) on this disk\directory is "
    ?? LEN(dir_files)
    ?
    WAIT "Press any key to get a listing of those files...."
    ?
    FOR x = 1 TO LEN(dir_files)
       ? dir_files[x]
    NEXT
    ?
    ? "End of Listing"
* End of File
```

AFILL()

Syntax: AFILL(<expC>, <exp> [, <expN> [, <expN>]])

Pass: <character expression>, <expression> [, <numeric expression>
               [, <numeric expression>]]

Return: nothing

Description: <expC> is the name of an array into which <exp> is filled. The
               first optional parameter is the beginning element for the fill opera-
               tion (the default is 1). The second optional parameter is the count
               parameter (the default is the length of the array).

               All elements from the first optional <expN> to the second optional
               <expN> will be filled with the same fill value <exp>.

The fill character < exp > may be of any valid data type (other than memo).

Function: Clipper enhanced - Autumn '86 only.

Autumn 86:   In order to use this function, the DBU.LIB library file must be linked in with your application and must appear in your link list after CLIPPER.LIB.

Sample:

```
********************
* Name        AFILLTEST.prg
* Date        December 1, 1986
* Notice      Copyright 1986, Stephen J. Straley
* Note        This sample program demonstrates how the AFILL()
*             function will fill an array with a given <exp>,
*             starting at the first <expN> position, and continuing
*             for <expN> positions.
*
*             In this demonstration, a portion of an array list
*             is put through the AINS() function, and then filled
*             with the AFILL() function
*
*             In order for this function to work, the Autumn '86
*             version must be used and the DBU.LIB file
*             must be linked in with the CLIPPER.LIB.
*
********************

CLEAR
DECLARE counter[20]
FOR x = 1 TO 20
   counter[x] = DATE() + x
NEXT
@ 1,5 SAY "Here is a list of dates..."
?
FOR x = 1 TO 20
   ? counter[x]
NEXT
?
WAIT "Press any key to FILL the array list"
CLEAR
FOR x = 5 TO 14
AINS(counter, x)
NEXT

AFILL(counter, "ZZZZZZZZZ", 5, 10)

@ 1,5 SAY "Here is the new list..."
?
? "The number of elements in the array is "
?? LEN(counter)
?
```

```
FOR x = 1 TO 20
   ? counter[x]
NEXT
?
WAIT
?
TEXT
Note that the array length remained at 20 and that
the elements at the 5th - 14th positions were shifted down.
After that, note that the string of Z's was placed into the
new, empty positions by using the AFILL() function.

ENDTEXT
```
* End of File

AINS()

Syntax: AINS(<expC>, <expN>)

Pass: <character expression>, <numeric expression>
Return: nothing

Description: This function inserts a blank space in the array named <expC> at
                   the <expN>th position.

                   The new position opened by this function becomes an undefined ele-
                   ment.

                   All array elements starting with the <expN>th position will be
                   shifted down one position in the array list and the last item in the ar-
                   ray will be removed completely. In other words, the old fifth array
                   element will now become the sixth element.

                   The length of the array will not stay at its DECLAREd value.

Function: Clipper Enhanced - Autumn '86 only.

Autumn 86:   In order to use this function, the DBU.LIB library file must be linked
                   in with your application and must appear in your link list after CLIP-
                   PER.LIB.

Sample:

```
********************
* Name        AINSTEST.prg
* Date        December 1, 1986
* Notice      Copyright 1986, Stephen J. Straley
* Note        This sample program first demonstrates how the AINS()
*             function will insert a space within the array at the
*             <expN>th position.
*
*             In order for this function to work, the Autumn '86
*             version must be used and the DBU.LIB file
*             must be linked in with the CLIPPER.LIB.
*
********************

       CLEAR
       DECLARE counter[10]
       FOR x = 1 TO 10
          counter[x] = x
       NEXT
       @ 1,5 SAY "Here is a list of numbers..."
       ?
       FOR x = 1 TO 10
          ? counter[x]
       NEXT
       ?
       WAIT "Press any key to INSERT the 5th element in array list"
       CLEAR

       AINS(counter, 5)

       @ 1,5 SAY "Here is the new list..."
       ?
       ? "The number of elements in the array is "
       ?? LEN(counter)
       ?
       FOR x = 1 TO 10
          ? counter[x]
       NEXT
       ?
       ?
       TEXT
       Notice that the length of the array remained at 10 though there
       are only 9 elements showing on the screen.  Also notice that
       the 5th element is now blank and needs to have a value assigned
       to it.  Further, notice that all lower elements in the array
       were moved down one position, including the old 5th element,
       and that the last element in the array is removed from
       the list.

       ENDTEXT
* End of File
```

ALIAS()

Syntax: ALIAS(< expN >)

Pass: < numeric expression >
Return: < character expression >

Description: This function yields the alias name of the work area specified by
                 < expN >. If no parameter is passed then the alias name of the cur-
                 rent work area is returned. If no database is in use, a null string is
                 returned.

Function: Clipper enhanced - Autumn '86.

Sample:
```
USE History
? ALIAS()      && Displays the word 'History'
? ALIAS(2)     && Displays a null string
```

ALLTRIM()

Syntax: ALLTRIM(< expC >)

Pass: < character expression >
Return: < character expression >

Description: This function returns < expC > with leading and trailing blanks
                 removed.

Function: Clipper simulated.

Autumn 86:   In order to use this function, the EXTENDDB.PRG file must be
                 compiled and linked in with your application and must appear in
                 your link list with all other .OBJ files.

Note: This is identical to the function called DLTRIM() located in Chapter
                 12, Designing User Designed Functions (UDFs).

AMPM()

Syntax: AMPM(< expC >)

Pass: < character expression >
Return: < character expression >

Description: The passed <expC> must be in the form of a time string. The AMPM function yields an 11-byte character string based on the time string, and will be in the 12-hour AM/PM format.

Function: Clipper simulated.

Autumn 86: In order to use this function, the EXTENDDB.PRG file must be compiled and linked in with your application and must appear in your link list with all other .OBJ files.

ASC()

Syntax: ASC(<expC>)

Pass: <character expression>
Return: <numeric expression>

Description: The ASC() function returns the ASCII number for the left-most character of any character expression.

Function: Standard.

Sample:
```
CLEAR
@ 10,10 SAY ASC("This function")   && Will yield a 84
STORE "N" TO test
@ 12,10 SAY ASC(test)              && Will yield a 78
```

ASCII TABLE

Char.	Number	Char.	Number	Char.	Number	Char.	Number
NUL	0	SPACE	32	@	64	`	96
^A	1	!	33	A	65	a	97
^B	2	"	34	B	66	b	98
^C	3	#	35	C	67	c	99
^D	4	$	36	D	68	d	100
^E	5	%	37	E	69	e	101
^F	6	&	38	F	70	f	102
^G	7	'	39	G	71	g	103
^H	8	(	40	H	72	h	104
^I	9	)	41	I	73	i	105
^J	10	*	42	J	74	j	106
^K	11	+	43	K	75	k	107
^L	12	,	44	L	76	l	108
^M	13	-	45	M	77	m	109
^N	14	.	46	N	78	n	110
^O	15	/	47	O	79	o	111
^P	16	0	48	P	80	p	112

^Q	17	1	49	Q	81	q	113
^R	18	2	50	R	82	r	114
^S	19	3	51	S	83	s	115
^T	20	4	52	T	84	t	116
^U	21	5	53	U	85	u	117
^V	22	6	54	V	86	v	118
^W	23	7	55	W	87	w	119
^X	24	8	56	X	88	x	120
^Y	25	9	57	Y	89	y	121
^Z	26	:	58	Z	90	z	122
ESC	27	;	59	[	91	{	123
FS	28	<	60	\	92	|	124
GS	29	=	61	]	93	}	125
RS	30	>	62	^	94	~	126
US	31	?	63	_	95	DEL	127

ASCAN()

Syntax: ASCAN(< expC >, < exp > [, < expN > [, < expN >]])

Pass: < character expression >, < expression >
                 [, < numeric expression > [, < numeric expression >]]

Return: < numeric expression >

Description: This function scans the contents of an array named < expC > for
                 < exp >. The returned value is the position in the array in which it
                 was found. If < exp > is not found, 0 is returned.

                 The two optional < numeric expression > values are the beginning
                 element number to start the search and the count value. The begin-
                 ning default is 1 and the count default value is the length of the array.

                 SET EXACT ON/OFF does have an effect on the matching ability
                 of this function.

Function: Clipper enhanced - Autumn '86 only.

Autumn 86:   In order to use this function, the DBU.LIB library file must be linked
                 in with your application and must appear in your link list after CLIP-
                 PER.LIB.

Sample:

```
********************
* Name       ASCANTST.prg
* Date       December 1, 1986
* Notice     Copyright 1986, Stephen J. Straley
* Note       This sample program demonstrates how the
*            ASCAN() function scans through an array and
*            SEEKs a specific value.
*
*            In order for this function to work, the Autumn '86
*            version must be used and the DBU.LIB file
*            must be linked in with the CLIPPER.LIB.
*
********************
   CLEAR
   DECLARE name[10]
   AFILL(name, SPACE(20))
   FOR x = 1 TO 10
      wording = LTRIM(STR(x))
      @ 2, 4 SAY "Enter in number &wording. name => " GET name[x]
      READ
      @ 2, 4 SAY SPACE(70)
   NEXT
   DO WHILE .T.
      CLEAR
      search = SPACE(20)
      @ 4, 5 SAY "What name should I find? " GET search
      @ 6, 5 SAY "Leave Blank to QUIT"
      READ
      IF EMPTY(search)
         EXIT
      ENDIF
      IF ASCAN(name, search) = 0
         @ 10, 10 SAY TRIM(search) + " was not found in the list"
      ELSE
         @ 10, 10 SAY TRIM(search) + " was found in position "
         ?? ASCAN(name, search)
      ENDIF
      ?
      WAIT "Press any key to try another name...."
   ENDDO
   ?
* End of File
```

AT()

Syntax: AT(<eaxpC>,<expC>)

Pass: <character expression>,<character expression>
Return: <numeric expression>

Description: The AT() function searches the second string expression for the
                 starting position of the characters in the first string expression. If the
                 substring (i.e., the first character expression) is not contained within
                 the second expression, the substring function AT() returns a zero
                 (0).

Function: Standard.

Sample:
```
STORE "Bert" TO search
STORE "Bill Jim  SteveRogerRay  Bert David" TO string
STORE AT(search,string) TO which_one
?  "B in 'BERT' is the "
?? which_one                    && This will display a 26
?? "th character in the string."
```

BOF()

Syntax: BOF()

Pass: nothing
Return: < logical expression >

Description: The BOF() function determines if the Beginning of File marker has
                 been reached. If it has, the function will yield a logical true (.T.);
                 otherwise, a logical false (.F.) will be returned.

Function: Standard.

Sample:
```
USE file      & Any standard .DBF file
GO TOP
? "Have we reached the beginning of file marker?  "
?? IF(BOF(), "Yes", "No")
SKIP - 1
? "Now are we there?   "
?? IF(BOF(), "Yes", "No")
```

CDOW()

Syntax: CDOW(< expD >)

Pass: < date expression >
Return: < character expression >

Description: This function returns a character string of the day of the week (Mon-
                 day, Tuesday, etc.) from a date expression passed to the function.

Function: Standard.

Sample:
```
STORE DATE() TO indate
STORE indate + 4 TO indate
CLEAR
a 10,10 SAY "What do you have planned for this " + ;
CDOW(indate)
```

CHR()

Syntax: CHR(<expN>)

Pass: <expression number>
Return: <character expression>

Description: The CHR() function returns the ASCII character code for
                 <expN>. The number **must** be an integer within the range of 1 to
                 255, inclusive. These ASCII codes send their true value to whatever
                 device is set. The CHR() function can be used for special printing
                 codes as well as normal and graphics character codes.

Function: Standard.

Sample:
```
* This routine will set an Epson MS/RX/FX series printer
* to condensed print mode.

SET CONSOLE OFF
SET PRINT ON
?? CHR(15)
SET PRINT OFF
SET CONSOLE ON
```

CMONTH()

Syntax: CMONTH(<expD>)

Pass: <date expression>
Return: <character expression>

Description: This function returns a character string of the month (January, Feb-
                 ruary, etc.) from a date expression passed to the function.

Function: Standard.

Sample:
```
CLEAR
STORE CTOD("05/23/86") TO temp_date
@ 10,10 SAY "This is the merry month of " + CMONTH(temp_date)
```

COL()

Syntax: COL()

Pass: nothing
Return: < numeric expression >

Description: The COL() function returns the current cursor column position. The COL() value may be tested for or passed to a memory variable.

Function: Standard.

Sample:
```
sample = COL()
? REPLICATE("-",sample)

DO WHILE COL() < 65
    ?? values + "  "
ENDDO

CLEAR
@ 01,COL() + 10 SAY "This starts in position 10 on the screen."
```

CTOD()

Syntax: CTOD(< expC >)

Pass: < character expression >
Return: < date expression >

Description: This function converts a date which has been entered as a character expression to a date expression. The character expression must be in the form of "MM/DD/YY".

Function: Standard.

Sample:
```
STORE "03/23/64" TO indate
STORE CTOD(indate) TO outdate
? "The date 10 days from now will be: "
?? outdate + 10
```

DATE()

Syntax: DATE()

Pass: nothing
Return: < date expression >

Description: The DATE() function returns the current system date.

Function: Standard.

Notes: To change the system date, RUN the DOS DATE command.

Sample:
```
? "The system is set to: "
?? DATE()
newdate = DTOC(DATE() - 1)
RUN date &newdate.
? "The system is now set to: "
?? DATE()
```

DAY()

Syntax: DAY(< expD >)

Pass: < date expression >
Return: < numeric expression >

Description: The DAY() function returns the numeric value of the day of the
                   month from a date expression passed to the function.

Function: Standard.

Sample:
```
? "This is the "
?? DAY(DATE())
?? " of the month"

CLEAR
FOR x = 1 TO DAY(DATE())
   ?? x
   ?? " "
NEXT
```

DAYS()

Syntax: DAYS($<expN>$)

Pass: < numeric expression >
Return: < numeric expression >

Description: This function converts $<expN>$ seconds to the equivalent number of days. 86,399 seconds represents one day, 0 seconds being Midnight.

                    If you maintained a log of elapsed time using the SECONDS() function, DAYS() could calculate the number of elapsed days.

Function: Clipper simulated.

Autumn 86:   In order to use this function, the EXTENDDB.PRG file must be compiled and linked in with your application and must appear in your link list with all other .OBJ files.

DBF()

Syntax: DBF()

Pass: nothing
Return: < character expression >

Description: This function returns the alias name of the currently selected and active database. Thus, in Clipper, it does not differ from the ALIAS function.

Difference: In dBASE III, this function will actually yield the name of the database even if the alias name is different. In the Clipper simulated function, only the alias name will be returned.

Function: Clipper simulated.

Autumn 86:   In order to use this function, the EXTENDDB.PRG file must be compiled and linked in with your application and must appear in your link list with all other .OBJ files.

Sample:
```
USE Hist
? DBF()     && Yields 'Hist'
USE Hist ALIAS History
? DBF()     && Yields 'History'
```

DELETED()

Syntax: DELETED()

Pass: nothing
Return: < logical expression >

Description: The DELETED() function returns a logical true (.T.) if the current
                 record has been marked for deletion. Otherwise, this function will
                 return a logical false (.F.).

Function: Standard.

Sample:
```
USE File
GO 5
? DELETED()
DELETE
? DELETED()
GO TOP
DO WHILE .NOT. EOF()
    IF DELETED()
        ? RECNO()
    ENDIF
    SKIP
ENDIF
```

DISKSPACE()

Syntax: DISKSPACE([< expN >])

Pass: < numeric expression >
Return: < numeric expression >

Description: This function yields the number of bytes available on the specified
                 disk drive. The disk drive is designated by the < expN >, where 1 is
                 for A:, 2 for B:, 3 for C:, etc. If no < expN > is passed to the func-
                 tion, then the space available on the currently logged drive will be
                 returned.

Function: Clipper extended.

Autumn 86:   In order to use this function, the EXTENDC.OBJ file must be linked
                 in with your application and must appear in your link list after CLIP-
                 PER.LIB.

Sample:
```
IF DISKSPACE(1) < RECSIZE() * LASTREC()
?? "There is not enough room for this file on drive A:"
ENDIF
```

DOW()

Syntax: DOW(< expD >)

Pass: < date expression >
Return: < numeric expression >

Description: The DOW() function returns the number representing the day of
                 the week for the date expression passed to it.

                         1 = Sunday
                         2 = Monday
                         3 = Tuesday
                         4 = Wednesday
                         5 = Thursday
                         6 = Friday
                         7 = Saturday

Function: Standard.

Sample:
```
STORE DATE() TO indate
? DOW(indate)
```

DTOC()

Syntax: DTOC(< expd >)

Pass: < date expression >
Return: < character expression >

Description: The DTOC() function converts any date expression (field or vari-
                 able) to a character expression.

Function: Standard.

Sample:
```
STORE DTOC(DATE()) TO indate
CLEAR
a 10,10 SAY "Enter in the correct date: " ;
GET indate PICT "99/99/99"
READ
```

DTOS()

Syntax:	DTOS(< expD >)
Pass:	< date expression >
Return:	< character expression >
Description:	This function returns a string in year, month, day order.
Function:	Clipper enhanced.
Notes:	This function is extremely useful for indexing on dates plus character expressions.
Sample:	

```
STORE SUBSTR(DTOS(DATE()),1,4) TO in_year
STORE SUBSTR(DTOS(DATE()),5,2) TO in_month
STORE SUBSTR(DTOS(DATE()),7,2) TO in_day
? in_year
? in_month
? in_day
```

ELAPTIME()

Syntax:	ELAPTIME(< expC >, < expC >)
Pass:	< character expression >, < character expression >
Return:	< character expression >
Description:	This function returns a string which will show the difference between the starting time, the first < expC >, and the ending time, the second < expC >. If the starting time is greater than the ending time the function will assume that the day changed once.
Function:	Clipper simulated.
Autumn 86:	In order to use this function, the EXTENDDB.PRG file must be compiled and linked in with your application and must appear in your link list with all other .OBJ files.

EOF()

Syntax: EOF()

Pass: nothing
Return: < logical expression >

Description: The EOF() function determines if the End of File marker has been
               reached. If it has, the function will yield a logical true (.T.); other-
               wise, a logical false (.F.) will be returned.

Function: Standard.

Sample:
```
USE file      & Any standard .DBF file
GO BOTTOM
? "Have we reached the end of file marker?  "
?? IF(EOF(), "Yes", "No")
SKIP + 1
? "Now are we there?   "
?? IF(EOF(), "Yes", "No")
```

EMPTY()

Syntax: EMPTY(< exp >)

Pass: < expression >
Return: < logical expression >

Description: This function is used to test variables for an EMPTY condition.

Function: Clipper enhanced.

Notes: The following is a list of conditions for various types of variables that
               would yield a .T. if evaluated.

```
Character variable:   EMPTY() = .T.

                      IF variable = "" .OR.
                         variable = "        "

Numeric variable:     EMPTY()= .T.

                      IF variable = 0

Date variable:        EMPTY() = .T.

                      IF variable = CTOD("  /  /  ")

Logical variable:     EMPTY() = .T.

                      IF variable = .F.
```

EXP()

Syntax: EXP(<expN>)

Pass: <numeric expression>
Return: <numeric expression>

Description: The EXP() function returns the exponential of any given real num-
                 ber.

Function: Standard.

Variance: For a more accurate exponential of any number, the SET
                 DECIMAL TO command must be invoked to carry the results out
                 to the desired number of places. Remember that the default is 2.

                 In dBASE III, all that is needed to carry out the results is to pass a
                 number to the EXP() function with x number of places representing
                 the number of carried places.

                 Run the following example under dBASE III and Clipper and note
                 ahe difference.

Sample:
```
CLEAR
? EXP(1)
? EXP(1.000)
? EXP(1.000000)
SET DECIMAL TO 8
? EXP(1)
? EXP(1.000)
? EXP(1.000000)
```

FCOUNT()

Syntax: FCOUNT()

Pass: nothing
Return: <numeric expression>

Description: The FCOUNT() function returns the number of fields in the current
                 and active database. It is similar to the User Defined Function
                 named ENDFIELD() in Chapter 12.

Function: Clipper enhanced - Autumn '86.

Sample: USE History
                 FOR x = 1 TO FCOUNT()
                 ? FIELDNAME(x)
                 NEXT

FKLABEL()

Syntax: FKLABEL(< expN >)

Pass: < numeric expression >
Return: < character expression >

Description: This function returns the name assigned to the function key specified
                 by < expN >. If < expN > is less than 0 or greater than 40, a "[]" will
                 be returned.

Function: Clipper simulated.

Autumn 86:   In order to use this function, the EXTENDDB.PRG file must be
                 compiled and linked in with your application and must appear in
                 your link list with all other .OBJ files.

FKMAX()

Syntax: FKMAX()

Pass: nothing
Return: < numeric expression >

Description: This simulated function will always return 40, which is the number of
                 function keys available for the IBM PC/XT/AT.

Function: Clipper simulated.

Autumn 86:   In order to use this function, the EXTENDDB.PRG file must be
                 compiled and linked in with your application and must appear in
                 your link list with all other .OBJ files.

FIELDNAME()

Syntax: FIELDNAME(< expN >)

Pass: < numeric expression >
Return: < character expression >

Description: The FIELDNAME() function yields the name of the < expN > th
                    field within the currently active database. A null string is returned if
                    < expN > is greater than the number of the last field present.

Function: Clipper enhanced.

Sample:
```
* List names of the first six fields of the open
* database to the screen .
USE test
FOR x = 1 TO 6
   option = FIELDNAME(x)
   ? option
NEXT
```

FILE()

Syntax: FILE(< expC >)

Pass: < character expression >
Return: < logical expression >

Description: The FILE() function returns a logical true (.T.) if the given file name
                    exists on the default or specified drive/directory.

Function: Standard.

Sample:
```
STORE "C:" TO drive
? FILE(drive + "Employ.dbf")
? FILE("C:Employ.dbf")
STORE "A:Employee.dbf" TO file
? FILE(file)
```

FLOCK()

Syntax:	FLOCK()
Pass:	nothing
Return:	< logical expression >
Description:	This function returns a logical true (.T.) if a file lock is attempted and is successful. This function will also unlock all record locks placed by the same station while placing on the file lock.
Function:	Clipper enhanced - Autumn '86 only.
Autumn 86:	Network Environment function only.

FOUND()

Syntax:	FOUND()
Pass:	nothing
Return:	< logical expression >
Description:	The FOUND function is used to test if the previous SEEK, LOCATE, CONTINUE, or FIND was successful.
Function:	Clipper enhanced.
Notes:	Takes the place of setting logical variables if conditions were true and removes lines of code which otherwise would have to test for EOF() conditions.

Sample:

```
STORE "Los Angeles" TO temp_city
SEEK temp_city
IF FOUND()
  DO Edit_rec
ELSE
    @ 10,10 SAY "That city does not exist.  Please enter"
    @ 11,10 SAY "in database.  Any Key to Continue..."
    SET CONSOLE OFF
    WAIT
    SET CONSOLE ON
ENDIF
```

GETE()

Syntax: GETE(< expC >)

Pass: < character expression >
Return: < character expression >

Description: The GETE() function yields a string which is the value of the
                   environmental variable < expC >, stored at the DOS level with the
                   SET command.

Function: Clipper enhanced.

Autumn 86:   In order to use this function, the EXTENDC.OBJ file must be linked
                   in with your application and must appear in your link list after CLIP-
                   PER.LIB.

Note: With the Autumn '86 release, the allowed variable size for Clipper
                   programs can be checked with this function by issuing
                   GETE("CLIPPER"). If a null string is returned and there is not
                   enough room to run the application, a SET CLIPPER = vXXX may
                   be issued at the DOS level.

                   vXXX represents the allowed variable table size. XXX is the num-
                   ber of Kilobytes to be allowed. If none is issued, then 20 percent of
                   available memory will be allocated for the application, up to 44K
                   bytes. Each unique variable in an application will take up 22 bytes;
                   therefore, in applications with only 256 memory variables, the value
                   for XXX may be set to 006. If this is the case, 38K bytes will be saved
                   for the application.

HARDCR()

Syntax: HARDCR(< expC >)

Pass: < character expression >
Return: < character expression >

Description: This function replaces all soft carriage returns (CHR(141)) found in
                   the character expression with hard carriage returns (CHR(13)).

Function: Clipper enhanced - Autumn '86.

| Autumn 86: | In order for this function to work, the MEMO.LIB file must be linked in with your application. |

Sample: `? HARDCR(memostr)`

HEADER()

Syntax: HEADER()

Pass: nothing
Return: < numeric expression >

Description: The HEADER() function returns the number of bytes in the header of the currently active and selected database file.

Function: Clipper extended.

Autumn 86:   In order to use this function, the EXTENDC.OBJ file must be linked in with your application and must appear in your link list after CLIP-PER.LIB.

Notes: If used in conjunction with the RECCOUNT(), RECSIZE(), DISKSPACE() functions, this function may be useful for back-up/restoration routines.

IF()

Syntax: IF(< exp1 > , < exp2 > , < exp3 >)

Pass: < condition > , < expression > , < expression >
Return: < expression >

Description: This function is similar to dBASE III's imperative IIF function. This function returns < exp2 > if < exp1 > is true, or it returns < exp3 > if < exp1 > is false.

Function: Standard.

Notes: All three expressions are required and all three are evaluated. In other words, the IF() function **may not** be used in conjunction with a divide overflow situation. IF() may be used to prevent a value being divided by zero; i.e., IF(y = 0,0,x/y).

Sample:
```
STORE .T. TO dep_ded_fl  && dependent deduction flag
a 10,15 SAY "Deduct Dependents "
?? IF(dep_ded_fl, "Before", "After")
?? "Calculating Taxes"
```

INDEXKEY()

Syntax: INDEXKEY(<expN>)

Pass: <numeric expression>
Return: <character expression>

Description: This function returns the key expression of an active index file where
                 <expN> is the placement in the index list of that index file. If
                 <expN> is 0 (zero), the key of the current controlling index is
                 returned. A null string is returned if <expN> is greater than the
                 number of indexes in use.

Function: Clipper enhanced - Autumn '86.

Sample:
```
********************
* Name       INDEXKEY.prg
* Date       December 1, 1986
* Notice     Copyright 1986, Stephen J. Straley
* Note       This sample program demonstrates how the
*            INDEXKEY() function yields the index key
*            expression for the selected index file.
*
********************

    USE Client
    INDEX ON name TO client1
    INDEX ON phone TO client2
    INDEX ON location TO client3
    INDEX ON build_code TO client4
    INDEX ON acct_num TO client5

    USE Client INDEX Client1, Client2, Client3, Client4, Client5
    CLEAR
    FOR x = 1 TO 5
       ? "The index expression is: "
       ?? INDEXKEY(x)
    NEXT

    DO WHILE .T.
       store 1 to which
       a 10,10 SAY "Which index order? " GET which RANGE 0,5
       a 12,10 SAY "Enter 0 to Exit (or ESC key)"
       READ
```

```
                      IF EMPTY(which) .OR. LASTKEY() = 27
                         EXIT
                      ENDIF
                      SET ORDER TO which
                      @ 14,10 SAY "That key expression is set to: "
                      ?? INDEXKEY(0)
                      ?
                      WAIT "Press any key to try again..."
                      @ 10,00 CLEAR
                   ENDDO
                * End of File
```

INKEY()

Syntax: INKEY()

Pass: nothing
Return: < numeric expression >

Description: The INKEY() function allows direct input from the keyboard at
                specific times during an operation.

Function: Standard.

Notes: May be used for testing the cursor keys as well as the function keys.

Sample:
```
STORE 0 TO value
CLEAR
DO WHILE value = 0
   @ 10,10 SAY "Strike any key... "
   value = INKEY()
   IF value <> 0
      @ 15,10 SAY value
      STORE 0 TO value
   ENDIF
ENDDO
```

INKEY(0)

Syntax: INKEY(0)

Pass: < 0 >
Return: < numeric expression >

Description: This version of INKEY() is more like a WAIT command and
                returns the ASCII value of the key struck.

Function: Clipper enhanced.

Notes: The function remains in effect until a key is struck. Keep in mind
                   that with this variation the INKEY() function does not need to be
                   placed inside a loop in order to trap the keyboard input.

Sample:
```
CLEAR
STORE 0 TO value
DO WHILE .T.
   a 10,10 SAY "Strike any key... "
   value = INKEY(0)
   a 15,10 SAY value
ENDDO
```

INKEY(number)

Syntax: INKEY(expN)

Pass: < numeric expression >
Return: < numeric expression >

Description: With this variation, the function waits for < expN > seconds or any
                   keyboard input, whichever comes first, before continuing.

Function: Clipper enhanced.

Notes: This can be very useful for painting help screens and allotting a
                   specific time to wait for a specific key to continue.

Sample:
```
CLEAR
DO WHILE .T.
   a 10,10 SAY "Here is the first screen ... "
   a 12,10 SAY "This will wait for 10 seconds or until"
   a 13,10 SAY "the ESCAPE key is struck..."
   IF INKEY(10) = 27
      a 15,10 SAY "That routine has completed."
      WAIT
      CLEAR
   ENDIF
ENDDO
```

Inkey Values: Here are some of the INKEY() values of keys not necessarily ex-
                   pressed in the ASCII TABLE.

Key Pressed	Inkey Value	Key Pressed	Inkey Value	Key Pressed	Inkey Value
F1	28	Ctrl F1	- 20	Home	1
F2	- 1	Ctrl F2	- 21	Up Arrow	5
F3	- 2	Ctrl F3	- 22	Down Arrow	24
F4	- 3	Ctrl F4	- 23	Left Arrow	19
F5	- 4	Ctrl F5	- 24	Ctrl Home	29
F6	- 5	Ctrl F6	- 25	Ctrl Left Arrow	26
F7	- 6	Ctrl F7	- 26	Ctrl Right Arrow	2
F8	- 7	Ctrl F8	- 27	PrtSc	42
F9	- 8	Ctrl F9	- 28	Esc	27
F10	- 9	Ctrl F10	- 29	Ins	22
Shift F1	- 10	Alt F1	- 30	Space Bar	32
Shift F2	- 11	Alt F2	- 31	Tab	9
Shift F3	- 12	Alt F3	- 32	Del	7
Shift F4	- 13	Alt F4	- 33	Ctrl *	16
Shift F5	- 14	Alt F5	- 34	Back Tab	271
Shift F6	- 15	Alt F6	- 35	Ctrl Page Down	30
Shift F7	- 16	Alt F7	- 36	Ctrl Page Up	31
Shift F8	- 17	Alt F8	- 37	Cntl Scroll	3
Shift F9	- 18	Alt F9	- 38	-	45
Shift F10	- 19	Alt F10	- 39	+	43
End	6	Alt Right Arrow	6	Right Arrow	4
Ctrl End	23	Alt Page Down	3	Page Down	3
Enter	13	Alt Down Arrow	2	Page Up	18
Backspace	8	Alt End	1		

ISALPHA()

Syntax:	ISALPHA(< expC >)
Pass:	< character expression >
Return:	< logical expression >
Description:	This function returns a logical true (.T.) if the first character in < expC > is alphabetic.
Function:	Clipper simulated.
Autumn 86:	In order to use this function, the EXTENDDB.PRG file must be compiled and linked in with your application and must appear in your link list with all other .OBJ files.

Sample:

```
? ISALPHA("Yes")    && This would yield a .T.
? ISALPHA("212")    && This would yield a .F.
```

ISCOLOR()

Syntax:	ISLOWER(< expC >)
Pass:	nothing
Return:	< logical expression >

Description: This function returns a logical true (.T.) if a color graphics card has
                 been installed in the computer.

Function: Not standard prior to Autumn 86.

Sample:
```
IF ISCOLOR()
   SET COLOR TO R/B
ELSE
   SET COLOR TO U
ENDIF
```

ISLOWER()

Syntax: ISLOWER(< expC >)

Pass: < character expression >
Return: < logical expression >

Description: This function returns a logical true (.T.) if the first character in
                 < expC > is a lower-case alphabetic character.

Function: Clipper simulated.

Autumn 86:   In order to use this function, the EXTENDDB.PRG file must be
                 compiled and linked in with your application and must appear in
                 your link list with all other .OBJ files.

Sample:
```
? ISLOWER("Yes")    && Yields a .F.
? ISLOWER("212")    && Yields a .F.
? ISLOWER("no")     && Yields a .T.
```

ISPRINTER()

Syntax: ISPRINTER()

Pass: nothing
Return: < logical expression >

Description: This function yields a logical true (.T.) if a parallel printer is on line
                 and ready. Otherwise a logical false (.F.) is returned. This function
                 will not work with a serial printer.

Function: Clipper extended.

Autumn 86:   In order to use this function, the EXTENDA.OBJ file must be linked
             in with your application and must appear in your link list after CLIP-
             PER.LIB.

Sample:
```
IF !ISPRINTER()
   ? "Your Printer is not ready.  Any Key to Continue..."
   IF INKEY(0) = 0
   ENDIF
ENDIF
```

ISUPPER()

Syntax: ISUPPER(< expC >)

Pass: < character expression >
Return: < logical expression >

Description: This function returns a logical true (.T.) if the first character in
              < expC > is an upper-case alphabetic character.

Function: Clipper simulated.

Autumn 86:   In order to use this function, the EXTENDDB.PRG file must be
              compiled and linked in with your application and must appear in
              your link list with all other .OBJ files.

Sample:
```
? ISUPPER("Yes")   && Yields a .T.
? ISUPPER("212")   && Yields a .F.
? ISUPPER("no")    && Yields a .F.
```

LASTKEY()

Syntax: LASTKEY()

Pass: nothing
Return: < numeric expression >

Description: The LASTKEY() function returns a number representing the ASCII
              value of the last key pressed.

Function: Clipper enhanced.

Notes: This includes all control keys, and is helpful when used to determine
              how a READ was completed. Values of keys not in the ASCII table
              are listed in the INKEY() section above.

Sample:
```
USE File
FOR x = 1 TO 32
APPEND BLANK
NEXT
GO TOP
down = 1
DO WHILE .NOT. EOF()
    @ 5,1 SAY "Prompt Message " + LTRIM(STR(down)) + ;
         "-> " GET prompt PICT "XXXXXXXXXXXXXXXXXXXXXXXXXXXXXXXX"
    READ
    ****************************************************
    * If a Page Up key is pressed, then the previous
    * record is brought back and reentered
    *
    ****************************************************
    IF LASTKEY() = 18
      IF .NOT. BOF()
         down = down - 1
         SKIP - 1
      ENDIF
      LOOP
    ENDIF
    IF EMPTY(prompt) = 0 .OR. LASTKEY() = 27
      EXIT
    ENDIF
ENDDO
```

LASTREC()

Syntax: LASTREC()

Pass: nothing
Return: < numeric expression >

Description: The LASTREC() function returns the number of records present in
                 the active database.

Function: Clipper enhanced.

Notes: May be used in place of GO BOTTOM and STORing the RECNO()
                 of the database to a temporary memory variable.

                 It is not dependent on an INDEX file being opened.

Sample:
```
USE Test
? "The number of records on file is "
?? LASTREC()
GO BOTTOM
```

```
STORE RECNO() TO testing
IF testing = LASTREC()
    ? "It is equal to the last record number"
ELSE
    ? "It is NOT equal"
ENDIF
```

LEFT()

Syntax: LEFT(< expC >, < expN >)

Pass: < character expression >, < numeric expression >
Return: < character expression >

Description: This function returns the left-most < expN > characters of
                    < expC >.

Function: Clipper simulated.

Autumn 86:   In order to use this function, the EXTENDDB.PRG file must be
                    compiled and linked in with your application and must appear in
                    your link list with all other .OBJ files.

Sample: `? LEFT("This is a test", 4)   && This would yield 'This'`

LEN()

Syntax: LEN(< expC >)

Pass: < character expression >
Return: < numeric expression >

Description: The LEN() function returns the length of the string passed to it. If
                    < expC > is the name of an array, it returns the array length.

Function: Standard.

Sample:
```
STORE SPACE(20) TO name
CLEAR
@ 10,10 SAY "Enter a name: " GET name
READ
@ 12,10 SAY "You entered in "
?? LEN(name)
?? " characters..."
```

LENNUM()

Syntax: LENNUM(< expN >)

Pass: < numeric expression >
Return: < numeric expression >

Description: This function will yield the length of the given < expN >. It is useful
                 in determining relative column positions for numeric values.

Function: Clipper simulated.

Autumn 86:   In order to use this function, the EXTENDDB.PRG file must be
                 compiled and linked in with your application and must appear in
                 your link list with all other .OBJ files.

LUPDATE()

Syntax: LUPDATE()

Pass: nothing
Return: < date expression >

Description: This function returns the date DOS entered when the selected and
                 active database was last written to disk.

Function: Clipper extended.

Autumn 86:   In order to use this function, the EXTENDC.OBJ file must be linked
                 in with your application and must appear in your link list after CLIP-
                 PER.LIB.

Sample: USE Hist
                 ? LUPDATE()

LOG()

Syntax: LOG(< expN >)

Pass: < numeric expression >
Return: < numeric expression >

Description: The LOG() function returns the natural logarithm of the number
                passed to it.

Function: Standard.

Sample:
```
CLEAR
? LOG(2.72)
? LOG(EXP(1))
SET DECIMALS TO 8
? LOG(2.72)
? LOG(EXP(1))
? 1 = LOG(EXP(1))
```

LOWER()

Syntax: LOWER(< expC >)

Pass: < character expression >
Return: < character expression >

Description: The LOWER() function converts any character to its lower case rep-
                resentation.

Function: Standard.

Sample:
```
STORE "Clipper is 20 times FASTER than ....." TO show
CLEAR
? LOWER(show)
```

LTRIM()

Syntax: LTRIM(< expC >)

Pass: < character expression >
Return: < character expression >

Description: The LTRIM() function trims leading blanks from a character string.

Function: Standard.

Notes: This function is useful for formatting output in conjunction with
                numeric values and specific screen/printer formats.

Sample:

```
ə 10,10 SAY 1
ə 11,10 SAY STR(1)
ə 12,10 SAY LTRIM(STR(1))
? LEN(STR(1))
? LEN(LTRIM(STR(1)))
```

MEMOEDIT()

Syntax: MEMOEDIT(<expC>, <expN>,<expN>,<expN>,<expN>, [, <expL>])

Pass: <memo field> / <character expression>,<numeric expression>, <numeric expression>,<numeric expression>,<numeric expression> [, <logical expression>]

Return: <character expression>

Description: The MEMOEDIT() function expands the ability to edit a memo field or a character string. MEMOEDIT() is a function with its own built-in word processer. Additionally, the MEMOEDIT() function allows specific windowing areas to be partitioned for the edit.

The first parameter is the name of the memo field or the character string. The second, third, fourth, and fifth parameters provide the top, left, bottom, right coordinates of the window in which the edit will take place. The last parameter is an update flag. If the memo is to be edited, the flag should be set to TRUE; otherwise, to merely display the memo, the flag should be set to FALSE.

Function: Clipper enhanced.

Autumn 86:   If you are using this function with the Autumn '86 release, you must link in the MEMO.LIB with your application in your library list, after listing CLIPPER.LIB first.

Notes: MEMOEDIT() is a function and follows all standard conventions as such; therefore, it has a value and will need to be used accordingly.

The SET KEY TO and the KEYBOARD commands should not be used in conjunction with the MEMOEDIT() function.

For detailed information regarding memo fields and the MEMOEDIT() function, please refer to Chapter 7, Memo Fields.

Sample: REPLACE memo_fld WITH MEMOEDIT(memo_fld, 5, 20, 10, 60, .T.)

                                      or

                     IF "" = MEMOEDIT(memo_field, 5, 20, 10, 60, .F.)
                     ENDIF

                     Commands within Memoedit():

                     Cursor
                     Movement: Up one line.......................... ^E/Up Arrow
                                     Down one line...................... ^C/Down Arrow
                                     Left one character .... ^S/Left Arrow
                                     Right one character............... ^D/Right Arrow
                                     Left one word..................... ^A/^Left Arrow
                                     Right one word.................... ^F/^Right Arrow
                                     Beginning of current line .... HOME
                                     End of current line .... END
                                     Beginning of memo/string.................... ^HOME
                                     End of memo/string .... ^END
                                     Window Up .... PgUp
                                     Window Down .... PgDn
                                     Beginning of current window .... ^PgUp
                                     End of current window .... ^PgDn
                     Editing
                     Keys: Finish editing .... ^W
                                     Abort editing/keep old memo .... ESC
                                     Delete current line .... ^Y
                                     Delete word right .... ^T
                                     Reformat memo/string in window .... ^B

Addition: The MEMOEDIT() function will also scroll within a specific
                     windowed area, especially on one line. For example, if you want to
                     edit a field that is larger than a screen, try the following:

```
CLEAR
SET FUNCTION 10 TO CHR(23)
STORE "" TO test
@ 5,0 SAY "Enter:"
STORE MEMOEDIT(test,5,15,5,80,.T.) TO test
WAIT
CLEAR
test
```

                     With this, keep two things in mind:

                     1)   The arrow keys will work like PgUp / PgDn keys.

                     2)   HARDCR() or a User Defined Function to strip out soft
                          carriage returns (CHR(141)) is necessary if the output is
                          ever to be displayed **other than** by using the MEMOEDIT()
                          function.

MEMOREAD()

Syntax: MEMOREAD(<filename>)

Pass: < character expression >
Return: < character expression >

Description: This function retrieves the contents of <filename> from the disk.

Function: Clipper enhanced - Autumn '86 only.

Autumn 86:   When using this function, you must link in the MEMO.LIB library
                     file with the rest of your application and it must follow the CLIP-
                     PER.LIB in the link list.

Sample:
```
REPORT FORM Payhist TO FILE Outhist.txt
? MEMOREAD("Outhist.txt")
```

MEMORY(0)

Syntax: MEMORY(0)

Pass: 0
Return: < numeric expression >

Description: This function returns the amount of free memory in K bytes.

Function: Clipper enhanced - Autumn '86 only.

Sample:
```
IF MEMORY(0) < 60
   CLEAR
   ? "In order to run this application, you must have more
   ? "available memory.  Please check to see if there are any"
   ? "ram resident programs which can be removed."
   QUIT
ELSE
   DO Mainmenu
ENDIF
```

MEMOTRAN()

Syntax: MEMOTRAN(expC > [,hard-fix][, soft-fix])

Pass: < character expression > [, < character expression >] [, < character expression >]

Return: < character expression >

Description: This function returns < expC > with the hard carriage returns and/or the soft carriage returns replaced with a special value.

Hard Carriage Returns with Line Feed characters (CHR(13) + CHR(10)) will be replaced with a semicolon unless a different character is specified by the [hard-fix] option.

Soft Carriage Returns with Line Feed characters (CHR(141) + CHR(10)) will be replaced with a space unless a different character is specified by the [soft-fix] option.

To strip all formatting characters from a memo field or from a character string returned by the MEMOEDIT() function, a MEMOTRAN(string, " ", " ") may be used.

Function: Clipper enhanced - Autumn '86 only.

Autumn 86:   When using this function, you must link in the MEMO.LIB library file with the rest of your application and it must follow the CLIP-PER.LIB in the link list.

Sample:

```
newstring = MEMOTRAN(oldstr, CHR(252), CHR(251))
```

MEMOWRIT()

Syntax: MEMOWRIT(< filename >, < expC >)

Pass: < filename >, < character expression >

Return: < logical expression >

Description: This function writes < expC > to disk as < filename >. If no drive designator is given with < filename >, the currently logged in drive\directory will be assumed.

If the write operation to the disk is successful, then the function returns a logical true (.T.) value; otherwise, a false (.F.) will be returned.

Function: Clipper enhanced - Autumn '86 only.

Autumn 86:   When using this function, you must link in the MEMO.LIB library
                 file with the rest of your application and it must follow the CLIP-
                 PER.LIB in the link list.

Sample:
```
IF MEMOWRIT("C:Outfile.txt", newstring)
   WAIT "File has been written.  Any Key to continue."
ELSE
  WAIT "Write error.  Process aborted.  Any key to continue."
ENDIF
```

MOD()

Syntax: MOD(<expN>, <expN>)

Pass: <numeric expression>, <numeric expression>
Return: <numeric expression>

Description: This function returns the remainder of the first <expN> divided by
                 the second <expN>

Differences: Below is a list of numeric values passed to this function that yield a
                 different value from dBASE III.

```
Extended Clipper:          dBASE function:

 3 %  0 ::=  0.00         MOD( 3, 0) ::=  3
 3 % -2 ::=  1.00         MOD( 3,-2) ::= -1
-3 %  2 ::= -1.00         MOD(-3, 2) ::=  1
-3 %  0 ::=  0.00         MOD(-3, 0) ::= -3
-1 %  3 ::= -1.00         MOD(-1, 3) ::=  2
-2 %  3 ::= -2.00         MOD(-2, 3) ::=  1
 2 % -3 ::=  2.00         MOD( 2,-3) ::= -1
 1 % -3 ::=  1.00         MOD( 1,-3) ::= -2
```

Function: Clipper simulated.

Autumn 86:   In order to use this function, the EXTENDDB.PRG file must be
                 compiled and linked in with your application and must appear in
                 your link list with all other .OBJ files.

MONTH()

Syntax: MONTH(< expD >)

Pass: < date expression >
Return: < numeric expression >

Description: The MONTH() function returns a number that represents the month of the given date expression.

Function: Standard.

Sample:
```
CLEAR
? DATE()
? MONTH(DATE())
? 28 + MONTH(DATE())
```

NDX()

Syntax: NDX(< expN >)

Pass: < numeric expression >
Return: < character expression >

Description: This function just returns the < expN > string preceded by a "NTX".

Difference: In dBASE III, this function will actually return the name of the index file located in the < expN > th position in the index list.

Function: Clipper simulated.

Autumn 86:   In order to use this function, the EXTENDDB.PRG file must be compiled and linked in with your application and must appear in your link list with all other .OBJ files.

NETERR()

Syntax: NETERR()

Pass: nothing
Return: < logical expression >

Description: This function returns a logical true (.T.) if a USE, an APPEND

BLANK or a USE...EXCLUSIVE command is issued and fails in a network environment.

Function: Clipper enhanced - Autumn '86 only.

Autumn 86:   Network Environment function only.

NETNAME()

Syntax: NETNAME()

Pass: nothing
Return: < character expression >

Description: This function returns the text of the network station name in a 15 character string. If there is no network name, a null string is returned. In order to function properly, the IBM PC Local Area Network Program must be loaded.

Function: Clipper enhanced - Autumn '86 only.

Autumn 86:   Network Environment function only.

OS()

Syntax: OS()

Pass: nothing
Return: < character expression >

Description: The OS() function always returns "MS/PC-DOS".

Function: Clipper simulated.

Autumn 86:   In order to use this function, the EXTENDDB.PRG file must be compiled and linked in with your application and must appear in your link list with all other .OBJ files.

PCOL()

Syntax: PCOL()

Pass: nothing
Return: < numeric expression >

Description: The PCOL() function returns the current column position of the
                   print head on the printer.

Function: Standard.

Sample:
```
SET DEVICE TO PRINT
a 1,10 SAY "This is a test"
STORE PCOL() TO test
a 10,0 SAY "The previous line ended on column "
a 10,PCOL() + 1 SAY test
```

PCOUNT()

Syntax: PCOUNT()

Pass: nothing
Return: < numeric expression >

Description: This function returns the number of successful parameter matches
                   issued. It can be used to test if the parameter name is "U" (un-
                   defined).

Function: Clipper enhanced - Autumn '86 only.

Sample:
```
PARAMETERS a, b, c
DO CASE
CASE PCOUNT() = 3
? a
? b
? c
CASE PCOUNT() = 2
? a
? b
CASE PCOUNT() = 1
? a
OTHERWISE
? "No parameters were passed to this procedure/function"
ENDCASE
```

PROCLINE()

Syntax: PROCLINE()

Pass: nothing
Return: < numeric expression >

Description: This function returns the source code line number of the currently
                 running program or procedure.

Function: Clipper enhanced.

Notes: One warning with this function: the results may be unpredictable if
                 used in conjunction with source code compiled without line numbers
                 (the -l option on the compiler).

                 This function can be extremely useful when you want to trace flow of
                 operation through your program without the additional aid of
                 DEBUG.OBJ.

Sample: ```
                 ? "You are now at line "
                 ?? PROCLINE()
                 ?? " of your application"
                 ```

## PROCNAME()

Syntax:          PROCNAME()

Pass:            nothing
Return:          < expression string >

Description:     This function returns the name of the program or procedure current-
                 ly being executed.

Function:        Clipper enhanced.

Notes:           This function can be extremely useful in tracing the flow of opera-
                 tions through your program without the additional aid of
                 DEBUG.OBJ.  It also can add to your application if certain prompts
                 or messages are to appear in some areas and not in others.  The
                 name of the program/procedure may be tested and the prompt/
                 message may or may not appear accordingly.
                 ```

Sample:

```
IF PROCNAME() = "MAINMENU"
a 23,10 SAY "You are running in the Main Menu"
ELSE
a 23,10 SAY "You are NOT running in the Main Menu"
ENDIF
```

PROW()

Syntax: PROW()

Pass: nothing
Return: < numeric expression >

Description: The PROW() function returns the current row position of the print
               head on the printer.

Function: Standard.

Sample:
```
SET DEVICE TO PRINT
a 1,10 SAY "This is a test"
STORE PROW() TO test
a 10,0 SAY "The previous was printed on row "
a PROW(),PCOL() + 1 SAY test
```

READKEY()

Syntax: READKEY()

Pass: nothing
Return: < numeric expression >

Description: This function returns a number representing the key pressed to exit
               from any full-screen mode.

Differences: There are some differences in what dBASE III will return as a value
               and what this simulated function will return:

Exit Key:	dBASE:	Clipper:
Backspace	0	no exit
^D, ^L	1	no exit
Lt arrow	2	no exit
Rt arrow	3	no exit
Up arrow	4	no exit
Dn arrow	5	no exit
PgUp	6	18

PgDn	7	3
Esc, ^Q	12	27 (Esc only)
^End, ^W	14	23 (^W only)
type past end	15	ASCII of last char typed
Enter	15	13
^Home	33	no exit
^PgUp	34	no exit
^PgDn	35	no exit
F1	36	no exit

Function: Clipper simulated.

Autumn 86:   In order to use this function, the EXTENDDB.PRG file must be
                compiled and linked in with your application and must appear in
                your link list with all other .OBJ files.

READVAR()

Syntax: READVAR()

Pass: nothing
Return: < character expression >

Description: The READVAR() function returns the name of the variable pending
                in the current GET/MENU. If none is pending, a null string is
                returned.

Function: Clipper enhanced.

Notes: This function is used either in conjunction with Clipper's HELP fa-
                cility or a secondary procedure called by the SET KEY < expN >
                TO < procedure name >.

Sample:
```
CLEAR
STORE "Y" TO test
DO WHILE test = "Y"
  @  5,10 SAY "Please press F1"
  @ 10,10 SAY "Continue? (Y/N) " GET test ;
  PICT "!" VALID(test$"YN")
  READ
  @ 17,10 SAY "The current value is: "
  @ ROW(),COL() SAY READVAR()
ENDDO
```

```
********************

PROCEDURE Help

  PARAMETERS p,l,v

  @ 12,10 SAY "The help says the current value is: "
  @ ROW(),COL() SAY READVAR()
  WAIT
```

RECNO()

Syntax: RECNO()

Pass: nothing
Return: < numeric expression >

Description: The RECNO() function returns the position of the record pointer in
                   the currently selected area.

Function: Standard.

Notes: If the database is empty, RECNO() will return a value of 1.

Sample:
```
USE File
ZAP
? RECNO()                  && Will return a 1
? EOF()                    && Will return .T.
APPEND FROM Another        && Appending 10 records
GO TOP
SKIP + 5
? RECNO()
STORE RECNO() + 1 TO test
?
? "The next record will be record # " + STR(test)
```

RECSIZE()

Syntax: RECSIZE()

Pass: nothing
Return: < numeric expression >

Description: This function returns the number of bytes used by a single record in
                   the currently selected and active database file.

Function: Clipper extended.

Autumn 86:   In order to use this function, the EXTENDC.OBJ file must be linked
                 in with your application and must appear in your link list after CLIP-
                 PER.LIB.

REPLICATE()

Syntax: REPLICATE(< expC >, < expN >)

Pass: < character expression >, < numeric expression >
Return: < character expression >

Description: The REPLICATE() function returns a string composed of < expN >
                 repetitions of < expC >.

Function: Clipper enhanced.

Notes: Both parameters must be passed when calling this function and must
                 follow the format of a character followed by a number.

Sample: `@ 10,10 SAY REPLICATE("-",20)`

RIGHT()

Syntax: RIGHT(< expC >, < expN >)

Pass: < character expression >
Return: < numeric expression >

Description: The RIGHT() function returns the right-most < expN > characters
                 of < expC >.

Function: Clipper simulated

Autumn 86:   In order to use this function, the EXTENDDB.PRG file must be
                 compiled and linked in with your application and must appear in
                 your link list with all other .OBJ files.

Sample: `? RIGHT("Hello There", 5) + " it is"  && Yields 'There it is'`

RLOCK()

Syntax:	RLOCK()/LOCK()

Pass:	nothing
Return:	< logical expression >

Description: This function returns a logical true (.T.) on a successful attempt to lock a specific record in the currently active and selected file. This function will yield a false (.F.) if the file is currently locked or if the desired record is currently locked.

Function: Clipper enhanced - Autumn '86 only.

Autumn 86: Network Environment function only.

ROUND()

Syntax:	ROUND(< expN >, < expN >)

Pass:	< numeric expression >, < numeric expression >
Return:	< numeric expression >

Description: The ROUND() function rounds off the first < expN > to the number of decimal places specified by the second < expN >.

Function: Standard.

Sample:
```
? ROUND(12.422354, 2)    && prints 12.420000
? ROUND(164.23312, 3)    && prints 164.23300
```

ROW()

Syntax:	ROW()

Pass:	nothing
Return:	< numeric expression >

Description: The ROW() function returns the current cursor row location.

Function: Standard.

Sample: CLEAR
               a 10,10 SAY "Hello"
               ?? SPACE(10)
               ?? ROW()
               STORE ROW() + 10 TO down
               a down,10 SAY "Hello again..."

SECONDS()

Syntax: SECONDS()

Pass: nothing
Return: < numeric expression >

Description: The SECONDS() function returns a numeric value representing the
               number of seconds based on the current system time.

Function: Clipper enhanced.

Notes: The system time is considered to start at 0 (midnight) and continues
               up to 86399 seconds. The value of the expression is displayed in both
               seconds and hundreds of seconds. This function can be useful in
               maintaining time logs. (See DAYS().)

Sample: ? "We are currently "
               ?? SECONDS()
               ?? " seconds past midnight"

SECS()

Syntax: SECS(< expC >)

Pass: < character expression >
Return: < numeric expression >

Description: This function yields a numeric expression which is the number of sec-
               onds based on a time string given in < expC >. See SECONDS()
               above.

Function: Clipper simulated.

Autumn 86:   In order to use this function, the EXTENDDB.PRG file must be
               compiled and linked in with your application and must appear in
               your link list with all other .OBJ files.

SELECT()

Syntax: SELECT()

Pass: nothing
Return: < numeric expression >

Description: The SELECT() function returns the numeric value of the currently
                 selected area.

Function: Clipper enhanced.

Notes: If used in conjunction with user defined HELP system, the HELP
                 file can be placed in a separate database and toggled for use.

Sample:

```
********************
* Name            TEMPHELP.prg
* Date            August 6, 1986
* Notice          Copyright 1986, Stephen J. Straley
* Note            This program shows the SELECT() function
*                 in direct use.
*
********************

PARAMETERS p,l,v

IF p = "HELP" .OR. p = "VERIFY"
  RETURN
ENDIF

SAVE SCREEN
SET SCOREBOARD off
p = p + SPACE(10 - LEN(p))
v = v + SPACE(10 - LEN(v))
IF .NOT. FILE("HELP.DBF")
  @ 00,10,03,70 BOX scrframe
  @ 01,11 SAY "There is no HELP file available.   " + ;
              "Would you like a help "
  @ 02,27 SAY "file to be generated?"
  IF .NOT. VERIFY()
    RESTORE SCREEN
    RETURN
  ENDIF
  goback = SELECT()
  DO Dohelp
  tempgo = STR(goback)
  SELECT &tempgo
ENDIF

goback = SELECT()
```

```
SELECT 9
USE Help INDEX Help
SET FILTER TO search_p = p .AND. search_v = v
LOCATE FOR search_l = l
IF FOUND()
  ? helpscr
ELSE
  @ 23,10 SAY "Press Any key to Continue...."
ENDIF
qw = INKEY(0)
RESTORE SCREEN
tempgo = STR(goback)
SELECT &tempgo
RETURN
```

SETPRC()

Syntax: SETPRC(< expN > , < expN >)

Pass: < numeric expression > , < numeric expression >
Return: nothing

Description: This function sets the internal PROW() and PCOL() values to the
                   specified numeric expressions passed to this function. It is especially
                   useful when issuing printer control codes without altering the values
                   of PROW() or PCOL().

Function: Clipper enhanced - Autumn '86 only.

Autumn 86:   This version allows functions which perform operations to be called
                   without any other command syntax.

Sample:
```
new_row = PROW()
new_col = PCOL()
SET PRINT ON
?? CHR(15)        && Condense print for some printers.
SETPRC(new_row, new_col)
```

SOUNDEX()

Syntax: SOUNDEX(< expC >)

Pass: < character expression >
Return: < character expression >

Description:	This function yields a character expression that is derived from the given < expC >. This new < expC > will be a sound-like calculation based on the passed string. A code/simulation will be returned.
Function:	Clipper simulated.
Autumn 86:	In order to use this function, the EXTENDDB.PRG file must be compiled and linked in with your application and must appear in your link list with all other .OBJ files.

SPACE()

Syntax:	SPACE(< expN >)
Pass: Return:	< numeric expression > < character expression >
Description:	The SPACE() function generates a string consisting of < expN > blank spaces.
Function:	Standard.

Sample:

```
? LEN(SPACE(10))
? '"' + SPACE(10) + '"'
? LEN(TRIM(SPACE(10)))
```

SQRT()

Syntax:	SQRT(< expN >)
Pass: Return:	< numeric expression > < numeric expression >
Description:	The SQRT() function returns the square root of < expN >.
Function:	Standard.
Notes:	Clipper does not support the square root of a negative number. The results of SQRT() are restricted to the amount the SET DECIMALS TO command has been set to.

Sample:

```
CLEAR
? SQRT(4)
? SQRT(5)
```

```
SET DECIMAL TO 8
? SQRT(4)
? SQRT(5)
```

STR()

Syntax: STR(expN,[,<length>[,[decimals>]]])

Pass: <numeric expression>,<numeric expression>,<numeric expres-
                   sion>

Return: <character expression>

Description: This function converts any numeric expression (<expN>) into a
                   character string. The second parameter sets the length of the string,
                   and the third parameter sets the number of decimal places to be
                   included.

Function: Standard.

Notes: If the second and third parameters are not given, the function returns
                   a string with the length of 10, unless the number stipulated is longer
                   than 10 significant places with or without decimals. If the length of
                   10 is assumed, note that the string returned from the function will
                   have leading spaces.

Sample:
```
CLEAR
? STR(1)
? LEN(STR(1))
@ 10,10 SAY "|----|----|----|----|"
@ 11,10 SAY STR(1)
```

STRZERO()

Syntax: STRZERO(<expN> [, <expN> [, <expN>]])

Pass: <numeric expression> [,<numeric expression> [,<numeric ex-
                   pression>]]

Return: <character expression>

Description: This function returns a string based on the given <expN> with lead-
                   ing 0's instead of blank spaces. The second <expN>, which is op-
                   tional, is for the desired length of the returned <expC>. The third
                   <expN>, which is also optional, is for the number of decimals to be
                   included.

Function:	Clipper simulated.
Autumn 86:	In order to use this function, the EXTENDDB.PRG file must be compiled and linked in with your application and must appear in your link list with all other .OBJ files.

STUFF()

Syntax:	STUFF(< expC >, < expN >, < expN >, < expC >)
Pass:	< character expression >, < numeric expression >, < numeric expression >, < character expression >
Return:	< character expression >
Description:	This function returns a character expression of the first < expC > overlayed by the second < expC >, starting at the first < expN > character position and continuing on for the second < expN >.
Function:	Clipper simulated.
Autumn 86:	In order to use this function, the EXTENDDB.PRG file must be compiled and linked in with your application and must appear in your link list with all other .OBJ files.

SUBSTR()

Syntax:	SUBSTR(< expC >,< expN >[,< expN >])
Pass:	< character expression >,< numeric expression > [,< numeric expression >] >
Return:	< character expression >
Description:	The SUBSTR() function returns a character string composed of < expC >, starting at the position of the first < expN >, and continuing for a length of the second < expN > characters.
Function:	Standard.
Notes:	If the second numeric expression, which represents the number of characters to be returned, is left out, the SUBSTR() will continue its substring parse through the last character in the string.

Sample:
```
CLEAR
STORE "Dave    Bill    Jim     Stephen JenniferAl      " TO a
STORE 1 TO pass
DO WHILE pass <> 7
  ?  "-> "
  ?? SUBSTR(a,pass * 8 - 7,8)
  pass = pass + 1
ENDDO
```

TIME()

Syntax: TIME()

Pass: nothing
Return: < character expression >

Description: This function returns the system time represented as a character
                string.

Function: Standard.

Sample:
```
CLEAR
? TIME()
? SUBSTR(TIME(),1,2)
```

TRANSFORM()

Syntax: TRANSFORM(< exp >, < expC >)

Pass: < character expression > / < numeric expression >, < picture expres-
                sion >
Return: < character expression >

Description: This function returns < exp > in the format of the picture expression
                passed to the function as < expC >.

Function: Standard.

Notes: All picture options available in an @ ... SAY/GET command are
                also available with the TRANSFORM() function.

                The < exp > can be either a numeric expression or a character
                expression.

This function is extremely useful for formatting output to alternate files to appear as the output would look on the screen or printer.

Sample: `? TRANSFORM(3242312.23, "$ ###,###,###.##)`

TRIM()

Syntax: TRIM(< expC)

Pass: < character expression >
Return: < character expression >

Description: This function returns < expC > with any trailing blank spaces removed.

Function: Standard.

Sample:
```
STORE "This is a test         " TO test
? LEN(test)
? test + "to see where the end is."
? LEN(TRIM(test))
? TRIM(test) + "to see where the end is."
*
* And now for proper format...
*
? TRIM(test) + " " + "to see where the end is."
```

TSTRING()

Syntax: TSTRING(< expN >)

Pass: < numeric expression >
Return: < character expression >

Description: This function yields a time string of < expN > seconds.

Function: Clipper simulated

Autumn 86:   In order to use this function, the EXTENDDB.PRG file must be compiled and linked in with your application and must appear in your link list with all other .OBJ files.

TYPE()

Syntax:	TYPE(< expC >)
Pass:	< character expression >
Return:	< character expression >

Description: This function returns a single character code that indicates the data
type of < expC > as follows:

```
Character    =   C
Numeric      =   N
Date         =   D
Logical      =   L
Memo         =   M
Array        =   A
Undefined    =   U
```

Function: Standard.

Notes: This function is used to test the existence of a variable field or
expression.

              If an array subscript is passed to the function, it returns the code for
the type of that element.

Sample:
```
? TYPE("indate")
STORE DATE() TO indate
? TYPE("indate")
DECLARE indate[4]
? TYPE("indate")
? TYPE("indate[1]")
IF TYPE("outdate")="U"
   ? "outdate does not exist"
ELSE
   ? TYPE("outdate")
ENDIF
```

UPDATED()

Syntax:	UPDATED()
Pass:	nothing
Return:	< logical expression >

Description: This function tests if the last READ command changed any of the
data associated with the appropriate GETs. If so, this function
returns a logical true (.T.); otherwise, a false (.F.) is returned.

Function: Clipper enhanced.

Sample:

```
********************
* Name          UPSHOW.prg
* Date          August 6, 1986
* Notice        Copyright 1986, Stephen J. Straley
* Note          This program shows the use of the UPDATED()
*               function.
*
********************

CREATE Fire
USE Fire
APPEND BLANK
REPLACE field_name WITH "TEMP", field_type WITH "N"
REPLACE field_len WITH 10
USE
CREATE Ash FROM Fire
USE Ash
FOR x = 1 TO 30
   APPEND BLANK
   REPLACE temp WITH x
NEXT
STORE 1 TO whichone
DO WHILE .T.
CLEAR
   @ 10,20 SAY "Which Record to get ... " GET whichone RANGE 0,30
   READ
   IF whichone = 0
      EXIT
   ENDIF
   GO whichone
   @ 12,20 GET temp
 READ

   ****************************************************
   * The following is the actual demonstration of the *
   * use of the UPDATED() function.                    *
   ****************************************************

   IF UPDATED()
   @ 21,10 SAY "Now Indexing the File"
   INDEX ON temp TO Ash
   ELSE
      @ 21,10 SAY "No need to index ... not updated..."
   ENDIF

   WAIT
ENDDO
ERASE Ash.dbf
ERASE Ash.ntx
ERASE Fire.dbf
```

UPPER()

Syntax: UPPER(< expC >)

Pass: < character expression >
Return: < character expression >

Description: This function converts < expC > to upper-case characters.

Function: Standard.

Sample: `? UPPER("Nothing like 20 times faster!!")`

VAL()

Syntax: VAL(< expC >)

Pass: < character expression >
Return: < numeric expression >

Description: This function converts any number previously defined as a character
                   expression (< expC >) into a numeric expression.

Function: Standard.

Notes: Any non-numeric character expression is evaluated as a zero (0). In
                   Clipper, the VAL() function will also display the decimal portion of
                   a number.

Sample: `? VAL("Clipper")`
                   `? VAL("390.9095")`
                   `? VAL("20")`

VERSION()

Syntax: VERSION()

Pass: nothing
Return: < character expression >

Description: This function always returns "Clipper, Autumn '86"

Function: Clipper simulated - Autumn '86 only.

Autumn 86:   In order to use this function, the EXTENDDB.PRG file must be
                    compiled and linked in with your application and must appear in
                    your link list with all other .OBJ files.

WORD()

Syntax: CALL < procedure > WITH WORD(< expN >)

Pass: < numeric expression >
Return: < character expression >

Description: This function converts a numeric parameter (< expN >), passed to a
                    CALLed routine/procedure, from a data type DOUBLE to a type
                    INT, thus reducing the CALLed routine's overhead.

Function: Clipper enhanced.

Notes: Keep in mind that if the value of < expN > does not fall within the
                    range of -32K to + 32K, then there is no need to pass a larger para-
                    meter. **Do not use** WORD() if the variable is beyond this range!

YEAR()

Syntax: YEAR(< expD >)

Pass: < date expression >
Return: < numeric expression >

Description: The YEAR() function returns the numeric value for the year in
                    < expD >.

Function: Standard.

Sample:
```
STORE DATE() TO indate
CLEAR
? YEAR(indate)
? YEAR(DATE() + 300)
```

CHAPTER SIX

Clipper Features, Utilities and Expansions

The following utility programs are provided with the Winter '85 version of the Clipper compiler:

CREATE.EXE: A program to create a dBASE III/Clipper compatible data-base (.DBF) file.

REPORT.EXE: A program to create a dBASE III/Clipper compatible form (.FRM) file.

LABEL.EXE: A program to create a dBASE III/Clipper compatible label (.LBL) file.

DEBUG.OBJ: An object file which can be linked with any application in order to help debug it.

ANSI.OBJ: An object file which can be linked with any application in order to allow the application to run with the ANSI driver. This includes any other screen driver provided which can be more machine specific (e.g. TIPRO.OBJ, WANG.OBJ, etc.).

EXTEND.*:   A group of files containing functions which extend Clipper's capabilities to include dBASE III Plus commands and facilities.

These utilities were created to assist application developers in design, creation, and execution. Each utility program can be given to any end user without royalty or obligation to the Nantucket Corporation.

Some utilities are designed strictly for the execution of the application; that is, some utility programs either assist the program in running or assist the developer in finding problems with the application. Other utilities prepare certain conditions prior to the execution of the application. Each utility program is fully outlined in the following pages and tips and hints on using them in the "real world" are included.

CREATE.EXE

Execution Syntax: CREATE < d:filename >

Notes: d: = drive and directory designator. If no drive designator is given, the current drive and directory is assumed.

                         < filename > = the name of the database file to be CREATED or MODIFY STRUCTUREd.

This program creates a new database file or modifies an existing database file with the specified field names, field lengths, field types, and field decimal places. The CREATE program is similar to the CREATE command in dBASE III's interactive mode. Prompts are issued throughout this program and on-line help is available at any time by striking the F1 key.

Field names can have any combination of up to ten characters with the following exceptions:

1) Spaces are not allowed in the middle of a field name.
2) Field names must start with an alphabetic character (A-Z, a-z).
3) Field names cannot contain hyphens.

Field types are represented by the following symbols:

1) C   Character type
2) N   Numeric type
3) L   Logical type
4) D   Date type
5) M   Memo type

Field lengths (decimals not included):

1) Character fields: 37343 characters in length.
2) Numeric fields: 15 characters in length.
3) Logical fields: 1 character in length.
4) Date field: 8 characters in length.
5) Memo field: 10 characters in length. (The memo file is dynamic: it will only increase as characters are added, not when blanks are APPENDed to the main file.)

Even with all of the information there are a few drawbacks in this version of the CREATE utility program:

1. The file extension **must** be a .DBF extension. This prevents the developer from adapting his or her own descriptive style for tagging files with anything other than the .DBF extension. A viable work around for this is to rename an existing file prior to running this program, then again rename the file after using CREATE.

2. The file extension can not be given as part of the parameter. Since the file must have a .DBF extension, just pass the root name as the parameter to CREATE.

3. Make a copy of the file if records are present and you are going to modify the structure of the database. As in dBASE II, the utility program will not append the records from the old database to the new database.

Comments: This utility program is helpful when creating a file for testing or for meeting urgent schedules. For any total application, the ability to create databases should be coded into the application. In most cases, the user should not have access to a program that can alter the structure of a database (especially when that program could eliminate the records). The CREATE command in the Clipper Syntax Command Library gives applications the ability to self-generate database structures, thereby removing any possible need for this utility program. For further information regarding CREATing databases within an application, please refer to the CREATE and the INDEX commands in Chapter 4, Compiling.

REPORT.EXE

Execution Syntax: REPORT < d:filename >

Notes: d: = drive or directory designator. If no drive designator is given, the current drive or directory will be assumed.

< filename > = the name of the file that the REPORT utility program will generate. This file will have a .FRM extension.

This utility program creates a fresh report form or modifies an existing report form. It does not react the same way as the report generator in dBASE III. Do not enter an extension, if any at all, other than the expected .FRM. If you were to type

```
C>REPORT Test.new
```

you would see the following:

```
Clipper(tm) REPORT Generator, Winter '85
Copyright (c) Nantucket Inc. 1985
Developed by: B. Russell / J. Rognerud

REPORT:  unable to open test.new.frm
```

After typing in the file name (in this case TEST), the following menu will appear:

```
Date: 04/21/86    Clipper(tm) Report Generator       New file:  TEST.frm

              P A G E   H E A D I N G:


        Enter page width.......... 80
        Enter left margin.........  8
        Enter right margin........  0
        Enter no. lines per page.. 58
        Double spaced report?.....  N
```

Under the title PAGE HEADING, a shaded area of four lines is provided for the actual heading for each page of the report. Under this are five parameters which can be changed for the report.

Warning: These five parameters are not maintained when modifying the report form. They are the default values and will always come up as such. If you change their values, make a note of them for future use.

After this page, a second screen of information is displayed:

```
Date: 04/21/86     Clipper(tm) Report Generator          New file:  TEST.frm

Group/subtotal on...........:


Summary report only? (Y/N) N             Eject after each subtotal? (Y/N) N

Group/subtotal heading......:

Subgroup/subsubtotal on.....:


Subgroup/subsubtotal heading
```

The information required is self-explanatory.

Warning: If a field is specified for a subtotal or a subsubtotal, that field must be spelled exactly as it is in the database the report is being designed for. Unlike the interpreter, REPORT does not have the capability to check the validity of a field's existence or spelling. If there is a misspelling or if there is no field with the specified name, a run-time error message will appear.

Finally, a third screen of information will appear. In this screen, each specific field to be included in the report must be entered. If TOTALS are to be included, answer **Y**.

Warning: Again, the field names are not checked with the database for their existence and spelling. If a field listed in the report is not in the database or is misspelled, a run-time error will occur. Also, the lengths of the fields are not compared. Verify the lengths entered with the actual lengths.

Feature: One important feature of this utility program is that user defined functions are allowed. However, as with fields, these functions must be defined somewhere within the application, otherwise a runtime error – "undefined symbol exists" – will appear.

Example:

Subgroup/subsubtotal on.....:MYORDER(last_name)

```
Date: 04/21/86    Clipper(tm) Report Generator        New file:  TEST.frm
                                                      Field:   1
```

```
CONTENTS:

                      # decimal places    0  Totals? (Y/N) N
```

```
HEADER:   1
          2
          3
          4
```

```
Width:  10
```

Comments: REPORT.EXE is a quick utility program with some major loopholes. It would not be a good idea to give this utility program to a user inexperienced with dBASE III's report utility or with your program because column lengths are not totaled as you enter each field and field specs are not compared to what is entered. If you use this utility, be very careful and cross-check everything **before** running the report in a compiled application.

LABEL.EXE

Execution Syntax: REPORT < d:filename >

Notes: d: = drive and directory designator. If no drive designator is given, the current drive and directory will be assumed.

                         < filename > = the name of the file that the LABEL utility program generates. This file will have a .LBL extension.

This utility program is designed to create label format files with a .LBL extension to be used in conjunction with the Clipper LABEL command. If no extension is provided, the utility program adds the proper extension. If an extension is provided other than the expected .LBL (e.g., TEST.NEW), the LABEL program will not execute and the following message will appear:

```
Clipper(tm) LABEL Generator, Winter '85
Copyright (c) Nantucket Inc. 1985
Developed by: B. Russell / J. Rognerud

LABEL: unable to open test.new.lbl
```

The first screen of the LABEL program looks something like this:

```
Date: 04/21/85        Clipper(tm) Label Generator        New file: TEST.lbl



              Enter width of label              35
              Enter height of label             5
              Enter left margin                 0
              Enter lines between labels        1
              Enter spaces between labels       0
              Enter number of labels across     1
```

Comments: The six parameters above can be changed, and are saved with the file
                 (unlike the REPORT.EXE utility program).

Immediately following this screen, the final screen appears:

```
Date: 04/21/85          Label Contents:              New file: test.lbl



        1
        2
        3
        4
        5
```

If the height of the label, for example, is changed to 2, then only 2 lines will appear on
the second screen. A maximum of 6 lines are allowed.

Warning: Do not misspell the names of the fields to be used with the label file
                 or use a field not associated with the selected database file at execu-
                 tion. If so, a run-time error appears.

Feature: User defined functions are allowed in conjunction with the LABEL
                 file.

                 Example:

```
                    Label Contents:

        1       CENTR(address_1)
        2       CENTR(address_2)
        3       CENTR(city)
        4       CENTR(state + "    " + zip)
        5
```

Comments: The LABEL.EXE utility program is perhaps the simplest utility pro-
                 gram to use; however, it should not fall into the hands of an inex-

perienced user. Misspellings and nonexistent fields will prove to be fatal. The developer should be in control of all output as well as all input. However, for quick labels without the aid of dBASE III, this utility program does the job.

DEBUG.OBJ

Overview

One of the most difficult tasks in developing any application is making code error-free. Even when applications work under the interpreter there can be a hitch or two under the compiler. Error-free code on the first try is largely a fantasy. Invariably, bugs creep into code. The simplest bug is often the most difficult to locate. As a result, you should develop standard techniques that help you search for bugs. Techniques that work in interpretive environments may not be practical with compilers because of the need to recompile, re-link, and try again.

Clipper has several commands that provide additional information and insight as an application runs. A small front end module that can be invoked to test for certain conditions is necessary. This is precisely the function DEBUG.OBJ provides.

The Debugger

Make sure that the DEBUG.OBJ you are going to use is the correct debugger for the version of Clipper are using. For the Winter '85 release, the proper DEBUG.OBJ file has a date stamp of 1-28-86 and a time stamp of 3:30a. Contrary to what the manual and documentation that comes with Clipper might say, the file DEBUG.OBJ is already an object file. This file is just like all other object files generated by the compiler; therefore, all that you need to do is link the file with all your other object files. For example, to use PLINK86 with a LiNK file an extra command line (e.g., FI < \directory\DEBUG >) would be necessary in order for DEBUG to be present in your application. Running PLINK86 interactively, your screen should look like this:

```
C>plink86
PSA Linkage Editor (Nantucket Clipper) Version 1.46.c
Copyright (C) 1984 by Phoenix Software Associates Ltd.

=>fi cmenu
=>fi \dbase\debug
=>lib \dbase\clipper
=>;
```

If you prefer the MicroSoft Linker or DOS linker, the syntax is:

```
C>link
```

The following would then appear and you would enter the appropriate data:

```
Microsoft (R) 8086 Object Linker  Version 3.05
Copyright (C) Microsoft Corp 1983, 1984, 1985.  All rights reserved.

Object Modules [.OBJ]: cmenu \dbase\debug
Run File [CMENU.EXE]:
List File [NUL.MAP]:
Libraries [.LIB]: \dbase\/se:1024,,
```

or

```
C>link

IBM Personal Computer Linker
Version 2.20 (C)Copyright IBM Corp 1981, 1982, 1983, 1984

Object Modules [.OBJ]: cmenu \dbase\debug
Run File [CMENU.EXE]:
List File [NUL.MAP]:
Libraries [.LIB]: \dbase
```

The Can Do's and Can't Do's of DEBUG.OBJ

Before the DEBUG.OBJ command list is described in detail you need to know what you can and cannot do with the debugger:

1) You can view and change memory variables.
2) You can display all SETs.
3) You can continue execution or step through the application line-by-line.
4) You can establish specific breakpoints within the application which, when reached, will invoke the debugger.
5) You can evaluate expressions.
6) You can clear the screen.
7) You can trace all calling programs by name and by line number.
8) Depending on memory, you can leave the program temporarily and go to DOS.
9) You can direct output to the printer.
10) You can stop the debugger from fixing code automatically.
11) You can prevent the DISPLAY STATUS function for selected database or index files.

Using DEBUG.OBJ

You also need to know where to place the DEBUG object file in the listing of files and how to compile programs that are to be linked with the DEBUG.OBJ file:

1. The DEBUG object file

    a) must be located in the main load module area (if using overlays) and not in an overlay (BEGINAREA...ENDAREA), and

    b) must not be the first file listed in your link list: the name of your program must be first.

2. **Do not** compile any program/module using the -l option (omit line numbers) if the debugger is to be used with those program/modules.

Once the debugger is linked in and you begin to execute your application, the first thing you will see is the debugger's message on the top line of your screen:

```
proc:CMENU line:1  ([F1]-help,B,C,D,E,G,L,M,P,Q,R,S,T,V):
```

You can manually invoke the debugger at any time (without using the breakpoint scheme) by striking ALT-D. Even if an error occurs and the run-time message (Q/A/I) appears, the debugger can still be invoked by striking ALT-D a couple of times (or first type the letter "I", to ignore).

The Debug Commands

Press:	Command:	Description:
G	Go	Continues execution of the program.
S	Single-step	Continues execution up to the next source line.
B	Breakpoint	For breakpoint 0, specifies a conditional expression. With 1 to 9, specifies a procedure and line number. The default procedure is the current one and line numbers must match lines with commands (not blank lines).
Q	Quit	Stops execution, closes files, and returns to the system.

V	Variable Value	Enters the name of a memory variable. If it does not exist, a new PRIVATE is created. Its value is displayed and a new value is requested. Press < RETURN > to keep the old value.
R	Run	Runs a program from DOS.
T	Trace	Displays the names and line numbers of the procedures called to reach the current program line.
D	Display Status	Shows the status of the SET commands.
M	Memory Variables	Displays the PRIVATE memory variables for each procedure that has been called.
L	List Public	Lists all PUBLIC variables.
E	Expression Value	Enters an expression and prints its value.
P	Printer	Toggles PRINT ON and OFF.
C	Cls	Clears the screen.

CHAPTER SEVEN

Memo Fields

INTRODUCTION TO MEMO FIELDS

The basic concept of the memo field is to give the ability to enter string information relative to a specific record without increasing the size of the master database file every time a record is APPENDed. Memo files are *dynamic:* they grow only when something is added, not when the record is APPENDed. It would be very inefficient to allow a 4K character field to exist in a database, whether any information is there or not. It would be wasteful to use 4K for each record regardless of how much information is put in that field. For these reasons, memo fields are kept in a separate file.

This file has the same root name as the main database file but it has a .DBT file extension. In the main database, the memo field is ten characters in length and contains no more than a pointer tying that record to a record in the memo file. The memo file and fields are no more than an elongated string with a matching reference pointer.

Memo fields can be somewhat of a problem to work with in dBASE III. Many users ignored the word "memo" and treated the fields as description or short story fields. This use often pushed the product to its limit and invited disaster.

The memo field is just a note pad: a device by which short notes pertaining to a record can be added or viewed. One of the problems in dBASE III is that whenever a memo is worked on the entire screen is given over to the memo field. This visually defeats the concept of the memo. Additionally, it is extremely difficult to port outside information into a memo field, especially text information longer than 255 bytes. Also it is impossible to use string functions on a memo field. Sometimes a note is best placed in a short character field directly in the database.

Clipper provides solutions to all these memo field problems.

CLIPPER AND MEMO FIELDS

In Clipper, memos can look like text: a small bordered/windowed area on the screen that can suddenly appear and disappear as desired. Using memo fields in Clipper has many advantages including direct cursor addressing of the area for editing, extended storage capabilities, and the ability to store memo information to character fields as well as to memory variables.

Memos can be added to or replaced using strings in Clipper. If strings are to be removed from the memo fields, the memo fields must first be stored to a temporary variable, and then the appropriate string is removed with the use of the AT() function and the SUBSTR() function. Clipper also has a MEMOEDIT() function. This function partitions an area of the screen for the edit to take place in, passes the variable/field to be edited, and either allows you to edit it or simply view it. Six parameters are needed in order to make the function work:

```
MEMOEDIT(parameter1, parameter2, ... parameter6)
```

Parameter Description

1) The name of the memo field, variable, or character field

2) The row coordinate of the top of the window to be used for the memo

3) The column coordinate of the left side of the memo window

4) The row coordinate of the bottom of the memo window

5) The column coordinate of the right side of the memo window

6) A logical flag indicating whether the memo is to be edited or merely displayed (.T. allows editing, .F. allows viewing)

When using the MEMOEDIT function, several rules must be followed to maintain system integrity:

1. If using the MEMOEDIT() function in conjunction with a memory variable, first set the value of the variable to a null string ("").

2. If using the MEMOEDIT() function in conjunction with a character field, first TRIM() the field to a null string ("").

    If there are values present in either the variable or character field, first store them to a temporary variable and then wipe out the contents of the original variable or field with a null string. After the edit, add the temporary variable either to the beginning or to the end of the edited field or variable.

3. Do not allow the user to access HELP.PRG while using MEMOEDIT().

    To accomplish this, you **must** issue this command prior to calling the MEMOEDIT() function:

    SET KEY 28 TO

    This will turn the F1 key (INKEY() value of 28) off. Once the MEMOEDIT() function had been completed, reinstate help with the command:

    SET KEY 28 TO Help

    Keep in mind that the MEMOEDIT() function can be used inside HELP.PRG.

4. Never allow an active key to do a procedure while using the MEMOEDIT() function.

This is similar to rule number 3. Be sure to turn off any key that has been pre-viously SET to a procedure. To do this, issue the following:

```
SET KEY <expN> TO
```

Then when completed with the MEMOEDIT() function, reset the key by enter-ing:

```
SET KEY <expN> TO <procedure>
```

Again, the MEMOEDIT() function can be used within a procedure that was called by a key; however, all the rules still apply.

5.   Avoid using the KEYBOARD command when using an active and open MEMOEDIT() function.

Though rules 3, 4, and 5 may be violated and the routine can still work, I have included them based on input from many users. It's better to be safe and follow these guidelines.

DISPLAYING A MEMO

A memo field can be sent to the screen, the printer, or an ALTERNATE file. Showing a memo on the screen is simple, but the others are not so easy. Let's take a brief look at displaying memo fields.

The area parameters we define for the memo field at time of data entry are **not** permanent, but can be changed any time the MEMOEDIT() function is called.

Let's look at a specific example:

```
REPLACE memo_field WITH MEMOEDIT(memo_field,5,5,20,75,.T.)
```

Now we change it to the following:

```
REPLACE memo_field WITH MEMOEDIT(memo_field,5,15,20,70,.F.)
```

Because the last parameter in the second example is set to FALSE, the MEMOEDIT() function does not allow the memo field to be edited. However, what occurs is that the field is reformatted with the new border constraints. In order to ad-just to varying column positions and for word-wrapping, the MEMOEDIT() function places soft carriage return markers inside the field. When a border approaches the middle of a word, the MEMOEDIT() places a CHR(141), instead of the customary hard carriage return CHR(13), in front of the word to be wrapped, and continues. Using this high-bit graphic character allows the MEMOEDIT() to quickly reposition the contents to whatever row and column position is needed. The problem is that those high-bit characters remain inside the field. If we try to dump the contents directly out to the printer or to the screen by means other than the MEMOEDIT() function, we will be confronted with a startling discovery. This high-bit character plays havoc with form feeds and graphic characters on our printer. While these characters are not a problem for the screen, they can lock up the printer.

If we send the field contents to a file with the ALTERNATE command, we see all of the standard ASCII characters we typed into the memo field as well as all of the added CHR(141)s. The output problems remain both when using the MEMOEDIT() function and when not using it. We will discuss how to solve this problem later.

DISPLAYING MEMO FIELD CONTENTS USING MEMOEDIT()

Because MEMOEDIT() is a function, it returns a value that can be stored to a variable or to a field (e.g., STORE SUBSTR(a,1,3) TO x) or it can be tested for specific conditions (e.g., IF EOF()). It would be a waste to store the value of the memo field (via MEMOEDIT()) to a memory variable if it were never to be used as a variable.

Here is a way, using the MEMOEDIT() function, to print the memo field to the screen in the desired area without assigning the value of the function to a memory variable:

```
IF "" = MEMOEDIT(memo_field,5,5,20,75,.F.)
ENDIF
```

The function will be called first and with the .F. (FALSE) toggle, the memo field will be displayed in the given area. After expanding the MEMOEDIT() function, the value returned is actually the string of the memo field for the length of the given area. What occurs is that the memo field is displayed to the screen in the given area; after you leave the MEMOEDIT() function, the string is compared to a null string; since no other command is given within the IF...ENDIF command, the program flow continues.

Another major concern is how to treat a memo field which is larger than the prescribed window area on the screen. Because we used the FALSE operator, the cursor is not in the memo field area; hence, we can not page up or down within the MEMOEDIT() function. Only one full screen can be displayed. The answer to the problem lies **outside** the use of MEMOEDIT().

DISPLAYING MEMO FIELD CONTENTS WITHOUT USING MEMOEDIT()

In order to display a memo field larger than the screen, the MEMOEDIT() screen formatting high-order bit first must be stripped. The user defined function BIT-STRIP() will strip the field of these characters and replace them with hard carriage returns.

This function is discussed in a series of sample functions in Chapter 12, Designing User Defined Functions. The procedure below shows the problems that will occur if a memo field is directly displayed to the screen when it is larger than one specific screen.

```
********************
* Name          SHOWMEMO.prg
* Date          August 7, 1986
* Notice        copyright 1986, Stephen J. Straley
* Note          This shows some of the problems
*               encountered using the MEMOEDIT function and
*               large memo fields.
*
********************

STORE "Now is the time for all good men to come to the" TO mess
STORE mess + " aid of their country regardless of their" TO mess
STORE mess + " memo edit function --- or the word processor" TO   mess
STORE mess + " they happen to be using...." TO mess
CLEAR
@ 1,0 SAY "Now, here is the string for use..."
? mess
@ 7,0 SAY "Now here is a small screen of that...."
*********************************************************************
* The KEYBOARD() command shouldn't be used, but for demon-        *
* stration purposes, it becomes necessary!                       *
*********************************************************************
KEYBOARD CHR(23)
STORE MEMOEDIT(mess,18,20,20,60,.T.) TO mess
@ 24,0 SAY "Press Any Key to Continue..."
qw = INKEY(0)
@ 7,0 CLEAR
@ 7,0 SAY "Now here is the memo with the problems...."
? mess
@ 24,0 SAY "Press Any Key to Continue..."
qw = INKEY(0)
@ 15,0 CLEAR
@ 15,0 SAY "And here is the solution...."
? BITSTRIP(mess)
```

```
*********************

FUNCTION Bitstrip

   PARAMETERS c

   outstring = ""
   DO WHILE .NOT. EMPTY(c)
      IF AT(CHR(141),c) = 0
         outstring = outstring + SUBSTR(c, 1, LEN(c))
         c = ""
      ELSE
         outstring = outstring + SUBSTR(c, 1, AT(CHR(141), c) - 1) + CHR(13)
         scan = AT(CHR(141), c) + 1
         c = SUBSTR(c, scan, LEN(c) - scan + 1)
      ENDIF
   ENDDO
   RETURN(outstring)
* End of File.
```

WHEN TO USE MEMO FIELDS

Memo fields can be useful tools for such things as notes for salespeople regarding special orders, contextual HELP, or even basic text information. If you are going to use memo fields, code just for the compiler rather than trying to make your code fit both environments; it usually won't work. Be careful of memory usage. MEMOEDIT() is a memory-hungry function and saves the original memo field in memory as well as the edited version. For additional information on the use of the MEMOEDIT() function in an application, please review Chapter 13, The HELP Facility.

CHAPTER EIGHT

Clipper Procedures

A procedure is a set of commands that performs a specific task. In general, procedures are created and used for small routines an application does repeatedly. To avoid having to recode those routines, dBASE III allows the routines to be pulled out and labeled separately. Whenever the routine is needed, the program files need only DO the procedure, much like DOing any other ordinary program file. A group of procedures can reside together in what dBASE III terms a *procedure file*. This is the first real attempt to allow modular programming techniques within the dBASE III language.

Several benefits come from constructing procedure files. First, routines can be ported over from one application to the next, saving development time. Second, applications using well-developed procedure files become more polished and uniform in appearance. Finally, problems within procedures need only be corrected locally in order to cure system-wide dilemmas.

Clipper handles procedures somewhat differently, starting with the concept of the procedure itself. In Clipper, application code falls into one of two categories: *procedure* or *function*. If a routine **does** something, it is a procedure; if a routine has a **value**, then it is a function. Painting menu screens is a procedure, while converting a date to string representation is a function.

The more generic a procedure is (which normally means more parameter passing), the better it will be able to service an entire application as well as other programs. This can all be summed up in five rules covering procedures:

1.   There is no difference between a program and procedure.

     Clipper makes no distinction between a procedure and a program (.PRG) file. Technically, the compiler creates a symbol representing the name of a program file exactly as it does for a procedure.

2.   There are no separate procedure files.

     Clipper places all code in one executable (.EXE) file. There is no need to worry about whether a procedure file is open or not. There is also no limit on the level of DO statements.

3.   Procedure files cannot have the same name as a procedure being called.

4.   Procedures can call other procedures as well as themselves.

     This is commonly referred to as program recursion.

5.   Generalize to Utilize

     While procedures can be customized to closely fit a certain application, it is more practical to generalize procedures and have them react uniquely based on the parameters passed to them. By allowing for more parameter passing, applications can more strictly adhere to modular programming rules. The more modular the application, the easier it is to support, repair and change.

PROCEDURES IN CLIPPER

Program files should be short, concise, and to the point. They should call other routines that, when combined, perform the overall operation. Procedures that are specialized to a single or a few limited operations should reside within the calling file and should not be placed in a master library or procedure file.

As a matter of fact, the SET PROCEDURE TO < filename > command in a program signals the compiler to go out to the directory and find the designated file and compile it with the main application. After that point, the command is treated as a remark line and is totally ignored. Therefore, procedure files can be exclusively compiled and linked intact without the recourse to the SET PROCEDURE TO < filename > command.

Procedures files under Clipper should be structured generically. If a routine is generic enough to be used often, it warrants being placed in a master procedure library file. A master file is one large .PRG file with many procedures that, like functions, can be called upon to serve specific needs of an application. Be careful about what goes in that master library file. If a procedure is common to only a couple of routines, do not place it in the master library file. Actually, you may want to establish a primary procedure file and a secondary file and use the secondary file for those routines limited to a subset of procedures or program files.

Avoid placing a procedure at the end of a file if it is already at the end of another program file. Clipper won't have a problem compiling the procedures separately, but a DUPLICATE error message (Warning 11) will appear when linking the files together. To avoid this, map out which files will contain the procedures common for all or establish a secondary procedure file. Here is an illustration to help you understand this point.

Program Files:	Procedures:
A	F
B	G
C	H
D	I
E	J
	K
	L

For this example, let's say all the program files require procedures F, G, and H at some time; but files A, B and C also require procedures I, J, K, and L. Here are two possible ways of setting up the compilation:

Example 1:

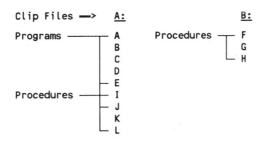

Compile @A, @B, @C

Linking A.OBJ + B.OBJ + C.OBJ + Clipper.lib = A.EXE

Example 2:

```
Clip Files ──>   A:                    B:
Programs ────────┬─ A     Procedures ──┬─ F
                 ├─ B                  │  G
                 ├─ C                  └─ H
                 ├─ D
                 ├─ E
Procedures ──────┼─ I
                 ├─ J
                 ├─ K
                 └─ L
```

Compile @A, @B

Linking A.OBJ + B.OBJ +.Clipper.lib = A.EXE

Example 1 has the advantage of having the second set of procedures (I,J,K, and L) in a secondary file for easy access and reference. The first set of procedures should always be in a separate file because they are our master procedure library file, a file we port from application to application. However, this approach generates a larger .EXE file size, as compared to Example 2, due to the additional object file for the linker to handle.

There are other approaches to this problem, but the main question is, which one is right? The answer depends upon the environment and the situation surrounding the application itself. On the surface, however, both are correct.

Consider the following pieces of code. Both procedures *do* the same thing; the difference is in the *way* they do it.

Sample 1:

```
********************
* Name       WHICHWY1.prg
* Date       August 7, 1986
* Notice     Copyright 1986, Stephen J. Straley
* Note       This demonstrates a specific procedure
*            approach.
*
********************

PARAMETERS screenprnt, outfile

    frame = CHR(201) + CHR(205) + CHR(201) + CHR(186) + CHR(188) + CHR(205) +;
            CHR(200) + CHR(186) + CHR(32)
    @  7,10,14,40 BOX frame
    @  9,15 PROMPT " 1>  Print to Screen "
    @ 10,15 PROMPT " 2>  Print to Printer "
    @ 11,15 PROMPT " 3>  Print to File "
    @ 12,15 PROMPT " 0>  or ESC to RETURN "
    MENU TO screenprnt

    DO CASE
    CASE screenprnt = 4 .OR. screenprnt = 0
       RETURN
    CASE screenprnt = 3
       @ 7,10,14,40 BOX frame
       @  9,15 SAY "Enter File Name..."
       @ 11,15 SAY "--> " GET outfile PICT "!!!!!!!!!!!!"
       READ
       IF LEN(TRIM(outfile)) = 0
          screenprnt = 1
       ELSE
          outfile = TRIM(outfile) + ".TXT"
       ENDIF
       * The two remaining options will be controlled by the
       * procedure calling WHICHWY1.
    ENDCASE
* End of File.
```

Sample Two:

```
********************
* Name       WHICHWY2.prg
* Date       August 7, 1986
* Notice     Copyright 1986, Stephen J. Straley
* Note       This demonstrates a general procedure
*            approach.
*
********************

PARAMETERS screenprnt, outfile, top, left

    frame = CHR(201) + CHR(205) + CHR(201) + CHR(186) + CHR(188) + CHR(205) +;
```

```
              CHR(200) + CHR(186) + CHR(32)
    @ top,left,top + 5, left + 40 BOX frame
    @ top + 1, left + 10 PROMPT " 1>  Print to Screen "
    @ top + 2, left + 10 PROMPT " 2>  Print to Printer "
    @ top + 3, left + 10 PROMPT " 3>  Print to File "
    @ top + 4, left + 10 SAY    "    ESC to RETURN"
    MENU TO screenprnt

    IF screenprnt = 3
       @ top + 1, left + 1, top + 4, left + 39 BOX SPACE(9)
       @ top + 1, left + 10 SAY "Enter File Name: "
       @ top + 3, left + 10 SAY "--> " GET outfile PICT "@!"
       READ
       screenprnt = IF(LEN(TRIM(screenprnt)) = 0, "", IF(AT(".",screenprnt) = ;
                       0, TRIM(SUBSTR(screenprnt,1,8)) + ".TXT", screenprnt))
          * the above line should be all on one line!
    ENDIF

    * Again, the first two options will be controlled by the
    * procedure calling WHICHWY2
  * End of File.
```

Notice the difference. By allowing the screen parameters to be passed in, the second sample procedure doesn't have to have the window in the same location every time it is called. Sometimes, the positioning of the BOX can overwrite an existing BOX or MENU. The first procedure would have to be recoded for every situation that needed different screen positioning. In the second procedure, the screen position can be controlled by the calling program. By adding just two parameters, we have made the specific procedure more generic.

In doing so, we have saved six lines of code. Multiply this number by the number of times another routine requires a different screen position and the savings go up tremendously.

The point to all of this is to get you to use a modular approach to programming. One way to accomplish this is by coding efficiently using parameter passing. As you code, ask yourself if you will be doing this procedure again in the application and if it will work the way it is currently coded. If not, add a parameter or two and watch your procedures assume a more modular and efficient style.

The last technique to master is *recursive program calling*. There is, however, a practical limit on the number of levels of DOs: the internal memory stack which manages the level of DOs is a finite size and can be corrupted by too many DOs being pushed onto the stack and not popped. Popping a DO is accomplished by the RETURN command.

In theory at least, procedures can "DO" themselves as many times as necessary. Again, the more generic the procedure, the more likelihood of this happening. When you can get your procedures to be so generic that they call themselves with *different results*, you are approaching the ultimate goal: concise, modular, efficient code.

Listed below is an example of embedding procedures at the end of a program file and using recursive program calling. Compile and execute it to learn more about embedded procedures and recursive procedure calling.

```
********************
* Name          REPEAT.prg
* Date          August 7, 1986
* Notice        copyright 1986, Stephen J. Straley
* Note          This program file shows:
*               a)  A procedure embedded in a program file
*               b)  Recursive procedure calling.
*
********************

SET SCORE OFF
CLEAR
STORE 0 TO times
@ 11,15 SAY "How many times do you want to pass through? " GET times ;
        PICT "###" RANGE 0,100
@ 13,26 SAY "0 to exit - Maximum is 100"
READ
IF times = 0
   @ 15,25 SAY "Exiting to operating system..."
   QUIT
ENDIF
@ 15,22 SAY "Press any key to begin processing..."
input = INKEY(0)
CLEAR
DO Recurse WITH (times)

********************

PROCEDURE Recurse

    PARAMETERS through

    ?? through
    ?? SPACE(5)
    through = through - 1
    IF through = 0
       ?
       ? "Press any key to go back..."
       input = INKEY(0)
       DO Repeat
    ELSE
       DO Recurse WITH (through)
    ENDIF
* End of File
```

Now, even though I showed this capability, keep in mind that with recursive procedure calling, the internal memory stack in Clipper is constantly pushed and never popped. Without returning to the preceding procedure in a normal fashion, a system memory fault will eventually appear and the application may crash.

It is important to remember to keep procedures small, direct, and simple. Huge program files are cumbersome. They should be broken up into several smaller procedures which collectively perform the same task.

PARAMETERS

Parameters Defined

A parameter is a set of one or more variables that is needed by the called procedure for the procedure to function properly. The parameters may be changed in value by the calling program or procedure and the new value passed to the called procedure. The called procedure will not run on its own because the value of the variable has not yet been established; that is the job of the calling procedure.

With proper parameter passing, procedures can be made more generic and thus more usable by other procedures. Assume, for example, that some data is to be displayed to the screen. This data must be displayed whether the operator is entering, scanning, editing, or deleting records. The small display is the same each time, yet it appears in different places on the screen depending upon the operation chosen by the operator. It would be foolish to recode this display four times, yet it is slightly different in each case. If we were to pass two parameters to a procedure, giving the row and the column at which we want the display to start, each operation could call the procedure with its own set of coordinates.

Under Clipper, parameters may be passed either by *reference* or by *value*.

Passing Parameters by Reference

Under most situations, parameters are passed by reference. The called procedure will refer to the parameter's value. In the compiler, a pointer to the address in memory that contains the value of the variable is passed to the called routine by the calling routine. This means that if the called procedure changes the value of the parameter, the address in memory which contains the variable's value is accessed and the data changed. The original value of that variable is lost. You should usually avoid using the PUBLIC command and initialize all variables in the top calling procedure file. This means that all variables can be referred to by the procedures below. This has the same effect as declaring the variables as public.

Even though a variable doesn't have to be passed to a specific procedure, if a lower procedure makes reference to a variable, that variable must be initialized at some prior point. Many times, however, for the sake of clarity, variables are renamed in subprocedures. In this case, the variable must be passed as a parameter by reference. Even though the variable name is different in the called procedure, the address of the original variable is maintained which allows changes to the original variable to be made.

In order to pass a parameter by reference, only the name of the variable has to be coded in the calling routine.

Passing Parameters by Value

Parameters can also be passed to a called routine by value. The actual value of the variable is passed to the subroutine, not the address at which the value resides. This means that a parameter's value can be changed within the called routine without altering the original value of the variable in the calling routine. Many times variables global to a system are needed to operate a procedure, such as screen painting. As the procedure performs the task (panning down the screen, for example), the value of the row position is altered. Upon completion, the procedure returns to the calling routine, where the original starting row position is preserved. This saves the few extra steps of saving the original value to another variable, altering the row variable, then restoring the row variable by storing the temporary variable to the row variable.

In order to pass a parameter to a routine by value only, the variable name must be placed within parentheses when it is passed by the calling routine.

Sample:

```
*********************
* Name           PARAM.prg
* Date           August 7, 1986
* Notice         copyright 1986, Stephen J. Straley
* Note           This program demonstrates differences in parameter
*                passing.  Involved are parameters passed by reference
*                and by value.
*
*********************

DO WHILE .T.
   STORE "Today is Sunny!" TO name
   STORE 1 TO y
   STORE "Y" TO option
   CLEAR
   @  2,20 SAY "Before the Routine"
   @  2,60 SAY "After the Routine"
   @  4,1 SAY "Name"
   @  4,20 SAY name
   @  6,1 SAY "Y"
   @  6,20 SAY y
   @ 20,10 SAY "Are you ready for the passing (Y/N)? " GET option ;
      PICT "!" VALID(option$"YN") *
   READ
   IF option = "N"
      QUIT
   ENDIF
   DO Sub_routin WITH (name), y
   @ 10,00 CLEAR
```

```
        @  4,60 SAY name
        @  6,60 SAY y
        @ 20,0 SAY "Press Any key when finished comparing..."
        qw = INKEY(0)
     ENDDO

     ********************

     PROCEDURE Sub_routin

        PARAMETERS a,b

        @ 20,0 CLEAR
        @ 10,10 SAY "   What do you want the NAME to be? " GET a
        READ
        @ 12,10 SAY "                        How about Y? " GET b
        READ
        @ 24,0 SAY "Press Any key to go back..."
        qw = INKEY(0)
     * End of File
```

Below is a sample program using arrays in parameter passing. If you do not have any experience in using arrays, you may want to read Chapter 11, Macros and Arrays, before studying the sample code below.

Sample:

```
        ********************
        * Name          PARA.prg
        * Date          August 7, 1986
        * Notice        copyright 1986, Stephen J. Straley
        * Note          This program demonstrates differences in parameter
        *               passing.  Involved are parameters passed by
        *               reference, by value, and arrays.
        *
        ********************
        DECLARE z[5]      && This is an array to be passed as a parameter
        FOR x = 1 TO 5
           STORE DATE() to z[x]
        NEXT
        DO WHILE .T.
           STORE " " to option
           STORE 1 TO x
           STORE "A" to y
           CLEAR
           @ 10,20 SAY "Before the Routine"
           @ 10,60 SAY "After the Routine"
           @ 12,1 SAY "X"
           @ 12,20 SAY x
           @ 14,1 SAY "Y"
           @ 14,20 SAY y
           FOR q = 1 TO 5
              @ 15+q,1 SAY "Date #"
```

```
        @ ROW(),COL() SAY q
        @ 15+q,20 SAY z[q]
    NEXT
    @ 5,10 SAY "Are you ready for the passing (Y/N)? " GET option ;
               PICT "!" VALID(option$"YN")
    READ
    IF option = "N"
       QUIT
    ENDIF
    DO Sub_routin WITH (x), y, "I am now here", z
    @ 12,60 SAY x
    @ 14,60 SAY y
    FOR q = 1 TO 5
       @ 15+q,60 SAY z[q]
    NEXT
    @ 24,0 SAY "Press Any key when finished comparing..."
    qw = INKEY(0)
ENDDO


********************

PROCEDURE Sub_routin

    PARAMETERS a,b,c,d

    SAVE SCREEN
    CLEAR
    @ 10,10 SAY "   What do you want X to be: " GET a
    READ
    @ 12,10 SAY "                 How about y? " GET b
    READ
    @ 14,10 SAY "     What about this string? " GET c
    READ
    @ 16,10 SAY "Enter into the array these -> "
    position = COL()
    FOR q = 1 TO 5
       @ 15 + q, position GET d[q]
       READ
    NEXT
    @ 24,0 SAY "Press Any key to go back..."
    qw = INKEY(0)
    RESTORE SCREEN
* End of File
```

An entire array can be passed as a parameter to another routine by just passing the
identifier, which is the array name without any subscripts. Please note that if this is
done the called routine has complete access to the array and can change values accordingly. Specific values in an array follow all other conventions described earlier.

Also, note that in this sample a literal was passed to the procedure which had no bear-
ing on the original routine. There are cases where this is extremely important. A
routine which prints a header, for example, needs only the name for the header. The

header can vary from routine to routine and does need not be placed in a variable and manipulated; in such a case just pass the string "as is" to the subroutine and print it.

A Final Thought

In all of this discussion there is one main point I have emphasized: modularizing. To take full advantage of Clipper's resources you must program in modules. Clipper allows programming methods to grow and develop. Procedures reduce entire applications to many single thoughts which, when combined, finish the application.

CHAPTER NINE

Extend Files

OVERVIEW

A few supplemental programs came with the Winter '85 release of Clipper. Among these programs are a few written by Tom Rettig which provide an expanded command set that emulates dBASE III Plus using User Defined Functions, written in dBASE, C and 8086 Assembler. These files are labeled with an EXTEND... beginning. Those UDFs written in dBASE syntax are located in Chapter 12, Designing User Defined Functions (UDFs). The functions are contained in the following files which came with your compiler:

EXTENDDB.prg	-	Functions in dBASE syntax
EXTENDA.asm	-	Functions in 8086 Assembler
EXTENDC.c	-	Functions in C
EXTEND.h	-	The header file for EXTENDC.c

Using these files increases the size of the executable file by less than 6,000 bytes. All of the added functions are listed at the end of this chapter.

EXTENDDB

This file has five sections: 1) functions which precisely emulate their dBASE III Plus counterparts; 2) dBASE III Plus functions which have embedded literal values or constants; 3) functions which are present in dBASE III Plus but with different names; 4) functions which do not exist in dBASE III Plus; and 5) functions which are EXTERNAL declarations for functions written in other languages that are linked separately.

EXTENDC.C

There is a module within Clipper that acts like an interface which allows some of the internal functions to be extended to the developer. In this group of files, there are three important files written in the C language:

EXTEND.C
EXTEND.H
EXTENDC.C

EXTENDC.C includes the section of the compiler's source code, in C, which contains the parameter passing function used by C programs that interface with normal Clipper applications. In EXTEND.C, the developer is allowed to write user defined functions in C and to interface with applications.

The second file, EXTEND.H, is a header file to be used when compiling EXTEND.C. This file takes care of constant definitions and variable declarations.

There is a specific convention used when writing code that interfaces with the library. All functions internal to the compiler begin with an underscore, such as in saving screens with _SAVESCR or restoring screens with _RESTSCR. Also, dBASE III functions are listed in upper case. In some cases, function names have been shortened in order not to conflict with key words in other languages, such as Lattice C.

PARAMETER PASSING

All parameters passed to a user defined function are tested by the _parinfo() function which returns the number of parameters passed. The syntax is _parinfo(n) where n is the number of parameters as it appears in the user defined function parameter list. EXTEND.H establishes several parameter check macros which are used for parameter checking in the IF statements in the EXTENDC.C file. The other "_par" functions are *type specific* and are used to place the incoming user defined function parameters appropriately in the *stack* internal to Clipper. For further information, please refer to the file entitled EXTEND.DOC on the same disk as the other EXTEND files. Each _par() function has an associated data type:

_parc()	=	character
_parl()	=	logical
_pards()	=	date (initially as string YYYYMMDD)
_parni()	=	numeric - integer
_parnl()	=	numeric - long
_parnd()	=	numeric - double

The functions beginning as "_ret" are functions for passing return values back to the compiler. One of these functions must be called prior to exiting from any C program in order to maintain the integrity of Clipper's internal stack.

_retc()	=	character
_retl()	=	logical
_retds()	=	date (initially as string YYYYMMDD)
_retni()	=	numeric from integer
_retnl()	=	numeric from long
_retnd()	=	numeric from double
_ret()	=	return to execution - no value passed

In order to maintain the stack with procedures that do not return a value, use the _ret() function.

EXTENDA.ASM

There are two basic functions in this file: ISCOLOR() and ISPRINTER(), neither of which requires a parameter. These functions have complete access to DOS, to the

BIOS, and to the Clipper library. The same functions used by the EXTENDC.C file are now called as procedures to return values.

_RETC	=	character
_RETL	=	logical
_RETDS	=	date (initially a string YYYYMMDD -- > date type)
_RETNI	=	word as numeric
_RETNL	=	double word as numeric
_RETND	=	floating point as numeric

The value returned is the first value PUSHed onto the stack before calling the return value procedure, which then places it on the internal stack of the compiler. _RET is not required, which means a FAR return is required in order to maintain system integrity.

If more user defined functions are added to the appropriate file, then you need the IBM Macro Assembler to produce a new object file from EXTENDA.ASM. For the EXTENDC.C file, you must have Lattice C (preferably a version prior to version 3.0) or a Lattice compatible version of C in order to produce a new object file. When using the Lattice compiler, three compiler options must be used: -ml, -v, and -n.

These symbols stand for the following: -ml = "large model"; -v = "no stack checking"; and -n = "greater than eight characters in identifiers".

The extended functions add great capabilities and power to all Clipper applications, but if you intend to add to or modify this extended library, you should have a sound understanding of both Assembly Language and Lattice C.

LIST OF FUNCTIONS IN THE EXTENDED LIBRARY

The following is a table listing of the functions provided by the extended library. An asterisk denotes that the function was implemented directly into the Autumn '86 release of Clipper. For a complete description of each of the functions, please refer to Chapter 5, Functions.

Function:	Description:
* ABS()	Returns absolute value of a number
* MAX()	Returns the higher of two numbers
* MIN()	Returns the lower of two numbers
ALLTRIM()	Trims leading and trailing blanks
AMPM()	Converts time to a 12-hour AM or PM format

DAYS()	Converts number of seconds into days
DBF()	Returns the name of the selected and open database
DISKSPACE()	Returns amount of remaining space on disk
ELAPTIME()	Calculates number of seconds between two time strings
FKLABEL()	Returns name of the <expN>th function key
FKMAX()	Returns 40, the number of function keys on an IBM XT
GETE()	Returns the environmental variables from operating system
HEADER()	Returns size of a database header
ISALPHA()	Determines if first character is alphabetic
ISCOLOR()	Determines if an active color card is found
ISPRINTER()	Determines if a parallel printer is on line and ready
ISUPPER()	Determines if first character is upper case
LEFT()	Selects the left-most portion of a string
LENNUM()	Calculates the length of <expN>
LUPDATE()	Determines the date of the last update of a database file
MOD()	Returns remainder of the first number divided by the second
NDX()	Returns the name of the index file in the <expN> position
OS()	Returns "MS/PC DOS"
RECSIZE()	Determines the size of a record in a database file
RIGHT()	Selects the right-most portion of a string
SECS()	Returns the number of seconds as a single numeric entity
SOUNDEX()	Creates a coded string which is based on a soundex algorithm
STRZERO()	Creates a string with leading zeros instead of blanks
STUFF()	Creates a string with a portion overlayed by a second string
TSTRING()	Creates a string based on a number of seconds
VERSION()	Returns the version of Clipper which contained this Extend library

CHAPTER TEN

Assembly and C Routines and the Call Command

THE CALL COMMAND

Clipper by itself can deal with most of the data management and screen handling situations you will face. There are, however, some tasks for which Clipper needs to use routines programmed in other languages. The CALL command allows you to program in C or in Assembler those routines the compiler is unable to handle directly. These routines then can be linked in with the rest of the application and CALLed as required. For details on the specific restrictions, please review the section on command syntax under CALL in Chapter Four, Commands.

Some sample programs written in other languages are listed below. These routines perform distinct tasks, normally machine-specific, that Clipper cannot handle. Each routine is defined, documented, and includes examples that demonstrate their use.

BOOT.ASM	This routine warm-boots the computer. This routine can be used to chain two large applications together through the use of the AUTOEXEC.BAT file.
LOCK.ASM	This routine checks if the insert, caps lock, scroll lock and num lock keys are on or off.
CURSOR.ASM	This routine toggles the cursor on and off.
DRSTATUS.ASM	This routine checks the status of a drive.
NODRIVES.ASM	This routine checks the number of drives in the system.
PRSTATUS.ASM	This routine checks the printer status.
DESCEND.C	This routine allows a descending index/sort to be performed.

BOOT.ASM

```
;--------------------
; Name         BOOT.asm
; Date         August 10, 1986
; Notice       Copyright 1986, Stephen J. Straley
; Note         Written in part by Fred Ho, this is the assembly
;              routine that reboots the computer upon command.
;
;
;--------------------

public  BOOTIT                          ; warm boot
;
_prog   segment byte                    ; byte aligned
```

```
        assume cs:_prog
        ;
        BOOTIT proc    far
               push    bp
               mov     bp,sp

               int     19h

               pop     bp
               ret
        BOOTIT endp
        ;
        _prog  ends
               end
        ;
        ;End of File
```

LOCK.ASM

```
        ;------------------
        ; Name          LOCKASM.asm
        ; Date          August 10, 1986
        ; Notice        Copyright 1986, Stephen J. Straley
        ; Note          Written in part by Fred Ho, this is to be used for
        ;               IBM PC's or absolutely 100% compatibles.
        ;
        ;
        ;               This routine checks the status of the four keys:
        ;               caps, insert, num lock, and scroll lock.  If the values
        ;               returned are in capital letters, the keys are ON,
        ;               otherwise, they are OFF.
        ;
        ;
        ;               Call LCKTAB with any 4 character field
        ;
        ;------------------


        ;
        public LCKSTAT
        ;
        datasg segment para    'DATA'

        LCKTAB db      'icnS'
               db      'icNs'
               db      'icNS'
               db      'iCns'
               db      'iCnS'
               db      'iCNs'
               db      'iCNS'
               db      'Icns'
               db      'IcNs'
               db      'IcNs'
               db      'IcNS'
               db      'ICns'
```

```
        db      'ICnS'
        db      'ICNs'
        db      'ICNs'
        db      'ICNS'
;
NUMB1   db      10h
FOUR    db      04h
;
datasg  ends
;
;

_prog   segment byte    ; byte aligned
assume  cs:_prog,ds:datasg,es:datasg
;
LCKSTAT proc    far
        push    bp
        mov     bp,sp
        push    ds
        push    es
        sub     ax,ax
        push    ax
        mov     ax,datasg
        mov     es,ax
        mov     ds,ax

        mov     ah,02
        int     16h
        xor     bx,bx
        mov     bl,al

        mov     ax,bx
        div     NUMB1
        lea     si,LCKTAB
        dec     al
        mul     FOUR
        add     si,ax
        cld
        les     di,[bp + 6]
        mov     cx,04
        rep     movsb

        stosb
        pop     ax
        pop     es
        pop     ds
        pop     bp
        ret
LCKSTAT endp
;
;
_prog   ends
        end
```

```
********************
* Name        PRNTLOCK.prg
* Date        August 10, 1986
* Notice      Copyright 1986, Stephen J. Straley
* Note        Uses an assembly routine to check to see if the insert,
*             the caps lock, the num lock, the scroll lock keys are
*             set on or off.
*
********************

a = "abcd"
DO WHILE .T.
   CLEAR
   CALL Lckstat WITH a
   ?
   ? "The INSERT KEY is set " + IF(ISUPPER(SUBSTR(a,1,1)), "ON", "OFF")
   ?
   ? "The CAPS LOCK KEY is set " + IF(ISUPPER(SUBSTR(a,2,1)), "ON", "OFF")
   ?
   ? "The NUM LOCK KEY is set " + IF(ISUPPER(SUBSTR(a,3,1)), "ON", "OFF")
   ?
   ? "The SCROLL LOCK KEY is set " + IF(ISUPPER(SUBSTR(a,4,1)), "ON", "OFF")
   ?
   ?
   WAIT
ENDDO


********************

FUNCTION Isupper

   PARAMETERS a

   RETURN a $ [ABCDEFGHIJKLMNOPQRSTUVWXYZ]
```

CURSOR.ASM

```
;--------------------
; Name        CURSOR.asm
; Date        August 10, 1986
; Notice      Copyright 1986, Stephen J. Straley
; Note        Written in part by David Dodson, this is to be used
;             for IBM PC's or 100% compatibles which allow direct video
;             mapping.
;             This routine acts as a toggle, for it will
;             turn the cursor on/off whenever called.
;
;--------------------
;
;
;
;
;--------------------
```

```
        PUBLIC  cursw
;
video           EQU     10h
curlin          EQU     01h
offlin          EQU     0FF00h
colcur          EQU     0A0Bh
eqpchk          EQU     11h
off             EQU     0FFh
on              EQU     00h
bw              EQU     30h
;
_PROG   SEGMENT BYTE
        ASSUME  CS:_PROG
;
cursw   PROC    FAR
        push    bp
        mov     bp,sp
        push    ds
        push    es
        cld
        cmp     byte ptr cs:[fstpas],0
        jnz     docurs
        mov     byte ptr cs:[fstpas],1
        int     eqpchk
        and     ax,bw
        cmp     ax,bw
        jnz     docurs
        mov     word ptr cs:[onlin],colcur
docurs:
        mov     ah,curlin
        lds     si,dword ptr [bp + 6]
        mov     bx,si
        push    cs
        pop     es
        mov     di,offset cs:oncmd
        mov     cx,3
        rep     cmpsb
        jnz     offtst
        mov     byte ptr cs:[curflg],off
        mov     cx,cs:[onlin]
        jmp     short curon
offtst:
        mov     si,bx
        mov     di,offset cs:offcmd
        mov     cx,4
        rep     cmpsb
        jnz     switch
        mov     byte ptr cs:[curflg],on
        mov     cx,offlin
        jmp     short curon
switch:
        mov     cx,cs:[onlin]
        cmp     byte ptr cs:[curflg],off
        jz      curon
        mov     cx,offlin
```

```
curon:
        int     video
        not     byte ptr cs:[curflg]
        pop     es
        pop     ds
        pop     bp
        ret
cursw   ENDP
;
curflg          DB      00h
fstpas          DB      00h
oncmd           DB      'ON',0
offcmd          DB      'OFF',0
onlin           DW      0707h
;
_PROG   ENDS
        END


; End of File
```

```
********************
* Name           SAMPCURS.prg
* Date           August 10, 1986
* Notice         Copyright 1986, Stephen J. Straley
* Note           This program, linked in with the CURSOR.obj file,
*                demonstrates how the cursor can be turned on/off.
*
********************

X = " "
DO WHILE x <> "X" .AND. x <> "x"
    CLEAR
    CALL CURSW
    WAIT "CURSOR IS NOW OFF...." TO x
    CALL CURSW
    WAIT "CURSOR IS NOW ON....." TO x
ENDDO
X = " "
DO WHILE x <> "X" .AND. x <> "x"
    CLEAR
    CALL CURSW WITH "OFF"
    WAIT "CURSOR OFF (WITH <param>)...." TO x
    CALL CURSW WITH "ON"
    WAIT "CURSOR ON (WITH <param>)....." TO x
ENDDO
* End of File
```

DRSTATUS.ASM

```
;------------------
; Name          DRSTATUS.asm
; Date          August 10, 1986
; Notice        Copyright 1986, Stephen J. Straley
; Note          Written in part by David Dodson, this is to be
;               used for IBM PC's or 100% compatibles
;
;               This routine needs a single byte parameter in
;               capital letters only, the drive designator. The returned
;               value follows the following format:
;
;
;
;
;
;             0 |     DRIVE READY - READ / WRITE
;             1 |     DRIVE READY - WRITE PROTECTED
;             2 |     DRIVE NOT READY - DOOR OPEN
;             3 |     DRIVE NOT READY - NON - DOS DISK
;             4 |     DRIVE NOT READY - MISC. ERROR
;
;------------------
;
PUBLIC  drstat
;
dskint          EQU     13h
read            EQU     02h
write           EQU     03h
dskrst          EQU     00h
wrprot          EQU     03h
door            EQU     80h
nondos          EQU     02h
;
_PROG   SEGMENT BYTE
        ASSUME  CS:_PROG
;
drstat  PROC    FAR
        push    bp
        mov     bp,sp
        push    es
        push    ds
        lds     si,dword ptr [bp + 6]
        push    cs
        pop     es
        mov     bx,offset cs:buffer
        lodsb
        sub     al,'A'
        mov     dl,al
        mov     dh,0
        mov     cx,1
        mov     al,1
        mov     ah,read
```

```
        int     dskint
        jc      error
        mov     ah,write
        mov     al,1
        int     dskint
        jc      error
        mov     al,'0'
        jmp     done
error:
        mov     al,'1'
        cmp     ah,wrprot
        jz      reset
        inc     al
        cmp     ah,door
        jz      reset
        inc     al
        cmp     ah,nondos
        jz      reset
        inc     al
reset:
        push    ax
        mov     ah,dskrst
        int     dskint
        pop     ax
done:
        les     di,dword ptr [bp + 10]
        stosb
        pop     ds
        pop     es
        pop     bp
        ret
drstat  ENDP
;
buffer  DB      1024 DUP(0)
;
_PROG   ENDS
        END
; End of File


********************
* Name       DRVESTAT.prg
* Date       August 10, 1986
* Notice     Copyright 1986, Stephen J. Straley
* Notes      This program shows the status of the disk drive.
*
********************

STORE " " TO x, st
CLEAR
DO WHILE UPPER(x) <> "X"
    IF ROW() > 20
        CLEAR
    ENDIF
```

```
          which = " "
          WAIT "Which drive? " TO which
          CALL DRSTAT WITH which, st
          DO CASE
          CASE st = "0"
             ?? " <= Drive is ready in READ/WRITE mode"
          CASE st = "1"
             ?? " <= Drive is ready, but is write protected"
          CASE st = "2"
             ?? " <= Drive is NOT ready, the door is open"
          CASE st = "3"
             ?? " <= Drive is NOT read, it is NOT a DOS disk"
          OTHERWISE
             ?? " <= Drive is NOT ready due to a miscellaneous error"
          ENDCASE
          ?
          WAIT "   ENTER X TO EXIT OR ANY OTHER KEY TO CONTINUE....  " TO x
          ?
       ENDDO
       * End of File
```

NODRIVES.ASM

```
;-------------------
; Name          NODRIVES.asm
; Date          August 10, 1986
; Notice        Copyright 1986, Stephen J. Straley
; Note          Written in part by David Dodson, this is to be
;               used for IBM PC's or 100% compatibles
;
;
;               This routine returns the number of logical drives available
;               on the machine in question.  Call with 2 byte string, returns
;               ASCII 2 digit value equal to the number of logical drives.
;               Use VAL() to convert to numeric.
;
;-------------------
;
PUBLIC   numdsk
;
dos            EQU      21h
seldsk         EQU      0Eh
curdsk         EQU      19h
;
_PROG    SEGMENT BYTE
         ASSUME   CS:_PROG
;
numdsk   PROC     FAR
         push     bp
         mov      bp,sp
         push     es
         cld
         les      di,dword ptr [bp + 6]
```

```
          mov      ah,curdsk
          int      dos
          mov      dl,al
          mov      ah,seldsk
          int      dos
          mov      ah,0
          aam
          add      ax,3030h
          xchg     ah,al
          stosw
          pop      es
          pop      bp
          ret
numdsk    ENDP
_PROG     ENDS
          END
; End of File
```

```
********************
* Name        NUMBDRVS.prg
* Date        August 10, 1986
* Notice      Copyright 1986, Stephen J. Straley
* Note        This program tests the number of drives available.
*
********************
```

```
ndrv = "  "
CALL NUMDSK WITH ndrv
n = VAL(ndrv)
? n
* End of File
```

PRSTATUS.ASM

```
;--------------------
; Name        PRSTATUS.asm
; Date        August 10, 1986
; Notice      Copyright 1986, Stephen J. Straley
; Note        Written in part by David Dodson, this is to be used
;             for IBM PC's or 100% compatibles.
;
;             This routine is to be CALLed to determine the current status
;             of the parallel printer on IBM compatibles. This routine is a
;             simple go or no go status report.  Its usefulness stems from
;             the fact that program termination to the operating system can
;             be avoided; i.e., instead of a DOS error message, provide
;             an internal program error message if the printer is not
;             available.  The program will then return to the
;             application instead of DOS.  Call with a single byte string
;             as a parameter. Returned in this string will be:
;
;
```

```
;                               0 = ON LINE, READY
;                               1 = PRINTER OFF LINE OR NOT READY
;
;               This routine assumes parallel port 1.
;
;------------------

PUBLIC  prstat
;
CHECK   EQU     2                       ; status check command
PNUM    EQU     0                       ; parallel port 1
PRNT    EQU     17h                     ; bios printer interrupt
REDY    EQU     90h                     ; printer ready
;
_PROG   SEGMENT BYTE
        ASSUME  CS:_PROG
;
prstat  PROC    FAR
        push    bp                      ; standard setup, param's
        mov     bp,sp                   ;
        push    es                      ;
        les     di,dword ptr [bp + 6]   ; address of return status byte
        mov     ah,CHECK                ; status check
        mov     dx,PNUM                 ; port 1
        int     PRNT                    ;
        mov     al,'0'                  ; returned if O.K.
        cmp     ah,REDY                 ; ready ?
        jz      done                    ; yes
        inc     al                      ; ascii 1
done:
        stosb                           ; place return byte
        pop     es                      ; restore state
        pop     bp                      ;
        ret
prstat  ENDP
_PROG   ENDS
        END
; End of File
```

```
********************
* Name         PRINTSTT.prg
* Date         August 10, 1986
* Notice       Copyright 1986, Stephen J. Straley
* Note         This program reports the status of the printer.
*
********************

STORE " " TO is_ready
CALL Prstat WITH is_ready
CLEAR
? "The printer is "
?? IF(is_ready = "0", "ready!", "not ready")
* End of File
```

DESCEND.C

```
/********************
* Name          DESCEND.C
* Date          August 10, 1986
*
* Note          Written in part by David Dodson; this C function is used
*               to "complement" a string, date, number or logical "value"
*
*               This must be compiled in Lattice C, version 2.15
*               (Do not use any higher version or any other C compiler)
*
*               This function allows Clipper indexes to be created in
*               descending order.  It can be used on any field type and
*               returns the same field type in a complemented form.  For
*               example, DESCEND(123.4 + 0) will return -123.4.  The function
*               does not alter the data base or numeric expression unless an
*               assignment is made by the user.  To use the function in an
*               index expression, use the following syntax:
*
*                      INDEX ON DESCEND(sales_date) TO date_dwn
*
*               To SEEK on the descending index use the following:
*
*                      SEEK DESCEND(find_date)
*
*     Warning!  If this function is used on a constant, it will
*               permanently alter that constant.  To ensure that you
*               are not using a constant, add (+"") to any constant
*               string, (+0) to any numeric constant and (.and. .T.)
*               to any logical constant.  Examples:
*
*       CORRECT                              INCORRECT
*
*       SEEK descend(123.4 + 0)              SEEK descend(123.4)
*       SEEK descend(.T. .and. .T.)          SEEK descend(.T.)
*       SEEK descend("California"+"")        SEEK descend("California")
*       SEEK descend(<fieldname>)
*       SEEK descend(<expression>)
*
*           NOTE:  number = 123.4
*                  SEEK descend(number)
*           is the same as the first INCORRECT example.  Use
*                  number = 123.4 + 0
*                  SEEK descend(number)
*
********************/

#include <extend.h>      /* included with your Clipper disks */

extern int *_tos;
```

```
descend()

{
    char *str;

    /*        Treat MEMO and CHARACTER types identically */
    switch (_parinfo(1))
    {
        case CHARACTER:
        case MEMO:
            /*        Get the pointer to the string */
            str = _parc(1);

            /*        Invert character bytes */
            while (*str)
            {
                *str = (char)(256 - *str);
                str++;
            }

            /*        Return the translated string */
            _retc(_parc(1));
            break;

        case DATE:
            /*        40903090 is the result of adding the numeric values of
                      the maximum and minimum dates   (12/31/2099) +
                      (01/01/1900) */

            _retnd((double)4903090.0 - _parnd(1));

            /*        Fudge data type */
            *_tos = DATE;
            break;

        case LOGICAL:
            _retl(!(_parl(1)));
            break;

        case NUMERIC:
            /*        Get the numeric value and rotate around 0 */
            _retnd(-(_parnd(1)));
            break;
    }
    return;
}
```

CHAPTER ELEVEN

Macros and Arrays

THE WORLD OF MACRO SUBSTITUTION

A macro is a symbol which tells the compiler to look for the associated definition for that symbol and to act upon those values accordingly.

Generally the programmer places a series of command verbs in a macro. When it is executed, the macro is expanded and the true representation of the macro is evaluated and executed. For example, a dBASE developer may program an application so that the user can choose which fields to LIST and the order in which they are to be LISTed. A simple LIST command followed by a macro (&) could refer to as few as one field or as many as all of the fields. In Clipper, this would have to be coded differently. Although macros have many advantages, there are restrictions on their use in the compiler environment.

SOME GUIDELINES FOR USING MACROS

1. Macros are allowed in DO WHILE...ENDDO and FOR...NEXT loops.

2. Macros can be used in conjunction with arrays.

3. Macros cannot contain any part of the syntactical structure of a command.

4. Macros can contain operators.

5. Macros can have up to sixteen parses.

MACROS IN A DO WHILE

The ability to have macro substitution in a DO WHILE...ENDDO loop, a valuable tool for programming introduced in dBASE II, was initially abandoned in dBASE III. The abandonment of this feature in dBASE III brought widespread disappointment. However, Clipper allows macro substitution in DO WHILE...ENDDO and in FOR... NEXT loops.

USING MACROS AND ARRAYS

With the advent of arrays in Clipper, macros assumed a new importance. Especially necessary for developing matrixes, macro substitution with arrays can build complex memory structures. Consider the following:

```
DECLARE database[15]
FOR x = 1 TO 15
   temp = LTRIM(STR(x))
```

```
* There will be a new array established for each database
* name present.  These new arrays (name1[], name2[], name3[],
* ... name15[] are built relating to each database
* (database[1], database[2], database[3], ... database[15].
* The macro varies as the loop executes, which in turn
* varies the name of the array.

  DECLARE name&temp[99]
  DECLARE type&temp[99]
  DECLARE len&temp[99]
  DECLARE dec&temp[99]
  DECLARE indx&temp[7]
NEXT
```

A series of arrays is established in this example, each with a unique root name with common numbered extensions and based on a main array. As the array named DATABASE pans down through its elements ([]), the corresponding subscript number is converted to a string and placed in a macro. This then points to the next appropriate array pertaining to that subscript number. Further information will be found later in this chapter in the section on arrays.

MACROS AND THE STRUCTURE OF A COMMAND

At compile time, the commands which are in a macro are not defined as such; the macro is defined, but not the contents. If, for example, a user is allowed to choose to LIST one field or five fields, the compiler must know in advance which case will occur, one field or five. Normally, the command structure looks like this:

```
STORE SPACE(40) TO list_input
@ 01,01 SAY "Enter Field to List: " GET list_input
READ
LIST &list_input
```

An interpreter finds this satisfactory, but a compiler does not. At the time of compiling, the macro has no value assigned to it. The value comes at run time. The compiler establishes a symbol which is referenced for expansion when the application is executed. So the compiler doesn't know whether one field is to be listed or five. When establishing the code for the LIST command, the compiler must know how many fields to list. This is determined by the comma, which in turn is part of the syntactical structure of the LIST command. In order to call upon the necessary library routines to make the command work, the compiler must have all of the necessary information before execution. Consider the following:

```
STORE "CLEAR" TO com_line
&com_line
```

The compiler has no problem with the first line. The string "CLEAR" is stored to the symbol defined as com_line. The compiler sees the second line as a macro expansion:

it establishes another symbol to hold the expanded value of com_line. The compiler does not know what command will be in the expanded macro; in this case what should be established is a symbol that will CLEAR the screen. To do this, the compiler has to interpret the previous command, which is what dBASE III does and which is precisely what slows down applications running under interpreters.

To sum up, remove command syntax from macros and, if applicable, establish multiple macros for the varying parts of the command. Otherwise, hard-code any commands that you might have put in a macro.

OPERATORS IN A MACRO

Even though command syntax is not legal in macros, operators are. Any mathematical operator (i.e. +, -, *, /) or logical operator (i.e. .OR., .NOT., .AND.) is not considered as part of the syntactical structure of the command and is allowed in a macro.

PARSING A MACRO

In the compiler, a macro is parsed into logical sections. Each section is then given a representing token (please see Chapter 2, Compiling) and is linked accordingly. In Clipper, macros may only be parsed sixteen times. If too many parses have occurred, the following error message will normally appear at the top of the screen when the application is executing:

```
MACRO EXPANSION ERROR
```

To avoid this, you should limit your macros to separate entities. However, it can be difficult to plan what is a separate entity and what is not. The basic rules are as follows:

1) Functions
2) Field / variable names
3) Mathematical operators
4) Conditional operators (.AND., .NOT., .OR.)

You can also get a Macro Expansion Error message if there isn't sufficient parsing of the macro, causing a problem with the macro syntax. For example:

```
STORE "LEN(TRIM(proc_name)) > 0 " TO show
STORE show + "row + col > 0" TO show
SET FILTER TO &show
GO TOP
LIST
```

This yields a Macro Expansion Error because there is no conditional operator either at the end of the first or the beginning of the second STORE TO command separating the two operations.

However, Macro Expansion Errors normally occur when too many parses (more than sixteen) have occurred on one macro. Consider the following:

Sample 1:

```
USE Multy
STORE "INT(RECNO()/2) = RECNO()/2 .AND. " TO show
STORE show + "(LEN(TRIM(proc_name)) > 0 .AND. top > 0 " TO show
STORE show + ".AND. left > 0 .AND. bottom > 0 .AND. " TO show
STORE show + "right > 0) .OR. (row_mess > 0 .AND. " TO show
STORE show + "col_mess > 0 .AND. row_esc > 0 .AND. " TO show
STORE show + "col_esc > 0) .OR.  (LEN(TRIM(STR(search))) > 0 " TO show
STORE show + ".AND.  LEN(TRIM(variable)) > 0)" TO show
SET FILTER TO &show
GO TOP
LIST
```

This extensive macro causes a Macro Expansion Error on the line with the SET FILTER TO command. The problem is that all the code in the macro is necessary for the application. If too much is being parsed, break the macro into separate macros, and use both macros on the SET FILTER TO command. Now consider the following variation on the above code fragment:

Sample 2:

```
USE Multy
STORE "INT(RECNO()/2) = RECNO()/2 .AND. " TO show1
STORE show1 + "(LEN(TRIM(proc_name)) > 0 .AND. top > 0 " TO show1
STORE show1 + ".AND. left > 0 .AND. bottom > 0 .AND. " TO show1

STORE "right > 0) .OR. (row_mess > 0 .AND. " TO show2
STORE show2 + "col_mess > 0 .AND. row_esc > 0 .AND. " TO show2
STORE show2 + "col_esc > 0) .OR.  (LEN(TRIM(STR(search))) > 0 " TO show2
STORE show2 + ".AND.  LEN(TRIM(variable)) > 0)" TO show2

SET FILTER TO &show1. &show2
GO TOP
LIST
```

In the first sample there were too many parses in one macro. In the second sample the macro was broken up into two separate macros. Remember that each macro can be parsed up to sixteen times.

The above guidelines may indicate that macros do not perform the same functions in the compiler as they do in the interpreter. That is not exactly the case, but it is true that programmers have to pay more attention to code structure when working with compilers than with interpreters.

If an application is "macro intensive", then look at how you use the macros before frustrating yourself with the compiler. If the syntax of command is spelled out as a literal and not in a macro, your chances for success are high. If you run into problems with macros and the way they are expanded, remember that there is always more than one way to code any given situation.

ARRAYS AND MATRIXES

An array is a database with only one field, held in memory. The name of the array is also the name of the field and the subscript is used as the record pointer. Before discussing the purpose and use of arrays, let's first examine the syntax used to declare an array in Clipper:

```
DECLARE array_name[x]

DECLARE: The Clipper command which initializes the array.

array_name: The name of the array; also known as the identifier.

[x]: The subscript; in a DECLARATION this sets the number of
     elements contained in the array.
```

The following guidelines pertaining to arrays will help in your planning:

1. An array without any elements takes up approximately 2K of memory space.

2. Each element in an array takes up additional memory space dependent on the size of that element type and whether or not it can fit in the pre-allocated space.

Date elements:	22 bytes
Logical elements:	22 bytes
Numeric elements:	22 bytes
Character elements:	22 bytes or the length of the string, if > 22 bytes.

3. Memo fields cannot be stored directly in arrays. Since the contents of a memo field are character data with a length dependent on the length of the string, a memo field can be stored first as a string variable and then placed in the array.

4. Arrays can contain mixed data types.

5. Arrays are always private.

6. Arrays cannot be SAVEd to memory files.

7. A memory variable assigned to the same name as an array destroys the array and all elements contained in it and also releases corresponding memory.

8. The TYPE(array_name) function returns an "A" representing the array if only the array name (without brackets) is used with this function.

    If specific elements are pointed to with the TYPE() function, such as TYPE(array_name[pointer]), the TYPE() function performs as expected on that element of the array.

9. The LEN(array_name) function returns the number of elements in the array if only the array name (without brackets) is used.

    If specific elements are pointed to with the LEN() function, such as LEN(array name[pointer]), the LEN() function performs as expected on that element of the array.

10. Macros can be used in conjunction with arrays; however, macros cannot be used to DECLARE the array if the command syntax is in the macro.

    Wrong:
    ```
    temp = "array_name[10]"
    DECLARE &temp
    ```

    Right:
    ```
    temp = "array_name"
    DECLARE &temp.[10]
    temp = "array_name[10]"
    STORE 1 TO &temp
    ? &temp
    ```

AN ILLUSTRATION OF AN ARRAY

The array automatically establishes 22 bytes per element. The full size of the array is dependent on the number of elements called for by the DECLARE command.

If, for example, 1000 elements are DECLAREd in an array named "legions", the actual size of legions[] is 22 bytes times 1000, or roughly 21.5K. If a string 30 characters long is stored in the array, then an address is stored that points to the actual position in memory. The array then indirectly consumes an additional 30 bytes for that string. This is what the code looks like:

```
STORE "HI" to temp
STORE 7 TO top
DECLARE legions[5]
STORE "This is a test" TO legions[1]
```

```
STORE .T. TO legions[2]
STORE 43 TO legions[3]
STORE CTOD("09/08/86") TO legions[4]
STORE "now is the time for all good men to come to the aid of ";
      TO legions[5]
```

Pre-Allocated Memory

```
Memvar  top        [7        ]
        temp       [HI       ]
        legions    [BDEFA    ] — which points to ⌐
                                                 │
       ┌─────────────────────────────────────────┘
       V
    [<------22 bytes------>]  BDEFA

    ["This is a test"......]  <- position 1
    [.T...................]  <- position 2
    [43...................]  <- position 3
    [09/08/86.............]  <- position 4
    [address A6EFF........]  <- position 5
                 │
                 │      which points in memory to that
                 │      address
                 V
A6EFF ["now is the time for all good men to come to the aid of "]
```

A SMALL SAMPLE

Let's say we wish to STORE 25 numbers to an array.

```
DECLARE choice[25]        && Line 1
FOR x = 1 TO 25           && Line 2
    choice[x] = x * 2     && Line 3
NEXT                      && Line 4
```

Line 1 establishes an array called choice[] which has 25 elements. Any previous memory variable or array with the name "choice" is destroyed. Immediately after the DECLARE command is the beginning of a FOR ... NEXT loop with 25 iterations, 1 through 25. Line 3, therefore, will be executed 25 times with the variable x incrementing by one on each pass. The value stored to the array at position x is 2 times x. The first pass points to the first position in the array and STOREs 2 to the array at position 1, the second pass STOREs 4 to the array at position 2, and so on until the 25th pass which STOREs 50 to the array at position 25.

ARRAYS AND PROCEDURES

Arrays, as well as specific elements in the array, can be passed to procedures. Since arrays are always private they must be passed to procedures by reference. This is done by passing only the array identifier or name to the procedure. Any change made to the array in the called procedure changes values in the array in the calling procedure. Specific elements in an array can be passed by value to a procedure as long as the subscript is used in conjunction with the identifier and the subscript points to the correct element in the array.

The following procedure demonstrates some of the many uses of an array as well as some of the functions (e.g., LEN() and TYPE()) that can be used on an array. It also shows how arrays are passed as parameters.

```
********************
* Name        SAMPARRY.prg
* Date        August 4, 1986
* Notice      Copyright 1986, Stephen J. Straley
* Note        This program initializes the months and the
*             days of the week to two memory variables and
*             passes them to procedures.
*
*******************

DECLARE month_a[12], day_a[7], date_a[50], numb_a[25], hodge_a[100]

****************************************
* The following initializes the arrays *
****************************************

FOR x = 1 TO 50
   DO CASE
      CASE x <= 7
         day_a[x]   = CDOW(DATE() + (1 *x))
         month_a[x] = CMONTH(DATE() + (30 * x))
         numb_a[x]  = x * 324
         date_a[x]  = DATE() + x * 84
      CASE x > 7 .AND. x <= 12
         month_a[x] = CMONTH(DATE() + (30 * x))
         numb_a[x]  = x * 324
         date_a[x]  = DATE() + x * 84
      CASE x > 12 .AND. x <= 25
         numb_a[x]  = x * 324
         date_a[x]  = DATE() + x * 84
      CASE x > 25
         date_a[x]  = DATE() + x * 84
   ENDCASE
NEXT
CLEAR
```

```
*****************************************************
* This section displays the values of the arrays *
*****************************************************

@ 01,05 SAY "Days of the week are ... "
FOR x = 1 TO 7
   ? day_a[x]
   hodge_a[x] = day_a[x]
NEXT
WAIT
CLEAR

@ 01,05 SAY "Months of the year are ... "
FOR x = 1 TO 12
   ? month_a[x]
   hodge_a[x + 7] = month_a[x]
NEXT
WAIT
CLEAR

STORE 1 TO temp_col
STORE 3 TO temp_row

@ 01,05 SAY "A random set of 25 numbers are ... "
FOR x = 1 TO 25
   @ temp_row, temp_col SAY numb_a[x]
   DO Chngescr
   hodge_a[x + 19] = numb_a[x]
NEXT
WAIT
CLEAR

STORE 1 TO temp_col
STORE 3 TO temp_row

@ 01,05 SAY "A random of 50 dates are ... "
FOR x = 1 TO 50
   @ temp_row, temp_col say date_a[x]
   DO Chngescr
   hodge_a[x + 44] = date_a[x]
NEXT
WAIT
CLEAR

STORE 1 TO temp_col
STORE 3 TO temp_row

@ 01,05 SAY "The total is ... "
FOR x = 1 TO 100
   @ temp_row, temp_col SAY hodge_a[x]
   DO Chngescr
NEXT
WAIT
CLEAR
```

```
**************************************************************
* The following displays information using the LEN() and *
* TYPE() functions.                                       *
**************************************************************

@ 10,15 SAY "The following will show the depth of each array ... "
@ 12,10 SAY "The number of elements in the Month Array   "
?? LEN(month_a)
@ 13,10 SAY "The number of elements in the Day Array      "
?? LEN(day_a)
@ 14,10 SAY "The number of elements in the Number Array  "
?? LEN(numb_a)
@ 15,10 SAY "The number of elements in the Date Array     "
?? LEN(date_a)
@ 16,10 SAY "The number of elements in Hodge Podge Array "
?? LEN(hodge_a)
@ 20,10 SAY "The type of the arrays are ...              "
?? TYPE("month_a")
WAIT
CLEAR
STORE "" TO in_temp

*****************************************************************
* This section passes an array element to a procedure by value *
*****************************************************************

DO Passarry WITH month_a[3]
@ 14,10 SAY "Month_a[3] is out of the procedure and equal to: "
@ 14,60 SAY month_a[3]
WAIT

**********************************************************
* This section passes the array element by value and *
* shows how to reassign the value back to the array. *
*                                                    *
**********************************************************

DO Passarry WITH month_a[3]
month_a[3] = in_temp
@ 14,10 SAY "Month_a[3] is out of the procedure and equal to: "
@ 14,60 SAY month_a[3]
WAIT

**********************************************************
* This section passes the entire array to a procedure by *
* reference.                                             *
**********************************************************

DO Anotarry WITH numb_a
CLEAR

STORE 3 TO temp_row
STORE 1 TO temp_col
```

```
@ 01,05 SAY "The numbers are now set to ... "
FOR x = 1 TO 25
   @ temp_row, temp_col SAY numb_a[x]
   DO Chngescr
NEXT

********************

PROCEDURE Passarry

   PARAMETERS in_val

   CLEAR
   @ 04,23 SAY "The value of the passed array is ... "
   @ 04,60 SAY in_val
   @ 06,23 SAY "Let us change the value ... " GET in_val
   READ
   @ 08,23 SAY "The new value is ... "
   @ 08,60 SAY in_val
   @ 10,20 SAY ""
   in_temp = in_val
   WAIT

********************

PROCEDURE Anotarry

   PARAMETERS b

   CLEAR
   temp_col = 1
   temp_row = 3
   @ 01,05 say "You may edit this Number Array ... "
   FOR x = 1 TO 25
      @ temp_row, temp_col GET b[x]
      DO Chngescr
   NEXT
   READ

********************

PROCEDURE Chngescr

   temp_col = temp_col + 15
   IF temp_col > 65
      temp_col = 1
      temp_row = temp_row + 1
   ENDIF
* End of File
```

ARRAYS AND MATRIXES

Arrays in Clipper are one-dimensional. In some languages, more than one subscript can be passed to the array, in which case it is referred to as a two-dimensional array or the beginnings of a matrix. A matrix is a multidimensional array in which the elements are interwoven and tied to one another.

To illustrate the structure of an array, let's say we want to establish up to ten individual databases, each with 99 possible field names, field types, field lengths, and, if applicable, field decimal places. The field descriptors must in some way relate to the appropriate database much like a relation established between databases. However, since this all needs to be entirely in memory, the SET RELATION TO command does not work. As each database is given a name, the pointer for that name must somehow refer to other arrays which will carry the detailed information; however, each detailed array has many pieces of information. In other languages, such as BASIC, the array declaration would look something like this:

```
DIM array_name(2,4)
```

This tells the computer that there will be 4 y elements for each element of x, and that there are 2 x elements. Somewhat graphically,

```
x        y
1        1,2,3,4
2        1,2,3,4
```

Since this is not legal in Clipper, we must somehow simulate it.

Simulating a Matrix: Part 1

The following procedures establish in memory 15 database structures including database names, field names, field type, their lengths, and the number of decimal places to be used. Only 99 field names, types, etc. are allowed due to memory restrictions. Users can employ this routine to create structures interactively without any other utility programs. This code demonstrates the use of arrays in conjunction with macros.

```
**********************
* Name        CREATEIT.prg
* Date        August 10, 1986
* Notice      Copyright 1986, Stephen J. Straley
* Note        This procedure creates several databases
*             in memory (15 maximum) as well as the structures
*             for each.  This is done using arrays and macros
*             to simulate matrixes.  Then the actual .DBF file
*             is written with the CREATEIT command.
*
**********************
```

```
SET CONFIRM ON
SET SCOREBOARD OFF
CLEAR
scrframe = CHR(201) + CHR(205) + CHR(187) + CHR(186) + ;
           CHR(188) + CHR(205) + CHR(200) + CHR(186) + CHR(32)
DECLARE database[15]
FOR x = 1 TO 15
   temp = LTRIM(STR(x))

   **********************************************************
   * Below, a separate array is created based on the       *
   * database[] array.  The idea is that as the pointer    *
   * in database[] advances, the subscript pointer         *
   * in essence points to the 4 arrays that contain the    *
   * detailed information on the database[] array.         *
   **********************************************************

   DECLARE name&temp[99], type&temp[99], len&temp[99], dec&temp[99]
NEXT
@ 0,0,23,79 BOX SUBSTR(scrframe,1,8)
@ 0,30 SAY " Create Databases "
FOR x = 1 TO 15
   STORE SPACE(12) TO database[x]
   @ 2,3 SAY "Enter Database Name: " GET database[x] PICT "@!"
   READ
   IF !EMPTY(database[x])
      temp = LTRIM(STR(x))
      trow = 8
      tcol = 0
      FOR y = 1 TO 99
         STORE SPACE(10) TO name&temp[y]
         STORE SPACE(1) TO type&temp[y]
         STORE 0 TO len&temp[y], dec&temp[y]
         @ 3,3 SAY "   Enter Field Name: " GET name&temp[y] PICT "@!"
         @ 4,3 SAY "               Type: " GET type&temp[y] PICT "!" ;
               VALID(type&temp[y]$"NCLDM ")
         @ 5,3 SAY "             Length: " GET len&temp[y] PICT "####" ;
               RANGE 0, 255
         @ 6,3 SAY "           Decimals: " GET dec&temp[y] PICT "##" ;
               RANGE 0,15
         READ
         IF EMPTY(name&temp[y])
            y = 100
         ELSE
            DO CASE
            CASE type&temp[y] = "D"
               len&temp[y] = 8
               dec&temp[y] = 0
            CASE type&temp[y] = "L"
               len&temp[y] = 1
               dec&temp[y] = 0
            CASE type&temp[y] = "M"
               len&temp[y] = 10
               dec&temp[y] = 0
```

```
                    CASE type&temp[y] = "N"
                        IF len&temp[y] > 15
                            len&temp[y] = 15
                        ENDIF
                    OTHERWISE
                        dec&temp[y] = 0
                    ENDCASE
                    IF trow > 22
                        trow = 8
                        FOR steve = 8 TO 22
                            @ steve,3 SAY SPACE(47)
                        NEXT
                    ENDIF
                    @ trow,5 SAY name&temp[y]
                    @ trow,COL() + 2 SAY type&temp[y]
                    @ trow,COL() + 2 SAY len&temp[y]
                    @ trow,COL() + 2 SAY dec&temp[y]
                    trow = trow + 1
                ENDIF
            NEXT
            FOR steve = 1 TO 22
                @ steve, 3 SAY SPACE(47)
            NEXT
            @ x, 52 SAY LTRIM(STR(x)) + "-> "
            @ x, COL() SAY database[x]
        ELSE
            x = 17
        ENDIF
    NEXT
    @ 0,0,23,79 BOX scrframe
    @ 10,26 SAY "Now Creating the Databases....."
    x = 1
    DO WHILE !EMPTY(database[x])
        z = LTRIM(STR(x))
        CREATE Temp
        USE Temp
        FOR y = 1 TO 99
            APPEND BLANK
            REPLACE field_name WITH name&z[y]
            REPLACE field_type WITH type&z[y]
            REPLACE field_len WITH len&z[y]
            REPLACE field_dec WITH dec&z[y]
            IF EMPTY(name&z[y+1])
                y = 100
            ENDIF
        NEXT
        USE
        temp_name = database[x]
        CREATE &temp_name FROM Temp
        ERASE Temp.dbf
        CLOSE DATABASES
        x = x + 1
    ENDDO
    CLEAR
    * End of File
```

Simulating a Matrix: Part 2

There is another way to simulate a matrix condition. Because an array can contain a mixture of any data types (except for the memo type), it is possible to write a user defined function that will take two numbers (the two numbers normally found in a matrix statement) and generate a single number that points to a position in a one-dimensional array that is **equivalent** to a given element from a two-dimensional array.

To better understand this technique, think of a card file in the library. Each file box (an array) has index cards (the x dimension) with several cards on individual books behind each of them (the y dimension). If every index card had the same number of book cards behind it, it would be simple to come up with a formula to tell the user what absolute position in the card file yields the *yth* card in the *xth* index.

The example DIMEN.PRG below is a simulation of this technique. Keep in mind that the formula for a three-dimensional array is similar to but more complex than that for a two-dimensional array.

```
********************
* Name          DIMEN.prg
* Date          August 10, 1986
* Notice        Copyright 1986, Stephen J. Straley
* Note          This program is designed to simulate a multidimensional
*               array construct using macros to simulate the condition.
*               A user defined function was created to point to the proper
*               position in the one-dimensional array.
*
********************
DO WHILE .T.
   STORE 0 TO x,y
   CLEAR
   @ 5,10 SAY "What is x range? " GET x PICT "###" RANGE 0,999
   @ 7,10 SAY "What is y range? " GET y PICT "###" RANGE 0,999
   READ
   IF EMPTY(x) .OR. EMPTY(y)
      EXIT
   ENDIF
   *********************************************
   *   The maximum number of elements in the   *
   *   array will always be the value of x      *
   *   times the value of y.                    *
   *********************************************
   DECLARE master[(x*y)]
   DECLARE names[x]
   FOR outside = 1 TO x
      STORE SPACE(30) TO names[outside]
      @ 10,10 SAY "Enter Name Number " + TRANSFORM(outside, "99") + ;
              " => " GET names[outside]
      READ
```

```
   *
   *  By TRANSFORMing the 'outside' variable, the user will know which
   *  subscript value he is working with while entering in information
   *
   FOR inside = 1 TO y
      ************************************************************
      *  outside is the current xth position while inside *
      *  is the current yth position.                     *
      ************************************************************
      STORE 0 TO master[DIM(outside, inside)]
      @ 11 + inside,10 SAY "Enter number: " ;
        GET master[DIM(outside, inside)]
      READ
   NEXT
   WAIT
   @ 10,0 CLEAR
NEXT
WAIT "Now for the list:"
@ 10,0 CLEAR
FOR outside = 1 TO x
   ? names[outside]
   ? SPACE(5)
   FOR inside = 1 TO y
      ?? master[DIM(outside, inside)]
   NEXT
NEXT
WAIT "This is it ..."
ENDDO


********************

FUNCTION Dim

   PARAMETERS a, b

   **********************************************************************
   *  a is only a private variable with the value of outside as passed *
   *  b is only a private variable with the value of inside as passed  *
   *  the y value is looked at publicly in order to determine the      *
   *  limits of the calculations.  Otherwise, the y value would        *
   *  have to passed as a parameter, thus altering the look of the     *
   *  two dimensional function, or the user defined function must      *
   *  be hard-coded to fit the y value.                                *
   **********************************************************************

   temp = ((a * y) - y) + b
   RETURN(temp)
```

LAST WORDS ON ARRAYS

The importance of the previous examples is that they show the limitations of some of
Clipper's extended features and demonstrate some conditions where using an array

may be more useful than using a disk file. Keep in mind that arrays have limitations. When you use an array construct to build a database rather than using the disk (increasing speed of execution by avoiding constant disk I/O) you are limited by available memory. You still have to consider disk space because at some time you probably will need to write the information in memory out to the disk.

CHAPTER TWELVE

Designing User Defined Functions (UDFs)

One of Clipper's most powerful features is that it gives you the ability to create a set of commonly used routines and treat them as functions. User defined functions (UDFs) can be great programming time savers and can also reduce system maintenance time. When you fix or modify a user defined function, all applications using that function can be changed by recompiling the function file and relinking that new file with all other relevant files.

Some examples of commonly needed features that lend themselves well to user defined functions are error messages, screen formats, password generation and verification, and check conversion routines (taking numbers and converting them into words). Once you develop a set of user defined functions, system development and · maintenance is drastically reduced. When designing your own functions you should strive for consistency and unity, especially if they will be used by others.

Functions often are said to have a *value*. The value of the function is that which the function returns to the calling program. If a function returns either a .T. or a .F., the function is said to have a *logical* value.

SYNTAX OF UDFS

While functions can appear at the end of program files, it's advisable to keep all generic functions together in one file to be compiled separately and later linked in with the other object files. But whether you append your functions to a program file or keep them all in one library, they must be defined in the same way.

Syntax:

    FUNCTION < Function name >

    PARAMETERS < variables >   && This is optional

    [Body of function]

    RETURN(< value or variable >)

SAMPLE FUNCTIONS

The following is a list of functions for which I have provided source code in this chapter. In some cases, sample code in an application environment is also provided for clarity.

Bitstrip():   Strips all of the high-order bits set for word-wrapping in a memo field.

Center():   Centers a string in a given screen width.

Centr():   Used in conjunction with the MESSAGE clause in the SET MES-
                   SAGE TO/PROMPT commands. This function centers the prompt
                   on the row.

Chkamnt():   Returns the worded value for any numeric value. Useful in check-
                   writing routines.

Chkpass():   Checks that the string passed to it equals the proper value for the
                   password generated by GENPASS().

Chng_prmpt()
Scan_prmpt()
Delt_prmpt():   These three functions are used for scrolling through a database,
                   depending upon whether the operation called for a CHANGE, a
                   SCAN, or a DELETION.

Day_Word():   Returns the name of the day. If a number is passed to the function
                   rather than a date, the function will convert that number to a string
                   representation.

Divide0():   Traps for and avoids Divide by Zero run-time errors; this is especial-
                   ly useful when running REPORT FORM commands.

Dltrim():   Returns a string with leading and trailing blank spaces deleted.

Endfield():   Returns the number of fields in any given database.

Expand():   Used for report generation, this function expands a given string with
                   spaces.

Fill_array():   Fills an array with the field values of a database.

Fill_out():   Returns a string padded with spaces. To be used in conjunction with
                   the CENTR() function, for report formatting, and for the SET MES-
                   SAGE TO command.

Genpass():   Generates a numeric value for any string given to it. Used for gener-
                   ating passwords, it can be modified for each application/use.

Goodfile():   Tests whether a file is a dBASE III database file. This function can
                   be modified to test for the value of the other related files.

Got():   Works in conjunction with POP(). It yields the value for a specific
                   file, field, and record number.

Great_zero(): Similar to MUST_FILL() in that the number being checked must be greater than zero.

Lookup(): Demonstrates the usefulness of a UDF in conjunction with the VALID clause.

Make_empty(): Makes an empty value depending on the data type involved. This function may be used independently; however, it was designed to work in conjunction with GOT().

Must_fill(): Used for a field that MUST be filled. Optional parameters are the row and column positions for the message.

Percent(): Yields a string in percent format from the two numbers passed to it.

Pop(): In conjunction with GOT(), it returns the record number of a set of valid choices (such as zip codes) which may be located in another file or in the current file. It will also display the values in a pop-up window and will allow the cursor keys to move through the window and choose the correct value.

Prntdate(): Converts the printed date format based on a pointer passed to the function along with the date to be converted.

Prnttime(): Generates the time in standard format, designates AM or PM, converts military time to standard time, and offers the option of including seconds in the output.

Qwait(): Designed for user interface, this function checks to see if the "Q" was input, and returns a .T. or .F.. This function is quite like verify; however, with this function, options like "Q to Quit" can be checked instead of "Y for Yes". Both functions (Verify() and Qwait()) can be modified and combined.

Roundit(): Specifically designed for two-digit numeric input. It is better than the existing rounding features in CLIPPER.

Upperlower(): Returns a string with the first character in upper-case and all others in lower-case.

Verify(): Checks for true/false conditions and returns the proper value.

BITSTRIP()

Syntax: BITSTRIP(< expC > [, < expN >])

Pass: < character expression > [, < numeric expression >]
Return: < character expression >

Notice: Copyright 1986, Stephen J. Straley

Description: The BITSTRIP() function strips the high-order bits which help wrap
                words around inside a memo field or long string variable. The
                returned value is the string representation of the memo field with
                hard returns (CHR(13)) replacing soft returns (CHR(141)).

                This function will not work directly with an @ ...SAY/GET com-
                mand: the graphic symbols for carriage return and line feed will dis-
                play.

Function: User Defined Function.

Code:
```
FUNCTION Bitstrip

PARAMETERS c, padding

IF TYPE("padding") = "U"
   padding = 0
ENDIF
outstring = ""
DO WHILE !EMPTY(c)
   IF AT(CHR(141),c) = 0
      outstring = outstring + SUBSTR(c, 1, LEN(c))
      c = ""
   ELSE
      outstring = outstring + ;
        SUBSTR(c, 1, AT(CHR(141), c) - 1) + CHR(13)
      outstring = outstring + SPACE(padding)
      scan = AT(CHR(141), c) + 1
      c = SUBSTR(c, scan, LEN(c) - scan + 1)
   ENDIF
ENDDO

RETURN(outstring)
```

Usage:
```
USE Database
GO TOP
SET PRINT ON
DO WHILE .NOT. EOF()
   ? BITSTRIP(memo_field)
   SET PRINT OFF
```

```
                    WAIT
                    ? SPACE(10) + BITSTRIP(memo_field,10)
                    WAIT
                    SET PRINT ON
               ENDDO
               SET PRINT OFF
```

CENTER()

Syntax: CENTER(< expC >)

Pass: < character expression >
Return: < numeric expression >

Notice: Copyright 1986, Stephen J. Straley

Description: The CENTER() function was designed to help center strings
                 within a given area. If no length is given, the function assumes a
                 width of 80.

Function: User Defined Function.

Code:
```
FUNCTION Center

PARAMETERS in_string, in_length

IF TYPE("in_length") = "U"
   in_length = 80
ENDIF

RETURN(in_length/2 - LEN(in_string)/2)
```

Usage: `@ 23,CENTER(EXPAND("The End")) SAY EXPAND("The End")`

CENTR()

Syntax: CENTR(< expC >)

Pass: < character expression >
Return: < character expression >

Notice: Copyright 1986, Stephen J. Straley

Description: The CENTR() function works in conjunction with the SET MES-
                 SAGE TO and the PROMPT command. The CENTR() function
                 centers the character expression found in the MESSAGE clause for

each PROMPT command by padding the front of the expression with blank spaces.

Function: User Defined Function.

Code:
```
FUNCTION Centr

PARAMETERS a

temp = 40 - INT(LEN(a)/2)

RETURN(SPACE(temp) + a)
```

Usage:
```
a 4, 8, 15, 72 BOX SUBSTR(scrframe,1,8)
SET MESSAGE TO 24
a 3, 29 SAY "Legal Billing Main Menu"
a 6, 10 PROMPT " 1>  Client Information " ;
    MESSAGE CENTR("Basic Information on Clients")
a 8, 14 PROMPT " 2>  Matter Information " ;
    MESSAGE CENTR("Matter Information Based on Client")
a 10, 18 PROMPT " 3>  Transactions " ;
    MESSAGE CENTR("Transactions Based on Matter Information")
a 11, 18 PROMPT " 4>  Disbursements " ;
    MESSAGE CENTR("Disbursements Based on Matter Information")
a 12, 18 PROMPT " 5>  Payments " ;
    MESSAGE CENTR("Payments Based on Matter Information")
a 6, 48 PROMPT " 6>  Codes " ;
    MESSAGE CENTR("Disbursements/Attorney/Matter Type Codes")
a 8, 48 PROMPT " 7>  Reports " ;
    MESSAGE CENTR("Print Lists and Reports")
a 10, 48 PROMPT " 8>  EOP Processing " ;
    MESSAGE CENTR("End Of Period Processing")
a 12, 48 PROMPT " 9>  Utilities " ;
    MESSAGE CENTR("File and Program Utilities")
a 14, 31 SAY "ESC to Exit Program"
    MENU TO option
```

CHKAMNT()

Syntax: CHKAMNT(< expN >)

Pass: < numeric expression >
Return: < character expression >

Notice: Copyright 1986, Stephen J. Straley

Description: The CHKAMNT() function is designed to give the worded value for any two-decimal positive numeric value. Specifically applicable in writing checks or vouchers. This function also calls upon another function, GRP_EXPAND(), to further narrow down the value of the input.

Function: User Defined Function.

Code:

```
FUNCTION Chkamnt

PARAMETERS figure

final = ""
IF figure < 0
   final = "Unable to Print"
   RETURN(final)
ELSE
   cents = SUBSTR(STR(figure, 15, 2), 14, 2)
   new = INT(figure)
ENDIF

***********************
* Check for BILLIONS *
***********************
temp = INT(new/1000000000)
IF temp > 0
   final = final + GRP_EXPAND(temp_ + " Billion "
   new = new - (temp * 1000000000)
ENDIF

**********************
* Check for MILLIONS *
**********************
temp = INT(new/1000000)
IF temp > 0
   final = final + GRP_EXPAND(temp) + " Million "
   new = new - (temp * 1000000)
ENDIF

***********************
* Check for THOUSANDS *
***********************
temp = INT(new/1000)
IF temp > 0
   final = final + GRP_EXPAND(temp) + " Thousand "
   new = new - (temp * 1000)
ENDIF
temp = new

*******************
* Check for UNITS *
*******************
IF temp > 0
   final = final + GRP_EXPAND(temp)
ENDIF
```

```
      IF SUBSTR(final,1,3) = "One" .AND. LEN(final) = 3
         final = final + " Dollar and " + cents + "/100"
      ELSE
         final = final + " Dollars and " + cents + "/100"
      ENDIF

      RETURN(final)
```

GRP_EXPAND()

Syntax: GRP_EXPAND(< expN >)

Pass: < numeric expression >
Return: < character expression >

Notice: Copyright 1986, Stephen J. Straley

Description: The GRP_EXPAND() function is the second half of the
                   CHKAMNT() function.

Function: User Defined Function.

Code:
```
FUNCTION Grp_expand

PARAMETERS group_val

one_unit = "One      Two      Three    Four     Five     "
one_unit = one_unit+"Six      Seven    Eight    Nine     Ten
"
one_unit = one_unit+"Eleven    Twelve    Thirteen Fourteen Fifteen
"
one_unit = one_unit+"Sixteen  SeventeenEighteen Nineteen"
ten_unit = "Twenty Thirty Forty  Fifty  Sixty  "
ten_unit = ten_unit + "SeventyEighty Ninety "
group_str = ""

IF group_val > 99
   new1 = INT(group_val/100)
   group_str = group_str + TRIM(SUBSTR(one_unit, (new1*9_-8,9)))
   group_val = group_val - (new1 * 100)
   group_str = group_str + " Hundred "
ENDIF
IF group_val > 19
   new1 = INT(group_val/10)-1
   group_str = group_str + TRIM(SUBSTR(ten_unit,(new1*7)-6,7))
   new1 = INT(group_val/10)*10
   group_val = group_val - new1
   IF group_val > 0
      group_str = group_str + "-"
   ENDIF
```

```
                    ENDIF
                    IF group_val > 0
                       group_str = group_str + ;
                       TRIM(SUBSTR(one_unit,(group_val*9)-8,9))
                    ENDIF

                    RETURN(group_str)
```

Usage: ```
                    amount = 735.45
                    @ 10,10 SAY CHKAMNT(amount)
                    ```

## CHKPASS()

Syntax:             CHKPASS( < expN >, < expN >)

Pass:               < numeric expression >, < numeric expression >
Return:             < logical expression >

Notice:             Copyright 1986, Stephen J. Straley

Description:        The CHKPASS() function displays a window at the positions given,
                    along with the prompt in the proper location. Available for
                    reference to the function are the following variables:

                    scrtimes (the number of times to execute the function) scrframe (the
                    outline of the chosen frame for BOX()) scrpass (the value of the
                    password generated by GENPASS())

                    If the input given passes the CHKPASS() function, the function
                    returns a .T. value; otherwise it will be .F.(false). If passwords are
                    not wanted, scrtimes is set to 0.

Function:           User Defined Function.

Code:               
```
FUNCTION Chkpass

PARAMETERS row, col

IF scrtimes = 0
   RETURN(.T.)
ENDIF
FOR x = 1 TO scrtimes
   in_pass = SPACE(15)
   @ row-3, col-5, row+3, col+34 BOX scrframe
   @ row,col SAY "Password --> " ;
   GET in_pass PICT "XXXXXXXXXXXXXXX"
   READ
   IF !EMPTY(in_pass)
```
```

```
                    temp_count = GENPASS(in_pass)
                    IF temp_count = scrpass
                        RETURN(.T.)
                    ENDIF
                ENDIF
            NEXT

            RETURN(.F.)
```

Usage: ```
                CASE option = 7
                IF CHKPASS(20,5)
                    DO Subopt
                ELSE
                    @ 17,0,23,39 BOX scrframe
                    @ 19, 3 SAY "Attempt to Access Utility Sub-Menu"
                    @ 20, 3 SAY "   without proper access code."
                    @ 21, 3 SAY "   Any Key to Continue ...."
                    IF INKEY(0)
                    ENDIF
                ENDIF
                ENDCASE
                ```

# CHNG_PRMPT()
# SCAN_PRMPT()
# DELT_PRMPT()

Syntax:         CHNG_PRMPT(<expN>)
                SCAN_PRMPT(<expN>)
                DELT_PRMPT(<expN>)

Pass:           < numeric expression >
Return:         < numeric expression >

Notice:         Copyright 1986, Stephen J. Straley

Description:    These three functions are used to help pan through a database based
                on the desired operation. The number passed to the functions is the
                row number for the choices to appear on. What makes them unique
                is that while they perform a task, their values can be tested and
                appropriate action can be taken based on the answer.

Function:       User Defined Function.

Sample:         ```
                FUNCTION Chng_prmpt

                    * This is the MENU prompt at the passed
                    * coordinates for CHANGE information
                ```

```
PARAMETERS a_row

temp_var = 3
@ a_row,10 SAY ;
  "< >ext - < >revious - < >dit - < >hoose Again - < >uit"
@ a_row,11 PROMPT "N"
@ a_row,20 PROMPT "P"
@ a_row,33 PROMPT "E"
@ a_row,42 PROMPT "C"
@ a_row,59 PROMPT "Q"
MENU TO temp_var

RETURN(temp_var)

********************

FUNCTION Scan_prmpt

   * This is the MENU prompt at the passed
   * coordinates for SCAN information

PARAMETERS a_row

temp_var = 1
@ a_row, 17 SAY ;
   "< >ext - < >revious - < >hoose Again - < >uit"
@ a_row, 18 PROMPT "N"
@ a_row, 27 PROMPT "P"
@ a_row, 40 PROMPT "C"
@ a_row, 57 PROMPT "Q"
MENU TO temp_var

RETURN(temp_var)

********************

FUNCTION Delt_prmpt

   * This is the MENU prompt at the passed
   * coordinates for DELETE information

PARAMETERS a_row

temp_strng = "< >ext - < >revious - < >" + ;
             IF(DELETED(), "ecall", "elete") + ;
             " - < >hoose Again - < >uit"
temp_var = 3
@ a_row,10 SAY temp_strng
@ a_row,11 PROMPT "N"
@ a_row,20 PROMPT "P"
@ a_row,33 PROMPT IF(DELETED(), "R", "D")
@ a_row,44 PROMPT "C"
@ a_row,61 PROMPT "Q"
MENU TO temp_var
RETURN(temp_var)
```

Usage:

```
USE Multy
GO TOP
DO WHILE .T.
   DO Paint_it
   which_way = DELT_PRMPT(18)
   DO CASE
   CASE which_way = 1
      SKIP
   CASE which_way = 2
      SKIP -1
   CASE which_way = 3
      DO Delt_it
   CASE which_way = 4
      EXIT
   OTHERWISE
      KEYBOARD CHR(13)
      EXIT
   ENDCASE
   DO Adjust
ENDDO
```

DAY_WORD()

Syntax: DAY_WORD(<exp>)

Pass: <date expression> or <numeric expression>
Return: <character expression>

Notice: Copyright 1986, Stephen J. Straley

Description: The DAY_WORD() function returns the string of any date variable
                   or field with the value of the 1st, the 2nd, the 3rd, the 4th, etc.

Function: User Defined Function.

Code:
```
FUNCTION Dayword

PARAMETERS in_date

IF TYPE("in_date") = "D"
   in_day = STR(DAY(in_date),2)
   in_val = VAL(in_day)
ELSE
   in_day = STR(in_date, 2)
   in_val = in_date
ENDIF

IF in_val > 3 .AND. in_val < 21
   in_day = in_day + "th"
ELSE
```

```
                        in_val = VAL(SUBSTR(in_day,2,1))
                        in_day = in_day + ;
                        SUBSTR("thstndrdthththththth"), (in_val * 2) + 1, 2)
                     ENDIF

                     RETURN(in_day)
```

Usage:
```
                     wording = DAY_WORD(DATE())
                     ? "Today is the " + wording
```

DIVIDE0()

Syntax: DIVIDE0(< expN >, < expN >)

Pass: < numeric expression >, < numeric expression >
Return: < numeric expression >

Notice: Copyright 1986, Stephen J. Straley

Description: The DIVIDE0() function returns the results of the first parameter
                 (the numerator) divided by the second parameter, or 0 if the second
                 parameter (the divisor) is equal to zero.

Function: User Defined Function.

Code:
```
                 FUNCTION Divide0

                 PARAMETERS top_numb, bot_numb

                 IF bot_numb == 0
                     RETURN(0)
                 ENDIF

                 RETURN(top_numb / bot_numb)
```

Usage:
```
                 in  = 7
                 out = 0
                 ? "The results are as follows:  " + STR(DIVIDE0(in, out))
```

DLTRIM()

Syntax: DLTRIM(< expC >)

Pass: < character expression >
Return: < character expression >

Notice: Copyright 1986, Stephen J. Straley

Description: The DLTRIM() function is primarily used immediately after a
                numeric field/variable has been converted to a string. In Clipper, as
                in dBASE III, numbers converted to strings are padded with blank
                spaces to concatenate the string for indexing purposes. However, in
                most cases a TRIM() or an LTRIM() will not suffice; the spaces
                have to be completely removed from the string.

Function: User Defined Function.

Code:
```
FUNCTION Dltrim

PARAMETER in_string

RETURN(LTRIM(TRIM(in_string)))
```

Usage:
```
x = 4
*
* here x is initialized to a numeric to make it easier
* to show how the STR() function puts in preceding blanks
* and Dltrim() eliminates them
*
findit = last_name + DLTRIM(STR(x)) + phone_num
SEEK findit
```

ENDFIELD()

Syntax: ENDFIELD(<expC>)

Pass: <character expression>
Return: <numeric expression>

Notice: Copyright 1986, Stephen J. Straley

Description: The ENDFIELD() function returns the number of fields in the given
                database. This function does a binary search to determine the posi-
                tion of the last field in the database.

Function: User Defined Function.

Code:
```
FUNCTION Last_field

PARAMETERS Filename

USE &filename
first  = 1
last   = 1024
middle = INT(last/2)
```

```
* The basis of a binary search is to take a
* beginning (first) and an ending (last) and find
* the midpoint (middle).  Once done, the actual
* search is to check if the value in question
* is above or below the midpoint value.  Depending
* upon the outcome of the test, the first, last, and
* middle are adjusted accordingly.  Once the value in
* question is equal to the midpoint, then the value
* is found.  The purpose of a binary search is simple:
* to search for a value by taking the halves of the
* extremes.  Binary searches are one of the
* fastest types of searches used: if a database being
* searched doubles in size, the binary search still has
* only one additional pass to make.

DO WHILE first <> last
    * Check the length of the field at the middle
    * position.  IF the value is 0, then there
    * is no field at position middle and make the value
    * of last equal to middle.  ELSE, there is a value
    * at position middle and then make the value of first
    * equal to middle.  Once this is done, then
    * recalculate the value of middle based on the new
    * values of first and last.

    IF LEN(FIELDNAME(middle)) = 0
       last = middle
    ELSE
       first = middle
    ENDIF
    middle = first + INT((last - first)/2)
    IF LEN(FIELDNAME(middle)) > 0 .AND. ;
       LEN(FIELDNAME(middle + 1)) = 0
       last  = middle
       first = middle
    ENDIF
ENDDO

RETURN(last)
```

Usage:
```
howmany = ENDFIELD("MULTY")
? "There are " + TRANSFORM(howmany, "9999) + "fields "
?? "in Multy.dbf"
```

EXPAND()

Syntax: EXPAND(< expC >)

Pass: < character expression >
Return: < character expression >

Notice: Copyright 1986, Stephen J. Straley

Description: The EXPAND() function is designed for screen formatting as well as
                 for report generation. It expands a string with a blank space between
                 each character.

Function: User Defined Function.

Code:
```
FUNCTION Expand

PARAMETER in_string

length  = LEN(in_string)
counter = 1
out_str = ""

DO WHILE counter <= length
   out_str = out_str + SUBSTR(in_string, counter,1) + " "
   counter = counter + 1
ENDDO
RETURN(TRIM(out_str))
```

Usage: @ 2,23 SAY EXPAND("Enter Customer")

FILL_ARRAY()

Syntax: FILL_ARRAY(< expC >, < expN >, < expN >, < expC >,
                 < expN > [, < expC >])

Pass: < character expression >, < numeric expression >,
                 < numeric expression >, < character expression >,
                 < expression numeric [, < character expression >]
Return: < logical expression >

Notice: Copyright 1986, Stephen J. Straley

Description: The FILL_ARRAY() function was designed to load a range of fields
                 from a database into an array. The array must be DECLARED
                 prior to the issuance of the function and must be set to the maximum
                 number of possible elements. The first parameter is the name of the
                 array; the send is the starting counter within the array; the third para-
                 meter is the ending counter within the array; the fourth is for the
                 name of the database; the fifth parameter is for the field number to
                 be used; and the sixth, which is optional, is any filter condition to be
                 placed on the newly selected and active database. You may alter the

values of the beginning and ending counters in order to fill an array only partially with field values. If you do, the function will still start at the top of the file and replace the values accordingly.

Function: User Defined Function.

Code:

```
FUNCTION Fill_array

PARAMETERS the_array, start, end_at, the_file, the_field, the_filt

go_back = SELECT()
IF !FILE(the_file)
   RETURN(.F.)
ENDIF
SELECT 9
USE &the_file
IF TYPE("the_filt") <> "U"
   SET FILTER TO &the_filt.
ENDIF
GO TOP
temp_val = FIELDNAME(the_field)
DO WHILE !EOF()
   the_array[start] = &temp_val.
   start = start + 1
   IF start > end_at
      EXIT
   ENDIF
   SKIP
ENDDO
return_to = TRIM(LTRIM(STR(go_back)))
SELECT &return_to.

RETURN(.T.)
```

Usage:

```
********************
* Name        FILLIT.prg
* Date        December 1, 1986
* Notice      Copyright 1986, Stephen J. Straley
* Note        This program shows how to use the FILL_ARRAY()
*             function. Notice that the same database is
*             opened twice. This is allowed in Clipper.
*             The ramifications of this are numerous,
*             including the use of data-dictionaries and
*             Clipper SQL routines with immediate cross-
*             checking.
*
********************

USE Client
DECLARE mast_list[LASTREC()]
IF FILL_ARRAY(mast_list, 1, LASTREC(), "Client.dbf", 3)
   CLEAR
```

```
        FOR x = 1 TO LEN(mast_list)
           ? mast_list[x]
        NEXT
     ELSE
        ? "File Not Found!!"
     ENDIF

     ********************

     FUNCTION Fill_array

     PARAMETERS the_array, start, end_at, the_file, the_field, the_filt

     go_back = SELECT()
     IF !FILE(the_file)
             RETURN(.F.)
     ENDIF
     SELECT 9
     USE &the_file
     IF TYPE("the_filt") <> "U"
        SET FILTER TO &the_filt.
     ENDIF
     GO TOP
     temp_val = FIELDNAME(the_field)
     DO WHILE !EOF()
        the_array[start] = &temp_val.
        start = start + 1
        IF start > end_at
           EXIT
        ENDIF
        SKIP
     ENDDO
        return_to = TRIM(LTRIM(STR(go_back)))
        SELECT &return_to.
        RETURN(.T.)
     * End of File
```

FILL_OUT()

Syntax: FILL_OUT(<expC> [,<expN>])

Pass: <character expression> [,<numeric expression>]
Return: <character expression>

Notice: Copyright 1986, Stephen J. Straley

Description: The FILL_OUT() function is designed for screen and report format-
                   ting. It fills out the given string with blank spaces, defaulting to a
                   width of 79. May be used in conjunction with the CENTR() function
                   to properly center a message for the SET MESSAGE TO /
                   PROMPT...MESSAGE commands.

Function: User Defined Function.

Code:
```
FUNCTION Fill_out

PARAMETERS a, b

IF TYPE("b") = "U"
   b = 79
ENDIF
c = b - LEN(a)
RETURN(a + SPACE(c))
```

Usage:
```
a 2,23 PROMPT " 1> Chart of Accounts " ;
MESSAGE CENTR(FILL_OUT("This is for the Chart of Accounts"))
```

GENPASS()

Syntax: GENPASS(< expC >)

Pass: < character expression >
Return: < numeric expression >

Notice: Copyright 1986, Stephen J. Straley

Description: The GENPASS() function provides a password generation scheme
                 for any application. It may be modified to any extreme for protection
                 purposes. It returns a numeric value for any string, based on the
                 ASCII value of each character multiplied by its relative position in
                 the string.

Function: User Defined Function.

Code:
```
FUNCTION Genpass

PARAMETERS in_string

count = LEN(TRIM(in_string))
final = 0
FOR beginning = 1 to (count + 1)
   final = final + ;
      ASC(SUBSTR(in_string, beginning, 1)) * beginning
NEXT

RETURN(final)
```

Usage:
```
password = SPACE(15)
a 10, 3 SAY "What Password do you wish to use?  " ;
      GET password PICT "XXXXXXXXXXXXXXX"
READ
scrpass = GENPASS(password)
```

GOODFILE()

Syntax: GOODFILE(<expC>)

Pass: <character expression>
Return: <logical expression>

Notice: Copyright 1986, Stephen J. Straley

Description: The GOODFILE() function determines if the file is a legitimate
                     dBASE III file. It may be modified to search for an ASCII 83 which
                     would signal that the file is not only a dBASE III database but that it
                     contains a memo field. This may be useful when copying files to be
                     sure the memo file gets copied.

Function: User Defined Function.

Code:
```
FUNCTION Goodfile

PARAMETERS file

CREATE Temp
USE Temp
APPEND BLANK
REPLACE field_name WITH "HEADER", ;
        field_type WITH "C", field_len WITH 32
USE
CREATE Header FROM Temp
CLOSE DATABASE
ERASE Temp.dbf
USE Header
APPEND FROM &file SDF
GO TOP
DO WHILE ASC(SUBSTR(header,1,1)) == 3 .OR. ;
         ASC(SUBSTR(header,1,1)) == 83
  x = ASC(SUBSTR(header,3,1))
  IF x > 12
     EXIT
  ENDIF
  x = ASC(SUBSTR(header,4,1))
  IF x > 32
     EXIT
  ENDIF
  USE
  ERASE Header.dbf
  RETURN(.T.)
ENDDO
USE
ERASE Header.dbf

RETURN(.F.)
```

Usage:

```
********************
* Name          GOOD.prg
* Date          August 11, 1986
* Notice        Copyright 1986, Stephen J. Straley
* Note          This program shows how to use a function like GOOD-
*               FILE().  This can also be used to test if a data-
*               base file has a .DBT file with it (the first byte
*               will be an 83, not a 3).  If it is, then when using
*               the COPY TO command, you can be sure to copy the
*               memo file with it.
*
********************

DO WHILE .T.
   CLEAR
   STORE SPACE(12) TO lookfor
   @ 6,10 SAY "Enter ? for directory..."
   @ 8,10 SAY "Enter name of file with extension: " ;
           GET lookfor PICT "@!" VALID(DODIR())
   READ
   @ 9,0 CLEAR
   IF EMPTY(lookfor)
       QUIT
   ENDIF
   IF AT(".",lookfor) = 0
       WAIT " Please enter an extension..."
       LOOP
   ENDIF
   lookfor = LTRIM(lookfor)
   lookfor = TRIM(lookfor)
   IF .NOT. FILE(lookfor)
      WAIT "Please enter a good file name, or leave blank to
quit.."
       LOOP
   ENDIF
   @ 11,10 SAY "That file "
   ?? IF(GOODFILE(lookfor), "IS", "IS NOT") + " a dBASE III file"
   ?
   WAIT "Press any key for next entry..."
ENDDO

********************

FUNCTION Dodir

   IF SUBSTR(lookfor,1,1) = "?"
      ?
      RUN DIR /W
      RETURN(.F.)
   ENDIF
   RETURN(.T.)
```

```
********************

FUNCTION Goodfile

PARAMETERS file

CREATE Temp
USE Temp
APPEND BLANK
REPLACE field_name WITH "HEADER", ;
        field_type WITH "C", field_len WITH 32
USE
CREATE Header FROM Temp
CLOSE DATABASE
ERASE Temp.dbf
USE Header
APPEND FROM &file SDF
GO TOP
DO WHILE ASC(SUBSTR(header,1,1)) == 3 .OR. ;
         ASC(SUBSTR(header,1,1)) == 83
   x = ASC(SUBSTR(header,3,1))
   IF x > 12
      EXIT
   ENDIF
   x = ASC(SUBSTR(header,4,1))
   IF x > 32
      EXIT
   ENDIF
   USE
   ERASE Header.dbf
   RETURN(.T.)
ENDDO
USE
ERASE Header.dbf
RETURN(.F.)
* End of File
```

GOT()

Syntax: GOT(<expC>, <expN>, <expN>)

Pass: <character expression>, <numeric expression>,
               <numeric expression>
Return: <expression>

Notice: Copyright 1986, Stephen J. Straley

Description: The GOT() function was created to give the user a chance to view
                valid choices (such as zip codes) which may be located in another file
                or in the current file. The first parameter is the name of the file to be

used; the second is the field to focus on within the file; and the third parameter is the specific record number this function will look at. This function was designed to be used with the POP() and MAKE_EMPTY() functions.

Function: User Defined Function.

Code:

```
FUNCTION Got

PARAMETERS file, field_no, record

SELECT 9
USE &file
IF record = 0
   GO TOP
   in_betw = FIELDNAME(field_no)
   give_it = &in_betw
   RETURN(MAKE_EMPTY(give_it))
ELSE
   GO record
ENDIF
in_betw = FIELDNAME(field_no)
output = &in_betw

RETURN(output)
```

Usage: Sample code is in the section entitled "Using GOT(), POP(), and MAKE_EMPTY()" at the end of the User Defined Function section.

GREAT_ZERO()

Syntax: GRET_ZERO(< expN >, < expN >, < expN >)

Pass: < numeric expression >, < num. expression >, < num. expression >
Return: < logical expression >

Notice: Copyright 1986, Stephen J. Straley

Description: The GREAT_ZERO() function returns a .T. if the field or variable expressed in the third < expN > is greater than 0. The first two numeric expressions are the row and column position on which to put an error message if the third < expN > fails the test.

Function: User Defined Function.

Code:

```
FUNCTION Great_zero

PARAMETERS arow, acol, value

IF value < 0
   arow, acol SAY "Number is too low!"
   RETURN(.F.)
ENDIF
arow, acol SAY SPACE(20)

RETURN(.T.)
```

LOOKUP()

Syntax: LOOKUP()

Pass: nothing
Return: < logical expression >

Notice: Copyright 1986, Stephen J. Straley

Description: The LOOKUP() function demonstrates how to use a user defined
               function in conjunction with the VALID clause. The concept, rather
               than the actual code, is important.

Function: User Defined Function.

Code:

```
FUNCTION Lookup
* This function is designed to always return a .T.
* so that if the zip code is found, the state variable
* will be manipulated by the function; otherwise, it is
* left alone and may be manipulated by the operator.

DO CASE
CASE inzip = "98234"
   instate = "CA"
CASE inzip = "76233"
   instate = "GA"
CASE inzip = "12009"
   instate = "NY"
ENDCASE
RETURN(.T.)
```

Usage:

```
DO WHILE .T.
STORE SPACE(2) TO instate
STORE SPACE(5) TO inzip
CLEAR
TEXT
```

Try entering either your own zip code or one of the following choices:

```
                98234   -   (CA)

                76233   -   (GA)

                12009   -   (NY)

ENDTEXT
a 12,10 SAY "Enter Zip Code: " GET inzip VALID(LOOKUP())
a 14,10 SAY "          State: " GET instate PICT "!!"
READ
a 18,10 SAY "Do you want to continue? "
IF !VERIFY()
    QUIT
ENDIF
ENDDO
```

MAKE_EMPTY()

Syntax: MAKE_EMPTY(< exp >)

Pass: < expression >
Return: < expression >

Notice: Copyright 1986, Stephen J. Straley

Description: The MAKE_EMPTY() function will evaluate an expression, determine its data type, and return an empty value of that type. This function can be used to initialize an array based on a data base. It was originally designed to be used with the GOT() and POP() functions to allow a user to escape out of the pop-menu and yield a null answer to GOT().

Function: User Defined Function.

Code:
```
FUNCTION Make_empty

PARAMETER in_s

DO CASE
CASE TYPE("in_s") = "C"
   RETURN(SPACE(LEN(in_s)))
CASE TYPE("in_s") = "D"
   RETURN(CTOD("  /  /  "))
CASE TYPE("in_s") = "N"
   RETURN(0.00)
OTHERWISE
   RETURN(.F.)
ENDCASE
```

Usage: Sample code is in the section entitled "Using GOT(), POP(), and
                MAKE_EMPTY()" at the end of the User Defined Function section.

MUST_FILL()

Syntax: MUST_FILL(<expC> [, <expN>, <expN>])

Pass: <character expression> [, <numeric expression>,
                            <numeric expression>]

Return: <logical expression>

Notice: Copyright 1986, Stephen J. Straley

Description: The MUST_FILL() function returns a logical .T. if the name of the
                field or variable expressed in <expC> has something in it. If the
                field is EMPTY(), then an error message is displayed and a false is
                returned. If the row, the first <expN>, and the column, the second
                <expN>, are given, then the error message appears at that position;
                otherwise, the error message appears on the same row as the GET.

Function: User Defined Function.

Code:
```
FUNCTION Must_fill

PARAMETERS a, b, c

IF EMPTY(a)
   IF TYPE("b") = "U"
      ??   "This field MUST be filled"
   ELSE
      @ b, c SAY "This field MUST be filled"
   ENDIF
   RETURN(.F.)
ELSE
   IF TYPE("b") = "U"
      ?? SPACE(26)
   ELSE
      @ b, c SAY SPACE(26)
   ENDIF
   RETURN(.T.)
ENDIF
```

Usage:
```
STORE SPACE(12) TO filename
@ 10,10 SAY "Enter File Name => " GET filename ;
   VALID(MUST_FILL(filename))
READ
STORE 0 TO age
@ 12,10 SAY "Now enter your age => " GET age;
   VALID(MUST_FILL(age,14,25))
READ
```

PERCENT()

Syntax: PERCENT(< expN >, < expN >)

Pass: < numeric expression >, < numeric expression >
Return: < character expression >

Notice: Copyright 1986, Stephen J. Straley

Description: The PERCENT() function returns a character string in the format of
                 a percentage. The calculation is based on the first < expN > divided
                 by the second < expN >. The function also traps for a zero in the
                 divisor (the second < expN >).

Function: User Defined Function.

Code:
```
FUNCTION Percent

PARAMETERS a, b

IF b = 0
   RETURN("  0.00%")
step_one = a / b * 100
step_two = ROUNDIT(step_one)

RETURN(TRANSFORM(step_two, "999.99%"))
```

Usage:
```
CLEAR
? PERCENT(5, 0)
STORE 10 TO a, b
?
? PERCENT(a, b)
```

POP()

Syntax: POP (< expN >, < expN >, < expN >, < expN >, < expC >,
                 < expN > [, < expC >]

Pass: < numeric expression >, < numeric expression >,
                 < numeric expression >, < numeric expression >,
                 < character expression >, < numeric expression >
                 [, < character expression >]
Return: < numeric expression >

Notice: Copyright 1986, Stephen J. Straley

Description: The POP() function will return the record number of a set of valid
                choices (e.g., zip codes) which may be located in another file or in
                the current file. The first parameter is the top-row coordinate for
                the pop menu; the second is the top-column coordinate; the third is
                rows down from the top-left coordinate the pop menu should use;
                the fourth one is the columns over from the top-left coordinate the
                pop menu should use; the fifth parameter is the name of the file to
                use (this may be the currently active file, as well); the sixth parameter
                is the field number to focus on in the selected database; and finally,
                the last parameter, which is optional, may be used to set a specific fil-
                ter on the file to be used. The field_number may be a different num-
                ber from the field number in the GOT() function.   This will allow
                the developer to display code names for the user while the GOT()
                function will yield the actual code value. This function was designed
                to be used with the GOT() and MAKE_EMPTY() functions.

Function: User Defined Function.

Code:

```
FUNCTION Pop

PARAMETERS top, left, down, over, file, field_no, filt

DECLARE pointer[down]
STORE SPACE(4000) TO backscr, frontscr -
CALL _scrsave WITH backscr
scrframe = CHR(201) + CHR(205) + CHR(187) + CHR(186) + ;
          CHR(188) + CHR(205) + CHR(200) + CHR(186) + CHR(32)
@ top, left, top+down, left+over BOX scrframe
CALL _scrsave WITH frontscr
SELECT 9
USE &file
IF TYPE("filt") = "U"
   SET FILTER TO
ELSE
   SET FILTER TO &filt
ENDIF
GO TOP
hit_bottom = .T.
starting = RECNO()
option = 1
screen_no = 1
DO WHILE .T.
   CALL _scrrest WITH frontscr
   beg_set = RECNO()
   FOR x = 1 TO down - 3
      pointer[x] = RECNO()
      inbetw = FIELDNAME(field_no)
      showit = &inbetw
      IF LEN(showit) >= over-2
         showit = SUBSTR(showit, 1, over-3)
```

```
                        showit = SUBSTR(showit, 1, over-3)
                     ENDIF
                     @ top+x, left+1 PROMPT " " + FILL_OUT(showit,over-2)
                     SKIP
                     IF EOF()
                        hit_bottom = .T.
                        x = down - 2
                     ENDIF
                  NEXT
                  next_set = RECNO()
                  DO CASE
                  CASE EOF()                        && Last Screen Full
                     IF screen_no > 1               && Not the first screen
                        IF over <= 8
                           top+down+1, left+2 SAY "ESC for UP"
                        ELSE
                           @ top+down-2, left+2 SAY "ESC for UP"
                        ENDIF
                     ENDIF
                  OTHERWISE                         && Somewhere else
                     IF screen_no > 1               && Not the first screen
                        IF over <= 8
                           @ top+down+1, left+2 SAY "ESC for UP"
                           @ top+down+2, left+2 PROMPT "Down Page"
                        ELSE
                           @ top+down-2, left+2 SAY "ESC for UP"
                           @ top+down - 1, left+2 PROMPT "Down Page"
                        ENDIF
                     ELSE
                        IF over <= 8
                           @ top+down + 2, left+2 PROMPT "Down Page"
                        ELSE
                           @ top+down - 1, left+2 PROMPT "Down Page"
                        ENDIF
                     ENDIF
                  ENDCASE

                  GO starting
                  MENU TO option
                  DO CASE
                  CASE option = 0
                     IF hit_bottom
                        hit_bottom = .F.
                     ENDIF
                     IF screen_no > 1
                        screen_no = screen_no - 1
                        GO beg_set
                        backward = (down - 3) * -1
                        SKIP backward
                     ELSE
                        RETURN(0)
                     ENDIF
                  CASE option = down - 2
```

```
            option = 1
            GO next_set
            screen_no = screen_no + 1
        OTHERWISE
            pass_to = pointer[option]
            CALL _scrrest WITH backscr
            STORE SPACE(4000) TO backscr, frontscr
            USE
            RETURN(pass_to)
    ENDCASE
ENDDO
```

Usage: Sample code is in the section entitled "Using GOT(), POP(), and
              MAKE_EMPTY()" at the end of the User Defined Function section.

PRNTDATE()

Syntax: PRNTDATE(< expD >, < expN >)

Pass: < date expression >, < numeric expression >
Return: < character expression >

Notice: Copyright 1986, Stephen J. Straley

Description: The PRNTDATE() function converts a date to a string in a special
              format mainly used in report writing. The < expN > determines
              which string format will be returned:

< expN >:	Date Format:
1	February 7th, 1987
2	Saturday, the 7th of February, 1987
3	Saturday, the 7th of February
4	The 7th of February, 1987
5	Saturday, February 7, 1987
6	February 7, 1987
7	1987-02-07
other	02/07/87

Function: User Defined Function.

Code:
```
FUNCTION Printdate

PARAMETERS in_date, date_opt

DO CASE
CASE date_opt = 1
    out_str = CMONTH(in_date) + " " + DAYWORD(in_date) + ;
```

```
                                  ", " + DLTRIM(STR(YEAR(in_date)))
                    CASE date_opt = 2
                       out_str = CDOW(in_date) + ", the " + DAYWORD(in_date) +;
                                  " of " + CMONTH(in_date) + ", " + ;
                                  DLTRIM(STR(YEAR(in_date)))
                    CASE date_opt = 3
                       out_str = CDOW(in_date) + ", the " + DAYWORD(in_date) +;
                                  " of " + CMONTH(in_date)
                    CASE date_opt = 4
                       out_str = "The " + dayword(in_date) + " of " + ;
                                  CMONTH(in_date) + ", " + ;
                                  DLTRIM(STR(YEAR(in_date)))
                    CASE date_opt = 5
                       out_str = CDOW(in_date) + ", " + CMON(in_date) + " "
                       out_str = out_str + DLTRIM(STR(DAY(in_date),2)) + ;
                                  ", " + STR(YEAR(in_date),4)
                    CASE date_opt = 6
                       out_str = CMONTH(in_date) + " " + ;
                                  DLTRIM(STR(DAY(in_date))) + ", " + ;
                                  DLTRIM(STR(YEAR(in_date)))
                    CASE date_opt = 7
                       out_str = SUBSTR(DTOS(in_date),1, 4) + "-" + ;
                                  SUBSTR(DTOS(in_date), 5,2) + "-" + ;
                                  SUBSTR(DTOS(in_date),7)
                    OTHERWISE
                       out_str = DTOC(in_date)
                    ENDCASE

                    RETURN(out_str)
```

Usage: ? PRINTDATE(DATE(), 1)

PRNTTIME()

Syntax: PRNTTIME(<expL>)

Pass: <logical expression>
Return: <character expression>

Notice: Copyright 1986, Stephen J. Straley

Description: The PRNTTIME() function returns the system time as a string. It
                   converts military (24 hour) time to standard time as well as desig-
                   nating "AM" or "PM". If <expL> is .T., then the seconds are
                   returned as well; otherwise, the string does not contain the seconds.

Function: User Defined Function.

Code: FUNCTION Prnttime

                   PARAMETERS with_secs

```
temptime = SECONDS()
hours    = INT(temptime / 3600)
minutes  = INT((temptime - hours * 3600) / 60)
secs     = INT(temptime - (hours * 3600) - (minutes * 60))

DO CASE
CASE hours = 0 .AND. minutes = 0
   comptime = "Midnight"
CASE hours = 12 .AND. minutes = 0
   comptime = "Noon"
OTHERWISE
   hours    = IF(hours > 12, hours - 12, hours)
   comptime = LTRIM(STR(hours)) + ":" + ;
              IF(minutes < 10, "0", "") + ;
              LTRIM(STR(minutes)) + " " + ;
              IF(hours > 11, "Pm", "Am")
ENDCASE
IF with_secs
   comptime = comptime + " and " + ;
              LTRIM(STR(secs)) + " seconds"
ENDIF

RETURN(comptime)
```

Usage:
```
FOR y = 1 TO 100
   CLEAR
   out_flag = IF(y/2 = INT(y/2), .T., .F.)
   @ 12,10 SAY "The current time is: " + PRNTTIME(out_flag)
   FOR x = 1 TO 200
   NEXT
NEXT
```

QWAIT()

Syntax: QWAIT()

Pass: nothing
Return: < logical expression >

Notice: Copyright 1986, Stephen J. Straley

Description: The QWAIT() function is similar to VERIFY() except that this
               checks for the letter Q rather than the letter Y.

Function: User Defined Function.

Code:
```
FUNCTION Qwait

SET FUNCTION off
WAIT TO temp
SET FUNCTION on
```

```
                    IF UPPER(temp) = "Q"
                       RETURN(.T.)
                    ENDIF
                    RETURN(.F.)
```

Usage:
```
                    @ 10,10 SAY "Press Any Key to Continue or Q to QUIT"
                    IF QWAIT
                       EJECT
                       RETURN
                    ENDIF
```

ROUNDIT()

Syntax: ROUNDIT(< expN >)

Pass: < numeric expression >
Return: < numeric expression >

Notice: Copyright 1986, Stephen J. Straley

Description: The ROUNDIT() function was created because it is more predictable and consistent than the ROUND() function in Clipper.

Function: User Defined Function.

Code:
```
FUNCTION Roundit

PARAMETER in_amount

in_amount = INT(in_amount * 100 + .5) / 100.00

RETURN(in_amount)
```

Usage:
```
x = 10.756 / 11.234
answer = ROUNDIT(x)
```

UPPERLOWER()

Syntax: UPPERLOWER(< expC >)

Pass: < character expression >
Return: < character expression >

Notice: Copyright 1986, Stephen J. Straley

Description: The UPPERLOWER() function reformats any character string with the first character capitalized and the rest lower-case.

Function:	User Defined Function.

Code:

```
FUNCTION Upperlower

PARAMETERS a

front = SUBSTR(a,1,1)
back  = SUBSTR(a,2)

RETURN(UPPER(front)+LOWER(back))
```

Usage:

```
a 10,10 SAY UPPERLOWER("mr. ") + UPPERLOWER("SMITH")
```

VERIFY()

Syntax: VERIFY()

Pass: nothing
Return: < logical expression >

Notice: Copyright 1986, Stephen J. Straley

Description: The VERIFY() function is used for checking the console for either a
               "Yy" or a "Nn" response to a question.

Function: User Defined Function.

Code:

```
FUNCTION Verify

SET CONSOLE OFF
STORE "" TO verify_var
DO WHILE .NOT. verify_var$"YyNn"
   WAIT TO verify_var
ENDDO
SET CONSOLE ON
IF UPPER(verify_var) = "Y"
   ?? "Yes"
   RETURN(.T.)
ELSE
   ?? "No "
   RETURN(.F.)
ENDIF
```

Usage:

```
a 10,10 SAY DATE()
a 13,10 SAY "Is this the correct date? (Y/N) "
IF VERIFY()
   DO Rest_of_prog
ELSE
   DO Change_Date
ENDIF
```

USING GOT(), POP(), and MAKE_EMPTY()

Below is a program that will generate two databases, fill one database with valid choices, and leave the other empty. Then a data entry screen will appear. If you enter either an invalid code or a "?" in the CODE field, a pop-up menu will appear to the right with all of the valid choices for that field, based on the CODE.DBF previously established. The GOT() function assigns the GET variable the value of the field in the CODE.DBF file based on the RECNO() that was passed back from the POP() function. The POP() function displays the pop-up menu in the bordered area and allows direct cursor control through the CODES.DBF over the desired fields. The MAKE_EMPTY() function makes an EMPTY() GET variable if the user should escape completely out of the pop-up menu.

```
********************
* Name          GOT_POP.prg
* Date          February 1, 1986
* Notice        Copyright 1987, Stephen J. Straley
* Note          This program demonstrates the use of the user
*               defined functions POP(), GOT(), MAKE_EMPTY(),
*               and FILL_OUT().
*
********************

* Creating Dummy Information

CREATE Template
USE Template
APPEND BLANK
REPLACE field_name WITH "CODES", field_type WITH "C", field_len WITH 5
APPEND BLANK
REPLACE field_name WITH "STATE", field_type WITH "C", field_len WITH 2
USE
CREATE Codes FROM Template
USE Codes
APPEND BLANK
REPLACE codes WITH "90350", state WITH "CA"
APPEND BLANK
REPLACE codes WITH "06854", state WITH "CT"
APPEND BLANK
REPLACE codes WITH "10017", state WITH "NY"
APPEND BLANK
REPLACE codes WITH "40047", state WITH "GA"
APPEND BLANK
REPLACE codes WITH "10376", state WITH "NJ"
APPEND BLANK
REPLACE codes WITH "98765", state WITH "OE"
USE
CREATE Template
USE Template
APPEND BLANK
REPLACE field_name WITH "CCODES", field_type WITH "C", field_len WITH 5
```

```
APPEND BLANK
REPLACE field_name WITH "CSTATE", field_type WITH "C", field_len WITH 2
APPEND BLANK
REPLACE field_name WITH "CNAME", field_type WITH "C", field_len WITH 10
USE
CREATE Client FROM Template
USE
ERASE Template.dbf
USE Client

* A Dummy Data Entry Screen

DO WHILE .T.
   CLEAR
   temp_code = SPACE(5)
   temp_state = SPACE(2)
   @ 5,5 SAY "       Enter State Zip Code => " GET temp_code PICT "XXXXX"
VALID(GOOD_STATE(temp_code))
   @ 7,5 SAY "       Press ESC to Escape"
   READ
   IF LASTKEY() = 27 .OR. EMPTY(temp_code)
      EXIT
   ENDIF
   SELECT 1
   APPEND BLANK
   REPLACE ccodes WITH temp_code, cstate WITH temp_state
   CLEAR
   @ 5,5 SAY "           State Zip Code => " GET ccodes
   CLEAR GETS
   @ 7,5 SAY "               State Code => " GET cstate PICT "!!"
   @ 9,5 SAY "              Client Name => " GET cname PICT "@X"
   READ
ENDDO

********************

FUNCTION Good_state

PARAMETER in_temp

IF EMPTY(in_temp) .AND. LASTKEY() = 27
   RETURN(.T.)
ENDIF
SAVE SCREEN
SELECT 2
USE Codes
LOCATE FOR codes = in_temp
IF FOUND()
   @ 7, 40 SAY "                        "
   temp_code = codes
   temp_state = state
   RETURN(.T.)
ELSE
```

```
      @ 7, 40 SAY "Move Cursor keys for Codes"
      a_file = "CODES.DBF"
      temp_code = GOT(a_file, 1, POP( 9, 45, 10, 9, a_file, 1))
      IF !EMPTY(temp_code)
         KEYBOARD CHR(13)
      ELSE
         RESTORE SCREEN
      ENDIF
      RETURN(.F.)
ENDIF

********************

FUNCTION Got

PARAMETERS file, field_no, record

SELECT 9
USE &file
IF record = 0
   GO TOP
   in_betw = FIELDNAME(field_no)
   give_it = &in_betw
   RETURN(MAKE_EMPTY(give_it))
ELSE
   GO record
ENDIF
in_betw = FIELDNAME(field_no)
output = &in_betw
RETURN(output)

********************

FUNCTION Make_empty

PARAMETER in_s

DO CASE
CASE TYPE("in_s") = "C"
   RETURN(SPACE(LEN(in_s)))
CASE TYPE("in_s") = "D"
   RETURN(CTOD("  /  /  "))
CASE TYPE("in_s") = "N"
   RETURN(0.00)
OTHERWISE
   RETURN(.F.)
ENDCASE

********************

FUNCTION Pop

PARAMETERS top, left, down, over, file, field_no, filt
```

```
DECLARE pointer[down]
STORE SPACE(4000) TO backscr, frontscr
CALL _scrsave WITH backscr
scrframe =  CHR(201) + CHR(205) + CHR(187) + CHR(186) + ;
            CHR(188) + CHR(205) + CHR(200) + CHR(186) + CHR(32)
@ top, left, top+down, left+over BOX scrframe
CALL _scrsave WITH frontscr
SELECT 9
USE &file
IF TYPE("filt") = "U"
   SET FILTER TO
ELSE
   SET FILTER TO &filt
ENDIF
GO TOP
hit_bottom = .T.
starting = RECNO()
option = 1
screen_no = 1
DO WHILE .T.
   CALL _scrrest WITH frontscr
   beg_set = RECNO()
   FOR x = 1 TO down - 3
      pointer[x] = RECNO()
      inbetw = FIELDNAME(field_no)
      showit = &inbetw
      IF LEN(showit) >= over-2
         showit = SUBSTR(showit, 1, over-3)
      ENDIF
      @ top+x, left+1 PROMPT " " + FILL_OUT(showit,over-2)
      SKIP
      IF EOF()
         hit_bottom = .T.
         x = down - 2
      ENDIF
   NEXT
   next_set = RECNO()

   DO CASE
   CASE EOF()                              && Last Screen Full
      IF screen_no > 1                     && Not the first screen
         IF over <= 8
            @ top+down+1, left+2 SAY "ESC for UP"
         ELSE
            @ top+down-2, left+2 SAY "ESC for UP"
         ENDIF
      ENDIF
   OTHERWISE                               && Somewhere else
      IF screen_no  > 1                    && Not the first screen
         IF over <= 8
            @ top+down+1, left+2 SAY "ESC for UP"
            @ top+down+2, left+2 PROMPT "Down Page"
         ELSE
```

```
                        @ top+down-2, left+2 SAY "ESC for UP"
                        @ top+down - 1, left+2 PROMPT "Down Page"
                  ENDIF
            ELSE
               IF over <= 8
                        @ top+down + 2, left+2 PROMPT "Down Page"
               ELSE
                        @ top+down - 1, left+2 PROMPT "Down Page"
               ENDIF
            ENDIF
            ENDCASE

            GO starting
            MENU TO option
            DO CASE
            CASE option = 0
               IF hit_bottom
                  hit_bottom = .F.
               ENDIF
               IF screen_no > 1
                  screen_no = screen_no - 1
                  GO beg_set
                  backward = (down - 3) * -1
                  SKIP backward
               ELSE
                  RETURN(0)
               ENDIF
            CASE option = down - 2
               option = 1
               GO next_set
               screen_no = screen_no + 1
            OTHERWISE
               pass_to = pointer[option]
               CALL _scrrest WITH backscr
               STORE SPACE(4000) TO backscr, frontscr
               USE
               RETURN(pass_to)
            ENDCASE
         ENDDO


*********************

FUNCTION Fill_out

PARAMETERS a, b

IF TYPE("b") = "U"
   b = 79
ENDIF
c = b - LEN(a)

RETURN(a + SPACE(c))
* End of File
```

CHAPTER THIRTEEN

Clipper's HELP Utility

A BRIEF SYNOPSIS OF HELP

The compiler contains a way to build a tool that's useful both for developers and their customers of applications compiled with Clipper: *on-line help.*

No matter how much time and energy is spent in designing the ultimate "user-friendly" system, no matter how many error-trapping routines are provided, regardless of how clear, helpful, and extensive the documentation may be, end-users usually fit one or more of the following descriptions.

1) They always get confused, bewildered, lost, and frustrated.

2) They always manage to break a system regardless how hard you have tried to prevent this from happening.

3) They never read the documentation.

The entire purpose of on-line help is to provide a means by which the developer may provide assistance to the program user even if the documentation never gets read. A developer should know that **no matter** how clear the program, how extensive the manual, or how involved the training, that cry for HELP eventually arrives. Context sensitive on-line help doesn't always prevent this from occurring, but it doesn't hurt.

The idea behind the HELP scheme in Clipper is that you can build a structured CASE statement which tests for the program name, variable name, and line number when the F1 key is struck. If help is needed on a variable or field, the user can press F1 and get specific information on that element. Thus, at every question, field input, and menu item displayed, the user can be guided through the system by the system. Of course, all of this is only possible if you have built a file called HELP.PRG.

HELP.PRG

Clipper has a default that looks for a procedure marked HELP whenever the F1 Key is pressed. If no file is present in the executable file, then nothing will happen. Therefore, the first thing to do is to create a file named HELP.PRG.

Because this file is not directly referenced by any other programs, it must be compiled separately. If you do not compile this file separately, Clipper will not see this file when F1 is pressed and your HELP scheme will not work. Once compiled, HELP.PRG must be linked into your application as a separate object file: if you neglect this step, no help will be available. Finally, don't compile any program with the -l option. If no line numbers are generated with the object files, then HELP will not have anything to use for the second parameter it needs (as described in the following section).

The basic construct of the file is one massive DO CASE ... ENDDO structure where each branch of the CASE is a separate test and may then branch for further testing.

P,L,V - MORE THAN JUST THREE LETTERS

The HELP procedure needs to have a PARAMETER command as the very first command line. Three parameters are automatically passed to HELP, regardless of the type of HELP designed. These three parameters are

1) P = program/procedure name of the routine calling HELP; this is of character type.

2) L = the line number of the source code line number calling HELP; this is of numeric type. It is the line number of the READ command associated with the corresponding GET command.

3) V = variable name in the routine calling HELP; this is of character type.

Remember that these three variables need not be initialized in any routine nor declared PUBLIC in order to function. They are private variables germane only to the HELP file and are released upon RETURN from HELP. In addition, these three variables are not restricted to these names: P, L, and V are used for clarity and simplicity within this document. Follow basic coding techniques when choosing a name appropriate for you.

These three parameters **must** be passed to HELP, but they do not have to be evaluated/tested within the program. Obviously, the more specific the help generated, the more extensive the evaluation on these variables has to be.

GLOBAL POINTER VARIABLES

HELP is just another procedure, except it is called by a key rather than a specific command in the program. All variables initialized above the HELP routine can be accessed by it. Many times, a global variable is immediately initialized to an empty value. This value will be accessed at some time by the HELP procedure. These global variables can be used to help direct or control the information displayed by the HELP procedure far better than just the variables P, L, and V.

Generalized help is based on the idea that one variable used in different programs can refer to the same piece of helpful information. If this is true in your application, then a more generalized help is in order rather than context sensitive help. This method of HELP is treated further in the section entitled "Generalized Help"; however, the basic technique is to use global variables only when the three variables passed to the HELP procedure are not adequate or are too cumbersome to use effectively. Just make sure that the variables accessed by the HELP procedure have been established previously. Otherwise, an undefined symbol message will appear at run time.

HELP INSIDE OF HELP

Basic to the concept of the HELP feature is the idea that the user is free to use the HELP procedure at any time. But what happens if the user should press the F1 key while inside the HELP procedure? The system may be able to keep track of things on one or two levels with only a minor glitch on the screen; however, system integrity is jeopardized. Anything past one or two levels is taking an unwarranted risk. More than likely, the application will generate an error, such as a System Memory Error. The developer must prevent this from happening. There are two ways to accomplish this task.

First, you can test to see if the calling program's name is HELP; if it is, simply go back to the calling program, which in this case is HELP. To do this, insert these three lines of code immediately after the PARAMETER statement:

```
IF p = "HELP"
   RETURN
ENDIF
```

The other method is to simply deactivate the F1 key. Immediately after the PARAMETER command, type this command:

```
SET KEY 28 TO
```

This follows the SET KEY TO command syntax and turns off the F1 key. When the execution of the program is returned to the original calling procedure, remember to turn on the HELP facility with the following command:

```
SET KEY 28 TO Help
```

HELP NEEDING HELP

If you decide that you need some additional help for HELP, a minor modification is needed to the SET KEY TO solution. Simply redirect the F1 key to another procedure – let's say HELPHELP – which could be a HELP procedure for the HELP procedure. To do this, issue the following command immediately after the PARAMETER command in the first HELP procedure:

```
SET KEY 28 TO Helphelp
```

All of the same rules will apply to HELPHELP. At this point, it may be a good idea to turn off the F1 key to keep from going any further. Keep track of the current level of the application and SET the F1 key accordingly. If this step is not taken, at some point in the application HELP may be turned off unexpectedly.

MEMOEDIT() AND HELP

The MEMOEDIT() function is a convenient feature to use in conjunction with the HELP procedure. MEMOEDIT() allows quick windowing techniques for displaying text information. However, the F1 key **must** be turned **off** prior to the use of the MEMOEDIT() function. If it is not, the user could edit the HELP information while inside the HELP routine. Once the MEMOEDIT() function has returned its value, the F1 key may be reinstated.

HELP TEXT: IN THE PROGRAM OR A FILE?

As you will see in the sample code later on in this section, the text information for HELP can reside either in the program or in a file on the disk. Each method has an advantage and a disadvantage. If you design HELP to reside in the program itself, you need to keep a close watch on the amount of memory required by the application without HELP. If the application is small enough, then the HELP information can be coded in and compiled with the rest of the application. The advantage to this method is in execution speed. Since the HELP information is resident in memory with every-thing else, access to the information is virtually instantaneous.

If memory space is a problem, the text for on-line HELP should be in a database file on the disk. This saves memory and compiling time; however, access time to the specific information increases dramatically. Review your application without HELP and consider the environment in which it will be running before deciding which of the two methods is best for your application.

HELP IN AN OVERLAY

HELP is needed at all times. Regardless of the procedure that is being used, the user will eventually look for help. It is possible to place the HELP object file in a separate overlay section to be loaded into the system whenever it is called. The problem with this is that there is sure to be more than one overlay area. Since the rules of overlaying dictate that no section in an overlay can call any other section in that same overlay, this can cause major problems. In most situations, the programmer decides which files belong where. However, since the developer cannot foresee when the HELP utility will be used, this file must be accessible to all procedures at all times. If the HELP procedure is called by another section within the same overlay, an EXEC SEQUENCE ERROR is sure to follow. For this reason alone, the HELP should never be placed in an overlay section.

Always avoid placing the HELP file anywhere but the main load module.

THE CLEAR COMMAND IN HELP

Never use the CLEAR command by itself to clear the screen when using the HELP facility, whether it is context sensitive or general HELP. When you use CLEAR, all GETS are also cleared which means that when the HELP returns control to the calling program, your application goes past the variable you were inquiring about. This may disrupt an application's entire execution scheme. This is true for **any** procedure called by the SET KEY < expN) TO < procedure >, since the calling of HELP is no more than a SET KEY 28 TO Help. To circumvent this, instead of using CLEAR by itself, add an appropriate @ SAY command such as:

```
@ 0,0 CLEAR
```

This clears the entire screen and positions the cursor to the top-left corner of the screen, but does **not** clear the GETS in the system.

SAVE SCREEN IN HELP

In order to take full advantage of the HELP system, use the SAVE SCREEN command to save the screen prior to displaying any HELP information. Then, once the information is displayed, RESTORE the SCREEN to its original display and continue with the execution of the program. The SAVE SCREEN command should be the first command prior to any structured DO CASE...ENDCASE statements or IF...ENDIF command other than the IF...ENDIF command testing for the HELP procedure.

CONSTRUCTING CONTEXT SENSITIVE HELP

Context specific help provides information on specific variables and fields throughout your application. Operational flow may be described best in a manual, but specific help on variables and user input is handled best by on-line HELP.

In using this technique, it is advisable to develop the application first and then use these lines of code:

```
PROCEDURE Help

PARAMETERS p, l, v

SET KEY 28 TO
SAVE SCREEN
@ 10,10 SAY "The calling program is:  "
?? p
@ 12,10 SAY "The source code line is:  "
?? l
@ 14,10 SAY "The variable is:          "
?? v
```

```
?
?
?
WAIT
SET KEY 28 TO Help
RESTORE SCREEN
```

Then, at every variable for which you want to write specific HELP, just press the F1 key and jot down the three values displayed on the screen. Once you have all of the values you need, construct the DO CASE...ENDCASE command as follows:

1) Group all of the P values together and build the initial level of DO CASE... ENDCASE. Establish an OTHERWISE statement to display a message informing the user that "No Help is Available".

2) Group all of the V values together and build a secondary, nested DO CASE...ENDCASE structure. Establish an OTHERWISE statement to display a message informing the user that "No Help is Available".

3) Only if absolutely necessary (normally this occurs with memory variables in the main application rather than fields) the L values may be tested and grouped together. If applicable, build a third nested DO CASE...END-CASE structure or an IF...ENDIF structure. Additionally establish an OTHERWISE or ELSE statement to display a message informing the user that "No Help is Available".

The following sample code demonstrates these principles:

```
********************
* Name          SHOWHELP.prg
* Date          August 11, 1986
* Notice        Copyright 1986, Stephen J. Straley
* Note          This program shows how context sensitive help works,
*               how a database pertaining to HELP works, and how
*               to create your own help "on-the-fly".
*
********************

CLEAR
TEXT

    A series of screens and variables will appear, as well as a menu
    choice. Choose a menu option, build a help screen for each level
    and note the coding techniques involved.

    Please press any key to begin demonstration ...
ENDTEXT
IF INKEY(0) = 0
ENDIF
```

```
scrframe = CHR(201) + CHR(205) + CHR(187) + CHR(186) + ;
           CHR(188) + CHR(205) + CHR(200) + CHR(186) + CHR(32)
DO WHILE .T.
   CLEAR
   option1 = 0
   @ 4, 8, 12, 72 BOX SUBSTR(scrframe,1,8)
   @ 3, 29 SAY "Legal Billing Main Menu"
   @ 6, 10 PROMPT " 1>  Client Information "
   @ 8, 14 PROMPT " 2>  Matter Information "
   @ 6, 48 PROMPT " 3>  Codes "
   @ 8, 48 PROMPT " 4>  Reports "
   @ 10, 31 SAY "ESC to Exit Program"
   MENU TO option1
   IF option1 = 0
      QUIT
   ELSE
      off = TRANSFORM(option1, "9")
      DO Branch&off.
   ENDIF
ENDDO


********************

PROCEDURE Branch1

   CLEAR
   STORE 1 TO this, that
   @ 10, 0 SAY "Enter in ages or F1 => " GET this
   @ 11, 0 SAY "                       " GET that
   READ


********************

PROCEDURE Branch2

   CLEAR
   @ 10,10 SAY "A new procedure for the same variable"
   @ 12,10 SAY "               Enter a new value => " GET option1
   READ


********************

PROCEDURE Branch3

   CLEAR
   @ 10,10 SAY "Press any key to go to Branch2 "
   IF INKEY(0) = 0
   ENDIF
   DO Branch2
```

```
********************

PROCEDURE Branch4

    CLEAR
    STORE .T. TO yes
    @ 10,10 SAY  "This option should yield 'No Help Available' .. " GET yes
    READ


********************

PROCEDURE Help

    PARAMETERS p,l,v

    SET KEY 28 TO
    SAVE SCREEN
    IF v = "YES"
       @ 00,10,03,70 BOX scrframe
       @ 01,15 SAY "There is no help available!  Any Key to continue..."
       IF INKEY(0) = 0
       ENDIF
       RESTORE SCREEN
       RETURN
    ENDIF
    SET SCOREBOARD OFF
    IF .NOT. FILE("HELP.DBF")
       @ 00,10,03,70 BOX scrframe
       @ 01,11 SAY "There is no HELP file available.    Would you like a help "
       @ 02,11 SAY "            file to be generated? "
       IF !VERIFY()
          RESTORE SCREEN
          SET KEY 28 TO Help
          RETURN
       ENDIF
       DO Dohelp
    ENDIF
    SELECT 9
    USE Help INDEX Help
    search = SUBSTR(p,1,10) + SUBSTR(v,1,10) + TRANSFORM(l, "9999")
    SEEK search
    IF FOUND()
       @ top,left,bottom,right BOX scrframe
       IF "" = MEMOEDIT(helpscr,top+1,left+1,bottom-1,right-1,.F.)
       ENDIF
       @ bottom-1,left+1 SAY "Any Key to Continue..."
    ELSE
       @ 00,10,03,70 BOX scrframe
       @ 01,11 SAY "There is no HELP for this section.  Would you like to
make"
       @ 02,11 SAY "            a HELP screen for this? "
       IF !VERIFY()
          RESTORE SCREEN
```

```
            SET KEY 28 TO Help
            RETURN
         ENDIF
         APPEND BLANK
         REPLACE lookit WITH SUBSTR(p,1,10) + SUBSTR(v,1,10) +;
                 TRANSFORM(l,"9999")
         STORE SPACE(4000) TO in_help, full_scr
         CALL _scrsave WITH full_scr
         STORE 0 TO temp_top, temp_left, temp_bot, temp_right
         DO WHILE .T.
            CALL _scrrest WITH full_scr
            @ 00,10,03,70 BOX scrframe
            @ 01,20 SAY "Position cursor with arrow for TOP, LEFT corner."
            cursor = 0
            newcur = CHR(201)
            CALL _scrsave WITH in_help
            @ 12,40 SAY newcur
            trow = 12
            tcol = 40
            DO WHILE.T.
               cursor = INKEY(0)
               DO CASE
               CASE cursor = 5
                  IF trow - 1 > 0
                     trow = trow - 1
                  ENDIF
               CASE cursor = 4
                  IF tcol + 1 < 79
                     tcol = tcol + 1
                  ENDIF
               CASE cursor = 19
                  IF tcol - 1 > 0
                     tcol = tcol - 1
                  ENDIF
               CASE cursor = 24
                  IF trow + 1 < 24
                     trow = trow + 1
                  ENDIF
               CASE cursor = 13 .OR. cursor = 27
                  EXIT
               ENDCASE
               CALL _scrrest WITH in_help
               @ trow, tcol SAY newcur
            ENDDO
            STORE trow TO temp_top
            STORE tcol TO temp_left
            @ 00,10,03,70 BOX scrframe
            @ 01,14 SAY "Position cursor with arrow for BOTTOM, RIGHT corner."
            cursor = 0
            CALL _scrsave WITH in_help
            newcur = CHR(188)
            trow = temp_top + 2
            tcol = temp_left + 5
```

```
@ trow, tcol SAY newcur
DO WHILE.T.
   cursor = INKEY(0)
   DO CASE
   CASE cursor = 5
      IF trow - 1 > temp_top
         trow = trow - 1
      ENDIF
   CASE cursor = 4
      IF tcol + 1 < 79
         tcol = tcol + 1
      ENDIF
   CASE cursor = 19
      IF tcol - 1 > temp_left + 3
         tcol = tcol - 1
      ENDIF
   CASE cursor = 24
      IF trow + 1 < 24
         trow = trow + 1
      ENDIF
   CASE cursor = 13 .OR. cursor = 27
      EXIT
   ENDCASE
   CALL _scrrest WITH in_help
   @ trow, tcol SAY newcur
ENDDO
STORE trow TO temp_bot
STORE tcol TO temp_right
CALL _scrsave WITH in_help
DO Temphelp
@ 00,10,03,70 BOX scrframe
@ 02,25 SAY "Is this what you wanted?   "
IF !VERIFY()
   CALL _scrrest WITH in_help
   LOOP
ELSE
   @ 00,10,03,70 BOX scrframe
   @ 01,20 SAY "     Ctrl-W to SAVE / Ctrl-Q to Abandon"
ENDIF
REPLACE top WITH temp_top, bottom WITH temp_bot, left WITH
temp_left, right WITH temp_right
EXIT
ENDDO
DO WHILE .T.
   @ top,left,bottom,right BOX scrframe
   REPLACE helpscr WITH MEMOEDIT(helpscr,top+1,left+1,bottom-1,right-
1,.T.)
   @ top,left,bottom,right BOX scrframe
   IF "" = MEMOEDIT(helpscr,top+1,left+1,bottom-1,right-1,.F.)
   ENDIF
   @ bottom-1,left+1 SAY "IS THIS CORRECT?    "
   IF !VERIFY()
      LOOP
```

```
               ENDIF
               EXIT
            ENDDO
            @ bottom-1,left+1 SAY "Press Any key to Continue...."
         ENDIF
         IF INKEY(0) = 0
         ENDIF
         RESTORE SCREEN
         SET KEY 28 TO Help
         RETURN


*******************

PROCEDURE Dohelp

   PARAMETER p1, l1, v1

   SELECT 9
   CREATE Temp
   USE Temp
   APPEND BLANK
   REPLACE field_name WITH "LOOKIT", field_type WITH "C", field_len WITH 24
   APPEND BLANK
   REPLACE field_name WITH "TOP", field_type WITH "N", field_len WITH 2
   APPEND BLANK
   REPLACE field_name WITH "LEFT", field_type WITH "N", field_len WITH 2
   APPEND BLANK
   REPLACE field_name WITH "BOTTOM", field_type WITH "N", field_len WITH 2
   APPEND BLANK
   REPLACE field_name WITH "RIGHT", field_type WITH "N", field_len WITH 2
   APPEND BLANK
   REPLACE field_name WITH "HELPSCR", field_type WITH "M", field_len WITH 10
   USE
   CREATE Help FROM Temp
   ERASE Temp
   USE Help
   INDEX ON lookit TO Help


*******************

PROCEDURE Temphelp

   SET COLOR TO W*
   @ temp_top, temp_left, temp_bot, temp_right BOX SUBSTR(scrframe,1,8)
   SET COLOR TO 7


*******************

FUNCTION Verify

   SET CONSOLE OFF
   STORE "" TO inertemp
   DO WHILE .NOT. inertemp$"YyNn"
```

```
         WAIT TO inertemp
      ENDDO
      SET CONSOLE ON
      IF UPPER(inertemp) = "Y"
         ?? "Yes"
         te = INKEY(.25)
         RETURN(.T.)
      ENDIF
      ?? "No "
      te = INKEY(.25)
      RETURN(.F.)
   * End of File
```

SAMPLE OF CONTEXT SENSITIVE HELP

The following program demonstrates one way to design a help scheme that is specific
to the calling program's name, the variable name, and the line number. Note that this
information is kept in the program file, increasing its overall size.

```
********************
* Name              DOMENU1.prg
* Date              August 12, 1986
* Notice            Copyright 1986, Stephen J. Straley
* Note              This program demonstrates how context specific
*                   HELP can be implemented.
*
********************

CLEAR
DO Domen1

********************

PROCEDURE Domen1

   DO WHILE .T.
      CLEAR
   scrframe =  CHR(201) + CHR(205) + CHR(187) + CHR(186) + ;
               CHR(188) + CHR(205) + CHR(200) + CHR(186) + CHR(32)
      STORE SPACE(4000) TO ascreen, bscreen, cscreen
      STORE 0 TO option
      @ 6, 1, 17, 75 BOX SUBSTR(scrframe,1,8)
      @ 5, 30 SAY "M A I N    M E N U"
      @ 8, 7 PROMPT " 1> Chart of Accounts "
      @ 10, 7 PROMPT " 2> Transactions "
      @ 12, 7 PROMPT " 3> Posting / Balancing "
      @ 14, 7 PROMPT " 4> Print Listings "
      @ 8, 48 PROMPT " 5> Print Reports "
      @ 10, 48 PROMPT " 6> Transfers "
      @ 12, 48 PROMPT " 7> Utilities "
      @ 14, 48 PROMPT " 8> End of Period "
      @ 16, 33 SAY "ESC to RETURN"
```

```
      MENU TO option
      CALL _scrsave WITH ascreen
      DO CASE
      CASE option = 0
         @ 18, 15 SAY "All Files Closed, Returning to Operating System"
         QUIT
      CASE option = 1
         DO Domen11
      OTHERWISE
         *************************
         * Do sub-procedure here *
         *************************
      ENDCASE
   ENDDO


*********************

PROCEDURE Domen11

   DO WHILE .T.
      IF !EMPTY(bscreen)
         CALL _scrrest WITH bscreen
      ENDIF
      STORE 0 TO option1
      @ 9, 39, 22, 64 BOX scrframe
      @ 10, 46 SAY "COA Sub-Menu"
      @ 12, 43 PROMPT " 1> Enter Account "
      @ 14, 43 PROMPT " 2> Edit Account "
      @ 16, 43 PROMPT " 3> Scan Accounts "
      @ 18, 43 PROMPT " 4> Delete Accounts "
      @ 21, 46 SAY "ESC to RETURN"
      MENU TO option1
      CALL _scrsave WITH bscreen
      DO CASE
      CASE option1 = 0
         EXIT
      CASE option1 = 1
         STORE SPACE(10) TO in_name, in_descpt
         STORE 0 TO in_bal, in_accnt
         @ 14,5,20,75 BOX scrframe
         @ 16,10 SAY "Enter Account Number: " GET in_accnt PICT "#####.##"
         @ 18,10 SAY "        Account Name: " GET in_name PICT "@X" ;
               VALID(!EMPTY(in_name))
         @ 16,46 SAY "    Balance: $" GET in_bal PICT "###,###,###.##"
         @ 18,46 SAY "Description: " GET in_descpt
         READ
      OTHERWISE
         *************************
         * Do sub-procedure here *
         *************************
      ENDCASE
   ENDDO
```

```
********************

PROCEDURE Help

  PARAMETERS p, l, v

     SET KEY 28 TO
     SAVE SCREEN
     DO CASE
     CASE p == "DOMEN1"
        DO CASE
        CASE v == "OPTION"
           @ 18, 7,23,72 BOX scrframe
           @ 19,12 SAY "This is the MAIN MENU.  Choose the menu item with the"
           @ 20,12 SAY "cursor keys, striking the RETURN key or first character"
           @ 21,12 SAY "string for immediate response.  Otherwise, the ESCape"
           @ 22,12 SAY "will return to Operating System."
           hrow = ROW()
           hcol = COL() + 1
        OTHERWISE
           @ 0,0,4,79 BOX scrframe
           @ 2,5 SAY "No Help is Available.  "
           hrow = ROW()
           hcol = 40
        ENDCASE
     CASE p == "DOMEN11"
        DO CASE
        CASE v == "OPTION1"
           @ 18, 7,23,72 BOX scrframe
           @ 19,12 SAY "This is the sub menu for the CHART OF ACCOUNTS. Move"
           @ 20,12 SAY "cursor keys for appropriate item, or first character"
           @ 21,12 SAY "string for immediate response.  Otherwise, the ESCape"
           @ 22,12 SAY "will return to the Main Menu. "
           hrow = ROW()
           hcol = COL() + 1
        CASE v == "IN_ACCNT"
           @ 1,5,5,75 BOX scrframe
           @ 2,11 SAY "Please enter the Account Number being entered into the"
           @ 3,11 SAY "Chart of Accounts.  To exit this routine, strike the"
           @ 4,11 SAY "PgDn Key when returned."
           hrow = ROW()
           hcol = COL() + 1
        CASE v == "IN_NAME"
           @ 1,5,5,75 BOX scrframe
           @ 2,11 SAY "Please enter the Account Name for the entered Account"
           @ 3,11 SAY "Number.  This is a field MUST be contain a value."
           hrow = ROW() + 1
           hcol = 17
        CASE v == "IN_BAL"
           @ 1,5,5,75 BOX scrframe
           @ 2,11 SAY "Please enter the Account Balance for the entered Ac-
count"
           @ 3,11 SAY "Number.  Leave blank for empty balance."
```

```
                  hrow = ROW()
                  hcol = COL() + 2
              CASE v == "IN_DESCPT"
                  a 1,5,5,75 BOX scrframe
                  a 2,11 SAY "Please enter the Description for the entered Account"
                  a 3,11 SAY "Number.  Leave blank for an empty field"
                  hrow = ROW()
                  hcol = COL() + 5
              OTHERWISE
                  a 0,0,4,79 BOX scrframe
                  a 2,5 SAY "No Help is Available.  "
                  hrow = ROW()
                  hcol = 40
              ENDCASE
          OTHERWISE
              a 0,0,4,79 BOX scrframe
              a 2,5 SAY "No Help is Available.  "
              hrow = ROW()
              hcol = 40
          ENDCASE
          a hrow, hcol SAY "[Any Key to RETURN]"
          STORE INKEY(0) TO tempkey
          RESTORE SCREEN
          SET KEY 28 TO Help
    * End of File
```

GENERAL HELP

General HELP is designed to provide the user with a sense of the flow of operation of
the program rather than with specific information on the fields or variables.

In order to establish General HELP, a global variable is set at the very top-level procedure. This variable – call it "help_code" – is initialized as available to all subprocedures, including HELP. As you proceed through the application, change the
value of "help_code". Then, inside HELP, test only for the value of the "help_code"
and build the help screen accordingly.

One approach would be to initialize "help_code" to a value of zero in the first routine
of the application. Inside HELP, if the value of "help_code" is found equal to 0, display the "No Help is Available" message.

Whatever HELP scheme you choose, make sure to:

1) Initialize the global variable at the very top level program/procedure.

2) Still pass the parameters.

3) SAVE the screen prior to execution and RESTORE it when leaving the
   routine.

4)   Disengage the F1 key before entering HELP and reinstate it upon leaving, or test for calling program = "HELP".

SAMPLE OF GENERAL HELP

The following program is a sample implementation of GENERAL HELP.

```
********************
* Name        DOMENU2.prg
* Date        August 11, 1986
* Notice      Copyright 1986, Stephen J. Straley
* Note        This program demonstrates how generalized HELP
*             can be implemented.
*
********************

CLEAR
DO Domen1

********************

PROCEDURE Domen1

DO WHILE .T.
   CLEAR
   scrframe =  CHR(201) + CHR(205) + CHR(187) + CHR(186) + ;
               CHR(188) + CHR(205) + CHR(200) + CHR(186) + CHR(32)
   STORE SPACE(4000) TO ascreen, bscreen, cscreen
   STORE 0 TO option, help_code
   @ 6, 1, 17, 75 BOX scrframe
   @ 5, 30 SAY "M A I N    M E N U"
   @ 8, 7 PROMPT " 1> Chart of Accounts "
   @ 10, 7 PROMPT " 2> Transactions "
   @ 12, 7 PROMPT " 3> Posting / Balancing "
   @ 14, 7 PROMPT " 4> Print Listings "
   @ 8, 48 PROMPT " 5> Print Reports "
   @ 10, 48 PROMPT " 6> Transfers "
   @ 12, 48 PROMPT " 7> Utilities "
   @ 14, 48 PROMPT " 8> End of Period "
   @ 16, 33 SAY "ESC to RETURN"
   MENU TO option
   CALL _scrsave WITH ascreen
   DO CASE
   CASE option = 0
      @ 18, 15 SAY "All Files Closed, Returning to Operating System"
      QUIT
   CASE option = 1
      DO Domen11
```

```
   OTHERWISE
      *************************
      * Do sub-procedure here *
      *************************
   ENDCASE
ENDDO

*********************

PROCEDURE Domen11

DO WHILE .T.
   IF !EMPTY(bscreen)
      CALL _scrrest WITH bscreen
   ENDIF
   @ 9, 39, 22, 64 BOX scrframe
   STORE 0 TO option1
   @ 10, 46 SAY "COA Sub-Menu"
   @ 12, 43 PROMPT " 1> Enter Account "
   @ 14, 43 PROMPT " 2> Edit Account "
   @ 16, 43 PROMPT " 3> Scan Accounts "
   @ 18, 43 PROMPT " 4> Delete Accounts "
   @ 21, 46 SAY "ESC to RETURN"
   MENU TO option1
   CALL _scrsave WITH bscreen
   DO CASE
   CASE option1 = 1
      STORE SPACE(10) TO in_name, in_descpt
      STORE 0 TO in_bal, in_accnt
      STORE 1 TO help_code
      @ 14,5,20,75 BOX scrframe
      @ 16,10 SAY "Enter Account Number: " GET in_bal  PICT "#####.##"
      @ 18,10 SAY "       Account Name: " GET in_name PICT "@X" ;
                 VALID(!EMPTY(in_name))
      @ 16,46 SAY "    Balance: $" GET in_bal PICT "###,###,###.##"
      @ 18,46 SAY "Description: " GET in_descpt
      READ
   CASE option1 = 2
      *************************
      * Do sub-procedure here *
      *************************
   CASE option1 = 3
      *************************
      * Do sub-procedure here *
      *************************
   CASE option1 = 4
      *************************
      * Do sub-procedure here *
      *************************
   CASE option1 = 0
      EXIT
   ENDCASE
ENDDO
```

```
********************

PROCEDURE Help

PARAMETERS p, l, v

    SET KEY 28 TO
    SAVE SCREEN
    DO CASE
    CASE help_code = 0
        @ 18, 7,23,72 BOX scrframe
        @ 19,12 SAY "Move the cursor to the proper menu option then strike the"
        @ 20,12 SAY "RETURN key, or strike the first character in the menu"
        @ 21,12 SAY "string for immediate response.  Otherwise, the ESCape will"
        @ 22,12 SAY "Return to the Main Menu."
        hrow = ROW()
        hcol = COL() + 1
    CASE help_code = 1
        @ 3,10,10,70 BOX scrframe
        @ 5,12 SAY "This is the ENTER ACCOUNT INFORMATION sub-menu...."
        @ 7,12 SAY "    Enter in the appropriate information and strike the"
        @ 8,12 SAY "    RETURN key to complete the entry."
        hrow = ROW()
        hcol = COL() + 1
    OTHERWISE
        @ 0,0,4,79 BOX scrframe
        @ 2,5 SAY "No Help is Available.  "
        hrow = ROW()
        hcol = 40
    ENDCASE
    @ hrow, hcol SAY "[Any Key to RETURN]"
    STORE INKEY(0) TO tempkey
    RESTORE SCREEN
    SET KEY 28 TO Help
* End of File
```

USING MEMOEDIT() AND A DISK FILE

There is another way to approach the subject of on-line help: using disk files. As more and more information is added to the HELP procedure, the size of your executable file increases and, in some cases, becomes too big to manage. In the technique shown in this example, the HELP procedure is larger than any of the other examples, but the program file will not increase further, regardless of the amount of information recorded for HELP.

Another feature of this technique is the use of the MEMOEDIT() function. In this example, the user can design a custom help screen based on the variable or program involved. This type of HELP is more like an on-line notepad.

The following code demonstrates context specific HELP using a disk file:

```
********************
* Name         DOMENU3.prg
* Date         August 12, 1986
* Notice       Copyright 1986, Stephen J. Straley
* Note         This program demonstrates how specific HELP
*              can be instituted in conjunction with the MEMOEDIT()
*              function and writing the context specific HELP to a
*              disk file.
*
*              To make this program work, you must link in the assembler
*              file CURSOR.OBJ (see Chapter 10) in order to turn off the
*              cursor.  Of course, this program then can only run on 100%
*              IBM compatibles.
*
********************

CLEAR
DO Domen1

********************

PROCEDURE Domen1

   DO WHILE .T.
      CLEAR
      scrframe = CHR(201) + CHR(205) + CHR(187) + CHR(186) + ;
                 CHR(188) + CHR(205) + CHR(200) + CHR(186) + CHR(32)
      STORE SPACE(4000) TO ascreen, bscreen, cscreen
      STORE 0 TO option
      SET FUNCTION 10 TO CHR(23)    && This is to write the memo
      @ 6, 1, 17, 75 BOX SUBSTR(scrframe,1,8)
      @ 5, 30 SAY "M A I N    M E N U"
      @ 8, 7 PROMPT " 1> Chart of Accounts "
      @ 10, 7 PROMPT " 2> Transactions "
      @ 12, 7 PROMPT " 3> Posting / Balancing "
      @ 14, 7 PROMPT " 4> Print Listings "
      @ 8, 48 PROMPT " 5> Print Reports "
      @ 10, 48 PROMPT " 6> Transfers "
      @ 12, 48 PROMPT " 7> Utilities "
      @ 14, 48 PROMPT " 8> End of Period "
      @ 16, 33 SAY "ESC to RETURN"
      MENU TO option
      CALL _scrsave WITH ascreen
      DO CASE
      CASE option = 0
         @ 18, 15 SAY "All Files Closed. Returning to Operating System"
         QUIT
      CASE option = 1
         DO Domen11
      OTHERWISE
         **************************
         * Do sub-procedure here *
         **************************
      ENDCASE
   ENDDO
```

```
********************

PROCEDURE Domen11

   DO WHILE .T.
      IF !EMPTY(bscreen)
         CALL _scrrest WITH bscreen
      ENDIF
      STORE 0 TO option1
      @ 9, 39, 22, 64 BOX scrframe
      @ 10, 46 SAY "COA Sub-Menu"
      @ 12, 43 PROMPT " 1> Enter Account "
      @ 14, 43 PROMPT " 2> Edit Account "
      @ 16, 43 PROMPT " 3> Scan Accounts "
      @ 18, 43 PROMPT " 4> Delete Accounts "
      @ 21, 46 SAY "ESC to RETURN"
      MENU TO option1
      CALL _scrsave WITH bscreen
      DO CASE
      CASE option1 = 1
         STORE SPACE(10) TO in_name, in_descpt
         STORE 0 TO in_bal, in_accnt
         @ 14,5,20,75 BOX scrframe
         @ 16,10 SAY "Enter Account Number: " GET in_accnt PICT "#####.##"
         @ 18,10 SAY "        Account Name: " GET in_name PICT "@X"
VALID(!EMPTY(in_name))
         @ 16,46 SAY "    Balance: $" GET in_bal PICT "###,###,###.##"
         @ 18,46 SAY "Description: " GET in_descpt
         READ
      CASE option1 = 2
         **************************
         * Do sub-procedure here *
         **************************
      CASE option1 = 3
         **************************
         * Do sub-procedure here *
         **************************
      CASE option1 = 4
         **************************
         * Do sub-procedure here *
         **************************
      CASE option1 = 0
         EXIT
      ENDCASE
   ENDDO

********************

PROCEDURE Help

   PARAMETERS p, l, v

      SET KEY 28 TO
      SAVE SCREEN
      SET SCOREBOARD OFF
```

```
            scrframe = CHR(201) + CHR(205) + CHR(187) + CHR(186) + ;
                       CHR(188) + CHR(205) + CHR(200) + CHR(186) + CHR(32)
         IF .NOT. FILE("HELP.DBF")
            @ 00,10,03,70 BOX scrframe
            @ 01,11 SAY "There is no HELP file available. Would you like a help"
            @ 02,27 SAY "file to be generated? "
            IF .NOT. VERIFY()
               RESTORE SCREEN
               SET KEY 28 TO Help
               RETURN
            ENDIF

            NOTE If a data base is open, its selected area must be noted
            goback = SELECT()
            DO Dohelp
            NOTE Once the help has been performed, the previously selected area
            NOTE is reselected.
            tempgo = STR(goback)
            SELECT &tempgo

         ENDIF
         goback = SELECT()
         SELECT 9
         USE Help INDEX Help
         search = SUBSTR(p,1,10) + SUBSTR(v,1,10) + TRANSFORM(l, "9999")
         SEEK search
         IF FOUND()
            @ top,left,bottom,right BOX scrframe
            IF "" = MEMOEDIT(helpscr,top+1,left+1,bottom-1,right-1,.F.)
            ENDIF
            @ bottom-1,left+1 SAY "Any Key to Continue..."
         ELSE
            @ 00,10,03,70 BOX scrframe
            @ 01,11 SAY "There is no HELP for this section.  Would you like to
make"
            @ 02,28 SAY "a HELP screen for this? "
            IF .NOT. VERIFY()
               RESTORE SCREEN
               SET KEY 28 TO Help
               RETURN
            ENDIF
            APPEND BLANK
            REPLACE lookit WITH SUBSTR(p,1,10) + SUBSTR(v,1,10) + TRANS-
FORM(l,"9999")
            STORE SPACE(4000) TO in_help, full_scr
            STORE 0 TO temp_top, temp_left, temp_bot, temp_right
            CALL _scrsave WITH full_scr
            DO WHILE .T.
               CALL _scrrest WITH full_scr
               @ 00,10,03,70 BOX scrframe
               @ 01,20 SAY "Position cursor with arrow for TOP, LEFT corner."
               cursor = 0
               newcur = CHR(201)
```

```
      CALL _scrsave WITH in_help
      @ 12,40 SAY newcur
      trow = 12
      tcol = 40
      CALL cursw
      DO WHILE.T.
         cursor = INKEY(0)
         loop_again = MOVECURS()
         IF !loop_again
            EXIT
         ENDIF
         CALL _scrrest WITH in_help
         @ trow, tcol SAY newcur
      ENDDO
      STORE trow TO temp_top
      STORE tcol TO temp_left
      @ 00,10,03,70 BOX scrframe
      @ 01,14 SAY "Position cursor with arrow for BOTTOM, RIGHT corner."
      cursor = 0
      CALL _scrsave WITH in_help
      newcur = CHR(188)
      trow = temp_top + 2
      tcol = temp_left + 5
      @ trow, tcol SAY newcur
      DO WHILE.T.
         cursor = INKEY(0)
         loop_again = MOVECURS()
         IF !loop_again
            EXIT
         ENDIF
         CALL _scrrest WITH in_help
         @ trow, tcol SAY newcur
      ENDDO
      CALL cursw
      STORE trow TO temp_bot
      STORE tcol TO temp_right
      CALL _scrsave WITH in_help
      DO Temphelp
      @ 00,10,03,70 BOX scrframe
      @ 02,25 SAY "Is this what you wanted?  "
      IF .NOT. VERIFY()
         CALL _scrrest WITH in_help
         LOOP
      ELSE
         EXIT
      ENDIF
   ENDDO
   @ 00,10,03,70 BOX scrframe
   @ 01,15 SAY "Enter in HELPful information.  Keep to ONE screen"
   @ 02,15 SAY "     of text.  Press F10 when finished."
   REPLACE top WITH temp_top, bottom WITH temp_bot
   REPLACE left WITH temp_left, right WITH temp_right
   DO WHILE .T.
```

```
                @ top,left,bottom,right BOX scrframe
                REPLACE helpscr WITH MEMOEDIT(helpscr,top+1,left+1,bottom-1,right-
1,.T.)
                @ top,left,bottom,right BOX scrframe
                IF "" = MEMOEDIT(helpscr,top+1,left+1,bottom-1,right-1,.F.)
                ENDIF
                @ bottom-1,left+1 SAY "IS THIS CORRECT?    "
                IF .NOT. VERIFY()
                    LOOP
                ENDIF
                EXIT
            ENDDO
            @ bottom-1,left+1 SAY "Press Any key to Continue..."
        ENDIF
        qw = INKEY(0)
        RESTORE SCREEN
        tempgo = STR(goback)
        SELECT &tempgo
        SET KEY 28 TO Help
        RETURN


    ********************

    PROCEDURE Dohelp

        SELECT 9
        CREATE Temp
        USE Temp
        APPEND BLANK
        REPLACE field_name WITH "LOOKIT", field_type WITH "C", field_len WITH 24
        APPEND BLANK
        REPLACE field_name WITH "TOP", field_type WITH "N", field_len WITH 2
        APPEND BLANK
        REPLACE field_name WITH "LEFT", field_type WITH "N", field_len WITH 2
        APPEND BLANK
        REPLACE field_name WITH "BOTTOM", field_type WITH "N", field_len WITH 2
        APPEND BLANK
        REPLACE field_name WITH "RIGHT", field_type WITH "N", field_len WITH 2
        APPEND BLANK
        REPLACE field_name WITH "HELPSCR", field_type WITH "M", field_len WITH 10
        USE
        CREATE Help FROM Temp
        USE
        ERASE Temp
        USE Help
        INDEX ON lookit TO Help

    ********************

    PROCEDURE Temphelp

        SET COLOR TO W*
        @ temp_top, temp_left, temp_bot, temp_right BOX SUBSTR(scrframe,1,8)
        SET COLOR TO 7
```

```
****************************

FUNCTION VERIFY

    SET CONSOLE off
    WAIT TO inertemp
    SET CONSOLE on
    IF UPPER(inertemp) = "Y"
       ?? "Yes"
       te = INKEY(.25)
       RETURN(.T.)
    ENDIF
    ?? "No "
    te = INKEY(.25)
    RETURN(.F.)


*********************

FUNCTION Movecurs

    DO CASE
    CASE cursor = 5
       IF trow - 1 > 0
          trow = trow - 1
       ENDIF
    CASE cursor = 4
       IF tcol + 1 < 79
          tcol = tcol + 1
       ENDIF
    CASE cursor = 19
       IF tcol - 1 > 0
          tcol = tcol - 1
       ENDIF
    CASE cursor = 24
       IF trow + 1 < 24
          trow = trow + 1
       ENDIF
    CASE cursor = 13 .OR. cursor = 27
       RETURN(.F.)
    ENDCASE
    RETURN(.T.)
* End of File
```

MULTIPLE LEVEL HELP, EVERYTHING AT ONCE

The following example is the expanded version of the HELP utility. Basically, it is
everything at once, including multiple levels of HELP. Notice the ability to inquire for
more HELP within the HELP procedure. A second level of HELP is established and
the appropriate key (the F1 Key) is set accordingly.

```
********************
* Name          DOMENU4.prg
* Date          August 12, 1986
* Notice        Copyright 1986, Stephen J. Straley
* Note          This program demonstrates how HELP can
*               can have another level of HELP in it.
*               Also, this example shows practically
*               every aspect of the Clipper HELP facility.
*
*               To make this program work, you must link in the assembler
*               file CURSOR.OBJ (see Chapter 10) in order to turn off the
*               cursor.   Of course, this program then can only run on 100%
*               IBM compatibles.
*
********************

CLEAR
DO Domen1

********************

PROCEDURE Domen1

   DO WHILE .T.
      CLEAR
      scrframe = CHR(201) + CHR(205) + CHR(187) + CHR(186) + ;
                 CHR(188) + CHR(205) + CHR(200) + CHR(186) + CHR(32)
      STORE SPACE(4000) TO ascreen, bscreen, cscreen
      STORE 0 TO option
      SET FUNCTION 10 TO CHR(23)   && This is to write the memo
      @ 6, 1, 17, 75 BOX SUBSTR(scrframe,1,8)
      @ 5, 30 SAY "M A I N    M E N U"
      @ 8, 7 PROMPT " 1> Chart of Accounts "
      @ 10, 7 PROMPT " 2> Transactions "
      @ 12, 7 PROMPT " 3> Posting / Balancing "
      @ 14, 7 PROMPT " 4> Print Listings "
      @ 8, 48 PROMPT " 5> Print Reports "
      @ 10, 48 PROMPT " 6> Transfers "
      @ 12, 48 PROMPT " 7> Utilities "
      @ 14, 48 PROMPT " 8> End of Period "
      @ 16, 33 SAY "ESC to RETURN"
      MENU TO option
      CALL _scrsave WITH ascreen
      DO CASE
      CASE option = 0
         @ 18, 15 SAY "All Files Closed. Returning to Operating System"
         QUIT
      CASE option = 1
         DO Domen11
      OTHERWISE
         *************************
         * Do sub-procedure here *
         *************************
      ENDCASE
   ENDDO
```

```
********************

PROCEDURE Domen11

    DO WHILE .T.
       IF !EMPTY(bscreen)
          CALL _scrrest WITH bscreen
       ENDIF
       STORE 0 TO option1
       @ 9, 39, 22, 64 BOX scrframe
       @ 10, 46 SAY "COA Sub-Menu"
       @ 12, 43 PROMPT " 1> Enter Account "
       @ 14, 43 PROMPT " 2> Edit Account "
       @ 16, 43 PROMPT " 3> Scan Accounts "
       @ 18, 43 PROMPT " 4> Delete Accounts "
       @ 21, 46 SAY "ESC to RETURN"
       MENU TO option1
       CALL _scrsave WITH bscreen
       DO CASE
       CASE option1 = 0
          EXIT
       CASE option1 = 1
          STORE SPACE(10) TO in_name, in_descpt
          STORE 0 TO in_bal, in_accnt
          @ 14,5,20,75 BOX scrframe
          @ 16,10 SAY "Enter Account Number: " GET in_accnt PICT "#####.##"
          @ 18,10 SAY "        Account Name: " GET in_name PICT "@X" ;
                  VALID(!EMPTY(in_name))
          @ 16,46 SAY "    Balance: $" GET in_bal PICT "###,###,###.##"
          @ 18,46 SAY "Description: " GET in_descpt
          READ
       OTHERWISE
          *************************
          * Do sub-procedure here *
          *************************
       ENDCASE
    ENDDO

********************

PROCEDURE Help

    PARAMETERS p, l, v

       SET KEY 28 TO Help2
       SAVE SCREEN
       STORE 0 TO level
       @ 18,20,23,60 BOX scrframe
       @ 19,25 PROMPT "1> Design Custom Help"
       @ 20,25 PROMPT "2> Take Pre-designed Help"
       @ 22,25 SAY    "ESC Key to RETURN TO SYSTEM"
       MENU TO level
       RESTORE SCREEN
```

```
                IF level = 0
                   RETURN
                   ELSE
                   IF level = 1
                      DO Help3
                      RETURN
                   ENDIF
                ENDIF
                SAVE SCREEN
                DO CASE
                CASE p == "DOMEN1"
                   DO CASE
                   CASE v == "OPTION"
                      @ 18, 7,23,72 BOX scrframe
                      @ 19,12 SAY "This is the MAIN MENU.  Choose the menu item with the "
                      @ 20,12 SAY "cursor keys, striking the RETURN key or first character"
                      @ 21,12 SAY "in the string for immediate response.  Otherwise, ESCape"
                      @ 22,12 SAY " will return to Operating System. "
                      hrow = ROW()
                      hcol = COL() + 1
                   OTHERWISE
                      @ 0,0,4,79 BOX scrframe
                      @ 2,5 SAY "No Help is Available.  "
                      hrow = ROW()
                      hcol = 40
                   ENDCASE
                CASE p == "DOMEN11"
                   DO CASE
                   CASE v == "OPTION1"
                      @ 18, 7,23,72 BOX scrframe
                      @ 19,12 SAY "This is the sub menu for the CHART OF ACCOUNTS.  Move the"
                      @ 20,12 SAY "cursor keys for appropriate item, or first character"
                      @ 21,12 SAY "in the string for immediate response.  Otherwise, ESCape"
                      @ 22,12 SAY "will return to the Main Menu. "
                      hrow = ROW()
                      hcol = COL() + 1
                   CASE v == "IN_ACCNT"
                      @ 1,5,5,75 BOX scrframe
                      @ 2,11 SAY "Please enter the Account Number being entered into the"
                      @ 3,11 SAY "Chart of Accounts.  To exit this routine, strike the"
                      @ 4,11 SAY "PgDn Key when returned."
                      hrow = ROW()
                      hcol = COL() + 1
                   CASE v == "IN_NAME"
                      @ 1,5,5,75 BOX scrframe
                      @ 2,11 SAY "Please enter the Account Name for the entered Account"
                      @ 3,11 SAY "Number.  This a field MUST be contain a value."
                      hrow = ROW() + 1
                      hcol = 17
                   CASE v == "IN_BAL"
                      @ 1,5,5,75 BOX scrframe
                      @ 2,11 SAY "Please enter the Account Balance for the entered Account"
                      @ 3,11 SAY "Number.  Leave blank for empty balance."
```

```
               hrow = ROW()
               hcol = COL() + 2
           CASE v == "IN_DESCPT"
               @ 1,5,5,75 BOX scrframe
               @ 2,11 SAY "Please enter the Description for the entered Account"
               @ 3,11 SAY "Number.  Leave blank for an empty field"
               hrow = ROW()
               hcol = COL() + 5
           OTHERWISE
               @ 0,0,4,79 BOX scrframe
               @ 2,5 SAY "No Help is Available.  "
               hrow = ROW()
               hcol = 40
           ENDCASE
       OTHERWISE
           @ 0,0,4,79 BOX scrframe
           @ 2,5 SAY "No Help is Available."
           hrow = ROW()
           hcol = 40
       ENDCASE
       @ hrow, hcol SAY "[Any Key to RETURN]"
       STORE INKEY(0) TO tempkey
       RESTORE SCREEN
       SET KEY 28 TO Help


********************

PROCEDURE Help2

    PARAMETERS p2, l2, v2
    SET KEY 28 TO
    STORE SPACE(4096) TO screen2
    CALL _scrsave WITH screen2
    SET COLOR TO W*+
    @ 0,5 SAY "Design Help will allow the use to custom their HELP for the system"
    @ 2,5 SAY "Predesigned HELP is just that ... help already configured for system"
    @ 4,5 SAY "Press any key to return to Menu Choice...."
    intemp = INKEY(0)
    SET COLOR TO
    SET KEY 28 TO Help2
    CALL _scrrest WITH screen2


********************

PROCEDURE Help3

    PARAMETERS p3, l3, v3

       SET KEY 28 TO
       SAVE SCREEN
       SET SCOREBOARD OFF
       IF .NOT. FILE("HELP.DBF")
          @ 00,10,03,70 BOX scrframe
```

```
              @ 01,11 SAY "There is no HELP file available.   Would you like a help "
              @ 02,27 SAY "file to be generated? "
              IF .NOT. VERIFY()
                 RESTORE SCREEN
                 SET KEY 28 TO Help
                 RETURN
              ENDIF

              NOTE If a data base is open, its selected area must be noted
              goback = SELECT()
              DO Dohelp
              NOTE Once the help has been performed, the selected area is
              NOTE reselected.
              tempgo = STR(goback)
              SELECT &tempgo

       ENDIF
       goback = SELECT()
       SELECT 9
       USE Help INDEX Help
       search = SUBSTR(p,1,10) + SUBSTR(v,1,10) + TRANSFORM(l, "9999")
       SEEK search
       IF FOUND()
          @ top,left,bottom,right BOX scrframe
          IF "" = MEMOEDIT(helpscr,top+1,left+1,bottom-1,right-1,.F.)
          ENDIF
          @ bottom-1,left+1 SAY "Any Key to Continue..."
       ELSE
          @ 00,10,03,70 BOX scrframe
          @ 01,11 SAY "There is no HELP for this section.  Would you like to make"
          @ 02,28 SAY "a HELP screen for this? "
          IF .NOT. VERIFY()
             RESTORE SCREEN
             SET KEY 28 TO Help
             RETURN
          ENDIF
          APPEND BLANK
          REPLACE lookit WITH SUBSTR(p,1,10) + SUBSTR(v,1,10) + TRANSFORM(l,"9999")
          STORE SPACE(4000) TO in_help, full_scr
          STORE 0 TO temp_top, temp_left, temp_bot, temp_right
          CALL _scrsave WITH full_scr
          DO WHILE .T.
             CALL _scrrest WITH full_scr
             @ 00,10,03,70 BOX scrframe
             @ 01,20 SAY "Position cursor with arrow for TOP, LEFT corner."
             cursor = 0
             newcur = CHR(201)
             CALL _scrsave WITH in_help
             @ 12,40 SAY newcur
             trow = 12
             tcol = 40
             CALL cursw
             DO WHILE.T.
```

```
            cursor = INKEY(0)
            loop_again = MOVECURS()
            IF !loop_again
               EXIT
            ENDIF
            CALL _scrrest WITH in_help
            @ trow, tcol SAY newcur
         ENDDO
         STORE trow TO temp_top
         STORE tcol TO temp_left
         @ 00,10,03,70 BOX scrframe
         @ 01,14 SAY "Position cursor with arrow for BOTTOM, RIGHT corner."
         cursor = 0
         CALL _scrsave WITH in_help
         newcur = CHR(188)
         trow = temp_top + 2
         tcol = temp_left + 5
         @ trow, tcol SAY newcur
         DO WHILE.T.
            cursor = INKEY(0)
            loop_again = MOVECURS()
            IF !loop_again
               EXIT
            ENDIF
            CALL _scrrest WITH in_help
            @ trow, tcol SAY newcur
         ENDDO
         CALL cursw
         STORE trow TO temp_bot
         STORE tcol TO temp_right
         CALL _scrsave WITH in_help
         DO Temphelp
         @ 00,10,03,70 BOX scrframe
         @ 02,25 SAY "Is this what you wanted?  "
         IF .NOT. VERIFY()
            CALL _scrrest WITH in_help
            LOOP
         ELSE
            EXIT
         ENDIF
      ENDDO
      @ 00,10,03,70 BOX scrframe
      @ 01,15 SAY "Enter in HELPful information.   Keep to ONE screen"
      @ 02,15 SAY "     of text.  Press F10 when finished."
      REPLACE top WITH temp_top, bottom WITH temp_bot
      REPLACE left WITH temp_left, right WITH temp_right
      DO WHILE .T.
         @ top,left,bottom,right BOX scrframe
         REPLACE helpscr WITH MEMOEDIT(helpscr,top+1,left+1,bottom-1,right-
1,.T.)
         @ top,left,bottom,right BOX scrframe
         IF "" = MEMOEDIT(helpscr,top+1,left+1,bottom-1,right-1,.F.)
         ENDIF
```

```
                @ bottom-1,left+1 SAY "IS THIS CORRECT?    "
                IF .NOT. VERIFY()
                    LOOP
                ENDIF
                EXIT
            ENDDO
            @ bottom-1,left+1 SAY "Press Any key to Continue...."
        ENDIF
        qw = INKEY(0)
        RESTORE SCREEN
        tempgo = STR(goback)
        SELECT &tempgo
        SET KEY 28 TO Help
        RETURN


********************

PROCEDURE Dohelp

    SELECT 9
    CREATE Temp
    USE Temp
    APPEND BLANK
    REPLACE field_name WITH "LOOKIT", field_type WITH "C", field_len WITH 24
    APPEND BLANK
    REPLACE field_name WITH "TOP", field_type WITH "N", field_len WITH 2
    APPEND BLANK
    REPLACE field_name WITH "LEFT", field_type WITH "N", field_len WITH 2
    APPEND BLANK
    REPLACE field_name WITH "BOTTOM", field_type WITH "N", field_len WITH 2
    APPEND BLANK
    REPLACE field_name WITH "RIGHT", field_type WITH "N", field_len WITH 2
    APPEND BLANK
    REPLACE field_name WITH "HELPSCR", field_type WITH "M", field_len WITH 10
    USE
    CREATE Help FROM Temp
    USE
    ERASE Temp
    USE Help
    INDEX ON search_p + search_v TO Help


********************

PROCEDURE Temphelp

    SET COLOR TO W*
    @ temp_top, temp_left, temp_bot, temp_right BOX SUBSTR(scrframe,1,8)
    SET COLOR TO 7


**************************

FUNCTION VERIFY

    SET CONSOLE off
    WAIT TO inertemp
```

```
   SET CONSOLE on
   IF UPPER(inertemp) = "Y"
      ?? "Yes"
      te = INKEY(.25)
      RETURN(.T.)
   ENDIF
   ?? "No "
   te = INKEY(.25)
   RETURN(.F.)


********************

FUNCTION Movecurs

   DO CASE
   CASE cursor = 5
      IF trow - 1 > 0
         trow = trow - 1
      ENDIF
   CASE cursor = 4
      IF tcol + 1 < 79
         tcol = tcol + 1
      ENDIF
   CASE cursor = 19
      IF tcol - 1 > 0
         tcol = tcol - 1
      ENDIF
   CASE cursor = 24
      IF trow + 1 < 24
         trow = trow + 1
      ENDIF
   CASE cursor = 13 .OR. cursor = 27
      RETURN(.F.)
   ENDCASE
   RETURN(.T.)
* End of File
```

FINAL CONSIDERATIONS ON HELP FILES

Here are the file sizes for each of the HELP files we have studied:

1) General Help - 5K
2) Specific Help - 7K
3) Help to a File - 9K
4) Everything - 13K

The first two HELP files increase in size as more information is appended to the procedure. In large applications, where disk space and memory space is always a concern, these two examples may not be viable options.

The third example relies totally on the disk. The main disadvantage is speed (because of disk I/O), but speed may be a reasonable price to pay for virtually unlimited on-line help.

The last example is a combination of HELP files written both in the procedure and to the disk. The main advantage to this approach is that for most help routines the user or developer can write most of the information out to the disk. However, for additional information, especially for MUST FILL fields and variables, it may be best to write specific information directly in the procedure, or to write a general HELP as a guide to operations.

Finally, remember it is crucial to applications using an overlay memory format to keep the HELP.PRG file in the main load module at all times.

CHAPTER FOURTEEN

**Programming Structure
and
Application Layout**

This chapter outlines rules of programming, guides to developing applications, and considerations about user support. Because of the nature of the subject, sample coding is sparse in this section – the information is more about Clipper as a language than about tricks in using Clipper.

GUIDELINES FOR GOOD PROGRAMMING

There are several rules of programming listed below. They are practical principles to follow when programming. These rules are not inviolate, but they can lend some structure to an often confusing job.

If you are familiar with these principles, review them again. If you are not, study the examples and the rules and judge your coding techniques against them. In either case, look on these rules as merely guides and remember that they may be broken to accomplish some worthwhile point. The problem is distinguishing between valid violations and just common sloppiness. The ability to make this judgement well comes with experience.

KEEP THE USER IN MIND

This refers to backup support. Your application is only good if your user base can work with it. The best way to accomplish this is with careful screen handling and meticulous control.

Keep in mind that the proper screen actually should be determined by the user. In some cases, the proper screen can require as much as 70 percent custom coding and 30 percent generic code. In other cases, the opposite is true. The point is to know your audience!

Clipper saves time and code with certain screen routines, especially with the SAVE SCREEN, BOX, and MENU...PROMPT commands. However, it still takes ingenuity to make best use of these features. The use of color adds to applications; it enhances the final results and eases user interfacing. If color is used, allow an additional ten percent in development time. Give the user as many options as possible to alter the basics of the application, including setting the screen border, the data delimiter, forcing a carriage return for every field, ringing a bell for every filled field, and similar customized settings.

The following code provides a screen and system initialization generator which can become a standard tool for your future applications.

```
********************
* Name        SCRINIT.prg
* Date        August 11, 1986
* Notice      Copyright 1986, Stephen J. Straley
* Notes       This is a initialization menu for items that
*             pertain to the screen.  It writes a file named
*             "SCREEN.SYS"; all variables inside that file
*             pertaining to screen control begin with the
*             letters "scr".
*
*
********************

SET SCOREBOARD OFF

CLEAR
scrleft_1   = "Copyright 1985 - Stephen J. Straley "
scrleft_2   = "All Rights Reserved"
right_1     = "Terminal/System Setup Program"
right_2     = "Version 2.10"
tscreen     = SPACE(4000)
scrframe    = CHR(201) + CHR(205) + CHR(187) + CHR(186) + CHR(188) + ;
              CHR(205) + CHR(200) + CHR(186)
center      = "Drive Assignment Setup"
@ 0,0 SAY scrleft_1
@ 1,0 SAY scrleft_2
@ 0,80-LEN(right_1) SAY right_1
@ 1,80-LEN(right_2) SAY right_2
@ 3,40-LEN(center)/2 SAY center
@ 4,0,23,79 BOX scrframe
CALL _scrsave WITH tscreen
IF .NOT. FILE("SCREEN.SYS")
   STORE "C:" TO scrprog, scrdata
   STORE .F. TO scrconfirm, scrdelim, scrcolor, scrinten, scrbell, scrshow,;
               scrtype
   STORE "" TO scrframe, scrbar, scrlin
   STORE "::" TO scrdelimto
   STORE 1 TO option, scrtimes, scrpass
   STORE .T. scrsys
ELSE
   RESTORE FROM Screen.sys ADDITIVE
   STORE 1 TO option
ENDIF

DO WHILE .T.

   CALL _scrrest WITH tscreen

   @  7, 5 PROMPT " 1> System Configured for " + ;
                  IF(scrsys, "Hard", "Floppy") + " Disk "
   @  7,45 PROMPT " 2> Program Drive Set to " + scrprog + " "
   @  8,45 PROMPT " 3> Data Drive Set to " + scrdata + " "
   @ 10, 5 PROMPT " 4> Confirm is " + IF(scrconfirm, "ON ", "OFF ")
```

```
@ 11, 5 PROMPT " 5> Delimiters are " + IF(scrdelim, "ON ", "OFF ")
@ 12, 5 PROMPT " 6> Delimiters SET to " + scrdelimto + " "
@ 13, 5 PROMPT " 7> Screen " + IF(scrcolor, "Bright ", "Normal ")
@ 14, 5 PROMPT " 8> Field Color is " + IF(scrinten, "ON ", "OFF ")
@ 15, 5 PROMPT " 9> Bell " + IF(scrbell, "WILL", "WILL NOT") + " ring "
@ 10,40 PROMPT " A> Password " + IF(scrshow, "WILL", "WILL NOT") +;
                " echo to screen "
@ 12,40 PROMPT " B> Change Password "
@ 14,40 PROMPT " C> " + DLTRIM(STR(scrtimes)) + " tries at the Password "
@ 16,40 PROMPT " D> " + IF(scrtype, "Engage", "Disengage") +;
                " Type-Ahead Feature "
@ 18,33 PROMPT " 0> Save Values "
MENU TO option
DO CASE
CASE option = 1
   scrsys = IF(scrsys, .F., .T.)
   IF .NOT. scrsys
      KEYBOARD option = 2
   ENDIF
CASE option = 2
      @ 21,10 SAY "Enter Program Drive: " GET scrprog PICT "!";
                   VALID(SUBSTR(scrprog,1,1) $"ABCDEFGHIJKLMNOP")
      READ
      IF .NOT. scrsys
      IF scrprog = scrdata
         @ 21,10 SAY SPACE(50)
         @ 22,10 SAY "Data Drive and Program Drive NOT EQUAL " +;
                  " for Flppy System"
         @ 21,10 SAY "Enter Data Drive: " GET scrdata PICT "!";
                   VALID(SUBSTR(scrdata,1,1) $"ABCDEFGHIJKLMNOP";
                   .AND.  scrprog <> scrdata)
         READ
      ENDIF
   ENDIF
CASE option = 3
   @ 21,10 SAY "Enter Data Drive: " GET scrdata PICT "!";
              VALID(SUBSTR(scrdata,1,1) $"ABCDEFGHIJKLMNOP")
   READ
      IF .NOT. scrsys
      IF scrprog = scrdata
         @ 21,10 SAY SPACE(50)
         @ 22,10 SAY "Program Drive and Data Drive NOT EQUAL for " +;
                  "Floppy System"
         @ 21,10 SAY "Enter Program Drive: " GET scrprog PICT "!";
                   VALID(SUBSTR(scrprog,1,1) $"ABCDEFGHIJKLMNOP";
                   .AND.  scrdata <> scrprog)
      ENDIF
   ENDIF
CASE option = 4
      scrconfirm = IF(scrconfirm, .F., .T.)
CASE option = 5
      scrdelim = IF(scrdelim, .F., .T.)
CASE option = 6
```

```
               STORE " " TO choice
               @ 21,10 SAY "Set Left Delimiter:    " GET choice PICT "X"
               READ
               STORE choice TO scrdelimto
               STORE " " TO choice
               @ 21,10 SAY "Set Right Delimiter: " GET choice PICT "X"
               READ
               STORE scrdelimto + choice TO scrdelimto
      CASE option = 7
         scrcolor = IF(scrcolor, .F., .T.)
      CASE option = 8
         scrinten = IF(scrinten, .F., .T.)
      CASE option = 9
         scrbell = IF(scrbell, .F., .T.)
      CASE option = 10
         scrshow = IF(scrshow, .F., .T.)
      CASE option = 11
         STORE SPACE(15) TO password
         @ 21,10 SAY "What Password do you want to use? " GET password;
                    PICT "XXXXXXXXXXXXXXX"
         READ
         scrpass = GENPASS(password)
      CASE option = 12
         @ 21,10 SAY "How may tries for a correct password? " GET scrtimes;
                    PICT "##" range 0,99
         READ
      CASE option = 13
         scrtype = IF(scrtype, .F., .T.)
      OTHERWISE
         EXIT
      ENDCASE

ENDDO
CALL _scrrest WITH tscreen
@ 3,3 SAY SPACE(60)
@ 3,29 SAY "Installing the Border"
CALL _scrsave WITH tscreen
in_choice = 4
prmpt_4 = scrframe
prmpt_5 = REPLICATE(CHR(177), 8) + " "
prmpt_6 = CHR(218) + CHR(196) + CHR(191) + CHR(179) + ;
          CHR(217) + CHR(196) + CHR(192) + CHR(179) + CHR(32)
prmpt_7 = CHR(222) + CHR(223) + CHR(221) + CHR(221) + ;
          CHR(221) + CHR(220) + CHR(222) + CHR(222) + CHR(32)
prmpt_9 = REPLICATE(CHR(15), 8) + " "
DO WHILE .T.
   CALL _scrrest WITH tscreen
   @ 6,5   PROMPT " 1>    ********* "
   @ 6,32  PROMPT " 2>    ========= "
   @ 6,59  PROMPT " 3>    --------- "
   @ 8,5   PROMPT " 4>    &prmpt_4. "
   @ 8,32  PROMPT " 5>    &prmpt_5. "
   @ 8,59  PROMPT " 6>    &prmpt_6. "
```

```
a 10,5   PROMPT  " 7>   &prmpt_7. "
a 10,32  PROMPT  " 8>        "
a 10,59  PROMPT  " 9>   &prmpt_9. "
a 13,20  SAY "Move Cursor to choose preferred border"
MENU TO in_choice

DO CASE
CASE in_choice = 1
   scrframe = "******** "
   scrbar   = REPLICATE("*",80)
   scrlin   = "*"
CASE in_choice = 2
   scrframe = "======== "
   scrbar   = REPLICATE("=",80)
   scrlin   = "="
CASE in_choice = 3
   scrframe = "-------- "
   scrbar   = REPLICATE("-",80)
   scrlin   = "|"
CASE in_choice = 4
   scrframe = CHR(201) + CHR(205) + CHR(187) + CHR(186) + CHR(188) + ;
              CHR(205) + CHR(200) + CHR(186) + CHR(32)
   scrbar   = CHR(204) + REPLICATE(CHR(205), 78) + CHR(185)
   scrlin   = CHR(186)
CASE in_choice = 5
   scrframe = REPLICATE(CHR(177), 8) + " "
   scrbar   = REPLICATE(CHR(177),80)
   scrlin   = CHR(177)
CASE in_choice = 6
   scrframe = CHR(218) + CHR(196) + CHR(191) + CHR(179) + CHR(217) + ;
              CHR(196) + CHR(192) + CHR(179) + CHR(32)
   scrbar   = CHR(195) + REPLICATE(CHR(196), 78) + CHR(180)
   scrlin   = CHR(179)
CASE in_choice = 7
   scrframe = CHR(222) + CHR(223) + CHR(221) + CHR(221) + CHR(221) + ;
              CHR(220) + CHR(222) + CHR(222) + CHR(32)
   scrbar   = CHR(222) + REPLICATE(CHR(220),78) + CHR(221)
   scrlin   = CHR(222)
CASE in_choice = 8
   scrframe = "  "
   scrbar   = REPLICATE("",80)
   scrlin   = ""
CASE in_choice = 9
   scrframe = REPLICATE(CHR(15), 8) + " "
   scrbar   = REPLICATE(CHR(15), 80)
   scrlin   = CHR(15)
ENDCASE
CALL _scrrest WITH tscreen
a 8,10,16,69 BOX SUBSTR(scrframe,1,8)
a 12,10 SAY SUBSTR(scrbar,1,1) + SUBSTR(scrbar,2,58) + SUBSTR(scrbar,80,1)

a 19,25 SAY "Is this the border you want?  "
IF VERIFY(0)
```

```
        EXIT
    ENDIF

ENDDO
writefile = scrprog + "SCREEN.SYS"
@ 22,24 SAY "Now Saving parameters to " + writefile
SAVE ALL LIKE scr* TO &writefile
CALL _scrrest WITH tscreen
@ 12,18 SAY  "Finished with Terminal/System Initialization"
@ 24,00 SAY ""
QUIT


*****************

FUNCTION Genpass

    PARAMETERS in_string

    COUNT = LEN(TRIM(in_string))
    final = 0
    FOR beginning = 1 TO (COUNT + 1)
        final = final + ASC(SUBSTR(in_string,beginning,1)) * beginning
    NEXT

    RETURN(final)

*******************

FUNCTION Verify

    * This is for 'Is this Correct? (Y/N)' *

    SET CONSOLE OFF
    STORE "" TO verify_var
    DO WHILE .NOT. verify_var$"YyNn"
        WAIT TO verify_var
    ENDDO
    SET CONSOLE ON
    IF UPPER(verify_var) = "Y"
        ?? "Yes"
        RETURN(.T.)
    ENDIF
    ?? "No "
    RETURN(.F.)

******************

FUNCTION Dltrim

    PARAMETERS a

    RETURN(LTRIM(TRIM(a)))
* End of File
```

BE MODULAR (ONLY ONE SCREEN AT A TIME)

Requiring the user to scroll up another screen to get more information thwarts the flow of action. If a particular action in your program extends beyond the scope of one screen, you have set up road blocks to smooth running and introduced user frustration. Cut the code down by being more modular. Force yourself to keep things in one coherent screen and you will have happier users and more effective, cleaner, and tighter code.

Clipper has several techniques which facilitate modular coding. One such feature is that procedures can call one another. Procedures which are recursive in nature reduce the basic code size a great deal. However, if you use some of Clipper's extended features, remember that they are only available in the compiled environment and not under the interpreter.

BUILD A LIBRARY

You save time by developing code for the future. Spend a little time now for future projects and assemble a function and procedure library. No matter what industry you are programming for, many routines are always the same. For example, a check always requires numeric values to be converted to character string output.

When you have an extensive library, repetitive coding becomes a thing of the past. When repetitive coding is eliminated, many simple errors (the most frustrating kind) disappear. A well developed function library supports the concepts of modular programming. If you find a bug in a library function, recode the function and relink it to all other applications calling it.

KEEP IT SIMPLE

There is often a strong tendency to develop applications in an overly complicated fashion. Remember that coding applications is very much like writing for a newspaper. Write clearly, say what you mean, keep to the point, and be as simple as you can. Do not try to be too clever and sacrifice clarity for fancy routines that only muddle your application.

In line with the rule of simplicity, choose the names you use carefully. Consider the variable names in the following example:

```
STORE .T. TO hel_fr_ovr
DO WHILE hel_fr_ovr
    <commands>
ENDDO
```

This is cute, but the variable name would make more sense if it were labeled something like "top_loop" or "looping". Naming variables is a question of style and technique, but the point is that variables should have names that either describe their location or operation. This makes code maintenance much easier.

THE TELEPHONE TECHNIQUE

The telephone technique helps to keep code 1) clear and easy to read; 2) compact and concise and 3) true to the overall structure of the application. The telephone technique is very simple. Take a section of your code and see if you can read it to someone over a telephone, line by line, command by command. If the person on the other side of the line can understand what you are trying to accomplish in your procedure and what the major branches, tests, and values are, then your code is understandable and direct, and adheres to many of the fundamental rules of good programing.

If the person on the other end of the conversation does not understand your code and your intent, then the code may be too verbose, cryptic, vague, or simply may miss the point. If your code has any of these problems, do not patch it, rewrite it.

Make sure that for each section of your code you know what you are trying to accomplish and what steps are necessary in order to get you there. Speaking out loud while you program may also be helpful. Use some means of communication to test the validity of your code. If it fails these simple tests, it will surely fail in the computer.

The telephone technique tests the strength of your code. If there are too many problems with it, start over and try again.

AVOID EXCESS BRANCHING ON IF

This rule is difficult to adhere to because no one starts out intending to use branching excessively. The main point is one of control. If an IF branch is necessary (and the IF() function is inappropriate) then keep control of it. One simple IF command can easily leads to another embedded IF command, which in turn yields a few more embedded IF commands. Sooner or later, if you use proper indenting, your code will wander off the right side of the screen.

If there is a situation which generates several testing conditions, break up the IF ... ENDIF commands into a more structured DO CASE...ENDCASE followed by the necessary IF... ENDIF command. Nesting several layers of IF commands only complicates your code. The basic structure for the IF... ELSE...ENDIF command is two branches, one for a true condition and one for a false. If multiple logical testing conditions exist and you do not wish to use a DO CASE...ENDCASE structure, then use nested IF() function calls.

DO NOT PATCH; REWRITE

Programmers often get too attached to their code, and in an attempt to save some faulty part, keep sticking in more lines of code. What normally evolves is a quilted pattern of several halfhearted attempts at one major thought, none of which ever seems to get the job done.

Bad code comes from bad design. Go back to the beginning and rework the design to improve the code. **Do not try to patch bad code!** Too much time is wasted on code with bad technique or design.

ESTIMATE THREE TIMES MORE TIME

This is more of a rule of planning than a rule of coding. Always estimate three times more time for application development than you think you need. Developers invariably leave out time for bad coding, revisions, modifications, and, of course, documentation. There are several variables that need to be figured into the time equation, including working with the compiler, working in a different environment, testing, and planning. Generally speaking, you should establish a time schedule, multiply that figure by three, and you will be closer to the truth.

CODING AND CUTENESS DON'T MIX

Developing clever or cute routines is wonderful on the surface, but it invariably has a cost in clarity. Even if you document your code heavily, cute code is confusing months later when you have to make modifications. In addition, cute code tends to restrict alterations. Write code clearly and concisely with enough comments to maintain readability.

If you code for yourself as well as for your customers you will save countless hours in debugging, recoding, and in alterations.

FOLLOW A LOGICAL FLOW

Computers are based on logic, specifically boolean logic. Programs should flow logically as well. In some languages where line numbers are allowed, it is easy to get caught in a spaghetti mush of GOTO and GOSUB statements. Many applications look like they started with a clear basic idea, then were given a quick addition here and there, including a few interfacing routines and a couple of slapped together functions, and then released. The application **may** work, but it is still sloppy.

Programming should flow from one distinct module to another without confusion or ambiguity.

AVOID SENSELESS ERRORS

The time spent on careful planning is almost always less than time spent fixing mistakes that result from rushing through the coding for an application. Some mistakes are inevitable, but the goal is to cut down on the mistakes that happen because of carelessness.

COMMENTS AND NOTATIONS

Whenever you are programming, assume that someone else will eventually read your code. You can help that reader by writing clearly. However, no matter how well you label variables, plan the program flow and define your structure; code alone isn't enough. Use comments and internal notations to explain structural elements, important variables, calling routines and functions. Comment lines are not compiled, so the execution of the generated object file will not be slowed down by commented information.

Treat comments like the code, be direct and to the point.

Finally, do not comment bad code; rewrite it!

ELEVEN RULES FOR SUCCESS IN PROGRAMMING

1. Write first in easy-to-understand pseudo-code, then translate into Clipper code.

    -   Do not stop with your first draft.
    -   Do not patch bad code; rewrite it.
    -   Do not strain to reuse code; just reorganize it.
    -   Make sure special cases are really special cases.
    -   Write and test a big program in small pieces.
    -   Do not stop at one bug; find others.
    -   Watch out for off-by-one errors:
        -   10.0 times 0.1 is hardly ever 1.0: test to make sure that calculations are correct.
        -   Do not compare floating point numbers just for equality.
    -   Be in control. Measure the effect of any change before making the change for the sake of efficiency.

2. Write clearly.

    -   Do not be too clever.
    -   Make your programs read from top to bottom.
    -   Let the data structure the program.
    -   Do not diddle with code to make it faster -- find a better algorithm.
    -   Format a program to help the reader understand it.
    -   Indent code to show the logical structure of a program.

3. Say what you mean, simply and directly.

- Make sure your code "does nothing" gracefully. Too often developers, when asked what their routine does, say "it does nothing." If this is the case, check it again. "Does nothing" code has a tendency to do plenty!
- Program defensively.
- Make it right before making it faster.
- Keep it right when making it faster.
- Make it clearer before making it faster.
- Do not sacrifice clarity for small gains in "efficiency".
- Keep it simple to make it faster.

4. Modularize.

- Use subroutines.
- Make the coupling between modules clearly visible.
- Each module should do one thing, and do it **well**.
- Use recursive procedures for recursively-defined structures.

5. Use library functions.

- Replace repetitive expressions with calls to a common function.

6. Avoid too many temporary variables.

- Choose variable names that cannot be confused.
- Choose procedure names that describe their basic purpose.
- Choose function names that describe their basic purpose.
- Choose field names that make the program simple.
- Use variable names that mean something.
- Create labels that mean something.

7. Let the machine and language do the dirty work.

8. Avoid unnecessary branches.

- Do not use conditional branches as a substitute for a logical expression.
- Use IF...ELSE...ENDIF to emphasize that only one of two actions is to be performed.
- Use the fundamental control flow constructs.
- Follow each division and its associated action as closely as possible.
- Avoid multiple exits from loops.
- Use the good features of the language and avoid the bad ones.
- Use data arrays to avoid repetitive control sequences.

9. Use DO WHILE and indenting to delimit groups of statements.

- Use DO and DO WHILE to emphasize the presence of loops.
- Use DO CASE to implement multi-way branches.

10.   Initialize all variables before use.

11.   Make sure comments and code agree.

-   Do not just echo the code with comments. Make the comments count!
-   Do not comment bad code; rewrite it!
-   Do not over-comment.

A STRUCTURED FORM FOR APPLICATION DEVELOPMENT

One of the most difficult things to do is to estimate the amount of time it takes to create an application. It's human to expect to devote far less time than reality demands. This is especially true for consultants who base their livelihood on the time they bill out for projects.

Getting clients and projects is based in part on reputation and in part on the ability to bid a project properly and then to bring in the project on time and on budget. To control time and budgeting, good developers should use a checklist of items that includes all of the features that make up an application.

DEVELOPMENT CHECKLIST:

	Hours	Cost

1.   System Environment Generation
   a.   Screen Design
      i.   Help
      ii.   Color
      iii.   Menus
   b.   Application Parameters
      i.   Passwords
      ii.   Borders
      iii.   Check Numbers
      iv.   Miscellaneous
2.   Creating Databases and Indexes
   a.   Fields
   b.   Memos (If Applicable)
   c.   Key Fields
   d.   Relations
3.   Data Control
   a.   Entering
   b.   Editing
   c.   Viewing
   d.   Deleting (If Applicable)
4.   Calculation
   a.   Totaling

   b.   Summing / Averaging
   c.   Balancing
5. Reporting and Listing
   a.   Screen
   b.   Printer
   c.   File
6. System Maintenance
   a.   Sorting and Re-Indexing
   b.   Backup / Restoring Data
   c.   Data Cleanup
   d.   Reconfiguring System
   e.   Miscellaneous
7. Data Interface (If Applicable)
   a.   Importing
   b.   Exporting
   c.   Across Systems
8. Multi-user Control (If Applicable)
9. Testing
10. Documentation

SCREEN DESIGN AND LAYOUT IN CLIPPER

SCREEN DESIGN THEORY

The most sophisticated programs can be worth absolutely nothing if screens are designed and handled poorly. An application's screens are the programmer's way of interacting cohesively, progressing logically, and eliminating confusion for the user. The following are not absolutes, but rather guidelines and suggestions for screen design.

Several user interfacing techniques have come to light in the microcomputer world. One example is the surface-sensitive device commonly known as a *mouse*. This device is a small peripheral attached to the computer which is either controlled by a roller ball underneath or is sensitive to a special pad. When the mouse is moved, a corresponding arrow on the screen moves in the same direction. Choices or options are selected by pushing a button on the mouse. The mouse guides users both visually and physically. Another method designed to increase user understanding is the *pull-down menu*. After the user chooses an option from a command line, a new frame or *window* shows up on the screen with further choices or options. This technique can give the user a sense of progress as he or she goes through each screen. The user gets the feeling that the computer is doing something as each window is pulled-down from the command line.

A final example is similar to pull-down menus. The user is presented with only one menu at a time, and an item chosen from one menu brings up another menu with additional selections. The user is never confronted with too many choices and can slowly work through the program. This is an old technique but it is still effective if it is used well.

There are many variations on the use of windows. You can take a dull menu and make it far more effective by just highlighting the previously selected menu item. Keeping previous menus visible while overlapping new menus also adds clarity to the program and maintains a sense of progress. The construction of menus and windows is covered in the next section of this chapter. The principles of interfacing with users are universal, however, no matter what method you employ.

THE PRINCIPLES OF USER INTERFACING

Keep a Standard Format for Screens and Prompts

Consistency is extremely important. Menus should read top to bottom, then left to right; numbers are also better than letters. Whatever your preference, decide upon one method of screen layout and stick to it. This simple but important rule of screen consistency is ignored much too often. If you decide that the number 0 is used to exit from the application, then the number 0 should also be used to exit from all sub-menus to higher menus. If numbers are used to select menu options, maintain that format and never switch to letters.

Prompts and messages, as well as menu headers if used, should be kept uniform from menu to menu. Normally, headers are used to contain the developing company's name, the name of the company using the product, a company logo, copyright declaration and date, the product name and possibly its developer, and the current version number. Again, be consistent. If the main menu title is centered on line 5 of the screen, then all menu titles should follow suit. Users get accustomed to looking at the same places on the screen for certain pieces of information. Users are creatures of habit out of necessity. Time lost searching for the "right" option on a screen is time wasted.

Many Menus, Few Options

Group similar options together to make submenus. Group general items as options which lead to submenus.

Many developers try to fit as many options on one screen as possible. The user cannot absorb all of that information at one time. Even though it may seem more convenient to add just one or two more options to a higher level menu screen rather than take the time to program an entire new screen, it's worth the extra programming time. Users can follow the logic of the program far easier if menus have only the minimum number of choices.

Show the Progression of Options

Inform the users of the current level of operation, how they got there, and what is going to happen next.

Users are left too often with screens that have no indication of what preceded or what follows, leading to confusion and getting lost in the application. Highlighting previous choices is a good practice, leaving the higher menu on the screen, while drawing the next sub-menu in a smaller section on the screen with the new choices and standard prompt. This method shows previous screens, preventing a user from getting lost especially if selected items are highlighted, and shows the next steps in a clear, concise manner. Pull-down menus are similar in that previous choices are expanded into new frames and new choices appear.

Keep the Wording Simple

Unnecessary use of big words adds to confusion and confusion adds to lost time.

Maintain a Sense of Operation

Whenever the computer is doing something, show it. Don't let the user assume that something is going on when there could be a problem or, conversely, that there is a problem when none exists.

All too often, the user is left in the dark when the computer is doing something that takes time. Relying on the disk drive light is not effective, as most operations are performed in memory before going to the disk drive. The use of a benevolent "One Moment Please" message on the screen that stays there for several hours is not sufficient because it doesn't reflect the actual operation taking place.

Maintain Easy Escape Methods

Allow the user to escape from wrong choices without having to wait for an operation to complete. Keep in mind that the user may make a mistake in choosing an item from a menu. Users poke and plod through menu choices, looking for the right path or the right menu. Allow this to happen. Getting into the system is important, but getting out is equally important. Choose an escape key or method and stick to it throughout the application.

Provide as Much Help as Possible

The key to providing effective user help is to give as much information as possible without cluttering the screen.

Use Clipper's HELP.PRG facility. Remember that users generally do not read manuals. Take the time to set up on line help whenever possible. While doing so, remember there is a fine line between sufficient help and too much clutter.

The type of help that should be on the screen at all times with the menus either shows the user how to get more help or how to move between menus.

There are two ways of approaching the development of HELP.PRG. One way is to create HELP.PRG with all of the text information that you will provide with your application. This is easy to develop, but takes space. The other way to develop help screens is to have the help screens available separately, yet maintain the option for the user to invoke them at any time.

WINDOWING WITH CLIPPER

Using the Box Command to Draw Boxes

Syntax: @ <t,l,b,r> BOX <string>

The BOX command is no more than two separate @...SAY, or @...GET statements combined. The first two coordinates <t,l> are the top-left positions for the BOX. The following two numbers are the bottom-right coordinates. The top and bottom coordinates must be in the range of 0 to 24, and the left and right coordinates must be in the 0 to 79 range. The <string> portion of the command is the section where you specify the design of the border of the BOX as well as the "fill" character. These characters must be in the following order:

    1.   the top-left corner character;
    2.   the character used across the top;
    3.   the top-right corner character;
    4.   the character down the right side;
    5.   the bottom-right corner character;
    6.   the character across the bottom;
    7.   the bottom-left corner character;
    8.   the character up the left side;
    9.   the character used to fill the box.

Generally, in designing menus, the fill character will be the space (CHR(32)). In the following sample, the fill character, as well as all of the other characters comprising the frame, are from the IBM graphic character set.

Sample:

```
frame = CHR(201) + CHR(205) + CHR(187) + CHR(186) +;
            CHR(188) + CHR(205) + CHR(200) + CHR(186) +;
            CHR(176)

@ 0,0,23,79 BOX frame
```

The screen is surrounded by a frame and filled with graphic blocks.

Here's a tip: to clear the BOXed area quickly, use the BOX command with a null string in place of the character set and the area specified by the four coordinates will be cleared.

Sample: `@ 0,0,23,79 BOX ""`

Sample Code Using the BOX Command:

```
********************
* Name        DRAWBOX.prg
* Date        August 12, 1986
* Notice      Copyright 1986, Stephen J. Straley
* Note        This shows the use of boxes o the screen and
*             how they can be incremented and decremented.  The
*             last screen takes advantage of the fill character
*             whereas all other BOXes are just frames.
*
********************

STORE CHR(218) + CHR(196) + CHR(191) + CHR(179) + CHR(217) +;
      CHR(196) + CHR(192) + CHR(179) + CHR(176) TO frame

CLEAR
STORE 1 TO counter, top, left
STORE 23 to bottom
STORE 78 to right
DO WHILE counter <> 11

   @ top, left, bottom, right BOX SUBSTR(frame,1,8)

   STORE top + 1 TO top
   STORE left + 3 TO left
   STORE bottom - 1 TO bottom
   STORE right - 3 TO right
   STORE counter + 1 to counter
ENDDO

@ top, left, bottom, right BOX frame
@ top + (bottom - top) / 2, left + (right - left) / 2 - 3 SAY ;
```

```
    "Finished"
STORE 1 TO counter
DO WHILE counter <> 500
    STORE counter + 1 TO counter
ENDDO
a 23,00 SAY ""
* End of File
```

Windows for Menus and Submenus

When developing menus and submenus, set a style and always use it. In many of my
applications, for example, I use the zero (0) to exit from submenus to higher level
menus and to exit the application. The escape method does not change from menu to
menu and the user feels more at ease. Also state menu options clearly, limiting the
number of options on the screen and panning from top to bottom and left to right.

Overlap submenus, with the background (usually the main menu) overlapped by submenus, which overlap each other. An additional technique is to have previous menu
choices remain on screen in inverse video. Screens should be saved as the operator
goes down through the application and the user should have the option to "pop" up to
the previous menu without going back to the main menu. The following sample code
shows other ways of using screen saving with ARRAYS, MENU...PROMPT commands, and the BOX command.

Sample Code for Windowing Menus:

```
********************
* Name        DRAWMEN1.prg
* Date        August 12, 1986
* Notice      Copyright 1986, Stephen J. Straley
* Note        This sample code shows how to develop menus as
*             they move down to more specific options; how screens
*             can be saved and recalled (especially in conjunction
*             with arrays); and how BOXes are drawn.
*
********************

STORE CHR(201) + CHR(205) + CHR(187) + CHR(186) + ;
      CHR(188) + CHR(205) + CHR(200) + CHR(186) + " " TO scrframe
SET INTENS on
SET DELIM off
prompt  = "Enter Choice:  "
disp0_1 = " 1>    Chart Of Accounts "
disp0_2 = " 2>    Transactions "
disp0_3 = " 3>    Posting & Balancing "
disp0_4 = " 4>    Transfers "
disp0_5 = " 5>    Print Lists / Checks "
disp0_6 = " 6>    Print Reports "
disp0_7 = " 7>    Utilities "
disp0_8 = " 8>    End of Period "
```

```
disp0_0 = " 0>    Exit Program "
disp1_1 = " 1>    Enter an Account "
disp1_2 = " 2>    Edit an Account "
disp1_3 = " 3>    Examine Accounts "
disp1_4 = " 4>    Delete an Account "
disp1_0 = " 0>    Return to Main Menu "
disp2_1 = " 1>  Enter Transaction "
disp2_2 = " 2>  Edit Transaction "
disp2_3 = " 3>  Delete Transaction "
disp2_0 = " 0>  Return to Main Menu "
disp5_1 = " 1>    Chart of Account Info. "
disp5_2 = " 2>    Print/Reprint Checks "
disp5_3 = " 3>    Transaction Information "
disp5_4 = " 4>    Heading Listings "
disp5_0 = " 0>    Return to Main Menu "
DO WHILE .T.
   option = "0"
   CLEAR
   @ 5,0,20,79 BOX SUBSTR(scrframe,1,8)
   @  4,33 SAY "M A I N   M E N U"
   @  7,10 SAY "1>    Chart Of Accounts"
   @ 10,10 SAY "2>    Transactions"
   @ 13,10 SAY "3>    Posting & Balancing"
   @ 16,10 SAY "4>    Transfers"
   @  7,50 SAY "5>    Print Lists / Checks"
   @ 10,50 SAY "6>    Print Reports"
   @ 13,50 SAY "7>    Utilities"
   @ 16,50 SAY "8>    End of Period"
   @ 18,30 SAY "0>    Exit Program"
   @ 22,30 SAY prompt GET option PICT "9" VALID(option $"012345678")
   READ
   DO CASE
   CASE option = "1"
      @ 7,9 GET disp0_1
      CLEAR GETS
      @ 12,37,22,76 BOX scrframe
      @ 13,44 SAY "Chart Of Accounts Sub-Menu"
      @ 15,46 SAY "1>    Enter an Account"
      @ 16,46 SAY "2>    Edit an Account"
      @ 17,46 SAY "3>    Examine Accounts"
      @ 18,46 SAY "4>    Delete an Account"
      @ 19,46 SAY "0>    Return to Main Menu"
      @ 21,47 SAY prompt GET option PICT "9" VALID(option $"0")
      READ

   CASE option = "3"
      STORE "0" TO option
      @ 13, 9 GET disp0_3
      CLEAR GETS
      @ 10,37,18,76 BOX scrframe
      @ 11,47 SAY "Post/Balance Sub-Menu"
      @ 13,45 SAY "1>  Post Transactions"
      @ 14,45 SAY "2>  Balance Accounts"
```

```
      @ 15,45 SAY "0>  Return to Main Menu"
      @ 17,47 SAY prompt GET option PICT "9" VALID(option $"0")
      READ

   CASE option = "5"
      STORE "0" TO option, suboption
      @  7,49 GET disp0_5
      CLEAR GETS
      @ 9,3,19,43 BOX scrframe
      @ 10,11 SAY "Print Lists/Checks Sub-Menu"
      @ 12,10 SAY "1>    Chart of Account Info."
      @ 13,10 SAY "2>    Print/Reprint Checks"
      @ 14,10 SAY "3>    Transaction Information"
      @ 15,10 SAY "4>    Heading Listings"
      @ 16,10 SAY "0>    Return to Main Menu"
      @ 18,12 SAY prompt GET option PICT "9" VALID(option $"01234")
      READ
      DO CASE
      CASE option = "0"
         @ 16,09 GET disp5_0
         CLEAR GETS
         LOOP
      CASE option = "1"
         @ 12, 9 GET disp5_1
         CLEAR GETS
         @ 6,40,16,77 BOX scrframe
         @  7,46 SAY " Printing Chart of Accounts"
         @  9,49 SAY "1>  Account Listing"
         @ 10,49 SAY "2>  Account History"
         @ 11,49 SAY "3>  Budget Listing"
         @ 12,49 SAY "0>  Return to Main Menu"
         @ 14,49 SAY prompt GET suboption PICT "9" VALID(suboption $"0123")
         READ

      CASE option = "2"
         @ 13, 9 GET disp5_2
         CLEAR GETS
         @ 6,37,15,76 BOX scrframe
         @ 7, 43 SAY "        Re/Print Checks"
         @ 9, 45 SAY "1>  Print Checks"
         @ 10,45 SAY "2>  Reprint Checks"
         @ 11,45 SAY "3>  Print Check Register"
         @ 12,45 SAY "0>  Return to Main Menu"
         @ 14,46 SAY Prompt GET suboption PICT "9" VALID(suboption $"0123")
         READ

      CASE option = "3"
         @ 14, 9 GET disp5_3
         CLEAR GETS
         @ 6,37,17,76 BOX scrframe
         @  7,43 SAY "      Print Transaction List"
         @  9,45 SAY "1>  By Transaction Code"
         @ 10,45 SAY "2>  By Transaction Source"
```

```
            @ 11,45 SAY "3>  By Date of Transaction"
            @ 12,45 SAY "4>  By Account Order"
            @ 13,45 SAY "5>  All Transactions"
            @ 14,45 SAY "0>  Return to Main Menu"
            @ 16,48 SAY prompt GET suboption PICT "9" VALID(suboption $"012345")
            READ

        CASE option = "4"
            @ 15, 9 GET disp5_4
            CLEAR GETS
            @ 6,37,15,76 BOX scrframe
            @  7,42 SAY "  List General Headings Sub-Menu"
            @  9,42 SAY "1>  List Master/Sub Masters"
            @ 10,42 SAY "2>  List Subheadings/Subtotals"
            @ 11,42 SAY "3>  List All"
            @ 12,42 SAY "0>  Return to Sub Menu"
            @ 14,45 SAY prompt GET suboption PICT "9" VALID(suboption $"0123")
            READ

        ENDCASE

    CASE option = "7"

    CASE option = "2"
        STORE "0" TO option
        @ 10, 9 GET disp0_2
        CLEAR GETS
        @ 8,37,17,76 BOX scrframe
        @  9,47 SAY "Transaction Sub-Menu"
        @ 11,45 SAY "1>  Enter Transaction"
        @ 12,45 SAY "2>  Edit Transaction"
        @ 13,45 SAY "3>  Delete Transaction"
        @ 14,45 SAY "0>  Return to Main Menu"
        @ 16,48 SAY prompt GET option PICT "9" VALID(option $"0")
        READ

    CASE option = "4"
        STORE "0" TO option
        @ 16, 9 GET disp0_4
        CLEAR GETS
        @ 9,37,22,76 BOX scrframe
        @ 10,47 SAY "Transfer Data Sub-Menu"
        @ 12,41 SAY "1>   Transfer Accounts Receivable"
        @ 13,41 SAY "2>   Transfer Payroll"
        @ 14,41 SAY "3>   Transfer Accounts Payable"
        @ 15,41 SAY "4>   Transfer Inventory"
        @ 16,41 SAY "5>   Transfer Other Systems"
        @ 17,41 SAY "6>   Transfer Outside Systems"
        @ 18,41 SAY "7>   Post Transfers"
        @ 19,41 SAY "0>   Return to Main Menu"
        @ 21,45 SAY prompt GET option PICT "9" VALID(option $"0")
        READ
```

```
      CASE option = "6"
         STORE "0" TO option
         @ 10,49 GET disp0_6
         CLEAR GETS
         @  9,3,18,43 BOX scrframe
         @ 10,12 SAY "Print Reports Sub-Menu"
         @ 12, 8 SAY "1>   Print Trial Balance"
         @ 13, 8 SAY "2>   Print Statement of Income"
         @ 14, 8 SAY "3>   Print Balance Sheet"
         @ 15, 8 SAY "0>   Return to Main Menu"
         @ 17,11 SAY prompt GET option PICT "9" VALID(option $"0")
         READ

      CASE option = "8"
         STORE "0" TO option
         @ 16,49 GET disp0_8
         CLEAR GETS
         @ 7,2,17,38 BOX scrframe
         @  8, 8 SAY "End of Period Processing"
         @  9,16 SAY "Sub-Menu"
         @ 11,10 SAY "1>  End of Month"
         @ 12,10 SAY "2>  End of Quarter"
         @ 13,10 SAY "3>  End of Year"
         @ 14,10 SAY "0>  Return to Main Menu"
         @ 16,11 SAY prompt GET option PICT "9" VALID(option $"0123")
         READ

      CASE option = "0"
         @ 18,29 GET disp0_0
         CLEAR GETS
         CLOSE
         @ 22,17 SAY "All Files Closed.  Returning to Operating System"
         QUIT
      ENDCASE
ENDDO
* End of File
```

SCREEN SAVING

The ability to save screens carries the responsibility of monitoring the size of an application. Two questions arise:

1.   How many screens should one save?
2.   Does saving screens really help the user?

The answer to the second question is, without a doubt, yes! But menus aren't the only things that should be saved. In many applications, previous data entry screens are more important to save than the menus. Don't forget that the bottom line to saving screens is saving time. If data-entry and data-processing are performed 65 percent of the time, then saving data-entry screens would be more beneficial than saving menus.

Why not save both? It would be nice to save all screens, but the reality is that it takes 4K of memory per screen. It would be nice to be able to save 20 screens (menus, processing screens, and help screens) in an application but with a total of 80K in additional overhead to the system many applications can't afford that luxury!

Sample Code for Windowing Menus

To illustrate the windowing techniques in conjunction with saving screens and using arrays, the previous windowing example is elaborated upon in the following code. Notice that this program uses a lot of memory. Even though the .EXE program is relatively small, the total amount of RAM required is about 384K.

```
********************
* Name          DRAWMEN2.prg
* Date          August 13, 1986
* Notice        Copyright 1986, Stephen J. Straley
* Note          Shows how menus are created in conjunction with
*               saving screens and the use of arrays.   This is
*               developed from DRAWMEN1.prg
*
********************

STORE CHR(201) + CHR(205) + CHR(187) + CHR(186) + CHR(188) +;
      CHR(205) + CHR(200) + CHR(186) + CHR(32) TO scrframe
SET INTENS on
SET DELIM off


***********************************************************
* The following arrays are established for all of the    *
* possible screens to follow.  The "shown[x]" array  is  *
* used to test  if the sub-menu had been shown            *
* before.  If it had, then shown[x] is true and the       *
* appropriate screen will be called back from the         *
* screen[x] array.  If not, then the BOX command and the  *
* proper displays are drawn; the screen is saved to       *
* screen[x], and shown[x] is set to true.                 *
***********************************************************

DECLARE screen[15], shown[15]
FOR x = 1 TO 15
   STORE .F. TO shown[x]
NEXT

STORE "Enter Choice:" TO prompt
STORE SPACE(4000) TO tempscreen


***********************************************************
* The following are the menu variables for inverse video *
***********************************************************
```

```
disp0_1 = " 1>    Chart Of Accounts "
disp0_2 = " 2>    Transactions "
disp0_3 = " 3>    Posting & Balancing "
disp0_4 = " 4>    Transfers "
disp0_5 = " 5>    Print Lists / Checks "
disp0_6 = " 6>    Print Reports "
disp0_7 = " 7>    Utilities "
disp0_8 = " 8>    End of Period "
disp0_0 = " 0>    Exit Program "
disp1_1 = " 1>  Enter an Account "
disp1_2 = " 2>  Edit an Account "
disp1_3 = " 3>  Examine Accounts "
disp1_4 = " 4>  Delete an Account "
disp1_0 = " 0>  Return to Main Menu "
disp2_1 = " 1> Enter Transaction "
disp2_2 = " 2> Edit Transaction "
disp2_3 = " 3> Delete Transaction "
disp2_0 = " 0> Return to Main Menu "
disp5_1 = " 1>  Chart of Account Info. "
disp5_2 = " 2>  Print/Reprint Checks "
disp5_3 = " 3>  Transaction Information "
disp5_4 = " 4>  Headings Listings "
disp5_0 = " 0>  Return to Main Menu "
option = "0"


***********************************
* Now for the actual operation... *
***********************************


CLEAR
@ 5,0,20,79 BOX SUBSTR(scrframe,1,8)
@ 4,33 SAY "M A I N   M E N U"

DO WHILE .T.

   ***********************************
   *  This section is the main menu *
   ***********************************
   IF shown[15]
      CALL _scrrest WITH screen[15]
   ELSE
      @  7,10 SAY "1>    Chart Of Accounts"
      @ 10,10 SAY "2>    Transactions"
      @ 13,10 SAY "3>    Posting & Balancing"
      @ 16,10 SAY "4>    Transfers"
      @  7,50 SAY "5>    Print Lists / Checks"
      @ 10,50 SAY "6>    Print Reports"
      @ 13,50 SAY "7>    Utilities"
      @ 16,50 SAY "8>    End of Period"
      @ 18,30 SAY "0>    Exit Program"
      CALL _scrsave WITH tempscreen
      STORE tempscreen TO screen[15]
      STORE .T. TO shown[15]
```

```
ENDIF
@ 22,30 SAY prompt GET option PICT "9" VALID(option $"012345678")
READ

DO CASE

CASE option = "1"

   ******************************
   * This is the first sub-menu *
   ******************************
   STORE "0" TO option
   IF shown[1]
      CALL _scrrest WITH screen[1]
   ELSE
      @  7, 9 GET disp0_1
      CLEAR GETS
      @ 12,37,22,76 BOX scrframe
      @ 13,44 SAY "Chart Of Accounts Sub-Menu"
      @ 15,46 SAY "1>    Enter an Account"
      @ 16,46 SAY "2>    Edit an Account"
      @ 17,46 SAY "3>    Examine Accounts"
      @ 18,46 SAY "4>    Delete an Account"
      @ 19,46 SAY "0>    Return to Main Menu"
      CALL _scrsave WITH tempscreen
      STORE tempscreen TO screen[1]
      STORE .T. TO shown[1]
   ENDIF
   @ 21,47 SAY prompt GET option PICT "9" VALID(option $"0")
   READ

CASE option = "2"

   *******************************
   * This is the second sub-menu *
   *******************************
   STORE "0" TO option
   IF shown[2]
      CALL _scrrest WITH screen[2]
   ELSE
      @ 10, 9 GET disp0_2
      CLEAR GETS
      @ 8,37,17,76 BOX scrframe
      @  9,47 SAY "Transaction Sub-Menu"
      @ 11,45 SAY "1>  Enter Transaction"
      @ 12,45 SAY "2>  Edit Transaction"
      @ 13,45 SAY "3>  Delete Transaction"
      @ 14,45 SAY "0>  Return to Main Menu"
      CALL _scrsave WITH tempscreen
      STORE tempscreen TO screen[2]
      STORE .T. TO shown[2]
   ENDIF
   @ 16,48 SAY prompt GET option PICT "9" VALID(option $"0")
   READ
```

```
CASE option = "3"

   ******************************
   * This is the third sub-menu *
   ******************************
   STORE "0" TO option
   IF shown[3]
      CALL _scrrest WITH screen[3]
   ELSE
      @ 13, 9 GET disp0_3
      CLEAR GETS
      @ 10,37,18,76 BOX scrframe
      @ 11,47 SAY "Post/Balance Sub-Menu"
      @ 13,45 SAY "1>  Post Transactions"
      @ 14,45 SAY "2>  Balance Accounts"
      @ 15,45 SAY "0>  Return to Main Menu"
      CALL _scrsave WITH tempscreen
      STORE tempscreen TO screen[3]
      STORE .T. TO shown[3]
   ENDIF
   @ 17,47 SAY prompt GET option PICT "9" VALID(option $"0")
   READ

CASE option = "4"

   *******************************
   * This is the fourth sub-menu *
   *******************************
   STORE "0" TO option
   IF shown[4]
         CALL _scrrest WITH screen[4]
      ELSE
         @ 16, 9 GET disp0_4
         CLEAR GETS
         @ 9,37,22,76 BOX scrframe
         @ 10,47 SAY "Transfer Data Sub-Menu"
         @ 12,41 SAY "1>    Transfer Accounts Receivable"
         @ 13,41 SAY "2>    Transfer Payroll"
         @ 14,41 SAY "3>    Transfer Accounts Payable"
         @ 15,41 SAY "4>    Transfer Inventory"
         @ 16,41 SAY "5>    Transfer Other Systems"
         @ 17,41 SAY "6>    Transfer Outside Systems"
         @ 18,41 SAY "7>    Post Transfers"
         @ 19,41 SAY "0>    Return to Main Menu"
         CALL _scrsave WITH tempscreen
         STORE tempscreen TO screen[4]
         STORE .T. TO shown[4]
      ENDIF
      @ 21,45 SAY prompt GET option PICT "9" VALID(option $"0")
      READ
```

```
    CASE option = "5"

    *******************************
    * This is the fifth sub-menu *
    *******************************
    DO WHILE .T.

        STORE "0" TO option, suboption
        IF shown[5]
            CALL _scrrest WITH screen[5]
        ELSE
            @  7,49 GET disp0_5
            CLEAR GETS
            @ 9,3,19,43 BOX scrframe
            @ 10,11 SAY "Print Lists/Checks Sub-Menu"
            @ 12,10 SAY "1>    Chart of Account Info."
            @ 13,10 SAY "2>    Print/Reprint Checks"
            @ 14,10 SAY "3>    Transaction Information"
            @ 15,10 SAY "4>    Headings Listings"
            @ 16,10 SAY "0>    Return to Main Menu"
            CALL _scrsave WITH tempscreen
            STORE tempscreen TO screen[5]
            STORE .T. TO shown[5]
        ENDIF
        @ 18,12 SAY prompt GET option PICT "9" VALID(option $"01234")
        READ

        DO CASE

        CASE option = "0"
            @ 16,09 GET disp5_0
            CLEAR GETS
            EXIT

        CASE option = "1"
            IF shown[10]
                CALL _scrrest WITH screen[10]
            ELSE
                @ 12, 9 GET disp5_1
                CLEAR GETS
                @ 6,40,16,77 BOX scrframe
                @  7,46 SAY " Printing Chart of Accounts"
                @  9,49 SAY "1>  Account Listing"
                @ 10,49 SAY "2>  Account History"
                @ 11,49 SAY "3>  Budget Listing"
                @ 12,49 SAY "0>  Return to Sub Menu"
                CALL _scrsave WITH tempscreen
                STORE tempscreen TO screen[10]
                STORE .T. TO shown[10]
            ENDIF
            @ 14,49 SAY prompt GET suboption PICT "9" VALID(suboption $"0")
            READ
```

```
CASE option = "2"
   IF shown[11]
      CALL _scrrest WITH screen[11]
   ELSE
      @ 13, 9 GET disp5_2
      CLEAR GETS
      @ 6,37,15,76 BOX scrframe
      @ 7, 43 SAY "        Re/Print Checks"
      @ 9, 45 SAY "1>  Print Checks"
      @ 10,45 SAY "2>  Reprint Checks"
      @ 11,45 SAY "3>  Print Check Register"
      @ 12,45 SAY "0>  Return to Sub Menu"
      CALL _scrsave WITH tempscreen
      STORE tempscreen TO screen[11]
      STORE .T. TO shown[11]
   ENDIF
   @ 14,46 SAY Prompt GET suboption PICT "9" VALID(suboption $"0")
   READ

CASE option = "3"
   IF shown[12]
      CALL _scrrest WITH screen[12]
   ELSE
      @ 14, 9 GET disp5_3
      CLEAR GETS
      @ 6,37,17,76 BOX scrframe
      @ 7,43 SAY "      Print Transaction List"
      @ 9,45 SAY "1>  By Transaction Code"
      @ 10,45 SAY "2>  By Transaction Source"
      @ 11,45 SAY "3>  By Date of Transaction"
      @ 12,45 SAY "4>  By Account Order"
      @ 13,45 SAY "5>  All Transactions"
      @ 14,45 SAY "0>  Return to Sub Menu"
      CALL _scrsave WITH tempscreen
      STORE tempscreen TO screen[12]
      STORE .T. TO shown[12]
   ENDIF
   @ 16,48 SAY prompt GET suboption PICT "9" VALID(suboption $"0")
   READ

CASE option = "4"
   IF shown[13]
      CALL _scrrest WITH screen[13]
   ELSE
      @ 15, 9 GET disp5_4
      CLEAR GETS
      @ 6,37,15,76 BOX scrframe
      @ 7,42 SAY " List General Headings Sub-Menu"
      @ 9,42 SAY "1>  List Master/Sub Masters"
      @ 10,42 SAY "2>  List Subheadings/Subtotals"
      @ 11,42 SAY "3>  List All"
      @ 12,42 SAY "0>  Return to Sub Menu"
      CALL _scrsave WITH tempscreen
```

```
                        STORE tempscreen TO screen[13]
                        STORE .T. TO shown[13]
                     ENDIF
                     @ 14,45 SAY prompt GET suboption PICT "9" VALID(suboption $"0")
                     READ
                  ENDCASE
               ENDDO

         CASE option = "6"

            ******************************
            * This is the sixth sub-menu *
            ******************************
            STORE "0" TO option
            IF shown[6]
               CALL _scrrest WITH screen[6]
            ELSE
               @ 10,49 GET disp0_6
               CLEAR GETS
               @  9,3,18,43 BOX scrframe
               @ 10,12 SAY "Print Reports Sub-Menu"
               @ 12, 8 SAY "1>    Print Trial Balance"
               @ 13, 8 SAY "2>    Print Statement of Income"
               @ 14, 8 SAY "3>    Print Balance Sheet"
               @ 15, 8 SAY "0>    Return to Main Menu"
               CALL _scrsave WITH tempscreen
               STORE tempscreen TO screen[6]
               STORE .T. TO shown[6]
            ENDIF
            @ 17,11 SAY prompt GET option PICT "9" VALID(option $"0")
            READ

         CASE option = "7"

         CASE option = "8"

            ******************************
            * This is the eighth sub-menu *
            ******************************
            STORE "0" TO option
            IF shown[8]
               CALL _scrrest WITH screen[8]
            ELSE
               @ 16,49 GET disp0_8
               CLEAR GETS
               @ 7,2,17,38 BOX scrframe
               @  8, 8 SAY "End of Period Processing"
               @  9,16 SAY "Sub-Menu"
               @ 11,10 SAY "1> End of Month"
               @ 12,10 SAY "2> End of Quarter"
               @ 13,10 SAY "3> End of Year"
               @ 14,10 SAY "0> Return to Main Menu"
               CALL _scrsave WITH tempscreen
```

```
            STORE tempscreen TO screen[8]
            STORE .T. TO shown[8]
        ENDIF
        @ 16,11 SAY prompt GET option PICT "9" VALID(option $"0")
        READ

    OTHERWISE

        @ 18,29 GET disp0_0
        CLEAR GETS
        CLOSE
        @ 22,17 SAY "All Files Closed.  Returning to Operating System"
        QUIT

    ENDCASE
ENDDO
* End of File
```

THE TOTAL PICTURE

What follows should give you the total picture of saving menu screens and processing screens for better user interaction. Not every screen has been developed – only enough to give an overall view of the final picture.

The code listed below builds on the sample menus drawn before. In this sample, we take advantage of the PROMPT command. Following this sample is a final sample of how to develop menus, in which all of the techniques previously mentioned are incorporated.

```
****************
*  Sample Menu *
****************

CLEAR
STORE SPACE(4000) TO mainscreen, listscreen
STORE CHR(201) + CHR(205) + CHR(187) + CHR(186) + CHR(188) + ;
      CHR(205) + CHR(200) + CHR(186) + " " TO scrframe
center = "M A I N    M E N U"
message = " <ESC> Key for Main Menu "
@ 5,0,20,79 BOX SUBSTR(scrframe,1,8)
CALL _scrsave WITH mainscreen

DO WHILE .t.
    ********
    *  Set up the environment
    ********
    CALL _scrrest WITH mainscreen
    @  7,10 PROMPT " 1>     Chart Of Accounts "
    @ 10,10 PROMPT " 2>     Transactions "
    @ 13,10 PROMPT " 3>     Posting & Balancing "
```

```
@ 16,10 PROMPT " 4>    Transfers "
@  7,50 PROMPT " 5>    Print Lists / Checks "
@ 10,50 PROMPT " 6>    Print Reports "
@ 13,50 PROMPT " 7>    Utilities "
@ 16,50 PROMPT " 8>    End of Period "
@ 18,30 SAY    "Press <ESC> to Exit"
MENU TO option
STORE 1 TO sub_option

DO CASE
CASE option = 1
   @ 8,38,22,77 BOX scrframe
   @ 10,45 SAY "Chart Of Accounts Sub-Menu"
   @ 12,47 PROMPT " 1>   Enter an Account "
   @ 14,47 PROMPT " 2>   Edit an Account "
   @ 16,47 PROMPT " 3>   Examine Accounts "
   @ 18,47 PROMPT " 4>   Delete an Account "
   @ 20,47 SAY message
   MENU TO sub_option
   IF sub_option = 0
      LOOP
   ENDIF

CASE option = 3
   @ 12,38,22,77 BOX scrframe
   @ 14,48 SAY "Post/Balance Sub-Menu"
   @ 16,45 PROMPT " 1>  Post Transactions "
   @ 18,45 PROMPT " 2>  Balance Accounts "
   @ 20,45 SAY message
   MENU TO sub_option

CASE option = 5
   @ 8,2,23,42 BOX scrframe
   @ 10,12 SAY "Print Lists/Checks Sub-Menu"
   @ 12, 9  PROMPT " 1>   Chart of Account Info. "
   @ 14, 9  PROMPT " 2>   Print/Reprint Checks "
   @ 16, 9  PROMPT " 3>   Transaction Information "
   @ 18, 9  PROMPT " 4>   Headings Listings "
   @ 20, 9  SAY message
   MENU TO sub_option

CASE option = 7

CASE option = 2
   @  6,38,18,77 BOX scrframe
   @  8,48 SAY "Transaction Sub-Menu"
   @ 10,46 PROMPT " 1> Enter Transaction "
   @ 12,46 PROMPT " 2> Edit Transaction "
   @ 14,46 PROMPT " 3> Delete Transaction "
   @ 16,46 SAY message
   MENU TO sub_option

CASE option = 4
   @ 7,38,18,77 BOX scrframe
   @  8,48 SAY "Transfer Data Sub-Menu"
   @ 10,40 PROMPT " 1>  Transfer Accounts Receivable "
```

```
        @ 11,40 PROMPT " 2>    Transfer Payroll "
        @ 12,40 PROMPT " 3>    Transfer Accounts Payable "
        @ 13,40 PROMPT " 4>    Transfer Inventory "
        @ 14,40 PROMPT " 5>    Transfer Other Systems "
        @ 15,40 PROMPT " 6>    Post Transfers "
        @ 16,43 SAY message
        MENU TO sub_option

    CASE option = 6
        @ 11,2,22,42 BOX scrframe
        @ 12,11 SAY "Print Reports Sub-Menu"
        @ 14, 7 PROMPT " 1>    Print Trial Balance "
        @ 16, 7 PROMPT " 2>    Print Statement of Income "
        @ 18, 7 PROMPT " 3>    Print Balance Sheet "
        @ 20, 7 SAY message
        MENU TO sub_option
        IF sub_option = 0
            LOOP
        ENDIF
        row = 16
        col = 45
        screenprnt = 0
        outfile = SPACE(10)
        DO Whichway WITH screenprnt, outfile
        IF screenprnt = 0
            LOOP
        ENDIF

    CASE option = 8
        @ 7,2,22,42 BOX scrframe
        @  9,10 SAY "End of Period Processing"
        @ 10,18 SAY "Sub-Menu"
        @ 12,12 PROMPT " 1>  End of Month "
        @ 14,12 PROMPT " 2>  End of Quarter "
        @ 16,12 PROMPT " 3>  End of Year "
        @ 18,12 SAY     " <ESC> Key for Main Menu "
        MENU TO sub_option
        IF sub_option = 4
            LOOP
        ENDIF

    OTHERWISE
        CLOSE
        @ 22,17 SAY "All Files Closed.  Returning to Operating System"
        QUIT
    ENDCASE
ENDDO

********************

PROCEDURE Whichway

    PARAMETERS screenprnt, outfile
```

```
      @ row, col, row + 7, col + 30 BOX scrframe

      @ row+2, col+5 PROMPT " 1>  Print to Screen "
      @ row+3, col+5 PROMPT " 2>  Print to Printer "
      @ row+4, col+5 PROMPT " 3>  Print to File "
      @ row+5, col+5 SAY     "   RETURN to Menu "
      MENU TO screenprnt

      DO CASE
      CASE screenprnt = 0
         RETURN
      CASE screenprnt = 3
         @ row, col, row + 7, col + 30 BOX scrframe
         @ row+2,col+5 SAY "Enter File Name.."
         @ row+4,col+5 SAY "--> " GET outfile PICT "!!!!!!!!!!!"
         READ
         IF LEN(TRIM(outfile)) = 0
            screenprnt = 1
         ELSE
            outfile = TRIM(outfile) + ".TXT"
         ENDIF
      ENDCASE
  * End of Program
```

A FINAL MENU

The following code incorporates all the techniques we have studied up to now. This code was basically generated by GENMEN.prg (see Appendix H) and then modified and commented further.

```
      ********************
      * Name          DRAWMEN3.prg
      * Date          August 13, 1986
      * Notice        Copyright 1986, Stephen J. Straley
      * Note          This is a sample of a menu generated by the menu
      *               generator.
      *
      ********************

      CLEAR
      DO Domen1

      ********************

      PROCEDURE Domen1

         DO WHILE .T.
            CLEAR
            *RESTORE FROM Screen.sys
            * Since there is no screen file 'SCREEN.SYS', the following
            * are the codes for the frame.
            STORE CHR(201) + CHR(205) + CHR(187) + CHR(186) + CHR(188) +;
```

```
        CHR(205) + CHR(200) + CHR(186) + CHR(32) TO scrframe
SET INTENS on
SET DELIM off
  STORE SPACE(4000) TO ascreen, bscreen, cscreen, dscreen, escreen,
fscreen
*DO Setup
STORE 0 TO option
@ 5, 0, 20, 77 BOX SUBSTR(scrframe,1,8)
@ 4, 30 SAY "M A I N    M E N U"
@ 8, 7 PROMPT " 1>    Chart of Accounts "
@ 11, 7 PROMPT " 2>    Transactions "
@ 14, 7 PROMPT " 3>    Posting & Balancing "
@ 17, 7 PROMPT " 4>    Transfers "
@ 8, 43 PROMPT " 5>    Print Lists / Checks "
@ 11, 43 PROMPT " 6>    Print Reports "
@ 14, 43 PROMPT " 7>    Utilities "
@ 17, 43 PROMPT " 8>    End of Period "
@ 19, 33 SAY "ESC to RETURN"
MENU TO option
CALL _scrsave WITH ascreen
*
* Another acceptable method would be as follows
* DO CASE
* CASE option = 0
*    @ 21, 18 SAY "All Files Closed, Returning to Operating System"
*    QUIT
* OTHERWISE
*    branch = TRANSFORM(option, "9")
*    DO Domen1&branch.
* ENDCASE
*
DO CASE
CASE option = 1
   DO Domen11
CASE option = 2
   DO Domen12
CASE option = 3
   DO Domen13
CASE option = 4
   DO Domen14
CASE option = 5
   DO Domen15
CASE option = 6
   DO Domen16
CASE option = 7
   *************************
   * Do sub-procedure here *
   *************************
CASE option = 8
   DO Domen18
CASE option = 0
   @ 21, 18 SAY "All Files Closed, Returning to Operating System"
   QUIT
```

```
        ENDCASE
ENDDO

********************

PROCEDURE Domen11

    DO WHILE .T.
       IF !EMPTY(bscreen)
          CALL _scrrest WITH bscreen
       ENDIF
       STORE 0 TO option1
       a 7, 39, 24, 73 BOX scrframe
       a 8, 43 SAY "Chart of Accounts Sub-Menu"
       a 11, 44 PROMPT " 1>  Enter an Account "
       a 14, 44 PROMPT " 2>  Edit an Account "
       a 17, 44 PROMPT " 3>  Examine an Account "
       a 20, 44 PROMPT " 4>  Delete an Account "
       a 23, 50 SAY "ESC to RETURN"
       MENU TO option1
       CALL _scrsave WITH bscreen
       DO CASE
       CASE option1 = 1
          ************************
          * Do sub-procedure here *
          ************************

       CASE option1 = 2
          ************************
          * Do sub-procedure here *
          ************************

       CASE option1 = 3
          ************************
          * Do sub-procedure here *
          ************************

       CASE option1 = 4
          ************************
          * Do sub-procedure here *
          ************************

       CASE option1 = 0
          EXIT
       ENDCASE
    ENDDO

********************

PROCEDURE Domen12

    DO WHILE .T.
       IF !EMPTY(bscreen)
          CALL _scrrest WITH bscreen
       ENDIF
       STORE 0 TO option1
       a 8, 39, 22, 72 BOX scrframe
```

```
     @ 9, 46 SAY "Transaction Sub-Menu"
     @ 12, 44 PROMPT " 1>  Enter Transaction "
     @ 15, 44 PROMPT " 2>  Edit Transaction "
     @ 18, 44 PROMPT " 3>  Delete Transactions "
     @ 21, 49 SAY "ESC to RETURN"
     MENU TO option1
     CALL _scrsave WITH bscreen
     DO CASE
     CASE option1 = 1
        *************************
        * Do sub-procedure here *
        *************************
     CASE option1 = 2
        *************************
        * Do sub-procedure here *
        *************************
     CASE option1 = 3
        *************************
        * Do sub-procedure here *
        *************************
     CASE option1 = 0
        EXIT
     ENDCASE
ENDDO


********************

PROCEDURE Domen13

DO WHILE .T.
   IF !EMPTY(bscreen)
      CALL _scrrest WITH bscreen
   ENDIF
   STORE 0 TO option1
   @ 12, 39, 22, 71 BOX scrframe
   @ 13, 45 SAY "Post/Balance Sub-Menu"
   @ 15, 43 PROMPT " 1>  Post Transactions "
   @ 18, 43 PROMPT " 2>  Balance Accounts "
   @ 21, 49 SAY "ESC to RETURN"
   MENU TO option1
   CALL _scrsave WITH bscreen
   DO CASE
   CASE option1 = 1
      *************************
      * Do sub-procedure here *
      *************************
   CASE option1 = 2
      *************************
      * Do sub-procedure here *
      *************************
   CASE option1 = 0
      EXIT
   ENDCASE
```

```
ENDDO

********************

PROCEDURE Domen14

DO WHILE .T.
   IF !EMPTY(bscreen)
      CALL _scrrest WITH bscreen
   ENDIF
   STORE 0 TO option1
   a 6, 38, 24, 67 BOX scrframe
   a 7, 42 SAY "Transfer Data Sub-Menu"
   a 9, 41 PROMPT " 1>  Accounts Receivable "
   a 11, 41 PROMPT " 2>  Payroll "
   a 13, 41 PROMPT " 3>  Accounts Payable "
   a 15, 41 PROMPT " 4>  Inventory "
   a 17, 41 PROMPT " 5>  Other Systems "
   a 19, 41 PROMPT " 6>  Outside Systems "
   a 21, 41 PROMPT " 7>  Post Transfers "
   a 23, 46 SAY "ESC to RETURN"
   MENU TO option1
   CALL _scrsave WITH bscreen
   DO CASE
   CASE option1 = 1
      **************************
      * Do sub-procedure here *
      **************************
   CASE option1 = 2
      **************************
      * Do sub-procedure here *
      **************************
   CASE option1 = 3
      **************************
      * Do sub-procedure here *
      **************************
   CASE option1 = 4
      **************************
      * Do sub-procedure here *
      **************************
   CASE option1 = 5
      **************************
      * Do sub-procedure here *
      **************************
   CASE option1 = 6
      **************************
      * Do sub-procedure here *
      **************************
   CASE option1 = 7
      **************************
      * Do sub-procedure here *
      **************************
   CASE option1 = 0
```

```
        EXIT
     ENDCASE
ENDDO

********************

PROCEDURE Domen15

DO WHILE .T.
   IF !EMPTY(bscreen)
      CALL _scrrest WITH bscreen
   ENDIF
   STORE 0 TO option1
   a 9, 5, 21, 44 BOX scrframe
   a 10, 12 SAY "Print Lists/Checks Sub-Menu"
   a 12, 11 PROMPT " 1>  Chart of Accounts Info. "
   a 14, 11 PROMPT " 2>  Print/Reprint Checks "
   a 16, 11 PROMPT " 3>  Transaction Information "
   a 18, 11 PROMPT " 4>  Heading's Listings "
   a 20, 19 SAY "ESC to RETURN"
   MENU TO option1
   CALL _scrsave WITH bscreen
   DO CASE
   CASE option1 = 1
      DO Domen151
   CASE option1 = 2
      DO Domen152
   CASE option1 = 3
      DO Domen153
   CASE option1 = 4
      DO Domen154
   CASE option1 = 0
      EXIT
   ENDCASE
   STORE SPACE(4000) TO cscreen
ENDDO

********************

PROCEDURE Domen151

DO WHILE .T.
   IF !EMPTY(cscreen)
      CALL _scrrest WITH cscreen
   ENDIF
   STORE 0 TO option2
   a 13, 40, 23, 73 BOX scrframe
   a 14, 44 SAY "Printing Chart of Accounts"
   a 16, 46 PROMPT " 1>  Account Listing "
   a 18, 46 PROMPT " 2>  Account History "
   a 20, 46 PROMPT " 3>  Budget Listing "
   a 22, 51 SAY "ESC to RETURN"
   MENU TO option2
```

```
            CALL _scrsave WITH cscreen
            DO CASE
            CASE option2 = 1
               *************************
               * Do sub-procedure here *
               *************************

            CASE option2 = 2
               *************************
               * Do sub-procedure here *
               *************************

            CASE option2 = 3
               *************************
               * Do sub-procedure here *
               *************************

            CASE option2 = 0
               EXIT
            ENDCASE
      ENDDO


      *********************

      PROCEDURE Domen152

      DO WHILE .T.
         IF !EMPTY(cscreen)
            CALL _scrrest WITH cscreen
         ENDIF
         STORE 0 TO option2
         @ 11, 42, 22, 74 BOX scrframe
         @ 12, 50 SAY "Re/Print Checks"
         @ 14, 46 PROMPT " 1>  Print Checks "
         @ 16, 46 PROMPT " 2>  Reprint Checks "
         @ 18, 46 PROMPT " 3>  Print Check Register "
         @ 21, 52 SAY "ESC to RETURN"
         MENU TO option2
         CALL _scrsave WITH cscreen
         DO CASE
         CASE option2 = 1
            *************************
            * Do sub-procedure here *
            *************************

         CASE option2 = 2
            *************************
            * Do sub-procedure here *
            *************************

         CASE option2 = 3
            *************************
            * Do sub-procedure here *
            *************************

         CASE option2 = 0
            EXIT
         ENDCASE
      ENDDO
```

```
********************

PROCEDURE Domen153

DO WHILE .T.
   IF !EMPTY(cscreen)
      CALL _scrrest WITH cscreen
   ENDIF
   STORE 0 TO option2
   @ 10, 42, 24, 75 BOX scrframe
   @ 11, 48 SAY "Print Transaction List"
   @ 13, 46 PROMPT " 1>  By Transaction Code "
   @ 15, 46 PROMPT " 2>  By Transaction Source "
   @ 17, 46 PROMPT " 3>  By Date of Transaction "
   @ 19, 46 PROMPT " 4>  By Account Order "
   @ 21, 46 PROMPT " 5>  All Transactions "
   @ 23, 53 SAY "ESC to RETURN"
   MENU TO option2
   CALL _scrsave WITH cscreen
   DO CASE
   CASE option2 = 1
      **************************
      * Do sub-procedure here *
      **************************
   CASE option2 = 2
      **************************
      * Do sub-procedure here *
      **************************
   CASE option2 = 3
      **************************
      * Do sub-procedure here *
      **************************
   CASE option2 = 4
      **************************
      * Do sub-procedure here *
      **************************
   CASE option2 = 5
      **************************
      * Do sub-procedure here *
      **************************
   CASE option2 = 0
      EXIT
   ENDCASE
ENDDO

********************

PROCEDURE Domen154

DO WHILE .T.
   IF !EMPTY(cscreen)
      CALL _scrrest WITH cscreen
   ENDIF
```

```
      STORE 0 TO option2
      @ 12, 41, 22, 75 BOX scrframe
      @ 13, 43 SAY "List General Headings Sub-Menu"
      @ 15, 43 PROMPT " 1> List Master/Sub Masters "
      @ 17, 43 PROMPT " 2> List Subheadings/Subtotals "
      @ 19, 43 PROMPT " 3> List All "
      @ 21, 52 SAY "ESC to RETURN"
      MENU TO option2
      CALL _scrsave WITH cscreen
      DO CASE
      CASE option2 = 1
         **************************
         * Do sub-procedure here *
         **************************

      CASE option2 = 2
         **************************
         * Do sub-procedure here *
         **************************

      CASE option2 = 3
         **************************
         * Do sub-procedure here *
         **************************

      CASE option2 = 0
         EXIT
      ENDCASE
ENDDO


********************

PROCEDURE Domen16

DO WHILE .T.
   IF !EMPTY(bscreen)
      CALL _scrrest WITH bscreen
   ENDIF
   STORE 0 TO option2
   @ 9, 4, 21, 42 BOX scrframe
   @ 11, 13 SAY "Print Report Sub-Menu"
   @ 13, 8 PROMPT " 1>  Print Trial Balance "
   @ 15, 8 PROMPT " 2>  Print Statement of Income "
   @ 17, 8 PROMPT " 3>  Print Balance Sheet "
   @ 19, 17 SAY "ESC to RETURN"
   MENU TO option2
   CALL _scrsave WITH bscreen
   DO CASE
   CASE option2 = 1
      **************************
      * Do sub-procedure here *
      **************************

   CASE option2 = 2
      **************************
      * Do sub-procedure here *
      **************************
```

```
      CASE option2 = 3
         **************************
         * Do sub-procedure here *
         **************************
      CASE option2 = 0
         EXIT
      ENDCASE
   ENDDO


   *********************

   PROCEDURE Domen18

   DO WHILE .T.
      IF !EMPTY(bscreen)
         CALL _scrrest WITH bscreen
      ENDIF
      STORE 0 TO option1
      @ 9, 6, 19, 38 BOX scrframe
      @ 10, 12 SAY "End of Period Sub-Menu"
      @ 12, 12 PROMPT " 1>  End of Month "
      @ 14, 12 PROMPT " 2>  End of Quarter "
      @ 16, 12 PROMPT " 3>  End of Year "
      @ 18, 17 SAY "ESC to RETURN"
      MENU TO option1
      CALL _scrsave WITH bscreen
      DO CASE
      CASE option1 = 1
         **************************
         * Do sub-procedure here *
         **************************
      CASE option1 = 2
         **************************
         * Do sub-procedure here *
         **************************
      CASE option1 = 3
         **************************
         * Do sub-procedure here *
         **************************
      CASE option1 = 0
         EXIT
      ENDCASE
   ENDDO
 * End of File
```

WINDOWING BUT NOT MENUS

The ability to create and manipulate windows in Clipper offers a powerful tool to the developer. Imagination and creativity are the only limits to the uses you can put this to. In the following code, we have opened a window that allows the display of some text and then scrolls it backwards.

```
********************
* Name        WINDOW.prg
* Date        August 28, 1986
* Notice      Copyright 1986, Stephen J. Straley
* Note        This program shows how the screen can be parsed and
*             manipulated and made to scroll backwards.  Though
*             this routine as it's written has no real purpose, it shows the
*             ability of Clipper to handle windowing without
*             the aid of another language.  In other words, this
*             routine simulates windowing with no Assembly required.
*
*             It should also be noted that the SUBSTR() function is
*             parsing the screen in 160 character sections.   That
*             is to allow for the 80 characters on each line, and each
*             accompanying attribute byte.   An attribute byte is a
*             character that tells the computer to throw the next
*             character displayed into a specific mode, such
*             as red, blue, bright, underlining, or flashing.
*
********************

STORE SPACE(4000) TO temp
CALL _scrsave WITH temp
FOR x = 25 TO 1 STEP - 1
   window  = SUBSTR(temp,3841,160)
   partial = window + temp
   temp    = SUBSTR(partial,1,4000)
   CALL _scrrest WITH temp
NEXT
* End of file
```

FORMATTING FOR HARD COPY

CONSIDERATIONS ON OUTPUT

Screen handling is just one part of an application. Data input to get information into the system and data manipulation to crunch numbers and arrange or modify the information are also necessary. Output is the final concern of application building.

All output considerations should include three destinations: the screen, the printer, and the disk drive. Many systems fail to allow output to an alternative file. By porting the information to a disk file, the user can use that data later.

You need to decide whether to use the REPORT form utility or to design custom reports. It gets to be a problem to constantly port over .FRM and .LBL files from a master floppy disk. Also, a lot of code must be added which checks that the files are available on the disk. Finally, there is the problem of security: the .FRM and .LBL files can be altered by the user. This defeats one purpose of the compiler -- to protect the developers ideas and code from the rest of the world. Should the user have access to the output code or should the output generator be embedded in the rest of the application? This is a serious question that must be addressed completely.

Below is a brief synopsis of three ways to output information.

SCREEN REPORTS

The two main considerations for all reports to the screen are the amount of space available and the amount of information required. The two are often in conflict. There are many times when the limit in the screen's capacity restricts the amount of information that can be given. If too much information is included, the screen becomes unreadable. Be careful to send only vital information to the screen. Screen output should be for quick reference and verification, not for complete reports. Balances are fine for screen reports, for example, but complete invoice detail is probably excessive. Each system's requirements change, but keep the restrictions of the screen and the purpose of the report in mind.

Allow an easy escape back to some entry or menu point. The user defined function QWAIT() which we discussed earlier was designed for this specific purpose. It allows the user to press any key for the next screen of information or the letter 'Q' to go back. This function can be made standard for all screen reports. For example:

```
USE Temp
SET FILTER TO .NOT. posted
GO TOP
DO WHILE .NOT. EOF()
   @ 6,1,22,78 BOX SPACE(9)
   @ 8, 5 SAY "Name of account:  " GET accnt_name
   @ 9, 5 SAY "         Number:  " GET accnt_numb
   @ 11,12 SAY "Current Balances"
   @ 11,52 SAY "Previous Balances"
   @ 13, 2 SAY "  Month-> "
   @ 14, 2 SAY "Quarter-> "
   @ 15, 2 SAY "   Year-> "
   @ 13,12 GET current_m
   @ 14,12 GET current_q
   @ 15,12 GET current_y
   @ 13,47 GET previous_m
   @ 14,47 GET previous_q
   @ 15,47 GET previous_y
   CLEAR GETS
   @ 18,10 SAY "Press any key to continue or 'Q' to Quit..."
   IF QWAIT()
      QUIT
   ENDIF
ENDDO
```

```
********************

FUNCTION Qwait

   SET CONSOLE OFF
   WAIT TO intemp
   SET CONSOLE ON
   IF UPPER(intemp) = "Q"
      RETURN(.T.)
   ENDIF
   RETURN(.F.)
```

As with the design of menus, be consistent with screen report formats.

PRINTER REPORTS

You should also understand and work within the limits of the hard-copy format. Some printers can produce condensed print. For example, to condense the print on an Epson printer, use the following set of commands (which you could put into a user defined function in your library file along with a Reset function):

```
SET PRINT ON
SET CONSOLE OFF
?? CHR(15)
SET PRINT OFF
SET CONSOLE ON
```

As with screen control, you should allow an easy escape route. Users change their minds; with the compiler's added features it's very easy to provide for these changes. For example, the application should allow for single sheet or continuous paper reports, as well as normal sized or condensed print reports. As another option, the program might be designed to ask the user to press any key for the next page after each page of printout. However, if there are quite a few pages to print, this option shouldn't be used. Additionally, the program should allow the user to abort printing. Listed below is a simple printing control routine.

```
DO WHILE .T.
   CLEAR
   FOR x = 1 To 200
      @ 10,10 SAY x
   NEXT
   IF LASTKEY() <> ASC("c") .OR. LASTKEY() = ASC("C")
      WAIT "ESC to Abort - 'C' to continue - or any key..."
   ENDIF
   IF NO_PRINT()
      @ 20,20 SAY "All complete"
      QUIT
   ENDIF
ENDDO
```

```
*******************

FUNCTION No_print

   IF LASTKEY() = 27
      RETURN(.T.)
   ENDIF
   RETURN(.F.)
```

FILE REPORTS

In printing out reports to an alternate file, several obstacles vanish immediately. Format, pausing for a change of paper, and escape routines are no longer problems. One new problem to be concerned with is disk space.

Possible options may be to allow for a few notes to be entered before or after the report, as well as a change of the default drive for the report. In either case, be consistent. Allow all options to be available for all reports, and not just for a few. The user will have trouble remembering which reports allow certain features and which do not. If possible, use the TRANSFORM() function universally for screen, paper, and file reports.

A FINAL WORD ON OUTPUT

In many cases the REPORT utilities of both dBASE III and Clipper are not sufficient. With the added ability of multiple-child relations as well as user defined functions, the REPORT utility program almost becomes obsolete. Judge the system size carefully as well. Applications grow with each report. It may be adequate to allow for some standard REPORT forms as well as some additional customized reports.

Study the following code as a sample of code which outputs to the printer. The code outputs a text file stored on your disk. It breaks for pages as designated and generates line numbers.

```
*******************
* Name         OUTPUT.prg
* Date         August 1, 1986
* Notice       Copyright 1986, Stephen J. Straley
* Note         This program prints out any text file to the printer
*              prompting the user for page numbers, line numbers,
*              pauses, file extension, and program name
*
*******************

CREATE Temp
APPEND BLANK
```

```
REPLACE field_name WITH "LINEPUT", field_type WITH "C", field_len WITH 132
USE
CREATE Reading FROM Temp
USE Reading
ERASE Temp
DO WHILE .T.
   CLEAR
   STORE SPACE(35) TO drive
   STORE SPACE(40) TO input
   @ 10,10 SAY "Name of File to Print => " GET input PICT "@!"
   READ
   IF LEN(TRIM(input)) = 0
      CLOSE DATABASES
      ERASE Reading
      QUIT
   ENDIF
   @ 12, 5 SAY "What drive/direcrtory to look on => " GET drive PICT "@!"
   @ 14, 5 SAY "Leave blank for logged drive/directory default"
   READ
   IF AT(".",input) = 0
      input = TRIM(input) + ".PRG"
   ENDIF
   the_file = TRIM(drive) + input
   IF .NOT. FILE(the_file)
      @ 19,CENTER(the_file) SAY the_file
      @ 20,CENTER("is not present on disk.  Please choose again, or") ;
         SAY "is not present on disk.  Please choose again, or"
      @ 21,CENTER("leave blank to exit program...") ;
         SAY "leave blank to exit program..."
      LOOP
   ENDIF
   @ 14, 5 SAY SPACE(69)
   @ 20,10 SAY SPACE(69)
   @ 21,10 SAY SPACE(69)
   GO TOP
   @ 24,10 SAY "Now Reading Information...."
   APPEND FROM &the_file. SDF
   @ 24,10 SAY SPACE(69)
   STORE 0 TO times
   DO WHILE times = 0
      @ 14,10 SAY "Number of lines per page to print?? " GET times PICT "##"
      READ
      IF times > 66
         STORE 0 TO times
         @ 22,10 SAY "Only 66 lines per page are allowed.  Please reenter!!!"
         LOOP
      ENDIF
   ENDDO
   @ 14,00 CLEAR
   @ 18,10 SAY "Do you wish to PAUSE after each page? "
   pause = VERIFY()
   @ 19,10 SAY "Do you wish to print page numbers? "
   pages = VERIFY()
```

```
   IF pages
      times = times - 4
   ENDIF
   @ 20,10 SAY "Do you wish to print line numbers? "
   lprint = VERIFY()
   amount = 1
   @ 0,0,24,79 BOX SPACE(9)
   @ 12,10 SAY "Press Any Key to Begin Printing... or Q to Quit..."
   IF QWAIT()
      LOOP
   ENDIF
   @ 12,10 SAY "          Now Printing.  One Moment Please...        "
   down = 0
   SET DEVICE TO PRINT
   GO TOP
   DO WHILE .NOT. EOF()
      IF lprint
         @ down,00 SAY RECNO() PICT "@B"
         @ down,10 SAY TRIM(lineput)
      ELSE
         @ down,0 SAY TRIM(lineput)
      ENDIF
      IF RECNO()/times = INT(RECNO()/times)
         IF pages
            @ down + 2,0 SAY "Page"
            @ PROW(),PCOL()+2 SAY amount PICT "@B"
         ENDIF
         EJECT
         amount = amount + 1
         down = 1
         IF pause
            SET DEVICE TO SCREEN
            @ 12,10 SAY "Press Any Key to Begin Printing... or Q to Quit..."
            IF QWAIT()
               EXIT
            ENDIF
            @ 12,10 SAY "          Now Printing.  One Moment Please...        "
            SET DEVICE TO PRINT
         ENDIF
      ENDIF
      down = down + 1
      SKIP
   ENDDO
   EJECT
   SET DEVICE TO SCREEN
   ZAP
   CLEAR
ENDDO

*******************************

FUNCTION pause
* This function pauses for a given length of time as specified and returns
* a null value.
```

```
PARAMETERS i

FOR x = 0 TO i
   mtime = TIME()
   DO WHILE mtime = TIME()
   ENDDO
NEXT

RETURN("")

********************

FUNCTION Qwait

   SET CONSOLE OFF
   WAIT TO intemp
   SET CONSOLE ON
   IF UPPER(intemp) = "Q"
      RETURN(.T.)
   ENDIF
   RETURN(.F.)


********************

FUNCTION Verify

   SET CONSOLE OFF
   STORE "" TO verify_var
   DO WHILE .NOT. verify_var$"YyNn"
      WAIT TO verify_var
   ENDDO
   SET CONSOLE ON
   IF UPPER(verify_var) = "Y"
      ?? "Yes"
      IF INKEY(0) = 0
      ENDIF
      RETURN(.T.)
   ENDIF
   ?? "No "
   IF INKEY(0) = 0
   ENDIF
   RETURN(.F.)


********************

FUNCTION Center

   PARAMETERS a

   result = INT(LEN(a)/2)
   RETURN(40-result)
* End of File
```

APPENDIX A

Command Syntax

The following is a quick reference to all of the Clipper commands, the proper syntax, and the associated clauses/phrases. Those commands preceded by an asterisk are included only with the Autumn '86 release.

MATHEMATICAL, RELATIONAL AND LOGICAL OPERATIONS

Operation Desired	Operator	Syntax	Special Notes
Addition or concatenation.	+	<exp> + <exp>	
Subtraction	-	<exp> - <exp>	
Multiplication	*	<expN> * <expN>	
Division	/	<expN> / <expN>	
Exponentiation	**	<expN> ** <expN>	
Modulus	%	<expN> % <expN>	
Less Than	<	<exp> < <exp>	
Greater Than	>	<exp> > <exp>	
Equal	=	<exp> = <exp>	Not to be used with !
Not Equal	# or <>	<exp> # <exp>	
Less Than or Equal To	<=	<exp> <= <exp>	
Greater Than or Equal To	>=	<exp> >= <exp>	
Evaluate Variables	==	<exp> == <exp>	SET EXACT ON has effect
And	.AND.	<exp>.AND.<exp>	Both <exp>'s MUST be true
Not	.NOT. or !	.NOT.<exp> or !<exp>	<exp> must NOT be true. Not to be used with =.
Or	.OR.	<exp> .OR. <exp>	One <exp> MUST be true.

Below is a *truth table*. Given the following possibilities within a command line with two separate conditions, the tables below show how each condition should be viewed in relation to the operator being used.

.AND.	Y	!Y	
X :	True	False	If the X condition is .T. .AND. the Y condition is .T., only then is the expression evaluated to a .T. condition.
!X :	False	False	

.OR.	Y	!Y	
X :	True	True	If either the Y condition is .T. .OR. the X condition is .T., .OR. BOTH conditions evaluate to .T., then the .OR. evaluates to a .T. Only when both X and Y are .F. will the .OR. expression evaluate to .F.
!X :	True	False	

DATA DISPLAY OPERATIONS

Operation Desired	Command	Syntax
Display to Screen/Printer	@	@ <row,column> [SAY<exp> [PICTURE <clause>]] [GET<exp> [PICTURE <clause>]] [RANGE<exp,exp>[VALID <exp>]] [CLEAR]

	* @	* @ <row,column>[CLEAR] TO<row2, col2>[DOUBLE]
	?	? <expression list>
	??	?? <expression list>
Print Labels	LABEL	LABEL FORM <filename> [<scope>][SAMPLE] [TO PRINT] [FOR/WHILE <condition>] [TO FILE <filename>]
Print Report	REPORT FORM	REPORT FORM <filename> [<scope>] [FOR <condition>] [WHILE <condition>] [PLAIN][HEADING <expC>][NOEJECT] [TO PRINT][TO FILE <filename>]
Show Fields/Records	DISPLAY	DISPLAY [OFF][scope] FIELDS <field list> [FOR/WHILE <condition>]
	LIST	LIST [OFF] [scope]<field list>[FOR<condition>] [WHILE <condition>] [TO PRINT/TO FILE <filename>]
Show Text	TEXT	TEXT [TO PRINT/TO FILE <filename>] <text> ENDTEXT
Type File	TYPE	TYPE <filename> [TO PRINT] [TO FILE<filename>]

ADDITION/CHANGING OF DATA

Operation Desired	Command	Syntax
Change Data	REPLACE	REPLACE [<scope>] <field> WITH <exp> [, <field> WITH <exp> ...] [FOR <condition>] [WHILE <condition>]
Input Data	ACCEPT	[<prompt message>] TO <memvar>
	INPUT	INPUT [<expC>] TO <memvar>

DATABASE MANIPULATION

Operation Desired	Command	Syntax
Choose Work Area	SELECT	SELECT <expN> SELECT <expC>
Close Files	CLOSE	CLOSE <file type>
Copy Records from a Database	APPEND FROM	APPEND [scope][FIELDS <field list>] FROM <filename> [FOR/WHILE <condition>] [SDF/Delimited]
Create File	CREATE	CREATE <database filename>
	CREATE FROM	CREATE <newfile> FROM <structure extended file>
Join Databases	JOIN	JOIN WITH <alias> TO <new filename> FOR <condition> [FIELDS <field list>]
Open a database	USE	USE [<filename>][INDEX <index list>] [ALIAS <expC>]

Reconstruct Index	REINDEX	REINDEX
Remove Data Marked for deletion	PACK	PACK
Sort Database	SORT	SORT <scope> TO [<newfile>] ON <field> [/A] [/C] [/D] [,<field2>] [/A] [/C] [/D] [FOR <condition>] [WHILE <condition>]
Unlock a database	*UNLOCK	UNLOCK [ALL]
Unmark Data Marked for deletion	RECALL	RECALL <scope> [[FOR]/ [WHILE] <condition>]
Update fields	UPDATE ON	UPDATE ON <key field> FROM <Alias> REPLACE <field> WITH <exp> [,<field2> WITH <exp> ...]
Wipe out Data in file	ZAP	ZAP

MANIPULATING MEMORY VARIABLES

Operation Desired	Command	Syntax
Change contents of memory variable	STORE	STORE <expression> TO <memory variable> [, <memory variable list>]
Clear Memory	CLEAR MEMORY RELEASE	CLEAR MEMORY RELEASE <memory variable> RELEASE <memory variable list> RELEASE ALL [LIKE / EXCEPT <skeleton>]
Clear Open GETS on Active READ	CLEAR GETS	CLEAR GETS
Compute Average of values	AVERAGE	AVERAGE <field list> TO <memvar list> [FOR/WHILE <condition>]
Count values	COUNT	COUNT [<scope>] [FOR/WHILE <condition>] TO <memvar>
Establish Array	DECLARE	DECLARE <memvar> [<expN>] [,<array list>]
Establish Variables	PUBLIC	PUBLIC Clipper
Recover Memory File	RESTORE FROM	RESTORE FROM <filename> [ADDITIVE]
Sum of values	SUM	SUM <field list> TO <memvar list> [FOR/WHILE <condition>]
Total of fields/values	TOTAL ON	TOTAL ON <key field> TO <newfile> [<scope>] FIELDS <field list> [FOR <condition>] [WHILE <condition>] RANDOM

POSITIONING WITHIN DATABASE

Operation Desired		Command	Syntax
Find Record:	Literal	FIND	FIND <expC>/<expN>
	Condition	LOCATE	LOCATE [<scope>] FOR <condition> [WHILE <condition>]
	Variable	SEEK	SEEK <expression>

Move Record Pointer	SKIP	SKIP [expN] [ALIAS <expN><expC>]
Position Record Pointer	GO / GOTO	GO / GOTO <exp>/TOP/BOTTOM
Resume Searching After Locate	CONTINUE	CONTINUE

MANIPULATING RECORDS

Operation Desired	Command	Syntax
Add Blank Records to Database	APPEND BLANK	APPEND BLANK
Mark Record for Deletion	DELETE	DELETE [<scope>][FOR <condition>] [WHILE <condition>]

CREATION/MANIPULATION OF FILES

Operation Desired	Command	Syntax
Build Index File	INDEX	INDEX ON <key expression> TO <filename>
Copy File	COPY FILE	COPY FILE <filename> TO <filename>
Copy File Structure	COPY STRUCTURE	COPY STRUCTURE TO <filename> [FIELDS <field list>]
	COPY STRUCTURE	COPY TO <filename> STRUCTURE EXTENDED
Erase File	ERASE	ERASE <filename>
Rename File	RENAME	RENAME <filename> TO <filename>
Save Memory File	SAVE TO	SAVE TO <filename> [ALL LIKE / EXCEPT <skeleton>]

PROGRAM CONTROL

Operation Desired	Command	Syntax
Branch for Multiple Testing	DO CASE	DO CASE CASE <condition> <commands> CASE <condition> <commands> OTHERWISE <commands> ENDCASE
Call outside program	CALL	CALL <process> [WITH <parameter list>]
Complete a GET	READ	READ
Declare a Procedure/Function Outside Current program name	EXTERNAL	EXTERNAL <procedure list> (May not be in the procedure list)
Define Code as FUNCTION	FUNCTION	FUNCTION <name> [PARAMETERS <expC>] <commands> RETURN(<value>)
Define Condition	IF	IF <condition> <commands>

		[ELSE]
		<commands>
		ENDIF
Establish Process	PROCEDURE	PROCEDURE <procedure name>
Go Back to Calling Program	RETURN	RETURN
Jump to top of DO WHILE	LOOP	LOOP
Menu Options	MENU TO	MENU TO <memvar>
	PROMPT...	@ <row>,<col> PROMPT <expC>
	MESSAGE	[MESSAGE <expC>]
Notation	NOTE, *, &&	NOTE / * <text>
		<command line> && <text>
Pass Values to Procedures	PARAMETERS	PARAMETERS <parameter list>
Pause	WAIT	WAIT [<expC>][TO <memvar>]
Perform Task	DO	DO <file name>
		[WITH <parameter(s)>]
Premature Terminate	EXIT	EXIT
of DO WHILE		
Repeat Task	DO WHILE	DO WHILE <condition>
		<commands>
		ENDDO
	FOR...NEXT	FOR <memvar> = <expN> TO <expN>
		[STEP <expN>]
		<commands>
		NEXT
Run another program	RUN / (!)	RUN <filename>
		! <filename>
Stop Processing	CANCEL	CANCEL
	QUIT	QUIT
Stuff the Keyboard	KEYBOARD	KEYBOARD <expC>

SYSTEM CONTROL PARAMETERS

Operation Desired	Command	Syntax
SET System Conditions	SET ALTERNATE	SET ALTERNATE TO [<filename>]
		SET ALTERNATE TO
		SET ALTERNATE ON/OFF
	SET COLOR TO	SET COLOR TO
		[<standard>[,<enhanced>
		[<border>]]]
	SET CONFIRM	SET CONFIRM ON/OFF
	SET CONSOLE	SET CONSOLE ON/OFF
*	SET CENTURY	SET CENTURY ON/OFF
	SET DECIMALS TO	SET DECIMALS TO <expN>
	SET DEFAULT TO	SET DEFAULT TO <disk drive>
	SET DELETED	SET DELETED ON/OFF
	SET DELIMITERS	SET DELIMITERS ON/OFF
		SET DELIMITERS TO

```
                                       [<expC>] [DEFAULT]
              SET DEVICE               SET DEVICE TO <PRINT/SCREEN>
              SET ESCAPE               SET ESCAPE ON/OFF
              SET EXACT                SET EXACT ON/OFF
         *    SET EXCLUSIVE            SET EXCLUSIVE ON/OFF
              SET FILTER TO            SET FILTER TO [<expression>]
              SET FIXED                SET FIXED ON/OFF
              SET FORMAT TO            SET FORMAT TO <file name>
              SET FUNCTION             SET FUNCTION <expN> TO <expC>
              SET INDEX                SET INDEX TO [<file list>]
              SET INTENSITY            SET INTENSITY ON/OFF
              SET KEY TO               SET KEY <expN> TO [<proc.>]
              SET MARGIN TO            SET MARGIN TO <expN>
              SET MESSAGE TO           SET MESSAGE TO <expN>
         *    SET ORDER TO             SET ORDER TO [<expN>]
              SET PATH TO              SET PATH TO <expC>
              SET PRINT                SET PRINT ON/OFF
         *    SET PRINTER TO           SET PRINTER TO
                                       [<device>/<filename>]
              SET PROCEDURE TO         SET PROCEDURE TO <filename>
              SET RELATION TO          SET RELATION TO
                                       <key exp> / RECNO()
                                       / <expN> INTO <alias>
                                       [,TO <key exp> / RECNO()
                                       / <expN>
                                       INTO <alias> ...]
              SET UNIQUE               SET UNIQUE ON/OFF
```

SCREEN HANDLING OPERATIONS

Operation Desired	Command	Syntax
Draw Window on Screen	BOX	@ <top,left,bottom,right> BOX <string>
Clear the Screen	CLEAR	CLEAR
Clear the System	CLEAR ALL	CLEAR ALL
Recover Screen	RESTORE SCREEN	RESTORE SCREEN
Save Screen	SAVE SCREEN	SAVE SCREEN

MISCELLANEOUS

Operation Desired	Command	Syntax
Directory	DIR	DIR [<drive>] [<path>] [<skeleton>]
Issue Page Eject	EJECT	EJECT

APPENDIX B

Functions

The following pages contain a quick reference to all of the Clipper functions, their proper syntax, and the data type returned. Included with this list are all proper definitions of syntax words and operators. The functions are grouped by category. Those preceded by an asterisk are available either only in the Autumn '86 release, or in the Extended File, or in additional libraries.

MATHEMATICAL FUNCTIONS

Operation	Function	Syntax	Value Returned
* Absolute Value of a Number	ABS()	ABS(<expN>)	Numeric
Exponential of number	EXP()	EXP(<expN>)	Numeric
Logarithm of number	LOG()	LOG(<expN>)	Numeric
* Remainder of two numbers	MOD()	MOD(<expN>, <expN>)	Numeric
Round off numeric value	ROUND()	ROUND(<expN>, <expN>)	Numeric
Square Root	SQRT()	SQRT(<expN>)	Numeric

OPERATING SYSTEM FUNCTIONS

Operation	Function	Syntax	Value Returned
* Amount of available memory	MEMORY(0)	MEMORY(0)	Numeric
* Available Disk Space	DISKSPACE()	DISKSPACE(<expN>)	Numeric
* Date of last update to database	LUPDATE()	LUPDATE()	Date
File Existence	FILE()	FILE(<expC>)	Logical
Last key pressed at console	LASTKEY()	LASTKEY()	Numeric
Length of a database header	HEADER()	HEADER()	Numeric
* Name of the function key label	FKLABEL()	FKLABEL(<expN>)	Character
* Name of the operating system	OS()	OS()	Character
* Number of maximum function keys available	FKMAX()	FKMAX()	Numeric
* Read the value of the last key pressed	READKEY()	READKEY()	Numeric
* Value of environmental variable	GETE()	GETE(<expC>)	Character
Waiting for keyboard input	INKEY()	INKEY() or INKEY(<expN>)	Numeric

STRING FUNCTIONS

Operation	Function	Syntax	Value Returned
Ascii value of character string	ASC()	ASC(<expC>)	Numeric
Blank space	SPACE()	SPACE(<expN>)	Character
Character representation of ascii value	CHR()	CHR(<expN>)	Character
Convert character type to numeric type	VAL()	VAL(<expC>)	Numeric

Operation	Function	Syntax	Value Returned
* Convert numeric zero to string	STRZERO()	STRZERO(<expN> [, <expN>][, <expN>]])	Character
* Delete all leading and trailing blanks	ALLTRIM()	ALLTRIM(<expC>)	Character
Display expression with specified picture	TRANSFORM()	TRANSFORM(<exp>,<expC>)	Character
* Length of a number	LENNUM()	LENNUM(<expN>)	Numeric
Length of a string	LEN()	LEN(<expc>)	Numeric
Lower case the string/character	LOWER()	LOWER(<expC>)	Character
Left trim the string	LTRIM()	LTRIM(<expC>)	Character
* Left-most portion of a string	LEFT()	LEFT(<expC>, <expN>)	Character
Position in main string of substring	AT()	AT(<expC>, <expC>)	Numeric
Repeat a character expression, x times	REPLICATE()	REPLICATE(<expC>, <expN>)	Character
* Replace portion of string with another	STUFF()	STUFF(<expC>, <expN>, <expN>, <expC>)	Character
* Replace soft carriage returns for hard	HARDCR()	HARDCR(<expC>)	Character
* Right-most portion of a string	RIGHT()	RIGHT(<expC>, <expN>)	Character
Substring selection	SUBSTR()	SUBSTR(<expC>, <expN> [, <expN>])	Character
* Test for alphabetic character	ISALPHA()	ISALPHA(<expC>)	Logical
* Test for lower-case character	ISLOWER()	ISLOWER(<expC>)	Logical
* Test for upper-case character	ISUPPER()	ISUPPER(<expC>)	Logical
Trim blank spaces off of string	TRIM()	TRIM(<expC>)	Character
Upper case the string/character	UPPER()	UPPER(<expC>)	Character

DATABASE FUNCTIONS

Operation	Function	Syntax	Value Returned
* Alias name of a work area	ALIAS()	ALIAS(<expN>)	Character
Field name in database	FIELDNAME()	FIELDNAME(<expn>)	Character
* Found record after locate, seek, or find	FOUND()	FOUND()	Logical
* Key expression in active index	INDEXKEY()	INDEXKEY(<expN>)	Character
Last read changed any data in gets	UPDATED()	UPDATED()	Logical
Last record number in active database	LASTREC()	LASTREC()	Numeric
* Name of current/selected database	DBF()	DBF()	Character
* Name of the index position	NDX()	NDX(<expN>)	Character
* Number of fields in active database	FCOUNT()	FCOUNT()	Numeric
Record number at current position	RECNO()	RECNO()	Numeric

Operation	Function	Syntax	Value Returned
Record positioned is marked for deletion	DELETED()	DELETED()	Logical
Record positioned at beginning of file	BOF()	BOF()	Logical
Record positioned at eof of file	EOF()	EOF()	Logical
Selected area currently open	SELECT()	SELECT()	Numeric
* Size of record in selected database	RECSIZE()	RECSIZE()	Numeric
* Sound-like interpretation of character	SOUNDEX()	SOUNDEX(<expC>)	Character

DATE / TIME FUNCTIONS

Operation	Function	Syntax	Value Returned
Calendar Month	CMONTH()	CMONTH(<expD>)	Character
Character to Date conversion	CTOD()	CTOD(<expC>)	Date
* Convert numeric seconds to time string	TSTRING()	TSTRING(<expN>)	Character
Date to Character conversion	DTOC()	DTOC(<expD>)	Character
Date to String conversion	DTOS()	DTOS(<expD>)	Character
Date of system	DATE()	DATE()	Date
Day of the Week	DOW()	DOW(<expD>)	Numeric
Day of week	CDOW()	CDOW(<expD>)	Character
Day of the Month	DAY()	DAY(<expD>)	Numeric
* Elapsed Days passed	DAYS()	DAYS(<expN>)	Numeric
* Elapsed Time passed	ELAPTIME()	ELAPTIME(<expC>, <expC>)	Character
Month of the Year	MONTH()	MONTH(<expD>)	Numeric
* Number of seconds from time string	SECS()	SECS(<expC>)	Numeric
System time as seconds/hundreds	SECONDS()	SECONDS()	Numeric
Time of system	TIME()	TIME()	Character
* Worded time expression	AMPM()	AMPM(<expC>)	Character
Year	YEAR()	YEAR(<expD>)	Numeric

NETWORKING FUNCTIONS

Operation	Function	Syntax	Value Returned
* Availability to share file	NETERR()	NETERR()	Logical
* Lock a File	FLOCK()	FLOCK()	Logical
* Lock a Record	RLOCK()	RLOCK()	Logical
* Name of the network work station	NETNAME()	NETNAME()	Character

MEMO FIELD FUNCTIONS

Operation	Function	Syntax	Value Returned
* Character replacement of Memo field	MEMOTRAN()	MEMOTRAN(<expC> [, <expC>] [, <expC>]	Character
Memo edit/display in a given area	MEMOEDIT()	MEMOEDIT(<exp>, <expN>, <expN>, <expN>, <expN>, <expL>)	
* Read a file from disk to character string	MEMOREAD()	MEMOREAD(<expC>)	Character
* Write a memo field/character string to disk	MEMOWRIT()	MEMOWRIT(<expC>, <expC>)	Character
			Logical

DISPLAY / PRINTER FUNCTIONS

Operation	Function	Syntax	Value Returned
Column position of printer	PCOL()	PCOL()	Numeric
Column position of screen	COL()	COL()	Numeric
* Test for on-line/ready printer status	ISPRINTER()	ISPRINTER()	Logical
Row position of printer	PROW()	PROW()	Numeric
Row position of screen	ROW()	ROW()	Numeric
* Set the printer row and column position	SETPRC()	SETPRC(<expN>, <expN>)	--------

ARRAY FUNCTIONS

Operation	Function	Syntax	Value Returned
* Deleting an element from an array	ADEL()	ADEL(<expC>, <expN>)	--------
* Fill an array with a specific element	AFILL()	AFILL(<expC>, <exp> [, <expN> [, <expN>]])	--------
* Insert an element into an array	AINS()	AINS(<expC>, <expN>)	--------
* Look for an element in an array	ASCAN()	ASCAN(<expC>, <exp> [, <expN> [, <expN>]])	--------
* Store DIRectory pattern/names in an array	ADIR()	ADIR(<expC> [, <expC>])	Numeric Numeric

PROGRAMMING FUNCTIONS

Operation	Function	Syntax	Value Returned
Convert numeric double type to integer type	WORD()	WORD(<expN>)	Numeric
Empty filed or variable	EMPTY()	EMPTY(<exp>)	Logical
If testing of two conditions	IF()	IF(<exp>,<exp>,<exp>)	<expression list>
Line number of program/procedure/function	PROCLINE()	PROCLINE()	Numeric
Name of current GET/MENU variable	READVAR()	READVAR()	Character
Name of program/procedure/function	PROCNAME()	PROCNAME()	Character
* Number of parameters passed	PCOUNT()	PCOUNT()	Numeric
Type of variable/field	TYPE()	TYPE(<exp>)	Character
* Version of program	VERSION()	VERSION()	Character

APPENDIX C

Error Messages

Each version of Clipper has had different error messages. To document all of the possible error messages from all of the versions would be a momentous task. Below, therefore, is a brief look at the possible error conditions (and where applicable, the error messages). Try to find your problem on the list. The errors are broken into three categories: *compiling, linking,* and *execution* errors.

Compiling error messages are normally straight-forward. If an error occurs during compiling treat it according to the message displayed. Sometimes the messages are a bit cryptic, but in time their meaning will become clearer. If multiple errors occur, fix the first error before all others. Often one error will generate three or four subsequent error messages.

Linking errors are much like compiling errors, once you get the hang of it, they make perfect sense. Unfortunately, it can seem to take an eternity to understand them. Most linking errors are due to one or more of the following three reasons:

1) Mismatching compiler and library versions.
2) Linking duplicate procedures.
3) Misspelling function names

Execution errors are more difficult to figure out than compiling or linking errors. Any number of factors may be the cause of the problem, ranging from the subtle differences between the environment of an interpreter and that of the compiler, to hardware inconsistencies, to problems with the code, the compiler, or both.

If you have a problem, first link in the DEBUGger with the rest of your application. Try to pinpoint the line on which the error is occurring. If the line number is far greater than any line number in your application, look for the last reasonable line number you recognize before the error. These large line numbers are due to calls to the Clipper library.

If the problem persists, try to duplicate the problem outside your application. Small test programs specifically designed to isolate a problem are good DEBUGging techniques. Finally, if, *after* trying all logical methods (which includes reading all "READ_ME" files and the documentation) you still can't locate the error, call Nantucket. You may have a problem with the compiler and their additional insight and current information may get to the root of the matter.

One word of advice: **never** say "But it works in dBASE..." It is understood that most people are converting existing dBASE III code into Clipper. Because of that, the technicians approach all problems as problems attributable to the differences between a compiler and an interpreter. If, however, there is a problem with the compiler, the technicians are the first to test, document, and admit to the problem.

Your best bet is probably never to assume that the problem you are experiencing is due to the compiler. Arrange your questions/problems as specifically as you can and always note all error messages, whether they are compile, link, or execution error messages.

COMPILING ERRORS

TOO MANY CONSTANTS - NEGATIVE CONSTANTS IN TABLE

Since the compiler tries to pull in all associated program, procedure, and format files, the constant table may have exceeded its capacity. Currently, only 32K worth of constants can be assigned in one compilation. In older versions, if the constant table was overloaded, then the message TOO MANY CONSTANTS appeared and the compiled code was be incomplete. Linking the object module and execution yielded unpredictable results.

In an attempt to increase the size of all of the tables, the error message was taken out, but the table space for the code, the symbols, and the constants remained at 32K. However, in the reference, if the constant table did become overloaded during the compile, in the end it would generate an object file with a negative constant table size (i.e. -35738 symbols).

The solution remains: break down the amount of source code that the compiler is looking at one time. In order to facilitate this, the use of CLiP files is necessary.

TOO MANY LABELS - TOO MANY SYMBOLS

As with the TOO MANY CONSTANTS problem, there is a specific size for the symbol and code tables. If too many procedures or functions are called, eventually, the appropriate tables overload. Again, just as with the constant table situation, if this should occur the only solution is to break up the amount of a compile into smaller sections and then to link them back together.

ASSIGNMENT ERRORS

A variable has been assigned an improper value. An example is the following:

```
STORE x TO "This is a test"
```

This is an ASSIGNMENT ERROR because it is impossible to give the string "This is a test" the value of x.

Another possible cause of an ASSIGNMENT ERROR is the use of a semicolon in a string. In dBASE III, the semicolon tells the interpreter that the remaining characters for this command line are on the following line. This can be in the middle of a string. For example:

```
CLEAR
STORE "Now is the time for all good men to come to the aid of their ;
country!" TO x
? x
```

In dBASE III, here is the result:

```
. ? x
Now is the time for all good men to come to the aid of their country!
```

But in Clipper, if you tried to compile the same code, the following would occur:

```
C>clipper test
The Cliper Compiler, Winter '85
Copyright (c) 1985, 1986 Nantucket Inc., All Rights Reserved.

Compiling TEST.PRG
line      7:  missing 2nd quote
STORE "Now is the time for all good men to come to the aid of their ;
          ^

line      7:  STORE error
STORE
    ^

line      8:  ASSIGNMENT error
country!" TO x
      ^

line      8:  ASSIGNMENT error
country       ^
4 errors detected
Code size:31     Symbols:64     Constants:112

C>
```

In Clipper, the work-around would be to split up the sentence and assign it to two separate variables and then add them together later.

Another possible error, similar to the previous example, is with command lines, which have the wraparound character (soft carriage return) in them. This high-bit character can not be in any program file to be compiled. The compiler acts the same way as it did with the semicolon. The solution is to remove those characters.

UNBALANCED PARENTHESES

This message is precise: too many parentheses are in a line. Be careful if you use parentheses to separate conditions for clarity. Also, if using multiple functions, the same problem may arise: too many or too few parentheses are in the command line.

The compiler gives a little help by flagging the area where the extraneous parenthesis appears. Consider the following example:

```
? SUBSTR(DTOC(DATE(),1,2) + SUBSTR(DTOC(DATE(),7,2))
```

This causes two major error messages, a TOO MANY ARGUMENTS error and a UNBALANCED PARENTHESIS error. Both would eventually yield a FATAL AT 0 - invalid code error.

In the first function, the DTOC() function only requires one parameter, yet by the structure of the command line, it appears that three parameters are being passed. Because of this, the whole sequence of parentheses are unbalanced, which yields the second error. And the final error is due to no code being generated at all, ending at line 0 (the top of the program file) because nothing makes sense to the compiler. In order to correct the problem, go through the command line character by character. If you have to, start from the innermost function and work your way out. In our example, the correct structure is:

```
. ? SUBSTR(DTOC(DATE()),1,2)+SUBSTR(DTOC(DATE()),7,2)
```

PROBLEMS WITH DO, IF, DO CASE and FOR/NEXT

The compiler is **very** strict with the use of these commands. Not only must there be a proper number of terminators for them (ENDDO, ENDIF, and ENDCASE), they must also be balanced properly.

Just because you may get a "enddo w/o while" does not necessarily mean that there is a problem with your DO's and your ENDDO's.

There is a special stack table inside the compiler. Every time a DO, an IF, FOR, or a DO CASE appear, a marker is placed on the stack. Each marker is unique and the compiler keeps track of what it was that caused this counter to be placed on the stack. Every time the compiler sees an ENDDO, ENDIF, NEXT, or an ENDCASE it removes a marker from the stack. The marker that is removed from the stack must coincide with the command that placed the marker on the stack in the first place. If there is an imbalance between the number of commands that placed markers on the stack and the number of commands that removed markers from the stack, an error will occur. Additionally, if a marker is removed by an improper matching command, the series of markers that follows will not match correctly, which will cause an UNBAL-ANCED or MISSING error message.

The compiler is very precise in finding these errors, but it only tells you that an imbalance exists. Check all of the markers and make sure that they are properly offset by the corresponding command. dBASE is tolerant of some of these errors because only 1K worth of source code is really kept in memory; if an UNBALANCED error exists, but its marker would have been more than 5K of source code away, dBASE III will not find it! Clipper, as you may learn to your dismay, allows no such sloppiness.

FATAL AT < > - ILLEGAL SYMBOL MODE

Normally this messages appears in conjunction with a PHASE ERROR. It means that when it tried to compile the code at the second pass, the compiler couldn't understand the symbolic tokens. The line number given often indicates the general area of the problem, but don't count on it. The best way to decipher this error is to break down your application into specific programs and try to compile them separately, thus narrowing down the possible choices.

FATAL AT < > - ILLEGAL SYMBOL MODE

Check to make sure that the procedure list in your EXTERNAL command does not include the name of the procedure being compiled. You cannot tell the compiler that it is **not** to compile the very program it is compiling!

PHASE ERRORS

Most PHASE ERRORS are brought on by one or more previously found FATAL ERRORS. If this is not the case, then remember that Clipper is a 2-pass compiler: on the first pass the compiler turns the source code into representing tokens, and on the second pass, it tries to turn the tokens into machine level object code. Somehow, the tokens generated by the first pass are not decipherable by the second pass. This out-of-sync symptom causes a phase error. If the problem does not go away after a recompile, call for technical assistance.

INVALID PARAMETERS

The number of parameters passed to a function is not right. For an example, please refer to the example above on Unbalanced Parenthesis. Make sure that you are passing exactly as many parameters as are required by the function -- no more and no less.

HYPHENS AND NUMBERS IN PROGRAM NAMES

Many application generators and programs use hyphens in the name of the program or procedure in order to better identify its purpose. Although this practice is allowed in dBASE III, it isn't allowed in Clipper. The reason for this is that the same routine that checks for the validity of field names also checks for program names as well.

FORMAT FILES AND CLIP FILES

If CLiP files are being used, then FORMAT files are ignored. With CLiP files, all that will be looked at are files with a .PRG extension. Since FORMAT files have a .FMT extension, the compiler will not even attempt to locate them. What needs to be done if CLiP files are used is to rename all FORMAT file extensions from .FMT to .PRG, and to change the code in the procedures that call them from SET FORMAT TO < Filename > to DO < Filename >.

LINKING ERRORS

UNDEFINED SYMBOLS IN A WEIRD MODULE
(NORMALLY BEGINNING WITH IO)

This indicates that the object code generated by the version of Clipper you are using is not of the same as the library the linker is referring to. Make sure that you are using the right version of the library. With the WINTER '85 version of the compiler, only two libraries may be used, one dated 01-29-86, and one dated 05-01-86. If using the Autumn '86 compiler, the date stamp of the appropriate library should 10-31-86.

If you are using the correct libraries, then check the version of the compiler you are using. To do this, just type in Clipper at the DOS prompt and note the version statement that appears.

Finally, make sure that no object file being linked in has been compiled with an older version. Once you use a new version of the compiler (not the library) on **any** program, procedure, format, or function file, then **all** program, procedure, format, and function files must be recompiled in order to maintain system-wide integrity.

The error codes listed below are in reverse numerical order:

Error 59

This is like Error 58. If you get this message please refer to the section in this text pertaining specifically to Plink86 Error Messages.

Error 58

This is saying that the amount of one object module is too large for the linker to handle. The maximum stack segment (roughly half the size of the object module being linked in) is 64K bytes.

Error 57

You have a problem with the OVERLAY.LIB file. Please make sure that the correct version of this library is being linked in with the appropriate version of PLINK86. If you are using PLINK86.EXE (64,320 bytes) with a date stamp of 01-29-86, you should be using the OVERLAY.LIB file (23,040 bytes) with a date stamp also of 01-29-86. This version was used for versions prior to the Autumn '86 release. With the Autumn '86 release, the proper date stamp for PLINK86 (78,688 bytes) should be 10-31-86 and the corresponding date stamp for the OVERLAY.LIB (6,932 bytes) will be 10-31-86.

Error 54

This says that there is not enough available memory to load and run PLINK86. The minimum requirement for PLINK86 is 256K bytes.

Error 52

A symbol (a function call, a procedure name, or a memory variable) used in an object module is "self-defined." In other words, the DEFINE command was used to define a symbol that is relative to another symbol. This defining process can continue until eventually, the original symbol is reached in this cycle.

Error 51

Normally, this is brought on with the use of the BUILD and DEFINE commands which are not supported in the special version of Plink86 provided with the Clipper compiler.

Error 50

This says that PLINK86 can not create the memory map on the disk. Check to see if the disk is full or if it is write protected.

Error 49

Again, this error pertains to the disk. It simply means that PLINK86 can not close the designated output file. Either the disk is write protected or there is a general hardware error.

Error 48

A fatal disk read error was detected in the output file. This is probably due to an irrecoverable hardware error.

Error 47

A fatal disk write error has occurred in the output file. Possibly the disk is full or write protected, or there has been some other type of hardware related error.

Error 46

This says that an invalid output file type has been specified. If one is given, it must either be .EXE or .CMD (for CP/M 86 machines).

Error 45

A general error that detects that PLINK86 can not create the output disk file. Check to see if the disk directory is full or if the disk is write protected.

Error 43

The object module specified in the link list could not be located. Check to see if indeed the file is located on the designated directory path or if you have spelled the name of the object file correctly.

Error 42

A fatal read error in the object file was detected.

Error 41

A premature end of file was detected. This is usually preceded with an "Unknown record type 7." Basically, the linker is attempting to link non-object files with the Clipper library. This is usually brought on when the CL.BAT batch file is used and the .PRG is passed along with the file name as a parameter. Clipper assumes that procedure files have the extension .PRG, so the .PRG is redundant. However, when the linking process starts, the .PRG is still passed as a parameter into the linker. When the linker tries to link the .PRG file, and not the .OBJ file, it chokes. To get around this, don't pass the file extension if you use CL.BAT.

EXECUTION ERRORS

SCREEN DISPLAYS IN THE WRONG PLACE

This error is due to a bad compile. The only solution is to recompile. If the problem persists, add a few remark lines and try again. If that does not solve the problem, call technical support.

VALUES DO NOT EQUAL

Because of a rounding problem internal to Lattice C, Clipper also has an internal rounding problem. This means that in many cases, values that should equal one another, do not. This is especially true when the ROUND() or INT() functions are used or math-intensive calculations are performed. To get around this, either use the User-Defined ROUNDIT() function in Chapter 12, be more specific in the INT() function, or use the double equal sign (= =) whenever possible.

CLIPPER ERROR MESSAGE (Q/A/I)

This message is issued by Clipper at runtime when Clipper or DOS finds an unrecoverable error when it tries to execute a command or function. It means:

Q - Quit the program, closing all files properly and return to DOS.
A - Abort to DOS immediately.
I - Ignore error, and try to continue with the program.

The user must enter either Q, A, or I from the keyboard in order to continue. If "I" is entered, keep in mind that the system integrity may be corrupted.

INDEX ERROR READ/WRITE

This error normally means one of two things:

1)   The "motherboard" is set for 640K of RAM while the expansion board is set for 256K of RAM.

2)   The disk drive is full.

INDEX ERROR UPDATE

Make sure that you are using a library dated 05-01-86 when using Winter '85 release. If you have not received this error with the library date stamp of 01-29-86 when using the Winter '85 release, then it is not necessary to acquire the 05-01-86 library. Otherwise, contact Nantucket for this library. The updated library resolves this problem.

DOS ERROR 0

This error is **not** an error from DOS. Whenever the application experiences an error during execution that the internal mechanisms installed by Clipper cannot understand, it attempts to go to the operating system and to find the cause of the problem. If it cannot find the associated DOS error to the problem, it assigns a 0 error code.

More than likely, the cause of this error is an object file with a negative sized constant table. If that is the case, check the section on COMPILING ERRORS / NEGATIVE CONSTANTS earlier in this section for the solution.

This error is only known to occur in the WINTER '85 version of the compiler.

DOS ERROR 2

This means that the file you are trying to use, find, or do something with cannot be found. If you are using macro substitution for file names, make sure that the macros have the proper dot terminators and that their values are what you expect them to be.

DOS ERROR 3

This error indicates that the path designated and passed to DOS was invalid. If you are using macro substitution for the path, make sure that the macros have the proper dot terminators and that their values are what you expect them to be. Also, make sure that the path really exists.

DOS ERROR 4

This message means that you have tried to open too many files for DOS to handle. If this error appears, check the CONFIG.SYS file. Remember, the CONFIG.SYS should be set to at least the following number of files and buffers:

```
FILES   = 20
BUFFERS = 8
```

Once you've fixed the CONFIG.SYS file, reboot the system and try again. If the problem persists, contact the technical support staff.

PROGRAM TOO BIG TO FIT INTO MEMORY

This message is quite literal and is generated by the operating system, not by Clipper. It means what it says, the program you are trying to load is too big to fit properly into memory. Even though it may seem that there is plenty of room for the program, Clipper has additional requirements (please see the section on memory requirements) and these restrictions may be part of the problem.

Another possible cause for this problem is when the computer's *motherboard* is set for 640K of RAM while the expansion board is set for 256K. Make sure that all internal hardware configurations are set properly.

MACRO EXPANSION ERROR

This error is one of the most difficult to trap, decipher and solve. A Macro Expansion Error occurs when the macro library is trying to expand an expression beyond its means. All macros are limited to 15 parses. This means that an expression can have only 15 logical parts for the macro library to understand at one time. Symbols, operators, and expressions are all items for the macro library to parse and interpret.

IF an ALIAS is used a macro can only handle 9 parses.

In some cases this error occurs on lines where no macro exists. The reason for this is commands that pertain to REPORTS, LABELS, or INDEXing are processed through the macro library.

In either case, try to break up the amount of information being processed on the command line. For normal macros, split the one macro into two separate macros. For all others, use a combination of other commands to help set database conditions, scopes and ranges on separate command lines.

MAC RELEASE ERROR

Like the Macro Expansion Error, the MAC Release Error indicates that the Macro library is trying to release an expression which is not a macro, or is not understood by the macro library. Think of it like trying to release a CLEAR command. How does one go about releasing a CLEAR command? This type of conflict disrupts the compiler at run time. Link in the DEBUGger and step through the application to the command line just prior to the occurrence of the error. Double check the validity of all variables and fields. If everything appears satisfactory, try to duplicate the error in a smaller test environment. If you are able to duplicate the error, contact the Technical Support Staff with the problem. If the problem disappears in the test, then go back to the original code and recode the problem area a little differently, combining a couple of commands, or separating one command into a couple. If a macro is involved, try hard coding a portion of the macro or evaluating the macro in the DEBUGger.

JOIN WITH A WHILE CLAUSE

It's an error because this combination is not allowed.

CURSOR / FUNCTION KEYS WITH ANSI.OBJ

Whenever using an application with the ANSI driver (or any other driver), the cursor keys and function keys will not work. Be careful because keys which were taken for granted (e.g., F1 for HELP and CTRL C to break out of a routine) will not work. In some cases, the SET KEY TO procedure may work, but only one key at a time. They may be redefined via your operating; however, be careful not to define a key to a value of another key. You could lock yourself out of solution and into a problem. Please consult your DOS manual for proper instructions.

DIVIDE OVERFLOW

This is a message interrupt from DOS which signals that the integrity of the command processor is in question. Link in the DEBUG object file and step through the application to pinpoint the line on which the error occurs. If that yields no help or further indications, call for technical assistance.

DIVIDE BY ZERO

Because Clipper is a compiler, the error trapping routines inside dBASE (the interpreter) are not present. In many REPORTs, massive divisions are globally enacted, even on fields where the denominator is zero. Division by zero is not allowed. Build a routine or User Defined Function to avoid this problem.

SYSTEM ERROR MEMORY ERROR / FAULT

Normally, one of two things can cause this problem. The first involves using the MEMOEDIT() function and trying to access HELP or any other SET KEY TO procedure. In order to avoid any problem that may creep up if this function is used, set all keys off including the HELP key. To turn off the HELP key, type in SET KEY 28 TO. After the MEMOEDIT() function has completed its operation, reset help with SET KEY 28 TO Help. Follow the same procedures for all other SET KEY TO commands.

The other situation which can cause this error message to appear also concerns the SET KEY TO and the HELP functions. If the three PARAMETERS (p, l, and v) are not passed to the procedure, regardless of their use, the stack is eventually corrupted and an error occurs. Make sure that the procedures being called by the SET KEY TO command have the proper PARAMETERS.

GETS AND READS IN CALLING PROGRAM ARE CLEARED

This normally occurs when implementing Context Sensitive Help with all SET KEY TO procedures. If the CLEAR command is issued to clear the screen, it will also CLEAR the GETS/READs as well -- even those on the calling end of the application. In order to CLEAR the screen and keep all GETs and READs active, the following work-around must be used:

```
a 0,0 CLEAR
```

DATA OFF ONE POSITION

This problem is normally due to either dBASE II database files having been converted to dBASE III via dCONVERT or you are using the SUMMER '85 version of Clipper on databases created under dBASE III Plus. In either case, if the data is being displayed offset by one character, rewrite the headers of the databases for true dBASE III files: either under version 1.0/1.1 or Plus. Keep in mind that if the files are rewritten under PLUS, the WINTER '85 version (or later versions) of the compiler MUST be used to get proper results. To rewrite the headers, use dBASE and USE the data files, then COPY TO a new file. Delete the old database from the disk and rename the new file to the name of the old file. This will ensure that the file has the proper dBASE III header.

CAN NOT FIND/SEEK DATA ELEMENTS

There are two possible reasons for this message:

First, if the indexes were created from databases which were either dCONVERTed or created under dBASE III PLUS (and you are not using the WINTER '85 version), then the FIND/SEEK commands will probably not work properly. To remedy this, rewrite the headers properly (please see the section on Data Displaying off one character) and rebuild the indexes.

Second, if the indexes were built from fields which were TRIMmed, the FIND/SEEK commands will not work properly. In Clipper, indexes are generated based on a blank record. TRIMming a blank record would generate a null byte for the index space. A space is required to allow the FIND/SEEK command to work and to allow the proper index key structure. Consider the following:

```
last_name    C   20
first_name   C   20
mid_init     C   1

USE File
INDEX ON TRIM(last_name) + ", " + TRIM(first_name) + " " + mid_init
```

The index key is generated with enough space for 4 characters: two for the ", ", one for the second " ", and one for the middle initial. To open up enough space for the fields being TRIMmed, you must use the SPACE() function to pad the index key. The new syntax would look like this:

```
USE File
INDEX ON TRIM(last_name) + ", " + TRIM(first_name) + " " + ;
        mid_init + SPACE(LEN(last_name) + LEN(first_name))
```

If the FIND or SEEK still does not work, especially if the file is a secondary file, refer to Chapter 4 for specific examples on using the INDEX command with a SUBSTR(TRIM()) combination.

This is also true for the INDEX ON CMONTH(date). In order to get it to INDEX and FIND or SEEK properly, the proper number of blank spaces must be added:

```
USE File
INDEX ON SUBSTR(CMONTH(datefield) + SPACE(10)) 1, 10)
```

PROBLEMS WITH SUM OR TOTAL

If TOTALs are not coming out quite right, or if fields are not being APPENDED properly, it is probably due to the lack of a FIELDs list. These commands require that a FIELDs list be included with the command. In some cases where the entire database is being SUMmed or TOTALed, all fields cannot be listed on the same command line. Macro substitution is the best solution for this problem.

ONLY ONE FIELD LISTING

Check to see if you are LISTing with a macro substitution which contains a comma in the string. If so, remember that syntactical structures of commands can not be placed inside a macro; they must be in place as a literal. During compilation, no comma is seen, therefore the compiler only allows the first field in the macro list to be printed.

EXECUTION IS SLOWER THAN IN DBASE

Most of the time this is due to the poor use of macro substitution. Consider the following:

```
instead_of = "state = 'CA' .AND. SUBSTR(zip,1,2) = '91'"
SET FILTER TO &instead_of
DO WHILE .NOT. EOF()
   DO Printit
ENDDO
```

As each record in the database is looked at in the Printit procedure, it is tested against the FILTERed condition. With each test to the FILTER, the macro is completely expanded. This sequence would speed up greatly if the macro were hard coded.

If any part of a macro is being expanded repetitively, find some means to change those command clauses as literals in a command line, thus leaving the rest for a macro.

EXEC SEQUENCE ERROR

This is due to a section in one overlay directly or indirectly calling another section in the same overlay. The problem is in the way the linker maintains control of the operation; the calling procedure is wiped out of memory as the second procedure comes into operation. Once the called procedure is finished, it tries to go back to the original procedure. The EXEC SEQUENCE ERROR pops up at this time, when the program realizes that it does not know where to go.

A FEW THINGS TO WATCH OUT FOR...

USING THE STR() FUNCTION

If a string conversion on a numeric value is performed, an extra placement must be allowed for the integer to the left of the decimal place.

For example, consider the following:

```
STORE .9823615 TO temp_var
a  3, 5 SAY STR(temp_var,8,7)
```

The results would be a complete string of asterisks (********).

To work-around this problem, make the length of the string one greater:

```
a  3, 5 SAY STR(temp_var,9,7)
```

DISPLAY COMMAND

Rather than being an error, this is more of a difference. Nevertheless, the DISPLAY command acts like the LIST command and will not stop to prompt the user that the screen is full.

APPENDIX D

Clipper and Networking

NETWORKING VS. MULTITASKING

There is a big difference between multi-user and multitasking software. Back in the days of CP/M and MP/M, the concepts of multi-user and multitasking seemed to coexist. In that era, everything was basically multi-tasking. This meant that the main computer, or server, was performing several different tasks at one time, much like the idea of timesharing on main frame systems. However, multitasking's biggest restriction was the inability for true file and record locking. The entire concept focused on having the same files, normally data-based files, open and shared by all. If a record became altered or "updated," the changes should then reflect as such to all users on the system. With multitasking systems, this was simulated by having multiple files on many drives and collating the data at the end of work day. A true PC based multi-user system was yet to come.

Today, both concepts are possible. There are several packages available which attach many "computer terminals" to a main computer called a *server*. This computer services all the file handling needs for the users. However, no two users can access a file at the same time. Even on multi-user systems, the files must be locked, preventing other users from gaining access to the system. With multi-user based systems, the server can *lock* specific files, records, and fields from other users. These routines are normally handled by a secondary software package, residing in memory, between DOS and the application. When software is called upon, for example, to lock a record, it goes "out to DOS" and invokes the necessary interrupts to perform the task, via the operating system.

In reality, neither the application nor the operating system "talks" to one another to perform these operations. Software packages like Novell and PC Net, reside in memory and handle all of the locking for the developer and the user. The trick is to call the necessary Assembly or C routines that do the trick.

Since Clipper's open architecture allows user defined functions and outside routines, written in Assembly or C, to be brought into the application, the implementation of file, record, and field locking is quite simple. Many who know both the Novell software and Assembly language have made libraries in Assembler which activate the necessary file, record, and field locking commands. These libraries are then linked into applications. On the application side, user defined functions (like RLOCK(), FLOCK(), and FDLOCK()) are created which have the proper CALL commands which go out to the Assembly routines, which in turn go to the operating system. Throughout the application, once the functions have been established and the library CALLs linked in, the developer needs only to issue simple dBASE-like commands to activate a multi-user application.

The Autumn '86 release of Clipper has those library routines built in as well as the functions predefined in the instruction set. However, additional libraries may be obtained and added to Clipper to yield even more power and flexibility in a networking environment. One such library is offered by Neil Weicher of Communication Horizon. Neil helped Brian Russel develop some of the library calls in the next Clipper and has a library ready-made for the current version. An additional feature Clipper developers may take advantage of is the ability to lock MEM files as well as REPORT and LABEL files, and even text files. Additionally, buffers can be flushed at will and active databases will be re-read.

Make sure that the network software is not engaged while trying to install the compiler.

Listed below are a few companies and individuals with third-party software and information concerning networking and Clipper:

Novell Netware Information

Neil Weicher - Communication Horizon Software
701 7th Ave., - 9th Floor
New York, NY 10036

3COM Ethernet

Donald Radle - Radle Computer Systems
5751 Darrow Road
Hudson, OH 44236

Neil Weicher - Communication Horizon Software
701 7th Ave., - 9th Floor
New York, NY 10036

APPENDIX E

Screen Drivers and the ANSI.OBJ File

One of the ways Clipper increases speed is the manner in which it displays information on the screen. The compiler calls the video RAM directly. Video RAM is the internal video addressing for IBM and fully compatible computers. Computers that follow this standard have no problem running an application that was compiled with Clipper.

There are some computers, however, that require a specific screen driver to handle the video addressing. A driver is like a converter: a video driver converts the code for direct video mapping into escape-sequence based code. This code emulates the video addressing normally performed by the computer. Because of this additional processing step before the information is displayed to the screen, the output appears to execute more slowly.

One sequence of escape codes, the ANSI (American National Standards Institute) codes, established a specific sequence of characters to display information to the screen. Most PC's that can't handle IBM video mapping can use the ANSI codes the following command line is present in the CONFIG.SYS file in root directory:

```
DEVICE = [d:] [path/]ANSI.SYS
```

The file ANSI.SYS (which comes with DOS) must be available in the root directory or in the PATH. The ANSI.OBJ file, which was provided with your copy of Clipper, must be linked into your application just as if it were any other object file compiled by Clipper. Remember not to link in the ANSI object file in an overlay area. This object file must reside in the main load module.

If the ANSI.OBJ file is used, the cursor keys and other related keys will not work, unless they have been redefined by the operating system before running the application. There are specific DOS commands and utility programs which allow you to do this. Please refer to your DOS manual for the appropriate syntax.

Some computers don't follow the standards of the ANSI sequence but have their own screen driver sequences. The ANSI.OBJ file will not work with these computers, even if DEVICE was set to ANSI in the CONFIG.SYS file. Special screen drivers need to be created in order for applications to work with these computers. The developer needs to keep in mind that if an application is to be installed on a WANG computer, for example, then the object files of the application need to be re-linked with a WANG screen driver. Applications need to be linked with drivers for the proper environment, and this responsibility rests with the developer. Currently, there are drivers available from Nantucket for the standard ANSI computers, TI Professional, WANG, and DEC Rainbow.

APPENDIX F

Simulating dBASE III Commands

Many dBASE III commands are intended for the interpretive environment and are not included in the Clipper language. However, there are times when they would be useful to have. Using the built-in power of Clipper, they can be simulated. The following simulations use User Defined Functions and customized procedures found in previous chapters. It is possible to take those functions and procedures and create a separate 'SIMULATE.PRG' file for all of these simulations. Then, after compiling that file separately, link it with the examples listed below. The alternative method is to compile each simulation as is.

DISPLAY STRUCTURE

```
********************
* Name          DISPSTRU.prg
* Date          August 18, 1986
* Notice        Copyright 1986, Stephen J. Straley
* Note          A Procedure which simulates dBASE III's
*               Display Structure command in Clipper.
*
********************

PARAMETERS Infile

    IF EMPTY(infile)
       infile = SPACE(30)
       @ ROW(),0 SAY "No data base in USE.  Enter filename: " GET infile
       READ
       IF EMPTY(infile)
          QUIT
       ENDIF
    ENDIF
    *****
    * Check to see if the clause 'TO PRINT' is added to the simulation
    *****
    search = AT("TO PRINT",UPPER(infile))  && <= Check for the words...
    IF search <> 0                         && <= There is no clause
       toggle = .T.
       infile = SUBSTR(infile,1,search-1)  && <= There is the clause
    ELSE
       toggle = .F.
    ENDIF
    search = AT(".",infile)                && check for file extension
    IF search = 0
       infile = TRIM(infile) + ".DBF"
    ENDIF
    IF !FILE(infile)
       ? "File Not Found"
       QUIT
    ENDIF
    RUN DIR &infile > Tempfile.txt
    CREATE Temp
```

```
USE Temp
APPEND BLANK
REPLACE field_name WITH "LINE", field_type WITH "C", field_len WITH 80
USE
CREATE Template FROM Temp
USE Template
ERASE Temp
APPEND FROM Tempfile.txt SDF
ERASE Tempfile.txt
GO 3
search = AT("of ",line)
direct = SUBSTR(line,search+3)
GO 5
search = AT("-",line)
datein = SUBSTR(line,search - 2,8)
USE &infile
ERASE Template
COPY STRUCTURE EXTENDED TO Template
USE Template
record = STR(LASTREC())
count  = 1
IF toggle
   SET PRINTER ON          && Turn printer on due to PRINT clause
ENDIF
? "Structure for database: " + TRIM(direct) + "\" + infile
? "Number of data records: " + record
? "Date of Last update   : " + datein
? "Field        Name      Type      Width     Dec"
GO TOP
DO WHILE .NOT. EOF()
   ?  RECNO()
   ?? SPACE(3)
   ?? field_name
   ?? SPACE(5)
   ?? TYPENAME()
   ?? SPACE(5)
   ?? field_len
   ?? SPACE(5)
   IF field_dec > 0
      ?? field_dec
   ENDIF
   SKIP
   count = count + 1
   IF count > 16       && Allowing only 16 fields to be displayed
      count = 1        && before the WAIT message appears
      WAIT
   ENDIF
ENDDO
USE
ERASE Template.dbf
ERASE Temp.dbf
IF toggle              && Turn the printer off
   SET PRINT OFF
ENDIF
```

```
***********************
** Function Typename **
***********************

FUNCTION Typename

DO CASE
CASE field_type = "N"
   RETURN("Numeric  ")
CASE field_type = "D"
   RETURN("Date     ")
CASE field_type = "M"
   RETURN("Memo     ")
CASE field_type = "C"
   RETURN("Character")
CASE field_type = "L"
   RETURN("Logical  ")
ENDCASE
RETURN("Undefined")
*** End of file
```

RETURN TO MASTER

There are two ways to simulate the RETURN TO MASTER command. The first involves using the KEYBOARD command to stuff the keyboard with the keystrokes that would come from a sub-level, one at a time.

The other method is to treat everything as a procedure, including the top level program. When the top level of the program is desired, the procedure is called directly. The problem with this approach is that as procedures are placed onto the internal memory stack (pushed), they are never removed from the stack (popped). Eventually, once the stack is full, a system memory error occurs.

1. STUFFING THE KEYBOARD

```
********************
* Name      MASTER1.prg
* Date      August 18, 1986
* Notice    Copyright 1986, Stephen J. Straley
* Note      This procedure simulates RETURN TO MASTER
*
********************

   DO WHILE .T.
      CLEAR
      STORE 1 TO option
      @ 0,0 SAY "This is the top menu..."
      @ 1,0 PROMPT " 1> Go Down to the Next Level "
      @ 2,0 PROMPT " 0> Exit to Operating System "
      MENU TO option
```

```
     IF option = 2
        QUIT
     ENDIF
     DO Level2
ENDDO

PROCEDURE Level2

   DO WHILE .T.
      a 3,0 CLEAR
      STORE 1 TO subopt
      a 4,5 PROMPT " 1>  Go Down to the Next Level "
      a 5,5 PROMPT " 0>  Go Up a Level "
      MENU TO subopt
      IF subopt = 2
         RETURN
      ENDIF
      DO Level3
   ENDDO

PROCEDURE Level3

   DO WHILE .T.
      a 6,0 CLEAR
      STORE 1 TO subopt2
      a 7,10 PROMPT " 1> Go down yet another level "
      a 8,10 PROMPT " 2> Go up one level "
      a 9,10 PROMPT " 3> RETURN TO MASTER "
      MENU TO subopt2
      DO CASE
      CASE subopt2 = 1
         DO Level4
      CASE subopt2 = 2
         RETURN
      OTHERWISE
         KEYBOARD "0"
         RETURN
      ENDCASE
   ENDDO

PROCEDURE Level4

   DO WHILE .T.
      a 10,0 CLEAR
      STORE 1 TO subopt3
      a 11,15 PROMPT " 1> Go Up a Level "
      a 12,15 PROMPT " 0> Go to top "
      MENU TO subopt3
      IF subopt3 = 2
        KEYBOARD "3"
       ENDIF
      RETURN
   ENDDO
* End of MASTER1.prg
```

2. EVERYTHING IS A PROCEDURE

```
********************
* Name          MASTER2.prg
* Date          August 18, 1986
* Notice        Copyright 1986, Stephen J. Straley
* Note          This procedure simulates RETURN TO MASTER
*
********************

    DO Level1

    PROCEDURE Level1

       DO WHILE .T.
          CLEAR
          STORE 1 TO option
          @ 0,0 SAY "This is the top menu..."
          @ 1,0 PROMPT " 1> Go Down to the Next Level "
          @ 2,0 PROMPT " 0> Exit to Operating System "
          MENU TO option
          IF option = 2
             QUIT
          ENDIF
          DO Level2          && Go down to the next procedure
       ENDDO

    PROCEDURE Level2

       DO WHILE .T.
          @ 3,0 CLEAR
          STORE 1 TO subopt
          @ 4,5 PROMPT " 1>  Go Down to the Next Level "
          @ 5,5 PROMPT " 0>  Go Up a Level "
          MENU TO subopt
          IF subopt = 2     && This "pops" the stack by going back
             RETURN
          ENDIF
          DO Level3          && Going down to the next level
       ENDDO

    PROCEDURE Level3

       DO WHILE .T.
          @ 6,0 CLEAR
          STORE 1 TO subopt2
          @ 7,10 PROMPT " 1> Go down yet another level "
          @ 8,10 PROMPT " 2> Go up one level "
          @ 9,10 PROMPT " 3> RETURN TO MASTER "
          MENU TO subopt2
          DO CASE
          CASE subopt2 = 1
             DO Level4       && "Push" down yet another level
```

```
         CASE subopt2 = 2
            RETURN              && "Pop" up to another level
         OTHERWISE
            DO Level1           && Go directly to the top, "pushing"
         ENDCASE                && another level onto the stack
      ENDDO

PROCEDURE Level4

   DO WHILE .T.
      @ 10,0 CLEAR
      STORE 1 TO subopt3
      @ 11,15 PROMPT " 1> Go Up a Level "
      @ 12,15 PROMPT " 0> Go to top "
      MENU TO subopt3
      IF subopt3 = 2
         DO Level1   && This "pushes" another procedure onto the stack
      ENDIF
      RETURN           && This "pops" the stack one level
   ENDDO
* End of MASTER2.prg
```

CREATE STRUCTURE

```
********************
* Name          CREATE.prg
* Date          August 18, 1986
* Notice        Copyright 1986, Stephen J. Straley
* Note          This procedure creates several databases (15 maximum)
*               as well as the structures for each, all in memory.
*               This is done using arrays and macros to simulate
*               matrixes.
*
********************

   SET CONFIRM ON
   SET SCOREBOARD OFF
   CLEAR
   DECLARE database[15]
   FOR x = 1 TO 15
      temp = LTRIM(STR(x))
      **********************************************************
      * Below, a separate array is created based on the      *
      * database[] array.  The idea is that as the pointer   *
      * in the database[] array passes down, the subscript   *
      * pointer will point to the appropriate                *
      * 4 arrays that contain the detailed information on     *
      * the database[] array.                                 *
      **********************************************************
```

```
***********************************************************
* Below, the arrays are set to 99 due to a restriction  *
* in memory.  Since most databases do not use more than *
* just a few fields, 99 should suffice.                 *
***********************************************************

   DECLARE name&temp[99], type&temp[99], len&temp[99], dec&temp[99]
NEXT
scrframe = CHR(201) + CHR(205) + CHR(187) + CHR(186) + ;
           CHR(188) + CHR(205) + CHR(200) + CHR(186) + CHR(32)
@ 0,0,23,79 BOX SUBSTR(scrframe,1,8)
@ 0,30 SAY " Create Databases "
FOR x = 1 TO 15
   STORE SPACE(12) TO database[x]
   @ 2,3 SAY "Enter Database Name: " GET database[x] PICT "@!"
   READ
   IF AT(".", database[x]) = 0
      database[x] = TRIM(SUBSTR(database[x],1,8)) + ".DBF"
   ENDIF
   IF EMPTY(database[x])
      temp = LTRIM(STR(x))
      trow = 8
      tcol = 0
      FOR y = 1 TO 99
         STORE SPACE(10) TO name&temp[y]
         STORE SPACE(1) TO type&temp[y]
         STORE 0 TO len&temp[y], dec&temp[y]
         @ 3,3 SAY "   Enter Field Name: " GET name&temp[y] PICT "@!"
         @ 4,3 SAY "               Type: " GET type&temp[y] PICT "!" ;
               VALID(type&temp[y]$"NCLDM ")
         @ 5,3 SAY "   Length: " GET len&temp[y] PICT "####" RANGE 0, 3000
         @ 6,3 SAY " Decimals: " GET dec&temp[y] PICT "##" RANGE 0,15
         READ
         IF LEN(TRIM(name&temp[y])) = 0     && This is equal to the EMPTY()
            y = 100                          && function. If it is,
         ELSE                                && increment the FOR counter
            DO CASE                          && beyond the range.
            CASE type&temp[y] = "D"
               len&temp[y] = 8
               dec&temp[y] = 0
            CASE type&temp[y] = "L"
               len&temp[y] = 1
               dec&temp[y] = 0
            CASE type&temp[y] = "M"
               len&temp[y] = 10
               dec&temp[y] = 0
            CASE type&temp[y] = "N"
               IF len&temp[y] > 15
                  len&temp[y] = 15
               ENDIF
            OTHERWISE
               dec&temp[y] = 0
            ENDCASE
```

```
            IF trow > 22
               trow = 8
               ************************************************************
               * The BOX command (@ 8,3,22,50 BOX " ") could have been   *
               * used in place of the following FOR...NEXT loop. This     *
               * loop is here because in an older version of the compiler*
               * the BOX command would clear an area in a spiral motion   *
               * rather than just straight down from top to bottom        *
               ************************************************************
               FOR steve = 8 TO 22
                  @ steve,3 SAY SPACE(47)
               NEXT
            ENDIF
            @ trow,5 SAY name&temp[y]
            @ trow,COL() + 2 SAY type&temp[y]
            @ trow,COL() + 2 SAY len&temp[y]
            @ trow,COL() + 2 SAY dec&temp[y]
            trow = trow + 1
         ENDIF
      NEXT
      FOR steve = 1 TO 22
         @ steve, 3 SAY SPACE(47)
      NEXT
      @ x, 52 SAY LTRIM(STR(x)) + "-> "
      @ x, COL() SAY database[x]
   ELSE
      x = 17
   ENDIF
NEXT
@ 0,0,23,79 BOX scrframe
@ 10,26 SAY "Now Creating the Databases....."
x = 1
DO WHILE LEN(TRIM(database[x])) <> 0
   z = LTRIM(STR(x))
   CREATE Temp
   USE Temp
   FOR y = 1 TO 99
      APPEND BLANK
      REPLACE field_name WITH name&z[y], field_type WITH type&z[y]
      REPLACE field_len WITH len&z[y], field_dec WITH dec&z[y]
      IF LEN(TRIM(name&z[y+1])) = 0
         y = 100
      ENDIF
   NEXT
   USE
   temp_name = database[x]
   CREATE &temp_name FROM Temp
   ERASE Temp.dbf
   CLOSE DATABASES
   x = x + 1
ENDDO
CLEAR
* End of CREATE.prg
```

BROWSE

```
********************
* Name          BROWSE.prg
* Date          August 18, 1986
* Notice        Copyright 1986, Stephen J. Straley
* Notes         This program tries to emulate the BROWSE feature/function
*               of dBASE III.  Cursor movement moves the display bar around.
*               However, to edit a record that the display bar is on,
*               the "B" key first must be pressed.
********************

PARAMETER file

IF AT("." file) = 0
   file = UPPER(TRIM(file)) + ".DBF"
ENDIF
DO Openfile
frame = CHR(201) + CHR(205) + CHR(187) + CHR(186) + ;
        CHR(188) + CHR(205) + CHR(200) + CHR(186) + CHR(32)
STORE SPACE(4000) TO tempscr, screen
DO Drawbord
CALL _scrsave WITH screen
SET FUNCTION 10 TO CHR(23)
DO Startup


********************

PROCEDURE Startup


****************************************************************************
* Setting Up the variables:
*
*
*
*   ending     :   the number of fields available in given file.
*   current    :   current record number of database
*
*   col_count  :   column position of the cursor on screen
*
*   row_count  :   row position of the cursor on screen
*
*   position   :   the field number BROWSE currently is resting on in
*                  CURRENT record of used FILE.
*
*   redraw     :   logical flag for a redraw of records on screen
*
*   advance    :   logical flag to allow for advancement of record number
*
*   last_posit :   the field number allowed to be shown in the last
*                  column position
*
```

```
*    frst_posit  :    the field number allowed to be shown in the first
*                     column position
*
*    in_val      :    the name of the field at any given position
*
*    in_command  :    the variable to store the INKEY()
*
*******************************************************************************

     ending      = ENDFIELD(file)
     current     = RECNO()
     bottom_rec  = LASTREC()
     col_count   = 2
     position    = 1
     row_count   = 9
     redraw      = .F.
     advance     = .F.
     last_posit  = 0
     frst_posit  = 1
     in_val      = ""


     ********************************************
     * Setting the variables to the file given *
     ********************************************
     last_posit = HOWMANY()
     DO Colmdraw
     DO Redraw
     GO current
     DO Fieldsho

     DO WHILE .T.
        @ 0,15 SAY RECNO() PICT "@B"
        in_command = 0
        in_command = INKEY()
        DO CASE
        CASE in_command = ASC("q") .OR. in_command = ASC("Q") .OR. in_command =
             65 .OR. in_command = 97
           @ 24,00 SAY ""
           CLOSE DATABASES
           QUIT

        CASE in_command = 29                      && Go to top of the file
           GO TOP
           DO Startup

        CASE in_command = 4                       && For the Right arrow key
           IF position < ending
              IF position < last_posit
                 position = position + 1
                 DO U_feldlt
              ELSE
                 frst_posit = last_posit
                 last_posit = HOWMANY()
```

```
            DO Colmdraw
            DO Redraw
            GO current
            col_count = 4 + FIELD_LEN(FIELDNAME(frst_posit))
            position = position + 1
            row_count = 9
         ENDIF
         DO Fieldrt
      ENDIF

   CASE in_command = 19                && For the left arrow key
      IF position > 1
         IF position > frst_posit
            position = position - 1
            DO U_feldrt
         ELSE
            frst_posit = frst_posit - 1
            last_posit = HOWMANY()
            position = position - 1
            DO Colmdraw
            DO Redraw
            col_count = FIELD_LEN(FIELDNAME(frst_posit)) + 4
            col_count = 2
            row_count = 9
         ENDIF
         DO Fieldlt
      ENDIF

   CASE in_command = 89 .OR. in_command = 121
      in_val = FIELDNAME(position)
      temp   = FIELD_LEN(in_val)
      DO CASE
      CASE TYPE(in_val) = "C"
         REPLACE &in_val WITH SPACE(temp)
      CASE TYPE(in_val) = "N"
         REPLACE &in_val WITH 0.00
      CASE TYPE(in_val) = "D"
         REPLACE &in_val WITH CTOD("  /  /  ")
      CASE TYPE(in_val) = "L"
         REPLACE &in_val WITH .F.
      ENDCASE
      DO Fieldsho
   CASE in_command = 18                && For screen up
      IF current > 7
         row_count = row_count - 7
         DO Upsevrl
         SKIP - 7
         current = RECNO()
         DO Showrec
         DO Fieldsho
      ENDIF

   CASE in_command = ASC("B") .OR. in_command = ASC("b")    && Begin to
      Edit
```

```
      IF TYPE(in_val) <> "M"                              && the
      highlighted
      a row_count, col_count SAY &in_val              && field/record
      a 23,0 SAY SPACE(159)
      a 23,0 GET &in_val
      READ
      tempin = FIELDNAME(position)
      REPLACE &tempin WITH &in_val
      a row_count, col_count GET &in_val
      CLEAR GETS
      a 23,0 CLEAR
   ELSE
      SAVE SCREEN
      a row_count, col_count SAY "memo"
      STORE &in_val TO editing
      tempin = FIELDNAME(position)
      a 20,5,24,75 BOX frame
      REPLACE &tempin WITH MEMOEDIT(editing,21,6,23,74,.T.)
      RESTORE SCREEN
   ENDIF

CASE in_command = 3                          && For down screen
   IF current + 7 < bottom_rec
      row_count = row_count + 7
      DO Dwnsevrl
      SKIP + 7
      current = RECNO()
      DO Showrec
      DO Fieldsho
   ENDIF

CASE in_command = 85 .OR. in_command = 117      && To delete a record
   IF DELETED()
      RECALL
      a row_count,0 SAY " "
   ELSE
      DELETE
      a row_count,0 SAY "*"
   ENDIF

CASE in_command = 1
   GO TOP
   current = RECNO()
   DO Redraw
   row_count = 9
   GO current
   DO Showrec
   DO Fieldsho

CASE in_command = 6                          && Go to bottom of the screen
   current = bottom_rec
   GO current
   DO Redraw
```

```
               row_count = 9
               GO current
               DO Showrec
               DO Fieldsho

          CASE in_command = 24                    && Go Down one record
             SKIP
             IF EOF()
                SKIP - 1
             ELSE
                SKIP - 1
                row_count = row_count + 1
                DO Downrec
                SKIP
                current = RECNO()
                DO Showrec
                DO Fieldsho
             ENDIF

          CASE in_command = 5                     && Go up one record
             SKIP - 1
             IF BOF()
                GO current
             ELSE
                SKIP + 1
                row_count = row_count - 1
                DO Uprec
                SKIP - 1
                current = RECNO()
                DO Showrec
                DO Fieldsho
             ENDIF
          ENDCASE

     ENDDO

****************

PROCEDURE Openfile

***********************************************************************
* This procedure opens the file entered.  If none, the expected message *
* is displayed.                                                       *
***********************************************************************

IF file = "."
   file = SPACE(14)
   @ ROW(),0 SAY "No database is in USE.  Enter file name: " GET file PIC-
       TURE "@!"
   READ
   file = TRIM(file)
   x = AT(".",file)
   IF X = 0
```

```
           file = file + ".DBF"
      ENDIF
   ENDIF
   IF .NOT. FILE("&file")
      ? file + " not found"
      WAIT
      QUIT
   ENDIF
   USE &file
   CLEAR
   SET SCOREBOARD OFF
   GO TOP
   RETURN


****************

PROCEDURE Drawbord

   *********************************************
   * Draw the border of BROWSE and help menu *
   *********************************************

   @ 0,1 SAY "Record No. "
   @ 0,50 SAY TRIM(file)
   @ 1,0,6,79 BOX frame
   FOR aa = 20 to 60 STEP 20
      @ 1,aa SAY CHR(203)
      @ 6,aa SAY CHR(202)
   NEXT
   FOR aa = 2 to 5
      @ aa,20 SAY CHR(186)
      @ aa,40 SAY CHR(186)
      @ aa,60 SAY CHR(186)
   NEXT
   @ 2,2 SAY "CURSOR <--  -->"
   @ 3,2 SAY "Char:  <-    ->"
   @ 4,2 SAY "Field: <-    ->"
   @ 2,22 SAY "     UP   DOWN"
   @ 3,22 SAY "Rec:    " + CHR(24) + "     " + CHR(25)
   @ 4,22 SAY "Page: PgUp  PgDn"
   @ 5,22 SAY "File: Home  End"
   @ 2,42 SAY "        DELETE"
   @ 3,42 SAY "Char:   DEL"
   @ 4,42 SAY "Field:   Y"
   @ 5,42 SAY "Record:  U"
   @ 2,62 SAY "       BROWSE"
   @ 3,62 SAY "Begin:      B"
   @ 4,62 SAY "Save/Quit   Q"
   @ 5,62 SAY "Abort:      A"
   RETURN
```

```
************

PROCEDURE COLMDRAW

************************************************************************
* Colmdraw draws the field names of the file in use                   *
*           just below the menu.                                      *
************************************************************************
* temp     : a temporary variable to start the draw of colmdraw out   *
*             at the TEMP position                                    *
*                                                                     *
* start    : a FOR - NEXT counter to move across the fields in a      *
*             file within the parameters of frst_posit and last_posit *
************************************************************************
temp = 2
CALL _scrrest WITH screen
FOR start = frst_posit TO last_posit
   in_val = FIELDNAME(start)
   IF TYPE(in_val) = "M"
      @ 7,temp SAY SUBSTR(in_val,1,4)
      temp = temp + 6
   ELSE
      @ 7,temp SAY in_val
      temp = temp + FIELD_LEN(in_val)+2
   ENDIF
NEXT
@ 8,0 SAY REPLICATE("ë",80)
RELEASE temp, start
RETURN


************

PROCEDURE Redraw

************************************************************************
* Redraw redraws the screen for the fields/records of the file in use  *
*         between the rows of 9 and 20 inclusive, for the number of fields *
*         allowed by HOWMANY()                                        *
* starthere : the starting field position for the draw.  Does not     *
*             change the value of position                            *
* down      : a temporary variable to start the drawing of the rows   *
*             between 9 and 20                                        *
* across    : a temporary variable to start the drawing of the columns *
*             between 2 and the value of HOWMANY()                    *
* start     : the counter to go across the screen                     *
************************************************************************
starthere = position
FOR down = 9 TO 20
   across = 2
   IF DELETED()
      @ down,0 SAY "*"
   ENDIF
   FOR start = frst_posit TO last_posit
```

```
            in_val = FIELDNAME(start)
            IF TYPE(in_val) = "M"
                @ down,across SAY "memo"
            ELSE
                @ down,across SAY &in_val
            ENDIF
            across = across + 2 + FIELD_LEN(in_val)
        NEXT
        starthere = starthere +1
        IF starthere > LASTREC()
            down = 21
        ELSE
            SKIP
        ENDIF
    NEXT
    SKIP - 12
    RETURN


*******************

PROCEDURE FIELDSHO

    ****************************************************************************
    * Fieldsho is a procedure that GETS the field at position and          *
    * displays it accordingly to the screen at row_count and col_count     *
    ****************************************************************************
    in_val = FIELDNAME(position)
    IF TYPE(in_val) = "M"
        tempit = "memo"
        @ row_count,col_count GET tempit
    ELSE
        @ row_count,col_count GET &in_val
    ENDIF
    CLEAR GETS
    RETURN


**************

PROCEDURE Downrec

    *************************************************************
    * Downrec gets things ready to go down and then goes ahead *
    *************************************************************
    IF row_count > 20
        CALL _scrrest WITH screen
        DO Colmdraw
        SKIP
        DO Redraw
        GO current
        row_count = 9
    ELSE
        IF TYPE(in_val) = "M"
            @ row_count-1,col_count SAY "memo"
```

```
        ELSE
           @ row_count-1,col_count SAY &in_val
        ENDIF
     ENDIF
     RETURN

***********

PROCEDURE Uprec

   **************************
   * Uprec goes up a record *
   **************************
   IF row_count < 9
      CALL _scrrest WITH screen
      DO Colmdraw
      SKIP - 1
      DO Redraw
      GO current
      row_count = 9
   ELSE
      IF TYPE(in_val) = "M"
         @ row_count+1,col_count SAY "memo"
      ELSE
         @ row_count+1,col_count SAY &in_val
      ENDIF
   ENDIF
   RETURN
*************

PROCEDURE Showrec

   ***************************************************************
   * Showrec displays the current record number to the screen *
   ***************************************************************
   @ 0,15 SAY SPACE(8)
   @ 0,15 SAY current PICT "@B"
   RETURN

***************

PROCEDURE Upsevrl

   *****************************
   * Upsevrl goes up 7 records *
   *****************************
   IF row_count < 9
      CALL _scrrest WITH screen
      DO Colmdraw
      SKIP - 7
      DO Redraw
      GO current
      row_count = 9
```

```
   ELSE
      IF TYPE(in_val) = "M"
         @ row_count+7,col_count SAY "memo"
      ELSE
         @ row_count+7,col_count SAY &in_val
      ENDIF
   ENDIF
   RETURN


***************

PROCEDURE Dwnsevrl

   ********************************************************************
   * Dwnsevrl gets things ready to go down 7 records and goes ahead *
   ********************************************************************
   IF row_count > 20
      CALL _scrrest WITH screen
      DO Colmdraw
      SKIP + 7
      DO Redraw
      GO current
      row_count = 9
   ELSE
      IF TYPE(in_val) = "M"
         @ row_count-7,col_count SAY "memo"
      ELSE
         @ row_count-7,col_count SAY &in_val
      ENDIF
   ENDIF
   RETURN


*****************

PROCEDURE U_feldlt

   *********************************************
   * U_FELDLT will unshow a field to the left *
   *********************************************
   IF TYPE(in_val) = "M"
      @ row_count, col_count SAY "memo"
      col_count = col_count + 6
   ELSE
      @ row_count,col_count SAY &in_val
      col_count = col_count + 2 + FIELD_LEN(in_val)
   ENDIF
   RETURN


**************

PROCEDURE Fieldrt

   **********************************************
   * FIELDRT will GET the field to the right... *
   **********************************************
```

```
   in_val = FIELDNAME(position)
   IF TYPE(in_val) = "M"
      tempit = "memo"
      @ row_count,col_count GET tempit
   ELSE
      @ row_count,col_count GET &in_val
   ENDIF
   CLEAR GETS
   RETURN

***********

PROCEDURE U_feldrt

   *******************************************
   * U_FELDRT will show field to the right *
   *******************************************
   IF TYPE(in_val) = "M"
      @ row_count, col_count SAY "memo"
   ELSE
      @ row_count,col_count SAY &in_val
   ENDIF
   in_val = FIELDNAME(position)
   col_count = col_count - 2 - FIELD_LEN(in_val)
   RETURN

***************

PROCEDURE Fieldlt

   *********************************************
   * FIELDLT will GET the field to the left *
   *********************************************
   in_val = FIELDNAME(position)
   IF TYPE(in_val) = "M"
      tempit = "memo"
      @ row_count,col_count GET tempit
   ELSE
      @ row_count,col_count GET &in_val
   ENDIF
   CLEAR GETS
   RETURN

***************

FUNCTION Endfield

   *****************************************************
   * This function determines the number of the last *
   * field in database given, using a binary search  *
   * algorithm.                                       *
   *****************************************************
```

```
PARAMETERS File

Use &File
x = 1
y = 1024
z = int(y/2)
DO WHILE X <> Y
   IF LEN(FIELDNAME(z)) = 0
      y = z
   ELSE
      x = z
   ENDIF
   z = x + int((y-x)/2)
   IF LEN(FIELDNAME(z)) > 0 .AND. LEN(FIELDNAME(z+1)) = 0
      y = z
      x = z
   ENDIF
ENDDO
RETURN(Y)
```

```
********************
```

```
FUNCTION Howmany
```

```
************************************************************
* Determines how many fields can be shown on the screen *
************************************************************
```

```
length = 0
FOR rover = position TO ending
   in_val = fieldname(rover)
   IF TYPE(in_val) = "M"
      length = length + 6
   ELSE
      length = length + FIELD_LEN(in_val)+2
   ENDIF
   IF length > 77
      RETURN(rover - 1)
   ENDIF
NEXT
* The remaining fields all fit on the screen
RETURN(rover)
```

```
***************
```

```
FUNCTION Fieldshow
```

```
IF advance
   @ row_count, col_count SAY &in_val
   col_count = col_count + 2 + FIELD_LEN(in_val)
   position = position + 1
   IF col_count > 80
      col_count = 2
```

```
        @ 9,0,20,79 BOX SPACE(9)
        col_count = REDRAW()
     ENDIF
  ENDIF
  in_val = FIELDNAME(position)
  @ row_count, col_count GET &in_val
  CLEAR GETS
  RETURN("")
```

****

```
FUNCTION Fieldminus

  IF advance
     @ row_count,col_count SAY &in_val
     col_count = col_count - 2 - FIELD_LEN(in_val)
     IF col_count < 2
        position = position - 1
        col_count = COLMDRAW()
        col_count = REDRAW()
     ENDIF
     position = position - 1
     in_val = fieldname(position)
     @ row_count,col_count GET &in_val
     CLEAR GETS
  ENDIF
  RETURN("")
```

****

```
FUNCTION Nowait

  SET CONSOLE OFF
  WAIT
  SET CONSOLE ON
  RETURN("")
```

****

```
FUNCTION FIELD_LEN

  *************************************
  * Field_len function               *
  *                                   *
  * Returns LEN() for character strings *
  * Returns LEN(STR()) for numeric    *
  * Returns 1 for logical             *
  * Returns 8 for date                *
  * Returns 4 for memo                *
  *************************************
  PARAMETER field_name

  IF TYPE(field_name) = "C"
```

```
        IF LEN(field_name) > LEN(&field_name)
            RETURN(LEN(field_name))
        ELSE
            RETURN(LEN(&field_name))
        ENDIF
    ENDIF
    IF TYPE(field_name) = "N"
        RETURN(LEN(STR(&field_name)))
    ENDIF
    RETURN( AT(TYPE(field_name), "L  M   D") )
    * Logical type returns an "L", since it is in the 1st position AT returns 1
    * Memo type returns an "M", since it is in the 4th position AT returns 4
    * Date type returns an "D", since it is in the 8th position AT returns 8


* End of BROWSE.prg
```

EDIT

```
********************
* Name          EDIT.prg
* Date          August 18, 1986
* Notice        Copyright 1986, Stephen J. Straley
* Note          This program emulates the EDIT command of dBASE III.
*               One exception is on a field larger than the width
*               of the screen: this program will allow a window
*               in which the edit can take place.
*
*               A limitation to this program is that it will only work
*               with 15 or fewer fields.  However, minor modifications
*               can be made allowing it to accept databases with
*               more fields.
*
*               Additionally, the way Memos and lengthy string fields
*               are handled are a bit different in this simulation from
*               dBASE III/Plus.
*
********************

PARAMETER file

file = UPPER(TRIM(file)) + ".DBF"
DO Openfile
frame = CHR(201) + CHR(205) + CHR(187) + CHR(186) + ;
        CHR(188) + CHR(205) + CHR(200) + CHR(186) + CHR(32)
DO Drawbord
```

```
************************************************************************
* Variable Declaration                                                *
*                                                                     *
*   howmany   = the number of fields in database                      *
*   screens   = the number of screens                                 *
*   pan       = this variable was set up to test for which screen     *
*               position.                                             *
*   recnumb   = was initialized to store the current record number    *
*   good_time = a logical variable to allow for an update or not      *
*   nullstr   = a null string variable that is to be global and       *
*               used for multiple-purposes                            *
************************************************************************

howmany = ENDFIELD()
* The operator is an addition that shows the modulus of two
* numbers
screens = INT(IF(howmany % 15 > 0, howmany / 15 + 1, howmany / 15))
recnumb = 1
pan     = 1
nullstr = ""
good_time = .T.

SET KEY 28 TO                      && Turns off On-Line Help
SET KEY -1 TO Deltit
SET KEY -9 TO Quitit
SET KEY  5 TO Upit
SET KEY 24 TO Dwit
DECLARE tempdata[15]               && This array holds the data for one
*                                  && screen
GO TOP
STORE SPACE(4000) TO newscr
CALL _scrsave WITH newscr
DO WHILE .T.
   DO Adjust
   CALL _scrrest WITH newscr
   DO Dispstat
   DO Scrnstat
   x = 1
   DO WHILE x <= 15
      good_time = .T.
      intemp   = FIELDNAME(x)
      tempdata[x] = &intemp
      IF EMPTY(intemp)
         EXIT
      ENDIF
      DO CASE
      CASE TYPE(intemp) = "M"
         @ 6+x,12 SAY ""
         tempvar = INKEY(0)
            IF tempvar = 5
               x = x - 1
               LOOP
            ENDIF
         good_time = .F.
```

```
      CASE TYPE(intemp) = "C"
         IF LEN(tempdata[x]) > 60
            a 6+x,12 SAY ""
            tempvar = INKEY(0)
            IF tempvar = 5
               x = x - 1
                  LOOP
            ENDIF
            good_time = .F.
         ELSE
            a 6+x,12 GET tempdata[x]
            READ
         ENDIF

      CASE TYPE(intemp) = "D"
         dat_disp = DTOC(tempdata[x])
         a 6+x,12 GET dat_disp PICT "99/99/99" VALID(GOOD_DATE())
         READ
         tempdata[x] = CTOD(dat_disp)

      OTHERWISE
         a 6+x,12 GET tempdata[x]
         READ
      ENDCASE
      IF good_time
         REPLACE &intemp WITH tempdata[x]
      ENDIF
      DO CASE
      CASE LASTKEY() = 3
         x = 15
      CASE LASTKEY() = 18
         x = 15
         SKIP - 1
      CASE LASTKEY() = 27 .OR. LASTKEY() = 17
         a 24,00 SAY ""
         QUIT
      CASE LASTKEY() = 29
          IF TYPE(intemp) = "M" .OR. (TYPE(intemp) = "C" .AND.
         LEN(tempdata[x]) > 60)
          newtemp = &intemp
          DO Editit
          REPLACE &intemp WITH newtemp
         ENDIF
      CASE LASTKEY() = 5
         x = x - 1
      ENDCASE

   x = x + 1

ENDDO
DO CASE
CASE LASTKEY() = 13 .OR. LASTKEY() = 24 .OR. LASTKEY() = 3
   SKIP
```

```
      CASE LASTKEY() = 5
         SKIP - 1
      ENDCASE

   ENDDO

********************

PROCEDURE Scrnstat


   FOR y = 1 TO 15

      intemp   = FIELDNAME(y)
      tempdata[y] = &intemp

      IF EMPTY(intemp)          && check to see if the field
         RETURN                 && is actually there.  If not,
      ENDIF                     && then return to calling proc

      a 6+y,00 SAY FIELDNAME(y)
      SET COLOR TO 0/7
      DO CASE
      CASE TYPE(intemp) = "M"
         a 6+y,12 SAY "memo"
      CASE TYPE(intemp) = "C"
         IF LEN(tempdata[y]) > 60
            a 6+y,12 SAY "string"
         ELSE
            a 6+y,12 SAY tempdata[y]
         ENDIF
      CASE TYPE(intemp) = "D"
         dat_disp = DTOC(tempdata[y])
         a 6+y,12 SAY dat_disp
      OTHERWISE
         a 6+y,12 SAY tempdata[y]
      ENDCASE
      SET COLOR TO

   NEXT

********************

FUNCTION GOOD_DATE

   IF dat_disp = "  /  /  "
      outval = .T.
   ELSE
      outval = IF(CTOD(dat_disp) == CTOD("  /  /  "), .F., .T.)
   ENDIF
   IF outval
      tempdata[x] = CTOD(dat_disp)
   ELSE
```

```
      SAVE SCREEN
      a 00,35 SAY SPACE(44)
      a 00,35 SAY "Invalid date.  (Press SPACE)"
      IF INKEY(0) = 0
      ENDIF
      RESTORE SCREEN
   ENDIF
   RETURN(outval)


********************

PROCEDURE Editit

   SAVE SCREEN
   a 2,62 SAY "  Memo  Edit  "
   a 3,62 SAY "Begin Edit ^Home"
   a 4,62 SAY "Abort Edit ESC"
   a 5,62 SAY "Save/Quit  F10"
   SET COLOR TO 0/7
   SET FUNCTION 10 TO CHR(23)
   SET KEY -1 TO
   SET KEY -9 TO
   SET KEY  5 TO
   SET KEY 24 TO
   newtemp = MEMOEDIT(newtemp,6+x,12,6+x,70,.T.)
   RESTORE SCREEN
   SET FUNCTION 10 TO
   SET COLOR TO 7/0
   SET KEY -1 TO Deltit
   SET KEY -9 TO Quitit
   SET KEY  5 TO Upit
   SET KEY 24 TO Dwit


********************

PROCEDURE Openfile

  IF file = "."
     file = SPACE(14)
     a ROW(),0 SAY "No database is in USE.  Enter file name: " GET file PIC-
           TURE "a!"
     READ
     file = TRIM(file)
     x = AT(".",file)
     IF X = 0
        file = file + ".DBF"
     ENDIF
  ENDIF
  IF .NOT. FILE("&file")
     ? file + " not found"
     WAIT
     QUIT
  ENDIF
```

```
USE &file
CLEAR
SET SCOREBOARD OFF
GO TOP
RETURN


********************

PROCEDURE Drawbord

   *
   * Draw the border of EDIT
   *

   @ 0,1 SAY "Record No. "
   @ 0,60 SAY TRIM(file)
   @ 1,0,6,79 BOX frame
   FOR aa = 20 to 60 STEP 20
      @ 1,aa SAY CHR(203)
      @ 6,aa SAY CHR(202)
   NEXT
   FOR aa = 2 to 5
      @ aa,20 SAY CHR(186)
      @ aa,40 SAY CHR(186)
      @ aa,60 SAY CHR(186)
   NEXT
   @ 2,2 SAY "CURSOR <--  -->"
   @ 3,2 SAY "Char:  <-    ->"
   @ 4,2 SAY "Field: ^<-   ^->"
   @ 2,22 SAY "     UP   DOWN"
   @ 3,22 SAY "Rec:   " + CHR(24) + "    " + CHR(25)
   @ 4,22 SAY "Page: PgUp  PgDn"
   @ 5,22 SAY "File: Home  End"
   @ 2,42 SAY "      DELETE"
   @ 3,42 SAY "Char:   DEL"
   @ 4,42 SAY "Field:   ^Y"
   @ 5,42 SAY "Record:  F2"
   @ 2,62 SAY "      EDIT"
   @ 3,62 SAY "Begin Edit ^Home"
   @ 4,62 SAY "            "
   @ 5,62 SAY "Save/Quit  F10"
   RETURN


********************

PROCEDURE Deltit

   PARAMETERS p,l,v

   IF DELETED()
      @ 00,38 SAY "      "
      RECALL
   ELSE
```

```
      @ 00,38 SAY "*DEL*"
      DELETE
   ENDIF

********************

PROCEDURE Upit

   PARAMETERS p,l,v

      good_time = .F.
      REPLACE &intemp WITH tempdata[x]
      CLEAR GETS
      x = x - 1
      IF x < 1
         x = 18
      ENDIF

********************

PROCEDURE Dwit

      PARAMETERS p,l,v

      KEYBOARD CHR(13)

********************

PROCEDURE Quitit

      PARAMETERS p, l, v

      CLEAR
      CLOSE DATABASES
      QUIT

********************

PROCEDURE Endmemo

      PARAMETERS p, l, v

      * This procedure is called by a SET KEY TO command and simulates
      * a control W key being pushed, thus completing a MEMOEDIT().

      KEYBOARD CHR(23)

********************

PROCEDURE Dispstat

      * This procedure displays a message if the record in the active
      * and selected database is deleted.
```

```
@ 00,15 SAY LTRIM(STR(RECNO()))
IF DELETED()
   @ 00,38 SAY "*DEL*"
ENDIF
```

****

PROCEDURE Adjust

```
* This should be done with most applications.  This simple routine
* readjusts the pointer of the currently selected and active database
* to the proper position.  Sometimes, when going through a database,if
* the EOF() or BOF() markers have been hit, and a READ is performed, a
* false record or an "image" of a record may show up. The solution is to
* check for either a BOF() or EOF() condition and move off the image.
* This procedure does just that.

IF BOF()
   GO TOP
ELSE
   IF EOF()
      GO BOTTOM
   ENDIF
ENDIF
```

****

PROCEDURE Loadarry

```
FOR x = 1 TO howmany
   temp  = FIELDNAME(x)     && because we can't go directly to the array
   atype[x]  = TYPE(temp)
   names[x] = temp
   DO CASE
   CASE atype[x] = "C"
      length[x] = LEN(temp)
   CASE atype[x] = "D"
      length[x] = 8
   CASE atype[x] = "N"
      length[x] = 10
   ENDCASE
NEXT
```

****

FUNCTION Endfield

```
* This function determines the number of the last field in database given
PARAMETERS File

x = 1
y = 1024
z = int(y/2)
```

```
    DO WHILE X <> Y
       IF LEN(FIELDNAME(z)) = 0
          y = z
       ELSE
          x = z
       ENDIF
       z = x + int((y-x)/2)
       IF LEN(FIELDNAME(z)) > 0 .AND. LEN(FIELDNAME(z+1)) = 0
          y = z
          x = z
       ENDIF
    ENDDO
    RETURN(Y)


********************

FUNCTION Bitstrip

    PARAMETERS c

    outstring = ""
    beginning = 1
    DO WHILE .NOT. EMPTY(c)
       IF AT(CHR(141),c) = 0
          outstring = outstring + SUBSTR(c,beginning,LEN(c))
          c = ""
       ELSE
          outstring = outstring + SUBSTR(c,beginning,AT(CHR(141),c)-1)
          beginning = AT(CHR(141),c)+1
          c = SUBSTR(c,beginning,LEN(c) - beginning + 1)
          beginning = 1
       ENDIF
    ENDDO
    RETURN(outstring)


********************

FUNCTION Big_screen

    PARAMETERS temp_row

    SET KEY 13 TO Endmemo
    data[x] = MEMOEDIT(data[x],temp_row,10,temp_row,80,.T.)
    SET KEY TO
    data[x] = BITSTRIP(data[x])
    RETURN(.T.)

* End of EDIT.prg
```

CENTURY ADJUSTING

```
********************
* Name           CENTURY.prg
* Date           August 31, 1986
* Notice         Copyright 1986, Stephen J. Straley
* Note           This program shows how you can adjust the internal
*                year mechanisms for Clipper.  This is only necessary
*                if there is a string of a date which is to be converted
*                back into the date format.  If the string contains
*                the century part of the year, then it will make no
*                difference to ADJ2000, which is the C sub-routine
*                in Clipper which actually makes the adjustment to the
*                date.
*
*                This section is really necessary for those applications
*                which require string manipulations on dates outside of
*                the currently adjusted century.  Such applications would
*                be those involving mortgages and insurance policies, for
*                example.
*
*                Two other notes:  This routine MUST be activated with a
*                DO and not a CALL.  In order for the DO to work properly,
*                the EXTERNAL command must be added to the routine.
*                Secondly, the variable being passed to the ADJ2000 routine
*                must be passed by VALUE and not by REFERENCE.  To do this,
*                use parentheses when passing it.
*
********************

STORE 0 TO year_rng
EXTERNAL _adj2000
atime = DTOC(DATE())                && Turning today's date to character type
DO WHILE .T.
   CLEAR
   TEXT
   Enter in the beginning year of the century to adjust the internal
   mechanisms of Clipper.  For example, if the year is 1986 and the
   beginning year of the century is set to a value less than or equal to
   86, then 86 will be considered in the 20th century.  If, on the other
   hand, the beginning number for the century is greater than the current
   year, then the century for the year will be considered as the 21st
   century.
   ENDTEXT
```

```
@ 10,10 SAY "Enter beginning year of the century: " GET year_rng PICT "###"
READ
newstff = year_rng
DO _ADJ2000 WITH (newstff)
btime = CTOD(atime)
@ 12,10 SAY "The String today is: " + STR(YEAR(btime))
WAIT
IF EMPTY(year_rng)
   QUIT
ENDIF
ENDDO
* End of CENTURY.prg
```

APPENDIX G

Program Generators

There is a set of standard tasks a complete application always does: set up system parameters, create databases, prompting functions, and enter, change, scan, and delete data. These tasks become tedious to generate over and over again for even the most enthusiastic developer.

To ease this, there are many programs available, such as Viewgen, HiLite, Quickcode, and Genifer, which either create basic core code for an application, or menu code for the front end of an application. However, most of these do not create code specifically for use with Clipper. They, too, have a marketing scheme and must appeal to both the developing market using Clipper and the market using dBASE.

Listed below is source code which generates the front end to an application, to be used strictly with Clipper. It is not intended to compete with other products and should be viewed solely as a demonstration of many of the things we have covered in this book. Pay particular attention to the techniques involved: not only does this program generate Clipper code, it runs under Clipper. Major sections to notice are the creation of the databases and the code for it, a sign-on message routine, and a set of standard procedures and functions.

When this code is combined with MENUGEN, which you will find immediately following GENCODE2, you have a fairly complete application generator.

A PROGRAM GENERATOR FOR CLIPPER

Create a CLiP file named GEN1.CLP containing the following one line:

```
Gencode1
```

Even though there is only one file in this CLiP file, this is one way to prevent an AS-SUMED EXTERNAL message from appearing at the end of the compile when Clipper would try to compile Eleven.prg in with the rest of this code.

```
********************
* Name        GENCODE1.prg
* Date        August 20, 1986
* Notice      Copyright 1986, Stephen J. Straley
* Note        The following source is the first half of the code that
*             creates the basic front-end of an application.
*             The code generated can then be modified to the
*             needs of the client/user. The second half is in GENCODE2.prg.
*
```

```
*                The following is a listing of the procedures and their
*                purpose as they relate to the code they generate.
*
*          First:    Writes a standard header to the text/prg file.
*          Second:   Asks for the names of the files that must
*                    be present on the disk in order to prevent the
*                    application from regenerating the data files.
*          Third:    This writes the code for the procedure named
*                    SCRINIT.  That procedure eventually sets up
*                    the screen and system parameters for the
*                    application.
*          Fourth:   Here the name of the application is entered,
*                    any special name for it, the designer's name,
*                    and the code for the initial message for the
*                    application
*          Fifth:    This section writes out the function library
*                    that is standard to most applications.
*          Sixth:    This section creates the Setup Procedure
*          Seventh:  This section creates the Redraw Procedure; this
*                    redraws the top 4 lines of the application.
*          Eight:    The WHICHWAY function allows a user to choose
*                    which way reports for the application are to
*                    print out.
*          Nine:     Here, 15 databases, each with 99 fields maximum,
*                    are created in memory using arrays and macros.
*                    These databases are specific to the application
*                    being developed.
*          Ten:      This procedure writes the initialization code
*                    for all of the databases created in memory, as
*                    well as writing out memory variables for the
*                    databases.  These variables may be used for a
*                    possible Report Generator.
*
********************

*
* All this does is display an initial message.
*
STORE SPACE(4000) TO Screen
CLEAR
CALL _scrsave WITH screen
SET COLOR TO 7+
STORE "Welcome to the Clipper Code Generator" TO message
over = 5
FOR y = 1 TO 2
   FOR x = 2 TO 18
      @ x,over SAY message
      CALL _scrrest WITH screen
      over = over + 3
   NEXT
   FOR x = 18 TO 2 STEP -1
      @ x,over SAY message
      CALL _scrrest WITH screen
      over = over + 3
   NEXT
NEXT
```

```
FOR y = COL() TO 20 STEP -1
   @ 2,y SAY message
   CALL _scrrest WITH screen
NEXT
FOR y = 2 TO 12
   @ y,20 SAY message
   CALL _scrrest WITH screen
NEXT
@ 12,20 SAY message
@ 14,28 SAY "Press Any Key to Begin!"
IF INKEY(0) = 0
ENDIF

SET CONFIRM ON
SET SCOREBOARD OFF
scrframe = CHR(201) + CHR(205) + CHR(187) + CHR(186) + ;
           CHR(188) + CHR(205) + CHR(200) + CHR(186) + CHR(32)
STORE SPACE(8) TO file
STORE SPACE(30) TO name
CLEAR
@ 0,0,22,79 BOX SUBSTR(scrframe,1,8)
@ 10,10 SAY "What is the name of the Application? " GET file PICT "@!"
@ 12,10 SAY "Enter your ame => " GET name PICT "@X"
READ
pref = SUBSTR(file,1,1) + LOWER(SUBSTR(file,2,1))
file = TRIM(file) + ".PRG"
name = "Copyright - " + SUBSTR(DTOS(DATE()),1,4) + " " + name
SET ALTERNATE TO &file
SET CONSOLE OFF
DO First


********************

PROCEDURE First

   SET ALTERNATE ON
   ? "*********************"
   ? "* Name     " + file
   ? "* Date     " + DTOC(DATE())
   ? "* Author   " + name
   ? "* Note     This is an application"
   ? "*"
   ? "*********************"
   ?
   ? "CLEAR"
   ? '? "Loading Program..."'
   ? "DO Beginit"
   ? "DO Draw"
   ? "DO " + pref + "menu"
   SET ALTERNATE OFF
   DO Second
```

```
********************

PROCEDURE Second

   CLEAR
   @ 0,0,22,79 BOX SUBSTR(scrframe,1,8)
   STORE SPACE(12) TO database1, database2, database3
   system1 = pref + SPACE(10)
   @ 4,5 SAY "Enter the Names of the Databases that MUST"
   @ 5,5 SAY "be on the disk in order to prevent the"
   @ 6,5 SAY "application from initializing all of the"
   @ 7,5 SAY "databases.   Give an extension if other than"
   @ 8,5 SAY "a .DBF extension."
   @ 10,20 SAY "->" GET database1 PICT "@!"
   @ 11,20 SAY "  " GET database2 PICT "@!"
   @ 12,20 SAY "  " GET database3 PICT "@!"
   READ
   database1 = TRIM(database1) + IF(AT(".",database1) = 0, ".DBF", "")
   database2 = TRIM(database2) + IF(AT(".",database2) = 0, ".DBF", "")
   database3 = TRIM(database3) + IF(AT(".",database3) = 0, ".DBF", "")
   *
   * Sometimes, an application requires special values to be written to
   * the disk.   Values such as the system date, end-of-year processing
   * date, check numbers, etc.
   *
   @ 15, 5 SAY "Will there be a special system file? "
   IF VERIFY()
      @ 17,10 SAY "Enter full name -> " GET system1 PICT "@!"
      READ
      system1 = TRIM(system1) + IF(AT(".",system1) = 0, ".MEM", "")
      system1 = SUBSTR(system1,1,1) + LOWER(SUBSTR(system1,2))
   ENDIF
   SET CONSOLE OFF
   @ 19,20 SAY "Just a sec...."
   SET ALTERNATE ON
   DO Prochead WITH "Beginit"          && PROCHEAD writes the basic header
   ? '   IF .NOT. FILE("SCREEN.SYS")'   && for a procedure
   ? '      DO Scrinit'
   ? '   ENDIF'
   ? '   RESTORE FROM Screen.sys'
   IF LEN(TRIM(system1)) > 2
      ? '   IF .NOT. FILE(scrdata + "' + UPPER(system1) + '")'
      ? "      DO " + LTRIM(SUBSTR(system1,1,5)) + "int"
      ? "   ENDIF"
   ENDIF
   ? "   IF .NOT. FILE(scrdata + " + CHR(34) + database1 + CHR(34) + ")"
   IF LEN(TRIM(database2)) > 4
      ?? " .OR. .NOT. FILE(scrdata + " + CHR(34) + database2 + CHR(34) + ")"
   ENDIF
   IF LEN(TRIM(database3)) > 4
      ?? " .OR. .NOT. FILE(scrdata + " + CHR(34) + database3 + CHR(34) + ")"
   ENDIF
   ? "      DO " + pref + "init"
```

```
? "    ENDIF"
SET ALTERNATE OFF
DO Third

*********************

PROCEDURE Third

   CLEAR
   a 0,0,22,79 BOX SUBSTR(scrframe,1,8)
   a 2,5 SAY "Writing SCRINIT to alternate file"
   SET ALTERNATE ON
   DO Prochead WITH "Scrinit"
   ?
   ? "    SET SCOREBOARD OFF"
   ?
   ? '    scrleft_1   = "Copyright 1986 - GLOBAL SOFTWARE"'
   ? '    scrleft_2   = "All Rights Reserved"'
   ? '    right_1     = "Terminal/System Setup Program"'
   ? '    right_2     = "' + CMONTH(DATE()) + ' - 1986"'
   ? '    temscreen   = SPACE(4000)'
   ?      scrframe    = CHR(201) + CHR(205) + CHR(187) + CHR(186) + ;
   ?                    CHR(188) + CHR(205) + CHR(200) + CHR(186) + CHR(32)
   ? '    CLEAR'
   ? '    center = "Drive Assignment Setup"'
   ? '    a  0,0 SAY scrleft_1'
   ? '    a  1,0 SAY scrleft_2'
   ? '    a  0,80-LEN(right_1) SAY right_1'
   ? '    a  1,80-LEN(right_2) SAY right_2'
   ? '    a  3,40-LEN(center)/2 SAY center'
   ? '    a  4,0,23,79 BOX scrframe'
   ? '    topspot = "          Move cursor to appropriate option.  Strike RETURN
            key to change          "'
   ? '    a  5, 1 GET topspot'
   ? '    CLEAR GETS'
   ? '    a  6, 0 SAY CHR(204) + REPLICATE(CHR(205),78) + CHR(185)'
   ? '    CALL _scrsave WITH temscreen'
   ? '    IF .NOT. FILE("SCREEN.SYS")'
   ? '       STORE "C:" TO scrprog, scrdata'
   ? '       STORE .F. TO scrconfirm, scrdelim, scrinten, scrbell, scrtype'
   ? '       STORE .T. TO scrsys, scrshow, scrcolor'
   ? '       STORE "" TO scrframe, scrbar, scrlin'
   ? '       STORE "::" TO scrdelimto'
   ? '       STORE 0 TO scrtimes, scrpass'
   ? '    ELSE'
   ? '       RESTORE FROM Screen.sys ADDITIVE'
   ? '    ENDIF'
   ? '    STORE 4 TO option'
   ?
   ? '    DO WHILE .T. '
   ? '       CALL _scrrest WITH temscreen'
   ? '       a  7, 5 PROMPT " 1> System Configured for " + IF(scrsys, "Hard",
            "Floppy") + " Disk "'
```

```
? '        @  7,45 PROMPT " 2> Program Drive Set to " + scrprog + " "'
? '        @  8,45 PROMPT " 3> Data Drive Set to " + scrdata + " "'
? '        @ 10, 5 PROMPT " 4> Confirm is " + IF(scrconfirm, "ON ", "OFF") +
        " "'
? '        @ 11, 5 PROMPT " 5> Delimiters are " + IF(scrdelim, "ON", "OFF") +
        " "'
? '        @ 12, 5 PROMPT " 6> Delimiters SET to " + scrdelimto + " "'
? '        @ 13, 5 PROMPT " 7> Screen " + IF(scrcolor, "Bright", "Normal") +
        " "'
? '        @ 14, 5 PROMPT " 8> Field Color is " + IF(scrinten, "ON", "OFF") +
        " "'
? '        @ 15, 5 PROMPT " 9> Bell " + IF(scrbell, "WILL", "WILL NOT") + "
        ring "'
? '        @ 10,40 PROMPT " A> Password " + IF(scrshow, "WILL", "WILL NOT") +
        " echo to screen "'
? '        @ 12,40 PROMPT " B> Change Password "'
? '        @ 14,40 PROMPT " C> " + DLTRIM(STR(scrtimes)) + " tries at the
        Password "'
? '        @ 16,40 PROMPT " D> " + IF(scrtype, "Engage", "Disengage") + "
        Type-Ahead Feature "'
? '        @ 18,33 SAY    "<ESC> to Save Values"'
? '        MENU TO option'
? '        DO CASE'
? '        CASE option = 1'
? '           scrsys = IF(scrsys, .F., .T.)'
? '           IF .NOT. scrsys'
? '              KEYBOARD "2"'
? '           ENDIF'
? '        CASE option = 2'
? '           @ 21,10 SAY "Enter Program Drive: " GET scrprog PICT "!";
                          VALID(SUBSTR(scrprog,1,1) $"ABCDEFGHIJKLMNOP")'
? '           READ'
? '           IF .NOT. scrsys'
? '              IF scrprog = scrdata'
? '                 @ 21,10 SAY SPACE(50)'
? '                 @ 22,10 SAY "Data Drive and Program Drive NOT EQUAL for
        Floppy System"'
? '                 @ 21,10 SAY "Enter Data Drive: " GET scrdata PICT "!";
                              VALID(SUBSTR(scrdata,1,1) $"ABCDEFGHIJKLMNOP"
        .AND. scrprog <> scrdata)'
? '                 READ'
? '              ENDIF'
? '           ENDIF'
? '        CASE option = 3'
? '           @ 21,10 SAY "Enter Data Drive: " GET scrdata PICT "!";
                          VALID(SUBSTR(scrdata,1,1) $"ABCDEFGHIJKLMNOP")'
? '           READ'
? '           IF .NOT. scrsys'
? '              IF scrprog = scrdata'
? '                 @ 21,10 SAY SPACE(50)'
? '                 @ 22,10 SAY "Program Drive and Data Drive NOT EQUAL for
        Floppy System"'
? '                 @ 21,10 SAY "Enter Program Drive: " GET scrprog PICT "!";
```

```
                                VALID(SUBSTR(scrprog,1,1) $"ABCDEFGHIJKLMNOP"
              .AND. scrdata <> scrprog)'
?  '              ENDIF'
?  '            ENDIF'
?  '         CASE option = 4'
?  '             scrconfirm = IF(scrconfirm, .F., .T.)'
?  '         CASE option = 5'
?  '             scrdelim = IF(scrdelim, .F., .T.)'
?  '         CASE option = 6'
?  '             STORE " " TO choice'
?  '             a 21,10 SAY "Set Left Delimiter:    " GET choice PICT "X"'
?  '             READ'
?  '             STORE choice TO scrdelimto'
?  '             STORE " " TO choice'
?  '             a 21,10 SAY "Set Right Delimiter: " GET choice PICT "X"'
?  '             READ'
?  '             STORE scrdelimto + choice TO scrdelimto'
?  '         CASE option = 7'
?  '             scrcolor = IF(scrcolor, .F., .T.)'
?  '         CASE option = 8'
?  '             scrinten = IF(scrinten, .F., .T.)    '
?  '         CASE option = 9'
?  '             scrbell = IF(scrbell, .F., .T.)'
?  '         CASE option = 10'
?  '             scrshow = IF(scrshow, .F., .T.)'
?  '         CASE option = 11'
?  '             STORE SPACE(15) TO password'
?  '             a 21,10 SAY "What Password do you want to use? " GET password
              PICT "XXXXXXXXXXXXXXX"'
?  '             READ'
?  '             scrpass = GENPASS(password)'
?  '         CASE option = 12'
?  '             a 21,10 SAY "How may tries for a correct password? " GET
              scrtimes PICT "##" range 0,99'
?  '             READ'
?  '         CASE option = 13'
?  '             scrtype = IF(scrtype, .F., .T.)'
?  '         OTHERWISE'
?  '             EXIT'
?  '         ENDCASE'
?  '     ENDDO'
?

prmpt_4 = CHR(201) + CHR(205) + CHR(187) + CHR(186) + ;
          CHR(188) + CHR(205) + CHR(200) + CHR(186) + CHR(32)
prmpt_5 = REPLICATE(CHR(177), 8) + " "
prmpt_6 = CHR(218) + CHR(196) + CHR(191) + CHR(179) + ;
          CHR(217) + CHR(196) + CHR(192) + CHR(179) + CHR(32)
prmpt_7 = CHR(222) + CHR(223) + CHR(221) + CHR(221) + ;
          CHR(221) + CHR(220) + CHR(222) + CHR(222) + CHR(32)
prmpt_9 = REPLICATE(CHR(15), 8) + " "

?  '    CALL _scrrest WITH temscreen'
?  '    a 3,3 SAY SPACE(60)'
```

```
? '    @ 3,29 SAY "Installing the Border"'
? '    CALL _scrsave WITH temscreen'
? '    in_choice = 4'
?
? '    DO WHILE .T.'
? '       CALL _scrrest WITH temscreen'
? '       @  8, 5 PROMPT  "1>    **********"'
? '       @  8,32 PROMPT  "2>    =========="'
? '       @  8,59 PROMPT  "3>    ----------"'
? '       @ 10, 5 PROMPT  "4>    &prmpt_4."'
? '       @ 10,32 PROMPT  "5>    &prmpt_5."'
? '       @ 10,59 PROMPT  "6>    &prmpt_6."'
? '       @ 12, 5 PROMPT  "7>    &prmpt_7."'
? '       @ 12,32 PROMPT  "8>    "'
? '       @ 12,59 PROMPT  "9>    &prmpt_9."'
? '       @ 14,20 SAY "Move Cursor to choose preferred boarder"'
? '       MENU TO in_choice'
? '       DO CASE'
? '       CASE in_choice = 1'
? '          scrframe = "******** "'
? '          scrbar   = REPLICATE("*",80)'
? '          scrlin   = "*"'
? '       CASE in_choice = 2'
? '          scrframe = "======== "'
? '          scrbar   = REPLICATE("=",80)'
? '          scrlin   = "="'
? '       CASE in_choice = 3'
? '          scrframe = "-------- "'
? '          scrbar   = REPLICATE("-",80)'
? '          scrlin   = "|"'
? '       CASE in_choice = 4'
? '          scrframe = CHR(201) + CHR(205) + CHR(187) + CHR(186) + CHR(188)
         + ;'
? '                     CHR(205) + CHR(200) + CHR(186) + CHR(32)'
? '          scrbar   = CHR(204) + REPLICATE(CHR(205), 78) + CHR(185)'
? '          scrlin   = CHR(186)'
? '       CASE in_choice = 5'
? '          scrframe = REPLICATE(CHR(177), 8) + " "'
? '          scrbar   = REPLICATE(CHR(177),80)'
? '          scrlin   = CHR(177)'
? '       CASE in_choice = 6'
? '          scrframe = CHR(218) + CHR(196) + CHR(191) + CHR(179) + CHR(217)
         + ;'
? '                     CHR(196) + CHR(192) + CHR(179) + CHR(32)'
? '          scrbar   = CHR(195) + REPLICATE(CHR(196), 78) + CHR(180)'
? '          scrlin   = CHR(179)'
? '       CASE in_choice = 7'
? '          scrframe = CHR(222) + CHR(223) + CHR(221) + CHR(221) + CHR(221)
         + ;'
? '                     CHR(220) + CHR(222) + CHR(222) + CHR(32)'
? '          scrbar   = CHR(222) + REPLICATE(CHR(220),78) + CHR(221)'
? '          scrlin   = CHR(222)'
? '       CASE in_choice = 8'
```

```
? '        scrframe = " "'
? '        scrbar   = REPLICATE("",80)'
? '        scrlin   = ""'
? '     CASE in_choice = 9'
? '        scrframe = REPLICATE(CHR(15), 8) + " "'
? '        scrbar   = REPLICATE(CHR(15), 80)'
? '        scrlin   = CHR(15)'
? '     ENDCASE'
?
? '     CALL _scrrest WITH temscreen'
? '     @ 8,10,16,69 BOX SUBSTR(scrframe,1,8)'
? '     @ 12,10 SAY SUBSTR(scrbar,1,1) + SUBSTR(scrbar,2,58) + SUB-
         STR(scrbar,80,1)'
? '     @ 19,25 SAY "Is this the border you want?  "'
? '     IF VERIFY()'
? '        EXIT'
? '     ENDIF'
? '  ENDDO'
?
? '  writefile = scrprog + "SCREEN.SYS"'
? '  @ 22,24 SAY "Now Saving parameters to " + writefile'
? '  SAVE ALL LIKE scr* TO &writefile'
? '  CALL _scrrest WITH temscreen'
? '  @ 12,18 SAY  "Finished with Terminal/System Initialization"'
? '  IF INKEY(.5) = 32'
? '     RETURN'
? '  ENDIF'
SET ALTERNATE OFF
@ 2,COL() SAY REPLICATE(".",64-COL()) + "FINISHED!"
DO Fourth


********************

PROCEDURE Fourth

   STORE SPACE(30) TO message1, message2, message3, message4
   @ 15,5 SAY "    Enter Name of Company: " GET message1
   READ
   message1 = TRIM(message1)
   @ 15,5 SAY "Enter Name of Application: " GET message2
   READ
   message2 = TRIM(message2)
   @ 15,5 SAY "    Enter Name of Module: " GET message3
   READ
   message3 = TRIM(message3)
   @ 15,5 SAY "    Enter Designer's Name: " GET message4
   READ
   message4 = TRIM(message4)
   @ 15,5 SAY SPACE(65)
   @ 3,5 SAY "Writing DRAW to alternate file"
   IF LEN(TRIM(system1)) > 2
      endposit = AT(".",system1)-1
      passing = SUBSTR(system1,1,endposit) + "int"
```

```
      SET ALTERNATE ON
      ?
      DO Prochead WITH passing
      temp = pref + "right_"
      ? '     ' + temp + '1 = "' + message2 + '"'
      ? '     ' + temp + '2 = "' + message3 + '"'
      ? '    SAVE ALL LIKE *&pref TO &system1'
      ?
      SET ALTERNATE OFF
ENDIF

SET ALTERNATE ON
DO Prochead WITH "Draw"
?
? '    CLEAR'
? '    RESTORE FROM SCREEN.SYS additive'
? '    IF scrcolor'
? '       SET COLOR TO 7+'
? '    ELSE'
? '       SET COLOR TO 7'
? '    ENDIF'
IF LEN(message1) > 0
    ? '    @ 1,20,7,60 BOX scrframe'
    ? '    @ 3,28 SAY "    GLOBAL SOFTWARE"'
    ? '    @ 4,28 SAY " in conjunction with"'
    ? '    @ 5,40-LEN("' + message1 + '")/2 SAY ' + '"' +  message1 + '"'
ELSE
    ? '    @ 3,20,7,60 BOX scrframe'
    ? '    @ 5,28 SAY "    GLOBAL SOFTWARE"'
ENDIF
IF LEN(message2) > 0
    ? '       @  9,40-LEN("' + message2 + '")/2 SAY ' + '"' + message2 + '"'
ENDIF
IF LEN(message3) > 0
    ? '       @ 11,40-LEN("' + message3 + '")/2 SAY ' + '"' + message3 + '"'
ENDIF
? '       @ 21,11 SAY "                  Designed by Stephen J. Straley
    "'
IF LEN(message4) > 0
    ? '       @ 22,40-LEN("with " + "' + message4 + '")/2 SAY "with " + "' +
    message4 + '"'
ENDIF
?
? '    DO WHILE .T. '
? '       STORE "Today' + CHR(39) + 's Date is " + CDOW(DATE()) + ", " +
      CMON(DATE()) TO prompt'
? '       STORE prompt + " " + STR(DAY(DATE()),2) + ", " +
      STR(YEAR(DATE()),4) TO prompt'
? '       @ 14,40-LEN(prompt)/2 SAY prompt'
? '       @ 18,25 SAY "Is this the Correct Date?  "'
? '       IF .NOT. VERIFY()'
? '          mdate = DATE()'
? '          @ 18, 0 SAY SPACE(80)'
```

```
? '          @ 18,28 SAY "Enter in Date:  " GET mdate'
? '          READ'
? '          mdate = DTOC(mdate)'
? '          RUN DATE &mdate'
? '          @ 18,25 SAY SPACE(40)'
? '       ELSE'
? '          EXIT'
? '       ENDIF'
?
? '    ENDDO'
SET ALTERNATE OFF
@ 3,COL() SAY REPLICATE(".",64-COL()) + "FINISHED!"
DO Fifth


********************


PROCEDURE Fifth

SET ALTERNATE ON
@ 4,5 SAY "Writing FUNCTION FILE to alternate file"
DO Funchead WITH "Dltrim"
?
? '    PARAMETER in_string'
?
? '       RETURN(LTRIM(TRIM(in_string)))'
?
DO Funchead WITH "Endfield"
?
? '    PARAMETER File'
?
? '       USE &File'
? '       x = 1'
? '       y = 1024'
? '       z = INT(y/2)'
?
? '       DO WHILE x <> y'
? '          IF LEN(FIELDNAME(z)) = 0'
? '             y = z'
? '          ELSE'
? '             x = z'
? '          ENDIF'
? '          z = x + int((y-x)/2)'
? '          IF LEN(FIELDNAME(z)) > 0 .AND. LEN(FIELDNAME(z+1)) = 0'
? '             y = z'
? '             x = z'
? '          ENDIF'
? '       ENDDO'
? '       RETURN(y)'
?
DO Funchead WITH "Dayword"
?
? '    PARAMETER in_date'
?
```

```
? '        in_day = STR(DAY(in_date),2)'
? '        in_val = VAL(in_day)'
? '        IF in_val > 3 .AND. in_val < 21'
? '            in_day = in_day + "th"'
? '        ELSE'
? '            in_val = VAL(SUBSTR(in_day,2,1))'
? '            in_day = in_day + SUBSTR("thstndrdthththththth", (in_val *
    2)+1,2)'
? '        ENDIF'
? '        RETURN(in_day)'
?
DO Funchead WITH "Expand"
?
? '    PARAMETER in_string'
?
? '        length  = LEN(in_string)'
? '        counter = 1'
? '        out_str = ""'
?
? '        DO WHILE counter <= length'
? '            out_str = out_str + SUBSTR(in_string,counter,1) + " "'
? '            counter = counter + 1'
? '        ENDDO'
? '        RETURN(TRIM(out_str))'
?
DO Funchead WITH "Qwait"
?
? '    SET CONSOLE OFF'
? '    WAIT TO intemp'
? '    SET CONSOLE ON'
? '    IF UPPER(intemp) = "Q"'
? '        RETURN(.T.)'
? '    ENDIF'
? '    RETURN(.F.)'
?
DO Funchead WITH "Chkamt"
?
? '    PARAMETERS figure'
?
? '        final = ""'
? '        IF figure < 0'
? '            final = "Unable to Print"'
? '            RETURN(final)'
? '        ENDIF'
? '        cents = SUBSTR(STR(figure, 15, 2), 14, 2)'
? '        new = INT(figure)'
? '        ********************'
? '        * check for BILLIONS'
? '        ********************'
? '        temp = INT(new/1000000000)'
? '        IF temp > 0'
? '            final = final + GRP_EXPAND(temp) + " Billion "'
? '            new = new - (temp*1000000000)'
```

```
?  '      ENDIF'
?  '      *********************'
?  '      * check for MILLIONS'
?  '      *********************'
?  '      temp = INT(new/1000000)'
?  '      IF temp > 0'
?  '         final = final + GRP_EXPAND(temp) + " Million "'
?  '         new = new - (temp*1000000)'
?  '      ENDIF'
?  '      *********************'
?  '      * check for THOUSANDS'
?  '      *********************'
?  '      temp = INT(new/1000)'
?  '      IF temp > 0'
?  '         final = final + GRP_EXPAND(temp) + " Thousand "'
?  '         new = new - (temp*1000)'
?  '      ENDIF'
?  '      temp = new'
?  '      ******************'
?  '      * check for UNITS'
?  '      ******************'
?  '      IF temp > 0'
?  '         final = final + GRP_EXPAND(temp)'
?  '      ENDIF'
?  '      IF SUBSTR(final,1,3) = "One" .AND. LEN(final) = 3'
?  '         final = final + " Dollar and " + cents + "/100"'
?  '      ELSE'
?  '         final = final + " Dollars and " + cents + "/100"'
?  '      ENDIF'
?  '      RETURN(final)'
?
DO Funchead WITH "Grp_expand"
?
?  '   PARAMETER group_val'
?
?  '      one_unit = "One     Two     Three   Four    Five    Six
             Seven   Eight   Nine    Ten     Eleven  Twelve  Thirteen
             FourteenFifteen Sixteen SeventeenEighteen Nineteen"'
?  '      ten_unit = "Twenty Thirty Forty  Fifty  Sixty  SeventyEighty
             Ninety "'
?  '      group_str = ""'
?  '      IF group_val > 99'
?  '         new1 = INT(group_val/100)'
?  '         group_str = group_str + TRIM(SUBSTR(one_unit,(new1*9)-8,9))'
?  '         group_val = group_val - (new1 * 100)'
?  '         group_str = group_str + " Hundred "'
?  '      ENDIF'
?  '      IF group_val > 19'
?  '         new1 = INT(group_val/10)-1'
?  '         group_str = group_str + TRIM(SUBSTR(ten_unit,(new1*7)-6,7))'
?  '         new1 = INT(group_val/10)*10'
?  '         group_val = group_val - new1'
?  '         IF group_val > 0'
```

```
? '            group_str = group_str + "-"'
? '          ENDIF'
? '        ENDIF'
? '        IF group_val > 0'
? '            group_str = group_str + TRIM(SUBSTR(one_unit,(group_val*9)-
        8,9))'
? '        ENDIF'
? '        RETURN(group_str)'
?
DO Funchead WITH "Chktest"
?
? '    in_check = "Y"'
? '    @ 12,10 SAY "Would you like to print a test check? "'
? '    IF VERIFY()'
? '        RETURN(.T.)'
? '    ENDIF'
? '    RETURN(.F.)'
?
DO Funchead WITH "Verify"
?
? '    SET CONSOLE OFF'
? '    STORE "" TO inertemp'
? '    DO WHILE .NOT. inertemp$"YyNn"'
? '        WAIT TO inertemp'
? '    ENDDO'
? '    SET CONSOLE ON'
? '    IF UPPER(inertemp) = "Y"'
? '        ?? "Yes"'
? '        te = INKEY(.25)'
? '        RETURN(.T.)'
? '    ENDIF'
? '    ?? "No "'
? '    te = INKEY(.25)'
? '    RETURN(.F.)'
?
DO Funchead WITH "Prntpage"
?
? '    PARAMETERS normal'
?
? '        IF normal'
? '            @ 63,35 SAY "Page"'
? '            @ PROW(),PCOL()+2 SAY page PICT "@B"'
? '            @ 64,0 SAY ""'
? '        ELSE'
? '            @ 63,65 SAY "Page"'
? '            @ PROW(),PCOL()+2 SAY page PICT "@B"'
? '            @ 64,0 SAY ""'
? '        ENDIF'
? '        RETURN(page)'
?
DO Funchead WITH "Signchng"
?
? '    PARAMETERS amount'
```

```
?
? '       IF amount >= 0'
? '           RETURN (STR(amount))'
? '       ENDIF'
? '       amount = amount * -1'
? '       newfig = "(" + TRIM(LTRIM(STR(amount,15,2))) + ")"'
? '       newfig = SPACE(16 - LEN(newfig)) + newfig'
? '       RETURN(newfig)'
?
DO Funchead WITH "Checking"
?
? '    IF EOF() .OR. BOF()'
? '       @ 22,8 SAY "Can not continue past end.  Press any key to return to
          the menu."'
? '       te = INKEY(0)'
? '       RETURN(.T.)'
? '    ENDIF'
? '    RETURN(.F.)'
?
DO Funchead WITH "Genpass"
?
? '    PARAMETERS in_string'
?
? '       count = LEN(TRIM(in_string))'
? '       final = 0'
? '       FOR beginning = 1 to (count + 1)'
? '           final = final + ASC(SUBSTR(in_string,beginning,1)) * beginning'
? '       NEXT'
? '       RETURN(final)'
?
DO Funchead WITH "Chkpass"
?
? '    PARAMETERS row, col'
?
? '       IF scrtimes = 0'
? '           RETURN(.T.)'
? '       ENDIF'
? '       IF scrshow'
? '           SET COLOR TO 7/0, 0/7'
? '       ELSE'
? '           SET COLOR TO 7+/0, 0+/0'
? '       ENDIF'
? '       FOR x = 1 to scrtimes'
? '           in_pass = SPACE(15)'
? '           @ row-3,col-5,row+3,col+34 BOX scrframe'
? '           @ row,col SAY "Password --> " GET in_pass PICT "@X"'
? '           READ'
? '           IF LEN(TRIM(in_pass)) <> 0'
? '               temp_count = GENPASS(in_pass)'
? '               IF temp_count = scrpass'
? '                   x = 1000'
? '               ENDIF'
? '           ENDIF'
```

```
? '      NEXT'
? '      IF scrcolor'
? '         SET COLOR TO 7+/0, 0/7'
? '      ELSE'
? '         SET COLOR TO 7/0, 0/7'
? '      ENDIF'
? '      IF scrinten'
? '         SET INTEN ON'
? '      ELSE'
? '         SET INTEN OFF'
? '      ENDIF'
? '      RETURN(x > 101)'
?
DO Funchead WITH "Roundit"
?
? '   PARAMETERS in_amount'
?
? '      in_amount = INT(in_amount * 100 + .5) / 100.00'
? '      RETURN(in_amount)'
?
DO Funchead WITH "Printdate"
?
? '   PARAMETERS in_date, whichone'
?
? '   DO CASE'
? '   CASE whichone = 1'
? '      out_str = CMONTH(in_date) + " " + DAYWORD(in_date) + ", " +
          DLTRIM(STR(YEAR(in_date)))'
? '   CASE whichone = 2'
? '      out_str = CDOW(in_date) + ", the " + DAYWORD(in_date) + " of ";
               + CMONTH(in_date) + ", " + dltrim(STR(YEAR(in_date)))'
? '   CASE whichone = 3'
? '      out_str = CDOW(in_date) + ", the " + DAYWORD(in_date) + " of " +
          CMONTH(in_date)'
? '   CASE whichone = 4'
? '      out_str = "The " + DAYWORD(in_date) + " of " + CMONTH(in_date) +
          ", " + DLTRIM(STR(YEAR(in_date)))'
? '   CASE whichone = 5'
? '      out_str = CDOW(in_date) + ", " + CMON(in_date) + " "'
? '      out_str = out_str + STR(DAY(in_date),2) + ", " +
          STR(YEAR(in_date),4)'
? '   OTHERWISE'
? '      out_str = DTOC(in_date)'
? '   ENDCASE'
? '   RETURN(out_str)'
?
```

```
DO Prochead WITH "Typeahead"
?
? '   IF !scrtype'
? '      CALL _cclr'
? '   ENDIF'
?
DO Prochead WITH "Blink"
?
? '   PARAMETERS temp_row, temp_col'
?
? '      IF scrcolor'
? '         SET COLOR TO W*+'
? '      ELSE'
? '         SET COLOR TO W*'
? '      ENDIF'
? '      @ temp_row, temp_col SAY "Deleted Record"'
? '      IF scrcolor'
? '         SET COLOR TO W+'
? '      ELSE'
? '         SET COLOR TO W'
? '      ENDIF'
?
@ 4,COL() SAY REPLICATE(".",64-COL()) + "FINISHED!"
SET ALTERNATE OFF
DO Sixth


********************

PROCEDURE Sixth

   SET ALTERNATE ON
   @ 5,5 SAY "Writing SETUP to alternate file"
   ?
   DO Prochead WITH "Setup"
   ?
   ? '   SET FUNCTION  2 TO CHR(22)'
   ? '   SET FUNCTION  3 TO CHR(1)'
   ? '   SET FUNCTION  4 TO CHR(6)'
   ? '   SET FUNCTION  5 TO CHR(3)'
   ? '   SET FUNCTION  6 TO CHR(5)'
   ? '   SET FUNCTION  8 TO CHR(23)'
   ? '   SET FUNCTION  7 TO CHR(20)'
   ? '   SET FUNCTION  9 TO CHR(25)'
   ? '   SET FUNCTION 10 TO CHR(21)'
   ? '   IF scrinten'
   ? '      SET INTENS on'
   ? '   ELSE'
   ? '      SET INTENS off'
   ? '   ENDIF'
   ? '   IF scrdelim'
   ? '      SET DELIM TO "&scrdelimto"'
   ? '      SET DELIM on'
```

```
? '   ELSE'
? '       SET DELIM off'
? '   ENDIF'
? '   IF scrconfirm'
? '       SET CONFIRM on'
? '   ELSE'
? '       SET CONFIRM off'
? '   ENDIF'
? '   IF scrbell'
? '       SET BELL on'
? '   ELSE'
? '       SET BELL off'
? '   ENDIF'
? '   IF scrcolor'
? '       SET COLOR TO 7+'
? '   ELSE'
? '       SET COLOR TO 7'
? '   ENDIF'
SET ALTERNATE OFF
@ 5,COL() SAY REPLICATE(".",64-COL()) + "FINISHED!"
DO Seventh


********************

PROCEDURE Seventh

    @ 6,5 SAY "Writing REDRAW to alternate file"
    SET ALTERNATE ON
    ?
    DO Prochead WITH "Redraw"
    ?
    ? '   PARAMETERS center'
    ?
    ? '       @ 1,0 say scrleft_1'
    ? '       @ 2,0 say scrleft_2'
    IF LEN(TRIM(system1)) > 2
        ? '       RESTORE FROM &system1. ADDITIVE'
        ? '       @ 1,80-LEN(' + pref + 'right_1) SAY ' + pref + 'right_1'
        ? '       @ 2,80-LEN(' + pref + 'right_2) SAY ' + pref + 'right_2'
    ELSE
        ? '       @ 1,80-LEN("Generic Application") SAY "Generic Application"'
        ? '       @ 2,80-LEN("Version 1.00") SAY "Version 1.00"'
        ? '       @ 4,40-LEN(center)/2 SAY center'
    ENDIF
    SET ALTERNATE OFF
    @ 6,COL() SAY REPLICATE(".",64-COL()) + "FINISHED!"
    DO Eight


********************

PROCEDURE Eight

    @ 7,5 SAY "Writing WHICHWAY to alternate file"
```

```
      SET ALTERNATE ON
      ?
      DO Prochead WITH "Whichway"
      ?
      ? '    PARAMETERS file, way, d, c'
      ?
      ? '       way = 1'
      ? '       a d,c,d + 5, c + 40 BOX scrframe'
      ? '       a d + 1, c + 10 PROMPT " 1> Print to Screen "'
      ? '       a d + 2, c + 10 PROMPT " 2> Print to Printer "'
      ? '       a d + 3, c + 10 PROMPT " 3> Print to File "'
      ? '       a d + 4, c + 10 SAY    "   ESC to RETURN"'
      ? '       MENU TO way'
      ? '       IF way = 3'
      ? '          FOR fortemp = d + 1 TO d + 4'
      ? '             a fortemp, c + 5 SAY SPACE(30)'
      ? '          NEXT'
      ? '          a d + 1, c + 10 SAY "Enter File Name: "'
      ? '          a d + 3, c + 10 SAY "-> " GET file PICT "aX"'
      ? '          READ'
      ? '          IF LEN(TRIM(file)) = 0'
      ? '             way = 0'
      ? '          ENDIF'
      ? '          IF AT(".",file) = 0'
      ? '             file = TRIM(SUBSTR(file,1,8)) + ".TXT"'
      ? '          ENDIF'
      ? '       ENDIF'
      a 7,COL() SAY REPLICATE(".",64-COL()) + "FINISHED!"
      SET ALTERNATE OFF
      DO Nine


  ********************


  PROCEDURE Nine

      SET SCOREBOARD OFF
      SAVE SCREEN
      CLEAR
      DECLARE database[15]
      FOR x = 1 TO 15
         temp = LTRIM(STR(x))
         DECLARE name&temp[99]
         DECLARE type&temp[99]
         DECLARE len&temp[99]
         DECLARE dec&temp[99]
         DECLARE indx&temp[7]
      NEXT
      a 0,0,23,79 BOX SUBSTR(scrframe,1,8)
      a 0,30 SAY " Create Databases "
      FOR x = 1 TO 15
         STORE SPACE(12) TO database[x]
         a 2,3 SAY "Enter Database Name: " GET database[x] PICT "a!"
         READ
```

```
IF LEN(TRIM(database[x])) <> 0
   temp = LTRIM(STR(x))
   trow = 8
   tcol = 0
   FOR y = 1 TO 99
      STORE SPACE(10) TO name&temp[y]
      STORE SPACE(1) TO type&temp[y]
      STORE 0 TO len&temp[y], dec&temp[y]
      @ 3,3 SAY "   Enter Field Name: " GET name&temp[y] PICT "@!"
      @ 4,3 SAY "                Type: " GET type&temp[y] PICT "!"
      VALID(type&temp[y]$"NCLDM ")
      @ 5,3 SAY "              Length: " GET len&temp[y] PICT "####" RANGE
      0, 3000
      @ 6,3 SAY "            Decimals: " GET dec&temp[y] PICT "##" RANGE
      0,15
      READ
      IF LEN(TRIM(name&temp[y])) = 0
         y = 100
      ELSE
         DO CASE
         CASE type&temp[y] = "D"
            len&temp[y] = 8
            dec&temp[y] = 0
         CASE type&temp[y] = "L"
            len&temp[y] = 1
            dec&temp[y] = 0
         CASE type&temp[y] = "M"
            len&temp[y] = 10
            dec&temp[y] = 0
         CASE type&temp[y] = "N"
            IF len&temp[y] > 15
               len&temp[y] = 15
            ENDIF
         OTHERWISE
            dec&temp[y] = 0
         ENDCASE
         IF trow > 22
            trow = 8
            FOR steve = 8 TO 22
               @ steve,3 SAY SPACE(47)
            NEXT
         ENDIF
         @ trow,5 SAY name&temp[y]
         @ trow,COL() + 2 SAY type&temp[y]
         @ trow,COL() + 2 SAY len&temp[y]
         @ trow,COL() + 2 SAY dec&temp[y]
         trow = trow + 1
      ENDIF
   NEXT
   FOR steve = 1 TO 22
      @ steve, 3 SAY SPACE(47)
   NEXT
   @ x, 52 SAY LTRIM(STR(x)) + "-> "
```

```
            @ x, COL() SAY database[x]
        ELSE
            x = 17
        ENDIF
    NEXT
    DO Ten


********************

PROCEDURE Ten

    RESTORE SCREEN
    @ 8,5 SAY "Writing " + pref + "init to alternate file"
    SET ALTERNATE ON
    DO Prochead WITH pref + "init"
    ?
    ? '   DO ' + pref + 'inthd'
    FOR x = 1 TO 15
       IF LEN(TRIM(database[x])) <> 0
          tempstr = pref + "init" + LTRIM(STR(x))
          ? '   DO ' + tempstr
       ELSE
          x = 16
       ENDIF
    NEXT
    ?
    ? '   @ 12, 6 SAY "All Files/Indexes have been properly created.   Any Key
          to Continue..."'
    ? '   IF 0 = INKEY(0)'
    ? '   ENDIF'
    ? '   CLOSE DATABASES'
    ? '   @ 12, 2 SAY SPACE(70)'
    SET ALTERNATE OFF
    SET COLOR TO W*+
    SAVE SCREEN
    @ 0,0,20,79 BOX SUBSTR(scrframe,1,8)
    @ 19,15 SAY "Now writing memory file for Report Generator..."
    FOR x = 1 TO 15
       @ 21,00 CLEAR
       writeout = IF(LEN(LTRIM(STR(x))) = 1, "0" + LTRIM(STR(x)),
             LTRIM(STR(x)))
       name = "DB" + writeout
       &name = database[x]
       temp = LTRIM(STR(x))
       @ 21,24 SAY "Now working on data fie ..... " + temp
       FOR y = 1 TO 99
          newout = IF(LEN(LTRIM(STR(y))) = 1, "0" + LTRIM(STR(y)),
             LTRIM(STR(y)))
          fame = "FD" + newout
          tame = "TY" + newout
          lame = "LE" + newout
          dame = "DE" + newout
          &fame = name&temp[y]
```

```
        &tame = type&temp[y]
        &lame = len&temp[y]
        &dame = dec&temp[y]
        a 22,28 SAY "Now working on files .... " + newout
        IF EMPTY(name&temp[y+1])
             y = 100
        ENDIF
      NEXT
      SAVE ALL LIKE FD?? TO Name&temp
      SAVE ALL LIKE TY?? TO Type&temp
      SAVE ALL LIKE LE?? TO Leng&temp
      SAVE ALL LIKE DE?? TO Deci&temp
      RELEASE ALL LIKE FD??
      RELEASE ALL LIKE TY??
      RELEASE ALL LIKE LE??
    . RELEASE ALL LIKE DE??
      IF EMPTY(database[x+1])
         x = 16
      ENDIF
    NEXT
    SAVE ALL LIKE DB?? TO Datafile
    a 20,00 CLEAR
    SET COLOR TO 7+
    RESTORE SCREEN
    a 8,COL() SAY REPLICATE(".",64-COL()) + "FINISHED!"
    DO Eleven
    * End of Gencode1
```

Now create a second CLiP file, GEN2.CLP, which will contain the following one line:

```
    Gencode2
```

```
*********************
* Name        GENCODE2.prg
* Date        August 20, 1986
* Notice      Copyright 1986, Stephen J. Straley
* Note        The following source is the other half of the code
*             that creates the basic front-end of an application.
*             The code generated can then be modified to the
*             needs of the client/user.
*
*             The following is a listing of the procedures and their
*             purpose as they relate to the code they generate.
*
*             Eleven:   This writes the code for the indexing (if
*                       any) routines and their proper prompts.
*                       It also maintains the indexing/file values
*                       for the code that writes the RESORT procedure.
*             Twelve:   Writes the Initial Message and Header for the
*                       initialization procedure.
```

```
*              Thirteen:   This writes the code for user-created On-
*                          Line HELP.   This also can be used by the
*                          developer after the application has been
*                          designed to write the Help he will provide
*                          with the application.
*              Fourteen:   This code writes the REINITIALIZATION procedure.
*              Fifteen:    This section writes the code to allow the user
*                          of the application to change the sub-directory
*                          he or she is currently working in.   This option
*                          allows an application to be used for multiple-
*                          companies.
*              Sixteen:    This writes the code for a Password initialization
*                          code.
*            Seventeen:    This procedure write the procedures that
*                          allow the developer to have his application
*                          change the computer's internal system date.
*             Eighteen:    Writes the procedure which allows a user to UNMARK
*                          the records tagged for deletion.  The file names
*                          used are those previously entered when creating
*                          the system initially.
*             Nineteen:    Similar to the procedure for UNMARK, REMOVE actually
*                          removes those records the user has tagged to be
*                          deleted.  Again, the file names are automatically
*                          used from a previous section.
*               Twenty:    This routine writes the RESORT procedure which
*                          will rebuild the indexes and prompt the user on
*                          the screen as the process is underway.
*
********************

PROCEDURE Eleven

   parc_strng = ""
   a 9,5 SAY "Writing Initializing Procedures to alternate"
   screencnt = 6
   SET ALTERNATE ON
   DECLARE indexkey[105], indexmes[105], indexfil[105]
   FOR x = 1 TO 15
      temp = LTRIM(STR(x))
      IF !EMPTY(database[x])
         tempstr = pref + "init" + temp
         DO Prochead WITH tempstr
         ?
         ? '   SELECT 9'
         IF screencnt >= 22
            screencnt = 5
            ? '   5,0,23,79 BOX scrframe'
         ENDIF
         ? '   a ' + LTRIM(STR(screencnt)) + ', 5 SAY "Initializing ' +
           TRIM(database[x]) + ' File' + '"'
         ? '   CREATE Template'
         ? '   USE Template'
         FOR y = 1 TO 99
```

```
      IF !EMPTY(name&temp[y])
         ? '    APPEND BLANK'
         ? '    REPLACE field_name WITH "' + TRIM(name&temp[y]) + '", '
         ?? ' field_type WITH "' + type&temp[y] + '", '
         ?? ' field_len WITH ' + LTRIM(STR(len&temp[y])) + ', '
         ?? ' field_dec WITH ' + LTRIM(STR(dec&temp[y]))
      ELSE
         y = 100
      ENDIF
NEXT
? '   USE'
? '   CREATE ' + CHR(38) + 'scrdata.' + TRIM(database[x]) + ' FROM
   Template'
? '   USE ' + CHR(38) + 'scrdata.' + TRIM(database[x])
? '   ERASE Template'
? '   @ ' + LTRIM(STR(screencnt)) + ', 5 SAY SPACE(70)'
FOR z = 1 TO 7
   qaz = LTRIM(STR(x))
   STORE SPACE(20) TO indexmes[MATRIX1(x,z)]
   @ 15,2 SAY "Database: " + TRIM(database[x]) + " / " +
   LTRIM(STR(z)) + " Index-> "
   @ 17,COL()-15 SAY "Enter Prompt Message: " GET index-
   mes[MATRIX(x,z)]
   READ
   IF !EMPTY(indexmes[MATRIX1(x,z)])
      STORE SPACE(45) TO key
      @ 19,5 SAY "Enter Index Expression: " GET key
VALID(!EMPTY(key))
      READ
      indexkey[MATRIX1(x,z)] = key
      screencnt = screencnt + 1
      ? '    @ ' + LTRIM(STR(screencnt)) + ', 5 SAY "Creating ';
               + TRIM(indexkey[MATRIX1(x,z)]) + ' Index"'
      IF "."$database[x]
         posit = AT(".",database[x]) - 1
         tempname = IF(posit < 6, SUBSTR(database[x],1,posit), SUB-
STR(database[x],1,6))
      ELSE
         tempname = TRIM(database[x])
      ENDIF


      DO CASE
      CASE AT(".",database[x]) = 0
         tempextn = ".NTX"
      CASE ".DBF"$database[x]
         tempextn = ".NTX"
      OTHERWISE
         tempextn = ".DAT"
      ENDCASE
      indexfil[MATRIX1(x,z)] = tempname + "_" + LTRIM(STR(z)) +
tempextn
      ? '    temp = scrdata' + ' ' + '"' + indexfil[MATRIX1(x,z)] + '"'
```

```
                       ? '    INDEX ON ' + TRIM(key) + ' TO ' + CHR(38) + 'temp'
                       ? '    @ ' + LTRIM(STR(screencnt) ) + ', 2 SAY SPACE(70)'
                 ELSE
                    z = 8
                 ENDIF
                 @ 15,2 SAY SPACE(75)
                 @ 17,2 SAY SPACE(75)
                 @ 19,2 SAY SPACE(75)
           NEXT
           screencnt = screencnt + 1
        ELSE
           x = 16
        ENDIF
     NEXT
     SET ALTERNATE OFF
     @ 9,5 SAY "Writing Indexing Files" + REPLICATE(".",37) + "FINISHED!"
     DO Twelve


********************

PROCEDURE Twelve

     SET ALTERNATE ON
     @ 10,5 SAY "Writing Inthead Procedure to alternate file"
     ?
     DO Prochead WITH pref + "inthd"
     ?
     ? '    RESTORE FROM Screen.sys ADDITIVE'
     ? '    DO Setup'
     ? '    CLEAR'
     ? '    DO Redraw WITH "Initializing Databases"'
     ? '    @ 5,0,23,79 BOX SUBSTR(scrframe,1,8)'
     ?
     SET ALTERNATE OFF
     @ 10,COL() SAY REPLICATE(".",64-COL()) + "FINISHED!"
     DO Thirteen


********************

PROCEDURE Thirteen

     SET ALTERNATE ON
     @ 11,5 SAY "Writing HELP to alternate file"
     DO Prochead WITH "Help"
     ?
     ? '    PARAMETERS p,l,v'
     ?
     ? '    SAVE SCREEN'
     ? '    SET SCOREBOARD OFF'
     ? '    p = p + SPACE(10 - LEN(p))'
     ? '    v = v + SPACE(10 - LEN(v))'
     ? '    IF .NOT. FILE("HELP.DBF")'
     ? '       @ 00,10,03,70 BOX scrframe'
```

```
? '        @ 01,11 SAY "There is no HELP file available.    Would you like a
          help "'
? '        @ 02,27 SAY "file to be generated?"'
? '        IF .NOT. VERIFY()'
? '           RESTORE SCREEN'
? '           SET KEY 28 TO Help'
? '           RETURN'
? '         ENDIF'
? '         goback = SELECT()'
? '         DO Dohelp'
? '         tempgo = STR(goback)'
? '         SELECT &tempgo'
? '      ENDIF'
? '      goback = SELECT()'
? '      SELECT 9'
? '      USE Help INDEX Help'
? '      SET FILTER TO search_p = p .AND. search_v = v'
? '      LOCATE FOR search_l = l'
? '      IF FOUND()'
frame = CHR(201) + CHR(205) + CHR(187) + CHR(186) + CHR(188) + ;
        CHR(205) + CHR(200) + CHR(186) + CHR(32)
? '        @ top,left,bottom,right BOX "&frame."'
? '        IF "" = MEMOEDIT(helpscr,top+1,left+1,bottom-1,right-1,.F.)'
? '        ENDIF'
? '        @ bottom-1,left+1 SAY "Any Key to Continue..."'
? '      ELSE'
? '        @ 00,10,03,70 BOX scrframe'
? '        @ 01,11 SAY "There is no HELP for this section.  Would you like
          to make"'
? '        @ 02,28 SAY "a HELP screen for this? "'
? '        IF .NOT. VERIFY()'
? '           RESTORE SCREEN'
? '           SET KEY 28 TO Help'
? '           RETURN'
? '        ENDIF'
? '        APPEND BLANK'
? '        REPLACE search_p WITH p, search_l WITH l, search_v WITH v'
? '        STORE SPACE(4000) TO in_help'
? '        STORE 0 TO temp_top, temp_left, temp_bot, temp_right'
? '        DO WHILE .T.'
? '           @ 00,10,03,70 BOX scrframe'
? '           @ 01,20 SAY "Position cursor with arrow for TOP, LEFT
          corner."'
? '           cursor = 0'
? '           @ 12,40 SAY ""'
? '           DO WHILE.T.'
? '              cursor = INKEY(0)'
? '              DO CASE'
? '              CASE cursor = 5'
? '                 @ ROW() - 1, COL() SAY ""'
? '              CASE cursor = 4'
? '                 @ ROW(), COL() + 1 SAY ""'
```

```
? '              CASE cursor = 19'
? '                 @ ROW(),COL() - 1 SAY ""'
? '              CASE cursor = 24'
? '                 @ ROW() + 1,COL() SAY ""'
? '              CASE cursor = 13 .OR. cursor = 27'
? '                 EXIT'
? '              ENDCASE'
? '           ENDDO'
? '           STORE ROW() TO temp_top'
? '           STORE COL() - 1 TO temp_left'
? '           @ 00,10,03,70 BOX scrframe'
? '           @ 01,20 SAY "Position cursor with arrow for BOTTOM, RIGHT
          corner."'
? '           cursor = 0'
? '           @ 12,40 SAY ""'
? '           DO WHILE.T.'
? '              cursor = INKEY(0)'
? '              DO CASE'
? '              CASE cursor = 5'
? '                 @ ROW() - 1, COL() SAY ""'
? '              CASE cursor = 4'
? '                 @ ROW(), COL() + 1 SAY ""'
? '              CASE cursor = 19'
? '                 @ ROW(),COL() - 1 SAY ""'
? '              CASE cursor = 24'
? '                 @ ROW() + 1,COL() SAY ""'
? '              CASE cursor = 13 .OR. cursor = 27'
? '                 EXIT'
? '              ENDCASE'
? '           ENDDO'
? '           STORE ROW() TO temp_bot'
? '           STORE COL() TO temp_right'
? '           CALL _scrsave WITH in_help'
? '           DO Temphelp'
? '           @ 00,10,03,70 BOX scrframe'
? '           @ 02,25 SAY "Is this what you wanted?  "'
? '           IF .NOT. VERIFY()'
? '              CALL _scrrest WITH in_help'
? '              LOOP'
? '           ENDIF'
? '           REPLACE top WITH temp_top, bottom WITH temp_bot, left WITH
          temp_left, right WITH temp_right'
? '           EXIT'
? '        ENDDO'
? '        DO WHILE .T.'
? '           @ top,left,bottom,right BOX "&frame."'
? '           REPLACE helpscr WITH MEMOEDIT(helpscr,top+1,left+1,bottom-
          1,right-1,.T.)'
? '           @ top,left,bottom,right BOX "&frame."'
? '           IF "" = MEMOEDIT(helpscr,top+1,left+1,bottom-1,right-1,.F.)'
? '           ENDIF'
? '           @ bottom-1,left+1 SAY "IS THIS CORRECT?   "'
```

```
? '           IF .NOT. VERIFY()'
? '                LOOP'
? '            ENDIF'
? '            EXIT'
? '         ENDDO'
? '         @ bottom-1,left+1 SAY "Press Any key to Continue...."'
? '      ENDIF'
? '      qw = INKEY(0)'
? '      RESTORE SCREEN'
? '      SET KEY 28 TO Help'
? '      tempgo = STR(goback)'
? '      SELECT &tempgo'
? '      RETURN'
?
? '********************'
?
? 'PROCEDURE Dohelp'
?
? '      SELECT 9'
? '      CREATE Temp'
? '      USE Temp'
? '      APPEND BLANK'
? '      REPLACE field_name WITH "SEARCH_P", field_type WITH "C", field_len
           WITH 10'
? '      APPEND BLANK'
? '      REPLACE field_name WITH "SEARCH_V", field_type WITH "C", field_len
           WITH 10'
? '      APPEND BLANK'
? '      REPLACE field_name WITH "SEARCH_L", field_type WITH "N", field_len
           WITH 4'
? '      APPEND BLANK'
? '      REPLACE field_name WITH "TOP", field_type WITH "N", field_len WITH 2'
? '      APPEND BLANK'
? '      REPLACE field_name WITH "LEFT", field_type WITH "N", field_len WITH
           2'
? '      APPEND BLANK'
? '      REPLACE field_name WITH "BOTTOM", field_type WITH "N", field_len WITH
           2'
? '      APPEND BLANK'
? '      REPLACE field_name WITH "RIGHT", field_type WITH "N", field_len WITH
           2'
? '      APPEND BLANK'
? '      REPLACE field_name WITH "HELPSCR", field_type WITH "M", field_len
           WITH 10'
? '      USE'
? '      CREATE Help FROM Temp'
? '      ERASE Temp'
? '      USE Help'
? '      INDEX ON search_p + search_v TO Help'
?
? '********************'
?
```

```
? 'PROCEDURE Temphelp'
?
? '   IF scrcolor'
? '      SET COLOR TO W*+'
? '   ELSE'
? '      SET COLOR TO W+'
? '   ENDIF'
? '   @ temp_top, temp_left, temp_bot, temp_right BOX SUBSTR(scrframe,1,8)'
? '   IF scrcolor'
? '      SET COLOR TO 7+'
? '   ELSE'
? '      SET COLOR TO 7'
? '   ENDIF'
SET ALTERNATE OFF
@ 11,COL() SAY REPLICATE(".",64-COL()) + "FINISHED!"
DO Fourteen


********************

PROCEDURE Fourteen

SET ALTERNATE ON
@ 13,5 SAY "Writing Re-initializing Procedure to alternate file"
DO Prochead WITH "Reinitx"
?
? '   @ 19,25,23,65 BOX scrframe'
? '   tempscr = SPACE(4000)'
? '   CALL _scrsave WITH tempscr'
? '   @ 20,29 SAY " Data Files are present.  If you"'
? '   @ 21,29 SAY "continue, all data will be lost."'
? '   @ 22,29 SAY "Do you want to continue? "'
? '   IF .NOT. VERIFY()'
? '      RETURN'
? '   ENDIF'
? '   CALL _scrrest WITH tempscr'
? '   @ 20,29 SAY "Would you like to re-Create"'
? '   @ 21,29 SAY "ALL of the databases?"'
? '   IF VERIFY()'
? '      DO ' + pref + 'init'
? '      RETURN'
? '   ENDIF'
scan = 1
DO WHILE LEN(TRIM(database[scan])) <> 0
    ? '   CALL _scrrest WITH tempscr'
    ? '   @ 20,28 SAY "Do you wish to re-create the"'
    ? '   @ 21,40-LEN("' + TRIM(database[scan]) + '")/2 SAY "' +
      TRIM(database[scan]) + CHR(34)
    ? '   @ 22,28 SAY "Database? (Yes / No)"'
    ? '   IF VERIFY()'
    ? '      DO ' + pref + 'inthd'
    ? '      DO ' + pref + 'init' + LTRIM(STR(scan))
    ? '   ENDIF'
    scan = scan + 1
```

```
        ENDDO
        ? '    CLOSE DATABASES'
        SET ALTERNATE OFF
        a 13,COL() SAY REPLICATE(".",64-COL()) + "FINISHED!"
        DO Fifteen


********************

PROCEDURE Fifteen

        SET ALTERNATE ON
        a 14,5 SAY "Writing Change Default Procedure to alternate file"
        DO Prochead WITH "Default"
        ? '    a 19,25,23,65 BOX scrframe'
        ? '    whichone = 1'
        ? '    a 20,32 PROMPT " 1>  Change Directory "'
        ? '    a 21,32 PROMPT " 2>  Change System Defaults "'
        ? '    a 22,32 SAY     "    ESC to RETURN TO MENU"'
        ? '    MENU TO whichone'
        ? '    DO CASE'
        ? '    CASE whichone = 0'
        ? '        RETURN'
        ? '    CASE whichone = 2'
        ? '        DO Scrinit'
        ? '    OTHERWISE'
        ? '        a 20,26,22,64 BOX SPACE(9)'
        ? '        indir = SPACE(30)'
        ? '        a 20,28 SAY "Enter in new PATH..."'
        ? '        a 21,28 SAY "->" GET indir PICT "XXXXXXXXXXXXXXXXXXXXXXXXXXXXXX"'
        ? '        READ'
        ? '        DO WHILE .NOT. FILE(scrprog + "\COMMAND.COM")'
        ? '            a 20,26,22,64 BOX SPACE(9)'
        ? '            a 20,28 SAY "Please insert DOS disk in drive :"  + SUB-
        STR(scrprog,1,1)'
        ? '            a 21,28 SAY "Any key or Q to Quit ......."'
        ? '            IF QWAIT()'
        ? '                RETURN'
        ? '            ENDIF'
        ? '        ENDDO'
        ? '        indir = "CD " + TRIM(indir)'
        ? '        RUN &indir'
        ? '        DO Beginit'
        ? '        RETURN'
        ? '    ENDCASE'
        SET ALTERNATE OFF
        a 14,COL() SAY REPLICATE(".",64-COL()) + "FINISHED!"
        DO Sixteen


********************

PROCEDURE Sixteen

        SET ALTERNATE ON
```

```
@ 15,5 SAY "Writing Password Procedure to alternate file"
DO Prochead WITH "Password"
? '    @ 19,25,23,65 BOX scrframe'
? '    temp = SPACE(15)'
? '    @ 20,28 SAY "Leave Blank to keep old Password"'
? '    @ 21,28 SAY "Enter New Password: " GET temp PICT "XXXXXXXXXXXXXXX"'
? '    READ'
? '    IF LEN(TRIM(tem)) <> 0'
? '       scrpass = GENPASS(temp)'
? '    ENDIF'
? '    @ 20,26,22,64 BOX SPACE(9)'
? '    @ 21,27 SAY "Enter Times for Password: " GET scrtimes PICT "##"'
? '    READ'
? '    SET DEFAULT TO ' + CHR(38) + 'scrprog'
? '    SAVE ALL LIKE scr* TO Screen.sys'
? '    SET DEFAULT TO ' + CHR(38) + 'scrdata'
SET ALTERNATE OFF
@ 15,COL() SAY REPLICATE(".",64-COL()) + "FINISHED!"
DO Seventeen


********************

PROCEDURE Seventeen

   SET ALTERNATE ON
   @ 16,5 SAY "Writing Change System Date Procedure to alternate file"
   DO Prochead WITH "Olddate"
   ? '    @ 19,25,23,65 BOX scrframe'
   ? '    @ 20,29 SAY "Changing System Date"'
   ? '    STORE "Today'+ CHR(39) + 's Date is " + CDOW(DATE()) + ", " +
           CMON(DATE()) to prompt'
   ? '    STORE prompt + " " + STR(DAY(DATE()),2) + ", " + STR(YEAR(DATE()),4)
           to prompt'
   ? '    @ 21,40-LEN(prompt)/2 SAY prompt'
   ? '    mdate = DATE()'
   ? '    @ 22,40-LEN("Enter in Date:      ")/2 SAY "Enter in Date:  " GET
           mdate'
   ? '    READ'
   ? '    IF FILE(scrprog + "COMMAND.COM")'
   ? '       mdate = DTOC(mdate)'
   ? '       RUN DATE ' + CHR(38) + 'mdate'
   ? '    ENDIF'
   SET ALTERNATE OFF
   @ 16,COL() SAY REPLICATE(".",64-COL()) + "FINISHED!"
   DO Eighteen


********************

PROCEDURE Eighteen

   SET ALTERNATE ON
   @ 17,5 SAY "Writing Unmark Data Procedure to alternate file"
   DO Prochead WITH "Unmark"
```

```
? '    @ 19,25,23,65 BOX scrframe'
? '    tempscr = SPACE(4000)'
? '    CALL _scrsave WITH tempscr'
? '    updated = .F.'
scan = 1
DO WHILE LEN(TRIM(database[scan])) <> 0
    ? '    CALL _scrrest WITH tempscr'
    ? '    @ 20,27 SAY "Do you wish to UNMARK data in the "'
    ? '    @ 21,27 SAY "' + TRIM(database[scan]) + ' file? "'
    ? '    IF VERIFY()'
    ? '       SELECT 1'
    ? '       USE ' + CHR(38) + 'scrdata.' + TRIM(database[scan])
    ? '       RECALL ALL'
    ? '       updated = .T.'
    ? '    ENDIF'
    scan = scan + 1
ENDDO
? '  CALL _scrrest WITH tempscr'
? '  IF updated'
? '     @ 21,27 SAY "Process Complete.  Any Key to Resort"'
? '     IF INKEY(0) = 0'
? '     ENDIF'
? '     DO Resort'
? '  ELSE'
? '     @ 21,27 SAY "Process Complete.  Any Key to Continue"'
? '     IF INKEY(0) = 0'
? '     ENDIF'
? '  ENDIF'
SET ALTERNATE OFF
@ 17,COL() SAY REPLICATE(".",64-COL()) + "FINISHED!"
DO Nineteen


********************

PROCEDURE Nineteen

    SET ALTERNATE ON
    @ 18,5 SAY "Writing Remove Marked Data Procedure to file"
    DO Prochead WITH "Removeit"
    ? '    @ 19,25,23,65 BOX scrframe'
    ? '    tempscr = SPACE(4000)'
    ? '    CALL _scrsave WITH tempscr'
    ? '    updated = .F.'
    scan = 1
    DO WHILE LEN(TRIM(database[scan])) <> 0
        ? '    CALL _scrrest WITH tempscr'
        ? '    @ 20,27 SAY "Do you wish to REMOVE data in the "'
        ? '    @ 21,27 SAY "' + TRIM(database[scan]) + ' file? "'
        ? '    IF VERIFY()'
        ? '       SELECT 1'
        ? '       USE ' + CHR(38) + 'scrdata.' + TRIM(database[scan])
        ? '       PACK'
        ? '       updated = .T.'
```

```
    ? '   ENDIF'
    scan = scan + 1
ENDDO
? '  CALL _scrrest WITH tempscr'
? '  IF updated'
? '     @ 21,27 SAY "Process Complete.  Any Key to Resort"'
? '     IF INKEY(0) = 0'
? '     ENDIF'
? '     DO Resort'
? '  ELSE'
? '     @ 21,27 SAY "Process Complete.  Any Key to Continue"'
? '     IF INKEY(0) = 0'
? '     ENDIF'
? '  ENDIF'
SET ALTERNATE OFF
@ 18,COL() SAY REPLICATE(".",64-COL()) + "FINISHED!"
SAVE TO Prefix ALL LIKE pref
DO Twenty


********************

PROCEDURE Twenty

    SET ALTERNATE ON
    @ 19, 5 SAY "Writing Resort Procedure to File"
    DO Prochead WITH "Resort"
    ?
    ? 'SAVE SCREEN'
    ? 'DO Redraw WITH "Re-sorting Data Files"'
    ? '@ 5,0,23,79 BOX scrframe'
    ? 'SELECT 1'
    beg_row = 6
    scan = UNPARSE(parc_strng)
    DO WHILE !EMPTY(scan)

        ? 'USE ' + CHR(38) + 'scrdata.' + scan
        scan = UNPARSE(parc_strng)
        ? '@ &beg_row.,5 SAY "' + scan + '"'
        scan = UNPARSE(parc_strng)
        ? 'INDEX ON ' + scan + 'TO ' + CHR(38) + 'scrdata."'
        scan = UNPARSE(parc_strng)
        ?? scan + '"'
        ? '@ &beg_row.,5 SAY SPACE(70)'
        beg_row = beg_row + 1
        scan = UNPARSE(parc_strng)


    ENDDO
    ? '@ &beg_row,8 SAY "All Files have been RE-indexed.  Press Any Key to Con-
            tinue..."'
    ? 'IF 0 = INKEY(0)'
    ? 'ENDIF'
    ? 'RESTORE SCREEN'
```

```
   CLOSE ALTERNATE
   @ 19,5 SAY REPLICATE(".",69-COL()) + "FINISHED!"
   @ 23,20 SAY "Procedure All Finished.  Output to &file"
   QUIT

********************        && This is an internal procedure

PROCEDURE Prochead

   PARAMETERS a

   ?
   ? "**********************"
   ?
   ? "PROCEDURE " + a
   ?

********************        && This is an internal procedure

PROCEDURE Funchead

   PARAMETERS a

   ?
   ? "**********************"
   ?
   ? "FUNCTION " + a
   ?

**************************

FUNCTION VERIFY             && This is an internal function

   SET CONSOLE off
   WAIT TO inertemp
   SET CONSOLE on
   IF UPPER(inertemp) = "Y"
      ?? "Yes"
      te = INKEY(.25)
      RETURN(.T.)
   ENDIF
   ?? "No "
   te = INKEY(.25)
   RETURN(.F.)

********************

FUNCTION Unparse            && This is an internal function

   PARAMETERS string_in

   stop = AT("~",string_in)
   IF stop = 0
```

```
        RETURN("")
    ENDIF
    parc_strng = SUBSTR(parc_strng,stop+1)
    RETURN(SUBSTR(parc_strng,1,stop-1))


********************

FUNCTION Up_down              && This is an internal function

    PARAMETERS a

    front = UPPER(SUBSTR(a,1,1))
    back  = LOWER(SUBSTR(a,2))

    RETURN(front_back)

********************

FUNCTION Matrix1

    PARAMETERS left_one, right_one

    * This is for 15 databases and 7 indexes, so the array will be for
    * 105 elements.   The first 7 are for the first database, the second
    * 7 are for the second, and so on...

    * 1,1 = 1
    * 2,1 = 8
    * 3,1 = 15
    * 1,2 = 2
    * 2,2 = 9
    * 1,3 = 3
    * 2,3 = 10

    first_stop = (left_one * 7) - 7
    RETURN(first_stop + right_one)
* End of GENCODE2.prg
```

COMPILING AND LINKING THE GENCODE FILES

The batch file list below compiles and links the two files together. This assumes that the sub-directory which holds CLIPPER.LIB is \dbase\. This was linked with the MicroSoft linker (version 3.05) which is the reason for the extra code after the listing of the sub-directory.

```
        CLIPPER @gen1
        CLIPPER @gen2
        LINK gen1 gen2 ,GENER8,, \dbase\/se:1024,,;
```

This incorporates the correct syntax for linking with the MicroSoft linker, which is:

```
=>link <object file> [<object file>], [<EXE filename>], [<MAP filename>,
       <path\clipper library> [<all other libraries>]/se:1024,,;
```

In the above batch file, Gen1 and Gen2 are the object files created by Gen1.clp and Gen2.clp; Gener8.EXE will be the name of the executable file; the MAP file will assume a default name; and the CLIPPER.LIB is located in the \dbase\ sub-directory.

APPENDIX H

Menu Generator

This program can be used in a stand-alone mode, but was designed to be used with GENCODE to provide menus for the application generator. The structure and program flow can best be seen by studying the following flow chart:

PROGRAM FLOW / MAP

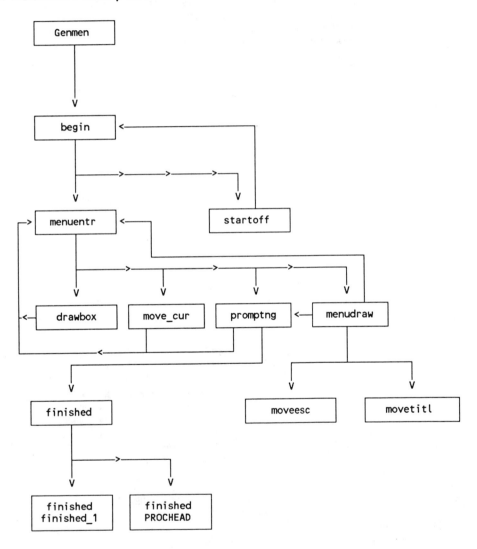

THE PROGRAM FILE

```
********************
* Name          GENMEN.prg
* Date          August 15, 1986
* Notice        Copyright 1986, Stephen J. Straley
* Note          This is a MENU GENerator.  It develops a file of procedures
*               which collectively can generate a menu with prompts and 4
*               sub-levels.  This writes information to a dBASE III file
*               which may be edited again by this program at a later date.
*               This program is the second half of the application generator;
*               however, it is also a stand-alone program.
********************

EXTERNAL Startoff, Begin, Promptng, Menuentr, Menudraw, Move_cur, Drawbox,;
Movetitl, Moveesc, Finished


CLEAR

TEXT



    Welcome to ......
ENDTEXT
IF INKEY(1) = 32
ENDIF
TEXT

        GGGGG      EEEEEEE NN      NN MM        MM EEEEEEE NN      NN
       GG   GG     EE      NNN     NN MMM     MMM EE       NNN     NN
       GG    GG    EE      NNNN    NN MMMM   MMMM EE       NNNN    NN
       GG          EEEEE   NN NN   NN MM MM MM MM EEEEE    NN NN   NN
       GG   GGGGG  EE      NN  NN NN MM  MMM  MM EE       NN  NN NN
       GG    GG    EE      NN   NNNN MM   M   MM EE       NN   NNNN
        GG   GG    EE      NN    NNN MM       MM EE       NN    NNN
        GGGGG      EEEEEEE NN      NN MM        MM EEEEEEE NN      NN
ENDTEXT
IF INKEY(1) = 32
ENDIF
frame  = CHR(201) + CHR(205) + CHR(187) + CHR(186) + CHR(188) + ;
         CHR(205) + CHR(200) + CHR(186) + CHR(32)
@ 2,0,22,79 BOX SUBSTR(frame,1,8)
@ 20,23 SAY "< Press Any Key to Continue >"
IF INKEY(0) = 0
ENDIF
@ 2,0,22,79 BOX frame
```

```
SET FUNCTION 9 TO CHR(25)
SET KEY -1 TO Doitagain
STORE SPACE(4000) TO xscreen
IF .NOT. FILE("Prefix.mem")
   @ 2,0,22,79 BOX frame
   @ 4,5 SAY "The Two Letter Prefix will be attached to the name of all"
   @ 5,5 SAY "procedures so created by this program.  For example,"
   @ 6,5 SAY "the file generated will be xxMENU, and all subsequent"
   @ 7,5 SAy "procedures will have the same root name with varied extensions."
   STORE "  " TO pref
   @ 12,15 SAY "Enter in Two Letter Prefix: " GET pref PICT "!X"
   READ
ELSE
   RESTORE FROM Prefix ADDITIVE
ENDIF
DO Begin

********************

FUNCTION Center

   PARAMETERS title, width

   midlen = INT(LEN(title) / 2)
   RETURN(width - midlen)

*******************

FUNCTION Short

   PARAMETERS qwert

   RETURN(LTRIM(STR(qwert,2)))

**************************

FUNCTION Verify

   SET CONSOLE OFF
   WAIT TO inertemp
   SET CONSOLE ON
   IF UPPER(inertemp) = "Y"
     ?? "Yes"
     te = INKEY(.25)
     RETURN(.T.)
   ENDIF
   ?? "No "
   te = INKEY(.25)
   RETURN(.F.)

*******************

PROCEDURE Prochead

   PARAMETERS a
```

```
        ?
        ? "********************"
        ?
        ? "PROCEDURE " + a
        ?

********************

PROCEDURE Doitagain

    PARAMETERS p, l, v

    KEYBOARD "0" + CHR(13) + "0" + CHR(13) + CHR(18) + CHR(13)

********************

PROCEDURE Chaina

    PARAMETERS a

    DO &a

********************

PROCEDURE Chainb

    PARAMETERS a, b

    DO &a. WITH &b

* End of GENMEN.prg


********************
* Name           STARTOFF.prg
* Date           August 15, 1986
* Notice         Copyright 1986, Stephen J. Straley
* Note           This section of the menu generator starts off
*                the program.   The rows, columns, prompts, and messages
*                are stored in two databases.  This section creates those
*                databases if they do not exist.
*
********************
    @ 18,5 SAY "Creating Files for Menus... One Moment Please...."
    CREATE Template
    USE Template
    APPEND BLANK
    REPLACE field_name WITH "PROC_NAME", field_type WITH "C", field_len WITH 10
    APPEND BLANK
    REPLACE field_name WITH "TOP", field_type WITH "N", field_len WITH 2
    APPEND BLANK
    REPLACE field_name WITH "LEFT", field_type WITH "N", field_len WITH 2
    APPEND BLANK
```

```
      REPLACE field_name WITH "BOTTOM", field_type WITH "N", field_len WITH 2
      APPEND BLANK
      REPLACE field_name WITH "RIGHT", field_type WITH "N", field_len WITH 2
      APPEND BLANK
      REPLACE field_name WITH "ROW_MESS", field_type WITH "N", field_len WITH 2
      APPEND BLANK
      REPLACE field_name WITH "COL_MESS", field_type WITH "N", field_len WITH 2
      APPEND BLANK
      REPLACE field_name WITH "MESSAGE", field_type WITH "C", field_len WITH 30
      APPEND BLANK
      REPLACE field_name WITH "ROW_ESC", field_type WITH "N", field_len WITH 2
      APPEND BLANK
      REPLACE field_name WITH "COL_ESC", field_type WITH "N", field_len WITH 2
      APPEND BLANK
      REPLACE field_name WITH "ESC_MESS", field_type WITH "C", field_len WITH 30
      APPEND BLANK
      REPLACE field_name WITH "SEARCH", field_type WITH "N", field_len WITH 5
      APPEND BLANK
      REPLACE field_name WITH "VARIABLE", field_type WITH "C", field_len WITH 8
      APPEND BLANK
      REPLACE field_name WITH "MENU", field_type WITH "L", field_len WITH 1,
              field_dec WITH 0
      APPEND BLANK
      REPLACE field_name WITH "SET_MESS", field_type WITH "N", field_len WITH 2,
              field_dec WITH 0
      USE
      CREATE Menu1 FROM Template
      CLOSE DATABASES
      CREATE Template
      USE Template
      APPEND BLANK
      REPLACE field_name WITH "SEARCH", field_type WITH "N", field_len WITH 5
      APPEND BLANK
      REPLACE field_name WITH "ROW_PROMPT", field_type WITH "N", field_len WITH 2
      APPEND BLANK
      REPLACE field_name WITH "COL_PROMPT", field_type WITH "N", field_len WITH 2
      APPEND BLANK
      REPLACE field_name WITH "PROMPT", field_type WITH "C", field_len WITH 30
      APPEND BLANK
      REPLACE field_name WITH "PROM_MESS", field_type WITH "C", field_len WITH 50
      USE
      CREATE Menu2 FROM Template
      ERASE Template.dbf
    * End of STARTOFF.prg
    **********************
    * Name       BEGIN.prg
    * Date       August 15, 1986
    * Notice     Copyright 1986, Stephen J. Straley
    * Note       This section of the menu generator checks to see if the
    *            menu databases exist.  If they do, then it uses them, else
    *            it runs STARTOFF to create them.  It also sets up the
    *            screen arrays and chains to the first functional procedure
    *            for menu generating, MENUENTR.
    *
    **********************
```

```
EXTERNAL Startoff, Promptng, Menuentr, Menudraw, Move_cur, Drawbox, Movetitl,
Moveesc, Finished

    IF .NOT. FILE("MENU?.DBF")
       DO Startoff
       CLOSE DATABASES
       SELECT 2
       USE Menu2
       SELECT 1
       USE Menu1
       APPEND BLANK
    ELSE
       SELECT 2
       USE Menu2
       SELECT 1
       USE Menu1
       GO TOP
    ENDIF
    SET SCORE OFF
    CLEAR
    frame  = CHR(201) + CHR(205) + CHR(187) + CHR(186) + CHR(188) + ;
             CHR(205) + CHR(200) + CHR(186) + CHR(32)
    STORE 1 TO menu, level, asearch
    STORE 0 TO down
    STORE pref + "men" TO name
    STORE SPACE(4000) TO ascreen, bscreen, cscreen, dscreen, tscreen
    STORE .T. TO which
    DECLARE screen[5]
    FOR qaz = 1 TO 5
       STORE SPACE(4000) TO screen[qaz]
    NEXT
    CALL _scrsave WITH ascreen

DO Menuentr
* End of BEGIN.prg


********************
* Name           PROMPTNG.prg
* Date           August 15, 1986
* Notice         Copyright 1986, Stephen J. Straley
* Note           This section of the menu generator paints the already
*                designed prompts to the screen and waits to see if
*                the drawn menu appears correct.  If it is and a new
*                sub-menu is chosen, a recursive procedure call is
*                made and a new menu is entered.  If an ESC key is
*                pressed and the program is at the top level of the program,
*                then the option to write the code is displayed.
*
********************

EXTERNAL Startoff, Begin, Menuentr, Menudraw, Move_cur, Drawbox, Movetitl,
Moveesc, Finished

    PARAMETERS p, l, v
```

```
@ 0,0 CLEAR
IF level = 1 .AND. LEN(TRIM(screen[level])) = 0
   * Just skip over and do nothing right now..
ELSE
   go_down = 1
   DO WHILE !EMPTY(screen[go_down])
      CALL _scrrest WITH screen[go_down]
      go_down = go_down + 1
   ENDDO
ENDIF
SELECT 1
IF .NOT. LASTKEY() = 27
   @ top, left, bottom, right BOX frame
   spot  = INT(LEN(TRIM(message))/2)
   point = INT(INT(right-left)/2)
   @ row_mess, col_mess SAY " " + TRIM(message) + " "
ENDIF
IF EMPTY(set_mess)
   SET MESSAGE TO
ELSE
   SET MESSAGE TO set_mess
ENDIF
SELECT 2
SET FILTER TO search = asearch
GO TOP
DO WHILE .NOT. EMPTY(prompt)
   IF !EMPTY(prom_mess)
      temp_mes = AT('("',prom_mess)
      IF temp_mes = 0
         @ row_prompt, col_prompt PROMPT " " + TRIM(prompt) + " " MES-
         SAGE(prom_mess)
      ELSE
         end_mes = AT(")", prom_mess)
         end_mes = end_mes - 2
         @ row_prompt, col_prompt PROMPT " " + TRIM(prompt) +;
                   " " MESSAGE(SUBSTR(prom_mess, temp_mes + 2, end_mes-
         temp_mes+2))
      ENDIF
   ELSE
      @ row_prompt, col_prompt PROMPT " " + TRIM(prompt) + " "
   ENDIF
   SKIP
ENDDO
IF .NOT. LASTKEY() = 27
   @ A->row_esc, A->col_esc SAY TRIM(A->esc_mess)
ENDIF
MENU TO option
IF option = 0
   level = level - 1
   STORE SPACE(4000) TO screen[level+1]
   IF level = 0
      DO Finished
      CLEAR
```

```
            a 12,30 SAY "Shall I REMOVE all Files?  "
            IF VERIFY()
                ERASE Prefix.mem
                ERASE Menu1.dbf
                ERASE Menu2.dbf
            ENDIF
            a 12,25 SAY "Thanks for using the Menu Generator!  "
            QUIT
        ENDIF
        asearch = INT(asearch/10)
        DO Promptng
    ELSE
        CALL _scrsave WITH tscreen
        screen[level] = tscreen
        level = level + 1
        asearch = (asearch * 10) + option
        APPEND BLANK
        SELECT 1
        lookfor = name + LTRIM(STR(asearch))
        LOCATE FOR proc_name = lookfor
        IF .NOT. FOUND()
            APPEND BLANK
        ENDIF
        DO Menuentr
    ENDIF
* End of PROMPTNG.prg


********************
* Name        MENUENTR.prg
* Date        August 15, 1986
* Notice      Copyright 1986, Stephen J. Straley
* Note        This part of the menu generator enters the
*             menu prompt messages.
*
********************
EXTERNAL Startoff, Begin, Promptng, Menudraw, Move_cur, Drawbox, Movetitl,
         Moveesc, Finished

    PARAMETERS p, l, v

    SELECT 1
    IF top + bottom + left + right > 0
        a 0,0 SAY SPACE(79)
        a 0,0 SAY "Do you want to edit the menu contents? "
        IF .NOT. VERIFY()
            DO Menudraw
        ENDIF
    ENDIF
    a 0,0 SAY SPACE(79)
    a 1,0 SAY SPACE(79)
    a 1,0 SAY "  Will this be a MENU (No for a data entry screen)? "
    IF VERIFY()
```

```
      REPLACE menu WITH .T.
ELSE
      REPLACE menu WITH .F.
ENDIF
@ 1,0 SAY SPACE(79)
@ 0,0 SAY "Choose the TOP, LEFT coordinates for the menu frame. Do so by
           moving the"
@ 1,0 SAY "the cursor with the arrow keys.    Strike the ESC key for retain
           values."
@ 3,0 SAY "Home"
@ 3,74 SAY "Pg Up"
@ 23,0 SAY "End"
@ 23,74 SAY "Pg Dn"
DO Drawbox WITH .T.
SET COLOR TO 7*/0
@ top, left SAY CHR(201)
SET COLOR TO
@ 0,0 SAY "Choose the BOTTOM, RIGHT coordinates for the menu frame. Do so
           be moving"
@ 1,0 SAY "the cursor with the arrow keys."
DO Drawbox WITH .F.
READ
@ 0,0 CLEAR
IF EMPTY(esc_mess)
   REPLACE esc_mess WITH "ESC to RETURN"
ENDIF
@ 0,0 SAY "Enter Menu Title: " GET message PICT "@X"
@ 1,0 SAY "  Escape Message: " GET esc_mess PICT "@X"
@ 0,50 SAY "Enter Variable: " GET variable
@ 1,50 SAY "Row for Message:" GET set_mess PICT "##" RANGE 0,24
READ
REPLACE search WITH asearch, proc_name WITH name + LTRIM(STR(asearch))
IF LEN(TRIM(variable)) = 0
   SELECT 2
   SET FILTER TO search = asearch
   GO TOP
   DELETE ALL
   PACK
   SELECT 1
   DELETE
   PACK
   DO Begin
ENDIF
SELECT 2
LOCATE FOR search = asearch
IF EOF()
   FOR x = 1 TO 32
      APPEND BLANK
      REPLACE search WITH asearch
   NEXT
ENDIF
SET FILTER TO search = asearch
GO TOP
```

```
        IF !EMPTY(prompt)
           @ 3,1 SAY "Do you want to EDIT the prompts? "
           IF .NOT. VERIFY()
              DO Menudraw
           ENDIF
           @ 3,1 SAY SPACE(40)
        ENDIF
        down = 1
        DO WHILE .NOT. EOF()
           @ 3,55 SAY SPACE(24)
           @ 3,1 SAY "   Menu Prompt " + TRANSFORM(down, "99") + "-> ";
                 GET prompt PICT "XXXXXXXXXXXXXXXXXXXXXXXXXXXXXX"
           @ 4,1 SAY "Prompt Message " + TRANSFORM(down, "99") + "-> " GET
                 prom_mess PICT "@X"
           READ
           IF LASTKEY() = 18
              IF .NOT. BOF()
                 down = down - 1
                 SKIP - 1
              ENDIF
              LOOP
           ENDIF
           IF LEN(TRIM(prompt)) = 0
              REPLACE col_prompt WITH 0, row_prompt WITH 0
              EXIT
           ENDIF
           IF row_prompt = 0 .AND. col_prompt = 0
              start_look = RECNO()
              SAVE SCREEN
              DO move_cur
              RESTORE SCREEN
           ELSE
              @ 3, 55 SAY "Row: " GET row_prompt
              @ 3, 65 SAY "Col: " GET col_prompt
              READ
           ENDIF
           @ 5,0 SAY SPACE(79)
           IF down > 16
              @ down - 16 + 7,45 SAY prompt
           ELSE
              @ down + 7, 0 SAY prompt
           ENDIF
           @ ROW(), COL()+1 SAY row_prompt
           @ row(), COL()+1 SAY col_prompt
           down = down + 1
           skip
        ENDDO
        DO Menudraw
      * End of MENUENTR.prg
```

```
********************
* Name        MENUDRAW.prg
* Date        August 15, 1986
* Notice      Copyright 1986, Stephen J. Straley
* Note        This section of the menu generator actually draws
*             the menu.
*
********************

EXTERNAL Startoff, Begin, Promptng, Menuentr, Move_cur, Drawbox, Movetitl,
         Moveesc, Finished

   PARAMETERS p, l, v

   @ 0,0 CLEAR
   CALL _scrrest WITH screen[level]
   SELECT 1
   @ top, left, bottom, right BOX frame
   IF row_mess = 0 .AND. col_mess = 0
      REPLACE row_mess WITH top+1
      REPLACE col_mess WITH CCOL(A->right,A->left,LEN(TRIM(message)))
   ENDIF
   @ row_mess, col_mess SAY " " + TRIM(message) + " "
   SELECT 2
   SET FILTER TO search = asearch
   GO TOP
   DO WHILE .NOT. EMPTY(prompt)
      @ row_prompt, col_prompt SAY " " + TRIM(prompt) + " "
      SKIP
   ENDDO
   SELECT 1
   IF row_esc = 0 .AND. col_esc = 0
      REPLACE row_esc WITH bottom-1
      REPLACE col_esc WITH CCOL(A->right,A->left,13)
   ENDIF
   @ row_esc, col_esc SAY TRIM(esc_mess)
   @ 0,0 SAY SPACE(79)
   SELECT 2
   @ 0,10 SAY "Are these the correct values? "
   IF VERIFY()
      @ 0,0 SAY SPACE(79)
      DO Promptng
   ELSE
      @ 0,0 SAY SPACE(79)
      @ 0,0 SAY "Do you want to move the Title Message? "
      IF VERIFY()
         @ 0,0 SAY SPACE(79)
         CALL _scrsave WITH dscreen
         DO Movetitl
      ENDIF
      @ 0,0 SAY SPACE(79)
      @ 0,0 SAY "Do you want to move the ESC message? "
      IF VERIFY()
```

```
            @ 0,0 SAY SPACE(79)
            CALL _scrsave WITH dscreen
            DO Moveesc
         ENDIF
         DO Menuentr
      ENDIF
* End of MENUDRAW.prg


********************
* Name          MOVE_CUR.prg
* Date          August 15, 1986
* Notice        Copyright 1986, Stephen J. Straley
* Note          This section of the menu generator moves the cursor on the
*               screen, positioning the menu option.
*
********************

EXTERNAL Startoff, Begin, Promptng, Menuentr, Menudraw, Drawbox, Movetitl,
         Moveesc, Finished

   PARAMETERS p, l, v

   SET KEY -9 TO
   CLEAR
   IF level > 1
      CALL _scrrest WITH screen[level-1]
   ENDIF
   @ A->top,A->left,A->bottom,A->right BOX frame
   GO TOP
   DO WHILE .NOT. EMPTY(prompt)
      @ row_prompt, col_prompt SAY " " + TRIM(prompt) + " "
      SKIP
   ENDDO
   GO start_look
   CALL _scrsave WITH dscreen
   cursor = 0
   STORE SPACE(LEN(TRIM(prompt))) TO moving
   @ CROW(A->top,A->bottom),CCOL(A->left,A->right, LEN(moving)) GET moving
   CLEAR GETS
   trow = ROW()
   tcol = COL() - LEN(moving)
   DO WHILE .T.
      cursor = INKEY(0)
      DO CASE
      CASE cursor = 5
         IF trow - 1 > A->top
            trow = trow - 1
         ENDIF
      CASE cursor = 4
         IF tcol + 1 + LEN(moving) < A->right
            tcol = tcol + 1
         ENDIF
```

```
        CASE cursor = 19
           IF tcol - 1 > A->left
              tcol = tcol - 1
           ENDIF
        CASE cursor = 24
           IF trow + 1 < A->bottom
              trow = trow + 1
           ENDIF
        CASE cursor = 13
           EXIT
        ENDCASE
        CALL _scrrest WITH dscreen
        a trow,tcol GET moving
        CLEAR GETS
     ENDDO
     REPLACE row_prompt WITH trow, col_prompt WITH tcol - 1
* End of MOVE_CUR.prg


********************
* Name        DRAWBOX.prg
* Date        August 15, 1986
* Notice      Copyright 1986, Stephen J. Straley
* Note        This section of the menu generator draws the box
*             around the menu.
*
********************
PARAMETERS whichone

EXTERNAL Startoff, Begin, Promptng, Menuentr, Menudraw, Move_cur, Movetitl,
         Moveesc, Finished

     PARAMETERS whichone

     IF whichone
        newcur = CHR(201)
     ELSE
        newcur = CHR(188)
     ENDIF
     STORE SPACE(4000) TO zscreen
     CALL _scrsave WITH zscreen
     cursor = 0
     trow = 12
     tcol = 40
     a trow,tcol SAY ""
     DO WHILE .T.
        cursor = INKEY(0)
        CALL _scrrest WITH zscreen
        DO CASE
        CASE cursor = 1
           trow = 4
           tcol = 1
        CASE cursor = 18
```

```
            trow = 4
            tcol = 79
         CASE cursor = 6
            trow = 22
            tcol = 1
         CASE cursor = 3
            trow = 22
            tcol = 79
         CASE cursor = 5
            IF trow > 4
               trow = trow - 1
            ENDIF
         CASE cursor = 4
            IF COL() < 78
               tcol = tcol + 1
            ENDIF
         CASE cursor = 19
            IF COL() > 1
               tcol = tcol - 1
            ENDIF
         CASE cursor = 24
            IF ROW() < 22
               trow = trow + 1
            ENDIF
         CASE cursor = 13 .OR. cursor = 27 .OR. cursor = 32
            EXIT
         ENDCASE
         @ trow, tcol SAY newcur
         @ trow, tcol SAY ""
      ENDDO
      IF LASTKEY() <> 27
         IF whichone
            REPLACE top WITH trow, left WITH tcol
         ELSE
            REPLACE bottom WITH trow, right WITH tcol
         ENDIF
      ENDIF
* End of DRAWBOX.prg



********************
* Name       MOVETITL.prg
* Date       August 15, 1986
* Notice     Copyright 1986, Stephen J. Straley
* Note       Like Menudraw.prg, this section of the menu generator
*            positions the menu title.
*
********************

EXTERNAL Startoff, Begin, Promptng, Menuentr, Menudraw, Move_cur, Drawbox,
         Moveesc, Finished

   PARAMETERS p, l, v
```

```
SELECT 1
cursor = 0
STORE SPACE(LEN(TRIM(message))) TO moving
@ row_mess, col_mess SAY ""
trow = ROW()
tcol = COL()
DO WHILE .T.
  cursor = INKEY(0)
  DO CASE
  CASE cursor = 5
    trow = trow - 1
  CASE cursor = 4
    tcol = tcol + 1
  CASE cursor = 19
    tcol = tcol - 1
  CASE cursor = 24
    trow = trow + 1
  CASE cursor = 13
    EXIT
  ENDCASE
  CALL _scrrest WITH dscreen
  @ trow, tcol GET moving
  CLEAR GETS
ENDDO
@ row_mess, col_mess SAY SPACE(LEN(TRIM(message)))+" "
REPLACE row_mess WITH trow, col_mess WITH tcol
@ row_mess, col_mess SAY TRIM(message)
SELECT 2
* End of MOVETITL.prg


*********************
* Name        MOVEESC.prg
* Date        August 15, 1986
* Notice      Copyright 1986, Stephen J. Straley
* Note        Similar to MOVETITL.prg, this section of the menu
*             generator moves the ESC message of the menu.
*
*********************

EXTERNAL Startoff, Begin, Promptng, Menuentr, Menudraw, Move_cur, Drawbox,
         Movetitl, Finished

  PARAMETERS p, l, v

  SELECT 1
  cursor = 0
  STORE SPACE(LEN(TRIM(esc_mess))) TO moving
  @ row_esc, col_esc SAY ""
  trow = ROW()
  tcol = COL()
  DO WHILE .T.
    cursor = INKEY(0)
```

```
   DO CASE
   CASE cursor = 5
      trow = trow - 1
   CASE cursor = 4
      tcol = tcol + 1
   CASE cursor = 19
      tcol = tcol - 1
   CASE cursor = 24
      trow = trow + 1
   CASE cursor = 13
      EXIT
   ENDCASE
   CALL _scrrest WITH dscreen
   @ trow, tcol GET moving
   CLEAR GETS
ENDDO
@ row_esc, col_esc SAY SPACE(LEN(TRIM(esc_mess)))
REPLACE row_esc WITH trow, col_esc WITH tcol
@ row_esc, col_esc SAY TRIM(esc_mess)
SELECT 2
* End of MOVEESC.prg
```

```
********************
* Name          FINISHED.prg
* Date          August 15, 1986
* Notice        Copyright 1986, Stephen J. Straley
* Note          This section of the menu generator asks the user if
*               all of the menus are entered.  If so, code is generated
*               based on the information in the two databases.   Some
*               of the procedures written in this section refer to
*               procedures generated by GENCODE.EXE.   This section does
*               not write the specific PROMPT commands.
*
*               Inside this .PRG is a procedure called FINISH_1.  This
*               procedure actually writes the PROMPT positions to the
*               alternate file opened by FINISHED.prg.  If a
*               menu option does not have a branch developed, then
*               a note will be generated in the code.
*
********************

EXTERNAL Startoff, Begin, Promptng, Menuentr, Menudraw, Move_cur, Drawbox,
         Movetitl, Moveesc

   PARAMETERS p, l, v

   CLEAR
   @ 12,15 SAY "Do you want to generate the code for the menus? "
   IF .NOT. VERIFY()
      RETURN
   ENDIF
   SELECT 1
```

```
GO TOP
SET CONSOLE OFF
STORE name +"u.prg" TO Outfile
SET ALTERNATE TO &Outfile
SET ALTERNATE ON
? "CLEAR"
? "DO " + name + "1"
DO WHILE .NOT. EOF()
   IF EMPTY(proc_name)
      SKIP
      LOOP
   ENDIF
   DO Prochead WITH A->proc_name
   tempstr = CHR(LEN(LTRIM(STR(A->search)))) + 96) + "screen"
   ? "DO WHILE .T."
   IF RECNO() = 1
      ? "   CLEAR"
      ? "   RESTORE FROM Screen.sys"
      ? "   STORE SPACE(4000) TO ascreen, bscreen, cscreen, dscreen, es-
        creen, fscreen"
      ? "   DO Setup"
      ? "   DO Redraw"
      STORE .T. TO topping
   ELSE
      ? "   IF !EMPTY(" + tempstr + ")"
      ? "      CALL _scrrest WITH " + tempstr
      ? "   ELSE"
      building = SHORT(top) + ", " + SHORT(left) + ", " + SHORT(bottom) +
        ", " +  SHORT(right) +;
               " BOX scrframe"
      ? '      STORE 0 TO ' + TRIM(variable)
      ? '      @ ' + building
      ? '      CALL _scrsave WITH ' + tempstr
      ? "   ENDIF"
      STORE .F. TO topping
   ENDIF
   ? "   SET MESSAGE TO " + IF(EMPTY(set_mess), "", TRANSFORM(set_mess,
     "99"))
   ? '   @ ' + SHORT(row_mess) + ', ' + SHORT(col_mess) + ' SAY "' +
     TRIM(message) + '"'
   asearch = search
   DO Finished_1
   ? "ENDDO"
   SKIP
ENDDO
? CHR(13) + CHR(12) + CHR(26) + CHR(26)
SET ALTERNATE OFF
CLOSE ALTERNATE
SET CONSOLE ON
```

```
********************

PROCEDURE Finished_1

   PARAMETERS p, l, v

   SELECT 2
   SET FILTER TO search = asearch
   GO TOP
   DO WHILE !EMPTY(prompt)
      ? '   @ ' + SHORT(row_prompt) + ', ' + SHORT(col_prompt) + ' PROMPT " '
           + TRIM(prompt) + ' "'
      IF !EMPTY(prom_mess)
         temp_mes = AT('("', prom_mess)
         IF temp_mes = 0
            ?? ' MESSAGE ' + '"' + TRIM(prom_mess) + '"'
         ELSE
            ?? ' MESSAGE ' + TRIM(prom_mess)
         ENDIF
      ENDIF
      SKIP
   ENDDO
   ? '   @ ' + SHORT(A->row_esc) + ', ' + SHORT(A->col_esc) + ' SAY "' +
           TRIM(A->esc_mess) + '"'
   ? '   MENU TO ' + TRIM(A->variable)
   ? '   CALL _scrsave WITH ' + tempstr
   GO TOP
   ? '   DO CASE'
   counter = 1
   DO WHILE !EMPTY(prompt)
      ? '   CASE ' + TRIM(A->variable) + ' = ' + SHORT(counter)
      temp = name + LTRIM(STR(search)) + LTRIM(STR(counter))
      SELECT 1
      back_to = RECNO()
      LOCATE FOR temp == TRIM(proc_name)
      IF .NOT. FOUND()
         ? '      ************************'
         ? '      * Do sub-procedure here *'
         ? '      ************************'
      ELSE
         ? '      DO ' + temp
      ENDIF
      GO back_to
      SELECT 2
      counter = counter + 1
      SKIP
   ENDDO
   ? '   CASE ' + TRIM(A->variable) + ' = 0'
   IF topping
      ? '      @ ' + SHORT(A->row_esc + 2) + ', 15 SAY "All Files Closed,
           Returning to Operating System"'
      ? '      QUIT'
   ELSE
```

```
        ? '        EXIT'
    ENDIF
    ? '   ENDCASE'
    ?
    ?
    SELECT 1


***********************

PROCEDURE Help

    PARAMETERS p,l,v

    IF p = "HELP"
        RETURN
    ENDIF
    hrow = 23
    hcol = 15
    CALL _scrsave WITH xscreen
    DO CASE
    CASE p = "CMENU"
        DO CASE
        CASE v = "PREF"
            @ 17,10,24,70 BOX frame
            @ 18,15 SAY "Since the CREATE program has not been executed prior"
            @ 19,15 SAY "to this program, you must enter the 2 letter prefix"
            @ 20,15 SAY "to be attached to all menus built as well as the"
            @ 21,15 SAY "prefix to the output."
        OTHERWISE
            @ 20,10,24,70 BOX frame
            @ 21,15 SAY "No help available...."
        ENDCASE
    CASE p = "PROMPTING"
        DO CASE
        CASE v = "OPTION"
            @ 18,10,24,70 BOX frame
            @ 19,13 SAY "Move the cursor to the menu choice on which to build"
            @ 20,13 SAY "the next menu.  If no menu exists, follow standard"
            @ 21,13 SAY "procedures; otherwise, edit previous menu items."
        OTHERWISE
            @ 20,10,24,70 BOX frame
            @ 21,15 SAY "No help available...."
        ENDCASE
    CASE p = "MENUENTR"
        DO CASE
        CASE v = "MESSAGE"
            @ 17,10,23,70 BOX frame
            @ 18,15 SAY "This will be the title for the menu you are about"
            @ 19,15 SAY "to draw.  For no menu title, please strike F9 to"
            @ 20,15 SAY "leave blank."
            hrow = 22
        CASE v = "VARIABLE"
            @ 18,10,24,70 BOX frame
```

```
          a 19,15 SAY "This will be the name of the variable used for the"
          a 20,15 SAY "'MENU TO' command.   Leaving blank or striking the F9"
          a 21,15 SAY "key will delete this menu from the entire system."
      CASE v = "PROMPT"
          a 17,10,24,70 BOX frame
          a 18,15 SAY "This will be the character string used for the PROMPT"
          a 19,15 SAY "command. If no coordinates exist, direct cursor posi-"
          a 20,15 SAY "tioning is possible by moving cursor within frame. If"
          a 21,15 SAY "they do exist, you may modify them directly."
      CASE v = "ROW_PROMPT"
          a 17,10,24,70 BOX frame
          a 18,12 SAY "This is the row number for the PROMPT message.  If al-
          ready"
          a 19,12 SAY "established with cursor keys.  Edit numbers directly or
          "
          a 20,12 SAY "strike F2 key to allow for re-direct cursor position-
          ing."
          hrow = 22
          hcol = 12
      OTHERWISE
          a 20,10,24,70 BOX frame
          a 21,15 SAY "No help available...."
      ENDCASE
  OTHERWISE
    a 0,0 CLEAR
    a  1,5 SAY "For all questions, either strike Y      F1:  On-line Help"
    a  2,5 SAY "for YES or any other key for NO.        F2:  To clear out row"
    a  3,5 SAY "                                        and column positions"
    a  4,5 SAY "If at any time there is a question      to allow direct cursor"
    a  5,5 SAY "as to what to enter, please strike      positioning for the"
    a  6,5 SAY "the F1 key.   If any help is            entered prompt message"
    a  7,5 SAY "available, instruction will appear."
    a  8,5 SAY "Otherwise, this screen will appear.     F9 :  Clear Field"
    a  9,5 SAY "                                        F10: Flash to Pre-"
    a 10,5 SAY "                                        vious screen."
    a 22,10 SAY "  Program name: "
    ?? p
    a 22,50 SAY "Line number: "
    ?? l
    a 23,10 SAY "Variable Name: "
    ?? v
    hrow = 24
  ENDCASE
  a hrow, hcol SAY "Any Key to Continue..."
  qwert = INKEY(0)

  CALL _scrrest WITH xscreen

********************

FUNCTION Crow

  PARAMETERS in_top, in_bottom
```

```
      tempin = in_bottom - in_top
      tempin = tempin / 2
      RETURN(in_top + INT(tempin))


*********************

FUNCTION Ccol

   PARAMETERS in_left, in_right, width

      tempin = in_right - in_left - width
      tempin = tempin / 2
      RETURN(in_left + INT(tempin))
* End of FINISHED.prg
```

COMPILING AND LINKING THE MENU GENERATOR

Create a batch file named GO.BAT with the commands to compile the menu generator program as follows:

```
GO.BAT:

   CLIPPER GENMEN
   CLIPPER BEGIN
   CLIPPER STARTOFF
   CLIPPER MENUENTR
   CLIPPER DRAWBOX
   CLIPPER MOVE_CUR
   CLIPPER PROMPTNG
   CLIPPER MENUDRAW
   CLIPPER MOVEESC
   CLIPPER MOVETITL
   CLIPPER FINISHED
```

To link the files enter the following command line:

```
C>LINK Genmen Begin Startoff Menuentr Drawbox Move_cur Promptng Menudraw
      Moveesc Movetitl Finished,,,/se:1024,,;
```

APPENDIX I

Call Tracking

AN OVERVIEW OF THE APPLICATION

This program is the beginning of a call tracking program for telephone support service organizations. The basic structure of the program was designed and generated by both the program generator and the menu generator provided within this text. To illustrate the potential time savings, the following code took a little less than **one hour** for coding, debugging, and testing!

Even though the project is far from complete and many more hours would be required for completion, the savings are still significant.

Basically, there are three files:

CALL.prg — generated by the program generator.

CAMENU.prg — generated by the menu generator.

CALLPROG.prg — generated in one hour, a massive procedure file.

THE BATCH FILE

The following should be included in a basic batch file to compile and link the program together. In this example, LINK was used instead of PLINK86.

```
CLIPPER Call
CLIPPER Callprog
LINK Call Callprog ,,,\Dbase\/SE:1024,,
CALL
```

THE PROGRAM FILES

CALL.PRG

```
*********************
* Name      CALL.prg
* Date      August 15, 1986
* Notice    Copyright 1986, Stephen J. Straley
* Note      This application was generated by GENCODE.
*
*********************

CLEAR
? "Loading Program..."
DO Beginit
DO Draw
DO Camenu
```

```
*******************

PROCEDURE Beginit

    IF .NOT. FILE("SCREEN.SYS")
       DO Scrinit
    ENDIF
    RESTORE FROM Screen.sys
    IF .NOT. FILE(scrdata + "LOG_CALL.DBF") .OR. .NOT. FILE(scrdata + "CON-
TRACT.DBF")
       DO Cainit
    ENDIF


*******************

PROCEDURE Scrinit

    SET SCOREBOARD OFF

    CLEAR
    scrframe    = CHR(201) + CHR(205) + CHR(187) + CHR(186) + CHR(188) + ;
                  CHR(205) + CHR(200) + CHR(186) + CHR(32)
    scrleft_1   = "Copyright 1986 - GLOBAL SOFTWARE"
    scrleft_2   = "All Rights Reserved"
    right_1     = "Terminal/System Setup Program"
    right_2     = "May - 1986"
    temscreen   = SPACE(4000)
    center      = "Drive Assignment Setup"
    @ 0,0 SAY scrleft_1
    @ 1,0 SAY scrleft_2
    @ 0,80-LEN(right_1) SAY right_1
    @ 1,80-LEN(right_2) SAY right_2
    @ 3,40-LEN(center)/2 SAY center
    @ 4,0,23,79 BOX SUBSTR(scrframe, 1, 8)
    topspot = "       Move cursor to appropriate option.  Strike RETURN key to
change        "
    @ 5, 1 GET topspot
    CLEAR GETS
    @ 6, 0 SAY CHR(204) + REPLICATE(CHR(205),78) + CHR(185)
    CALL _scrsave WITH temscreen
    IF .NOT. FILE("SCREEN.SYS")
       STORE "C:" TO scrprog, scrdata
       STORE .F. TO scrconfirm, scrdelim, scrcolor, scrinten, scrbell, scrtype
       STORE .T. TO scrsys, scrshow
       STORE "" TO scrframe, scrbar, scrlin
       STORE "::" TO scrdelimto
       STORE 0 TO scrtimes, scrpass
    ELSE
       RESTORE FROM Screen.sys ADDITIVE
    ENDIF
    STORE 4 TO option
```

```
        DO WHILE .T.
           CALL _scrrest WITH temscreen
           @  7, 5 PROMPT " 1> System Configured for " + IF(scrsys, "Hard", "Floppy")
+ " Disk "
           @  7,45 PROMPT " 2> Program Drive Set to " + scrprog + " "
           @  8,45 PROMPT " 3> Data Drive Set to " + scrdata + " "
           @ 10, 5 PROMPT " 4> Confirm is " + IF(scrconfirm, "ON ", "OFF") + " "
           @ 11, 5 PROMPT " 5> Delimiters are " + IF(scrdelim, "ON", "OFF") + " "
           @ 12, 5 PROMPT " 6> Delimiters SET to " + scrdelimto + " "
           @ 13, 5 PROMPT " 7> Screen " + IF(scrcolor, "Bright", "Normal") + " "
           @ 14, 5 PROMPT " 8> Field Color is " + IF(scrinten, "ON", "OFF") + " "
           @ 15, 5 PROMPT " 9> Bell " + IF(scrbell, "WILL", "WILL NOT") + " ring "
           @ 10,40 PROMPT " A> Password " + IF(scrshow, "WILL", "WILL NOT") + " echo
to screen "
           @ 12,40 PROMPT " B> Change Password "
           @ 14,40 PROMPT " C> " + DLTRIM(STR(scrtimes)) + " tries at the Password"
           @ 16,40 PROMPT " D> " + IF(scrtype, "Engage", "Disengage") + " Type-Ahead
Feature "
           @ 18,33 SAY     "<ESC> to Save Values"
           MENU TO option
           DO CASE
           CASE option = 1
              scrsys = IF(scrsys, .F., .T.)
              IF .NOT. scrsys
                 KEYBOARD "2"
              ENDIF
           CASE option = 2
              @ 21,10 SAY "Enter Program Drive: " GET scrprog PICT "!"
VALID(SUBSTR(scrprog,1,1) $"ABCDEFGHIJKLMNOP")
              READ
              IF .NOT. scrsys
                 IF scrprog = scrdata
                    @ 21,10 SAY SPACE(50)
                    @ 22,10 SAY "Data Drive and Program Drive NOT EQUAL for Floppy
System"
                    @ 21,10 SAY "Enter Data Drive: " GET scrdata PICT "!"
VALID(SUBSTR(scrdata,1,1) $"ABCDEFGHIJKLMNOP" .AND.;
                                scrprog <> scrdata)
                    READ
                 ENDIF
              ENDIF
           CASE option = 3
              @ 21,10 SAY "Enter Data Drive: " GET scrdata PICT "!"
VALID(SUBSTR(scrdata,1,1) $"ABCDEFGHIJKLMNOP")
              READ
              IF .NOT. scrsys
                 IF scrprog = scrdata
                    @ 21,10 SAY SPACE(50)
                    @ 22,10 SAY "Program Drive and Data Drive NOT EQUAL for Floppy
System"
                    @ 21,10 SAY "Enter Program Drive: " GET scrprog PICT "!"
VALID(SUBSTR(scrprog,1,1) $"ABCDEFGHIJKLMNOP" .AND.;
                                scrdata <> scrprog)
```

```
            ENDIF
          ENDIF
       CASE option = 4
          scrconfirm = IF(scrconfirm, .F., .T.)
       CASE option = 5
          scrdelim = IF(scrdelim, .F., .T.)
       CASE option = 6
          STORE " " TO choice
          a 21,10 SAY "Set Left Delimiter:   " GET choice PICT "X"
          READ
          STORE choice TO scrdelimto
          STORE " " TO choice
          a 21,10 SAY "Set Right Delimiter:  " GET choice PICT "X"
          READ
          STORE scrdelimto + choice TO scrdelimto
       CASE option = 7
          scrcolor = IF(scrcolor, .F., .T.)
       CASE option = 8
          scrinten = IF(scrinten, .F., .T.)
       CASE option = 9
          scrbell = IF(scrbell, .F., .T.)
       CASE option = 10
          scrshow = IF(scrshow, .F., .T.)
       CASE option = 11
          STORE SPACE(15) TO password
          a 21,10 SAY "What Password do you want to use? " GET password PICT
"XXXXXXXXXXXXXXX"
          READ
          scrpass = GENPASS(password)
       CASE option = 12
          a 21,10 SAY "How may tries for a correct password? " GET scrtimes PICT
"##" range 0,99
          READ
       CASE option = 13
          scrtype = IF(scrtype, .F., .T.)
       OTHERWISE
          EXIT
       ENDCASE
    ENDDO


    CALL _scrrest WITH temscreen
    a 3,3 SAY SPACE(60)
    a 3,29 SAY "Installing the Border"
    CALL _scrsave WITH temscreen
    in_choice = 4
    prmpt_4 = CHR(201) + CHR(205) + CHR(187) + CHR(186) + ;
            CHR(188) + CHR(205) + CHR(200) + CHR(186) + CHR(32)
    prmpt_5 = REPLICATE(CHR(177), 8) + " "
    prmpt_6 = CHR(218) + CHR(196) + CHR(191) + CHR(179) + ;
            CHR(217) + CHR(196) + CHR(192) + CHR(179) + CHR(32)
    prmpt_7 = CHR(222) + CHR(223) + CHR(221) + CHR(221) + ;
            CHR(221) + CHR(220) + CHR(222) + CHR(222) + CHR(32)
    prmpt_9 = REPLICATE(CHR(15), 8) + " "
```

```
DO WHILE .T.
   CALL _scrrest WITH temscreen
   @  8, 5 PROMPT  "1>    *********"
   @  8,32 PROMPT  "2>    ========="
   @  8,59 PROMPT  "3>    ---------"
   @ 10, 5 PROMPT  "4>    &prmpt_4."
   @ 10,32 PROMPT  "5>    &prmpt_5."
   @ 10,59 PROMPT  "6>    &prmpt_6."
   @ 12, 5 PROMPT  "7>    &prmpt_7."
   @ 12,32 PROMPT  "8>       "
   @ 12,59 PROMPT  "9>    &prmpt_9."
   @ 14,20 SAY "Move Cursor to choose preferred boarded"
   MENU TO in_choice
   DO CASE
   CASE in_choice = 1
      scrframe = "******** "
      scrbar   = REPLICATE("*",80)
      scrlin   = "*"
   CASE in_choice = 2
      scrframe = "======== "
      scrbar   = REPLICATE("=",80)
      scrlin   = "="
   CASE in_choice = 3
      scrframe = "-------- "
      scrbar   = REPLICATE("-",80)
      scrlin   = "|"
   CASE in_choice = 4
      scrframe = CHR(201) + CHR(205) + CHR(187) + CHR(186) + CHR(188) + ;
                 CHR(205) + CHR(200) + CHR(186) + CHR(32)
      scrbar   = CHR(204) + REPLICATE(CHR(205), 78) + CHR(185)
      scrlin   = CHR(186)
   CASE in_choice = 5
      scrframe = REPLICATE(CHR(177), 8) + " "
      scrbar   = REPLICATE(CHR(177),80)
      scrlin   = CHR(177)
   CASE in_choice = 6
      scrframe = CHR(218) + CHR(196) + CHR(191) + CHR(179) + CHR(217) + ;
                 CHR(196) + CHR(192) + CHR(179) + CHR(32)
      scrbar   = CHR(195) + REPLICATE(CHR(196), 78) + CHR(180)
      scrlin   = CHR(179)
   CASE in_choice = 7
      scrframe = CHR(222) + CHR(223) + CHR(221) + CHR(221) + CHR(221) + ;
                 CHR(220) + CHR(222) + CHR(222) + CHR(32)
      scrbar   = CHR(222) + REPLICATE(CHR(220),78) + CHR(221)
      scrlin   = CHR(222)
   CASE in_choice = 8
      scrframe = " "
      scrbar   = REPLICATE("",80)
      scrlin   = ""
   CASE in_choice = 9
      scrframe = REPLICATE(CHR(15), 8) + " "
      scrbar   = REPLICATE(CHR(15), 80)
      scrlin   = CHR(15)
   ENDCASE
```

```
      CALL _scrrest WITH temscreen
      @ 8,10,16,69 BOX SUBSTR(scrframe,1,8)
      @ 12,10 SAY SUBSTR(scrbar,1,1) + SUBSTR(scrbar,2,58) + SUBSTR(scrbar,80,1)
      @ 19,25 SAY "Is this the border you want?  "
      IF VERIFY()
         EXIT
      ENDIF
   ENDDO


   writefile = scrprog + "SCREEN.SYS"
   @ 22,24 SAY "Now Saving parameters to " + writefile
   SAVE ALL LIKE scr* TO &writefile
   CALL _scrrest WITH temscreen
   @ 12,18 SAY  "Finished with Terminal/System Initialization"
   IF INKEY(.5) = 32
      RETURN
   ENDIF


**********************

PROCEDURE Draw

   CLEAR
   RESTORE FROM SCREEN.SYS additive
   IF scrcolor
      SET COLOR TO 7+
   ELSE
      SET COLOR TO 7
   ENDIF
   @ 3,20,7,60 BOX scrframe
   @ 5,28 SAY "   GLOBAL SOFTWARE      "
      @ 9,40-LEN("Call Tracking")/2 SAY "Call Tracking"
      @ 21,11 SAY "           Designed by Stephen J. Straley           "

   DO WHILE .T.
      STORE "Today's Date is " + CDOW(DATE()) + ", " + CMON(DATE()) TO prompt
      STORE prompt + " " + STR(DAY(DATE()),2) + ", " + STR(YEAR(DATE()),4) TO
prompt
      @ 14,40-LEN(prompt)/2 SAY prompt
      @ 18,25 SAY "Is this the Correct Date?  "
      IF .NOT. VERIFY()
         mdate = DATE()
         @ 18, 0 SAY SPACE(80)
         @ 18,28 SAY "Enter in Date:  " GET mdate
         READ
         mdate = DTOC(mdate)
         RUN DATE &mdate
         @ 18,25 SAY SPACE(40)
      ELSE
         EXIT
      ENDIF
   ENDDO
```

```
********************

FUNCTION Dltrim

   PARAMETER in_string

   RETURN(LTRIM(TRIM(in_string)))

********************

FUNCTION Endfield

   PARAMETER File

      USE CALL.PRG
      x = 1
      y = 1024
      z = INT(y/2)

      DO WHILE x <> y
         IF LEN(FIELDNAME(z)) = 0
            y = z
         ELSE
            x = z
         ENDIF
         z = x + int((y-x)/2)
         IF LEN(FIELDNAME(z)) > 0 .AND. LEN(FIELDNAME(z+1)) = 0
            y = z
            x = z
         ENDIF
      ENDDO
      RETURN(y)


********************

FUNCTION Dayword

   PARAMETER in_date

      in_day = STR(DAY(in_date),2)
      in_val = VAL(in_day)
      IF in_val > 4 .AND. in_val < 21
         in_day = in_day + "th"
      ELSE
         in_val = VAL(SUBSTR(in_day,2,1))
         in_day = in_day + SUBSTR("thstndrdthththththth", (in_val * 2)+1,2)
      ENDIF
      RETURN(in_day)


********************

FUNCTION Expand

   PARAMETER in_string
```

```
      length  = LEN(in_string)
      counter = 1
      out_str = ""

      DO WHILE counter <= length
         out_str = out_str + SUBSTR(in_string,counter,1) + " "
         counter = counter + 1
      ENDDO
      RETURN(TRIM(out_str))


********************

FUNCTION Qwait

   SET CONSOLE OFF
   WAIT TO intemp
   SET CONSOLE ON
   IF UPPER(intemp) = "Q"
      RETURN(.T.)
   ENDIF
   RETURN(.F.)


********************

FUNCTION Chkamt

   PARAMETERS figure

      final = ""
      IF figure < 0
         final = "Unable to Print"
         RETURN(final)
      ENDIF
      cents = SUBSTR(STR(figure, 15, 2), 14, 2)
      new = INT(figure)
      ********************
      * check for BILLIONS
      ********************
      temp = INT(new/1000000000)
      IF temp > 0
         final = final + GRP_EXPAND(temp) + " Billion "
         new = new - (temp*1000000000)
      ENDIF
      ********************
      * check for MILLIONS
      ********************
      temp = INT(new/1000000)
      IF temp > 0
         final = final + GRP_EXPAND(temp) + " Million "
         new = new - (temp*1000000)
      ENDIF
      ********************
      * check for THOUSANDS
```

```
********************
temp = INT(new/1000)
IF temp > 0
   final = final + GRP_EXPAND(temp) + " Thousand "
   new = new - (temp*1000)
ENDIF
temp = new
*****************
* check for UNITS
*****************
IF temp > 0
   final = final + GRP_EXPAND(temp)
ENDIF
IF SUBSTR(final,1,3) = "One" .AND. LEN(final) = 3
   final = final + " Dollar and " + cents + "/100"
ELSE
   final = final + " Dollars and " + cents + "/100"
ENDIF
RETURN(final)


********************

FUNCTION Grp_expand

   PARAMETER group_val

   one_unit = "One     Two     Three   Four    Five    Six     Seven
Eight   Nine    Ten     Eleven  Twelve  Thirteen Fourteen Fifteen Sixteen
SeventeenEighteen Nineteen"
   ten_unit = "Twenty Thirty Forty  Fifty  Sixty  SeventyEighty Ninety "
   group_str = ""
   IF group_val > 99
      new1 = INT(group_val/100)
      group_str = group_str + TRIM(SUBSTR(one_unit,(new1*9)-8,9))
      group_val = group_val - (new1 * 100)
      group_str = group_str + " Hundred "
   ENDIF
   IF group_val > 19
      new1 = INT(group_val/10)-1
      group_str = group_str + TRIM(SUBSTR(ten_unit,(new1*7)-6,7))
      new1 = INT(group_val/10)*10
      group_val = group_val - new1
      IF group_val > 0
         group_str = group_str + "-"
      ENDIF
   ENDIF
   IF group_val > 0
      group_str = group_str + TRIM(SUBSTR(one_unit,(group_val*9)-8,9))
   ENDIF
   RETURN(group_str)
```

```
********************

FUNCTION Chktest

   in_check = "Y"
   @ 12,10 SAY "Would you like to print a test check? "
   IF VERIFY()
      RETURN(.T.)
   ENDIF
   RETURN(.F.)


********************

FUNCTION Verify

   SET CONSOLE OFF
   STORE "" TO inertemp
   DO WHILE .NOT. inertemp$"YyNn"
      WAIT TO inertemp
   ENDDO
   SET CONSOLE ON
   IF UPPER(inertemp) = "Y"
      ?? "Yes"
      te = INKEY(.25)
      RETURN(.T.)
   ENDIF
   ?? "No "
   te = INKEY(.25)
   RETURN(.F.)


********************

FUNCTION Prntpage

   PARAMETERS normal

      IF normal
         @ 63,35 SAY "Page"
         @ PROW(),PCOL()+2 SAY page PICT "@B"
         @ 64,0 SAY ""
      ELSE
         @ 63,65 SAY "Page"
         @ PROW(),PCOL()+2 SAY page PICT "@B"
         @ 64,0 SAY ""
      ENDIF
      RETURN(page)


********************

FUNCTION Signchng

   PARAMETERS amount
```

```
      IF amount >= 0
          RETURN (STR(amount))
      ENDIF
      amount = amount * -1
      newfig = "(" + TRIM(LTRIM(STR(amount,15,2))) + ")"
      newfig = SPACE(16 - LEN(newfig)) + newfig
      RETURN(newfig)


********************

   FUNCTION Prntdate

      PARAMETERS in_date

          out_date = CDOW(in_date) + ", " + "the " + DAYWORD(in_date) + " of " +
CMON(in_date) + ", " + STR(YEAR(in_date),4)
          RETURN(out_date)
********************

   FUNCTION Checking

      IF EOF() .OR. BOF()
          @ 22,8 SAY "Can not continue past end.  Press any key to return to the
menu."
          te = INKEY(0)
          RETURN(.T.)
      ENDIF
      RETURN(.F.)


********************

   FUNCTION Genpass

      PARAMETERS in_string

          count = LEN(TRIM(in_string))
          final = 0
          FOR beginning = 1 to (count + 1)
              final = final + ASC(SUBSTR(in_string,beginning,1)) * beginning
          NEXT
          RETURN(final)


********************

   FUNCTION Chkpass

      PARAMETERS row, col

          IF scrtimes = 0
              RETURN(.T.)
          ENDIF
          IF scrshow
              SET COLOR TO 7/0, 0/7
```

```
      ELSE
         SET COLOR TO 7+/0, 0+/0
      ENDIF
      FOR x = 1 to scrtimes
         in_pass = SPACE(15)
         @ row-3,col-5,row+3,col+34 BOX scrframe
         @ row,col SAY "Password --> " GET in_pass PICT "XXXXXXXXXXXXXXX"
         READ
         IF LEN(TRIM(in_pass)) <> 0
            temp_count = GENPASS(in_pass)
            IF temp_count = scrpass
               x = 1000
            ENDIF
         ENDIF
      NEXT
      IF scrcolor
         SET COLOR TO 7+/0, 0/7
      ELSE
         SET COLOR TO 7/0, 0/7
      ENDIF
      IF scrinten
         SET INTEN ON
      ELSE
         SET INTEN OFF
      ENDIF
      RETURN(x > 101)


********************

FUNCTION Roundit

   PARAMETERS in_amount

      in_amount = INT(in_amount * 100 + .5) / 100.00
      RETURN(in_amount)

********************

FUNCTION Printdate

   PARAMETERS in_date, whichone

   DO CASE
   CASE whichone = 1
      out_str = CMONTH(in_date) + " " + DAYWORD(in_date) + ", " +
DLTRIM(STR(YEAR(in_date)))
   CASE whichone = 2
      out_str = CDOW(in_date) + ", the " + DAYWORD(in_date) + " of " +
CMONTH(in_date) + ", " + dltrim(STR(YEAR(in_date)))
   CASE whichone = 3
      out_str = CDOW(in_date) + ", the " + DAYWORD(in_date) + " of " +
CMONTH(in_date)
   CASE whichone = 4
```

```
          out_str = "The " + DAYWORD(in_date) + " of " + CMONTH(in_date) + ", " +
DLTRIM(STR(YEAR(in_date)))
      CASE whichone = 5
          out_str = CDOW(in_date) + ", " + CMON(in_date) + " "
          out_str = out_str + STR(DAY(in_date),2) + ", " + STR(YEAR(in_date),4)
      OTHERWISE
          out_str = DTOC(in_date)
      ENDCASE
      RETURN(out_str)


********************

PROCEDURE Typeahead

   IF !scrtype
      CALL _cclr
   ENDIF


********************

PROCEDURE Blink

   PARAMETERS temp_row, temp_col

       IF scrcolor
          SET COLOR TO W*+
       ELSE
          SET COLOR TO W*
       ENDIF
       @ temp_row, temp_col SAY "Deleted Record"
       IF scrcolor
          SET COLOR TO W+
       ELSE
          SET COLOR TO W
       ENDIF


********************

PROCEDURE Setup

      SET FUNCTION  2 TO CHR(22)
      SET FUNCTION  3 TO CHR(1)
      SET FUNCTION  4 TO CHR(6)
      SET FUNCTION  5 TO CHR(3)
      SET FUNCTION  6 TO CHR(5)
      SET FUNCTION  8 TO CHR(23)
      SET FUNCTION  7 TO CHR(20)
      SET FUNCTION  9 TO CHR(25)
      SET FUNCTION 10 TO CHR(21)
      IF scrinten
         SET INTENS on
      ELSE
         SET INTENS off
```

```
    ENDIF
    IF scrdelim
       SET DELIM TO "&scrdelimto"
       SET DELIM on
    ELSE
       SET DELIM off
    ENDIF
    IF scrconfirm
       SET CONFIRM on
    ELSE
       SET CONFIRM off
    ENDIF
    IF scrbell
       SET BELL on
    ELSE
       SET BELL off
    ENDIF
    IF scrcolor
       SET COLOR TO 7+
    ELSE
       SET COLOR TO 7
    ENDIF


********************

PROCEDURE Redraw

    PARAMETERS center
       @ 1,0 say scrleft_1
       @ 2,0 say scrleft_2
       @ 1,80-LEN("Generic Application") SAY "Generic Application"
       @ 2,80-LEN("Version 1.00") SAY "Version 1.00"
       @ 4,40-LEN(center)/2 SAY center

********************

PROCEDURE Whichway

    PARAMETERS file, way, d, c

       way = 1
       @ d,c,d + 5, c + 40 BOX scrframe
       @ d + 1, c + 10 PROMPT " 1> Print to Screen "
       @ d + 2, c + 10 PROMPT " 2> Print to Printer "
       @ d + 3, c + 10 PROMPT " 3> Print to File "
       @ d + 4, c + 10 SAY     "    ESC to RETURN"
       MENU TO way
       IF way = 3
          FOR fortemp = d + 1 TO d + 4
             @ fortemp, c + 5 SAY SPACE(30)
          NEXT
          @ d + 1, c + 10 SAY "Enter File Name: "
          @ d + 3, c + 10 SAY "-> " GET file PICT "@X"
```

```
        READ
        IF LEN(TRIM(file)) = 0
            way = 0
        ENDIF
        IF AT(".",file) = 0
            file = TRIM(SUBSTR(file,1,8)) + ".TXT"
        ENDIF
    ENDIF
```

****

```
PROCEDURE Cainit

    DO Cainthd
    DO Cainit1
    DO Cainit2

    @ 12, 6 SAY "All Files/Indexes have been properly created.    Any Key to Con-
tinue..."
    qw = INKEY(0)
    CLOSE DATABASES
    @ 12, 2 SAY SPACE(70)
```

****

```
PROCEDURE Cainit1

    SELECT 9
    @ 6, 5 SAY "Initializing CONTRACT File"
    CREATE Template
    USE Template
    APPEND BLANK
    REPLACE field_name WITH "IN_DATE",  field_type WITH "D",  field_len WITH 8,
field_dec WITH 0
    APPEND BLANK
    REPLACE field_name WITH "SUPPORT_NO",  field_type WITH "N",  field_len WITH
6,  field_dec WITH 0
    APPEND BLANK
    REPLACE field_name WITH "COMPUTER",  field_type WITH "C",  field_len WITH 10,
field_dec WITH 0
    APPEND BLANK
    REPLACE field_name WITH "OP_SYSTEM",  field_type WITH "C",  field_len WITH 3,
field_dec WITH 0
    APPEND BLANK
    REPLACE field_name WITH "PURCHASED",  field_type WITH "C",  field_len WITH
20,  field_dec WITH 0
    APPEND BLANK
    REPLACE field_name WITH "SERIAL_NO",  field_type WITH "C",  field_len WITH 8,
field_dec WITH 0
    APPEND BLANK
    REPLACE field_name WITH "PAYMENT_M",  field_type WITH "C",  field_len WITH
10,  field_dec WITH 0
    APPEND BLANK
```

```
      REPLACE field_name WITH "PAYMENT_A",  field_type WITH "N",  field_len WITH 6,
field_dec WITH 2
      APPEND BLANK
      REPLACE field_name WITH "EXPIRES",  field_type WITH "C",  field_len WITH 5,
field_dec WITH 0
      APPEND BLANK
      REPLACE field_name WITH "END_OF_SUP",  field_type WITH "D",  field_len WITH
8,  field_dec WITH 0
      APPEND BLANK
      REPLACE field_name WITH "COMPANY", field_type WITH "C", field_len WITH 30
      APPEND BLANK
      REPLACE field_name WITH "NAME", field_type WITH "C", field_len WITH 25
      APPEND BLANK
      REPLACE field_name WITH "ADDRESS_1", field_type WITH "C", field_len WITH 25
      APPEND BLANK
      REPLACE field_name WITH "ADDRESS_2", field_type WITH "C", field_len WITH 25
      APPEND BLANK
      REPLACE field_name WITH "CITY", field_type WITH "C", field_len WITH 20
      APPEND BLANK
      REPLACE field_name WITH "STATE", field_type WITH "C", field_len WITH 2
      APPEND BLANK
      REPLACE field_name WITH "ZIP", field_type WITH "C", field_len WITH 5
      APPEND BLANK
      REPLACE field_name WITH "PHONE_NO", field_type WITH "C", field_len WITH 21
      USE
      CREATE &scrdata.CONTRACT FROM Template
      USE &scrdata.CONTRACT
      ERASE Template
      a 6, 5 SAY SPACE(70)
      a 7, 5 SAY "Creating Support Number Index"
      temp = scrdata + "CONTRA_1.DAT"
      INDEX ON support_no TO &temp
      a 7, 2 SAY SPACE(70)
      a 8, 5 SAY "Creating Phone Number Index"
      temp = scrdata + "CONTRA_2.DAT"
      INDEX ON phone_no TO &temp
      a 8, 2 SAY SPACE(70)
      a 9, 5 SAY "Creating Company Name Index"
      temp = scrdata + "CONTRA_3.DAT"
      INDEX ON company TO &temp
      a 9, 2 SAY SPACE(70)


********************

PROCEDURE Cainit2

      SELECT 9
      a 10, 5 SAY "Initializing LOG_CALL File"
      CREATE Template
      USE Template
      APPEND BLANK
      REPLACE field_name WITH "CONTROL_NO",  field_type WITH "N",  field_len WITH
6,  field_dec WITH 0
```

```
      APPEND BLANK
      REPLACE field_name WITH "CATEGORY",  field_type WITH "N",  field_len WITH 1,
field_dec WITH 0
      APPEND BLANK
      REPLACE field_name WITH "DATE_IN",  field_type WITH "D",  field_len WITH 8,
field_dec WITH 0
      APPEND BLANK
      REPLACE field_name WITH "WEEK_IN",  field_type WITH "N",  field_len WITH 2,
field_dec WITH 0
      APPEND BLANK
      REPLACE field_name WITH "TIME_IN",  field_type WITH "N",  field_len WITH 5,
field_dec WITH 0
      APPEND BLANK
      REPLACE field_name WITH "DATE_OUT",  field_type WITH "D",  field_len WITH 8,
field_dec WITH 0
      APPEND BLANK
      REPLACE field_name WITH "WEEK_OUT",  field_type WITH "N",  field_len WITH 2,
field_dec WITH 0
      APPEND BLANK
      REPLACE field_name WITH "TIME_OUT",  field_type WITH "N",  field_len WITH 5,
field_dec WITH 0
      APPEND BLANK
      REPLACE field_name WITH "ELAPSED",  field_type WITH "N",  field_len WITH 10,
field_dec WITH 2
      APPEND BLANK
      REPLACE field_name WITH "TIME_OF_CL",  field_type WITH "C",  field_len WITH
8,  field_dec WITH 0
      APPEND BLANK
      REPLACE field_name WITH "SUPPORT_NO",  field_type WITH "N",  field_len WITH
6,  field_dec WITH 0
      APPEND BLANK
      REPLACE field_name WITH "SERIAL_NO",  field_type WITH "C",  field_len WITH 8,
field_dec WITH 0
      APPEND BLANK
      REPLACE field_name WITH "COMPUTER",  field_type WITH "C",  field_len WITH 20,
field_dec WITH 0
      APPEND BLANK
      REPLACE field_name WITH "OP_SYSTEM",  field_type WITH "C",  field_len WITH 5,
field_dec WITH 0
      APPEND BLANK
      REPLACE field_name WITH "NAME",  field_type WITH "C",  field_len WITH 30,
field_dec WITH 0
      APPEND BLANK
      REPLACE field_name WITH "COMPANY",  field_type WITH "C",  field_len WITH 30,
field_dec WITH 0
      APPEND BLANK
      REPLACE field_name WITH "ADDRESS_1",  field_type WITH "C",  field_len WITH
25,  field_dec WITH 0
      APPEND BLANK
      REPLACE field_name WITH "ADDRESS_2",  field_type WITH "C",  field_len WITH
25,  field_dec WITH 0
      APPEND BLANK
      REPLACE field_name WITH "CITY",  field_type WITH "C",  field_len WITH 20,
field_dec WITH 0
```

```
      APPEND BLANK
      REPLACE field_name WITH "STATE",  field_type WITH "C",  field_len WITH 2,
field_dec WITH 0
      APPEND BLANK
      REPLACE field_name WITH "ZIP",  field_type WITH "C",  field_len WITH 5,
field_dec WITH 0
      APPEND BLANK
      REPLACE field_name WITH "PHONE_ONE",  field_type WITH "C",  field_len WITH
21,  field_dec WITH 0
      APPEND BLANK
      REPLACE field_name WITH "PHONE_TWO",  field_type WITH "C",  field_len WITH
21,  field_dec WITH 0
      APPEND BLANK
      REPLACE field_name WITH "PROBLEM_1",  field_type WITH "C",  field_len WITH
60,  field_dec WITH 0
      APPEND BLANK
      REPLACE field_name WITH "PROBLEM_2",  field_type WITH "C",  field_len WITH
60,  field_dec WITH 0
      APPEND BLANK
      REPLACE field_name WITH "PROBLEM_3",  field_type WITH "C",  field_len WITH
60,  field_dec WITH 0
      APPEND BLANK
      REPLACE field_name WITH "PERSONAL",  field_type WITH "C",  field_len WITH 15,
field_dec WITH 0
      USE
      CREATE &scrdata.LOG_CALL FROM Template
      USE &scrdata.LOG_CALL
      ERASE Template
      @ 10, 5 SAY SPACE(70)
      @ 11, 5 SAY "Creating Control Number Index"
      temp = scrdata + "LOG_CA_1.DAT"
      INDEX ON control_no TO &temp
      @ 11, 2 SAY SPACE(70)


*********************

PROCEDURE Cainthd

      RESTORE FROM Screen.sys ADDITIVE
      DO Setup
      CLEAR
      DO Redraw WITH "Initializing Databases"
      @ 5,0,23,79 BOX SUBSTR(scrframe,1,8)


*********************

PROCEDURE Help

      PARAMETERS p,l,v

      SAVE SCREEN
      SET SCOREBOARD OFF
      frame = CHR(201) + CHR(205) + CHR(187) + CHR(186) + ;
```

```
                    CHR(188) + CHR(205) + CHR(200) + CHR(186) + CHR(32)
p = p + SPACE(10 - LEN(p))
v = v + SPACE(10 - LEN(v))
IF .NOT. FILE("HELP.DBF")
   @ 00,10,03,70 BOX scrframe
   @ 01,11 SAY "There is no HELP file available.    Would you like a help "
   @ 02,27 SAY "file to be generated?"
   IF .NOT. VERIFY()
      RESTORE SCREEN
      SET KEY 28 TO Help
      RETURN
   ENDIF
   goback = SELECT()
   DO Dohelp
   tempgo = STR(goback)
   SELECT &tempgo
ENDIF
goback = SELECT()
SELECT 9
USE Help INDEX Help
SET FILTER TO search_p = p .AND. search_v = v
LOCATE FOR search_l = l
IF FOUND()
   @ top,left,bottom,right BOX frame
   IF "" = MEMOEDIT(helpscr,top+1,left+1,bottom-1,right-1,.F.)
   ENDIF
   @ bottom-1,left+1 SAY "Any Key to Continue..."
ELSE
   @ 00,10,03,70 BOX scrframe
   @ 01,11 SAY "There is no HELP for this section.  Would you like to make"
   @ 02,28 SAY "a HELP screen for this? "
   IF .NOT. VERIFY()
      RESTORE SCREEN
      SET KEY 28 TO Help
      RETURN
   ENDIF
   APPEND BLANK
   REPLACE search_p WITH p, search_l WITH l, search_v WITH v
   STORE SPACE(4000) TO in_help
   STORE 0 TO temp_top, temp_left, temp_bot, temp_right
   DO WHILE .T.
      @ 00,10,03,70 BOX scrframe
      @ 01,20 SAY "Position cursor with arrow for TOP, LEFT corner."
      cursor = 0
      @ 12,40 SAY ""
      DO WHILE.T.
         cursor = INKEY(0)
         DO CASE
         CASE cursor = 5
            @ ROW() - 1, COL() SAY ""
         CASE cursor = 4
            @ ROW(), COL() + 1 SAY ""
         CASE cursor = 19
```

```
                     a ROW(),COL() - 1 SAY ""
                 CASE cursor = 24
                     a ROW() + 1,COL() SAY ""
                 CASE cursor = 13 .OR. cursor = 27
                     EXIT
                 ENDCASE
             ENDDO
             STORE ROW() TO temp_top
             STORE COL() - 1 TO temp_left
             a 00,10,03,70 BOX scrframe
             a 01,20 SAY "Position cursor with arrow for BOTTOM, RIGHT corner."
             cursor = 0
             a 12,40 SAY ""
             DO WHILE.T.
                 cursor = INKEY(0)
                 DO CASE
                 CASE cursor = 5
                     a ROW() - 1, COL() SAY ""
                 CASE cursor = 4
                     a ROW(), COL() + 1 SAY ""
                 CASE cursor = 19
                     a ROW(),COL() - 1 SAY ""
                 CASE cursor = 24
                     a ROW() + 1,COL() SAY ""
                 CASE cursor = 13 .OR. cursor = 27
                     EXIT
                 ENDCASE
             ENDDO
             STORE ROW() TO temp_bot
             STORE COL() TO temp_right
             CALL _scrsave WITH in_help
             DO Temphelp
             a 00,10,03,70 BOX scrframe
             a 02,25 SAY "Is this what you wanted?  "
             IF .NOT. VERIFY()
                 CALL _scrrest WITH in_help
                 LOOP
             ENDIF
             REPLACE top WITH temp_top, bottom WITH temp_bot, left WITH temp_left,
right WITH temp_right
             EXIT
         ENDDO
         DO WHILE .T.
             a top,left,bottom,right BOX frame
             REPLACE helpscr WITH MEMOEDIT(helpscr,top+1,left+1,bottom-1,right-
1,.T.)
             a top,left,bottom,right BOX frame
             IF "" = MEMOEDIT(helpscr,top+1,left+1,bottom-1,right-1,.F.)
             ENDIF
             a bottom-1,left+1 SAY "IS THIS CORRECT?   "
             IF .NOT. VERIFY()
                 LOOP
             ENDIF
```

```
           EXIT
        ENDDO
        @ bottom-1,left+1 SAY "Press Any key to Continue...."
     ENDIF
     qw = INKEY(0)
     RESTORE SCREEN
     SET KEY 28 TO Help
     tempgo = STR(goback)
     SELECT &tempgo
     RETURN

********************

PROCEDURE Dohelp

   SELECT 9
   CREATE Temp
   USE Temp
   APPEND BLANK
   REPLACE field_name WITH "SEARCH_P", field_type WITH "C", field_len WITH 10
   APPEND BLANK
   REPLACE field_name WITH "SEARCH_V", field_type WITH "C", field_len WITH 10
   APPEND BLANK
   REPLACE field_name WITH "SEARCH_L", field_type WITH "N", field_len WITH 4
   APPEND BLANK
   REPLACE field_name WITH "TOP", field_type WITH "N", field_len WITH 2
   APPEND BLANK
   REPLACE field_name WITH "LEFT", field_type WITH "N", field_len WITH 2
   APPEND BLANK
   REPLACE field_name WITH "BOTTOM", field_type WITH "N", field_len WITH 2
   APPEND BLANK
   REPLACE field_name WITH "RIGHT", field_type WITH "N", field_len WITH 2
   APPEND BLANK
   REPLACE field_name WITH "HELPSCR", field_type WITH "M", field_len WITH 10
   USE
   CREATE Help FROM Temp
   ERASE Temp
   USE Help
   INDEX ON search_p + search_v TO Help

********************

PROCEDURE Temphelp

   IF scrcolor
      SET COLOR TO W*+
   ELSE
      SET COLOR TO W+
   ENDIF
   @ temp_top, temp_left, temp_bot, temp_right BOX SUBSTR(scrframe,1,8)
   IF scrcolor
      SET COLOR TO 7+
   ELSE
      SET COLOR TO 7
   ENDIF
```

```
********************

PROCEDURE Reinitx

   a 19,25,23,65 BOX scrframe
   tempscr = SPACE(4000)
   CALL _scrsave WITH tempscr
   a 20,29 SAY " Data Files are present.  If you"
   a 21,29 SAY "continue, all data will be lost."
   a 22,29 SAY "Do you want to continue? "
   IF .NOT. VERIFY()
      RETURN
   ENDIF
   CALL _scrrest WITH tempscr
   a 20,29 SAY "Would you like to re-Create"
   a 21,29 SAY "ALL of the databases?"
   IF VERIFY()
      DO Cainit
      RETURN
   ENDIF
   CALL _scrrest WITH tempscr
   a 20,28 SAY "Do you wish to re-create the"
   a 21,40-LEN("CONTRACT")/2 SAY "CONTRACT"
   a 22,28 SAY "Database? (Yes / No)"
   IF VERIFY()
      DO Cainthd
      DO Cainit1
   ENDIF
   CALL _scrrest WITH tempscr
   a 20,28 SAY "Do you wish to re-create the"
   a 21,40-LEN("LOG_CALL")/2 SAY "LOG_CALL"
   a 22,28 SAY "Database? (Yes / No)"
   IF VERIFY()
      DO Cainthd
      DO Cainit2
   ENDIF
   CLOSE DATABASES


********************

PROCEDURE Default

   a 19,25,23,65 BOX scrframe
   whichone = 1
   a 20,32 PROMPT " 1>  Change Directory "
   a 21,32 PROMPT " 2>  Change System Defaults "
   a 22,32 SAY     "    ESC to RETURN TO MENU"
   MENU TO whichone
   DO CASE
   CASE whichone = 0
      RETURN
   CASE whichone = 2
      DO Scrinit
```

```
        OTHERWISE
           @ 20,26,22,64 BOX SPACE(9)
           indir = SPACE(30)
           @ 20,28 SAY "Enter in new PATH..."
           @ 21,28 SAY "->" GET indir PICT "XXXXXXXXXXXXXXXXXXXXXXXXXXXXXX"
           READ
           DO WHILE .NOT. FILE(scrprog + "\COMMAND.COM")
              @ 20,26,22,64 BOX SPACE(9)
              @ 20,28 SAY "Please insert DOS disk in drive :"  + SUBSTR(scrprog,1,1)
              @ 21,28 SAY "Any key or Q to Quit ......."
              IF QWAIT()
                 RETURN
              ENDIF
           ENDDO
           indir = "CD " + TRIM(indir)
           RUN &indir
           DO Beginit
           RETURN
        ENDCASE


********************

PROCEDURE Password

   @ 19,25,23,65 BOX scrframe
   temp = SPACE(15)
   @ 20,28 SAY "Leave Blank to keep old Password"
   @ 21,28 SAY "Enter New Password: " GET temp PICT "XXXXXXXXXXXXXXX"
   READ
   IF LEN(TRIM(tem)) <> 0
      scrpass = GENPASS(temp)
   ENDIF
   @ 20,26,22,64 BOX SPACE(9)
   @ 21,27 SAY "Enter Times for Password: " GET scrtimes PICT "##"
   READ
   SET DEFAULT TO &scrprog
   SAVE ALL LIKE scr* TO Screen.sys
   SET DEFAULT TO &scrdata
*
********************

PROCEDURE Olddate

   @ 19,25,23,75 BOX scrframe
   @ 20,29 SAY "Changing System Date"
   STORE "Today's Date is " + CDOW(DATE()) + ", " + CMON(DATE()) to prompt
   STORE prompt +" "+ STR(DAY(DATE()),2) + ", " + STR(YEAR(DATE()),4) to
prompt
   @ 21,69 SAY prompt
   mdate = DATE()
   @ 22,29 SAY "Enter in Date:  " GET mdate
   READ
   IF FILE(scrprog + "\COMMAND.COM")
      mdate = DTOC(mdate)
      RUN DATE &mdate
   ENDIF
```

```
********************

PROCEDURE Unmark

   @ 19,25,23,65 BOX scrframe
   tempscr = SPACE(4000)
   CALL _scrsave WITH tempscr
   updated = .F.
   CALL _scrrest WITH tempscr
   @ 20,27 SAY "Do you wish to UNMARK data in the "
   @ 21,27 SAY "CONTRACT file? "
   IF VERIFY()
      SELECT 1
      USE &scrdata.CONTRACT
      RECALL ALL
      updated = .T.
   ENDIF
   CALL _scrrest WITH tempscr
   @ 20,27 SAY "Do you wish to UNMARK data in the "
   @ 21,27 SAY "LOG_CALL file? "
   IF VERIFY()
      SELECT 1
      USE &scrdata.LOG_CALL
      RECALL ALL
      updated = .T.
   ENDIF
   CALL _scrrest WITH tempscr
   IF updated
      @ 21,27 SAY "Process Complete.  Any Key to Resort"
      IF INKEY(0) = 0
      ENDIF
      DO Resort
   ELSE
      @ 21,27 SAY "Process Complete.  Any Key to Continue"
      IF INKEY(0) = 0
      ENDIF
   ENDIF


********************

PROCEDURE Removeit

   @ 19,25,23,65 BOX scrframe
   tempscr = SPACE(4000)
   CALL _scrsave WITH tempscr
   updated = .F.
   CALL _scrrest WITH tempscr
   @ 20,27 SAY "Do you wish to REMOVE data in the "
   @ 21,27 SAY "CONTRACT file? "
   IF VERIFY()
      SELECT 1
      USE &scrdata.CONTRACT
      PACK
```

```
              updated = .T.
           ENDIF
           CALL _scrrest WITH tempscr
           @ 20,27 SAY "Do you wish to REMOVE data in the "
           @ 21,27 SAY "LOG_CALL file? "
           IF VERIFY()
              SELECT 1
              USE &scrdata.LOG_CALL
              PACK
              updated = .T.
           ENDIF
        CALL _scrrest WITH tempscr
        IF updated
           @ 21,27 SAY "Process Complete.  Any Key to Resort"
           IF INKEY(0) = 0
           ENDIF
           DO Resort
        ELSE
           @ 21,27 SAY "Process Complete.  Any Key to Continue"
           IF INKEY(0) = 0
           ENDIF
        ENDIF


********************

PROCEDURE Resort

     @ 5,0,23,79 BOX scrframe
     SELECT 1
     USE &scrdata.CONTRACT
     @ 6, 5 SAY "Creating Support Number Index"
     temp = scrdata + "CONTRA_1.DAT"
     INDEX ON support_no TO &temp
     @ 6, 2 SAY SPACE(70)
     @ 7, 5 SAY "Creating Phone Number Index"
     temp = scrdata + "CONTRA_2.DAT"
     INDEX ON phone_no TO &temp
     @ 7, 2 SAY SPACE(70)
     @ 8, 5 SAY "Creating Company Name Index"
     temp = scrdata + "CONTRA_3.DAT"
     INDEX ON company TO &temp
     @ 8, 2 SAY SPACE(70)
     USE &scrdata.LOG_CALL
     @ 9, 5 SAY SPACE(70)
     @ 10, 5 SAY "Creating Control Number Index"
     temp = scrdata + "LOG_CA_1.DAT"
     INDEX ON control_no TO &temp
 * End of CALL.prg
```

CAMENU.PRG

```
*********************
* Name        CAMENU.prg
* Date        August 15, 1986
* Notice      Copyright 1986, Stephen J. Straley
* Note        This menu is for the CALL TRACKING application and
*             was generated by the GENMEN application
*
*********************

CLEAR
DO Camen1


*********************

PROCEDURE Camen1

DO WHILE .T.
   CLEAR
   CLOSE DATABASES
   RESTORE FROM Screen.sys
   STORE SPACE(4000) TO ascreen, bscreen, cscreen, dscreen, escreen, fscreen
   DO Setup
   STORE 0 TO option
   in_control = 1
   @  4,  2, 16, 73 BOX SUBSTR(scrframe,1,8)
   @  3, 28 SAY "M a i n    M e n u"
   @  7, 10 PROMPT " Support Contracts "
   @  6, 42 PROMPT " Register In-coming Calls "
   @  8, 42 PROMPT " Log-Out Calls "
   @ 10, 42 PROMPT " Print Lists "
   @ 12, 42 PROMPT " Generate Reports "
   @ 14, 42 PROMPT " Utility Sub-Menu "
   @ 17, 31 SAY "ESC to RETURN"
   MENU TO option
   CALL _scrsave WITH ascreen
   DO CASE
   CASE option = 1
      DO Camen11
   CASE option = 2
      SELECT 2
      USE &scrdata.Log_call INDEX &scrdata.Log_ca_1.dat
      SELECT 1
      USE &scrdata.Contract INDEX &scrdata.Contra_1.dat
      DO Call_enter
   CASE option = 3
      *************************
      * Do sub-procedure here *
      *************************
   CASE option = 4
      *************************
      * Do sub-procedure here *
      *************************
```

```
        CASE option = 5
           DO Camen15
        CASE option = 6
           DO Camen16
        CASE option = 0
           a 19, 15 SAY "All Files Closed, Returning to Operating System"
           QUIT
        ENDCASE
     ENDDO


     ********************

     PROCEDURE Camen11

     DO WHILE .T.
        IF LEN(TRIM(bscreen)) <> 0
           CALL _scrrest WITH bscreen
        ENDIF
        STORE 0 TO option1
        a 8, 11, 15, 27 BOX scrframe
        a 9, 8 SAY ""
        a 9, 15 PROMPT " 1> Enter "
        a 10, 15 PROMPT " 2> Edit "
        a 11, 15 PROMPT " 3> Scan "
        a 12, 15 PROMPT " 4> Delete "
        a 14, 13 SAY "ESC to RETURN"
        MENU TO option1
        CALL _scrsave WITH bscreen
        IF option1 > 0
           USE &scrdata.Contract INDEX &scrdata.Contra_1.dat, &scrdata.Contra_2.dat,
  &scrdata.Contra_3.dat
        ENDIF
        DO CASE
        CASE option1 = 1
           DO Support_ent
        CASE option1 = 2
           prom_acros = "< >ext - < >revious - < >dit -   < >hoose Again - < >uit"
           DO Support_edt
        CASE option1 = 3
           prom_acros = "< >ext - < >revious - < >can -   < >hoose Again - < >uit"
           DO Support_edt
        CASE option1 = 4
           prom_acros = "< >ext - < >revious - < >elete - < >hoose Again - < >uit"
           DO Support_del
        CASE option1 = 0
           EXIT
        ENDCASE
     ENDDO


     ********************

     PROCEDURE Camen15

     DO WHILE .T.
        IF LEN(TRIM(bscreen)) <> 0
           CALL _scrrest WITH bscreen
```

```
     ENDIF
     STORE 0 TO option2
     @ 6, 9, 14, 36 BOX scrframe
     @ 6, 15 SAY "Report Sub-Menu"
     @ 8, 13 PROMPT " Call Activity Log "
     @ 9, 13 PROMPT " Weekly Breakdown "
     @ 10, 13 PROMPT " Daily Call Totals "
     @ 11, 13 PROMPT " Non-responded Calls "
     @ 13, 16 SAY "ESC to RETURN"
     MENU TO option2
     CALL _scrsave WITH bscreen
     DO CASE
     CASE option2 = 1
         *************************
         * Do sub-procedure here *
         *************************
     CASE option2 = 2
         *************************
         * Do sub-procedure here *
         *************************
     CASE option2 = 3
         *************************
         * Do sub-procedure here *
         *************************
     CASE option2 = 4
         *************************
         * Do sub-procedure here *
         *************************
`    CASE option2 = 0
         EXIT
     ENDCASE
ENDDO

********************

PROCEDURE Camen16

DO WHILE .T.
     IF LEN(TRIM(bscreen)) <> 0
        CALL _scrrest WITH bscreen
     ENDIF
     STORE 0 TO option3
     @ 5, 5, 21, 40 BOX scrframe
     @ 5, 14 SAY "Utility Sub-Menu"
     @ 7, 9 PROMPT " 1> Backup/Restore Data "
     @ 8, 9 PROMPT " 2> Re-Index Data Files "
     @ 9, 9 PROMPT " 3> Remove Data "
     @ 10, 9 PROMPT " 4> Reset System Date "
     @ 11, 9 PROMPT " 5> Reset Screen Parameters "
     @ 12, 9 PROMPT " 6> Scan Entered Calls "
     @ 13, 9 PROMPT " 7> Reclaim Marked Data "
     @ 14, 9 PROMPT " 8> Dump Data "
     @ 15, 9 PROMPT " 9> Run a Program "
```

```
    a 16, 9 PROMPT " A> Enter/Edit Staff "
    a 17, 9 PROMPT " B> Merge Outside Data "
    a 18, 9 PROMPT " C> New Password "
    a 19, 9 PROMPT " D> Initialize Data Files "
    a 21, 16 SAY "ESC to RETURN"
    MENU TO option3
    CALL _scrsave WITH bscreen
    DO CASE
    CASE option3 = 1
       **************************
       * Do sub-procedure here *
       **************************
    CASE option3 = 2
       DO Resort
    CASE option3 = 3
       DO Removeit
    CASE option3 = 4
       DO Olddate
    CASE option3 = 5
       DO Scrinit
    CASE option3 = 6
       **************************
       * Do sub-procedure here *
       **************************
    CASE option3 = 7
       DO Unmark
    CASE option3 = 8
       **************************
       * Do sub-procedure here *
       **************************
    CASE option3 = 9
       **************************
       * Do sub-procedure here *
       **************************
    CASE option3 = 10
       **************************
       * Do sub-procedure here *
       **************************
    CASE option3 = 11
       **************************
       * Do sub-procedure here *
       **************************
    CASE option3 = 12
       **************************
       * Do sub-procedure here *
       **************************
    CASE option3 = 13
       DO Reinitx
    CASE option3 = 0
       EXIT
    ENDCASE
ENDDO
* End of CAMENU.prg
```

CALLPROG.PRG

```
********************
* Name        CALLPROG.prg
* Date        August 15, 1986
* Notice      Copyright 1986, Stephen J. Straley
* Note        This shows that everything is either a procedure
*             or a function to the compiler.  In this file there is
*             a series of procedures to be called from the CALL
*             TRACKING application.   No specific reference is made
*             to it so it has to be compiled separately and linked
*             with the other object files.
*
********************

PROCEDURE Support_ent

    @ 4,2,21,73 BOX scrframe
    @ 3,27 SAY "Enter Support Contract"
    CALL _scrsave WITH cscreen
    DO WHILE .T.
       CALL _scrrest WITH cscreen
       STORE 0 TO in_support
       @ 6,7 SAY "Enter Support Number " + CHR(205) + "> " GET in_support
VALID(LOOKUP())
       READ
       IF in_support = 0
          RETURN
       ENDIF
       CALL _scrrest WITH cscreen
       REPLACE in_date WITH DATE()
       @ 6,10 SAY "  Date Entered: " GET in_date VALID(CHNGEDATE())
       @ 8,10 SAY "Support Number: " GET support_no
       DO Fir_half
       READ
       DO Sec_half
       READ
    ENDDO


********************

PROCEDURE Support_edt

    @ 4,2,21,73 BOX scrframe
    IF option1 = 2
       @ 3,27 SAY "Edit "
    ELSE
       @ 3,27 SAY "Scan "
    ENDIF
    ?? "Support Contract"
    CALL _scrsave WITH cscreen
    DO WHILE .T.
       CALL _scrrest WITH cscreen
```

```
        STORE 0 TO in_support
        @ 6,7 SAY "Enter Support Number " + CHR(205) + "> " GET in_support
VALID(LOOKUP2())
        READ
        IF in_support = 0
           RETURN
        ENDIF
        DO WHILE .T.
           CALL _scrrest WITH cscreen
           @ 6,10 SAY "  Date Entered: " GET in_date VALID(CHNGEDATE())
           @ 8,10 SAY "Support Number: " GET in_support VALID(LOOKUP3())
           DO Checkdel
           DO Fir_half
           @ 22,11 SAY prom_acros
           passing = IF(option1 = 2, "E", "S")
           whichone = PROMPTING(passing)
           DO CASE
           CASE whichone = 1
              CLEAR GETS
              IF .NOT. EOF()
                 SKIP
              ENDIF
              in_support = support_no
           CASE whichone = 2
              CLEAR GETS
              IF .NOT. BOF()
                 SKIP - 1
              ENDIF
              in_support = support_no
           CASE whichone = 3
              IF option1 = 2
                 READ
                 REPLACE support_no WITH in_support
              ELSE
                 CLEAR GETS
              ENDIF
              DO Sec_half
              IF option1 = 2
                 READ
              ELSE
                 @ 19,5 SAY "Press any key to move on ... "
                 IF 0 = INKEY(0)
                 ENDIF
              ENDIF
           CASE whichone = 4
              CLEAR GETS
              EXIT
           OTHERWISE
              CLEAR GETS
              KEYBOARD "0" + CHR(13)
              EXIT
           ENDCASE
        ENDDO
     ENDDO
```

```
********************

PROCEDURE Support_de

    @ 4,2,21,73 BOX scrframe
    @ 3,25 SAY "Delete Support Contract"
    CALL _scrsave WITH cscreen
    DO WHILE .T.
       CALL _scrrest WITH cscreen
       STORE 0 TO in_support
       @ 6,7 SAY "Enter Support Number " + CHR(205) + "> " GET in_support
VALID(LOOKUP2())
       READ
       IF in_support = 0
          RETURN
       ENDIF
       DO WHILE .T.
          CALL _scrrest WITH cscreen
          @ 6,10 SAY "  Date Entered: " GET in_date VALID(CHNGEDATE())
          @ 8,10 SAY "Support Number: " GET in_support VALID(LOOKUP3())
          DO Checkdel
          DO Fir_half
          @ 22,11 SAY prom_acros
          whichone = PROMPTING("D")
          CLEAR GETS
          DO CASE
          CASE whichone = 1
             IF .NOT. EOF()
                SKIP
             ENDIF
             in_support = support_no
          CASE whichone = 2
             IF .NOT. BOF()
                SKIP - 1
             ENDIF
             in_support = support_no
          CASE whichone = 3
             IF DELETED()
                RECALL
             ELSE
                DELETE
             ENDIF
          CASE whichone = 4
             EXIT
          OTHERWISE
             KEYBOARD "0" + CHR(13)
             EXIT
          ENDCASE
       ENDDO
    ENDDO
```

```
********************

PROCEDURE Call_enter

    @ 4,2,21,73 BOX scrframe
    @ 3,27 SAY "  Enter Support Call  "
    CALL _scrsave WITH dscreen
    DO WHILE .T.
        SELECT 2
        GO TOP
        SELECT 1
        GO TOP
        CALL _scrrest WITH dscreen
        @ 8,10 SAY "        Do they have a Support Contract? (Y/N)  "
        IF .NOT. VERIFY()
            @ 10,10 SAY "Do you wish to enter a Support Contract?  (Y/N)  "
            IF VERIFY()
                SAVE SCREEN
                SELECT 1
                USE &scrdata.Contract INDEX &scrdata.Contra_1.dat,
&scrdata.Contra_2.dat, &scrdata.Contra_3.dat
                DO Support_ent
                SELECT 1
                USE &scrdata.Contract INDEX &scrdata.Contra_1.dat
                RESTORE SCREEN
            ELSE
                @ 10,10 SAY "Do you wish to RETURN to the Main Menu?  (Y/N)  "
                IF VERIFY()
                    RETURN
                ENDIF
                LOOP
            ENDIF
        ENDIF
        in_con = 0
        SET KEY -1 TO Scanname
        SET KEY -9 TO Scancall
        tempnumb = "F2 to SCAN Support Names   :  F10 TO SCAN Day's CALLS"
        @ 16,12 GET tempnumb
        CLEAR GETS
        @ 12,10 SAY "Enter Support Number: "
        @ 12,50 SAY "Enter 0 to RETURN"
        @ 12,35 GET in_con
        READ
        SET KEY -1 TO
        SET KEY -9 TO
        IF EMPTY(in_con)
            LOOP
        ENDIF
        SEEK in_con
        IF .NOT. FOUND()
            @ 12, 5 SAY SPACE(67)
            @ 12,15 SAY "The number entered is not valid.  Do you wish to"
            @ 13,15 SAY "continue with blank contract number? (Y/N)  "
```

```
         IF .NOT. VERIFY()
            LOOP
         ENDIF
         SELECT 2
         APPEND BLANK
         REPLACE date_in WITH DATE(), time_in WITH SECONDS(), support_no WITH 0
      ELSE
         IF DATE() > A->end_of_sup
            @ 14,10 SAY "Support Contract has expired!   Continue? (Y/N)  "
            IF .NOT. VERIFY()
               LOOP
            ENDIF
         ENDIF
         SELECT 2
         APPEND BLANK
         REPLACE date_in WITH DATE(), time_in WITH SECONDS(), support_no WITH
in_con
         REPLACE company WITH A->company, name WITH A->name, address_1 WITH A-
>address_1
         REPLACE address_2 WITH A->address_2, phone_one WITH A->phone_no, state
WITH A->state
         REPLACE zip WITH A->zip, serial_no WITH A->serial_no, control_no WITH
in_control
      ENDIF
      CALL _scrrest WITH dscreen
      @ 5,10 SAY "Support Number: " GET support_no
      CLEAR GETS
      @ 7,10 SAY " Serial Number: " GET serial_no
      @ 9,10 SAY "       Computer: " GET computer
      @ 9,COL() + 1 SAY "Operating System: " GET op_system
      @ 11,10 SAY "         Person: " GET name
      @ 12,10 SAY "        Company: " GET company
      @ 13,10 SAY "    Address(es): " GET address_1
      @ 14,10 SAY "                 " GET address_2
      @ 15,10 SAY "           City: " GET city
      @ 16,10 SAY "          State: " GET state PICT "!!"
      @ 16,COL()+1 SAY "Zip: " GET zip PICT "99999"
      @ 18,10 SAY "      Phone One: " GET phone_one PICT "(999)999-9999 [9999]"
      @ 19,10 SAY "            Two: " GET phone_two PICT "(999)999-9999 [9999]"
      @ 22,19 SAY "For Defaults, PRESS PgDn key or RETURN"
      READ
      FOR x = 13 TO 19
         @ x, 5 SAY SPACE(67)
      NEXT
      @ 14,33 SAY "Enter Problem"
      @ 15,05 SAY CHR(205) + "> " GET problem_1
      @ 16,05 SAY CHR(205) + "> " GET problem_2
      @ 17,05 SAY CHR(205) + "> " GET problem_3
      @ 19,10 SAY "Personnel Entering: " GET personal
      READ
      CALL _scrrest WITH dscreen
      @ 6,5 SAY "Call is Logged In.  Do you wish to skip the printing? (Y/N)    "
      IF VERIFY()
```

```
            @ 8,15 SAY "Call not printed.  Press Any Key to Continue...."
            in_control = in_control + 1
            IF 0 = INKEY(0)
            ENDIF
            LOOP
         ENDIF
         @  8,15 SAY "     Please check the printer!"
         @ 10,15 SAY "Press Any key to print or Q to QUIT!!   "
         IF QWAIT()
            in_control = in_control + 1
            LOOP
         ENDIF
         CALL _scrrest WITH dscreen
         @ 12,15 SAY EXPAND("Printing!")
         SET DEVICE TO PRINT
         @  2,10 SAY EXPAND("Software Support Message Form")
         @  4, 4 SAY "Memo: _____"
         @  4,50 SAY "Mail: _____"
         @  6, 4 SAY "Control: "
         @  6,PCOL() SAY control_no PICT "@B"
         @  6,50 SAY "Serial Number: "
         @  6,PCOL() SAY serial_no PICT "@B"
         @  8, 4 SAY "Date In: "
         @  8,PCOL() SAY date_in
         @  8,50 SAY "Time In: "
         @  8,PCOL() SAY TIME()
         @ 10, 4 SAY "Master/Visa #: _____    Expires:
         _____"
         @ 12, 4 SAY " Name/Company: "
         @ 12,PCOL() SAY TRIM(name) + "/" + TRIM(company)
         @ 14, 4 SAY "      Address: "
         tempnumb = PCOL()
         @ 14,tempnumb SAY address_1
         @ 16,tempnumb SAY address_2
         @ 18, 4 SAY "         City: "
         @ 18,PCOL() SAY IF(EMPTY(city), REPLICATE("_",25), city)
         @ 18,PCOL() + 2 SAY "State: "
         @ 18,PCOL() SAY IF(EMPTY(state), "_", state)
         @ 18,PCOL() + 2 SAY "Zip: "
         @ 18,PCOL() SAY IF(EMPTY(zip), "_____", zip)
         @ 20, 4 SAY phone_one
         @ 20,40 SAY phone_two
         @ 23, 4 SAY "Problem: "
         tempnumb = PCOL()
         @ 23,tempnumb SAY problem_1
         @ 25,tempnumb SAY problem_2
         @ 27,tempnumb SAY problem_3
         @ 29, 4 SAY "Technician: _____    Time In: _____   Time Out:
         _____"
         @ 31, 4 SAY "L/M #1 AT: _____   L/M #2: _____   N/A: _____
Sales: _____ "
         @ 33, 4 SAY "C/B #1 AT: _____   C/B #2: _____   Busy: _____
Wrong #: _____ "
```

```
       @ 37, 4 SAY REPLICATE("=",70)
       @ 39, 4 SAY "NOTES:      LOG [ ]          ANOMALY [ ]          COM-
MENTS [ ]"
       in_control = in_control + 1

       EJECT
       SET DEVICE TO SCREEN
    ENDDO

********************

PROCEDURE Scanname

    PARAMETERS p, l, v

    ret_record = RECNO()
    SAVE SCREEN
    @ 8,7,23,70 BOX scrframe
    @ 10,10 SAY ret_record
    WAIT
    RESTORE SCREEN

********************

PROCEDURE Scancall

    PARAMETERS p, l, v

    SAVE SCREEN
    past_scr = .T.
    temprow = 9
    tempcol = 8
    passthr = .T.
    SELECT 2
    SET FILTER TO date_in = DATE()
    GO TOP
    DO WHILE .NOT. EOF()
       IF past_scr
          @ 8,6,23,70 BOX scrframe
          past_scr = .F.
       ENDIF
       @ temprow, tempcol SAY control_no
       @ temprow, COL()+1 SAY name
       temprow = temprow + 1
       IF temprow > 22
          IF .NOT. passthr
             tempcol  = 8
             temprow  = 9
             passthr = .T.
             past_scr = .T.
             @ 23,10 SAY "  Press Any Key to Continue....   "
             IF 0 = INKEY(0)
             ENDIF
```

```
            ELSE
                tempcol = 30
                temprow = 9
                passthr = .F.
            ENDIF
        ENDIF
        SKIP
    ENDDO
    @ 23,10 SAY "  Press Any Key to Continue....   "
    IF 0 = INKEY(0)
    ENDIF
    SET FILTER TO
    GO TOP
    SELECT 1
    RESTORE SCREEN


********************

FUNCTION Chngedate

    REPLACE end_of_support WITH in_date + 90
    RETURN(.T.)


********************

FUNCTION Lookup

    IF in_support = 0
        RETURN(.T.)
    ENDIF
    SEEK in_support
    IF FOUND()
        @ 22, 9 SAY "That number is already entered.  Please choose another num-
ber"
        RETURN(.F.)
    ENDIF
    APPEND BLANK
    REPLACE support_no WITH in_support
    RETURN(.T.)


********************

FUNCTION Lookup2

    IF in_support = 0
        RETURN(.T.)
    ENDIF
    SEEK in_support
    IF .NOT. FOUND()
        @ 22,9 SAY "That number is not in database.  Please choose another number"
        RETURN(.F.)
    ENDIF
    RETURN(.T.)
```

```
********************

FUNCTION Lookup3

   tempval = support_no
   IF support_no = in_support
      RETURN(.T.)
   ENDIF
   SEEK in_support
   IF FOUND()
      @ 22,0 SAY SPACE(79)
      @ 22,13 SAY "That number is already present.  Please choose again!!"
      SEEK tempval
      RETURN(.F.)
   ENDIF
   SEEK tempval

********************

FUNCTION Prompting

   PARAMETER letter

   invalue = 1
   @ 22,12 PROMPT "N"
   @ 22,21 PROMPT "P"
   @ 22,34 PROMPT letter
   @ 22,45 PROMPT "C"
   @ 22,62 PROMPT "Q"
   MENU TO invalue
   RETURN(invalue)

********************

PROCEDURE Sec_half

   FOR x = 10 TO 18
      @ x,5 SAY SPACE(67)
   NEXT
   @ 10,10 SAY "         Computer: " GET computer
   @ 11,10 SAY " Operating System: " GET op_system
   @ 12,10 SAY "   Purchased From: " GET purchased
   @ 13,10 SAY "     Serial Number: " GET serial_no
   @ 14,10 SAY "Method of Payment: " GET payment_m
   @ 15,10 SAY "          Expires: " GET expires PICT "99/99"
   @ 16,10 SAY "         Amount $: " GET payment_a PICT "@Z"
   @ 18,10 SAY "    End of Support: " GET end_of_support

********************

PROCEDURE Fir_half

   @ 10,10 SAY "    Subscriber: " GET name
   @ 12,10 SAY "       Company: " GET company
   @ 13,10 SAY "    Address(es): " GET address_1
```

```
ə 14,10 SAY "                " GET address_2
ə 15,10 SAY "         City: " GET city
ə 16,10 SAY "        State: " GET state PICT "!!"
ə 16,COL()+1 SAY "Zip " GET zip PICT "99999"
ə 18,10 SAY "  Phone Number: " GET phone_no PICT "(999)999-9999 [9999]"


********************

PROCEDURE Checkdel

   IF DELETED()
      DO Blink WITH 5,30
   ELSE
      ə 5,35 SAY SPACE(20)
   ENDIF
* End of CALLPROG.prg
```

INDEX

V

W

X

Y

Z